Frommer's®

Brazil

5th Edition

by Shawn Blore & Alexandra de Vries

WILEY

Wiley Publishing, Inc.

Published by:

WILEY PUBLISHING, INC.

111 River St.
Hoboken, NJ 07030-5774

ISBN 978-0-470-59151-2

Editor: Matthew Brown (with *Melinda Quintero* and *Jennifer Reilly*)
Production Editor: Eric T. Schroeder
Cartographer: Roberta Stockwell
Photo Editor: Richard Fox
Production by Wiley Indianapolis Composition Services

Front cover photo: A man practicing *capoeira* on the beach ©Andrea Matone / Alamy Images
Back cover photo: Street scene in Salvador, Bahia ©Florian Kopp / PhotoLibrary

For information on our other products and services or to obtain technical support, please contact our Customer Care Department within the U.S. at 877/762-2974, outside the U.S. at 317/572-3993 or fax 317/572-4002.

Wiley also publishes its books in a variety of electronic formats. Some content that appears in print may not be available in electronic formats.

Manufactured in the United States of America

5   4   3   2   1

CONTENTS

9 SETTLING INTO SÃO PAULO   204

10 EXPLORING SÃO PAULO   226

11 SALVADOR & THE BEST OF BAHIA   248

12 RECIFE & OLINDA   307

BRAZIL

CONTENTS

13 NATAL   332

14 FORTALEZA   345

15 SÃO LUIS & THE LENÇOIS MARANHENSES   359

16 THE AMAZON: MANAUS & BELEM   376

17 BRASILIA 418

18 IGUAÇU & THE FALLS 431

19 THE PANTANAL 443

20 FERNANDO DE NORONHA 463

21 FLORIANÓPOLIS 473

LIST OF MAPS

HOW TO CONTACT US

In researching this book, we discovered many wonderful places—hotels, restaurants, shops, and more. We're sure you'll find others. Please tell us about them so we can share the information with your fellow travelers in upcoming editions. If you were disappointed with a recommendation, we'd love to know that, too. Please write to:

Frommer's Brazil, 5th Edition
Wiley Publishing, Inc. • 111 River St. • Hoboken, NJ 07030-5774

AN ADDITIONAL NOTE

Please be advised that travel information is subject to change at any time—and this is especially true of prices. We therefore suggest that you write or call ahead for confirmation when making your travel plans. The authors, editors, and publisher cannot be held responsible for the experiences of readers while traveling. Your safety is important to us, however, so we encourage you to stay alert and be aware of your surroundings. Keep a close eye on cameras, purses, and wallets, all favorite targets of thieves and pickpockets.

ABOUT THE AUTHORS

A native of California, **Shawn Blore** has lived and worked in a half dozen countries and traveled in at least 50 more (but who's counting?). Long a resident of Vancouver, Shawn has for the past few years made his home in Rio de Janeiro. He is an award-winning magazine writer and the author of *Vancouver: Secrets of the City* and coauthor of *Frommer's South America* and *Frommer's Portable Rio de Janeiro.*

Alexandra de Vries made her first journey to Brazil at the ripe old age of 1 month (alas, few of her food reviews from that trip survive). In recent years, Alexandra has returned many times to travel, explore, and live in this amazing country. Alexandra cowrites *Frommer's Portable Rio de Janeiro,* about her favorite place to live, and *Frommer's South America,* about her favorite places to visit.

FROMMER'S STAR RATINGS, ICONS & ABBREVIATIONS

Every hotel, restaurant, and attraction listing in this guide has been ranked for quality, value, service, amenities, and special features using a **star-rating system.** In country, state, and regional guides, we also rate towns and regions to help you narrow down your choices and budget your time accordingly. Hotels and restaurants are rated on a scale of zero (recommended) to three stars (exceptional). Attractions, shopping, nightlife, towns, and regions are rated according to the following scale: zero stars (recommended), one star (highly recommended), two stars (very highly recommended), and three stars (must-see).

In addition to the star-rating system, we also use **seven feature icons** that point you to the great deals, in-the-know advice, and unique experiences that separate travelers from tourists. Throughout the book, look for:

(Finds)	Special finds—those places only insiders know about
(Fun Facts)	Fun facts—details that make travelers more informed and their trips more fun
(Kids)	Best bets for kids, and advice for the whole family
(Moments)	Special moments—those experiences that memories are made of
(Overrated)	Places or experiences not worth your time or money
(Tips)	Insider tips—great ways to save time and money
(Value)	Great values—where to get the best deals

The following **abbreviations** are used for credit cards:

| **AE** | American Express | **DISC** | Discover | **V** | Visa |
| **DC** | Diners Club | **MC** | MasterCard | | |

TRAVEL RESOURCES AT FROMMERS.COM

Frommer's travel resources don't end with this guide. Frommer's website, **www.frommers.com,** has travel information on more than 4,000 destinations. We update features regularly, giving you access to the most current trip-planning information and the best airfare, lodging, and car-rental bargains. You can also listen to podcasts, connect with other Frommers.com members through our active-reader forums, share your travel photos, read blogs from guidebook editors and fellow travelers, and much more.

The Best of Brazil

There's a joke Brazilians like to tell: When the world was created, one of the archangels peered over God's shoulder at the work in progress and couldn't help noticing that one country had been especially favored. "You've given everything to Brazil," the archangel said. "It has the longest beaches, the largest river, the biggest forest, the best soil. The weather's always warm and sunny, with no floods, hurricanes, or natural disasters at all. Don't you think that's a little unfair?" "Ah," God replied, "just wait until you see the people I'm putting there."

Accuracy rarely comes with a punch line, but there's a significant grain of truth in that tale. Brazil as a nation *is* unusually blessed. Over 8,000km (5,000 miles) of coastline—some of it packed with cafes and partygoers, but long stretches blissfully empty. Rainforests and wetlands teem with exotic critters. Some of the oldest cities and civic architecture in the New World (and one of the newest cities in the entire world) are here. Restaurants match the snobbiest standards, with regional cuisines that have yet to be discovered in culinary capitals like New York or L.A. Music lovers could make Brazil a lifetime study. And let's not forget a little thing called Carnaval.

And about those Brazilians: They work as hard as anyone in the First World, and many a good deal harder. In recent years, Brazil has devoted time and resources to improving its tourism infrastructure, reflected in the new airports, hotels, and inns that have sprung up around the country. Yet no one could accuse Brazilians of worshiping efficiency. They'd much rather get along than get things done; the goal is, above all, harmony. Harmony can mean an entire Sunday spent watching soccer or afternoons off for quality time with your buddies at the beach. It can mean countless hours of effort for a single night's party. But above all, harmony mandates never taking anything all that seriously. And at this, Brazilians excel.

1 THE MOST UNFORGETTABLE TRAVEL EXPERIENCES

- **Attend Carnaval in Rio:** The biggest party in the world. Whether you dance in the streets, watch thousands participate with their elaborate costumes in the samba parade, or attend the fairytale Copacabana Palace ball, it's the one event not to miss! See chapter 6.
- **Watch a Soccer Game at Maracanã Stadium:** Nothing can prepare you for a game at the largest stadium in the world. Up to 100,000 fans sing, dance, and drum for hours in one of the biggest parties in town. See chapter 6.
- **Get to Know Pelourinho:** The historic center of Salvador is a treasure of baroque churches, colorful colonial architecture, steep cobblestone streets, and large squares. See chapter 11.
- **Hear the Drummers in Pelô:** At night the historic heart of Salvador comes alive with music. Most impressive are the Blocos Afro, the all-percussion bands that create a rhythm and beat with their drums so intense it sends shivers down your spine. See chapter 11.

Brazil

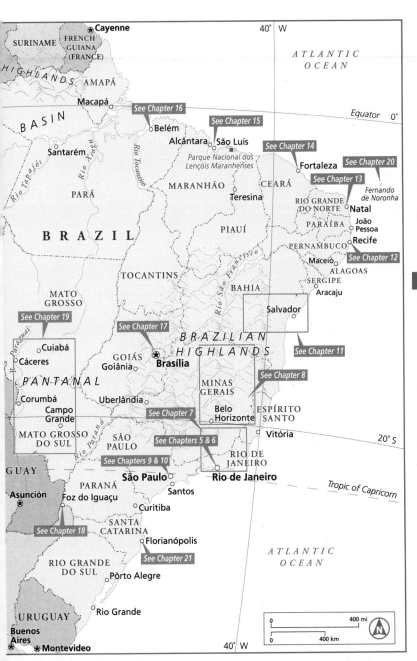

- **Watch the Sunset over the Lençóis Maranhenses:** The magical snow-white dunes interlaced with strings of turquoise, blue, and green lagoons make one of the most spectacular sights in all of Brazil. See chapter 15.

- **Herd Water Buffalo in Marajó:** The buffalo ranches on this island in the mouth of the Amazon offer city slickers a unique cowboy experience. Riding out on horseback, visitors to Fazenda Sanjo help round up the water buffalo herd and bring it back to the ranch. See chapter 16.

- **Kayak in the Amazon:** To explore the rainforest in depth, nothing beats a slow descent of an Amazon tributary; the kayak provides the freedom to view the rainforest at leisure, guides explain the workings of this ecosystem, and cooks prepare meals of delicious Amazon fish. See chapter 16.

- **Admire the Modernist Architecture of Brasilia:** Built from scratch in a matter of years on the red soil of the dry *cerrado,* Brasilia is an oasis of modernism in Brazil's interior. Marvel at the clean lines and functional forms and admire some of the best public art in the country. See chapter 17.

- **Get Drenched at Amazing Iguaçu Falls:** These falls consist of 275 cataracts along a 2.5km (1½-mile) stretch of the Iguaçu River. The water's power mesmerizes as you stare into the roiling cauldrons. See chapter 18.

- **Wildlife Viewing on Horseback in the Pantanal:** Richer in bird life by far than the Amazon, but far too soggy to hike, the wet fields of the Pantanal are best explored on horseback. And if you like it fast, there's nothing like galloping through the fields, as a flurry of colorful birds scatter and caiman scurry off underfoot. See chapter 19.

2 THE BEST BEACHES

- **Ipanema, Rio de Janeiro:** Yes, this is one of the most urban beaches in the world, but it's still one of the country's prime tanning spots. The long stretch of white sand is perfect for observing the tan and lovely (male and female alike). Or watch a game of volleyball while having a beer and some fresh seafood; if you feel like it, go for a swim or a stroll. See chapter 6.

- **Ilha Grande:** This former prison colony off the coast of Rio de Janeiro offers dozens of beaches. The nicest may well be **Lopes Mendes,** facing the ocean on the eastern tip of the island. This long stretch of strand is unspoiled by any development, and features fine soft sand, clear clean water, and excellent waves for surfing. See p. 172.

- **Boipeba, Bahia:** The perfect island getaway, Boipeba makes Morro de São Paulo seem busy and hectic. Just south of Morro, Boipeba offers glorious empty beaches framed by rows and rows of palm trees. At Boca da Barra, where the river Inferno meets the ocean, huge sand banks appear at low tide. You can choose whether to swim on the freshwater side or play in salty ocean. See chapter 11.

- **Porto de Galinhas, Pernambuco:** Development in Porto de Galinhas has been kept resolutely small-scale. No high-rises mar the unpretentious town of Porto de Galinhas, which has perhaps four streets—enough for a dozen restaurants, a bank, some surf shops, and a beachside bar or two. See chapter 12.

- **Ponta Negra, Manaus:** Not an ocean beach but a river beach, Ponta Negra, on the shores of Rio Negro, is the most popular tanning spot in the dry season. All the standard beach accouterments are present, including vendors plying food, drinks, and souvenirs. Beach kiosks serve up snacks until the wee hours. See chapter 16.

- **Fernando do Noronha:** The island archipelago of Fernando do Noronha has so many spectacular beaches, it's hard to single out just one. Praia do Leão offers wild crashing surf and sea turtle hatchings in season. The most gorgeously secluded is Praia da Baía do Sancho, a crescent of red sand on shimmering clear blue water that can only be reached by clambering down a rickety iron ladder through a chasm in the cliff side. See chapter 20.

- **Praia Mole, Florianópolis:** Praia Mole is one of the most popular beaches on the beautiful southern island of Santa Catarina (aka Florianópolis). Perfectly white fluffy sand, lush green vegetation, and rocky outcrops give the beach an isolated, paradisiacal feel. Yet, the strand is anything but quiet, packed with a bohemian crowd of locals from Floripa, yuppie tourists, surfers, gay and gay-friendly sunbathers, and families. See chapter 21.

3 THE BEST OUTDOOR ADVENTURES

- **Hang Gliding in Rio:** Running off the edge of a platform with nothing between you and the ground 800m (2,624 ft.) below requires a leap of faith, so to speak, but once you do, the views of the rainforest and beaches are so enthralling that you almost forget about the ground until your toes touch the sand at São Conrado beach. See chapter 6.

- **Hike or Bike the Chapada Diaman-tina:** These highlands inland from Salvador have rock formations similar to the buttes and mesas of the American Southwest. They also have waterfalls and natural water slides of smooth red marble, plus lots of great hiking and biking trails. See chapter 11.

- **Riding a Beach Buggy from Natal to Fortaleza:** The long coast from Natal to Fortaleza is one of the last places on earth with hundreds of kilometers of unobstructed sand. Make the 4-day journey by dune buggy and never once leave the beach, exploring vast towering dunes along the way. See chapter 13.

- **Kite Surfing in Jericoacoara:** From July to November, kite-surf fans from around the world gather in this tiny village to enjoy some of the best and most reliable kite-surf conditions in Brazil, suitable for both beginners and advanced surfers. Spend the day on the water and catch the stunning sunset at the top of the 60m (200-ft.) sand dune overlooking the town. See chapter 14.

- **Swimming in the Lençóis Maran-henses:** The end of the rainy season signals the best time of year to visit the dunes at Lençóis National Park. June to October, the dunes are full of crystal-clear freshwater lagoons. A swim is the best reward for hiking through the desert of dunes. See chapter 15.

- **Canoeing the Amazon:** Just you and a canoe in the jungle. Your senses heighten as you listen to the sounds of the forest, watch for splashes in the water, and peer into the trees to find birds, sloths, and monkeys. See chapter 16.

- **Tree Climbing in the Amazon Forest:** Get off the river and delve into the forest. Most visitors only see the trees from the bottom up. Actually climbing into the tree will give you a whole new perspective on the forest and its ecosystem. See chapter 16.

- **Swimming in the Waterfalls of Chapada dos Guimarães:** The red-rock formations of this minicanyon hide some spectacular waterfalls nestled in small stands of lush tropical forest. With dozens and dozens of falls and trails, it's not hard to find one all for yourself. See chapter 19.

- **Diving in Fernando de Noronha:** Brazil's best diving is found on this small archipelago off the coast of Pernambuco. See dolphins, turtles, manta rays, and lots of underwater caves. Crowds are limited, because only 420 visitors are allowed on the island at a time. See chapter 20.

4 THE BEST WILDLIFE ENCOUNTERS

- **Go, Turtles, Go!** (Bahia): From mid-February to April you have a good chance to watch turtle hatchings at Praia do Forte Tamar's turtle project. See how these tiny sea turtles crawl out of the egg, and cheer them on as they waddle to the ocean for their first swim. See p. 288.

- **Sea Horses in Porto de Galinhas:** The roots of the mangroves in Porto de Galinhas are home to one of the most magical sea creatures, the sea horse. Guides dive in the water to look for these delicate animals and are usually successful in scooping one up (literally, in a glass jar). Once you have had a chance to learn a little bit more about the animal it goes back into its natural habitat. See chapter 12.

- **Caiman Spotting** (the Amazon): Spotting caiman (alligators native to South America) involves setting out in a canoe after the sun has set. Boating through the dark Amazon forest is quite an experience, but nothing quite prepares you for the sight of those caiman eyes that light up in the beam of the spotlight. See chapter 16.

- **Butterflies in Iguaçu:** Everyone talks about the falls; few mention the butterflies. The lush rainforest provides the perfect environment for many colorful species, and everywhere you go lovely butterflies are aflutter. Hard to miss is the metallic-blue Morpho butterfly; it's about the size of your hand. See chapter 18.

- **Bird Spotting in the Pantanal:** Even if you're not a birder, the Pantanal has hundreds of species to spot, some as big as your little brother, others as colorful as Carnaval. Plus hungry caiman and giant river otters, and sometimes even jaguar, all of it best viewed from horseback. See chapter 19.

- **Red Araras:** The sunset over the red-rock formations in the Chapada dos Guimarães, north of Cuiabá, is a magical experience in itself. Even more special is the view of scarlet macaws working the thermals off the sheer cliffs in the warm glow of the setting sun. See chapter 19.

5 THE BEST MUSEUMS

- **Museu do Oratorio** (Ouro Preto; ℭ **031/3551-5369;** www.oratorio. com.br): Behind Ouro Preto's main square stands the town's loveliest museum, which houses a colorful collection of oratories, which are in fact little mini-altars, used by people so they could pray without having to go to church. The Afro-Brazilian oratories are decorated with flowers and shells from the Candomblé religion. See p. 194.

- **Museu de Arte Sacra** (Mariana; © 031/ 3551-4736): One of the best collections of sacred art in Brazil can be found in the small town of Mariana, just outside of Ouro Preto. The vast collection of impressive gold and silver works is displayed in a gorgeous old colonial mansion. See p. 199.
- **Monument to Latin America** (São Paulo; © 011/3823-4600; www. memorial.org.br): Designed by famed Brazilian architect Oscar Niemeyer, the monument is, well, *so* Niemeyer—shy of a visit to Brasilia, it's the best place to see Brazilian modernism in all its concrete austerity. See p. 231.
- **Pinacoteca do Estado** (São Paulo; © 011/3324-1000): The Pinacoteca in São Paulo is the place to come for

anyone who wants to see Brazilian art. The museum has an excellent collection of Brazilian art from the 19th and 20th centuries, including works by Alfredo Ceschiatti, the artist who designed many of the sculptures in Brasilia. See p. 227.

- **Museu de Arte Sacra** (Salvador; © 071/3243-6310): One of the finest museums in Salvador, the Arte Sacra displays one of Brazil's best collections of Catholic art. The artifacts are shown in the monastery adjoining the Igreja de Santa Teresa, a simple, beautiful building that is itself a work of art. The collection includes oil paintings, *oratorios* (small cabinets containing a crucifix or saint image), and amazing silver work. See p. 269.

6 THE BEST FESTIVALS & CELEBRATIONS

Well, Carnaval—*that's* an obvious choice (and already covered under "The Most Unforgettable Travel Experiences," above). Here are some other favorites:

- *Reveillon*/**New Year's Celebration** (Rio de Janeiro): Close to two million people gather for one of the most spectacular New Year's celebrations in the world. It starts on the evening of December 31 and continues well into the morning of January 1. The main event takes place on Copacabana Beach—live music, fireworks, and the muted Candomblé religious ceremonies. For details contact **Riotur** (© 021/2217-7575; www.rio. rj.gov.br/riotur) or **Alô Rio** (© 021/ 2542-8080). See chapter 6.
- **Washing of the Steps of Bonfim Church** (Salvador): One of the most important religious ceremonies in Salvador takes place on the third Thursday of January when hundreds of women in traditional Bahian dress form a procession and carry perfumed water to wash the church steps; 800,000 onlookers

and revelers accompany them. For details contact **Bahiatursa** (© 071/ 3321-2463; www.bahiatursa.ba.gov. br). See chapter 11.

- **Celebration of Yemanjá, the Goddess of the Sea** (Salvador): On February 2, watch the devotees throughout Brazil offer flowers, perfumes, and jewelry to the sea. It's celebrated on the beach with music and food. The largest celebration takes place in Salvador on Praia Vermelha. For details contact **Bahiatursa** (© 071/3321-2463; www.bahiatursa. ba.gov.br). See chapter 11.
- **The Passion Play** (Nova Jerusalem, near Recife): South America's largest passion play takes place at Nova Jerusalem, just outside of Recife in the Northeast of Brazil. Performances are daily in the 10 days leading up to Easter. For details contact **Recife Tourist Information** (© 081/3462-4960 or 3341-6090). See p. 320.
- **Bumba-meu-boi** (São Luis): A party that gets the whole city involved, the

bumba-meu-boi is a fascinating folk festival centered around the story of a bull that gets killed and resurrected. The festivities take place over several months as there are several stages to each part of the story. Contact the **São Luis Tourist Office** for details on what happens when (℗ **081/3462-4960**). See chapter 15.

7 THE BEST HOTELS

- **Hotel Sofitel** (Rio de Janeiro; ℗ **0800/ 241-232** or 021/2525-1232): Considered Rio's best hotel, the Sofitel combines old-world elegance and style with one of the city's best locations, across from the Copacabana Fort and steps from Ipanema. See p. 77.

- **Portinari** (Rio de Janeiro; ℗ **021/ 3222-8800**): Designed by eight different Brazilian designers and architects, the hotel offers a wonderful showcase of Brazilian style and inventiveness; everything from the furniture to the lighting and accessories is unique. Best of all, this style doesn't get in the way of comfort. See p. 78.

- **Insólito Boutique Hotel** (Búzios; ℗ **022/2623-2172;** www.insolito hotel.com.br): This new luxury boutique hotel clings to the rocks overlooking Ferradura beach. With only 12 rooms set amid lush tropical gardens and spectacular terraces, guests practically have the place to themselves. See p. 106.

- **Unique** (São Paulo; ℗ **011/3055- 4700**): Extraordinary high-design rooms and suites feature the cleanest-of-clean white-on-white decor, luscious bedding, sparkling bathrooms with Jacuzzi tubs, a plethora of room gadgets, plus a rooftop view of the Avenida Paulista's power skyscrapers and lush green Ibirapuera park. See p. 216.

- **Convento do Carmo** (Salvador; ℗ **071/3327-8400;** www.pousadas.pt): A 17th-century convent in the very heart of a 17th-century city has been restored to 21st-century luxury. Unforgettable. See p. 254.

- **Tropical Manaus** (Manaus; ℗ **0800/ 701-2670** or 092/3659-5000): The Tropical Manaus is without a doubt *the* hotel in town. Set in its own piece of rainforest on the banks of the Rio Negro, the hotel is built in an elegant colonial style. Rooms are spacious, and the amenities are top-notch; archery lessons, a zoo, wakeboard lessons, a wave pool, salon, and more await you in the middle of the Amazon. See p. 381.

- **Bourbon Cataratas** (Foz do Iguaçu; ℗ **0800/451-010** or 045/3521-3900): Make sure you don't forget to see the falls! The Bourbon Hotel has plenty to keep you busy. Over 3km (2 miles) of trails through orchards and tree nurseries are the perfect place to watch for toucans, butterflies, and parrots. The pool deck has three large pools to soak up those rays or an indoor wave pool and spa for a dreary day. Active types can play a game of tennis, try the climbing wall, and play volleyball or soccer. See p. 436.

8 THE BEST POUSADAS

- **Pousada do Mondego** (Ouro Preto; ℗ **031/3551-2040**): Wake up to the unforgettable view of Ouro Preto's most famous church, São Francisco de Assis, just outside your window. Early in the morning the surrounding hills are often shrouded in mist. See p. 196.

- **Solar da Ponte** (Tiradentes; ☎ **032/ 3355-1255**): In the heart of Tiradentes, one the most charming colonial villages, Pousada Solar da Ponte is a real retreat. The spacious antiques-furnished rooms look out over the cobblestone streets. The lovely garden, library, and sitting rooms are perfect for a relaxing day. A yummy breakfast is served in the dining room overlooking the garden. See p. 202.

- **Pousada Santa Clara** (Boipeba; ☎ **075/3653-6085**): For a romantic getaway or just a few days of blissful relaxation, there's no place better than this lovely pousada, on the small island of Boipeba south of Morro de São Paulo. Each room is uniquely decorated, and many feature a veranda and large windows looking out over the lush tropical garden. The nearly deserted beach is only 5 minutes away, if you walk slowly. See p. 298.

- **Vila Kalango** (Jericoacoara; ☎ **088/ 3669-2290;** www.vilakalango.com.br): You couldn't ask for a more idyllic setting on the edge of the village, overlooking the ocean and the large dune, perfect for watching the sunset. The rustic round bungalows on stilts let in the cool sea breeze and are tastefully decorated with local artwork. See p. 358.

- **Tabapitanga** (Porto de Galinhas; ☎ **081/3552-1037**): The oceanfront rooms of Tabapitanga are so close to the beach that light sleepers may want to close their veranda doors to keep the sound of the waves out. All rooms feature bright and cheerful artwork, king-size beds, and a veranda with hammock and lazy chair. See p. 329.

- **Manary Praia Hotel** (Natal; ☎ **084/ 3204-2900**): On the beach of Ponta Negra in Natal, the Manary Praia offers luxurious and comfortable accommodations. The hacienda-style mansion is an excellent home base for exploring some of the best beaches in the Northeast. See p. 336.

- **Araras Eco Lodge** (Pantanal; ☎ **065/ 3682-2800**): This lodge is the best in the Pantanal for wildlife viewing and experiencing the lifestyle of the *pantaneiro* cowboy. Accommodations are rustic but the quality of guides, the amazing food, and the unparalleled wildlife are worth it. The owner has a history of environmental work in the region and runs an excellent program. See p. 448.

9 THE BEST DINING EXPERIENCES

- **Experiencing** *Feijoada,* **the National Dish:** It's impossible to single out one restaurant in all of Brazil for its *feijoada.* Just try it and try it right. Start with a caipirinha (that potent, delicious lime and sugar-cane drink) and some *caldo* (soup), followed by steaming hot black beans with all the various meats. Side dishes include *farofa,* cabbage, orange slices, and white rice. Dab some *malagueta* peppers on the beans for an extra kick.

- **Street Food:** Whether you want prawns, chicken, tapioca pancakes, coconut sweets, or corn on the cob, it can all be purchased on the street for next to nothing. Don't be afraid to try some of the best snacks that Brazil has to offer.

- **All Beef, All the Time:** *Rodízio* churrascarias are all-you-can-eat meat orgies. The best cuts of beef are served up one after another; try one or two, or try them all. As long as you can take it they dish it out. Our favorite is surely *picanha,* the lean, tender rump steak—it will melt in your mouth. One of the country's most popular restaurants is **Porcão,** a nationwide chain. Their flagship location is in Rio's Flamengo neighborhood (© 021/2554-8535; p. 88), with views of the bay and Sugarloaf Mountain.

- **Sophisticated Amazonian Cuisine:** Don't miss this all Amazonian 10-course gourmet meal fit for a king (and presidents) at Sofitel's **Le Pré Catelan** (© 021/2525-1160). French top chef Roland Villard has outdone himself with this unique feast of ingredients unknown to even most Brazilians. See p. 91.
- **Colonial Coffee in Rio:** For the most elegant coffee experience, visit **Confeitaria Colombo** (© 021/2221-0107). This 19th-century Belle Epoque establishment is one of the most beautiful salons in all of Brazil. See p. 84.
- **Fine Dining in São Paulo:** Brazil's biggest, richest city is where you'll find the best chefs and the most demanding customers. It is the place in Brazil for sophisticated fine dining. Two places you won't go wrong, for service, ambience, or food are **Figueira Rubaiyat** (© 011/3063-3888) and **D.O.M.** (© 011/3088-0761), both in the Jardins. D.O.M. offers ultra-high-end dining, with one of the best wine lists in

the hemisphere. Figueira offers excellent food, and one of the nicest dining rooms anywhere, beneath the limbs of a huge fig tree. See p. 221 and 220 respectively.
- **_Moquecas_ in Salvador:** You can't say you've been to Salvador without trying _moqueca_, the tasty stew of fresh seafood with coconut milk, lime juice, cilantro, and red dendê palm oil. Try **Jardim das Delicias** (© 071/3321-1449). See p. 260.
- **Fine Dining in Porto de Galinhas: Beijupirá** (© 081/3552-2354), in a small resort town in Brazil's Northeast, is perhaps one of the most pleasant little restaurants in the country. The decorations are whimsical and rustic, the food an inspired Brazilian cuisine that makes use of fresh seafood, tropical fruit, and spices. See p. 330.
- **The Regional Cuisine of Belém:** Located in the Tropics, on the Amazon River but at the mouth of the ocean, Belém has access to a richer assortment of ingredients than almost anywhere else in Brazil. Local chefs make the most of the variety. For regional cuisine, try **Lá em Casa** (© 091/3212-5588). See p. 409.

10 THE BEST MARKETS

- **Antiques Fair** (São Paulo): Every Sunday from 10am to 5pm there's an antiques fair in the open space beneath the **MASP** building on Avenida Paulista. Dealers are registered, and the quality of the wares is often good. See p. 230.
- **Japanese Market** (São Paulo): One of the largest Asian street markets takes place every Sunday on the **Praça da Liberdade** (next to the Liberdade Metrô stop) in São Paulo's Liberdade neighborhood. The city's Japanese residents celebrate their heritage with an excellent and inexpensive selection of Japanese cuisine and arts and crafts. See p. 236.

- **Mercado Modelo** (Salvador; © 071/3243-6543): Souvenir junkies will think they've died and gone to heaven. In the former Customs building, this market has around 300 merchants selling a large variety of souvenirs: leather goods, hammocks, instruments, masks, carvings, paintings, lace, terra-cotta figurines, and jewelry. See p. 270.
- **Mercado Adolpho Lisboa** (Manaus; © 092/3233-0469): This beautiful iron-and-glass market hall is a great place to see exotic Amazonian fish, fruit, and vegetables. A number of stalls have indigenous handicrafts at reasonable prices. See p. 385.

- **The Ver-o-Peso Market** (Belém): The Ver-o-Peso market is a vast waterside cornucopia of outrageously strange Amazon fish, hundreds of species of Amazon fruit found nowhere else, traditional medicine love potions, and just about anything else produced in the Amazon, all of it cheap, cheap, cheap. See p. 412.

11 THE BEST NIGHTLIFE

- **Arco do Teles** (Rio de Janeiro): Tucked away in an alley just off the Praça XV, the Arco de Teles reveals perfectly preserved colonial buildings set on narrow cobblestone streets, lined with restaurants and cafes. With over 15 bars and botequins it doesn't matter which one you pick; walk around and see what's doing. If you get there after 10pm you'll be lucky to find a seat at all. See p. 14.
- **Centro Cultural Carioca** (Rio de Janeiro; ℰ **021/2252-6468;** www.centroculturalcarioca.com.br): This beautifully restored building from the 1920s hosts local musicians and big names who specialize in samba, MPB, *choro,* and *gafieira.* The room is cozy and intimate, and guests sit at small tables to watch the shows. See p. 139.
- **Carioca da Gema** (Rio de Janeiro; ℰ **021/2221-0043**): One of the hottest nightspots in the samba-rich sector of Lapa, Carioca da Gema offers some of the finest *pagode* and samba. Just steps from the Lapa aqueduct, Carioca da Gema is one of the many small music venues in this funky bohemian neighborhood. The best night is Thursday. See p. 139.
- **Rua das Pedras** (Búzios): The hottest beach resort close to Rio, Búzios is the place to go if you're on a mission to party. Nightlife central is on the Rua das Pedras where the pubs, bars, discos, and restaurants stay open on weekends until 3 or 4am. Enjoy a delicious cocktail at the **Anexo Bar and Lounge,** or dance until the early hours at popular Ibiza nightclub **Pacha.** See p. 163.
- **Skye** (São Paulo; ℰ 011/3055-4702): One of the city's trendiest bars, Skye also comes with one of the best views in the city. On the Unique Hotel's top floor, the bar's large glass windows and pool deck offer spectacular skyline views of South America's largest city. See p. 224.
- **Rabo do Peixe** (São Paulo; ℰ 011/3842-8666): If there is such a thing as a typical Brazilian pub, this is it. On a street corner, the patio fans out on all sides, and tables are packed every day. A great spot to kick off your evening with a cold beer and the best *picanha* in town. See p. 247.
- **Pelourinho** (Salvador): Many nights of the week Pelourinho transforms itself into one big music venue. Two of the most popular venues are the Praça Quincas Berro D'Agua and the Largo Pedro Archanjo. At the Praça do Reggae, there's always reggae playing. See chapter 11.
- **The Reviver** (São Luis): Now that it's been brought back to life, the historic downtown of São Luis has a new name—Reviver. It's packed with bars and restaurants that center around the Rua da Estrela. One of prettiest is **Antigamente** (ℰ 098/3232-3964). Grab a table outside and enjoy the bustling atmosphere. See p. 364.

Brazil in Depth

Brazil is a unique combination, simultaneously old and young. "Old" in the sense that, though charted and colonized by Europeans at roughly the same time as North America, European civilization took root faster and flowered far earlier here. While Virginia Company adventurers starved to death on the James River and Massachusetts Bay colonists subsisted in rude huts clustered around a single narrow church, Brazilian cities like Salvador and Olinda thrived with paved streets, walls and houses of stone, and high cathedrals gilt with gold. "Young" because Brazil as a country did not achieve independence until 1822, and didn't throw off the monarchy and proclaim itself a republic until 1888. In today's Brazil, elements of old and new coexist in every aspect of society: architecture, technology, culture, festivals, food, business attitudes—all mix the most modern with the most tradition-bound.

1 BRAZIL TODAY

Brazil is a land of incredible diversity, a place where native hunters, Pantanal cowboys, priests of West African gods, and city slickers with roots in Italy, Syria, Portugal, and Japan all happily call themselves Brazilian. An extraordinary ability to enjoy life may be the one and only thing they have in common. Making that first million by age 30, scaling a mountaintop because it's there—these aren't the things that animate Brazilians. Friends, and especially family, are what matter, plus beer and a beach, bar, or soccer stadium in which to enjoy it all. Whether this general disinterest in things political is the result or the cause of Brazil's rather painful 20th-century history is a chicken-and-egg question. What is certain is that having experienced both the giddy expansion of the "economic miracle" of the 1960s and the debt, recession, and inflation crises

that followed, Brazil has now settled into something approaching normality. Inflation is manageable, crime is decreasing, and the army is safely back in the barracks where it belongs.

Challenges in the future include getting a grip on corruption (not the petty kind that bothers tourists, but the lose-a-billion-dollars-in-a-Swiss-bank-account kind that bothers taxpayers); coping with growth as Brazil's already huge cities continue to expand; and finding a way to balance environmental preservation—particularly in the Amazon—with the demand for economic development. If Brazilians have learned the hard way that they can't solve these problems at the drop of a hat, they can at least behave like the rest of the democratic world and somehow muddle through—having fun even as they muddle.

2 LOOKING BACK AT BRAZIL

IN THE BEGINNING

No one is quite sure when or how Brazil's first inhabitants arrived. The long-favored

theory—that Native Americans arrived about 10,000 years ago, most likely from Asia via a land bridge over the Bering

Sea—is now under serious attack. Some archaeologists claim canoe-based cultures might have paddled their way down the coasts; others suggest seafaring peoples could have made the journey from Africa. The date of first arrival now varies from 10,000 to as far back as 30,000 years ago.

However and whenever they first arrived, by the year A.D. 1500 between one and eight million aboriginals lived in Brazil, speaking nearly 170 different languages. Unlike in the Inca territory across the Andes, Brazil's indigenous civilization was largely tribal: small groups living in villages making a subsistence living from the local environment.

THE PORTUGUESE ARRIVE

In 1500, the first Europeans arrived: 13 ships under the command of **Pedro Alvares Cabral,** a Portuguese explorer sent to find a Western trade route to India. Cabral tarried only briefly on the coast, but the reports he sent back were encouraging enough for other captains to set out. In particular, what the Europeans were after was **pau-brasil,** a type of wood that could be processed to yield a rich red dye. Coastal Indians were induced to cut and sell timber in return for metal implements such as axes. It was an efficient system, so much so that within a little over a generation the trees—which by then had given their name to the country—were all but nonexistent.

What worried Portuguese **King João III,** however, was the number of French and Spanish ships taking part in the trade. In an attempt to establish Portuguese authority (while saving the cost of a formal colony) the king divided the Brazilian coast into 15 parcels or **"captaincies,"** each of which was given to a Portuguese noble as his hereditary property, on the understanding he'd show the flag, build up a colony at his own expense, and maybe generate some tax revenue for the royal treasury.

A few of the newly arriving captains managed to establish themselves by forging alliances with local Indian tribes. Mostly, however, the Portuguese arrivals generated hostility. Many of the new settlements were burned out and destroyed, the would-be settlers killed. Perhaps the captaincies only lasting effect was on the political map—the borders of many Brazilian states still reflect the boundaries laid down for those first 15 captaincies. Establishing viable colonies in Brazil, however, was going to require the sort of armed force only a king could provide.

In 1549 King João revoked the captaincies and sent out a force of 1,500 men—soldiers, priests, artisans, and administrators—under the command of Brazil's first governor-general, **Tomé de Sousa.** Landing at **Salvador** in what is now the state of **Bahia,** de Sousa's force was large enough to turn the tide. Warfare with Brazil's native inhabitants would continue for another 200 years or so, but for the most part the Portuguese would have the upper hand.

SUGAR CANE & SLAVERY

What made the expense worthwhile—in the eyes of the crown—was **sugar.** The cash crop of the 16th century, it grew well in the tropical climate of northeast Brazil. **Salvador,** the new capital, was soon surrounded by rapidly expanding plantations of sugar cane.

Turning that cane into sugar, however, was backbreaking work, and the Portuguese were critically devoid of labor. Short of enslavement (also frequently attempted), local Indians were uninterested in the repetitive drudgery of cutting cane. In any case, disease had ripped through indigenous peoples, sending their population on a downward spiral. (One that didn't end, in fact, until the 1960s, at which time Brazilian Indians numbered just a few hundred thousand.)

So the Portuguese began to import **slaves,** captured or bought in West Africa.

Brazil was soon one leg on a lucrative maritime trade triangle: guns and supplies from Portugal to Africa, slaves from Africa to Brazil, sugar from Brazil back to Europe. Within a few decades, colonial cities such as Salvador and **Olinda** were fabulously rich.

A DUTCH THREAT & THE RISE OF RIO

Other European powers took note. In 1624 a **Dutch expedition** conquered and briefly occupied the Brazilian capital of Salvador, leaving a year later after a combined Portuguese-Spanish fleet counterattacked. The next year the Dutch were back, burning Olinda to the ground, taking control of **Pernambuco** and establishing their own capital city of **Recife.** Under the leadership of **Maurits van Nassau,** Dutch Brazil was soon a thriving colony, exporting ever-larger quantities of sugar. When internal politicking forced Nassau out of the colony in 1644, however, Dutch fortunes began to wane. A rebellion of the local Portuguese planters, followed by renewed attacks from Portugal, finally forced the surrender of Dutch forces in 1654. Never again would another European power successfully challenge Portuguese control of the country.

Free of external threat, the settlers turned their attention inland. Small expeditions of Brazilian adventures—called *bandeirantes* because they often carried the royal flag—began exploring westward seeking gold, minerals, or other treasure. **Gold** and diamonds were soon uncovered in what would later be the state of **Minas Gerais,** followed by further gold strikes farther west in Mato Grosso. The resulting flood of miners and other settlers gave effective control of the interior to Portugal—a fact recognized by the **1750 Treaty of Madrid,** which gave the entire Amazon basin and those lands east of the Rio Prata to Brazil.

In addition to the miners, the other main beneficiary of the Minas gold rush was **Rio de Janeiro,** the major transshipment point for gold and supplies. In recognition of this, in 1762 the **colonial capital** was officially transferred to Rio.

Stunning as its physical setting was, Rio was hardly then the cidade maravilhosa it would become. Indeed, it would likely have remained little more than a backwater colonial capital had it not been for **Napoleon.** In 1807, having overrun most of western Europe, the little French emperor set his sights on Portugal. Faced with the imminent conquest of Lisbon, Portuguese **Prince Regent João** (later **King João VI**) fled to his ships, opting to relocate himself and his entire court to Brazil. And so it was that in March 1808 the king and 15,000 of his nobles, knights, and courtiers arrived in the rather raw town of Rio.

INDEPENDENCE ARRIVES

The changes wrought by the royal presence were enormous: palaces, parks, and gardens were built all over the city. A new administrative class was formed. Indeed, the denizens of Rio got so used to being at the center of things that the king's return to Portugal in 1821 created no small outrage. Used to being at the heart of the empire, Brazilians—among them the king's 23-year-old son Pedro—were outraged at the prospect of being returned to the status of mere colony. In January 1822 Pedro announced he was remaining in Brazil. Initially, he planned on ruling as prince regent, but as the year wore on it became clear that Lisbon was not interested in compromise, so on September 7, 1822, Pedro declared **Brazil independent,** and himself **Emperor Pedro I.**

His reign lasted only 9 years. In acceding to the throne Dom Pedro had agreed to rule as a constitutional monarch, but in practice sharing power with a parliament of meddling politicians went against his aristocratic nature. A costly war with

Argentina—which led to the creation of **Uruguay** in 1828—only lessened his popularity. Finally in April 1832, Dom Pedro was presented with an ultimatum demanding he appoint a reformist cabinet. He chose instead to **abdicate.** His 5-year-old son became Emperor Pedro II.

Brazil in this period was a deeply conservative country, with a few very wealthy plantation owners, a tiny professional class, and a great mass of slaves indentured into cultivating either sugar or Brazil's new cash crop, **coffee.** Though the antislavery movement was growing powerful across the globe, Brazil's conservative landowning class was determined to hold on to slavery at all costs.

Taking power in 1840 at the tender age of 14, **Dom Pedro II** found himself in a political bind. Though he personally favored abolishing slavery, the conservative slave owners were also the chief supporters of the monarchy. The liberal abolitionists in the parliament were republicans to a man. Faced with this intractable situation, Dom Pedro opted to ally himself with the conservatives. He would move forward on the slavery issue, but at a glacial pace.

In the 1850s, under heavy pressure from Britain, Brazil finally moved to halt the **importation** of slaves from Africa. Slavery was still legal within the country, but its days were clearly numbered. Seeking a new source of labor, in 1857 Brazil opened itself up to **immigration.** Thousands poured in, mostly **Germans** and **Italians,** settling themselves in the hilly, temperate lands in the south of Brazil. Not only did they provide alternate labor on coffee plantations, but these newcomers also established their own small farms and vineyards, or else moved into Brazil's growing cities, giving the southern part of Brazil a very European flavor.

Through the 1860s and 1870s, the government showed little interest in confronting the slavery issue. A law passed in 1871 envisioned the legal end of slavery—but not until 1896. Another passed in 1885 promised to free only those slaves over the age of 65. As immigration continued, the plantation class became an increasingly tiny fraction of the populace, albeit one that maintained a stranglehold on Brazilian politics. Dom Pedro himself seemed to have lost interest in governing, spending much of his time on extended trips abroad. Finally in 1888, his daughter, the **Princess Regent Isabel,** passed the **Lei Aurea,** which set Brazil's slaves free. There were celebrations in the streets, but by this time the monarchy was so thoroughly associated with the plantation owners, it had little popular support. When reformist army officers and other liberals staged a coup in 1889, Pedro II's 57-year rule came to an end.

The republic that took its place had many of the same ills of the old regime. In a country with an increasingly large working class, the government remained in the hands of the coffee-growing elite. Corruption was endemic, rebellions a regular occurrence. Finally, in 1930, reformist army officers staged a **bloody coup.** After several days' fighting, a military-backed regime took charge, putting an **end to the Old Republic** and ushering in the 15-year reign of the fascinating, maddening figure of **Getulio Vargas.**

THE AGE OF VARGAS & A NEW CAPITAL IS BORN

A pol to his fingertips, Vargas managed to ride each new political wave as it swept in. He began his time in office as a **populist,** legalizing unions and investing in hundreds of projects designed to foster Brazil's industrial development. When the workers nevertheless looked set to reject him in renewed elections (and in the aftermath of a failed Communist revolt), Vargas tore up the constitution and instituted a **quasi-fascist dictatorship,** complete with a **propaganda ministry** that celebrated every action of the glorious leader Getulio. In the early 1940s when the **United States** made it clear Brazil had better cease its flirtation with Germany, Vargas dumped his fascist posturing, **declared war on the Axis powers,** and sent 20,000 Brazilian troops to take part in the **invasion of Italy.** When the troops came home at war's end, the contradiction between the fight for freedom abroad and the dictatorship at home proved too much even for Vargas's political skills. In 1945 in a very **quiet coup,** the army removed Getulio from power.

In 1950 **Vargas returned,** this time as the democratically elected president. His reign was a disaster. By 1954 there were riots in the streets, the army was on the verge of mutiny, and even his own vice president was calling for his resignation. Vargas, instead, retired to his office in the Catete Palace in Rio, and on the night of August 4, 1954, put a bullet through his heart.

In 1956, **Juscelino Kubitschek** (known as JK) took office, largely on the strength of a single bold promise: Within 4 years, he would **transfer the capital** from Rio de Janeiro to an entirely new city located somewhere in Brazil's vast interior. Few thought he could do it.

The site chosen in Brazil's high interior plateau—the *sertão*—was hundreds of miles from the nearest paved road, not to mention the nearest airport. Undaunted, JK assembled a team of Brazil's top **modernist architects**—among the best in the world at the time—and an astounding 4 years later, the new capital of **Brasilia** was complete.

DICTATORSHIP & AGAIN, DEMOCRACY

Democracy, unfortunately, did not fare well in the arid soil of the *sertão*. In 1964, the army took power in a coup, ushering in an ever more repressive **military dictatorship** that would last for another 20 years.

For a time, no one much complained. Thanks to massive government investment, the economy boomed. São Paulo, which had been little more than a market town in the 1920s, exploded in size and population, surpassing Rio to become the heart of Brazil's new manufacturing economy. These were the days of the Brazilian **"economic miracle."**

On the soccer field Brazil ruled. True, in the **1950 World Cup**—held in the specially built **Maracaná** stadium in Rio—Brazil lost in a 2-to-1 final to underdog Uruguay. (The shame of that defeat haunts Brazil to this day.) Brazil came back strong, however, taking the World Cup championships in 1958, 1962, and 1970, making Brazil the first **three-time champion** in World Cup history. (They won a fourth championship in 1994 and a fifth in 2002.)

In the early '70s, however, it became clear that much of the economic "miracle" had been financed on easy international loans, much of that invested in **dubious development projects** (roads that disappeared back into the forest, nuclear power plants that never functioned) or channeled directly into the pockets of various well-connected generals. The international banks now wanted their money back, with interest. As **discontent** with the regime spread, the military reacted with ever-stronger **repression.**

The 1980s were perhaps Brazil's worst decade. **Inflation** ran rampant, while growth was next to nonexistent. Austerity measures imposed by the International Monetary Fund left governments with little money for basic infrastructure—much less social services—and in big cities such as Rio and São Paulo, favelas (shantytowns) spread while crime spiraled out of control.

In the midst of this mess, the army began a **transition to democracy.** In **1988,** in the first direct presidential election in over 2 decades, Brazilians elected a good-looking millionaire named **Fernando Collor de Mello.** It proved to be a bad move. Not only did Collor seize the bank savings of private citizens via government fiat, he was also soon found lining his own pockets with government cash. The civilian government did prove capable of legally forcing him from office, however, paving the way in 1992 for the election of **Fernando Henrique Cardoso.**

Though an academic Marxist for much of his career, once in office FHC proved to be a cautious centrist. In his 8 years in office he managed to reign in **inflation,** bring some **stability** to the Brazilian currency, and begin a modest extension of social services to Brazil's many poor.

The main opposition throughout this period was the **Workers Party (PT),** lead by **Luiz Inácio Lula da Silva,** a charismatic trade unionist with a personal rags-to-riches story. Born into poverty in the Northeast, **Lula,** as he is usually known, left school to work as a shoeshine boy, got a job in a São Paulo factory, joined the metalworkers' union, and began to get involved in politics. During the waning days of Brazil's dictatorship he and others formed the Workers Party, and only just lost Brazil's first democratic election in 1988, thanks in large part to some blatant scare-mongering by the Globo print and television conglomerate. Lula persevered, however, contesting the following two elections against FHC, while refining and moderating policies to bring them into a form more acceptable to the Brazilian electorate. Finally in 2002, in his fourth attempt, Lula was elected Brazilian president, the first democratically elected leftist ever to hold power in Brazil.

Hopes for Lula's first term in office were enormous. Confounding expectations of financial markets and right-wing critics, Lula in office proved to be an economic moderate, continuing the tight-money policy of his predecessor. But to the disappointment of his supporters on the left,

Lula also proved to be a poor and often absent administrator. Many of the hoped-for reforms—from the distribution of land, to access to education and healthcare, to environmental policy—were never enacted. Worse, his government, which had pledged to clean up Brazilian politics, has been plagued by corruption scandals as bad as or worse than any of his predecessors.

On the positive side, Lula's government broadened Brazil's welfare system, extending a guaranteed basic income to the poorest families for the first time. Lula's government also eased credit terms on housing and durable consumer goods, sparking a consumer boom, particularly in the lower middle class. These measures, combined with gradually diminishing unemployment and steady but not spectacular growth, were enough, in 2006, to win Lula reelection to a second 4-year term in office.

In the cities, things have certainly improved since the 1980s. The **1992 Environment Conference** in Rio was a watershed for Brazil. Politicians woke up to the fact that the country was developing a reputation for crime and lawlessness. Governments, having paid off the worst of the '80s debts, now had funds available, which they proceeded to spend on increased policing, better street lighting, and on extending services such as sewers, water, and schooling to urban slum dwellers. In the shantytowns of Rio and São Paulo, gangs remain stubbornly entrenched, but the major cities of Brazil are nonetheless cleaner and safer than they've been in a generation. Though they're a few years yet from matching the new improved Manhattan for safety, Brazil's cities are far and away superior when it comes to sheer *joie de vivre.*

Brazil's steady growth, responsible public finances, and vast potential lead the gnomes of international finance to christen the country as one of the breakthrough nations of the 21st century, lumping Brazil together with Russia, India, and China to form the **BRIC** nations.

Brazil's own growing confidence in its future has lead it to reach out to the rest of the world, ramping up a campaign for a UN Security Council seat, at the same time bidding to host a variety of international sporting events. The first of these, the Pan American Games, was held in Rio in 2007. That proved to be just an audition. As a follow-up, Brazil bid successfully to host first the Soccer World Cup in 2014. Then in 2009, Rio de Janeiro was selected to host the 2016 Olympic Summer Games.

3 CULTURAL NOTES & BUSINESS ETIQUETTE

Be prepared for lots of skin-on-skin contact! Brazilians will often greet with a kiss or a hug, and both men and women will frequently touch you when speaking, either patting your shoulder or placing their hand on your hand or arm to make a point. In crowds, Brazilians maintain much less physical distance than North Americans normally find comfortable.

GREETINGS Shaking hands has become a more acceptable way of greeting someone, but don't be surprised if you are kissed on the cheek once (in São Paulo) or twice (in Rio and elsewhere), even when greeting someone to whom you have just been introduced. Men do not kiss each other, but greet with an open hug, using one hand to shake hands and the other to grab the man by the shoulder. These greetings are not only used between good friends and family members but are also quite common between business acquaintances.

DRESS Brazilians, and particularly Brazilian women, have a reputation for colorful and sexy outfits. This certainly holds true in Rio, but in the south and the interior, people are more conservative. Novelist Jorge Amado has some fun with this, describing the arrival of a flamboyant Carioca woman in a small Bahian town: *"The female creature, outfitted in totally exotic style, a kind of blue overalls with zippers and pockets and in the legs and arms, studded with flashy metallic grommets and nailheads, raised her helmet and revealed herself to be quite a dish. She drew off her gloves and with long fingers fluffed up auburn hair with a platinum streak in the middle, showing that she was either a Venusian or from Rio de Janeiro, and very exciting either way."*

In business settings—even in Rio— men are expected to wear full suits, even when the thermometer hits 43°C (110°F). Women will wear smart business suits (either a skirt or pants is acceptable). The only other dress code applies to churches and government buildings (loosely adhered to in most parts but enforced with un-Brazilian ferocity in Brasilia): No shorts, tank tops, flip-flops, or miniskirts allowed. Anywhere else, smart-casual attire is more than enough; even shorts and a tank top are enough to gain access to most shops and restaurants.

GETTING THINGS DONE As informal and casual as Brazilians are in social settings, they can be strangely formal in a business situation: Titles matter and hierarchy is followed strictly. Often people in lower positions will be reluctant to make decisions on sometimes (in our eyes) minor issues. (One front-desk clerk refused to provide the hotel's website— this was the marketing manager's responsibility.) Getting around such obstacles (Brazilians are famous for inventing seemingly pointless rules and procedures) involves a *jeitinho* (literally "finding a way"), a very Brazilian term used to describe the way one can get around a rule without really breaking it. Finding the appropriate *jeitinho* often requires creative problem solving; the best idea is usually to keep talking, keep suggesting things. Whatever you do, *don't* get angry. Brazilians avoid conflict and rarely raise their voices or show anger in public. This passive behavior can be frustrating in business situations, as Brazilians will rarely ever criticize or disagree with anyone.

Also note that unlike in much of Europe and North America, it can be nearly impossible to arrange anything over the phone. Most people do not have voice mail, and phone calls are often not returned. E-mail is becoming more common, but only as a follow-up. A personal visit is really the only effective way to get things done. Persistence usually pays off, and having a business card to introduce yourself or to leave behind can be helpful. Indeed, even when traveling to Brazil as a tourist, having some business cards with you can make a difference if you are trying to reach a hotel manager or an airline supervisor to solve a problem.

4 THE LAY OF THE LAND

Though continental in dimensions, Brazil has some six predominant ecosystems, each with representative flora and fauna. On the coast, from the north of Bahia south to Rio de Janeiro and São Paulo, it's Mata Atlantica, or Atlantic rainforest, said by scientists to be nearly as rich in biodiversity as the Amazon, but now sadly degraded by the heavy settlement and farming along Brazil's Atlantic coast. Only about 4% of the original Atlantic rainforest cover remains, with large intact stands in the south of Bahia and on islands such as Ilha Grande and Ilha Bela. The golden lion tamarin—a beautiful squirrel-size primate-is the signature species of Brazil's Atlantic ecosystem, now much endangered. Common tamarins can often be seen in trees and parks in Rio. The coast is also the only place you'll find truly significant mountains.

Inland, Brazil rises to a high plateau of from 1,000m to 1,500m (3,280–4,920 ft.) in altitude that rolls all the way to the western foothills of the Andes. In the southern parts of Brazil (Paraná, Santa Catarina, Rio Grande do Sul), this plateau was covered in subtropical rainforest, most of which has long since been converted to cropland.

In the center and center west where things are drier (Goiania, Brasilia, Mato Grosso do Sul, Mato Grosso, Tocantins), you'll find cerrado, dry scrubland forest reminiscent of California chaparral, dotted with beautiful branching Ipe trees-known for bright yellow or purple flowers. Farther west still, on the Paraguay river basin that forms the border with Bolivia, stands the Pantanal. This world's biggest wetland (about the size of Florida) is actually a seasonal flood plain that fills and then slowly drains in response to seasonal rains. It is home to a rich assortment of birdlife-jabiru storks, American woodstorks, red and hyacinth macaws-plus capybara, giant otters, anteaters, and caiman. In the north, the semidesert inland from the coast is known as sertão. This is cowboy country, with cattle, bandits (historically), cactus, and not much else.

In the north, covering about a third of the country (Amazonas, Acre, Mato Grosso, Para, Roraima), stands the Amazon rainforest, the richest assortment of plants and animals on earth. Deforestation rates have been reduced in recent years, though a chunk the size of Connecticut still falls to the chainsaw every year.

For more information on the country's regions, see "The Regions in Brief," in chapter 4.

5 BRAZILIAN CULTURE & RELIGION

CULTURAL MAKEUP

Modern Brazil's diverse population is a melting pot of three main ethnic groups: the indigenous inhabitants of Brazil, the white settlers from Portugal and other European countries, and the black slaves from Africa. Within Brazil the blending of various cultures and ethnic groups varies from region to region. Rio de Janeiro has a large population of **mulattos.** A mix of whites and blacks, people of this heritage are considered to have the "typically Brazilian" look—light brown skin, black hair, and brown, hazel, or green eyes. In Salvador, more than any other area of Brazil, the people are mostly of **African descent.** Many of the freed slaves settled in this area, and the African influence is reflected in the food, religion, and music. In the Amazon, the cities are populated by migrants from other parts of Brazil, while the forest is predominantly populated by *caboclos* (a mixture of white and Indian ethnicities) and indigenous tribes, many of whom still maintain their traditional culture, dress, and lifestyle. The south of Brazil was settled mostly by white **European immigrants,** with a few notable exceptions such as the large **Japanese** and **Middle Eastern** communities of São Paulo. Migration within Brazil has also had an influence on the cultural makeup of certain cities. Both Brasilia and São Paulo have had a large influx of workers from the poorer Northeastern regions. These so-called **Nordestinos** introduced their music (*forró*) and traditional foods to these cities.

RELIGION

Brazil is still officially the world's largest **Catholic** country, but the Church no longer influences day-to-day affairs the way it once did; even as late as the 1970s divorce remained illegal in Brazil. Catholicism remains a very strong cultural influence—Brazilian speech is peppered with phrases like *Graças a Deus* and exclamations such as *Nossa!* (short for Nossa Senhora, a reference to Mary)—and most Brazilians still take their children to be baptized, but fewer and fewer are making it to Mass on Sunday.

In recent years, evangelical Protestant churches have been making great strides in Brazil, particularly among poorer members of society. There are dozens of sects, many of which make use of sophisticated marketing and media techniques; some have their own radio and TV stations. Non–church members will often tell you these *evangélicas* are little more than moneymaking schemes; there have indeed been a number of well-reported financial scandals involving evangelical churches, but that hasn't dimmed their appeal. Perhaps the largest—the Igreja Universal de Reina de Deus—has dozens of churches in almost every sizable Brazilian city.

The other religion of note is **Candomblé.** Though uniquely Brazilian, its origins lie in West African religions brought to Brazil by imported slaves. Followers of Candomblé believe in a pantheon of spirits, or Orixás, who will if approached properly bring supplicants luck, or fortune or love. Each individual has a particular Orixá. Determining which one you belong to requires going to a Candomblé priest or priestess. The religion is particularly strong in Salvador and Rio, but the exact number of Candomblé followers is impossible to determine. The religion was officially forbidden until recently, and Candomblé followers remain reluctant to profess their beliefs openly.

6 BRAZIL IN POPULAR CULTURE: MUSIC, BOOKS & FILM

MUSIC

Ever since **Vinicius de Moraes** and **Tom Jobim** penned the bossa nova hit "The Girl from Ipanema," Brazil has been a player on the international music scene. The outside world, however, seems only able to absorb one Brazilian musical style at a time. Bossa nova and samba were hot in the '50s and '60s; Tropicalismo—spearheaded by Brazil's megastars **Caetano Veloso** and **Gilberto Gil**—was popular in the '70s. This movement paved the way for some of Brazil's most loved MPB (*musica popular brasileira*) stars to break through on the international stage: **Gal Costa, Milton Nascimento, Djavan, Maria Bethania.** Others such as **Jorge Ben, João Bosco, Chico Buarque,** and **Elis Regina** were huge in Brazil but never quite made the crossover. One style that did make it out of Brazil (and maybe shouldn't have) to briefly dominate the dance floors of the late '80s was the Lambada. In the '90s, a crop of new artists such as **Marisa Monte, Daniela Mercury,** and **Olodum** managed to get airtime outside of Brazil, while the "golden oldies" such as Caetano Veloso, Gilberto Gil, and Milton Nascimento continue to tour the global stages. In the past 10 years, samba has also made a strong comeback, with dozens of clubs opening up in Rio and São Paulo, and *pagode* (a type of samba) bands like **Revelação** selling double-platinum albums and touring to packed houses.

But if the outside world sees only a few artists at a time, inside Brazil the music scene is a whirlwind of activity with trends coming and going all the time. In the '80s, Brazil had its own share of local pop bands that were enormously popular, selling millions of albums. Among those who survived that decade and matured into excellent performers are **Legião Urbana, Os Titás,** and **Lulu Santos.** Another Brazilian icon is **Cazuza.** Originally the lead singer of the immensely popular **Barão Vermelho,** Cazuza had a successful solo career before dying of AIDS at a young age in 1990; he left a legacy of beautifully crafted songs and an increased AIDS awareness among the general public.

(Moments) Finding Forró

Wandering one night in the old Pelourinho section of Salvador, we came across the faint sound of an accordion. At first, we couldn't make out where it was coming from; our ears seemed to lead us into the lobby of an office building, but once out the back exit we found a passage that lead to a courtyard where an accordion player was squeezing out a light and almost indecently happy brand of *forró*. The beat was fast, and the dance floor was packed. There were teenagers, awkwardly trying to figure out how to move with a partner in their arms, as well as older, more confident dancers. But what really caught our eye was this couple in their '60s or '70s. They skipped across the dance floor like they owned it, dancing each new tune as if it was their special song. Likely, they'd been dancing together that way for 50 years.

(Fun Facts) Who is Brazil's Best-Selling Recording Artist?

Answer: Roberto Carlos. Alas. With all the great music is Brazil, it's just a little disappointing to discover that the country's most popular singer is this curly-headed crooner—the Brazilian answer to Paul Anka. However, you do have to respect the work that's gone into his success. Carlos started his singing career as a 9-year-old, becoming Brazil's first teen pop idol just a few years later. And for the ensuing half-century, Carlos produced an average of one original album every year, selling over 70 million copies in all. Now over 60, Carlos recently reached out to a younger audience, producing an all-acoustic recording with MTV.

Then there are the regional trends that almost never make it to the rest of the world, among them the uniquely Brazilian country sound known as **Sertanejo.** In smaller towns and rural communities, this style—which like its American counterpart is big on broken hearts and horses—is incredibly popular. Artists such as **Chitãozinho e Xororó** have sold over 30 million albums. In Bahia, beginning in the '90s and continuing until today there's been a huge revival of reggae and Afrorhythms. The Bahian group **Olodum** performs original tunes and old Bob Marley classics using massed percussion (15–30 people wielding six–seven kinds of drum). Also from Bahia but lighter and more pop-y is **axé,** a mélange of African, Caribbean, and Brazilian infused pop.

Likely the most unlooked-for trend is the mania for **forró** that has recently swept the country. A happy, upbeat, accordion-infused brand of country, *forró* began in Brazil's poorer northeastern regions, and came to the big cities as poor Nordestino migrants made their way south (in Portuguese it is often referred to as *musica nordestina*). Originally looked down upon by southern Brazilians, *forró* was confined to Nordestino dance halls where crowds of transplanted peasants would dance the night away doing a simple two-step. There was something about this infectious rhythm that would not be denied, however (for one thing it's incredibly dance-

able, and Brazilians love to dance), and *forró* grew and grew to the point where it has now taken over many of Rio and São Paulo's most sophisticated nightclubs. The grandfather of all *forró* is **Luiz Gonzaga,** a man who was never seen without his accordion.

And then there's **brega,** a kind of glam version of *forró,* with over-the-top costumes and shamelessly sentimental lyrics—the very word *brega* in Portuguese means "tacky," and *brega* is. It's also infectiously fun and danceable. Hailing from Belém and the northern Amazon, where Brazil edges close to the Caribbean, *brega* combines *forró* with a kind of reggaeton beat and the salsa band fixation with the horn section. The biggest Brazilian *brega* bands are **Calypso** and **Calcinha Preta.**

In the first decade of the millennium, the new music phenomenon has been **Funk,** a mix of funk and rap and hip-hop with a driving (and monotonous!) dance beat. Funk originated in the favelas and the other poor neighborhoods but has slowly made its way down from the hills and begun infiltrating the rest of the city. Performers, mostly male, surround themselves with scantily clad women who bump and grind to misogynist and sexually explicit lyrics. Usually performers play at large dance events called *bailes funk,* held in large warehouses or empty lots. Cities have tried to prohibit some of these events but, not surprisingly, the resulting controversy has only made both the events and the performers more popular, particularly among teenagers.

BOOKS

Fiction

Brazilians aren't great book lovers. Their great popular figures are singers, not writers. The most popular narrative form is not the novel but the *novela,* the nightly prime-time television soap opera. Despite this unpromising soil, Brazil has still managed to produce a substantial crop of important writers. Most popular among them is the Bahian novelist **Jorge Amado** who, until he passed away in 2001, was considered a serious candidate for the Nobel Prize. His greatest novels came in the 1950s after he set aside leftist polemics and got back to what he knew best, the colorful characters of his beloved Bahia. His best known works include *Dona Flor and Her Two Husbands, Tieta* (the story of a successful whore returning to the conservative town of her birth), and *Gabriela, Clove and Cinnamon* (the title works better in Portuguese: *Gabriela, cravo e canela*). In a previous generation, **Joaquim Maria Machado de Assis** wrote closely observed and fiercely ironic novels and short stories, many set in Rio toward the end of the 19th century. In recent years there's been renewed critical interest in Machado de Assis, including a new translation of his work by the renowned American literary translator Gregory Rabasa. Look for Rabasa's version of *Posthumous Memoirs of Bras Cubas* and *Quincas Borba.* Also available in English is the short-story collection *The Devil's Church and Other Stories.* Brazil's greatest social realist is **Graciliano Ramos.** His masterpiece *Barren Lives* is considered to be one of Brazil's finest novels. From the postwar generation, **Clarice Lispector** is another Brazilian author to be gaining renewed respect in the English-speaking world, including a new 2009 biography, *Why This World: A Biography of Clarice Lispector,* by Benjamin Moser. Lispector's most ambitious novel, *The Apple in the Dark,* has been translated into English by Gregory Rabasa. The success of the film *Cidade de Deus (City of God)* has spawned a whole subgenre of favela literature. Look for the original novel *City of God* by **Paulo Lins.**

Further Reading

There is no single good general history covering Brazil from 1500 to the present. *Colonial Brazil,* by Leslie Bethel, is a scholarly but readable account of Brazil under the Portuguese, while Peter Flynn's *Brazil: a Political Analysis* covers political history from the birth of the first republic to the close of the second dictatorship.

For a fascinating introduction to a whole range of topics in Brazil, pick up the truly excellent anthology *Travellers' Tales: Brazil.* Less varied but equally interesting is *Tristes Tropiques,* by the great French anthropologist Claude Lévi-Strauss. Levi-Strauss got his start teaching at the university of São Paulo in the '30s. His

---

ⓘ Tips Brazil Unplugged

MTV in Brazil has lately recorded a number of acoustic sessions with some of Brazil's best artists, and the results have been phenomenal. Many of Brazil's major artists or bands have gone into the studio to record an unplugged version of their biggest hits; check out those by **Marcelo D2, Kid Abelha, Capital Inicial, Cassia Eller, O Rappa, Jorge Ben Jor, Zeca Pagodinha,** or any other one you can lay your hands on.

description of that town before the monster boom of the '40s and '50s is fascinating. Even better, Levi-Strauss exhibits a wry sense of humor, the rarest of qualities for a French academic. Those who would like to learn more about Brazil's fascinating and convoluted race relations may want to pick up a copy of *The Masters and the Slaves (Casa Grande e Senzala),* by Gilberto Freyre. Even though it was written almost 80 years ago, it's still one of the more comprehensive efforts to explain Brazilian society.

FILM

Brazil has a long and impressive history of filmmaking, including a number of films by directors who have moved back and forth between Brazil and Hollywood. **Hector Babenco** is best known in Brazil for *Carandiru* (2003), his excellent film about life in a São Paulo maximum security prison. North American audiences are more likely to have seen his work in *At Play in the Fields of the Lord* or *Kiss of the Spider Woman* (1985). Hector Babenco directed the hard-hitting political thriller *Four Days in September* (1997) about the kidnapping of the U.S.

ambassador to Brazil in the 1970s, then followed it up with the fun and fluffy *Bossa Nova* (2000), a romantic comedy filmed in English and set in Rio, starring Amy Irving (Bebenco's wife) and many of the stars of Brazil's *novela* soap operas. Babenco's latest film is *Last Stop 174* (2008), a true story about the hijacking of a city bus in downtown Rio de Janeiro. Many of these films don't make it to North American screens. One that did was *Central Station* (1998), which was nominated for best foreign film Oscar in 1998.

Five years later, the extraordinary *City of God* (2003) exploded across screens in North America and around the world, with its powerful story of a young man growing up in one of Rio's ultraviolent favelas. Director **Fernando Meirelles** followed up that film with *The Constant Gardener* (2005) and *Blindness* (2008). The granddaddy of Brazilian crossover hits has to be *Black Orpheus,* a 1959 retelling of the myth of Orpheus and Euridice, set in a poor neighborhood in Rio during the glorious nights of Carnaval. (Worth it for the music alone; most songs were composed by Antonio Carlos Jobim.)

7 EATING & DRINKING IN BRAZIL

THE CUISINE

Brazilian cuisine comes in many regional varieties but the one truly national dish is *feijoada,* a black-bean stew that originated with African slaves who used leftovers to make a tasty meal. Traditionally served on Saturdays, the beans are spiced with garlic, onions, and bay leaves and left to stew for hours with a hodgepodge of meats that may include sausage, beef, dried meat, and obscure bits of pork. Accompanied with rice, *farofa* (manioc flour), slices of orange, and stir-fried cabbage, it's a meal by itself.

Brazil's most distinguished regional cuisine is found in coastal Bahia, a region with very strong African influences. (Most Brazilian slaves arrived first in Bahia, and after slavery was abolished many of them settled in that area.) **Bahian cuisine** mixes African spices with the fresh and bountiful local ingredients. Bahia's most famous dish is the *moqueca,* a rich stew made with fresh fish or seafood, coconut milk, lime juice, cilantro, spicy *malagueta* peppers, and flavored with the oil from a dendê palm, which gives this dish its characteristic red color.

(Moments) **You Say Farofa, I Say . . . Blech**

Shawn says: I never got *farofa*. What I mean is, I got it with *every* meal. Really, what is the point? *Farofa* (flour taken from ground manioc root, then baked with oil) has the dry, crumbly consistency of sawdust—and not coincidentally, that's what it tastes like. Brazilians painstakingly disguise the flavor, sometimes with raisins and dried fruit, but the end result tastes like . . . sawdust with raisins or dried fruit. Eating it made sense in the days when Brazilians lived in peasant huts; *farofa* was the sole source of carbohydrates. Like potatoes for the Irish, *farofa* kept them going. But Brazilian cooking now incorporates lots of carbs—like rice. Potatoes. French fries. Sometimes all three at once. But no matter how many starches are piled on your plate, *farofa* will be there to top it off.

Alexandra says: *Farofa*—what's not to like? The coarsely roasted flour of the manioc root is the perfect companion to a Brazilian meal. Served plain, *farofa*'s nutty flavor stands up, while allowing it to soak up the juices on your plate only enhances its flavor. Every Brazilian has his or her favorite *farofa* recipe. My mother makes the best sweet *farofa* with bananas and raisins; it tastes as delightful as some of the best stuffings I've had. Other cooks prefer a savory version, adding spicy chorizo sausage, olives, or bacon. A *feijoada* is just not the same without *farofa*. Next time skip those greasy french fries and add some *farofa* to your plate. *Bon appétit!*

In the **Amazon,** whatever food does not come from the forest or the river has to be shipped in and is therefore very expensive. Fortunately the region is blessed with a large variety of fish. Cast aside any preconceived notions you may have about freshwater fish. The Amazon fish are delicious—firm white meat that tastes best just plainly grilled with salt and herbs. Local names for the best fish vary from one part of the Amazon to the next, but look for *surubim, pacu, dourado,* and *pirarucu.* The forest also yields a large variety of fruit that are often unknown outside of the Amazon. The best way to try them is just to order something off the juice menu; point if you can't wrap your tongue around Indian names such as *cupuaçu, açai,* or *jabuticaba.*

In the **South** and **Southwest** of Brazil (the Pantanal, Iguaçu, and the south of Brazil) the cuisine is more European, and as the largest beef-producing region in Brazil, meat is always on the menu. *Churrascarias,* or Brazilian steakhouses, are everywhere; indeed it's sometimes hard to find anything else to eat. Often churrascarias operate on a *rodízio* system—all-you-can-eat meat BBQ. Endless waiters scurry from grill to tables bearing giant skewers of beautifully roasted beef or chicken or pork or sausage, from which they then slice off a succulent few slices onto your plate. The parade of meat continues until you throw up your hands and cry enough. If carnivorous overconsumption doesn't appeal, there are other places to get yourself a fine cut of beef. Neighborhood bars *(botequins)* and even street vendors also offer barbecued beef, often served with a side of vinaigrette sauce, rice, and *farofa.*

Also very popular in Brazil is the simple hearty fare from **Minas Gerais,** a state settled largely by European immigrants. Favorite dishes include *Tutu mineiro,* Brazil's version of refried beans, served with grilled pork sausage, pork tenderloin, crispy bacon bits, *couve mineiro* (green cabbage), and a boiled egg. Other dishes include a variety of stews made with chicken or beef, potatoes, carrots, and sometimes pumpkin.

In **Rio** and **São Paulo,** the restaurant scene is very cosmopolitan: excellent Japanese restaurants, fabulous Italian, traditional Portuguese, and Spanish food as well as popular restaurants that serve Brazilian food—rice, black beans, *farofa,* and steak.

DINING OUT

Brazilians love to eat out. There is no shortage of eateries, from beach vendors selling grilled cheese and sweets, to lunch-bars serving pastries and cold beers, to fine French cuisine complete with the elegance and pretensions of Paris. Most Brazilians eat a very small breakfast at home—usually café au lait and some bread—then go out for lunch. Traditionally, these lunches are full hot meals, but these days you can also find North American–style sandwiches and salads as a lighter alternative. Dinner is eaten late, especially when dining out. Most restaurants don't get busy until 9 or 10pm and will often serve dinner until 1 or 2am. The trick to lasting that long without fainting is to have a *lanche* or light meal—often a fruit juice and a pastry—around 5 or 6 pm.

In Brazil, portions often serve two people, especially in more casual restaurants. Always ask or you may well end up with an extraordinary amount of food. In Portuguese ask, *"Serve para dois?"* (pronounced *Sir*-vay p'ra doysh—"Does it serve two?").

The standard Brazilian menu comes close to what some restaurants label as international cuisine: pasta, seafood, beef,

and chicken. Except in Brazil, these are served with a local or regional twist. The pasta may be stuffed with catupiry cheese and *abôbora* (a kind of pumpkin); the chicken could have *maracujá* (passion-fruit) sauce. Brazilian beef comes from cows just like in the rest of the world, but in Brazil the cows are open-range and grass-fed, making for a very lean beef which comes in uniquely Brazilian cuts such as *picanha* (tender rump steak), *fraldinha* (bottom sirloin), or *alcatra* (top sirloin). And of course, for side dishes no Brazilian meal is complete without *farofa* and rice or black beans.

These days you will find more and more **kilo** (*quilo* in Portuguese) restaurants. The food is laid out in a large buffet, and at the better ones there's a grill at the back serving freshly cooked steaks, chicken, and sausage. Kilos aren't all-you-can-eat. Rather, you pay by weight (but the quality is *much* better than at American lunch buffets). If you're not familiar with Brazilian food, it's a great way to see all the dishes laid out in front of you; you can try as little or as much as you like. Even better, they often have a variety of salads and vegetables that are often hard to come by elsewhere in Brazil. The system works as follows: When you enter the restaurant, you're given a piece of paper on which all your orders are recorded. Don't lose this slip or you'll have to pay a ridiculously high penalty. You grab a plate, wander by the buffet and grill, filling up on whatever catches your eye (all items have the same per-kilogram cost, which is usually advertised both outside and inside the restaurant), and then take the plate to the scale to be weighed. The weigher records the charges on your bill, after which you find a table. Normally a waiter will then come by and take your drink order, adding these charges to your tally. On your way out the cashier sums it all up. *Tip:* Small cups of strong dark coffee (called *cafezinhos*) are usually served free by the cashier or exit. Look for a thermos and a stack of little plastic cups.

A *churrascaria* is a steakhouse that operates on the *rodízio* system, essentially all you can eat—though you'll pay extra for drinks and dessert. The set price buys you unlimited access to a massive salad-bar buffet, often also including fish and sushi, and the attention of an army of waiters all offering different cuts of meat, sliced directly onto your plate. All the typical and unique Brazilian cuts of beef are on offer, as well as chicken breast, chicken hearts, sausage, and on and on and on.

3

Planning Your Trip to Brazil

Brazil is a vast, sprawling country, with much to see and do—from the Amazon rainforests to the civilized beaches of Rio to the restored colonial buildings of Salvador and the hundreds of frolicking dolphins of Fernando de Noronha. This chapter helps you figure out where to begin: where and when to go; how to get there; what precautions to take; and best of all, how to save money on your trip.

For additional help in planning your trip and for more on-the-ground resources in Brazil, please see chapter 22, "Fast Facts."

1 WHEN TO GO

High season in Brazil lasts from the week before Christmas until Carnaval (which falls sometime in Feb or early Mar, depending on the year). Flights and accommodations are more expensive and more likely to be full during this period. Book well ahead of time for accommodations during New Year's and Carnaval. This is the most fun time to travel—towns and resorts are bustling as many Brazilians take their summer vacations, the weather's warm, and New Year's and Carnaval are fabulously entertaining. If you want to spend New Year's in Brazil, it's best to arrive after Christmas. The 25th is really a family affair, and most restaurants and shops will be closed.

Other busy times of the year include Easter week and the months of July, when Brazilian schools and universities take their winter break, and August, when most Europeans and North Americans visit during the summer vacation. This is probably the worst time of year to travel; prices go up significantly, and except for in the

north and parts of the Northeast, the weather can be iffy and downright chilly from Rio de Janeiro southward. One year in Rio, I suffered through 4 straight weeks of rain, and temperatures as low as 5 to 10 Celsius (40s–50s Fahrenheit) are not unheard of in the south. If you want to take advantage of the best deals and still have good weather, consider visiting Brazil in September or October. The spring weather means warm days in São Paulo, Iguaçu, and Rio, and tropical heat everywhere else; in the Amazon and the Pantanal, you'll be there just before the wet season starts. As an added bonus, in Rio you'll be able to attend some of the samba school rehearsals as they get ready for Carnaval (yes, they start 4 months early). Another good period for a visit is after Carnaval (early to mid-Mar, depending on the dates) through May, when you can take advantage of low-season prices, particularly in hotels, while still enjoying good weather.

Average Monthly Temperature (Celsius/Fahrenheit)

	Jan	Feb	Mar	Apr	May	June	July	Aug	Sept	Oct	Nov	Dec
Rio de Janeiro	28/83	28/84	27/82	26/79	23/75	22/73	22/72	22/73	23/74	24/76	26/79	27/81
Manaus	27/81	26/80	26/80	27/81	27/81	27/81	27/81	27/81	28/82	28/82	28/82	27/81

Average Precipitation (Centimeters/Inches)

	Jan	Feb	Mar	Apr	May	June	July	Aug	Sept	Oct	Nov	Dec
Rio de Janeiro	13/5.3	12/4.9	13/5.3	10/4.3	7/3.1	5/2.0	4/1.8	4/1.8	6/2.4	8/3.2	9/3.9	13/5.4
Manaus	25/64	27/69	30/76	29/74	26/66	10/25	8/20	5/13	7/18	10/25	15/38	20/51

WEATHER

As Brazil lies in the Southern Hemisphere, its seasons are the exact opposite of what Northern Hemisphere residents are used to: **summer is December through March** and **winter June through September.** Within the country the climate varies considerably from region to region. In most of Brazil the summers are very hot. Temperatures can rise to 43°C (110°F) with high humidity. The **Northeast** (from Salvador north) is warm year-round, often with a pleasant breeze coming off the ocean. Temperatures hover between the upper 20s to mid-30s Celsius (low 80s and mid-90s Fahrenheit). The winter months (June–July) are slightly wetter, but even then the amount of rain is limited—a quick shower that cools things down briefly before giving way to more sunshine.

As befits a rainforest, the **Amazon** is also hot and humid year-round, with temperatures hovering around the mid- to high 30s Celsius (mid-90s to low 100s Fahrenheit). The dry season lasts from June to December and is often called "summer" by the locals as it is hot and sunny. As the rivers recede, beaches and islands reappear. The wet season typically runs from December to May and is referred to as "winter." The humidity is higher in the rainy season, building up over the course of the day to produce a heavy downfall almost every afternoon. Even then, however, mornings and early afternoons can be clear and sunny.

The **Pantanal** is very hot in the rainy season, with temperatures climbing over the low 40s Celsius mark (100°F). Most of the rain falls December through March. The driest time of the year is May through October. In these winter months things cool down considerably, though nighttime temperatures will seldom drop below 20°C (68°F). **Rio** has very hot and humid summers—38°C (100°F) and 98% humidity are not uncommon. Rio winters are quite mild, with nighttime temperatures dropping as low as 19°C (66°F), and daytime temperatures climbing to the pleasant and sunny 30°C (86°F). Cariocas themselves find this lack of heat appalling, and will often throw on a coat or heavy sweater when the temperature drops below 21°C (70°F). In their defense, I should note that most houses and apartments are completely without heat, and many restaurants and stores lack windows or doors, so it can feel quite cool.

São Paulo has a similar climate to Rio's, hot in the summer and mild in winter. As São Paulo sits atop a plateau at approximately 700m (2,300 ft.) of elevation it can sometimes get downright chilly, with daytime lows June through September sometimes reaching 12°C (54°F). **South of São**

Paulo, things get even colder in the winter. In Florianópolis, many restaurants and even some hotels and pousadas shut down for the winter season. Also, in the mountain resort of **Petrópolis** and the historic towns of **Ouro Preto** and **Tiradentes,** it often gets cold enough to see your breath (5°C/41°F) in the fall and winter, and Brazilians will travel here to experience winter.

HOLIDAYS

The following holidays are observed in Brazil: New Year's Day (Jan 1); Carnaval (Mar 5–8, 2011, Feb 18–21, 2012); Easter (Apr 4, 2010, and Apr 24, 2011); Tiradentes Day (Apr 21); Labor Day (May 1); Corpus Christi (June 3, 2010, and June 23,

2011); Independence Day (Sept 7); Our Lady of Apparition (Oct 12); All Souls' Day (Nov 2); Proclamation of the Republic (Nov 15); and Christmas Day (Dec 25). On these days banks, schools, and government institutions will be closed, and some stores may be closed as well.

Brazil's biggest holidays are New Year's and Carnaval (see "Everything You Need to Know About Carnaval" and "Reveillon: New Year's Eve in Rio," both in chapter 6). Easter is also a big celebration in a number of towns around the country, particularly in the historic towns of Minas Gerais and Novo Jerusalem outside Recife. Reservations are recommended for those planning to attend these events.

BRAZIL CALENDAR OF EVENTS

For an exhaustive list of events beyond those listed here, check http://events. frommers.com, where you'll find a searchable, up-to-the-minute roster of what's happening in cities all over the world.

JANUARY

New Year's Celebration, Rio de Janeiro. Close to two million people gather for one of the most spectacular New Year's celebrations in the world. Starting on the evening of December 31 (**Reveillon,** New Year's Eve) and continuing well into the morning of January 1, the main event takes place on Copacabana beach with live music and fireworks, as well as Candomblé religious ceremonies. For details contact **Riotur** (© 021/2271-7000; www. riodejaneiro-turismo.com.br) or **Alô Rio** (© 021/2542-8080). See "Reveillon: New Year's Eve in Rio," p. 154. January 1.

Three Kings Festival, Salvador. Salvador celebrates the Three Kings Festival with a procession and events around the Praça da Sé in the old town. Contact **Bahiatursa** (© 071/3103-3103; www. bahia.com.br) for details. January 6.

Washing of the Steps of Bonfim Church, Salvador. This is one of the most important religious ceremonies in Salvador when hundreds of women in traditional Bahian dress form a procession and carry perfumed water to wash the church steps, accompanied by 800,000 onlookers and revelers. Contact **Bahiatursa** (© 071/3103-3103; www.bahia.com.br) for details. Third Thursday of January.

Saint Sebastian Day, Rio de Janeiro. The patron saint of Rio de Janeiro is honored in this regional holiday. The highlight is a procession to the city's modern cathedral. For details contact **Riotur** (© 021/2271-7000; www. riodejaneiro-turismo.com.br) or **Alô Rio** (© 021/2542-8080). January 20.

FEBRUARY

Celebration of Yemanjá, the Goddess of the Sea, Salvador. Devotees throughout Brazil offer flowers, perfumes, and jewelry to the sea. Celebrations take place on the beach with music and food. The largest celebration takes place in Salvador on Praia Vermelha. Contact **Bahiatursa** (℃ **071/3103-3103;** www. bahia.com.br) for details. February 2.

Carnaval. This event can take place anywhere from early February to mid-March. Carnaval begins the weekend before Ash Wednesday and ends on the morning of Ash Wednesday. For the next 2 years, the dates are as follows: March 5–8, 2011, February 18–21, 2012. The largest celebrations take place in Rio, Salvador, and Recife/Olinda. For details contact **Riotur** (℃ **021/2271-7000;** www.riode janeiro-turismo.com.br) or **Alô Rio** (℃ 021/2542-8080); in Salvador contact **Bahiatursa** (℃ **071/3103-3103;** www.bahia.com.br); the **Recife** tourist office (℃ **081/3232-8409**); and Olinda tourism (℃ **081/3439-9434**). Book ahead if you plan on attending this event.

MARCH

Passion Play, Nova Jerusalem. South America's largest Passion Play (daily) takes place in Nova Jerusalem, just outside of Recife in Brazil's Northeast. For more information contact **Recife Tourist Information** at (℃ **081/3232-8409**). Ten days preceding Easter.

APRIL

Easter Weekend (Semana Santa), Ouro Preto. This important Catholic holiday is celebrated with processions and concerts. Ouro Preto, with its 13 baroque churches, is a popular destination during Easter. Contact **Ouro Preto Tourist Information** (℃ **031/3551-1469;** www.ouropreto.org.br) for details. April 4, 2010, and April 24, 2011.

Week of the Inconfidência. Tiradentes Day on April 21 is a national holiday,

but only Ouro Preto has made it into a large event with celebrations, plays, and cultural events taking place. Contact **Ouro Preto Tourist Information** (℃ **031/3551-1469;** www.ouropreto.org.br) for details. April 16 to April 21.

JUNE

Bumba-meu-boi, São Luis. In São Luis in Maranhão, the peasant folklore festival bumba-meu-boi begins June 1 with the baptizing of the bull, and continues throughout the month, culminating with a large street party on June 30, the feast day of São Marçal. In São Luis, contact the **State Tourism Agency** (℃ **098/3231-2000;** www.turismo.ma.gov.br).

Festas Juninas. This folklore event in honor of saints Anthony, John, and Peter is celebrated throughout Brazil. The harvest festival offers country music, bonfires, hot-air balloons, and funfairs. For details contact **Riotur** (℃ 021/2271-7000; www.riodejaneiro-turismo.com.br) or **Alô Rio** (℃ 021/2542-8080). June 13 to June 14.

Bauernfest, Petrópolis. Petrópolis celebrates the German heritage of its many settlers with a week of German food, folklore, and music. Contact the **Petrópolis Foundation of Culture and Tourism** (℃ **0800/024-1516;** www.petropolis.rj.gov.br) for details. Last weekend of June and first week of July.

JULY

FLIP, Paraty. Don't miss **FLIP** (Festa Literária Internacional de Paraty). The Paraty International Literary Festival, held near the beginning of July, draws a cultured crowd to one of the most charming colonial towns in Brazil. See **www.flip.org.br** or contact the **Paraty tourist information** office (℃ **024/3371-1897**) or the **FLIP festival office** in Paraty (℃ **024/3371-7082**) for details. First week of July.

Independence Day. This is Brazil's national holiday. Most cities hold military parades. In Rio de Janeiro this impressive event takes place around Avenida Rio Branco. September 7.

Film Festival Rio BR, Rio de Janeiro. Rio's film festival showcases Brazilian and international films (**www.festivaldorio.com.br**). Subtitles are in Portuguese, but there is usually a good selection of international movies. For details contact **Riotur** (℃ **021/2271-7000;** www.riodejaneiro-turismo.com.br) or **Alô Rio** (℃ **021/2542-8080**). Late September to the first week of October.

OCTOBER

Free Jazz Festival, Rio de Janeiro and São Paulo. A 3-day jazz festival with national and international acts. For details contact **Riotur** (℃ **021/2271-7000;** www.riodejaneiro-turismo.com.br) or **Alô Rio** (℃ **021/2542-8080**). In São Paulo contact the **tourist information agency** (℃ **011/3231-4455** or 2226-0400). Mid- to late October.

Cirio of Nazaré, Belém. Hundreds of thousands of the faithful parade an icon of the Virgin of Nazaré through the streets and harbor of Belém. Contact **Paratur** (℃ **091/3212-0575;** www.paraturismo.pa.gov.br). Second Sunday of October (Oct 10, 2010, and Oct 9, 2011).

International Film Festival, São Paulo. The festival presents the best films of Brazil, Latin America, and the world. Most venues concentrate around the Avenida Paulista. Contact

℃ **011/3141-0413,** or check www.mostra.org. Last 2 weeks of October.

Grand Prix, São Paulo. Brazilians are car-racing fanatics; watching a big race in the company of Brazilian fans is an event in itself. The Grand Prix at Interlagos (a suburb of São Paulo) is the prime event in the country. Visit **www.gpbrasil.com.br** for more information, or call the tourist office in São Paulo (℃ **011/3231-4455** or 2226-0400). Third week of October. Check website for exact dates.

São Paulo Bienal. Art, theater, music, and architecture—the biggest arts event in Latin America takes place every even year in Ibirapuera Park. For schedules and information contact the Fundação Bienal de São Paulo (℃ **011/5576-7600;** www.bienalsaopaulo.org.br).

NOVEMBER

Aleijadinho Week, Ouro Preto. Special exhibits and presentations about the beloved sculptor. Contact Ouro Preto Tourist Information (℃ **031/3551-1469;** www.ouropreto.org.br) for details. November 14 to November 21.

DECEMBER

Santa Barbara, Salvador. This festival is celebrated with processions, music, and dance. Santa Barbara is the Candomblé equivalent of Iansã, the goddess of wind. Contact **Bahiatursa** (℃ **071/3103-3103;** www.bahia.com.br) for details. December 4.

Christmas Eve. Brazilians go to midnight Mass to celebrate Christmas. Mass is usually followed by a late-night supper with family. December 24.

2 ENTRY REQUIREMENTS

VISAS

Nationals of the United States, Canada, and Australia require a visa to visit Brazil. **British nationals** (and holders of an E.U. passport) and **New Zealand** passport holders do not require a visa, but do need a passport valid for at least 6 months and a return ticket. A number of visa types are available; cost, processing time, and documentation requirements vary. Visas for **Australians** cost A$90, plus local handling fees, and take about 2 weeks to process. For **Canadians** a similar visa costs C$72 and takes about the same processing time. **U.S. citizens** pay US$100 for a standard single-entry tourist visa valid for 90 days (add another US$10 for handling fees, passport photos, and courier costs if you don't live near a consulate). Count on at least 2 weeks of processing time.

Upon arrival in Brazil, visitors will receive a 90-day entry stamp in their passport and a stamped entry card. Hang on to the card for dear life, as losing it will result in a possible fine and a certain major hassle when you leave. If necessary, the visa can be renewed once for another 90 days. **Visa renewals** are obtained through the local Policia Federal. This is best done in large cities where the staff has experience with tourists. It's a good idea to print and fill in a copy of the requisite form, available at the following website: www.dpf.gov.br/web/formulario/form_cgpi/requerimento_de_prorrogacao_de_prazo.htm.

Children 17 and under must have their own passport and visa. Children from 3 months to 6 years of age must also show proof of vaccination for polio. If a child is traveling with people other than his, or even if the child is only traveling with one of parents, the child must have a notarized letter *from both parents* confirming permission for the child to travel. For a model of this letter, see www.consulatebrazil.org/autorizacaoviagemmenor.htm. Immigration authorities may well demand such a letter on entry or exit. Buses and airlines often demand such a letter before allowing a child to board.

Shortly after the United States began fingerprinting Brazilian visitors, Brazil, in a tit-for-tat bit of retaliation, implemented its own fingerprint program for U.S. visitors. In its first few months the system caused numerous long delays; nowadays the fingerprint requirement is fulfilled with a quick and efficient digital reading of a single thumb digit.

Note that Brazilian consulates in the U.S. often no longer offer multiple entry visas (though you can ask). However, this is not a problem for visitors to Iguaçu who wish only to travel over to the Argentine side for a few hours and return the same day. The Policia Federal at the Iguaçu border post inspect passports but let you exit and return without the need for a new visa.

For more information regarding visas and to obtain application details:

Australians can call © 02/6273-2372 (in Australia) or log on to www.brazil.org.au.

Canadians can apply through **Toronto**'s Brazilian consulate (© 416/922-2503; www.consbrastoronto.org).

In **New Zealand** inquiries can be made in Wellington at © 04/473-3516 or check www.brazil.org.nz.

In the **U.K.**, more information is available at © 020/7399-9000 (in the U.K.); www.brazil.org.uk.

U.S. citizens can contact the Brazilian consulate in **New York** (© 917/777-7791; www.brazilny.org); **Los Angeles** (© 323/651-2664; www.brazilian-consulate.org); or **Miami** (© 305/285-6200; www.brazilmiami.org). Links will connect you to the consulate closest to you.

CUSTOMS

What You Can Bring In

As a visitor you are unlikely to be scrutinized very closely by Brazilian Customs; however, there are random checks, and your luggage may be thoroughly inspected. Visitors are allowed to bring in whatever they need for personal use on their trip, including electronics such as a camera and laptop. If you are bringing in new electronic items you may be asked to register the item to ensure that you will take it with you when you leave. Gifts purchased abroad worth more than US$500 must be declared and are subject to duties for the value over US$500. Merchandise for sale or samples should also be declared upon arrival.

What You Can Take Home from Brazil

For information on what you're allowed to bring home, contact one of the following agencies:

Australian Citizens: Australian Customs Service at © **1300/363-263,** or log on to www.customs.gov.au.

Canadian Citizens: Canada Border Services Agency (© **800/461-9999** in Canada, or 204/983-3500; www.cbsa-asfc.gc.ca).

New Zealand Citizens: New Zealand Customs, The Customhouse, 17–21 Whitmore St., Box 2218, Wellington (© **04/473-6099** or 0800/428-786; www.customs.govt.nz).

U.K. Citizens: HM Customs & Excise at © **0845/010-9000** (from outside the U.K., 020/8929-0152), or consult their website at www.hmce.gov.uk.

U.S. Citizens: U.S. Customs & Border Protection (CBP), 1300 Pennsylvania Ave., NW, Washington, DC 20229 (© **877/287-8667;** www.cbp.gov).

MEDICAL REQUIREMENTS

Before going, check your vaccinations and get booster shots for tetanus and polio if required. Children ages 3 months to 6 years may be required to show proof of polio vaccination. One vaccination that is definitely recommended—and sometimes mandatory—for Brazil is **yellow fever.** Outbreaks are sometimes reported in the Amazon, the Pantanal, Brasilia, or even Minas Gerais. Make sure you get an international certificate of vaccination as Brazilian authorities sometimes require proof of vaccination for people going to or coming from an affected area. Travelers who have been to Colombia, Bolivia, Ecuador, French Guyana, Peru, or Venezuela within 90 days prior to their arrival in Brazil **must** show proof of yellow fever vaccination. Keep in mind that the vaccine takes 10 days to take effect.

3 GETTING TO & AROUND BRAZIL

GETTING TO BRAZIL BY PLANE

The major international gateway to Brazil is São Paulo's **Guarulhos international airport (GRU).** Most international airways have flights to Guarulhos, and it is possible to connect to all other cities in Brazil. The other major gateway is Rio de Janeiro's **Galeão International airport (GIG).** Though a modern international airport, Galeão has fewer direct flights to other Brazilian cities; you may have to connect through São Paulo or Brasilia.

The two big Brazilian airlines—**Gol/ Varig** and **TAM**—also operate a number of international flights. **TAM** (© **888/ 2FLY-TAM** [235-9826] in the U.S. and Canada, 020/8897-0005 in the U.K., or 0800/570-5700 in Brazil; www.tam.com. br) has the most international connections to North America, Europe, Asia, and the

> **Tips** **Don't Leave Home Without a Picture ID**
>
> Bring an alternative picture ID, like a driver's license or student ID. You are required to carry ID in Brazil, and it's sometimes requested when entering office buildings or even tourist sites. Your passport is safer in the hotel safe and not required except for official transactions.

rest of South America. Relative newcomer, low-budget carrier **Gol** (© **0300/115-2121** in Brazil; www.voegol.com.br) now offers service to a number of South American destinations (Argentina, Chile, Peru, and Bolivia), a good alternative for those traveling within South America.

GETTING AROUND

By Plane

The sheer vastness of Brazil (and the absence of rail travel) makes air travel the only viable option for those who want to visit a variety of cities and regions. However, the Brazilian airline industry has been experiencing turbulent times of late. The last 6 years has seen the bankruptcy of two Brazilian carriers, Transbrasil and Vasp, followed by the effective demise of the country's flagship carrier Varig. (A new, smaller Varig flew out of bankruptcy protection, only to merge with low-cost carrier Gol.) Disruptions by air-traffic controllers and delays at domestic airports lead the president to sack the head of the civilian air agency in mid-2007, and the new chief seems to be bringing order back to the skies. However, travelers should stock up on patience before entering a Brazilian airport. (It may well not be required, but you never know.) During peak travel times (holidays, high season) long delays are not an unlikely occurrence.

For those traveling larger distances in Brazil there is also the option of purchasing an **air pass** with Tam (much to the envy of Brazilians this pass is available to foreigners only). The pass offers travelers four flights within a 21-day period. Air

passes need to be purchased and booked outside of Brazil. Only limited changes are allowed once you arrive in the country. Also, it's a good idea to read the small print before choosing your pass. Often flights between Rio's and São Paulo's downtown airports are excluded (meaning you have to use the international airports) and the pass does not allow returns on the same stretch.

TAM (© **0800/123-100** in Brazil; www.tam.com.br) offers four segments for US$551 if you arrive on an international TAM flight (otherwise the pass costs US$635). The pass is valid for 21 days. Check TAM's special English-language site for more details on the air pass (www.tamairlines.com). If you're traveling to only one or two destinations within Brazil, it can be cheaper to skip the air pass and buy a separate ticket.

The big winner from much of the air chaos has been **Gol** (© **0300/789-2121** in Brazil; www.voegol.com.br). This airline has modeled itself after American discount carriers like Southwest Airlines—quick bookings online and no-frills flights, now between nearly every significant city in Brazil. Tickets can be purchased online—but only if you have an American Express card—or at the airport. The company flies brand-new Boeing 737s and provides friendly and efficient service.

In the past couple of years a number of lower-cost airlines have sprung up, offering competitive and often cheaper fares between Brazilian cities. These newcomers include **Azul** (© **011/3003-2985;** http://viajemais.voeazul.com.br); **Ocean Air**

(Tips) Domestic Travel Do's and Don'ts

There are a few tricks to avoiding delays and cancellations when flying domestically in Brazil. **First,** if at all possible, avoid flights stopping or connecting through São Paulo. That may be hard to do; the city serves as Brazil's major hub, and its airports as a result have a tendency to get clogged and backed up. **Second,** travel early in the day: Delays tend to accumulate throughout the day and lead to bigger and bigger backlogs. **Third,** don't book tight connections, especially if you have to transfer from the domestic airport in Rio or São Paulo to the international airport. For a simple connection within the same airport, give yourself an hour. For a transfer from domestic to international airports, allow for at least 2 hours in Rio and 3 hours in São Paulo.

(℃ **0300/789-8160;** www.oceanair.com. br); **TRIP** (℃ **011/3003-8747;** www. voetrip.com.br); and **Webjet** (℃ **0300/ 210-1234;** www.webjet.com.br).

Domestic departure tax is around R$21 at most airports, and international departures are a hefty R$108. Payment can only be made in cash with U.S. dollars or Brazilian currency but not in a combination of both.

By Car

Car rentals are expensive, and the distances are huge. From Recife to Brasilia is 2,121km (1,315 miles); Salvador to Rio is a 1,800km (1,116-mile) drive. Within Brazilian cities, renting a car is only for the confident driver. Brazilian drivers are aggressive, rules sporadically applied, and parking a competitive sport. That said, there are occasions—a side trip to the mountain resorts of Rio, a visit to the historic towns of Minas Gerais, or a drive to the Chapada dos Guimarães outside of Cuiabá—where a car makes sense. Local contact numbers for rental companies are given in each chapter.

Car rental in Brazil is more expensive than in North America. A two-door compact (Fiat Palio, Ford Ka) with air-conditioning and unlimited mileage costs about R$100 per day, plus some R$20 to R$30 for insurance. Most rental cars in Brazil will work on either unleaded gasoline,

gasohol, or pure alcohol (ethanol). Gasoline costs about R$2.70 per liter. Ethanol costs significantly less, about R$1.70 per liter, but burns more quickly. Still, ethanol winds up being cheaper overall.

Officially you need an international driver's license but we have never encountered any problems having a U.S., Canadian, or European license. To obtain an international license, contact your local automobile association. While expensive, the comprehensive insurance is probably a good idea as Brazilian drivers are not as gentle with their cars as folks in North America. Bumpers are meant to be used, Brazilians believe, and if a bit of nudging is required to get into that parking spot, so be it.

Speed limits within the cities range from 40kmph to 70kmph (25mph–43mph. Many cities have radar and automated monitoring. Fines are expensive—R$100 to R$500, depending on how fast you're going. Highway speed limits range from 90kmph to 120kmph (56mph–75mph), but are much less rigorously enforced.

Brazilians mark accident sites by leaving cut branches or small piles of leaves on the road. If you see such a pile of foliage on the tarmac, it means there's an accident ahead. Slow down. It's a good idea to seek local information about the state of the roads on the route you plan to travel.

Brazilian roads have been improving, but some can still be potholed and difficult. Locals and your local rental agency will know the road conditions, and be able to suggest alternatives.

The following agencies have bureaus in most airports and major cities in Brazil: **Avis** (© **0800/725-2847;** www.avis.com. br); **Hertz** (© **0800/701-7300;** www. hertz.com.br); **Localiza** (© **0800/ 979-2000;** www.localiza.com); **Unidas** (© **0800/121-121;** www.unidas.com.br). To rent a car you need a passport and valid drivers license. An international license is not required.

By Bus

Bus travel in Brazil is comfortable, efficient, and affordable. The only problem is, it's a long way from anywhere to anywhere else. A trip from Rio to São Paulo takes 6 to 8 hours, from Rio to Brasilia closer to 20 hours.

There are a vast number of bus companies, serving various regional routes. Unlike in North America, there is no nationwide bus company. To find out which bus company travels to your desired destination, you contact the bus station in your city of origin, and they pass on the number of the appropriate company. This can be tricky if you don't speak Portuguese. Fortunately, however, the bus stations in major cities now have websites, which allow you to select your destination from a drop-down menu, and then provide the departure times, price, and the name of the bus company. You can often also purchase tickets online. Tickets can be purchased ahead of time with reserved seats. All buses are nonsmoking. On many popular routes travelers can opt for a deluxe coach with air-conditioning and *leito* (seats that recline almost flat).

4 MONEY & COSTS

The Value of the Real vs. Other Popular Currencies

R$	US$	Can$	UK£	Euro (€)	Aus$	NZ$
1	$0.57	C$0.61	£0.34	0.39€	A$0.62	NZ$0.78

Frommer's lists exact prices in the local currency. The currency conversions quoted above were correct at press time. However, rates fluctuate, so before departing consult a currency exchange website such as **www. xe.com** to check up-to-the-minute rates.

The official unit of currency in Brazil is the **Real** (pronounced Ray-*all;* the plural is **Reais,** pronounced Ray-*eyes*), which the Brazilian government introduced in 1994 in an attempt to control inflation. International money speculations around the 2002 presidential elections sent the Real into a tailspin, arriving at a record low of nearly R$4 to the U.S. dollar. When it

became clear the new leftist president, Lula da Silva, was actually planning to follow a quite conservative monetary policy, the Real settled back around R$3 to the U.S. dollar. Since then, the U.S. dollar has been on a steady decline to its current level around R$1.70 to the dollar. For travelers this means that Brazil is still affordable, though not the bargain it was in years past.

Tip: When exchanging money, be it cash or traveler's checks, always keep the receipt. You will need it in case you want to change back any unused Reais at the end of your trip. See **www.xe.com** online for an easy currency converter.

What Things Cost in Brazil

Beer on the beach	R$2
Night in an inexpensive hotel in Rio de Janeiro	R$125
Night in a midrange hotel in Rio de Janeiro	R$225
Metrô ride in Rio de Janeiro	R$2.80
Metrô ride in São Paulo	R$2.55
Espresso at a snack bar	R$2
Midrange three-course dinner for two, no booze	R$130

THE U.S. DOLLAR

Up until 2004, many businesses based their rates on the U.S. dollar. With the dollar's fall, some businesses have lowered their Real prices to keep a steady dollar price, others have increased the Real rate, and still others have switched over to accounting in euros. For U.S. travelers, it means that Brazil has gotten a little bit more expensive. When prices are listed in U.S. dollars only, it's because these companies quote their prices directly in dollars. If in doubt, ask. And though it's a bad idea to carry large wads of cash, it can be helpful to bring a small amount of U.S. cash ($10s or $20s only, no $100s) as an emergency supply in case that ATM is broken or your credit card isn't working. Even in the smallest towns people will know the exchange rate, and someone will be happy to take the U.S. dollars off your hands.

TRAVELER'S CHECKS

Traveler's checks aren't a very good idea in Brazil. Most shops won't accept them, hotels give a miserable exchange rate (if they cash them), and many banks have a strange policy that they will not cash your traveler's checks unless you have an account at that branch of that bank. The Banco do Brasil is the only bank that will cash them with a minimum of hassle but will charge a US$20 service fee.

ATMS

The best way to get cash at a reasonable exchange rate is by withdrawing money from an ATM. Brazil's financial infrastructure is very sophisticated, and ATMs were common here even before they were used in western Europe. You will find them everywhere in Brazil, even in the smallest towns. The only trick is finding one that works with your card. ATMs are linked to a network that most likely includes your bank at home. **Cirrus** (© 800/424-7787; www.mastercard.com) and **PLUS** (© 800/843-7587; www.visa.com) are the two most popular networks in the U.S.; call or check online for ATM locations at your destination. You need to have a four-digit PIN to be able to access ATMs in Brazil. For most ATMs the limit is R$1,000 but depending on the machine these amounts may be lower.

The vast majority of travelers find they are able to use the HSBC and Banco do Brasil ATMs bearing a PLUS/Visa and Cirrus/MasterCard logo. Almost all Brazilian airports have HSBC and Banco do Brasil ATMs. However, it's not a bad idea to bring two different cards to increase your access options with other banks. (Small towns normally only have one ATM. It will be PLUS/Visa or Cirrus/MasterCard, but not always both.) Bradesco, Banco 24 Horas, and Citibank ATMs are often compatible with PLUS/Visa. If in doubt, check with your bank to find out which Brazilian bank networks are compatible with your card. Also, plan ahead to ensure that you have enough cash; for safety reasons many ATMs do not operate 24 hours. Often they will close after 10pm or only allow a small amount of cash to be withdrawn during the off-hours. Your best bets for late-night withdrawals are airports, malls, or gas stations.

Finally, make sure that during New Year's and Carnaval you get enough cash ahead of time, as machines often run out of money by the end of the holidays.

Tip: Before you leave home, write down all your card numbers, expiration dates, and contact phone numbers. Leave a copy with someone you can easily reach, and e-mail a copy to yourself and save it in an account that can be accessed anywhere, so you have the information at your fingertips in case of loss or theft.

CREDIT CARDS

The best exchange rates can be obtained through credit cards, which are accepted at most Brazilian shops and hotels and restaurants. Just keep in mind that you are sometimes able to negotiate a better discount on a room or in a store if you pay cash. The most commonly accepted cards are Visa and MasterCard. American Express and Diners Club are also often accepted. It's a good idea to have at least two cards as some stores and restaurants may only accept one card (usually Visa or MasterCard; Diners and Amex are less common, especially in small towns). Keep in mind that many banks now assess a 1% to 3% "transaction fee" on all charges you incur abroad (whether you're using the local currency or U.S. dollars). But credit cards still may be the smart way to go when you factor in things like exorbitant ATM fees and the higher exchange rates and service fees you'll pay with traveler's checks.

5 HEALTH

Standards for hygiene and public health in Brazil are generally high. Before leaving, however, check with your doctor or with the Centers for Disease Control (www.cdc.gov) for specific advisories. Use common sense when eating on the street or in restaurants.

COMMON AILMENTS

DENGUE FEVER Dengue fever is a viral infection transmitted by mosquitoes. It's unfortunately common in Rio de Janeiro. It's characterized by sudden-onset high fever, severe headaches, joint and muscle pain, nausea/vomiting, and rash. (The rash may not appear until 3–4 days after the fever.) Proper diagnosis requires a blood test. The illness may last up to 10 days, but complete recovery can take 2 to 4 weeks. Dengue is rarely fatal.

The risk for dengue fever is highest during periods of heat and rain, where stagnant pools of water allow mosquitoes to breed. Though it strikes most often in poorer communities, the disease has infiltrated Rio's more affluent neighborhoods. There is no vaccine for dengue fever. Symptoms can be treated with bed rest, fluids, and medications to reduce fever, such as acetaminophen (Tylenol); aspirin should be avoided. The most important precaution a traveler can take is to avoid mosquito bites in dengue-prone areas. Try to remain in well-screened or air-conditioned areas, use mosquito repellents (preferably those containing DEET) on skin and clothing, and sleep with bed nets. For up-to-date information on the status of dengue fever in Brazil, consult the Centers for Disease Control website (www.cdc.gov) before departing.

SUN EXPOSURE The Brazilian sun is very strong, particularly in summer (the North American winter, when many travelers from above the Equator can be quite pale). Sunscreen of at least SPF 15 should be applied frequently.

INSECT/ANIMAL BITES Tourists rarely encounter snakes and are even more rarely bitten. You'll find ticks most everywhere in Brazil, but the only place I considered them a nuisance was hiking in highland areas like the Chapada Diamantina inland from Salvador (see chapter 11) or the Chapada Guimarães near Cuiabá.

MALARIA There is malaria endemic to the Amazon or the Pantanal, though it's not very common. Still, a malaria prophylaxis (usually pills that you take daily) may be recommended.

AIDS & STDS According to recent UN statistics, Brazil has the dubious honor of ranking third in the world for total number of people with HIV infections. Though condom usage is becoming more accepted—thanks in part to the examples shown in popular nighttime soaps on TV—the reality is that some people still won't use them, and AIDS and other STDs are still being spread. So be careful and be safe—always insist on using a condom. Though condoms are readily available in Brazilian pharmacies, it's best to bring your own; brands are more reliable in North America and Europe. To purchase condoms in Brazil ask for a *preservativo* or a *camisinha* (kah-mee-*zeen*-ya), literally a small shirt; the latter word is the commonly used term for condom.

WHAT TO DO IF YOU GET SICK AWAY FROM HOME

If you worry about getting sick away from home, consider purchasing **medical travel insurance.** In most cases, however, your existing health plan will provide all the coverage you need. However it is wise to check any conditions and/or limitations on your coverage. Be sure to carry your identification card in your wallet.

Pack **prescription medications** in your carry-on luggage. Carry written prescriptions in generic, not brand-name, form, and dispense all prescription medications from their original labeled vials. Also bring along copies of your prescriptions in case you lose your pills or run out.

If you do wind up with traveler's tummy or some other ailment (upset stomach, diarrhea, sunburn, or rash), **Brazilian pharmacies** are a wonder. Each has a licensed pharmacist who is trained to deal with small medical emergencies and can make recommendations for treatment. The service is free and medication is fairly inexpensive. If you take medication that may need replacement while in Brazil, ask your doctor to write out the active ingredients of the prescription, as many drugs are sold under different trade names in Brazil. Many drugs available by prescription only in the U.S. and Canada are available over-the-counter in Brazil. While this is incredibly convenient, the downside is that Brazilians are the world's biggest pill-poppers who will happily "prescribe" drugs for themselves or their relatives or friends at the slightest whiff of sickness.

Contact the **International Association for Medical Assistance to Travelers (IAMAT; ✆ 716/754-4883** in the U.S. and Canada, or 416/652-0137; www.iamat.org). This organization offers tips on travel and health concerns in the countries you'll be visiting, and lists many local English-speaking doctors. When you're abroad, any local consulate can provide a list of area doctors who speak English (though it may be hard to find one with more than a basic knowledge of English, even in larger cities). If you do get sick, you may want to ask the concierge at your hotel to recommend a local doctor—even his or her own. This will probably yield a better recommendation than any 800 number would. If you can't find a doctor who can help you right away, try the emergency room at the local hospital.

We list additional emergency numbers in chapter 22, "Fast Facts."

6 SAFETY

Sometime in the 1980s Brazil began developing a world reputation for violence and crime. Rio especially was seen as the sort of place where walking down the street was openly asking for a mugging. Some of this was pure sensationalism, but there was a good measure of truth as well. Brazil at the time was massively in debt to First World banks, and the combination of crippling interest payments and International Monetary Fund austerity measures left governments at all levels with no money for basics, such as street lighting and police, much less schools and hospitals.

Fortunately, in the early '90s things began to turn around. The debt crisis eased, leaving governments with some discretionary spending, and with the advent of the 1992 World Environment Conference in Rio, Brazilians realized they had a serious image problem on their hands. Governments began putting money back into basic services, starting with policing. Cops were stationed on city streets, on public beaches, and anywhere else there seemed to be a problem. At the same time governments began working on extending water and sanitation to some of the city's poorer residents in the *favelas* (shantytowns).

The long expansion that followed made massive new investments in tourism infrastructure feasible. Many cities got brand-new airports. A domestic tourism boom ensued, making the protection of tourists even more of a political imperative. Nowadays, though still not perfect by any means, Rio, São Paulo, and Brazil's other big cities have bounced back to the point where they're as safe as some large international cities.

Statistically, of course, Rio and other big Brazilian cities still have very high crime rates, including high rates of violent crime. Most of that crime, however, takes place in the favelas and shantytowns of the far-off industrial outskirts. Brazil is a highly unequal society, and the burden of crime and violence falls disproportionately (and unfairly) on the country's poor. But unless you go wandering unaccompanied into a hillside favela (not recommended), you're unlikely to be affected.

That said, in large centers such as São Paulo, Rio, Salvador, and Recife, common-sense rules still apply. Don't flash your valuables. Diamond rings and Rolex wristwatches are a no-no. Always have a few small bills ready in your pocket or bag to avoid pulling out your wallet in public places. Plan your sightseeing trips to the city's central core during office hours when there are lots of people about. By all means bring your camera or video camera, but keep it inside a backpack or purse, and only take it out when you want to use it. Don't stroll Copacabana beach at 3am with R$1,000 in your pocket and a video camera pressed to your eyeball (a true story, alas). And though public transit is safe during the day and evening, watch for pickpockets when it gets really packed, and come nightfall, use taxis instead. Be careful at night; stick to the main streets where there is traffic and other pedestrians, and avoid dark alleys or deserted streets.

Perhaps even more importantly, *keep your wits about you in traffic!* Brazilian drivers (with a few exceptions) show no respect for pedestrians and there's no such thing as pedestrian right of way. So be very careful when crossing the street, particularly at night when drivers will often run red lights. Also pay special attention when crossing one-way streets; many drivers, especially those who drive motorcycles or delivery bicycles, think that the one-way rule does not apply to them and will happily go the wrong way.

Machismo is alive and well in Brazil, but it's a kinder, gentler machismo than in other parts of Latin America. Single women and a few women traveling together will undoubtedly attract masculine attention. There are upsides to this. It's usually fairly harmless and can sometimes lead to some fun conversations. Brazilian men, it seems, have an insurmountable urge to flirt. Perhaps because flirting is such a way of life, they take rejection well. Indeed, the object of the exercise lies mostly in the act of flirtation itself—actually making a conquest appears to be not terribly important. Wearing a wedding ring (fake or real) will throw up only the flimsiest of barriers; it will be either completely ignored, seen as a challenge, or solicit questions such as "How married are you?" or "What kind of husband would let you out of his sight?" However, if you are not interested, just say so or walk away if necessary and that is usually enough. The downside is that it's difficult for a woman to go out for a drink by herself and not receive attention. If you're not comfortable with this, you may want to form up a mixed group with other travelers or else stick to higher-end restaurants or hotel bars. Brazilian women in groups of two or three often link arms or hold hands as a sign that they are not interested in male attention. Use common sense to avoid situations where you may find yourself alone with someone giving you unwanted attention. At night, taking taxis is safer than walking by yourself.

DEALING WITH DISCRIMINATION

Outside of the big cities such as São Paulo, Rio de Janeiro, and Salvador, openly gay men or women will certainly draw attention and perhaps be subjected to comments or jokes. Brazil is still a macho culture and any open sign of affection between people of the same sex will meet with disapproval.

Black travelers shouldn't encounter much in the way of discrimination. However, mixed couples (particularly where the woman is black and the man is not) may encounter discrimination in hotels or bars because people may assume that the woman is a Brazilian prostitute who has hooked up with a gringo guy. Particularly in Rio and the Northeast such "temporary couples" are a common sight, and people will make assumptions based on appearances.

7 SPECIALIZED TRAVEL RESOURCES

FOR GAY & LESBIAN TRAVELERS

Gay and lesbian travelers will find small but vibrant gay communities in São Paulo, Rio de Janeiro, Salvador, and some of the other big cities, more often geared toward men than women. There are now gay pride parades in many of Brazil's big cities—Rio, São Paulo, Belo Horizonte, even Manaus in the Amazon. There are gay beach areas in Rio, and gay bars and clubs in most larger Brazilian cities. However, public displays of affection are not common among gays and lesbians even in the cities, and in small towns and communities the level of acceptance is significantly lower—rude remarks and jokes are almost guaranteed, though physical violence is thankfully rare.

One Brazilian travel agency in Rio that specializes in tours for gay and lesbian travelers is **Rio G Travel,** Rua Teixeira de Melo 16, Ipanema (✆ **021/3813-0003;** www.riog.com.br).

TRAVELERS WITH DISABILITIES

Travelers with disabilities will find Brazil challenging. Those who use a wheelchair to get around will find that very few places are accessible. In the large cities, increasing numbers of hotels, restaurants, and attractions are making themselves accessible. The trick lies in getting to them. Sidewalks are often uneven, ramps are usually absent, and buses and taxis are not adapted to handle a wheelchair. City Metrô systems in Rio and São Paulo are beginning to provide ramps and elevators, but not all stations are equipped.

FAMILIES

Brazilians love kids. They will go out of their way to please children, yours and everyone else's. In fact you will see children out and about a lot more than in the U.S. or Canada, even at restaurants, bars, or late-night events. Perhaps because Brazilian children are used to going out a lot more, they seem to always behave very well in public, playing with other kids or amusing themselves, with few of the hissy fits that sometimes accompany evenings out with North American youngsters. Traveling with children is a wonderful way to meet Brazilians, as people will be receptive, friendly, and inquisitive. Hotels are very accommodating but do usually charge 10% to 25% extra for children over the age of 6 or 12 who stay in the same room as a parent or guardian. In most hotels, the age limit and the amount of extra percentage charged can be flexible and is certainly worth bargaining over.

If a child is traveling with people other than his or her parents, or even if the child is only traveling with one of his or her parents, it is a good idea to have a notarized letter from the parents confirming permission for the child to travel. Buses and airlines sometimes demand such a letter before allowing a child to board. For even greater safety, have the notarized letter stamped by

the Brazilian consulate or embassy. (Please contact the Brazilian consulate or embassy for further information.) Brazilians can be incredibly picky (in moments of frustration in dealing with Brazilian bureaucrats we have used words other than "picky") when it comes to paperwork; showing an embassy stamp makes a difference because that means that somebody in authority has already approved it.

To locate accommodations, restaurants, and attractions that are particularly kid-friendly, refer to the "Kids" icon throughout this guide.

WOMEN TRAVELERS

Some hotels, particularly in larger cities, now offer women-only floors. The Metrô in Rio has women-only cars—painted pastel pink—for the exclusive use of women travelers during rush hours.

See also "For Women" in the "Safety" section above.

MULTICULTURAL TRAVELERS

Brazil is experiencing an increase in the number of African–North American visitors interested in learning about the African roots of Brazilian culture. Most of these travelers visit Salvador, the Brazilian city with the highest percentage of residents of African descent, as well as Rio, which is more of a melting pot but where Afro-Brazilian culture is also strong. **Brazil Nuts** (www.brazilnuts.com) offers several packages that focus on African religions, festivals, and culture. They can also customize a trip according to your requirements.

FOR SENIORS

Senior travelers can try and ask for discounts, though these are reserved for those over 60 or 65 years of age who can show Brazilian ID. Still, it's worth asking at tourist attractions if there's a discount. The phrase to use is "*Tem desconto para idosos?*"

TRAVELERS WITH FOOD ALLERGIES

If you are allergic to nuts you should be extra careful around certain dishes. Especially those with a seafood or shrimp allergy may want to check before ordering stews from the Northeast such as *moqueca, vatapá,* and *bobó.* These dishes often have ground-up shrimp or sometimes nuts in the sauce. Also, many fish dishes come with shrimp sauce, which may not be listed on the menu. Desserts often have nuts in them so always ask before digging in. Peanuts are *amendoim* (ah-man-doo-*een*), cashews in Portuguese are *castanha de caju* (ka-*stan*-ya de *ka*-zhoo) or *caju* for short, and Brazil nuts are known as *castanha do Pará* (ka-*stan*-ya doh pa-*rah*). The general word for nuts is *nozes* (no-*zhes*) and you can let people know that you have an allergy by saying *"Tenho alergia de amendoim"* (*Ten*-yo ah-lehr-*gee*-ah de ah-man-doo-*een*).

8 SUSTAINABLE TOURISM

A standard return flight from New York to São Paulo has a carbon footprint of some 3.75 global hectares (gha). Further domestic flights around Brazil, for example, from São Paulo to Rio, Rio to Salvador, Salvador to Manaus, and Manaus back to São Paulo, add another 1.75 gha, for a total carbon footprint for the trip of about 5.5gha. Carbon offsets, which balance the carbon released by a particular activity, either through reforestation or avoided deforestation, or investment in energy efficiency or carbon trading projects, can be purchased through the NGO **Carbon Fund** (www.carbonfund.org). They will offset the 24,000km (40,000 miles) of flights involved in a trip to Brazil for an astonishingly cheap US$75. Never was environmental expiation purchased so cheaply.

But how can you try to mitigate your local impact once you arrive? First and foremost, live like the locals. Brazilian cities are already far less energy-intensive and resource-hungry than most North American ones. Brazilians—even the middle class—tend to live in high-rise apartments in dense urban neighborhoods, and navigate their cities by public transport or small fuel-efficient car. Do as they do, stay in a high-rise near the beach, take the Metrô or a bus or even cabs, and your ecological impact for the weeks you're here will drop some 90%—from the U.S. average of 37.02 gha to the Brazil average of 3.04 gha.

Beyond that though, your options are somewhat limited. Brazilian resorts and tour operators do advertise "eco-tourism," but in Brazil this means anything that takes place in the outdoors, be it leave-only-footprints nature hikes or churn-up-the-wildlife ATV expeditions. It does not signify lodges or hotels with solar heating or clever ways of dealing with wastewater, or even outdoor operators that take particular care of their local ecosystems. "Eco-tourism" in Brazil is a term that has been stretched to and beyond the bounds of any useful meaning.

In Brazil's two most vulnerable remaining ecosystems—the Pantanal (chapter 19) and the Amazon (chapter 16)—there are tourism operators who strive to protect their local ecosystems. In the Pantanal the **Araras Eco Lodge** (p. 448) and the **Jaguar Ecological Reserve** (p. 448) have helped to popularize the private ecological reserve, a Brazilian program through which the government provides tax breaks in return for a landowner committing to preserving a portion of his in perpetuity. The presence of eco-tourism operators in the Pantanal—particularly Araras—has also provided a lobby to counter certain ill-advised development schemes, including the paving of the Transpantaneira highway, and the widening, straightening, and deepening of the Rio Paraguay, the better to transport soybeans to the coast.

In the Amazon, the **Pousada Uakarí** (p. 399) serves as an integral part of the **Mamiraua Sustainable Development Institute** (www.mamiraua.org.br), a project designed to preserve the habitat of the Uakarí monkey while improving the living standards of local human populations living in and around the Uakarí reserve. Other Amazon lodges come nowhere near this standard, though they do provide some local employment for guides and other lodge staff. Unfortunately, the minuscule scale of eco-tourism operations in comparison with the employment and revenues generated by the timber and cattle industries has rendered eco-tourism a nonplayer in the debate over preserving the Amazon.

However, one could argue that those who experience the Amazon become more likely to lobby to save it. Certainly, awareness of the importance of the Amazon, both globally and in Brazil, has lead to the passage in Brazil of a range of reasonably stringent preservation measures, including parks, reserves, Indian reservations, national forestlands, and restrictions on deforestation on private landholdings. The problem in Brazil is that these regulations are often not respected, while enforcement on the ground remains weak. Still, rates of deforestation in the Brazilian Amazon have declined, from a 2004 peak of 27,400 sq. km (an area somewhat larger than Vermont) to 12,911 sq. km (an area somewhat smaller than Connecticut) in 2008. For more on making an informed decision when booking your trip to the Amazon, see chapter 16.

9 SPECIAL-INTEREST TRIPS & ESCORTED GENERAL-INTEREST TOURS

ACADEMIC TRIPS & LANGUAGE CLASSES

Learning Portuguese will greatly enhance your travel experience in Brazil. "Knowing a bit of Spanish" usually won't cut it here, especially outside of the main tourist destinations. The better language programs are found in large cities where there is a constant supply of students. In addition to learning Portuguese, many programs will also include cultural outings (such as music and events) and provide a great opportunity to meet other travelers. **Languages in Action** (www.languagesinaction.com) offers individual and group courses in São Paulo and Salvador. A company with a language school in downtown Rio de Janeiro is **Bridge Brazil,** Rua da Quitanda 191, Rio de Janeiro (© **866/574-8606** in the U.S. and Canada, or 021/2220-8659 in Rio; www.bridgebrazil.com).

MEDICAL TOURISM

Brazil is emerging as one of the prime destinations for cosmetic and plastic surgery. Brazilian surgeons are second only to U.S. doctors in the number of procedures performed and therefore have extensive experience. Their training is top-notch (in fact, many foreign surgeons come to Brazil to train) and cities like Rio de Janeiro and São Paulo have outstanding medical facilities. In addition to plastic surgery, travelers can also opt for excellent dental care and other beauty treatments, like laser hair removal, botox, and peelings. Of course it pays to do your research. One company that offers a lot of information and a free consultation service to get you started is **Cosmetic Vacations,** 120 E. Oakland Park Blvd. 105-1A, Fort Lauderdale, FL 33334 (© **877/627-2556;** www.cosmetic vacations.com).

VOLUNTEER & WORKING TRIPS

For a different kind of travel experience consider donating some of your time as a volunteer to a local organization. One organization that is particularly well set up to accommodate foreign volunteers is **Iko Poran,** Rua do Oriente, 280/201, Rio de Janeiro (© **021/3852-2916;** www.iko poran.org). They can provide you with detailed information and help you decide if this is something you want to do. Although speaking Portuguese is not a prerequisite, some language knowledge will open up more interesting opportunities.

GENERAL-INTEREST TOURS & PACKAGES

Many travel agencies offer package tours to Brazil, but few have the knowledge to effectively customize your trip or make interesting recommendations. To book a package with Brazil travel experts, contact **Brazil Nuts,** 1854 Trade Center Way, Ste. 101A, Naples, FL 34109 (© **800/553-9959** or 914/593-0266; www.brazilnuts. com). The owners and staff are indeed nuts about Brazil and possess a vast amount of knowledge about the country and its attractions. Depending on your needs you can book just a flight and hotels, or you can add one or more group excursions in more inaccessible places such as the Amazon. Their website is a fount of

information, and staff can answer any questions you may have about Brazil.

Note: Brazilian travel agents still have a firm grip on the hotel market, and Brazilian hotels will usually offer their lowest rates to travel agents instead of posting them on their websites. Once you have narrowed down your hotel options, it can pay to contact an agency like Brazil Nuts to compare rates.

Another excellent resource on Brazil and South America travel in general is **South America Travel** (© **800/747-4540;** www.southamerica.travel). South America Travel offers packages customizable to whatever level you're comfortable with. A number of interesting add-ons are available—outdoors lovers will be pleased to see some great hiking and camping options.

Travelers planning a trip beyond Brazil, to Argentina and Chile, may want to consult with **Borello Travel & Tours,** 7 Park Ave., Ste. 21, New York, NY 10016 (© **800/405-3072** or 212/686-4911; www.borellotravel.com). This travel agency specializes in the Southern Cone and can help you plan a great itinerary to make the most of the region.

A good travel agency to book your ticket through is **Santini Tours,** 6575 Shattuck Ave., Oakland, CA 94609 (© **800/769-9669** or 510/652-8600; www.santours.com). The owner as well as many of the travel agents are Brazilian and can give you many useful suggestions on air pass routings and answer any questions you have about your itinerary. In addition to selling tickets and air passes, Santini can also arrange customized tours, including everything from airport transfers to sight-seeing and guided tours.

For more information on escorted general-interest tours, including questions to ask before booking your trip, see www.frommers.com/planning.

10 STAYING CONNECTED

As in most parts of the world, using the phone from your hotel room is an invitation to a gouging at the checkout desk. Premiums almost always apply, and can sometimes reach extraordinary levels. Public phones in Brazil can be found everywhere and are called *orelhões*. To use these phones you need a phone card, for sale at all newsstands. Ask for a *cartão telefonico*.

TELEPHONES
To call Brazil:
1. Dial the international access code (011 in the U.S. and Canada, 00 in the U.K., Ireland, and New Zealand, or 0011 from Australia).
2. Dial the country code: 55.
3. Then the area code without the 0 (for example, 21 for Rio, 11 for São Paulo).

To call within Brazil:
Dialing a **local number** is straightforward: dial the number without the area code. However, for **long-distance** dialing, telephone numbers are normally listed with a three-digit prefix, followed by the area code, followed by the seven- or eight-digit number (for example, 0XX-21-5555-5555). Since phones were deregulated, a number of very competitive companies have sprung up. The two digits that fill in the XX are the number of the appropriate service provider (in Portuguese this is called the *prestadora*). Any phone can be used to access any service provider. In some cities there may be a choice of two or three providers. The only code that works in all of Brazil (and the only *prestadora* code you need to remember) is the one for *Embratel*—21 (which also happens to be the area code of Rio). So, if you were dialing long distance to a number in Rio, you would dial 0-21 (selecting Embratel as your provider), 21 (Rio's area code), and 5555-5555 (the number). Dialing long

distance to a number in São Paulo, you'd dial 0-21-11-5555-5555.

To make international calls:
Dial 00 + 21 + the country code (U.S. or Canada 1, U.K. 44, Australia 61, New Zealand 64) + area code + phone number.

International collect calls can be requested by dialing **000-111,** or automatically by dialing 90 + 21 + country code (U.S. or Canada 1, U.K. 44, Australia 61, New Zealand 64) + area code + phone number. Major long distance company access codes are as follows: **AT&T** ✆ 0800/890-0288; **MCI** ✆ 0800/890-0012; **Sprint** ✆ 0800/888-8000; and **Canada Direct** ✆ 0800/890-0014.

CELLPHONES
International GSM cellphones work in most parts of Brazil. Charges can be high—usually US$1 to US$1.50 per minute. A better option is to buy a local SIM card, which gives you a local Brazilian number and allows you to pay local Brazilian rates (about R$1 per minute for local calls, R$1.40 for long distance). There is no charge to receive calls if you are in your home area. Outside your area code, roaming charges of about R$1 per minute apply. There are a number of cellphone providers that sell SIM chips in Brazil, but the only one that provides service throughout the country is **TIM** (www.tim.com.br). There are TIM kiosks in all major malls, and airports and department stores. Note that after you buy a TIM SIM chip, you will have to call and register your account (as part of its anti-crime laws Brazil does not allow anonymous cellphone accounts). You will need to give your name and passport number. Cards that allow you to add credit to your account are available at newsstands throughout Brazil.

INTERNET & E-MAIL

Wi-Fi is becoming increasingly common in Brazil. Many hotels offer it either in the lobby or the rooms, or both. A few hotels offer the service for free; many more charge a daily access fee. While Wi-Fi is becoming the norm, many hotels still only offer the old cable plug-in. Remember to bring your cable.

Wi-Fi hot spots are far less common. There is free Wi-Fi on Copacabana beach in Rio de Janeiro, and paid Wi-Fi in airports in Rio and São Paulo, and other sites (generally with an access fee) in some bookstores and cafes in the larger Brazilian cities.

Internet cafes (called *cyber cafés* in Brazil) are quite common everywhere in Brazil, from the Amazon to the big cities. Prices range from R$.55 to R$2 per hour; luxury hotels usually charge the most, anywhere up to R$30 per hour.

11 TIPS ON ACCOMMODATIONS

Brazil offers a wide range of accommodations. In the large cities there are modern high-rise hotels as well as apartment hotels (or rental flats for you Brits) known in Brazil as apart-hotels. The apart-hotels are often a better deal than regular hotel rooms, offering both cheaper rates and more space: a separate living room, bedroom, and kitchen. The drawback is that you sometimes don't get the pool, restaurants, and other amenities of a hotel.

Some of the better hotels that you will find in Brazil are among the **Accor Group** (www.accorhotels.com.br). This French company operates a number of brands such as the Sofitel luxury hotels, the excellent Parthenon apart-hotels, and the Mercure and Ibis. The last two are fairly new and most hotels are only a few years old. The Mercure offers more comfortable accommodations; the Ibis is the Motel 6 version, clean and reliable but no-frills.

A more high-end chain with numerous new properties is the **Meliá** (www.solmelia. com). The **Blue Tree** (www.bluetree.com. br) is also represented in many Brazilian cities. The older properties in the chain are not the best but the modern ones are excellent. A relative newcomer is the **Atlantica Hotels** (www.atlanticahotels.com.br) chain. Some of its best-known brands are the **Comfort Suites** and **Quality.** Both are good, affordable hotels with modern amenities and standards.

Outside of the large cities you will often find pousadas, essentially our equivalent of a bed-and-breakfast or small inn. Accommodations prices fluctuate widely. The rates posted at the front desk—the rack rate or *tarifa balcão*—are just a guideline. Outside of high season and on weekends you can almost always negotiate significant (20%–30%) discounts. High season is from mid-December to Carnaval (mid- to late Feb), Easter week, long weekends (see "Holidays," earlier in this chapter, for Brazilian holidays), and July (winter vacation). Notable exceptions are Brasilia and São Paulo, where business just dies during high season and weekends and rooms are heavily discounted.

Tip: Always check the quotes you have obtained from a hotel with a travel agency such as Brazil Nuts or South America Travel as many hotels will give their best rates to travel agents and stick it to individual travelers or those who book via the Internet. The Copacabana Palace quoted us a price of US$220 to US$450 for a room, whereas Brazil Nuts can sell you that same room for US$150.

Unlike North American hotels, Brazilian hotel rooms do not feature coffeemakers, irons, or ironing boards, although the latter can sometimes be delivered to your room upon request. Even in luxury hotels, the complimentary toiletries are usually very basic, so pack your own. On the other hand, **breakfast** *(café de manha)* at Brazilian hotels is almost always included in the room price and at most places includes a nice buffet-style spread including bread, meats, cheeses, fruit, eggs (sometimes), and *café com leite,* strong coffee served with hot milk. In recent years a few of the more expensive hotels have taken to charging for *café de manha;* if this is the case it's noted in the review.

Accommodations **taxes** range from nothing to 15%, varying from city to city and hotel to hotel. Always check in advance.

Suggested Brazil Itineraries

A vast, beautiful, sprawling country, Brazil covers nearly as much land area as the United States, and has regions as geographically different from each other as Arizona is from Vermont, and as culturally diverse as Boston and Salt Lake City. Getting even a taste of such an ocean of experiences requires time and air travel. Most of the itineraries below cover just over 2 weeks. If you have more time, by all means add destinations from other routes, or better yet, slow down and take things easy. It is a vacation, after all.

Obviously, the possibilities are endless. Itineraries below try to combine what is best in Brazil—its people, culture, and music, its history, and its natural wonders, be they beaches, islands, or vast tropical forest.

1 THE REGIONS IN BRIEF

Brazil's 190 million citizens inhabit the fifth-largest country in the world, a nation about 10% larger than the continental United States. The **Amazon** dominates the northern third of the country—a vast tropical rainforest with the river at its heart. The country's central interior is dominated by the *planalto,* a high dry plateau covered in *cerrado,* a type of dry savanna reminiscent of that of Southern Africa. The chief city in this region is the planned federal capital Brasilia. West of the *planalto* but south of the Amazon rainforest you find the **Pantanal,** a wetland the size of France that is one of the best places to see wildlife in the whole of South America. Brazil's **Northeast** is a land apart. Running roughly from São Luis to Salvador, the coast is dominated by midsize cities and sugar cane, the culture strongly Afro-Brazilian, while on the dry interior plateau those Nordestinos who haven't yet fled to the cities eke out a bare living on the land. Brazil's two chief cities, **Rio de Janeiro** and **São Paulo,** stand within a few hundred miles of each other close to the country's south coast. São Paulo is the larger and more important of the two, but Rio, the former capital and *cidade maravilhosa* (marvelous city), is by far the more interesting. The small southern tip of the country is inhabited largely by descendants of European immigrants. It's the most densely settled and best-organized part of Brazil. The area has the astonishing natural wonder of **Iguaçu Falls,** for many visitors a must-see. The island of Santa Catarina, also known as **Florianópolis,** has over 40 beaches and is the favorite summer destination in the south.

RIO DE JANEIRO Few cities are as striking as Rio. The city folds itself into the narrow bits of land between tropical beaches and mountains that leap to 750m (2,500-ft.) heights (one of these is crowned by the city's landmark statue of Christ). The city offers much in the way of sightseeing, from nature to sunbathing to museums and historic neighborhoods. The culture, perhaps best expressed in music and nightlife, is just as appealing. Samba is alive and well, augmented by many vibrant newer forms of distinctly Brazilian music. The event of the year is **Carnaval,** the biggest party of the world. And

BRAZIL IN 1 WEEK
- **1-3** Rio de Janeiro
- **4-5** Salvador
- **6-7** Iguaçu Falls

BRAZIL IN 2 WEEKS
- **1-3** Rio de Janeiro
- **4-6** Salvador
- **7-11** The Amazon
- **12** Transit
- **13-14** Iguaçu Falls

BRAZIL FOR FAMILIES
- **1-2** Rio de Janeiro
- **3-6** Olinda & Porto de Galinhas
- **7-11** Amazon
- **12-15** Belém & the Island of Marajó
- **16-17** Iguaçu Falls

BRAZIL FOR NATURE LOVERS
- **1-2** Rio de Janeiro
- **3-6** Pantanal
- **7-12** Amazon
- **13-16** Fernando de Noronha
- **17-18** Iguaçu Falls

believe me when I say that Cariocas—as Rio residents are known—know how to throw a party.

SÃO PAULO   Some 25 million people live in and around São Paulo, the largest city not only in Brazil but in all of South America. São Paulo is Brazil's New York. It's the melting pot that attracts the best and brightest to make their fortune. The city overflows with restaurants, including the best fine dining in Brazil. São Paulo has emerged as the cultural capital of Brazil, rich with art galleries and strong in new theater. And it's the best place in Brazil to shop.

THE NORTHEAST   Even in a country with such strong regional distinctions, Brazil's Northeast (Nordeste) stands apart. Roughly speaking, the Nordeste encompasses the area from Salvador to São Luis, including cities such as Recife, Natal, and Fortaleza. Everything Nordeste is different: the food richer, the cities more historic, the beaches longer and whiter, the music more vibrant, the politics more Byzantine and traditionally more corrupt. This was the first part of Brazil to be settled, the area where sugar cane and slavery dominated economy and society for more than 3 centuries. The downturn in the sugar economy left the area a backwater, and only with the recent advent of tourism have Nordeste fortunes really begun to pick up. For visitors, the Northeast offers a year-round tropical climate with long, white sandy beaches, historic cities, and a vibrant Afro-Brazilian culture, which is reflected in the cuisine, the festivals, and, especially, the music and dance. Olinda is a quiet colonial gem of a city, while Salvador's 16th-century colonial core has been transformed into a stroller's dream.

THE AMAZON   The largest rainforest in the world is so vast it defies easy description: All of western Europe would fit comfortably with room to spare beneath its leafy canopy. Thanks in large part to media coverage of the many threats to this region, interest in eco-tourism and visits to the Amazon have skyrocketed. The main staging ground for trips to the Brazilian Amazon is the city of Manaus, located where the Rio Negro joins the Rio Solimões to form the Amazon. Manaus itself is surprisingly modern. Moderately interesting in itself, its real interest is as the starting point for expeditions into the rainforest. Options include everything from day trips on the Amazon to multiday trips to virgin rainforest where one can catch sight of countless unique plants and animals. In contrast to Manaus, the city of Belém, located at the mouth of the Amazon, is an old and settled city, with numerous churches and a historic downtown, and the incredible Ver-o-Peso market, where the entire produce of the Amazon is bought and sold. Close to Belém in the mouth of the Amazon river is Marajó, an island larger than Switzerland, dotted with buffalo ranches and rich with bird life. Halfway between Manaus and Belém there is Santarem, and the astonishing white-sand beaches of Alter do Chão.

THE CENTER WEST   Brazil's center west is a broad flat plain, dotted here and there with craggy highlands, and populated chiefly by ranchers, cowhands, and increasingly by large commercial farms. It was in the midst of this vast and not especially intriguing region that nearly 50 years ago Brazil erected its striking modernist capital, Brasilia. While the capital may be the region's man-made wonder, the natural wonder is the Pantanal. A wetland the size of France, the Pantanal has traditionally been overlooked in favor of the Amazon, but that's changing as people become increasingly aware of the incredible wildlife-viewing opportunities the area offers. More than 600 bird species, anacondas, jaguars, caiman, giant otters, and anteaters are just some of the animals found in the wetlands. As this area lacks the dense foliage of the Amazon, the animals are much easier to spot.

The southern part of Brazil, made up of the states of Paraná, Santa Catarina, and Rio Grande do Sul, has a temperate climate and good soil, attributes that long attracted large numbers of European immigrants. It's a settled, well-organized region. The prime beach destination in the south is Florianópolis, a large island with over 40 beaches, clean waters, and excellent restaurants and nightlife. The Iguaçu Falls, a UNESCO World Heritage Site, are located on the border of Brazil, Argentina, and Paraguay. These spectacular falls are made up of 275 falls that cascade from 72m (240 ft.) down a 2.5km-wide (1½-mile) precipice in a fabulous jungle setting.

---

2 BRAZIL IN 1 WEEK

You've got a week, and you want to see Brazil? Your first step should be to talk your boss into giving you another week, preferably two. Failing that, the route below gives a quick taste of three of Brazil's highlights: Rio de Janeiro, the historic city of Salvador, and the natural wonder of Iguaçu Falls. It'll be a busy week, though. Those who like a more laid-back pace should skip either Salvador or Iguaçu.

Days ❶–❸: Rio de Janeiro ★★★

To get into the Brazilian spirit, start off your trip in **Rio de Janeiro** (chapters 5 and 6). After getting settled in your hotel, head for the beach. Enjoy the scene, tan a bit (but don't overdo it). Watch the sunset from **Arpoador.** You'll be tired from the flight, so take it easy with a good dinner in one of the top restaurants of **Ipanema** or **Leblon.** On day 2 get out and see the mountains. Take a tram up to the **Corcovado,** or take a jeep tour up through **Tijuca Forest.** Stop by **Cinelândia** in Rio's Centro in the afternoon. That night, discover the late-night Carioca lifestyle. Have dinner around 11pm, then catch some samba, played live in **Lapa.** You'll be sleeping late the next day, so spend some more time at the beach, or take a trolley up to explore the hillside neighborhood of **Santa Teresa.** All this should acclimatize you to the Brazilian way before you set off to explore the rest of the country.

Days ❹ & ❺: Salvador ★★★

Early on day 4, catch a flight for **Salvador** (chapter 11). This is the city where the country's African roots are strongest. Stay in one of the lovely pousadas in **Pelourinho** like the **Pousada do Pilar** (p. 255), or

pamper yourself with a stay in the restored 17th-century **Convento do Carmo** (p. 254). Wander through Pelourinho's 17th-century streets. In the evening, try some Bahian cuisine, then go out and enjoy the music in Pelourinho after dark. Next day, take the boat tour of the **Bay of All Saints,** or head out to the church of **Bonfim,** or tour the lovely **Museu de Arte Sacra.** Or if you're the Energizer Bunny, do all three.

Days ❻ & ❼: Iguaçu Falls ★★★

A final must-see—one of the most awe-inspiring natural wonders of the world—**Iguaçu Falls** (chapter 18). The early flight from Salvador should get you to Iguaçu before 2pm. Store your stuff and go see the falls. Today stick to the Brazilian side. Don't forget to take the **Macuco boat safari** (p. 438). Unforgettable.

Your next step the next day depends on flights. There are afternoon flights from Iguaçu that will get you to São Paulo in time to connect with your evening flight back to North America. Theoretically, you could get up early (again) and make the trip to the Argentine side and make it back in time for that 4pm flight. Or you could do the sensible thing and stay another night in Iguaçu. Get up a little later, and go explore the Argentine side at a leisurely pace. That night, have dinner somewhere in downtown Foz do Iguaçu.

Next morning, you can catch an early flight to São Paulo and spend the day exploring, or you can dawdle by the hotel pool in Iguaçu (or go see the **Bird Park,** p. 440), before catching a later flight to São Paulo and connecting to your evening flight home.

3 BRAZIL IN 2 WEEKS

In 2 weeks, you can get a good taste of Brazil at a pace that won't leave you with post-holiday stress disorder. The route below takes you to Rio de Janeiro and the historic city of Salvador. You then have the option of spending time in the Amazon or on a beautiful Bahian beach. The Amazon is fascinating, but it requires both money and travel time. This route includes Iguaçu Falls and a brief taste of the urban sophistication that is São Paulo.

Days ❶–❺: Same as Above

Day ❻: Salvador ★★★
With your extra day in Salvador, dig deeper into this city's treasures at a leisurely pace; head out to the church of **Bonfim,** or tour the lovely **Museu de Arte Sacra.** See the lighthouse and beaches of **Barra.**

Days ❼–⓫: The Amazon ★★★
Catch an early flight to **Manaus** (p. 376). It's time to experience a bit of the largest standing rainforest on earth, the Amazon. On your first day you should have time to see the highlights of Manaus, including the famous **Opera House.** The next morning, set off early for a jungle lodge (or better yet, if you have more time, go kayaking through the forest with **Amazon Mystery Tours,** p. 402). Choose a smaller lodge farther from the city. Don't go to the Ariaú. Although the area around Manaus is hardly unexplored, a few days will allow you to experience the fauna and flora of a tropical rainforest. Enjoy the trees, the monkeys, the caiman, and the bright pink dolphins.

Day ⓬: Transit
It's going to take a day of taxis, boats, and airplanes to get you to your next destination, Iguaçu.

Days ⓭ & ⓮: Iguaçu Falls ★★★
A final must-see—one of the most awe-inspiring natural wonders of the world—**Iguaçu Falls** (chapter 18). The early flight from Salvador should get you to Iguaçu before 2pm. Store your stuff and go see the falls. Stick to the Brazilian side today and perhaps take the **Macuco boat safari** (p. 438). The next day, go explore the falls from the Argentine side. You can catch an early flight to São Paulo and spend the next day exploring, or you can dawdle by the hotel pool in Iguaçu (or go see the **Bird Park,** p. 440), before catching a later flight to São Paulo and connecting to your evening flight home.

4 BRAZIL FOR FAMILIES

Brazilians love children nearly as much as they love beaches, beer, and music. Maybe more. This route combines Brazil's top destinations in ways that will allow both you and your kids to have fun.

Days ❶ & ❷: Rio de Janeiro ★★★

To get into the Brazilian spirit, start off your trip in **Rio de Janeiro** (p. 60). See the must-sees such as the **Corcovado, Sugar Loaf,** and **Copacabana beach,** while discovering the typically Brazilian *joie de vivre* and the late-night Carioca lifestyle— spend an afternoon at the beach, watch the sunset at **Arpoador,** drink beers in an old-fashioned bar in the hillside neighborhood of **Santa Teresa,** dance to samba in **Lapa,** start dinner after midnight (assuming you aren't traveling with small children). More than seeing the sights, it will acclimatize you to the Brazilian way before you set off to explore the rest of the country.

Days ❸–❻: Olinda & Porto de Galinhas ★★★

From Rio, it's only a short flight to **Recife** and **Olinda** (chapter 12). As historic as Salvador, Olinda is more lived in, full of artists, among them the famous puppet makers who show works in the **Puppet Museum** (p. 321). Spend a day here, then head south to the beachside village of Porto de Galinhas. Snorkel the shallow reef pools full of fish. Look for sea horses in the tidal mangroves.

Days ❼–⓫: Amazon ★★★

Catch an early flight to Manaus. It's time to experience a bit of the largest standing rainforest on earth, the **Amazon** (chapter 16). On your first day you should have time to see the highlights of Manaus, including the famous Manaus Opera House. Set off early the next morning for a jungle lodge. Choose a smaller lodge farther from the city. Don't go to the Ariaú. Although the area around Manaus is hardly unexplored, a few days will allow you to experience the fauna and flora of a tropical rainforest. Enjoy the trees, the monkeys, the caiman, and the bright pink dolphins.

Days ⓬–⓯: Belém & the Island of Marajó ★★

From Manaus, fly to **Belem** (p. 402), and hop on a ferry for the big river island of **Marajó** (p. 415). Spend a few days on a buffalo ranch—we recommend the **Fazenda Sanjo**—with a Marajó family, riding horses, herding buffalo, and seeing caiman and flocks of bright red roseate spoonbills (p. 416).

Days ⓰ & ⓱: Iguaçu Falls ★★★

A final must-see on a first-time visit—one of the most awe-inspiring natural wonders of the world—is **Iguaçu Falls** (chapter 18). You can easily spend 2 days exploring the falls from various angles and in various ways: on foot, by boat, by train, and by helicopter.

---

5 BRAZIL FOR NATURE LOVERS

Buildings, history, beautiful bodies—none of that interests the nature lover. What they want to see are trees, birds, butterflies, and animals lurking and playing in their native habitats.

Days ❶ & ❷: Rio de Janeiro ★★★

Yes, it's a city of 12 million. But it's one of those rare cities with an intimate relationship with nature. Instead of the busy beach neighborhoods, stay in one of **Rio de Janeiro**'s (chapter 5) small B&Bs in hilltop **Santa Teresa.** Take a guided hike through the **Tijuca** rainforest with **Rio Hiking** (p. 125). Take a walk below the Sugarloaf by **Praia Vermelha,** and admire the bird life and rainforest and with luck, the troupe of marmosets that make their home on the hillside. Go up to the **Corcovado,** look down at Rio, and see how ocean, beach, city, and forest merge into one.

Days ❸–❻: The Pantanal ★★★

Then catch a flight to **Cuiabá** and head down the **Transpantaneira** into the **Pantanal** (chapter 19). This flooded landscape is a bird-watcher's dream, so bring your binoculars and several pencils to keep track of all the new species you'll be seeing.

Days ❼–⓬: The Amazon ★★★

From the Pantanal, fly north to the **Amazon** (chapter 16). The species diversity is greater here, but the very richness of the foliage makes the animals and birds much harder to see. So enjoy the trees. And the monkeys, and dolphins, and parrots. Go out on a kayak trip on the upper Amazon with **Amazon Mystery Tours** (p. 402). Or head for one of the lodges far from **Manaus,** preferably the **Mamiraua Reserve** (p. 399).

Days ⓭–⓰: Fernando de Noronha ★★

From Manaus, catch a flight all the way out to **Fernando de Noronha** (chapter 20). A vastly different ecosystem, this semidesert tropical island is home to large schools of spinner dolphins, not to mention the sea turtles that lay their eggs on the island's long beaches. If you scuba dive, bring your gear. If you don't, there's still plenty to see above the surface of the water.

Days ⓱ & ⓲: Iguaçu Falls ★★★

Take the long flight all the way south to **Iguaçu Falls** (chapter 18), one of the natural wonders of the world. Astonishing enough in themselves, the falls create a misty microclimate perfect for toucans, dusky swifts (which actually nest on the cliff behind the waterfalls), and bright, colorful butterflies. In the rainy season, thousands of the colorful insects float and flutter at the edge of the roaring falls.

6 BRAZIL FOR THE ACTIVE TRAVELER

This is the itinerary for those who want to be out doing—hiking, climbing, swimming, diving. Brazil is rich in outdoor sports, be they on mountain peaks, on the beach, in the ocean, or underneath it. This route starts in Rio, then has three different options for hiking—in the mountains near the city, on an island covered in Atlantic rainforest, or farther north in the dry highlands of Bahia. The route then includes time in Fernando de Noronha and the Lençóis Maranhenses, two magical landscapes found nowhere outside Brazil.

Days ❶ & ❷: Rio de Janeiro ★★★

Arrive in **Rio de Janeiro** (chapters 5 and 6). Spend a half-day rock climbing up the **Sugarloaf,** or else hike the **Floresta de Tijuca,** a vast rainforest that wraps itself around the city. Or rent a board and catch the surf bus out to **Barra** for the city's best waves.

Days ❸–❻: Teresopolis to Petrópolis ★

The 2- to 3-day hike between the royal cities of **Teresopolis** and **Petrópolis** takes in the high mountain terrain (approx. 1,500m/4,900 ft.) in Serra dos Orgãos mountains close to Rio de Janeiro. Hiking specialists **Rio Hiking** can arrange transfer to and from the city, and make your trek more comfortable. See "Trekking," in chapter 6, and "Petrópolis," in chapter 7.

OR Days ❸–❻: Chapada Diamantina ★★

Fly to **Salvador** and get a bus or plane up to the **Chapada Diamantina** (p. 290). This magic highland area is full of bluffs, buttes, and waterfalls, and laced with stunning crystal caverns. Do day hikes from the city of **Lençóis,** or contract a guide to take you on a multiday trek past the Falls of Smoke (Cachoeira de Fumaça).

OR Days ❸–❻: Ilha Grande ★★

Take the bus and ferry to **Ilha Grande** (p. 169). This former prison colony has beaches for **surfing, swimming,** and **bodyboarding,** forest-covered mountains for **hiking,** wrecks for **diving,** little sheltered inlets for **snorkeling,** and wide-open seas for **kayaking.** Take 3 days and do it all.

Day ❼: Transit Day

Whether you start from Rio, Ilha Grande, or the Chapada Diamantina, it's going to take you most of a day to get to the island of Fernando de Noronha.

Days ❽–⓫: Fernando de Noronha ★★

Grab your scuba gear and go diving. This isolated archipelago (chapter 20) has the best underwater sea life in Brazil. **Atlantis Divers** (p. 470) is the company to go with. Don't forget to rent a buggy and explore the island. While you're there, try to see the baby sea turtles hatch.

Days ⓬–⓯: Lençóis Maranhenses ★★

From Fernando, fly to **São Luis** and catch a plane or bus for **Barreirinhas,** gateway to the **Lençóis Maranhenses** (chapter 15). An ecosystem unlike anything else on earth, the Lençóis is a vast desert of shifting white-sand dunes, chock-full of rainwater. In the wet season the rainwater collects to form countless crystal pools and lakes in the depressions between dunes. Best of all, the sand is so fine-grained that it's cool on your feet, even in the height of summer.

---

7 BRAZIL FOR ARCHITECTURE & HISTORY BUFFS

This is for those who like to stroll and observe and learn, understanding a country's culture by researching its history, and by close observation of that most enduring of the visual arts, architecture. The route takes in both of Brazil's former capitals (Rio de Janeiro and Salvador), the rich baroque cities of Minas Gerais, and the modern new city of Brasilia.

Days ❶–❸: Rio de Janeiro ★★★

Start in **Rio de Janeiro** (chapters 5 and 6). Brazil's former capital is rich in history. Tour the **Museu Histórico Nacional** and the **Quinta da Boa Vista** where the Emperor Pedro II lived in baroque splendor, collecting scientific specimens all the while. Wander the **Paço Imperial** where the emperor once ruled, and the nearby

Praça XV where rebellious army officers brought his reign to an end. Don't forget to have a look at the **Palácio Gustavo Capenema** in Rio's downtown. Designed by Le Corbusier and Oscar Niemeyer, this building is where the Brazilian love affair with modernism began, where the seeds of what became Brasilia were laid.

SUGGESTED BRAZIL ITINERARIES

4

BRAZIL BEACHES, BEACHES & BEACHES

Days ❹–❼: Historic Cities of Minas Gerais ★★★

Rent a car (or hop on a bus) and take a road trip through the historic cities of **Minas Gerais, Ouro Preto, Mariana,** and **Tiradentes** (chapter 8). These cities were awash in gold when the colonial baroque was at its height. Admire the churches and fine buildings, and the phenomenal sculpture works of crippled sculptor **Aleijadinho.**

Days ❽–❿: Salvador ★★★

Back in Rio, catch a flight to **Salvador** (chapter 11). Stay in one of the lovely pousadas in **Pelourinho** like the **Boqueirão.** Wander through the 17th-century streets of Pelourinho, and marvel at the wealth brought by sugar. Tour the **Museu de Arte Sacra** to see the fine artwork wrought from Brazilian silver.

Days ⓫–⓭: Recife & Olinda ★★

From Salvador fly north to **Recife** (chapter 12), a city founded not by the Portuguese but by the Dutch, who conquered northern Brazil for a time. For more on this period, tour the city's fine **history museum,** housed in the **Fort of Five Points.** To compare Dutch and Portuguese styles of city-building, travel but a few miles north to **Olinda** (p. 307), the former capital of the region, and a city built by the Portuguese. Olinda rivals Salvador for the quality of its churches and historic buildings.

Days ⓮ & ⓯: Brasilia ★★

Leave the 17th century behind and make a bold leap into the modern world. Fly to **Brasilia** (chapter 17). Admire the fluid and futuristic architecture of **Oscar Niemeyer.** Judge for yourself whether the world's first fully planned national capital has succeeded or failed in making Brazil the country of the future.

Day ⓰: São Paulo ★

From Brasilia, fly to **São Paulo** (chapters 9 and 10). See Niemeyer's later (and to my mind, inferior) works such as the **Monument to Latin America.** Then see what Brazilian architects are doing now. Walk the Avenida Paulista. If you can afford it, stay at the Hotel Unique. If you can't, have a drink on its rooftop bar. Admire the run of skyscrapers on the Avenida Paulista in the distance.

8 BRAZIL BEACHES, BEACHES & BEACHES

This is the trip for those who think white grains of silicon assembled together by the seaside is the sole and perfect definition of paradise. Brazil is especially blessed with beaches: urban beaches, party beaches, surfing beaches, and wild, desolate, and lonely beaches. This tour takes a short splash on all of them.

Days ❶–❸: Rio de Janeiro ★★★

Start in **Rio de Janeiro** (chapters 5 and 6), and spend a couple or a few days experiencing the beach culture of the cidade maravilhosa. Dozens of kilometers of beach are within the city limits. Key beaches to explore include **Copacabana, Ipanema, Leblon, São Conrado, Barra,** and the **Grumari.**

Days ❹ & ❺: Salvador ★★★

From Rio, take the plane to **Salvador** (chapter 11). Enjoy the colonial architecture and the music scene for a day, but don't forget to test out the music and dining on Salvador's best urban beach, **Stella Maris.**

Days ❻–❿: Morro de São Paulo & Boipeba

From the Bahian capital take the catamaran south 2 hours and party for a day or two in **Morro de São Paulo** (p. 294). In this little beach resort even the streets are made of sand. Then take a short boat trip one island south to relax for a day or two on **Boipeba** (p. 298), one of the most relaxed and isolated beaches on the Bahian coastline.

Days ⑪–⑯: Natal to Fortaleza by Dune Buggy

From Boipeba, take the boat back to Morro and catch a plane back to Salvador airport in time to make a connecting flight to **Natal** (chapter 13), a city surrounded by sand. Rent a dune buggy and explore the sand, sea, and massive sand dunes that stretch from the city's edge hundreds of kilometers north. Better yet, make a 4-day journey by beach buggy with **Buggy & Cia** to **Fortaleza** (p. 343).

OR Days ⑪–⑯: São Luis & Lençóis Maranhenses

Either way, your next leg should be by plane to **São Luis** (p. 359). It's worth spending a day wandering this historic city, before catching a plane or bus for the town of **Barreirinhas** (p. 371), gateway to the **Lençóis Maranhenses** (p. 370). The Lençóis are not so much beach as a vast Sahara-like desert of perfect white-sand dunes, laced with countless rainwater lakes. You can hike the dunes, swim in the lagoons, and visit the wild, untouched coast nearby.

Days ⑰–⑳: Florianópolis

Returning to São Luis, catch a long flight down to **Santa Catarina,** and spend some days on the southern, surf-crazy island of **Florianópolis** (chapter 21). Rent a car and drive to the southern tip of the island and feast on fresh oysters.

Settling into Rio de Janeiro

Say "Rio" and mental images explode: the glittering skimpy costumes of Carnaval; the statue of Christ, arms outspread on the mountaintop; the beach at Ipanema, crowded with women in minuscule bikinis; the rocky Sugarloaf; or the persistent rhythm of the samba.

Fortunately in Rio there's much more beyond the glitter: historic neighborhoods, compelling architecture, wildlife and nature, dining (fine and not so fine), nightspots, cafes, museums, and enclaves of rich and poor. In Rio, the more you explore, the more there is.

Stunning as the physical setting is—mountains tumbling down to sandy beaches and the sea—Rio was not always the *cidade maravilhosa* (marvelous city) it would become. The town grew up as a shipping center for gold and supplies during Brazil's 18th-century gold rush. In 1762, the colonial capital was transferred from Salvador to Rio, though the city remained a dusty colonial backwater.

In 1808, the Portuguese royal family fled Lisbon ahead of Napoleon's armies and moved court and the capital to Rio. Accustomed to the style of European capitals, the prince regent and the 12,000 nobles who accompanied him began to transform Rio into a city of ornate palaces and landscaped parks. High culture arrived in the form of a new library, an academy of arts and sciences, and the many glittering balls held by the imported elite. King João VI's son, Pedro, liked Rio so much that when the king returned to Lisbon, Pedro stayed on and declared Brazil independent.

Now the capital of a country larger and richer than many in Europe, Rio grew at a phenomenal pace; by the late 1800s it was one of the largest cities in the world. A sizable segment of the population were Brazilians of African descent who brought with them the musical traditions of Africa and the Brazilian Northeast.

A new "low culture" of distinctly Brazilian music began to develop in the city's poorer neighborhoods. The high point of the year for both high and low cultures was the celebration of Carnaval. In palace ballrooms the elite held elaborate costume balls. In the streets, poorer residents staged their own all-night parades. Not until the 1920s did the two celebrations begin to merge. Low culture influenced composer Heitor Villa-Lobos, who incorporated Brazilian rhythms and sounds into his classical compositions. Gowns and costumes at the elite balls got more elaborate, not to mention more risqué. At about the same time, the first road was punched through to Copacabana, and Cariocas (as Rio residents are called) flocked to the new community by the beach.

All of these elements came together in the 1930s with the opening of the Copacabana Palace hotel—a luxury hotel on Copacabana beach with a nightclub that featured exclusively Brazilian music. The 1933 Fred Astaire–Ginger Rogers musical *Flying Down to Rio* portrayed Rio as a city of beach, song, and beautiful, passionate people. The image held enough truth that the iconography has stuck through the end of the 20th century and beyond.

In the years following World War II, São Paulo took over as Brazil's industrial leader; the federal capital moved inland to Brasilia in the early 1960s. By the 1980s, violence and crime plagued the country, and Rio was perceived as the sort of place where walking down the street was asking for a mugging. Cariocas began to fear for the future of their city.

Fortunately, in the early 1990s, governments began putting money back into basic services; cops were stationed on city streets, on public beaches, and anywhere else there seemed to be a problem. Public and private owners began renovating the many heritage buildings of the city's colonial core. Rio's youth rediscovered samba, returning to pack renovated clubs in the old bohemian enclave of Lapa. Rio began reaching out to the rest of the world, with successful bids to host the Pan-American games in 2007, followed by soccer's World Cup in 2014, capped off with the city's selection to host the 2016 Olympic Summer Games.

A city of some seven million and growing, Rio remains one of Brazil's media capitals, an important business center, and Brazil's key tourist destination.

1 RIO DE JANEIRO ESSENTIALS

359km (223 miles) NE of São Paolo

ARRIVING

By Plane

GALEÃO AIRPORT Most major airlines fly to Rio de Janeiro, sometimes with a stop or connection in São Paulo. International passengers arrive at **Antônio Carlos Jobim Airport** (© 021/3398-5050), more commonly known as **Galeão Airport,** 20km (12 miles) from downtown.

On the third floor of Terminal 1 is a Banco do Brasil office (daily 8am–10pm), as well as ATMs of HSBC and Banco 24 Horas, both of which use the Visa/PLUS system. The American Express office (daily 6:30am–10pm) is in the second floor departure area of Terminal 1.

Taxis at Galeão are a challenge. Drivers will start to hassle you the minute you step through the sliding doors. The safer but more expensive bet is to buy a prepaid fare at the **TransCoopass** desk in the arrivals hall (© 021/2209-1555; www.transcoopass.com.br; all major credit cards accepted). Rates range from R$60 to Flamengo, and R$70 to R$80 to the beach hotels of Copacabana and Ipanema. These prepaid taxis are about 40% more expensive, but give you peace of mind; it doesn't matter if you get stuck in traffic or the driver takes the long route. On the other hand, if you know what you're doing (or can bluff), you can cut those prices significantly just by hailing a regular taxi out in front of the terminal. A ride to Copacabana should cost about R$45 in average traffic conditions. Note that if you don't know what you're doing, your friendly Rio taxi man may well take you on a detour long enough to double that price, or even claim the meter reads in dollars.

Gray Line (© 021/2512-9919; www.grayline.com) offers a minibus transfer service from Galeão to the hotels of the Zona Sul or Barra. Cost is US$21 (payable in advance online or the equivalent in Reals to the bus driver) one-way, with one bag free, extra bags R$5 (payable to the bus driver). Buses depart daily once an hour from 8am to 7pm. You meet the uniformed Gray Line driver by the RioTur booth in either Terminal 1 or Terminal 2. Transfers can be booked in advance on the Internet.

See "Where to Stay & Dine in São Conrado, Leblon, Ipanema & Copacabana" map

Morro dois Irmãos

Serra da Carioca

Jardim Botânico

JARDIM BOTÂNICO

LEBLON BEACH
Posto 11

LEBLON

L. Franca

Av. Padre

R. Mário Ribeiro

Av. B. Mitre

R. Jardim Botânico

Jockey Club

R. Gen. Goyês

Av. B. de Medeiros

Av. Lineu de Paula Machado

R. Jardim Botânico

Corcovado Railway

Corcovado

Posto 10

Av. Delfim Moreira

Av. Vieira Souto

Av. Prudente de Morais

Lagoa Rodrigo de Freitas

IPANEMA BEACH
Posto 9

IPANEMA

R. Visc. de Pirajá

Av. Epitácio Pessoa

Av. Epitácio Pessoa

SILVESTRE

Túnel Rebouças

Posto 8

Praça Gal Osório
G. OSÓRIO

Morro do Cantagalo

Morro dos Cabritos

ARPOADOR BEACH

Posto 7

R. P. Loureiro

R. B. Ribeiro

CANTAGALO

Av. Atlântica

R. V. da Pátria

R. Real Grandeza

Museu do Indio

R. das Palmeiras

R. Sorocaba

Museu Villa Lobos

R. Dona Mariana

R. Mena Barreto

Posto 6

Posto 5

R. Santa Clara

COPACABANA

São João Batista Cemetery

BOTAFOGO

Forte de Copacabana

Posto 4

Av. Atlântica

SIQUEIRA CAMPOS

Morro de São João

R. Muniz Barreto

BOTAFOGO

Praça Serzedelo Correia

CARDEAL ARCOVERDE

COPACABANA BEACH

Posto 3

Av. Atlântica

Av. Princesa Isabel

Av. Lauro Sodré

Botafogo Bay

ATLANTIC OCEAN

Posto 2

LEME

URCA

Museu Carmen Miranda

Posto 1

Av. Atlântica

Av. Portugal

LEME BEACH

Cable Car Station

Morro da Urca

URCA BEACH

VERMELHA BEACH

URCA

Morro do Leme

Morro do Urubu

Sugarloaf Cable Car

Sugarloaf

ATLANTIC OCEAN

Manaus
Belém

Natal

B R A Z I L
Amazon
Recife

Brasília
Salvador

Rio de Janeiro

São Paulo

500 mi
500 km

0   1 mi
0   1 km

Beach
M Subway Station
- - - Street Car
✈ Airport

SANTOS DUMONT AIRPORT Rio's second airport, **Santos Dumont,** Praça Senador Salgado Filho (© 021/3814-7070), is downtown, surrounded by the Baia de Guanabara. Most Brazilian airlines now use Santos Dumont for domestic flights. These airlines include **TAM** (© 021/4002-5700; www.tam.com.br), **Gol** (© 0300/115-2121; www.voegol.com.br), **Azul** (© 021/3003-2985; www.voeazul.com.br), **Webjet** (© 0300/210-1234; www.webjet.com.br), **TRIP** (© 021/3003-8747; www.voetrip.com.br), and **Ocean Air** (© 0300/789-8160; www.oceanair.com.br).

Taxis from Santos Dumont are less of a problem. Prepaid taxis are available from the **TransCoopass** (© 021/2209-1555; www.transcoopass.com.br) booth in the arrivals hall. The prepaid service costs about double what a metered taxi will cost. Better just to hail a cab from the taxi row in front of the terminal. Airport cabs are about 20% more expensive than a normal taxis (not officially, but almost universally so in practice), but distances from Santos Dumont are short enough that this won't make a huge difference. A metered taxi to Ipanema should cost around R$30.

A variety of bank machines, including a Banco do Brasil and HSBC, are located at the center entrance of the airport.

By Bus

All long-distance buses arrive at the **Novo Rio Rodoviaria,** Av. Francisco Bicalho 1, Santo Cristo (© 021/3213-1800; www.novorio.com.br), close to downtown near the old port. It's best to use a taxi traveling to or from the station. It's not the best part of town, particularly with all your bags. Prepaid taxi vouchers are available at the booth next to the taxi stand. A ride from the bus station to Ipanema costs about R$40.

By Cruise Ship

Cruise ships dock in the terminal almost opposite Praça Mauá. Downtown is an easy walk, and public transit is close by. If returning to the ship after dark, it's best to take a taxi. Praça Mauá becomes a somewhat seedy red-light district in the evening.

RIO'S NEIGHBORHOODS AT A GLANCE

Mountains and ocean are ever present in Rio. The city has essentially squeezed itself into any available space on the tiny littoral between the two. The city is traditionally divided into four zones: **North (Zona Norte), Center (Centro), West (Zona Oeste),** and **South (Zona Sul).** A much more detailed description of Rio's neighborhoods can be found in "Neighborhoods to Explore" in chapter 6.

ZONA NORTE Largest and least interesting from a visitor's perspective, the **Zona Norte** stretches from a few blocks north of Avenida Presidente Vargas all the way to the city limits. With only a few bright exceptions—the **Maracaná** stadium, the **Quinta da Boa Vista** gardens, the **Floresta da Tijuca** park, and **Galeão Airport**—the region is a dull swath of port, residential high-rise, industrial suburb, and favela. It's not the sort of place one should wander unaccompanied.

ZONA OESTE The Zona Oeste houses some of the poorest and richest neighborhoods of the city. Inland on one side of a wide lagoon there's Cidade de Deus—featured in the movie *City of God*—a huge low-income housing project built in the 1960s to relocate people from downtown slums out to what was then the far edge of the city. On the waterfront are the seaside condominium enclaves **Barra da Tijuca** and **Recreio.** Beyond Recreio is **Grumari,** a pristine beach on the city's outskirts.

CENTRO   Rio's **Centro** neighborhood, the oldest part of the city, is where you'll find most of the city's notable churches, squares, monuments, and museums, as well as the modern office towers where Rio's white-collar elite earn their daily bread. Roughly speaking, Centro stretches from the **São Bento Monastery** in the north to the seaside **Monument to the Dead of World War II** in the south, and from **Praça XV** on the waterfront east to the **Sambodromo** (near Praça XI). Bustling with life during the week, on weekends and particularly Sundays, this area becomes very deserted, and a little too spooky to warrant a visit.

ZONA SUL—THE BAY   Just to the south of Centro lies the fun and slightly bohemian hilltop neighborhood of **Santa Teresa,** and then one after the other the neighborhoods of **Glória, Catete,** and **Flamengo.** These last three were the fashionable sections of the city around the start of the 20th century, located as they were on flat ground by the edge of Guanabara Bay. Other neighborhoods in this section include **Botafogo** and **Urca** (nestled beneath the Sugarloaf), and in the narrow valley behind Flamengo the two residential neighborhoods of **Laranjeiras** and **Cosme Velho.** Today they're all still pleasant and walkable—Botafogo was more commercial, but has been undergoing a residential boom over the past few years; Catete and Flamengo contain a number of historic buildings—but their bloom faded in the 1920s when engineers cut a tunnel through the mountainside to Copacabana.

ZONA SUL—THE BEACHES   Then, as now, the big attraction was the ocean. Where Centro and Flamengo sit on Guanabara Bay, **Copacabana, Ipanema, São Conrado,** and **Barra de Tijuca** face the open Atlantic. The waves are bigger, the water cleaner, and the beaches more inviting. First to be developed, **Copacabana** officially covers only the lower two-thirds of the beach. The northern third (the bit closest to Urca, farthest from Ipanema) is known as **Leme.** Taking a 90-degree turn around a low headland, one comes to **Ipanema.** Like Copacabana, Ipanema is a modern neighborhood, consisting almost exclusively of high-rise apartments from the '60s and '70s. Here, too, the same stretch of beach is considered to be two neighborhoods: Ipanema sits next to Copacabana, while the area at the far end of the beach is known as **Leblon.** Again, the two ends of the beach are nearly indistinguishable, though Leblon has a few more restaurants. Behind Ipanema there's a lagoon, the **Lagoa Rodrigo de Freitas,** which is circled by a pleasant 8.5km (5¼-mile) walking/cycling trail. At its north end, farthest from the beach, stand the two quiet residential neighborhoods of **Lagoa** and **Jardim Botânico,** the latter named for the extensive botanical gardens around which the area grew.

At the far end of Ipanema stands a tall sheer double-pointed rock called the **Pedra Dois Irmãos (Two Brothers Rock).** The road carries on, winding around the cliff face to reach the tiny enclave of **São Conrado.** One of the better surfing beaches, this is also where the hang gliders like to land after swooping down from the 830m (2,700-ft.) **Pedra de Gâvea.**

At night, the wide beaches are dark and mostly deserted; if you're in the mood for a moonlit stroll, stick to the brightly lit and police-patrolled pedestrian walkway that parallels the beach.

BEYOND THE BEACHES   Beyond São Conrado, the road goes up on stilts to sneak beneath the cliffs until reaching **Barra da Tijuca.** More like Miami Beach than Rio, Barra—as it's usually called—is a land of big streets, big malls, big cars, and big condominium towers (see "Zona Oeste," above).

GETTING AROUND
By Public Transportation

Rio may seem like a large and sprawling city, but the neighborhoods in which visitors spend most of their time are very easy to get around in. From Centro south to São Conrado, the neighborhoods hang like beads on a string on the narrow strip of land between the ocean and the mountains. You can almost always see one or the other; with landmarks like these it's pretty hard to stray too far from where you want to go.

BY METRÔ   The easiest way to get around is by subway; in Centro and the Zona Sul it covers almost every major area of interest, particularly now that there are integrated bus/subway lines for the parts of the city where the Metrô has not yet reached. There are only two lines: **Line 1** goes north from downtown—it's useful for going to the Maracanã and the Quinta da Boa Vista—while **Line 2** begins at the Central Station and goes south, covering most of Centro, then swinging thorough Glória, Catete, Flamengo, and Botafogo before ducking through the mountain to its final destination in Ipanema. The trip takes about 20 minutes to move you from Centro to Copacabana (as compared to a 40–60-min. bus ride in rush hour). The system is very safe and efficient. You purchase a magnetic ticket card at the entrance of the station, either from a machine or from a ticket booth. You can buy a single ride card (R$2.80), or opt for a rechargeable magnetic card, to which you then add value, which gets deducted when you swipe the card passing through the turnstile. There is no charge for the magnetic card, but the minimum recharge value is R$10.

The subway system recently expanded its integrated **Metrô/bus service,** and now has new air-conditioned buses feeding into the Metrô system from all parts of the city. The more popular routes include: Metrô/Ipanema (to Ipanema; transfer at Siqueira Campos); Metrô/Gavea or Barra (to Leblon and Gavea or Barra; transfer at Siqueira Campos); Metrô/Rodoviaria (to the main bus terminal; transfer at Largo do Machado); Metrô-Urca (to the Sugarloaf; transfer at Botafogo); and Metrô-Cosme Velho (to the Corcovado; transfer at Largo do Machado). The price is R$3.60, cheaper than paying separately for the Metrô and bus. After you use the electronic ticket to enter the subway turnstile, the ticket is returned so that you can present it on the bus at the transfer station.

BY BUS   Rio's buses follow direct, logical pathways, sticking to the main streets along much the same route you'd take if you were driving. What's more, they're fast. Indeed, it's a good idea to wedge yourself in your seat; Rio drivers like to lean into the turns.

More than 30 different buses run from Centro to Copacabana alone. Figuring out which to take is straightforward. The route number and final destination are displayed in big letters on the front of the bus. Smaller signs displayed inside the front window (usually below and to the left of the driver) and posted on the side of the bus list the intermediate stops. Armed with that information and a map, it's fairly uncomplicated to figure out which route the bus will take and how close you will get to your destination.

 Know the Subway Hours

The Metrô operates Monday through Saturday from 5am to midnight. On Sundays and statutory holidays the Metrô runs from 7am to 11pm. Special schedules apply during New Year's and Carnaval when trains will run all night.

A bus going from Praça XV in Centro out to Copacabana, for example, would show COPACABANA as the final destination, and on the smaller sign list intermediate destinations such as CINELANDIA, GLORIA, LARGO DO MACHADO (in Flamengo), and RIO SUL (the big mall in Botafogo). *Tip:* If you're going from Ipanema or Copacabana all the way to Centro (or vice versa), look for a bus that says VIA ATERRO in its smaller window sign. These buses get on the waterfront boulevard in Botafogo and don't stop until they reach downtown.

Buses stop only if someone wants to board. If you see your bus coming, wave your hand at the driver. Most buses are boarded from the front and exited from the rear. Have your bus money ready—R$2.50 to R$3.50—as you will go through a turnstile right away. You pay for each ride; there are no transfers. Buses are safe during the day; just watch for pickpockets when it gets busy. In the evening, when fewer passengers ride, it is better to take a taxi.

By Taxi

Taxis are plentiful and relatively inexpensive. They're the perfect way to reach those out-of-the-way places and the best way to get around in the evening. Regular taxis can be hailed anywhere on the street. You will also find taxi stands throughout the city. A ride from Copacabana to Praça XV in Centro costs about R$25 to R$30; a ride from the main bus station to Leblon is about R$35, R$40 in traffic. Radio taxis are about 20% more expensive, often work with a set fee per destination, and can be contacted by phone; try **Coopertramo** (© 021/2209-9292) or **TransCoopass** (© 021/2209-1555). Most hotels work with radio taxis so if you don't want to pay extra just walk to the corner and hail your own regular taxi. Radio taxis are said to be more reliable (and they have air-conditioning as well), but—aside from at the airport—we've never had a problem with any regular taxi.

By Van

When you see the chaotic bus-ridden streets of Rio de Janeiro, it's hard to believe that there could be a shortage of buses. However, in the last few years the city has seen an explosion of additional bus services provided by Volkswagen vans and microbuses. Some of these vans are licensed, many more remain officially illegal. Fares range from R$2 to R$4.50 and quality ranges from downright scary to clean, modern vehicles. Those that circulate along the Zona Sul waterfront and farther out to Barra da Tijuca are generally quick and efficient. Vans can be hailed anywhere and will let you off anywhere on their route.

By Ferry

Rio has a number of ferries operated by **Barcas SA** (© 0800/704-4113; www.barcas-sa.com.br), departing from Praça XV downtown. The busiest routes link downtown Rio with downtown Niterói or Charitas (also in Niterói) across the bay—also reached by car and bus by crossing the 14km (8½-mile) bridge. The service to Niterói runs daily from 6am to 11:30pm; to Charitas the service is Monday to Friday 6:50am to 9pm; departures on both routes run at approximately half-hour intervals. On the Niterói route, the cheapest ferry (R$2.80) is the regular one, taking about 25 minutes to cross. The catamaran and *aerobarco,* a hydrofoil, cross the same route in less than 10 minutes and cost R$5. The Charitas ferry costs R$8. A popular ferry for tourists as well as Cariocas on the weekend is the route to Paquetá, a large car-free island in the Baia da Guanabara. The ferries to Paquetá depart Rio at 5:15, 7:10, 10:30am, 1:30, 3:30, 4, 7, 9, and 11pm; the fare is R$4.50.

By Car

A car is not required for exploring Rio; a combination of public transit (in the daytime and evening) and taxis (late at night) gets you pretty much anywhere in the city for very little money. But for information about renting a car, see the entry for "Car Rentals" under "Fast Facts: Rio de Janeiro," below.

The truth is, driving in Rio is not for the weak of heart. Traffic is hectic, street patterns confusing, drivers just a few shades shy of courteous, and parking next to nonexistent. Better to get used to the city traffic as a pedestrian first and rent a car only if you're going out to destinations such as Petrópolis and the historic towns of the Minas Gerais region (for more, see chapter 8).

SPECIAL DRIVING RULES The rule is, *there are no rules.* Okay, maybe we're exaggerating. Traffic has improved immensely in recent years since police began using photoradars. People now wear seat belts and stop at red lights during the day. However, Cariocas still drive aggressively. Lane dividers are either absent or ignored. Any space larger than 10 centimeters (4 in.) between your car and the one in front will be instantly occupied by another driver. Later at night red lights become optional. Be careful when approaching intersections.

VISITOR INFORMATION

Riotur (© 021/2271-7000; www.riodejaneiro-turismo.com.br) provides excellent information on the city of Rio de Janeiro and operates a number of offices and kiosks around town. At **Rio's international airport** booths in the international arrivals halls of both Terminal 1 (© 021/3398-4077), and Terminal 2 (© 021/3398-2245), plus the domestic arrivals hall (© 021/3398-3034) are all open daily 6am to midnight. At Rio's main bus station, **Rodoviaria Novo Rio,** there's a counter in the arrivals area, open daily 8am to 8pm (© 021/2263-4857). The main **Riotur Information Center** (© 021/2541-7522) is on Av. Princesa Isabel 183, Copacabana. Open Monday to Friday 9am to 6pm, this office has the largest selection of brochures and information. Riotur also operates an information line, **Alô Rio** (© 021/2542-8080), with English-speaking staff, Monday to Friday from 9am to 6pm.

A must-have is Riotur's *Guia do Rio–Rio Guide* booklet, published every 3 months. Written in both English and Portuguese, it lists all tourist attractions, events, and festivals, and has many other useful phone numbers. Riotur also publishes a number of brochures specifically on outdoor sports, museums, and Carnaval. The office in Copacabana is most likely to stock all these publications.

The Rio de Janeiro state tourism agency **TurisRio** (© 021/2215-0011; www.turisrio.rj.gov.br) offers information on destinations in both the city and state of Rio de Janeiro. Their office, on the ground floor of Rua Mexico 125, Centro, is open Monday to Friday from 9am to 6pm. They also run an information line, **Disque Turismo** (© 0800/282-2007), with English-speaking staff, available Monday to Friday 8am to 8pm.

(*Fast Facts*) Rio de Janeiro

Area Code The area code for Rio de Janeiro is **021.**

Banks & Currency Exchange **Banco do Brasil** has branches at Rua Joana Angelica, Ipanema (© **021/3544-9700**), Av. N.S. de Copacabana 594, Copacabana (© **021/3816-5800**), and international airport, Terminal 1, third floor (© **021/ 3398-3652**); all have 24-hour ATMs. For currency exchange, try **Casa Aliança Cambio,** Rua Miguel Couto 35, Centro (© **021/2224-4617**); **Citibank,** Rua da Assembleia 100, Centro (© **021/4009-8229**); and **Casa Universal Cambio,** Av. N.S. Copacabana 371, loja E, Copacabana (© **021/2548-6696**).

Car Rentals Antônio Carlos Jobim International Airport has **Hertz** (© 021/3398-2379), **Localiza** (© 021/3398-5445), and **Unidas** (© 021/3398-2286). Santos Dumont Airport has **Hertz** (© 021/2262-0612), **Localiza** (© 021/2220-5455), and **Unidas** (© 021/2240-6715). Copacabana has **Hertz,** Av. Princesa Isabel 500 (© 021/-7440), **Localiza,** Av. Princesa Isabel 150 (© 021/2275-3340), and **Unidas,** Av. Princesa Isabel 166 (© 021/3873-2521). Rates start at R$100 per day for a compact car with air-conditioning. Insurance adds R$30 per day.

Consulates **Australia,** Av. Presidente Wilson 231, Ste. 23, Centro (© **021/3824-4624**). **Canada,** Av. Atlântica 1130, fifth floor, Copacabana (© **21/2543-3004**). **Great Britain,** Praia do Flamengo 284, second floor, Flamengo (© **021/2555-9600**). **U.S.,** Av. Presidente Wilson 147, Centro (© **021/3823-2000**).

Dentist **Sorriclin,** Rua Visconde de Pirajá 207/209, Ipanema (© **021/2522-1220**).

Doctor **Clinica Galdino Campos,** Av. N.S. de Copacabana 492, Copacabana (© **021/2548-9966;** www.clinicagaldinocampos.com.br), offers 24-hour service, including house calls. English spoken. Ask your hotel for further recommendations, as they may have an arrangement with a doctor nearby.

Emergencies Police © **190;** fire and ambulance © **193;** tourist police, Av. Afrânio de Melo Franco 159, Leblon (contact line © **021/2332-2924** or 2332-2885 or 2332-2889).

Hospitals Public hospital emergency rooms can be found at Miguel Couto, Rua Bartolemeu Mitre 1108, Leblon (© **021/3111-3800**), or at Souza Aguiar, Praça da Republica 111, Centro (© **021/3111-2600**). Private emergency rooms can be found at the Cardio Trauma Ipanema, Rua Farme de Amoedo 86, Ipanema (© **021/2525-1900**), and at the city's best hospital, Copa D'or, Rua Figueiredo de Magalhães 875, Copacabana (© **021/2545-3600**).

Internet Access Internet cafes or Lan Houses can be found everywhere. There is also free public Wi-Fi on the entire beachfront, from Leme to Leblon.

Mail Look for the yellow-and-blue sign saying CORREIOS. **Downtown:** Av. Rio Branco 156, Centro (© **021/2240-8764**); **Copacabana:** Av. N.S. de Copacabana 540, Copacabana (© **021/2256-1439**); **Ipanema:** Rua Visconde de Pirajá 452, Ipanema (© **021/2567-6197**). The international airport also has a post office (© **021/3398-7024**), open Monday to Friday 9am to 9pm, Saturday till 1pm.

Maps **Riotur** (Av. Princesa Isabel 183, Copacabana) has helpful small maps of the main tourist areas.

Newspapers Your best bet for international papers is the newsstands along Visconde de Pirajá in Ipanema, and the bookstore Letras e Expressões, Visconde de Pirajá 276, Ipanema (© 021/2521-6110). The English-language Rio paper, the *Gringo Times* (www.thegringotimes.com) is mostly Web-based but has free distribution in some Zona Sul hotels.

Pharmacies In Copacabana, **City Farma,** Rua Toneleiro 153 D (© 021/3208-0000), delivers Monday to Saturday 7am to 10pm and Sunday 8am to 2pm. All major credit cards accepted. In Ipanema, **Drogaria Pacheco,** Rua Visconde de Pirajá 265, Ipanema (© 021/2287-7686), is open 24 hours.

Safety Rio retains a somewhat unsavory reputation for street violence, though things have improved significantly since their nadir in the late 1980s and early 1990s. That said, there are still several things to keep in mind. It's a bad idea to wander unaccompanied into any of the favelas (shantytowns) found in and around the city. In the ritzy areas like the Zona Sul, favelas cling to steep hillsides and ridge tops. It's also best to avoid the city center (Centro) on weekends and holidays when this part of town remains mostly empty, and more than a little eerie. Avoid the beaches at night, which are dark and mostly deserted (stick to the brightly lit and police-patrolled pedestrian walkway that borders the beach). At night, traveling by taxi is recommended—don't rely on public transportation. Finally, as in any large metropolitan area, it's wise to observe common-sense precautions: Don't flash jewelry and large amounts of cash, and stick to well-lit and well-traveled thoroughfares.

Taxes The city of Rio charges a 5% accommodations tax, collected by the hotel operators. This amount will be added to your bill. Hotels may also add a 10% service charge to your bill. There are no taxes on retail items.

Time Zones Rio de Janeiro is 3 hours behind GMT. During daylight saving Rio's time difference changes to 2 hours behind GMT.

Visa Renewal If you need to extend your visa, go to the **Policia Federal** at Galeão airport (top floor Terminal 1) (© 021/3398-3897), open Monday to Friday 10am to 5pm. The fee is R$75, and you may need to show evidence of sufficient funds for your stay and a return ticket.

Weather Rio's summers, from December to March, are hot and humid. Temperatures rise routinely above 40°C (105°F). In the spring and fall, the temperatures stay between the high 20s to low 30s Celsius (high 70s and low 90s Fahrenheit). In the winter, June to August, it can cool off at night to as low as 15°C (59°F), but during the day temperatures range from the 20s Celsius (70s to the mid-80s Fahrenheit). Rain falls in the summer in short, intense tropical showers, and in the winter in longer drizzly showers.

2 WHERE TO STAY

Though Rio has a good number of hotels, there's surprisingly little variety: There are few pousadas, boutique hotels, or fancy bed-and-breakfasts, at least not in the beach neighborhoods. (The exception is the hilltop neighborhood of Santa Teresa, which has pousadas in

Tips **Beware of Dengue Fever in Brazil**

Occasionally Brazil experiences outbreaks of dengue fever, a malaria-like illness transmitted by mosquitoes. Most of the cases were reported in the state of Rio de Janeiro, with additional outbreaks in São Paulo as well. See the section on "Health" in chapter 3 for more on dengue fever, and for the latest information on the situation in Rio, check the **Centers for Disease Control** website (www.cdc. gov) before you leave.

heritage buildings, fancy boutique hotels, and quaint historic B&Bs galore.) In Copacabana and Ipanema, the vast majority of hotels are in modern high-rises, many built in the '60s and '70s, most with a similar layout and design. The difference between hotels thus lies in the location, the room size, the amenities, and, of course, the view. The best rooms always face the ocean and are priced accordingly. Note that if you choose not to stay in a prime oceanview room, you often get much better value by staying at the best room in a less expensive hotel away from the beach than by paying for a cheaper room in an expensive beachfront hotel.

The best-known hotel area is **Copacabana,** with easy access via Metrô back to the city core, and a good selection of inexpensive hotels close to the beach. One beach over from Copacabana, **Ipanema** and **Leblon** have become increasingly popular over the past decade and now have better nightlife and trendier shopping than Copa. The area is much farther from the city core, but integrated Metrô/bus routes now connect the area to the subway, and there are lots of regular buses.

Farther out in **Barra da Tijuca** is where you will find the city's newest and most modern hotels. Hotels out here are close to the convention center and the big new malls and office complexes, but it's a 30- to 60-minute cab ride from Ipanema and Copacabana and the people and street life that make Rio so fascinating.

Back toward downtown you find the lively and more historic neighborhoods **Glória, Catete,** and **Flamengo.** Located a 15-minute subway ride from both downtown and Copacabana, they offer excellent budget options. The hilltop neighborhood of **Santa Teresa** now has a few wonderful pousadas, B&Bs, and boutique hotels, most of them in the gorgeous converted mansions of Rio's 19th-century elite. Santa Teresa offers cobblestone streets and terrific views in all directions, and a bohemian artistic feel. The only drawback is access; getting up to or down from Santa Teresa is a matter of a bus or taxi ride, and later in the evening some taxis are reluctant to go up the hill.

In the lobby, hotels always list the rack rates on a sign behind the desk, but you can expect to pay 50% to 80% of this amount, depending on the season, the staff person, and your bargaining skills. Prices are quite flexible; always negotiate. Sometimes just paying with cash can result in a 10% to 15% discount.

The only time of year when it's difficult to get a deal is during **high season,** from the week before Christmas through the end of Carnaval. The city overflows with visitors from all over the world, not to mention Argentines and Brazilians taking their summer holidays. New Year's and Carnaval are the tourism industry's cash cows, and during this time most hotels will only accept reservations for set package deals—usually a 2- or 3-night minimum stay for New Year's and a 5-night minimum stay for Carnaval—at highly inflated prices. Shop around in advance if you're going to be in Rio during these

SETTLING INTO RIO DE JANEIRO

5

WHERE TO STAY

Tips **Where Not to Stay in Rio**

The only neighborhood to avoid hotel-wise is downtown Rio. The Praça Mauá hotels may look like a bargain, but this area transforms into a red-light district at night when the office workers have gone home.

times; packages (*especially* the less expensive ones) sell out by October or November. Most hotels now have websites and will provide quick information upon request.

Make sure to ask about taxes that will be added to your bill. Most hotels charge a 10% service tax, a 5% city tax, and, if they are a member of the Rio Convention and Visitor's Bureau, a tourist tax of R$3 to R$9 per day. This can add up to a total of 18% extra on your bill.

SÃO CONRADO/BARRA DA TIJUCA

The only reason to stay beyond Leblon is if you prefer your hotel with a large leisure area such as tennis courts and large swimming pools. Close to the convention center and the new business centers, hotels in Barra usually have huge recreational areas. The drawback is that you're anywhere from 30 minutes to an hour or more from Ipanema and Copacabana (depending on traffic) and thus quite isolated. If you do choose Barra, resign yourself to long cab or bus rides.

Very Expensive

Sheraton Barra Hotel & Suites ★★★ **Kids**   Located on Barra's premier stretch of waterfront, the Sheraton offers the most modern and luxurious accommodations in Rio. Rooms all have balconies and face the ocean. Classic rooms are located on floors one to five. Preferred rooms take up floors 6 to 15. All rooms come with a large desk, a sitting area, and a wet bar. Beds are indulgent, with a firm king-size mattress, cozy fleece blanket, plump duvet, and five cushy pillows. What really sets this hotel apart is its leisure amenities, with two swimming pools and Jacuzzi tubs set in a beautifully landscaped garden, a state-of-the-art fitness center, squash courts, a fully equipped business center, and a trendy lounge. Guests also have access to the 18-hole Itanhangá golf course. There's a free shuttle to the Barra Shopping.

Av. Lúcio Costa 3150 (aka Av. Sernambetiba), Barra da Tijuca, 22630-011 RJ. ✆ **021/3139-8000.** Fax 021/3139-8085. www.sheraton-barra.com.br. 292 units. R$485 classic room double; R$725 preferred room double; R$925 junior suite double. Extra person R$155. Children 12 and under stay free in parent's room. AE, DC, MC, V. Bus: Metrô Integração Barra. **Amenities:** Restaurant; 2 bars; concierge; health club; 1 outdoor heated adult pool and 1 outdoor heated children's pool; room service; sauna; smoke-free rooms. *In room:* A/C, TV, fridge, hair dryer, Internet, kitchenette, minibar.

Sheraton Rio Hotel & Towers ★★★ **Kids**   The Sheraton is the only large luxury hotel with a fabulous leisure area that is still relatively close to the Zona Sul. You are only a 30-minute walk from Leblon or a 10-minute taxi ride from Ipanema. (The hotel offers a free regular shuttle along Ipanema and Copa beaches all the way to the Rio Sul mall.) It is also the place where Rio's societal divisions will stare you right in the face, or rather, into your room. Located directly on its own beautiful pocket beach, the Sheraton sits in the shadow of a hillside favela. Guests in the north-facing rooms awake to the calls of roosters roaming round the small brick shacks across the road. As sharp as the contrast may seem, there is a friendly mingling of tourists and locals on the beach (which is kept

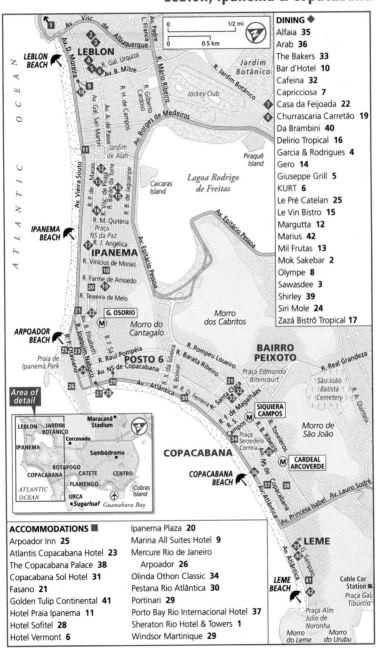

DINING ◆
Alfaia **35**
Arab **36**
The Bakers **33**
Bar d'Hotel **10**
Cafeina **32**
Capricciosa **7**
Casa da Feijoada **22**
Churrascaria Carretão **19**
Da Brambini **40**
Delirio Tropical **16**
Garcia & Rodrigues **4**
Gero **14**
Giuseppe Grill **5**
KURT **6**
Le Pré Catelan **25**
Le Vin Bistro **15**
Margutta **12**
Marius **42**
Mil Frutas **13**
Mok Sakebar **2**
Olympe **8**
Sawasdee **3**
Shirley **39**
Siri Mole **24**
Zazá Bistrô Tropical **17**

SETTLING INTO RIO DE JANEIRO

5

WHERE TO STAY

ACCOMMODATIONS ■
Arpoador Inn **25**
Atlantis Copacabana Hotel **23**
The Copacabana Palace **38**
Copacabana Sol Hotel **31**
Fasano **21**
Golden Tulip Continental **41**
Hotel Praia Ipanema **11**
Hotel Sofitel **28**
Hotel Vermont **6**
Ipanema Plaza **20**
Marina All Suites Hotel **9**
Mercure Rio de Janeiro
  Arpoador **26**
Olinda Othon Classic **34**
Pestana Rio Atlântica **30**
Portinari **29**
Porto Bay Rio Internacional Hotel **37**
Sheraton Rio Hotel & Towers **1**
Windsor Martinique **29**

very safe by hotel security). The hotel itself features three large swimming pools in a beautiful parklike setting, beachfront access, and sweeping ocean views. The rooms are bright and spacious, with verandas with a partial or full ocean view, large desks, and dual phone lines. The location is suitable for children, and the hotel staff offer lots of activities to keep little ones busy.

Av. Niemeyer 121, São Conrado, Rio de Janeiro, 22450-220 RJ. © **021/2274-1122.** Fax 021/2239-5643. www.sheraton-rio.com. 559 units. R$425–R$500 standard double; R$475–R$600 oceanview double; R$625–R$750 junior suite double. Check the website for specials. Extra person add 25%. Children 10 and under stay free in parent's room. Breakfast not included. AE, DC, MC, V. Free parking. No public transit. **Amenities:** 3 restaurants; bar; disco; babysitting; children's center; concierge; executive-level rooms; health club (extra charge); 3 outdoor heated pools; room service; sauna; smoke-free floors; spa (extra charge); tennis courts (extra charge); Wi-Fi (lobby only). *In room:* A/C, TV, fridge, hair dryer, Internet, minibar.

Windsor Barra ★★ (**Kids**)   Open since September 2005, the Windsor Barra is all modern design on the outside. Inside, rooms feature classic, elegant furnishings and color schemes that are easy on the eye—lots of beiges and moss greens. The superior apartments are on lower floors and have side views of the ocean. The best rooms are the spacious deluxe corner rooms on the higher floors—these have both side and full ocean views, plus a Jacuzzi tub. The best view in the house is reserved for the leisure area; the swimming pools and bar have a sweeping 360-degree view of Barra Beach and surroundings.

Av. Sernambetiba 2630 (aka Av. Lúcio Costa), Barra da Tijuca, 22620-170 RJ. © **021/2195-5000.** Fax 021/2195-5050. www.windsorhotels.com.br. 338 units. R$475 double superior; R$725 double deluxe. Extra person add 25%. Children 6 and under stay free in parent's room. AE, DC, MC, V. **Amenities:** 2 restaurants; 2 bars; concierge; health club; 1 outdoor heated adult pool and 1 outdoor heated children's pool; room service; sauna; smoke-free rooms. *In room:* A/C, TV, fridge, hair dryer, Internet, kitchenette, minibar.

IPANEMA/LEBLON

One beach over from Copacabana, **Ipanema** and **Leblon** offer some of the city's trendiest shopping and best dining options. Leblon, in particular, has become Rio's prime neighborhood for fine dining. There are both affordable hotel options and outstanding luxury accommodations.

Very Expensive

Fasano ★★★ (**Overrated**)   Overrated and three stars?? Well, the design sense in this hotel is truly lovely. This first ever hotel designed inside and out by the famous *enfant terrible* of the design world Philippe Starck, the Fasano features wood-paneled hallways accented with big Dr. Seuss chairs, giving the hotel a James Bond/Austin Powers shaggalicious kind of feel. The rooftop pool is a thing of beauty. That said, even the least expensive rooms (called Superior) come gussied up in high design—the queen-size beds are set off at an oblique angle to the room's basic rectangle, there's a small desk area, plus a bathroom with rainfall showers—all that decorative sense doesn't change the fact that they are small, and very expensive, and lack both balcony and ocean view. If design is not your thing, you can get much more room for the money staying somewhere else. If you are in the mood to splurge, the deluxe oceanview rooms are a much more comfortable size, offering a small sitting area and a balcony with a pair of lovely (high-design) deck chairs. The difference in feeling is significant. The oceanview suites are larger still, with a retractable silk curtain to separate off a comfortable little sitting area, which comes with its own separate bathroom facilities. The quality of everything in all rooms—bedding, bathroom products, bathrobes—is top-notch.

Av. Vieira Souto 88, Ipanema, Rio de Janeiro, 22420-000 RJ. ℂ **021/3202-4000.** Fax 021/3202-4010. www. fasano.com.br. 91 units. R$945 superior double; R$1,425 deluxe oceanview double; R$2,800 oceanview suite. Extra bed R$150. Children 12 and under stay free in parent's room. Inquire about seasonal discounts. AE, DC, MC, V. Valet parking. Metrô: General Osorio. **Amenities:** Restaurant; bar; babysitting; concierge; well-equipped fitness center; rooftop pool; room service; sauna; smoke-free floors; small spa. *In room:* A/C, TV, hair dryer, minibar, Wi-Fi.

Marina All Suites Hotel ★★★ (Finds) This place offers design with a capital D. The architects and decorators behind this hotel bought, gutted, and redecorated all the rooms, in the process reducing the original layout of six rooms per floor to a very spacious three. All are so precociously modern they positively squeak, with original pieces of art and a style unique to each unit. The two-bedroom Suite Diamante must be the most beautiful suite in Rio and is said to be Gisele Bündchen's favorite room when in town. The "basic" suites (basic being an understatement) are studio apartments. The design suites have a separate bedroom. All feature an American kitchen (microwave, fridge, and wet bar), ample desk space and sitting areas, spacious bathrooms, and luxurious furnishings, making this truly one of Rio's most outstanding hotels. The restaurant **Bar d'Hotel** is one Rio's more chic nightspots (p. 96).

Av. Delfim Moreira 696, Leblon, Rio de Janeiro, 22441-000 RJ. ℂ **021/2172-1100.** Fax 021/2294-1644. www.marinaallsuites.com.br. 38 units. R$765–R$1,030 basic suite; R$1,075–R$1,350 design suite; R$1,450 Suite Diamante. AE, DC, MC, V. Free parking. Bus: 474. **Amenities:** Restaurant; babysitting; concierge; excellent gym; outdoor pool; room service; sauna. *In room:* A/C, TV, fridge, hair dryer, kitchen, minibar, Wi-Fi.

Expensive

Hotel Praia Ipanema ★★★ Straddling the border between Ipanema and Leblon, the Praia Ipanema offers beachfront luxury accommodations, all within walking distance of Lagoa, the upscale shopping and restaurants of the Zona Sul, and the restaurants and bars of Leblon. All 105 units offer king-size beds and lovely bedding, plus balconies and ocean views. In the lowest category, Superior Master rooms offer either a front ocean view on a lower floor, or a side-view from an upper floor. (As the side-view rooms are actually a bit larger than the front-views, an upper-floor side view may well be the best deal.) One step up, the Deluxe (luxo) rooms offer a front view from a higher floor. Deluxe Master (luxo master) rooms offer the same front view from floors 10 and up—where views of sand and sea get ever more spectacular—plus extras like a DVD and flatscreen TV. Suites are large, and come with a front-view balcony and a separate comfortable sitting room.

Av. Vieira Souto 706, Ipanema, Rio de Janeiro, 22420-000 RJ. ℂ **021/2540-4949.** Fax 021/2239-6889. www.praiaipanema.com. 101 units. R$500 superior master double; R$550 Deluxe double; R$580 Deluxe Master double; R$780 suite. AE, DC, MC, V. No parking. Bus: 474 or 404. **Amenities:** Restaurant; 2 bars; small gym; rooftop pool; room service. *In room:* A/C, TV, fridge, hair dryer, minibar, Wi-Fi.

Ipanema Plaza ★ (Overrated) The fabulous location—just 1 block from Ipanema beach, in the heart of the neighborhood's trendy gay section—is why so many stay here. Unfortunately, the Plaza seems to be living solely off its spot by the sand. Rooms are a decent size, but the luxury extras you'd expect (considering you're paying luxury price) are absent: Bedding is run-of-the-mill, bathrooms are serviceable but old and a little worn, breakfast is nothing special, service (even by Brazilian standards) is more than a little lackadaisical. The junior suites—really just a larger room—don't justify the hefty markup. The exclusive Ipanema floor tries to emulate boutique hotel standards, but fails. All in all, you'll get much better quality at a similar price staying at the Praia Ipanema (or similar quality at a cheaper price, plus better service and genuine waterfront, staying at the Arpoador Inn).

Rua Farme de Amoedo 34, Ipanema, Rio de Janeiro, 22420-020 RJ. ✆ **021/3687-2000.** Fax 021/3687-2001. www.ipanemaplazahotel.com. 140 units. R$400 superior double; R$450 deluxe double (with veranda add R$25); R$550 junior suite; R$575 Ipanema floor double. Extra person add 25%. Children 9 and under stay free in parent's room. AE, DC, MC, V. Bus: 474 or 404. **Amenities:** Restaurant; bar; small gym; rooftop pool; room service. *In room:* A/C, TV/DVD, hair dryer, Internet, minibar.

Mercure Rio de Janeiro Arpoador ★★ (Value)
Here you'll find an excellent value for money, and a location that lets you choose between Ipanema and Copacabana. All units in this flat hotel are small suites—bedrooms come with comfortable queen-size beds, the sitting rooms have a fold-out couch and sizable desk, and there's a small but fully equipped adjoining kitchen. Both bedroom and sitting room have a TV/DVD, and there's free Wi-Fi throughout. They're great for a family, or if you have work to do and are spending more time in Rio. Note that though the hotel backs onto the beach (rooms higher up on the back side get a beach view), to reach the beach you have to exit the hotel and walk a full 100m (328 ft.) or so on the street.

Rua Francisco Otaviano 61, Arpoador, Rio de Janeiro, 22080-060 RJ. ✆ **021/2113-8600.** www.accorhotels.com.br. 56 units. R$350 standard double. Up to 25% discount in low season and weekends. AE, DC, MC, V. Parking R$15. Bus: 474. **Amenities:** Outdoor pool; room service; sauna. *In room:* A/C, TV/DVD, kitchen, Wi-Fi.

Moderate

Arpoador Inn ★ (Value)
The only moderately priced oceanfront hotel in Ipanema, the Arpoador Inn enjoys a privileged location on a quiet stretch of beach popular with the surf crowd, and just around the corner from Copacabana. Even better, the beach in front of the hotel is closed to cars and is therefore pleasantly quiet. The deluxe rooms all face the ocean. The furniture is simple but the rooms are bright and spotless. Obtaining these does require booking ahead; if they're full, the superior rooms, which look out over the street behind the beach, make an acceptable alternative. Avoid the standard rooms, which are small, dark, and look into an interior wall.

Rua Francisco Otaviano 177, Ipanema, Rio de Janeiro, 22080-040 RJ. ✆ **021/2523-0060.** Fax 021/2511-5094. www.arpoadorinn.com.br. 50 units. R$212 standard double; R$300 street-view superior double; R$440 deluxe ocean view. Extra person R$120. Children 6 and under stay free in parent's room. AE, DC, MC, V. No parking. Metrô: General Osorio. **Amenities:** Restaurant; room service. *In room:* A/C, TV, fridge.

Hotel Vermont ★
The Vermont sits smack in the middle of Ipanema's swankiest shopping district, and thanks to the rates at this small budget hotel, you'll have plenty of cash left for conspicuous consumption. All rooms have tile floors, new furniture, large mirrors, and clean, modern fixtures. Standard rooms face out the back and are simply furnished with two twins or a double bed, a closet, and a desk. Superior rooms are a little more spacious but they also get some street noise, although at night traffic slows down significantly. Most of the rooms have twin beds so if you want a double it's best to reserve in advance. Note that the hotel is a bad choice for those with limited mobility—access to the hotel elevators is up one flight of stairs.

Rua Visconde de Pirajá 254, Ipanema, Rio de Janeiro, 22410-000 RJ. ✆ **021/3202-5500.** Fax 021/2267-7046. www.hotelvermont.com.br. 84 units. R$240 standard or superior double. Extra person R$90. Children 2 and under stay free in parent's room. AE, DC, MC, V. No parking. Bus: 415. *In room:* A/C, TV, minibar, Wi-Fi.

COPACABANA

Copacabana may not be the upscale neighborhood that it was in the days when bossa nova was young, but there are still advantages to staying in this part of the city. Prices are lower than in Ipanema, and with Copacabana's strategic location, it's only a 10- to 15-minute cab ride to Ipanema or to downtown; there's excellent bus service and a Metrô line, which makes it easy to get downtown or to places farther out, such as the Sambodromo or the Maracanã soccer stadium. The best hotels are on the Avenida Atlântica and some of its cross streets. Avoid the hectic Nossa Senhora de Copacabana Avenue and Rua Barata Ribeiro.

The drawback to Copacabana is that you share the hood with seniors, lots and lots of other tourists, vendors, hawkers, hustlers and, in certain sections, street hookers and (mostly foreign) johns (it's particularly bad around Av. Prado Junior and in front of the Help discothèque). With some common precautions the neighborhood is just as safe as Ipanema, but you do get that extra local flavor. We find it quite colorful and a part of what makes Copa unique. However, it may not be for everybody. Leme, at the far end of Copa, could be the perfect alternative for those who want to have all the benefits of being close to Copa without sinking in the midst of it.

Very Expensive

The Copacabana Palace ★★   The spot where beachfront luxury in Rio began way back in the Jazz age, the 86-year-old Palace is still the place to splurge. Taking full advantage, however, requires approaching things with Gatsbyesque confidence. Take, for example, the city-view rooms and suites. Or rather, don't take them. Though slightly cheaper, they face a busy city street and offer not a drop of ocean view. Better to simply stay elsewhere. Deluxe beach-view rooms do give you that coveted ocean view but to get value for money at the Palace it's really a case of go big or go home: The pool or ocean-view suites are spacious, elegant, and tastefully decorated, each with its own private veranda overlooking the pool and Copacabana beach. One step up again and you've reached the penthouse suites, which are tasteful, sophisticated, and vast, each with a sitting room and bedroom and a private terrace looking down on the beach. The penthouse floor also has a private pool and bar. Now that is the life we were intended to live.

Av. Atlântica 1702, Copacabana, Rio de Janeiro, 22021-001 RJ. © **0800/211-533** or 021/2548-7070. Fax 021/2235-7330. www.copacabanapalace.com. 225 units. R$960 deluxe city-view double; R$1,170 deluxe oceanview double; R$1,960 pool/oceanview suite double; penthouse suite R$3,580. Extra person add about 25%. Children 12 and under stay free in parent's room. AE, DC, MC, V. Free parking. Metrô: Arcoverde. **Amenities:** 2 restaurants; bar; babysitting; concierge; executive-level rooms; health club; Jacuzzi; large outdoor pool; room service; sauna; rooftop tennis courts. *In room:* A/C, TV, hair dryer, minibar, Wi-Fi.

Hotel Sofitel ★★★   There may be newer, more trendy hotels in town, but when it comes to top-notch service and luxury accommodations, the Sofitel gets it right every time. Set on the edge of Copacabana directly opposite the Copacabana Fort, the flagship of the French Sofitel has recently renovated all of its rooms. "Standard" amenities in all rooms include elegant, modern furniture, efficient work spaces, a comfy lounge chair, top-notch lighting, flatscreen TVs, the Sofitel's signature mattresses and the finest linen, a pillow menu, fabulous showers, and luxurious l'Occitane amenities. But wait, there is more: two gorgeous swimming pools (one for the morning sun and the other for the afternoon rays), a state-of-the-art fitness center, a running kit for those who prefer to jog along the beach, and a killer oceanfront location with exclusive services for hotel guests. Sofitel also deserves kudos for offering the city's best rooms for travelers with disabilities. Special adaptations include sliding doors, extra-wide doorways, a wheel-in shower, accessible bathroom fixtures, and a bedroom large enough to allow a wheelchair to move freely around the room. The hotel's **Pré Catelan** restaurant (p. 91) offers one of the best dining experiences in town.

Av. Atlântica 4240, Copacabana, Rio de Janeiro, 22070-002 RJ. © **0800/241-232** or 021/2525-1232. Fax 021/2525-1200. www.accorhotels.com.br. 388 units. R$590 superior double; R$675 deluxe double; R$900 junior suite double. Children 12 and under stay free in parent's room. AE, DC, MC, V. Free parking. Bus: 474. **Amenities:** 2 restaurants; bar; babysitting; concierge; health club; 2 outdoor pools; room service; sauna; smoke-free floors. *In room:* A/C, TV, hair dryer, minibar, Wi-Fi.

Expensive

Olinda Othon Classic ★★ (Value A lovely heritage building, the Olinda has finally gotten a much-needed makeover. The lobby has been transformed into an elegant salon with a restaurant and piano bar. Elevators have been upgraded to the 21st century, and all the rooms have been renovated, the dark colonial furniture replaced by lighter woods, soothing pale colors, and stylish furniture. You should still avoid the standard rooms, which are smaller and face the back of the building. The deluxe oceanview rooms (luxo) feature a king-size bed, elegant 1950s detailing, and a view of the ocean. The luxo rooms with veranda are actually smaller, but have a lovely little veranda for two with a view out over the ocean. The spacious suites are one of the best deals in town; located on the top floor, they feature a large veranda with a view of the beach, a bedroom, and sitting room, all with lots of light and a lovely Art Deco feel.

Av. Atlântica 2230, Copacabana, 22041-001 RJ. ⓒ/fax **021/2545-9091.** www.hoteis-othon.com.br. 102 units. R$250 standard double; R$325 deluxe double; R$450 suite double. Extra person add 40%. Children 10 and under stay free in parent's room. AE, DC, MC, V. No parking. Metrô: Arcoverde. **Amenities:** Restaurant; bar; room service. *In room:* A/C, TV, minibar, Wi-Fi.

Pestana Rio Atlântica ★★★ Always one of the nicest hotels on the Avenida Atlântica, the Pestana looks brand-new thanks to a recent overhaul. The best rooms in the house are the Oceanic suites. These large rooms offer ocean views and large balconies, and come elegantly furnished with dark wooden furniture and splashes of yellow and beige. They are among the best in Copa, if you can afford the splurge. The standard and superior rooms are more plainly furnished, but still luxurious. Standard rooms look out over the buildings adjacent to the hotel. Superior rooms (on the 10th floor and higher) have a partial ocean view. There's a good fitness center and the rooftop pool area offers a massage room, sauna, and Jacuzzi. Breakfast costs R$36.

Av. Atlântica 2964, Copacabana, Rio de Janeiro, 22070-000 RJ. ⓒ **021/2548-6332.** Fax 021/2255-6410. www.pestana.com. 216 units. R$400 standard double; R$450–R$550 superior double; R$750–R$950 suite Oceanic. Children 10 and under stay free in parent's room. AE, DC, MC, V. Valet parking. Metrô: Arcoverde. **Amenities:** Restaurant; bar; babysitting; concierge; health club; Jacuzzi; outdoor pool; room service; sauna; smoke-free rooms. *In room:* A/C, TV, hair dryer, Internet, minibar.

Portinari ★★ The only thing that keeps this Rio design hotel from getting three stars is its location just off the busy Avenida N.S. de Copacabana; it lacks the sex appeal of a beach address. Inside, the hotel is fabulous. Each floor has a unique look. Styles range from classic-romantic with elegant furniture and pale colors to environmentally friendly rooms furnished with recycled wood and natural fabrics. Our favorites are the rooms designed by Marcia Muller. The design is sensuous with gorgeous indirect lighting and luxurious white linens. The shower is separated by a translucent wall from the bedroom. All rooms come with queen-size or twin beds with 200-thread linen and goose down pillows. The large suites feature large bathrooms (some with sauna or tub) and DVD players.

Rua Francisco de Sá 17, Copacabana, 22080-010 RJ. ⓒ **021/3222-8800.** Fax 021/3222-8803. www.hotel portinari.com.br. 66 units. R$320 double; R$385–R$450 suite. Extra person add 25%. Children 10 and under stay free in parent's room. AE, DC, MC, V. Valet parking R$30 per day. Bus: 415. **Amenities:** Restaurant; coffee shop; bar; concierge; small exercise room; rooftop pool; room service; sauna; smoke-free floors. *In room:* A/C, TV, hair dryer, minibar, Wi-Fi.

Porto Bay Rio Internacional Hotel ★★ The Porto Bay proves that you shouldn't judge a hotel by its cover. Behind the '80s-style black glass facade hides a remarkably pleasant hotel with friendly and attentive staff that welcome guests with a glass of champagne. A recent US$4-million overhaul equipped all guest accommodations with new, attractive furnishings, firm king- or queen-size beds, flatscreen TVs, and DVD and CD players. Thanks to the building's corner location, all rooms have at the bare minimum a partial ocean view. The prime rooms, the deluxe suites, have large panorama windows and a balcony—definitely worth the splurge. The hotel also has a lovely rooftop bar and swimming pool. Located next to the Copacabana Palace and 3 blocks from the subway, the Porto Bay makes an excellent base for exploring the city.

Av. Atlântica 1500, Copacabana, Rio de Janeiro, 22021-000 RJ. © **0800/021-1559** or 021/2546-8000. Fax 021/2542-5443. www.portobay.com. 117 units. R$460 superior double; R$600 deluxe double. Children 10 and under stay free in parent's room. AE, DC, MC, V. Parking. Metrô: Cardeal Arcoverde. **Amenities:** Restaurant; bar; exercise room; rooftop pool; room service; smoke-free floors. In room: A/C, TV/DVD, CD player, hair dryer, minibar, Wi-Fi.

Moderate

Atlantis Copacabana Hotel ★ Located between Ipanema and Copacabana on a quiet residential street, the Atlantis Copacabana Hotel is perfect for those who like to keep their options open. Either beach is within minutes from your hotel, and shopping and restaurants are easily accessible. The hotel offers basic accommodations; all 87 rooms are standard with only a small variation in size and layout; rooms ending in 07 and 08 (for example, nos. 107 and 108) are slightly larger. Rooms above the eighth floor that look out the back offer a view of Arpoador and Ipanema beach.

Rua Bulhões de Carvalho 61, Copacabana, Rio de Janeiro, 22081-000 RJ. © **021/2521-1142.** Fax 021/2287-8896. www.atlantishotel.com.br. 87 units. R$220–R$270 double. Extra person R$50. Children 5 and under stay free in parent's room. AE, DC, MC, V. Limited street parking. Bus: 128 or 474. **Amenities:** Concierge; rooftop pool; room service; sauna. In room: A/C, TV, fridge, minibar, Wi-Fi.

Copacabana Sol Hotel ★ If you don't mind being off the waterfront, the Copacabana Sol offers good value and pleasant accommodations only 4 blocks from Copacabana beach. The lobby, a positively funky space, features colorful furniture and modern art. Rooms don't quite live up to this standard, but are still pleasant and comfortable. Superior rooms overlook the street and have balconies and a small sitting area. The Rua Santa Clara is not too noisy (especially at night), making these rooms preferable to the alley-facing standard rooms. Both superior and standard rooms have very small bathrooms with showers only. The suites are often a great deal. Spacious and cool with granite floors, the suites have a comfortable sitting room and gorgeous bathrooms with Jacuzzi tubs and separate showers.

Rua Santa Clara 141, Copacabana, Rio de Janeiro, 22041-010 RJ. © **0800/025-4477** or 021/2549-4577. Fax 021/2255-0744. www.copacabanasolhotel.com.br. 70 units. R$195–R$250 standard and superior double; R$325 suite double. Extra person R$40. Children 5 and under stay free in parent's room. AE, DC, MC, V. Free parking. Bus: 128 or 474. **Amenities:** Restaurant; concierge; room service. In room: A/C, TV, fridge, minibar, Wi-Fi.

Golden Tulip Continental ★ (Value Located a block off the beach in green and quiet Leme, a residential neighborhood at the far end of Copacabana beach, the Continental offers outstanding value. Rates seldom top R$275 and online bookings can even be less than that. For that you get services that are worthy of a deluxe hotel: room service and business center, Wi-Fi, a large fitness room, and rooftop pool. The rooms themselves are comfortable albeit a tad on the plain side with a double bed or twins, a work counter,

Santa Teresa Bed & Breakfast Network ★★

Quite a change from most of Rio de Janeiro's high-rise accommodations, the **Santa Teresa Cama e Café B&B Network** (�C 021/2225-4366 or 2221-7635; www.camaecafe.com.br) offers beautiful rooms in one of the city's most charming neighborhoods. The participating homes are often quite spectacular and situated in some of Santa Teresa's finest locations. You can choose your bed for its price and size and location, or you can fill out a more detailed form and staff will match you to your host according to your hobbies, interests, and language skills. Hosts include a variety of resident artists, chefs, and academics, as well as specialists in Brazilian music, art, and history. Houses range from century-old mansions to Art Deco villas to spacious apartments with fab views. Prices range from R$120 to R$210. Even at the cheaper end you can book yourself into a fabulous house with great views, swimming pool, and garden. The drawback to Santa Teresa is its isolation. In the evening you need to rely on taxis to get around. However, in the daytime you can grab a bus and be at the Metrô or downtown in 20 minutes. Santa Teresa in itself is worth a day of exploration. It's a perfect retreat, away from the beach.

and small table and chairs. Though adjacent to busy Copacabana, Leme is a cul-de-sac with much lighter traffic. To make the most of the view, reserve a room on the 16th floor or higher that faces the ocean.

Rua Gustavo Sampaio 320, Leme, Rio de Janeiro, 22010-010 RJ. ℂ **021/3545-5300.** Fax 021/35445-5301. www.goldentulipcontinental.com. 275 units. R$210 standard double; R$275 deluxe double. Extra person add 25%. Children 12 and under stay free in parent's room. AE, DC, MC, V. No parking. Bus: 472. **Amenities:** Restaurant; bar; concierge; health club; outdoor pool; room service; sauna; smoke-free rooms. *In room:* A/C, TV, hair dryer, Internet, minibar.

Windsor Martinique ★ Value The Windsor Martinique offers excellent value in a great location, only a half-block off the Avenida Atlântica and within easy walking distance of Ipanema. The hotel consists of two side-by-side buildings that were gutted and then joined together, making for some mazelike hallways and some small rooms. On the plus side, the rooms are nearly new and the rates are affordable. The best rooms are the superior ones that look out over the street. Corner rooms ending in 13 (such as 413 and 513, and so on) even have a partial ocean view. The standard rooms look out at adjacent buildings. All are pleasantly furnished in bright colors and have comfortable beds. Nice details at this price level include the hair dryer, electronic safe, and high-speed Internet in each room. Most rooms are a tad on the small side and accommodate two people only. There's even a rooftop pool and sun deck, but with the beach only 91m (300 ft.) away you'd have to be pretty lazy not to make it out the door.

Rua Sá Ferreira 30, Copacabana, Rio de Janeiro, 22071-100 RJ. ℂ **021/2195-5200.** Fax 021/2195-5222. www.windsorhoteis.com. 116 units. R$220–R$275 double. Extra person add 25%. Children 10 and under stay free in parent's room. AE, DC, MC, V. Metrô: Cantagalo. **Amenities:** Restaurant; concierge; cardio equipment; rooftop pool; room service; smoke-free floors. *In room:* A/C, TV, hair dryer, minibar.

FLAMENGO, CATETE & GLORIA

These older neighborhoods just south of downtown offer a range of excellent accommodations. These neighborhoods are also architecturally interesting and offer many

Where to Stay & Dine in Botafogo, Flamengo, Catete, Glória & Santa Teresa

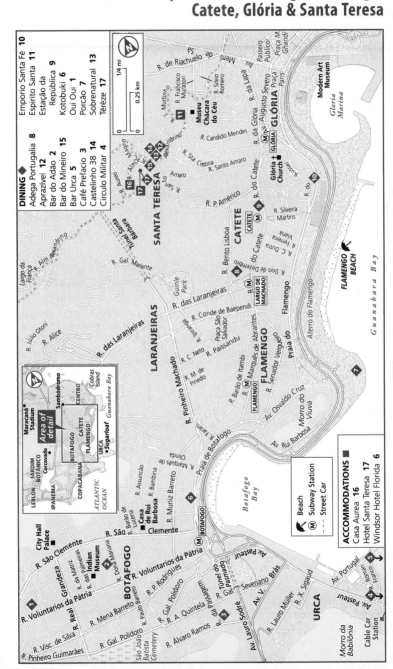

DINING ◆

Adega Portugalia **8**
Aprazível **12**
Bar do Adão **2**
Bar do Mineiro **15**
Bar Urca **5**
Café Prefácio **3**
Castelinho 38 **14**
Círculo Militar **4**

Emporio Santa Fé **10**
Espirito Santa **11**
Estação da
    República **9**
Kotobuki **6**
Oui Oui **7**
Porção **7**
Sobrenatural **13**
Térèze **17**

ACCOMMODATIONS ■
Casa Aurea **16**
Hotel Santa Teresa **17**
Windsor Hotel Florida **6**

Beach ⚓
Ⓜ Subway Station
- - - Street Car

glimpses into Rio's fascinating history. The chief drawback to the area is its distance from the ocean beaches.

Very Expensive

Hotel Santa Teresa ★★★ This is one of the most romantic small hotels in the whole city, standing head and shoulders above other boutique hotels in Santa Teresa neighborhood (comparable in price to the nearby Mama Ruisa, the Santa Teresa offers infinitely more bang for your splurging buck). Rooms are tastefully decorated with hardwood floors and king-size four poster beds, top-quality linens, and tasteful little touches of artwork and design. Deluxe rooms have a bit more space and better views of the city and surrounding hills. Suites are larger still, with sitting areas and designer bathrooms. The hotel spa features a variety of Amazon-themed treatments. The outdoor pool offers fabulous city views, as does the lounge bar. The hotel restaurant **Térèze** (p. 87) is one of the city's best. The Largo dos Guimarães, Santa Teresa's main square and "restaurant row," is only a 5-minute walk away.

Rua Almirante Alexandrino 660, Santa Teresa, Rio de Janeiro, 20241-260 RJ. ✆ **021/2222-2755.** Fax 021/2221-1406. www.santateresahotel.com. 44 units. R$650–R$725 double; R$800–R$1,600 suite. Children 10 and under stay free in parent's room. AE, DC, MC, V. No parking. Integrated Metrô/bus from Carioca Metrô stop. **Amenities:** Restaurant; outdoor pool; limited room service; spa. *In room:* A/C, TV, fridge, minibar, Wi-Fi.

Expensive

Windsor Hotel Florida ★★ (Finds) The Florida is popular with business travelers from São Paulo who know a good deal when they see it: On top of a reasonable room rate the Florida offers free parking, free local calls, and free Internet access. Built in the 1940s, the hotel doesn't suffer from the modern "small room" syndrome; rooms are spacious and pleasant, and though furnishings are a bit dated, there are good queen-size beds, hardwood floors, and ample workspace. The standard rooms overlook the rear or the side of the building. Both the superior and deluxe rooms offer views and have bathrooms with whirlpool tubs. The nicest rooms are those overlooking the lush gardens of the Palácio do Catete, Brazil's former presidential palace. The deluxe rooms are the most spacious, with a large entrance hall, king-size bed, sitting area, and desk. The hotel offers excellent discounts on weekends.

Rua Ferreira Viana 81, Flamengo, Rio de Janeiro, 22210-040 RJ. ✆ **021/2195-6800.** Fax 021/2285-5777. www.windsorhoteis.com. 312 units. R$275 standard double; R$275 superior double; R$325 deluxe double. Extra person add 25%. Children 10 and under stay free in parent's room. AE, DC, MC, V. Free parking. Metrô: Catete. **Amenities:** Restaurant; bar; concierge; weight room; rooftop pool; room service; sauna; smoke-free floors. *In room:* A/C, TV, fridge, hair dryer, minibar, Wi-Fi.

Moderate

Casa Aurea Only a short walk up the road from the main square in Santa Teresa, this affordable pousada is popular with sociable travelers and backpackers. Private rooms have ensuite bathrooms, and other rooms share a bathroom down the hall. All are simply furnished but very clean and pleasant with high ceilings and large windows with wooden shutters. The house has a gorgeous garden and patio, outdoor reading lounge, sitting room, and barbecue area, and is decorated with lovely artwork by some of the well-known artists from Santa Teresa.

Rua Aurea 80, Santa Teresa, Rio de Janeiro, 20240-210 RJ. ✆ **021/2242-5830.** www.casaaurea.com.br. 12 units. R$220–R$280 double; R$330–R$495 mini-apt double. Children 7 and under stay free in parent's room. No parking. **Amenities:** Bar; Wi-Fi. *In room:* Fan.

Castelinho 38 ★   A pretty two-story neoclassical mansion in the heart of Santa Teresa, the Castelinho offers airy ceilings, and a pretty garden and terrace overlooking the center of the city. Accommodations are quirky but comfortable. On the ground floor, facing the garden, are three rooms with private ensuite bathrooms. On the same floor are also two triple rooms (a double bed and a single) with private external bathrooms. Somewhat fancier, the two master suites on the first floor feature higher ceilings and a bit of view. The first floor also has a comfortable mini-apartment that can house up to five people. Best of all is the master suite—the *mangueira*—with air-conditioning and a lovely view of the city.

Rua Triunfo 38, Santa Teresa, Rio de Janeiro, 20240-320 RJ. ✆ **021/2252-2549.** Fax 021/2242-7511. www. castelinho38.com. 9 units. 25% discount in low season. Children 1 and under stay free in parent's room; children 2–7 R$60. MC, V. **Amenities:** Bar. *In room:* Fan, Wi-Fi.

---

3   WHERE TO DINE

Cariocas love to eat out. Better yet, they love to linger over their meals. Waiters in Rio would never dream of coming by to ask you to "settle up" so they can go off shift. So take your time. Dawdle. Savor. Enjoy.

Rio offers an endless variety of places to eat. There are the *chopperias,* the place for cold beer and casual munchies. Slightly more upscale are the botequins, many of which are open to the early hours. There are hundreds of food kiosks, each with its own specialty, be it barbecued prawns, Bahian finger food, or vegetarian sandwiches. And on top of all that, there's a wide variety of restaurants in all neighborhoods, ranging from inexpensive to very expensive, from simple sandwiches to delicious steaks, from fresh sushi to the complicated stews and sauces of Brazil's Northeast. There's no excuse for going hungry in Rio.

Most restaurants are open from around 11am until 4pm and then again from 7pm until midnight or later. There are also quite a few establishments that will stay open all day, especially on the weekends when people leave the beach at 4pm to go eat lunch. Sunday is often the busiest day for lunch as extended families get together for a meal. Many restaurants close Sunday evening. The exception to these hours is in Rio's downtown, where restaurants cater to the office crowd; only a few of them remain open evenings and weekends.

Note: For maps of restaurants in Leblon, Ipanema, Copacabana, Botafogo, Flamengo, and Catete, see the "Where to Stay & Dine" maps, earlier in this chapter.

CENTRO
Expensive
Cais do Oriente ★★ ASIAN/MEDITERRANEAN   This 19th-century warehouse has been transformed into a stunning restaurant and bar, complete with large gilt mirrors and opulent antique furniture. The menu travels from the Orient to the Mediterranean, including dishes such as sweet-and-sour duck and fried rice tossed with cashews and pistachio nuts, and prawn risotto with basil and grilled salmon served with a Gorgonzola-and-ricotta-stuffed pancake. The upstairs bar is a great venue for live music on Fridays or Saturdays.

Rua Visconde de Itaboraí 8, Centro. ✆ **021/2233-2531.** www.caisdooriente.com.br. Main courses R$32–R$58. AE, DC, MC, V. Tues–Sat noon–midnight; Sun–Mon noon–4pm. In the evenings, taxi recommended. Bus: 119. Get off 1 stop past the Praça XV.

(**Moments**) **Don't Shy Away from Street Food**

When it comes to street vendors and food, you read a lot of strange things in travel guides. Never eat meat. Don't touch fruit. Don't eat anything at all. Only drinks. In cans. Insist on ice cubes made from bottled water. Sheesh!

Rio is *not* Rangoon, nor the fetid fever swamps of 19th-century Benin. Yes, tap water is best avoided. It won't kill you; it's just so chlorine-saturated that it tastes like *eau de* swimming pool. Some of the best meals I've had in Brazil have been purchased from a street vendor. One night in Rio, on the Rua Ouvidor, we came across a man and his charcoal brazier, selling skewers of fresh-grilled prawns, lightly salted and doused with lemon. We bought two skewers, which lasted about 40 seconds . . . so we went back for four more . . . and then another four. The moral? Eating from street vendors is fine, as long as you take precautions. Does the vendor look clean and healthy? Is the food stored in a cooler? Are Brazilians queuing up? If so, odds are the food's good, and whatever supplies he has in his cooler haven't been hanging around long enough to go bad. So eat, enjoy, and don't have a cow. Or rather, *do*, if that's what they're selling.

Confeitaria Colombo ★★ BRAZILIAN/DESSERT   This stunning Victorian tearoom hasn't changed much since it opened in 1894. Two large counters at the entrance serve up sweets and snacks with coffee or other refreshments. The rest of the ground floor features an elegant tearoom, where a variety of teas, sandwiches, and sweets are served on fine china underneath a '20s stained-glass window. The upstairs is for full lunches—on Saturdays the *feijoada* (black beans and pork stew) is worth a trip downtown. *Tip:* A branch of the Confeitaria Colombo is inside the Forte Copacabana, with a smaller menu but fabulous views.

Rua Gonçalves Dias 32, Centro. ✆ **021/2505-1500.** www.confeitariacolombo.com.br. Tearoom snacks and lunches R$10–R$35; buffet lunch or Sat *feijoada* buffet R$55 including dessert. AE, DC, MC, V. Mon–Fri 8:30am–7pm; Sat 9am–5pm. Metrô: Carioca.

Sagrada Familia ★ BRAZILIAN   The second floor of a renovated 19th-century warehouse forms the site for one of Rio's most popular and innovative lunchtime spots. The menu focuses on meats—chicken, beef, duck—but tries to mix things up, thus the chicken filet with brie, and almond rice, or the filet mignon in a pepper crust, with Gorgonzola sauce. (There are also more traditional salads, pasta, and meat dishes.) The wine list offers one of Rio's larger selections by the glass or half-bottle, as well as a good selection of bottles below the R$80 mark, from South America, Portugal, and Spain.

Rua do Rosario 98 (upstairs), Centro. ✆ **021/2252-2240.** www.lasagradafamilia.com.br. Main courses R$20–R$38. AE, DC, V. Mon–Fri 11:30am–3:30pm. Metrô: Carioca.

Moderate

Bar Brasil BOTEQUIM   This bustling botequim on the busiest corner of the Lapa entertainment zone offers tasty *pastel* snacks—try the *bolinhos de bacalhau* (cod pastries)—meat-filled croquettes, and steaming little sausages with mustard. The draft beer

Airport

Ⓜ Subway Station

--- Street Car

Bar Brasil **2**
Bar Luiz **1**
Beco das Sardinhas **8**
Bistro do Paço **4**
Boteco Casual **5**
Cais do Oriente **6**
Confeitaria Colombo **3**
Paladino **9**
Sagrada Familia **7**

Sambódromo

R. Frei Caneca

Av. 31 de Março

R. B. Hipólito

Av. Presidente Vargas

Lad. Frei
Orlando

Túnel Mem de Sá

R. Frei

R. Marquês de Pombal

R. de Santana

R. Senador Pompeu

Central Station
(Central
do Brasil
Railway)

Praça Assunção
(Harmonia)

R. Matos

R. de

R. Riachuelo

R. Monconvo Filho

R. General Caldwell

Carioca

R. Barão de São Félix

Lad. do Livramento

R. do Livramento

R. do Resende

Av. Henrique

Av. Mem de Sá

R. do Senado

R. Carlos Sampaio

Av. 20
de Abril

Praça
República
(Campo de
Santana)

Ⓜ CENTRAL

R. Visc. de Gávea

R. C. Ferreira

R. R. Souza e
Sacadura

Venezuela

Silva

Praça Cruz
Vermelha

R. U. do Amaral

R. Frei Caneca

R. Visc. do
Rio Branco

Itamaraty
Palace

R. Alexandre Mackenzie

R. Camerino

Av. Barão de Tefé

R. Coelho e Castro

R. dos Inválidos

Av. Gomes Freire

R. da Relação

R. do Lavradio

R. Gonçalves Ledo

R. Senhor dos Passos

R. Buenos Aires

R. da Alfândega

PRESIDENTE
VARGAS
Ⓜ

Av. Marechal Floriano

R. Senador Pompeu

R. de Bola

Av. Rodrigues Alves

LAPA

Av. Rep. do Chile

Praça
Tiradentes

R. da Construção

Av. Passos

R. do Conceição

Morro da
Conceição

R. L. Martins

Lad. J. Homem

San Sebastião
Cathedral

2

Av. Rep. do Paraguai

7

Largo do
São Francisco

R. dos Andradros

URUGUAIANA
Ⓜ

9 CENTRO

8

R. do Acre

R. Visc. de

R. Dom Gerardo

R. Evaristo

Dantas

R. Uruguaiana

R. Gonçalves Dias

R. do Rosário

R. M. Couto

R. da Inhaúma

R. Teófilo Otoni

R. da Candelária

3

R. T. de
Freitas

R. do

Passeio
Público

Praça
Mahatma
Ghandi
Ⓜ

P. Senador...

R. 13 de Maio

CARIOCA
Ⓜ

CINELÂNDIA

Av. N. Peçanha

Av. Rio Branco

R. São José

R. 7 de Setembro

R. da Quitanda

R. da Assembléia

R. do Carmo

R. 1 de Março

7

R. do Ouvidor

CASTELO

R. do Mercado

Praça XV
de Novembro

6

Av. Pres. Kubitschek

Cobras
Island

Museu
de Arte
Moderna
(MAM)

Av. Infante Dom Henrique

Av. Beira Mar

Av. Pres. Wilson

Av. Pres. Antônio Carlos

Av. Graça Aranha

Av. México

R. Araújo Porto-Alegre

R. Debret

4

R. da Misericórdia

R. Erasmo Braga

R. São José

R. Santa Luzia

Av. Mal. Câmara

Av. Franklin Roosevelt

Av. Churchill

Museu
Histórico
Nacional

Ferry
Terminal

*Guanabara
Bay*

Av. General Justo

SANTOS DUMONT
AIRPORT

0   1/4 mi
0   0.25 km

Maracanã
Stadium

LEBLON

JARDIM
BOTÂNICO

Corcovado

IPANEMA

Area of
detail

Sambódromo

CENTRO

BOTAFOGO

COPACABANA

CATETE

FLAMENGO

*ATLANTIC
OCEAN*

URCA

Sugarloaf

Cobras
Island

Guanabara Bay

SETTLING INTO RIO DE JANEIRO

5

WHERE TO DINE

comes in clear and dark flavors, both cold with a thick topping of foam. There are tables inside, but for prime people-watching grab a stool on the patio.

Av. Mem de Sà 90, Lapa. ☏ **021/2509-5943.** R$10–R$25. DC, MC, V. Mon–Sat 11am–midnight; Sun 11am–6pm. Bus: 464.

Bistro do Paço ★ **Finds** BRAZILIAN   This is the perfect spot to escape the heat and noise in downtown. Inside the historic Paço Imperial, the thick whitewashed walls keep out the bustle while you recharge your batteries in the cool shade of the inner courtyard. The restaurant serves mostly bistro fare as well as a daily lunch special that will set you back R$15 to R$26 for a plate of roast beef with a side order of pasta, and spinach crepes with a ricotta-and-mushroom stuffing. For a light snack try a quiche, a freshly made sandwich with grilled vegetables, or a cold-cut plate. Desserts are strictly European: Austrian *linzertortes,* German fruit strudels, and Black Forest chocolate cakes, all of which go so well with a Brazilian *cafezinho.*

Praça XV 48 (inside the Paço Imperial), Centro. ☏ **021/2262-3613.** Main courses R$18–R$35; sandwiches and quiches R$10–R$22. AE, DC, MC, V. Mon–Fri 10am–8pm; Sat noon–7pm. Bus: 415.

Boteco Casual BOTEQUIM   In the heart of Rio's historic district just off Praça XV, this little bar-restaurant offers delicious cold beer and Portuguese specialties like stuffed octopus flavored with port, or salted grilled sardines. For dessert, try the *pastel de nata.* And if this little bar is packed, there's a bunch of others right alongside.

Rua do Ouvidor 26, Centro. ☏ **021/2232-0250.** Main courses R$10–R$25. AE, DC, MC, V. Mon–Fri 11am–2am; Sat 11am–6pm. Bus: 119 or 415 to Praça XV.

Inexpensive

Beco das Sardinhas (Rei dos Frangos Maritimos) ★ **Finds** BRAZILIAN   Known as "the sardine triangle," this corner in Rio's historic downtown is the perfect place to spend a Friday afternoon as locals gather to unwind from the workweek. It started in the '60s when the Portuguese owners of three small restaurants began selling fried sardines. They would cut open the fish and fry them like a filet, dubbed *frango maritimo* (chicken of the sea) by a jesting customer, and the name stuck to one of the restaurants. These days the triangle has expanded to include six restaurants in a pedestrian area between Rua do Acre and Rua Mayrink Veiga. Every Friday after 6pm it transforms into a giant TGIF party. The patio tables and counters fill up almost as quickly as the fried sardines, salted and breaded in manioc flour, come piping hot off the grill. Accompanied by a *loira gelada* ("icy blond," the local nickname for draft), it's the perfect way to start a weekend.

Rua Miguel Couto 139, Centro. ☏ **021/2233-6119.** Everything under R$15. No credit cards. Mon–Fri 11am–10pm. Metrô: Uruguaiana.

Paladino ★ BRAZILIAN   Is Paladino a deli, with racks of spices and jars of capers and artichoke hearts? Is it a liquor store, as the hundreds of glass bottles lined up in gleaming wooden cases seem to suggest? Or is it a bustling lunch bar with some of the best draft beer in town? Is an exact definition really important? What matters is that the beer is clear and cold and comes at the wave of a finger, the atmosphere is that of Rio in the Belle Epoque, and the sandwiches and snack plates are delicious. *Pratinhos,* as the latter are known in Portuguese, cost next to nothing—R$4 to R$8—and come loaded with sardines or olives, cheese, or great heaping stacks of smoked sausage. All this delectable nosh is served up by old-fashioned waiters in black pants and white shirts. Since 1907, an eclectic mix of lawyers, shopkeepers, workers, and executives has come here, and though none have ever succeeded in defining exactly what it is, they've never stopped coming.

Rua Uruguaiana 226, Centro. ✆ **021/2263-2094.** Reservations not accepted. Sandwiches and side dishes R$4–R$15. No credit cards. Mon–Fri 7am–8:30pm; Sat 8am–noon. Metrô: Uruguaiana.

SANTA TERESA
Expensive

Aprazível ★ **Finds** BRAZILIAN Much of the charm of this Santa Teresa fixture comes from its setting in a hilltop mansion. Tables spill out over the gardens and patios, offering views of downtown Rio by day, and warm and exotic lighting in the evening. View junkies should ask for a table on the house veranda, or on the patio tables outside by the bar. The food, while good, doesn't quite rise to the same standard. The kitchen serves up an intriguing variation on Brazilian cuisine, using many ingredients from the Nordeste region. Interesting starters include fresh grilled palm hearts, and pumpkin cream soup with prawns. The signature main is the *peixe tropical,* grilled fish in an orange sauce, served with coconut rice and baked banana.

Rua Aprazível 62, Santa Teresa. ✆ **021/2508-9174.** www.aprazivel.com.br. Reservations recommended. Main courses R$38–R$55. AE, MC, V. Thurs 8pm–midnight; Fri–Sat noon–midnight; Sun 1–6pm. Taxi recommended.

Espirito Santa ★★ BRAZILIAN Espirito Santa proves there's no great secret to success—a cute restaurant, a great patio looking out over Santa Teresa, and excellent and inventive Brazilian cuisine. Chef Natacha Fink hails from the Amazon, and it shows in her menu. The signature starter is the *tambaqui* "ribs"—made of *tambaqui* (a popular Amazonian fish) lightly breaded and served with a pesto of *jambu* herbs. The *mujica de piranha* (piranha soup) is thick and tasty. For salads, there's one with toasted Brazil nuts and a passion-fruit vinaigrette. The classic fish dish is a grilled *namorado* with a cashew crust, served on a bed of grilled fresh palm heart. Meat lovers should try the *bacuri* steak, grilled filet mignon served with a *bacuri* (Amazonian fruit) sauce and mashed sweet potatoes. Or try grilled filet of duck in *açai* sauce. For dessert, there's warm gâteau filled with guava cream and cheese, or ice cream of *cupuaçu.*

Rua Almirante Alexandrino 264, Santa Teresa. ✆ **021/2508-7095.** www.espiritosanta.com.br. Main courses R$28–R$55. AE, DC, MC, V. Mon, Wed, and Sun noon–7pm; Thurs–Sat noon–midnight. Bus: 214, or take the tram, getting off just before the Largo dos Guimarães.

Térèze ★★ ASIAN/MEDITERRANEAN Here you'll find sophisticated dining on a hilltop in the heights of Rio's most historic neighborhood, with a view of treetops, colonial houses, and the city and bay below. The menu offers an upscale take on fusion: miso-marinated lamb, grilled and served with wok-fried vegetables, *gyoza* with sweet-and-sour *maracujá* dipping sauce, or grilled *cherne* with cashew tapenade. Desserts can be equally creative, such as the macaroni-shaped chocolates with hazelnut *farofa* and vanilla ice cream. On Thursdays there's a tasting menu, featuring smaller portions and matched wines.

In the Hotel Santa Teresa (p. 82), Rua Almirante Alexandrino 660, Santa Teresa. ✆ **021/2222-2755.** www.tereze.com.br. Reservations recommended. Main courses R$38–R$65. AE, MC, V. Mon–Fri noon–5pm and 8pm–midnight; Sat noon–midnight; Sun noon–5pm. Taxi recommended.

Moderate

Sobrenatural **Overrated** SEAFOOD Things have gone downhill at this hilltop spot. For years, we recommended Sobrenatural for its seafood and spacious ambience, but over the past year or so prices have risen while quality has declined, and the restaurant has come to focus increasingly on the tourist trade at the expense of its local clientele. For better food at a comparable price, seek out Espirito Santa (see above) a few doors down, while for cheap and cheerful Brazilian cuisine, there's Bar do Mineiro (see below).

Rua Almirante Alexandrino 432, Santa Teresa. ✆ **021/2224-1003.** Main courses R$55–R$75 for 2. AE, DC, MC, V. Daily noon–midnight. Bus: 214, or take the tram, getting off at the Largo dos Guimarães.

Inexpensive
Bar do Mineiro (Finds) BRAZILIAN   Minas Gerais is looked on as the source of down-home hearty comfort food. Bar do Mineiro is a little piece of Minas in Santa Teresa. Meals are hearty and portions generous. Appetizers include sausages and *pasteis*—savory pastries with a variety of stuffings, including sausage, cheese, or cabbage. The *frango com quiabo* (stewed chicken with okra) is popular, as is the *Feijão tropeiro.* There's also a very good (and very Carioca) *feijoada.*

Rua Pascoal Carlos Magno 99, Santa Teresa. ✆ **021/2221-9227.** Main courses R$14–R$28. AE, V. Tues–Thurs 11am–2am; Fri–Sat 11am–3am; Sun 11am–midnight. Bus: 214, or take the tram, getting off at the Largo dos Guimarães.

URCA
Moderate
Bar Urca ★ BOTEQUIM   This tiny botequim has one of the best views in the city—or does if you make like the locals, and drink your beer and munch from the delicious selection of *pastels* on the sea wall overlooking Botafogo Bay. (Waiters used to cross the street and serve you *in situ,* but due to a recent crackdown customers now have to order in the restaurant and carry their wares to the sea wall themselves.) If you do go inside, sit upstairs with a window view and order one of the delicious seafood stews—fish or prawns or octopus in a rich broth, with rice and *pirão* on the side. Don't think of drinking anything but beer.

Rua Candido Gaffree 205, Urca. ✆ **021/2295-8744.** www.barurca.com.br. Main courses R$10–R$35. DC, MC, V. Daily 9am–11pm. Metrô: Integração from Botofogo.

Circulo Militar ★★ (Finds) BRAZILIAN   Whenever we hanker for dinner and a view we head to the Circulo Militar. This fabulous view of the Sugarloaf and Bay comes courtesy of the Brazilian armed forces. From the tree-shaded patio of a military club in Urca called the Circulo Militar, you look out across a tiny bay full of fishing boats to the sheer solid sides of the Sugarloaf. Civilians are completely welcome. The menu serves up standard Brazilian fare (the two stars are for the view, not for the food) such as the *churrasco* for two with beef, sausage, chicken, and pork served with fries and rice. In the evenings the kitchen fires up the wood-burning oven and turns out some decent pizzas. There's live music from 8pm onward, Tuesday through Sunday.

Praça General Tiburcio s/n, Praia Vermelha (on the far right, inside the military complex). ✆ **021/2275-7245.** www.cmpv.com.br. Main courses R$24–R$42. No credit cards. Daily noon–midnight. Bus: 107 from downtown, 512 from Ipanema and Copacabana.

FLAMENGO/GLORIA/CATETE
Very Expensive
Porcão ★★ BRAZILIAN/STEAK   A mass carnivorous orgy, Porcão is where you go not to sample or taste or nibble, but to munch and stuff and gorge yourself on some of the best beef the world has to offer—in this case served up with some of the best views

in the world. Porcão is a churrascaria (a chain, in fact; there are several in Rio, but this one has the best view) operating on the *rodízio* system. It's one price for all you can eat (dessert and drinks are extra), and once you sit down, an onslaught of waiters comes bearing all manner of meat (steak cuts, roast cuts, filet mignon, chicken breast, chicken hearts, sausage, and much more) which they slice to perfection on your plate. Oh, and don't forget the nonmeat dishes: Included in your meal is a buffet with dozens of antipasto items, hot and cold seafood dishes, and at least 15 different kinds of salads and cheeses. Alas, no doggy bags allowed.

Av. Infante Dom Henrique s/n, Parque do Flamengo. ⓒ 021/2554-8535. www.porcao.com.br. Reservations accepted. R$75 per person all-you-can-eat meat and buffet. 50% discount for children 6–9, free for children 5 and under. AE, DC, MC, V. Daily 11:30am–1am. Taxi recommended.

Expensive

Emporio Santa Fé ★★ BRAZILIAN/PASTA   This lovely two-story restaurant overlooking the Aterro do Flamengo is one of the best restaurants in Flamengo. The ground floor has a small wine bar and a few tables but you really want to head upstairs and, if possible, grab one of the window tables in the elegant L-shaped dining room. The chef's forte is pasta; all dishes are made fresh and combine some creative flavors. We loved the ravioli with prawns in a leek sauce with mushrooms as well as the *Tortele Tricolor,* pasta rounds stuffed with smoked ricotta, figs, and Parma ham. Steak lovers have plenty to choose from, including filet mignon medallions with grilled brie and potatoes, or grilled tournedos in a balsamic jus, served with rice and mushrooms. The wine list has over 400 options covering most of the world's regions, many reasonably priced (under R$70).

Praia do Flamengo 2, Flamengo. ⓒ 021/2245-6274. www.emporiosantafe.com. Reservations accepted. R$35–R$65 main courses. AE, DC, MC, V. Sun–Thurs noon–midnight; Fri–Sat noon–2am. Bus: Any bus to Praia do Flamengo.

Moderate

Adega Portugalia PORTUGUESE   This simple little bar/restaurant looks out on the Largo do Machado, a graceful Rio urban square. Sample a plate of appetizers—cheese, olives, spiced potatoes, octopus—from the counter deli, order a portion of *frango a pasarinho* (garlic baked chicken wings), or sample a steak or Portuguesa pizza. Make sure to order a chopp to go with the munchies.

Largo do Machado 30, Flamengo. ⓒ 021/2558-2821. Reservations not accepted. R$15–R$30. MC, V. Mon–Sat 10am–midnight; Sun 10am–6pm. Metrô: Largo do Machado.

Estação da República ★ (Kids) KILO   The Estação is top of the heap in that unique Brazilian category, the kilo restaurant. It offers a daily selection of at least 20 salads, a range of pastas, pizza, and many Brazilian favorites such as *feijoada* (bean stew), *vatapá* (seafood stew), and *bobó* (shrimp stew). Fancier dishes include carpaccio and sushi. The *pièce de résistance* is the grill in the back of the restaurant where skilled chefs serve you a choice of beef, chicken, and a wide assortment of fish. You can have your meat nearly raw or very well done; just ask the chef. It's a great place for children; they can see the food and try as much or as little as they like. Make your selection, weigh your plate, and find yourself a seat; drinks are served at your table.

Rua do Catete 104, Catete. ⓒ 021/2128-5650. www.estacaorepublica.com.br. Reservations not accepted. R$32 per kilo. AE, DC, MC, V. Daily 11am–midnight. Metrô: Catete.

Expensive

Kotobuki ★ JAPANESE The food at Kotobuki is good, very good even, but it's not really better than a number of other Japanese restaurants around Rio. What is outstanding is what you're watching while you eat. Kotobuki offers a sweeping view of Botafogo Bay with the pretty boats at anchor in the marina, and, backstopping it all, the soaring Pão de Açúcar. Located in the seventh-floor food court of the Botafogo Praia Shopping (I know, but food-court food is *different* in Brazil), Kotobuki offers lunchtime specials including the *prato executivo:* 15 pieces of sushi and sashimi with a miso soup (called *misoshuri* in Brazil), or beef stir-fry with rice and miso and a *sunomuno* salad. The teppanyaki for two is skillfully prepared at your table, as the chef cooks up thin slices of beef, tofu, and vegetables.

Praia de Botafogo 400, 7th floor, Botafogo. ✆ **021/3141-9595.** Reservations accepted, but window tables are on a first-come, first-served basis. Main courses R$22–R$48. AE, DC, MC, V. Daily 11:30am–midnight. Metrô: Botafogo.

Oui Oui ★★ FUSION Better late than never! Tapas has finally made it to Rio at Oui Oui, which has created a wonderful menu of 20 small dishes that can be combined into a very satisfying meal. Start off with a refreshing Moranguito cocktail (sparkling wine, strawberries, and mint) and a plate of spring rolls stuffed with fresh figs and shredded duck. Other interesting dishes include the vegetable risotto with mascarpone, spicy grilled beef with lemon grass, and the shrimp *moqueca* stew with cashew nuts and mango. The hands down (and finger-licking) winner was the portion of caramelized spareribs served with a pumpkin and goat cheese purée, topped with toasted almonds. It probably violates the cardinal rule of tapas eating, but next time I am not sharing that dish! The wine list is a tad overpriced, but does contain a few good deals such as a South African chenin blanc for R$64.

Rua Conde de Irajá 85, Humaitá. ✆ **021/2527-3537.** Main courses R$17–R$26. AE, DC, MC, V. Tues–Sun 7:30pm–1am. Metrô: Integração Botafogo.

Moderate

Café Prefacio CAFE Books. Wine. Food. Food. Books. Wine. No matter how you put the words together, it's a winning combination. This bookstore/cafe (or cafe/bookstore) in the Botofogo cinema zone offers good coffee, wine by the glass, and a simple menu of delicious sandwiches and salads. Seating is at the coffee bar in the front, or the mezzanines above the bookshelves, or in the small dining room at the back. Browse the titles while awaiting your order (there's an English-language section, and a wide selection of art books), or order up a bottle of Argentine Malbec (R$40 or so) and stay the night.

Rua Voluntarios de Patria 39, Botafogo. ✆ **021/2527-5699.** www.prefaciolivrarias.com.br. Reservations not accepted. Main courses R$15–R$30. MC, V. Mon–Sat 9am–11pm; Sun 4:30–11pm. Metrô: Botafogo.

Meza Bar ★★ TAPAS It may be time for a new review category: the gourmet bar. Meza has all the trappings of a hip bar: a beautiful heritage building in trendy Humaitá, modern and funky decorations that spill out over several rooms, a discreet DJ, free Wi-Fi, and awesome drinks. How about a "Hot Chip"—a *cachaça* or vodka cocktail with watermelon, cardamom, and basil, or the Apple Mojito, with premium rum, lime juice, mint, and caramelized apple? My favorite is the Bordello, sake with peach liquor, lychee, and basil. There is food and it's light-years ahead of your average pub grub. From the kitchen comes a steady flow of small dishes, like spicy chicken with lime and tequila, tuna *tartare*

Juice Magic

Rio's juice bars are a bit like a magician's hat. You peer into a hole-in-the-wall diner and think there's nothing there, then the guy behind the counter conjures up any kind of fruit juice you care to name, all of it made fresh to order. The menu in these often standing-room-only spots will typically list over 25 different kinds of fruit juice. There are the standards such as passion fruit *(maracujá)*, pineapple *(abacaxi)*, mango *(manga)*, or cashew fruit *(caju)*; there's *carambola* (star fruit), *goiaba* (guava), *jaca* (jack fruit), and *açerola* (red juice from the tiny *açerola* fruit). This is where things get fun. You can mix anything with anything else. Try *laranja com açerola* (orange juice with *açerola,* a very popular combination); *maracujá com mango;* or *pineapple e guava, cashew e açerola*. Some of these work, some don't. The magicians behind the counter are full of suggestions if you have any doubts. (Brazilians like to mix their fruit juice with milk.) You can also just throw caution to the wind and see what comes out of the hat.

Excellent juice bars include **Big Nectar,** Teixeira de Melo 34A, Ipanema. (no phone; www.bignectar.com.br; 24 hr.). Five other locations are in Ipanema, Copacabana, and Catete. Or try **Bibi Sucos,** Av. Ataulfo de Paiva 591, Leblon. (℮ **021/2259-4298;** www.bibisucos.com.br; daily 8am–2am), with 10 other locations in Rio.

with orange and Parmesan crisps, quinoa salad with a grilled squid skewer, or a spicy Thai salad with shrimp and mango.

Rua Capitão Salomão 69, Humaitá. ℮ **021/3239-1951.** www.mezabar.com.br. Main courses R$12–R$17. AE, DC, MC, V. Sun–Wed 6pm–1am; Thurs–Sat 6pm–3am. Bus: 176.

Inexpensive

Bar do Adão BOTEQUIM   This lovely heritage house in Botafogo houses an excellent bar that serves up the best *pasteis* in town, or the second-best *pasteis,* as the original Bar do Adão in the Zona Norte neighborhood of Grajau first developed their recipe for success. Made out of light fluffy dough, the *pasteis* come in an amazing variety of fillings, are quickly deep-fried, and arrive piping hot at your table. The 60 different flavors include brie and apricot, Gorgonzola and sun-dried tomato, prawns and cream cheese, shiitake mushrooms and more. On Tuesday nights it is two for one.

Rua Dona Mariana 81, Botafogo. ℮ **021/2535-4572.** www.bardoadao.com.br. Reservations not accepted. Main courses R$10–R$25. MC, V. Daily noon–midnight. Metrô: Botafogo.

COPACABANA/LEME
Very Expensive

Le Pré Catelan ★★★ FRENCH   Even after a decade as one of Rio's top celebrity chefs, Roland Villard still manages to offer diners a "wow" every time. After transforming the staid old hotel dining room into a stylish and trendy lounge overlooking Copacabana beach, it was time for the next challenge. Inspired by a trip to the Brazilian rainforest, he spent several years researching and preparing his latest project: a 10-course menu of exclusively Amazonian dishes. Guests receive a booklet with pictures and descriptions of all the ingredients and dishes, such as the Tucanaré *brandade* with coconut milk, roasted tapioca stuffed with freshwater crustaceans, *pirarucu* fish with a cashew crust served in a mouth-tingling *jambu* sauce. Other dishes include *tambaqui* "cutlets" in a red wine jus and the outstanding sparerib confit in a sweet-tangy *jabuticaba* sauce. Tropical fruit *granités* are served as palate cleansers between courses. Sommelier Jean Pierre pairs these fantastic flavors with some excellent wines. Guests can also order from the a la carte menu, but you would be foolish to miss this amazing Amazon dining experience!

Hotel Sofitel, Av. Atlântica 4240, Copacabana. ℂ **021/2525-1160.** Reservations required. Main courses R$88; Amazon 10-course tasting menu R$230. AE, DC, MC, V. Mon–Wed 7:30–11:30pm; Thurs–Sat 7:30pm–midnight. Bus: 415.

Marius STEAK   One of the better all-you-can-eat *rodízio* restaurants, Marius serves up prime cuts of beef. In addition to this carnivore's dream, the buffet also includes excellent seafood such as fresh oysters, shrimp, langoustines, smoked salmon, and paella, in addition to salads and other side dishes. But back to what we came for. Here at Marius, waiters will come out over and over with your favorite cuts of steak, whether it is juicy tender rib-eye, T-bone, rack of lamb, or any of the other kinds of typical Brazilian beef cuts such as *maminha, alcatra, picanha,* and *fraldinha.*

Av. Atlântica 290A, Leme. ℂ **021/2543-6363.** www.marius.com.br. Reservations accepted. R$119 per person, all-you-can-eat buffet. AE, DC, MC, V. Mon–Fri noon–4pm and 6pm–midnight; Sat–Sun noon–midnight. Bus: 472.

Expensive

Da Brambini ★ (Finds) ITALIAN   For traditional Italian food in a cozy little bistro, look no further than Da Brambini. To start off, indulge in the *couvert*—a tasty antipasto platter with olives, salami, tuna paste, grilled eggplant, and freshly baked breads. Other worthwhile appetizers include the polenta with fresh funghi or Gorgonzola. Main courses include veal with mushrooms, traditional *osso buco* (veal shanks stewed in wine), as well as a number of outstanding pasta dishes. Da Brambini certainly doesn't skimp on ingredients; the handmade ravioli with shrimp is just swimming with the little critters, all smothered in a creamy seafood sauce. The linguine with mussels, *sururu* (a tiny clam), and *vongole* are equally tasty. For wine, Da Brambini offers a good selection of Italian reds, starting at R$45 a bottle. The service is unhurried, and the staff is happy to let you linger over your dinner.

Av. Atlântica 514, Leme. ℂ **021/2275-4346.** www.dabrambini.com.br. Reservations recommended. Main courses R$28–R$55. AE, DC, MC, V. Daily noon–1am. Bus: 472.

Siri Mole ★★ BAHIAN   Siri Mole is one of the best Bahian restaurants in town. Although the location on the corner of the busy Rua Francisco Otaviano is less than inspired, the food is worth the trip. The *moquecas* are outstanding, perfectly balancing the mix of coconut milk, red dendê palm oil, and fresh cilantro that give this dish its signature flavor. Try a *moqueca* with prawns, octopus, fish, or lagoustine. The grilled seafood or fish are also excellent. Portions are a reasonable size and can often be shared. During Saturday's lunch buffet (noon–5pm) the restaurant serves up a variety of delicacies (R$42 per person, all you can eat). Make sure to save room for dessert. There's *quindim*, a creamy coconut pudding, or *cocada*—pure coconut mixed with pure cane sugar—then wash it down with a hot and black *cafezinho*. **Tip:** For the same excellent food in a waterfront location, try the Sire Mole in one of the new kiosks on the Copacabana beachfront, opposite the Rua Bolivar: **Siri Mole Prai** (ℂ **021/3684-6671;** www. sirimolepraia.com.br; Tues–Sun 9am–midnight).

Moderate

Alfaia ★★ (Finds PORTUGUESE   Portuguese cooking is a staple of Brazilian cuisine, but somewhat more rare in North America. This lovely neighborhood restaurant, tucked away off Avenida N.S. de Copacabana, is one of the best places in Rio to give Portuguese dishes a try. The house specialties always include *bacalhau* (salted codfish). Start off with the perfectly deep-fried *bolinhos de bacalhau* (codfish dumplings). The classic main dish here is the *bacalhau à Bras,* oven-baked codfish served with potatoes, scrambled egg, onion, and olives. Portions are huge, but half-portions are available. We found that with appetizers and dessert, a half-portion was plenty for two people. (For non–cod lovers, there's sole *á belle meuniére,* or grilled octopus with red peppers.) The wine list includes some excellent Portuguese whites and reds. For dessert there are delicious Portuguese pastries. Try the *pastel de nata,* a flaky pastry stuffed with creamy custard.

Rua Inhangá 30, Copacabana. ✆ **021/2236-1222.** Main courses R$46–R$85 for 2. AE, DC, MC, V. Mon–Sat noon–midnight; Sun noon–11pm. Metrô: Cardeal Arcoverde.

Arab ★ MIDDLE EASTERN   Arab has a terrific waterfront patio (on Copa beach) and delicious Middle Eastern cuisine. For lunch the kitchen puts on an excellent kilo buffet (R$42/kilo), great for trying a variety of dishes. Offerings include tasty salads with chickpeas, lentils, grilled vegetables, and outstanding main dishes such as the roasted chicken with apricots, couscous with cod, grilled lamb kabobs, and piping hot, fresh pita breads. In the evenings, dishes are a la carte. Our favorites include the tray of *mezzes* (appetizer plates). Perfect for sharing, these plates come with enough munchies for three or four people and include hummus, baba ghanouj, savory pastries with ground beef or lamb, and other finger food. Desserts are dangerously rich and include sweet pastries made with sugar, rosewater, and almonds or pistachios.

Av. Atlântica 1936, Copacabana. ✆ **021/2235-6698.** www.restaurantearab.com.br. Main courses R$25–R$42. AE, DC, MC, V. Mon 5pm–1am; Tues–Sun 8am–1am. Metrô: Cardeal Arcoverde.

Churrascaria Carretão (Kids (Value BRAZILIAN/STEAK   For a churrascaria meal without breaking the bank, try Carretão. It's an all-you-can-eat *rodízio* system: Meats are delivered to your table by a constant parade of waiters carrying a variety of cuts, and you can help yourself to a large buffet with a selection of 20 salads, sushi, and even grilled salmon or trout. Carretão also serves up a variety of pork, sausage, chicken, and turkey cuts. Children 4 and under eat free, those ages 5 to 9 pay only half price. Just keep them away from the fruit smoothies and desserts so eagerly pushed by the waiters; these aren't included in the price, and jack up the bill pretty quickly.

Rua Visconde de Pirajá 112, Ipanema. ✆ **021/2267-3965.** Reservations accepted. R$35 all-you-can-eat, drinks and desserts extra. AE, DC, MC, V. Daily 11am–midnight. Bus: 404 or 474 (corner Teixeira de Melo). Also in Copacabana: Rua Ronald de Carvalho 55, ✆ **021/2543-2666,** and Rua Siqueira Campos 23, ✆ **021/2236-3435.**

Shirley ★★ (Finds SPANISH   This hole-in-the-wall Spanish seafood restaurant has been packing them in for years. The restaurant is small, the tables close together, and the older waiters quaint, though not exactly perky, and the food is definitely worth the trip. When you finally nab a spot, order the *couvert* while perusing the menu; you get a plate of chunky sardines in tomato sauce, olives, and lots of pickled veggies. It's better than many of the appetizers, and goes nicely with the house sangria. The menu offers a range

> **(Finds) Where to Find the Finest Feijoada**
>
> For the best *feijoada* in town, try one of the following restaurants (on a Sat, of course—lunch only). **Confeitaria Colombo** serves an outstanding *feijoada* in the loveliest dining room in town, Rua Gonçalves Dias 32, Centro (© **021/2221-0107;** www.confeitariacolombo.com.br). **Galani,** on the 23rd floor of the plush Caesar Park Hotel, Av. Vieira Souto 460, Ipanema (© **021/2525-2525;** www.caesarpark-rio.com), is famous for its Saturday buffet. Even fancier is the spread at the Sheraton's **Mirador,** Avenida Niemeyer, São Conrado (© **021/2274-1122;** www.sheraton-rio.com). After lunch you'll welcome the 30-minute walk back to Leblon.

of fish and seafood dishes, including typically Spanish items such as paella and zarzuela, a souplike stew. The prawn dishes are made with the fresh, monster-size prawns you see in the display window. Fish lovers have the option of sole, sea bass, and snapper, which can be grilled, sautéed, broiled, or breaded. Plates come with generous side dishes of vegetables, potatoes, or rice and will easily feed two.

Rua Gustavo Sampaio 620, Leme. © 021/2275-1398. Main courses R$26–R$56; most are for 2 people. No credit cards. Daily 11am–midnight. Bus: 472.

Inexpensive

The Bakers SANDWICHES/DESSERT   The perfect combination of American-style sandwiches and Brazilian sweets and desserts. The sandwich menu includes breads not often seen in Rio, including ciabatta, eight-grain, whole wheat, and challah. The Al Pacino sandwich comes with Parma ham, mozzarella, sun-dried tomatoes, and a Mediterranean dressing. The Romeo and Juliet is a delicious combination of chicken breast, herb-flavored catupiry cheese, greens, and an apricot dressing. Once you've chewed through one of those, you can choose from a mouthwatering selection of cakes and pies, including the Ecstasy, a chocolate cake with fresh strawberries, whipped cream, and chocolate sauce, or for something more nutty, the chocolate mousse cake with cashews. The bakery also serves up a mean cappuccino.

Rua Santa Clara 86, Copacabana. © 021/3209-1212. www.thebakers.com.br. Everything under R$15. No credit cards. Daily 9am–8pm. Bus: 415.

Cafeina CAFE/BREAKFAST   There's excellent coffee and cappuccino here, home-made specialty breads, and a good selection of sandwiches, but what really draws folks in is the breakfast menu: There are waffles with honey or whipped cream or Nutella, delicious eggs and omelets, or the classic breakfast for two—fresh OJ, a basket of breads with jam and honey and cheese, cold cuts, cakes, papayas, yogurt with granola, and of course coffee (R$47 for two).

Rua Barata Ribeiro 507, Copacabana. © 021/2547-4390. www.cafeina.biz. Main courses R$8–R$30. MC, V. Daily 8am–11pm. Metrô: Cardeal Arcoverde. Plus 4 other locations in Copacabana, Ipanema, and Leblon.

IPANEMA
Very Expensive

Margutta ★★★ ITALIAN   Margutta offers Mediterranean cuisine with an emphasis on seafood. The room is cozy and intimately lit. Owner Paolo Neroni often greets guests at the door and provides a word or two of recommendation. We started off with deliciously sautéed mushrooms, followed by the *farfalle al gamberi e zafferano*, bow-tie pasta with prawns in creamy saffron. For our entree we tried the signature dish, the *Pesce alla Neroni* (oven-roasted fish with fine herbs and a side of roasted potatoes and tomatoes). What impresses is the simplicity of the dishes. No convoluted sauces, long lists of ingredients, or fancy fusion. Most dishes seem to consist of three or four ingredients and just the right amount of herbs to balance the flavors. The result is a simple and elegant cuisine that brings out the best of all ingredients.

Av. Henrique Dumont 62, Ipanema. ℂ 021/2259-3718. www.margutta.com.br. Reservations recommended. Main courses R$35–R$75. AE, DC, MC. Mon–Fri 6pm–1am; Sat and holidays noon–1am; Sun noon–midnight. Bus: 415.

Expensive

Gero ★★ ITALIAN The Rio branch of a highly successful São Paulo restaurant brings the same sophisticated styling to the room and the same meticulous preparation to the meals. Signature dishes include rack of lamb with a black truffle and foie gras sauce, or *osso buco* with mushrooms. Pastas include gnocchi with squid, and a ravioli of veal with a mushroom sauce. The room is open but warm, with a hardwood floor and exposed brick walls. Wines lean to the higher end—avoid the overpriced token Brazilian vintages, and seek out the midpriced Chilean and Argentine vintages.

Rua Anibal de Mendonça 157, Ipanema. ℂ **021/2239-8158.** www.fasano.com.br. Main courses R$35–R$65. AE, DC, MC, V. Mon–Fri noon–4pm and 7pm–1am; Sat noon–2am; Sun noon–midnight. Bus: 415.

Le Vin Bistro ★★ FRENCH This place offers French bistro cuisine, though perhaps a tad higher end than is normal in Paris. For starters, try the half-dozen oysters, the *mouilles et frites*, or the obligatory escargots, served dripping in garlic and adorned with parsley. For a main course, try the lamb in a red-wine reduction, or steak in béarnaise sauce, with baked potatoes. The wine list has an extensive selection by the glass, a good way to mix and match reds and whites to every dish. For dessert, try the traditional profiterole or petit gâteau. *Et voilà.*

Rua Barão de Torre 490, Ipanema. ℂ **021/3502-1002.** www.levin.com.br. Main courses R$35–R$55. AE, DC, MC, V. Mon–Sat noon–midnight; Sun noon–11pm. Bus: 415.

Zazá Bistrô Tropical ★★ BRAZILIAN/FUSION Zazá is Rio's funkiest eatery, serving up a creative menu of South American cuisine fused with Oriental flavors. Everything about Zazá is fun, from the playful and eclectic decorations to the unique and excellent dishes. Diners can choose from a table on the terrace or in the dining room. The more adventurous can ask for a spot upstairs where everyone sits on the floor, surrounded by candlelight, leaning back on silk-covered pillows. It feels like a palace from the *Arabian Nights.* The menu offers plenty of choices. Appetizers include a deliciously grilled squid salad served on a bed of greens with an orange vinaigrette, or an order of mini-*acarajés* (deep-fried dumplings made of mashed beans and spicy shrimp) served with tomato chutney instead of the usual hot-pepper sauce. Main courses also mix up the flavors. Try the *namorado* fish filet served with a purée of banana and palm heart, or a prawn ravioli served with grilled salmon in a saffron sauce. For vegetarians there is always an intriguing daily special.

Rua Joana Angelica 40, Ipanema. ℂ **021/2247-9101.** www.zazabistro.com.br. Main courses R$28–R$45. AE, DC, MC, V. Sun–Thurs 7:30pm–1am; Fri–Sat 7:30pm–1:30am. Bus: 415.

Casa da Feijoada ★ BRAZILIAN   There may be restaurants with better *feijoada* in town—there are certainly better-decorated ones—but what they can't offer you is *feijoada* any old day of the week. (Brazilian tradition dictates that the full-on *feijoada* meal is only served on Sat.) That's where the Casa da Feijoada comes to the rescue. Get off to a good start with the *caldo de feijão* (bean soup), washed down with a *batida de limão* (lime cocktail) to line your stomach, as the Brazilians would say. Next bring on the actual bean stew, served in a clay pot with whatever meat you've a hankering for, be it sausage, bacon, *carne seca* (dried meat), pork loin, pig's snout, and other more obscure cuts. Side dishes include white rice, stir-fried cabbage, *farofa* (roasted manioc flour), and orange slices. To spice it up, ask for *pimenta,* and they will bring you oil-soaked *malagueta* peppers to drizzle on the beans. Have another lime cocktail standing by in case you underestimate the heat.

Rua Prudente de Moraes 10, Ipanema. © **021/2523-4994.** www.cozinhatipica.com.br. R$25–R$42 main courses; *feijoada* meal R$55 per person, including appetizers, dessert, and drinks. AE, DC, MC, V. Daily noon–11pm. Metrô: General Osorio.

Delirio Tropical ★ BRAZILIAN   Stop here for a lighter and healthier snack. The menu includes delicious fresh salads such as the *caprese* (a layered tower of sliced tomatoes, basil, and mozzarella), *salpição* (shredded chicken with carrots and corn), pasta salads, and at least six other salads. You can put together a meal with a selection of salads alone, or you can add some grilled meat, or make a choice from the daily hot dish specials, often stuffed cannelloni or roast beef. The sandwich bar serves made-to-order sandwiches, with your choice of bread, filling, and salad. The service is cafeteria-style; you choose your dishes, load up your tray, and find a seat. Perfect brunch spot!

Rua Garcia d'Avila 48, Ipanema. © **021/3624-8164.** www.delirio.com.br. Main courses R$14–R$32. AE, MC, V. Daily 9am–9pm. Bus: 415.

LEBLON

Very Expensive

Bar d'Hotel ★★ (Finds) CONTEMPORARY   On the first floor of the Marina Hotel in Ipanema, this hip eatery overlooks the most famous beach in the world yet doesn't even try to cash in on the view. Artists, actors, soccer players, designers, and others too cool to look at the ocean compete for each other's attention, all the while trying not to look like they're looking. Fortunately, the food is also great—the creations of chef Felipe Bronze—so we mere mortals can remain happily oblivious and just enjoy. Appetizers include mini lamb burgers with foie gras. For mains there's a rich stew of ginger-scented prawns with jasmine rice, or filet mignon with a crust of caramelized macadamia nuts. The wine list is extensive; the drinks list is almost as long and far more creative. The restaurant is also a great place to just have a drink.

Av. Delfim Moreira 696, 2nd floor (inside the Marina All Suites Hotel, p. 75), Leblon. © **021/2540-4990.** Reservations recommended. Main courses R$24–R$48. MC, V. Daily noon–2am. Bus: 415.

Expensive

Giuseppe Grill ★★ STEAK   With outstanding steak, an affordably priced wine list, and excellent and attentive service, what's not to recommend? The house specialty is beef. You can choose from grilled beef or slowly roasted beef on a charcoal grill. Both options include numerous cuts—prime rib, Argentine chorizo steak, filet mignon, and rump steak as well as beef ribs, pork, and chicken. Each main course comes with a side dish; you can choose from salads, rice, and potatoes served fried, roasted, baked, or sautéed. In

Rio's Avenida Gourmet

We could probably fill half the Rio section with reviews of restaurants on the **Rua Dias Ferreira.** This windy street on the far edge of Leblon has become a one-stop shop for gourmands. Trendy vegetarians head straight for **O Celeiro** (no. 199; ✆ **021/2274-7843**). You pay by the weight so help yourself to the delicious offerings and grab a spot on the large patio. To enjoy a stylish afternoon tea with all the trimmings, head over to **Eliane Carvalho** (no. 242; ✆ **021/ 2540-5438;** closed Mon). For pasta there's **Quadrucci** (no. 233; ✆ **021/2512-4551**), which is open for lunch and dinner and has a great patio.

For fine dining there are a number of options, mostly only open in the evenings. **Zuka** (no. 233; ✆ **021/3205-7154**) offers creative seafood dishes such as crab in phyllo pastry or grilled tuna in a cashew-nut crust. Across the street you'll find **Carlota** (no. 64; ✆ **021/2540-6821**), chosen by *Condé Nast Traveler* as one of the 50 most exciting restaurants in the world. Chef Carlota opened this Rio restaurant after her original São Paulo digs became the toast of the town. As in the original, her Rio dishes are fresh and creative, but portions are tiny. Farther down on the corner of Rua Rainha Guilhermina is the sushi hot spot of the city, **Sushi Leblon** (✆ **021/2512-7830**). Thursday through Saturday evenings the lines can be long, but most people don't seem to mind the wait. If you're up on who's who in the Brazilian entertainment world, you can pass the time spotting artists and actresses. If a smaller and intimate sushi venue is more your style, check out **Minimok** (no. 116; ✆ **021/2511-1476**). By the same owners as the Mok Sakebar (below), this very stylish hole in the wall serves up great variety of sushi, sashimi, tempura, and rolls.

addition, the restaurant also serves up outstanding fresh seafood. There's shrimp and *namorado* and catch of the day—ask for the waiter's recommendation. We went with the octopus, grilled to perfection and served tossed with arugula as a warm salad. Best of all, a steak dinner for two with appetizers, a bottle of Argentine Malbec, and coffee barely cracked the US$100 mark.

Av. Bartolomeu Mitre 370, Leblon. ✆ **021/2249-3055.** www.bestfork.com.br. Main courses R$36–R$65. AE, DC, MC, V. Mon–Thurs noon–4pm and 7pm–midnight; Fri–Sat noon–1am; Sun noon–11pm. Bus: 415.

Mok Sakebar ★★★ JAPANESE   To do this restaurant justice would require three reviews. First there is the sushi bar, run by talented chef Takashi Kawamura. His creations alone are worth the trip. Try the tuna marinated in green apple wasabi or the dragon roll with eel and shiitake mushrooms. Then there is the sake bar with an amazing selection of sake, including gold-flecked, bubbly, lime-flavored or 30-year-old vintage sakes. No idea what to order? Try the sake sampler (three small shot glasses) and the knowledgeable staff will be happy to help get you drunk. They also mix up some mean cocktails, like a banana or ginger-mandarin caipirinha or spicy Lotus Mary with wasabi, basil, and lime. As *pièce de résistance,* there is the restaurant itself and the main courses created by French chef Pierre Landry, such as tender grilled duck breast or spicy seared tuna with avocado tempura. The perfect three-part harmony.

Rua Dias Ferreira 78, Leblon. ✆ 021/2512-6526. www.moksushi.com.br. Main courses R$42–R$70. AE, V. Mon 7pm–1am; Tues–Thurs noon–3:30pm and 7pm–1am; Sat noon–1:30am; Sun 1–11pm. Bus: 415.

Sawasdee ★★ THAI   Normally it's Rio restaurants that branch out, but in this case Buzios's best Thai restaurant made the trek in to the big city to set up shop in Leblon. The menu includes the tried and tested bestsellers, focusing on fresh, top-quality ingredients. Start off with the spicy chicken satay with peanut sauce or salmon fish cakes with a tangy dipping sauce. For main courses, we highly recommend bringing friends, ordering a variety of dishes, and sharing. Try at least one of the salads, like the mango salad with shrimp, a noodle dish (the pad Thai is outstanding), and perhaps a traditional green or red curry. The kitchen also serves a large variety of vegetarian dishes and prepares several child-friendly versions of Thai classics.

Rua Dias Ferreira 771, Leblon. ✆ 021/2511-0057. www.sawasdee.com.br. Main courses R$45–R$68. AE, MC, V. Tues–Thurs noon–midnight; Fri–Sat noon–1am; Sun noon–11pm. Bus: 415.

Moderate

Garcia & Rodrigues ★★ BISTRO   G&R features a deli, bakery, cafe, bistro, and wine bar. The cafe serves up an excellent breakfast, a great selection of sandwiches, cheese plates, and some of the finest baked goods in town. By noon, the bistro also offers risottos, pasta, grilled steak, and seafood, including a wonderful grilled salmon in orange-saffron sauce. You can also put a great spread together by ordering various deli appetizers such as the carpaccio, the bruschetta with brie, honey, and chutney, and a cold-cut or pâté plate, served with a basket of freshly baked bread. Luckily the wine cellar (or rather attic) remains; the maitre d' will happily help you choose an appropriate bottle.

Av. Ataulfo de Paiva 1251, Leblon. ✆ 021/3206-4100. www.garciaerodrigues.com.br. Main courses R$24–R$52. AE, DC, MC, V. Cafe and bakery daily 8am–midnight. Bistro Mon–Thurs noon–12:30am. Bus: 415.

Inexpensive

KURT ★ (Value) DESSERT   So what if Leblon has a higher than average number of dessert shops? This is one we couldn't leave out. German pastry maker Kurt passed away a few years ago but his legacy (and treats) live on in the hands of his grandsons (who obviously inherited the sweet gene; they run the pastry shop the Bakers, p. 94). This tiny shop in Leblon remains one of the best places in town to go for an *apfel strude,* pecan pie, or apricot cake. A famous Kurt creation is the "bee sting" *(picada de abelha),* a chocolate cake, the recipe of which is a closely guarded family secret.

Rua General Urquiza 117 (corner of Rua Ataulfo de Paiva), Leblon. ✆ 021/2294-0599. www.confeitaria kurt.com.br. Everything under R$15. No credit cards. Mon–Fri 8am–7pm; Sat 8am–5pm. Bus: 415.

Mil Frutas ★ DESSERT   One of the best ice-cream parlors in town, Mil Frutas offers a whole gamut of chocolate and fruit flavors, including some exotic ones from northern Brazil such as *açai, cupuaçu,* and *caja.* The staff is happy to give you a taste of several flavors before you decide on one, or two, or three.

Rua Garcia d'Avila 134, Ipanema. ✆ 021/2521-1584. www.milfrutas.com.br. Everything under R$12. No credit cards. Daily 10:30am–1am. Bus: 415.

JARDIM BOTANICO/LAGOA

Very Expensive

Mr. Lam ★★ CHINESE   What do you do when you're the richest man in Brazil but simply can't find any decent Chinese food? Make it yourself! Billionaire Eike Batista hired top Chinese chef Mr. Lam, from famed New York's Mr. Chow, and set him up in a swanky building overlooking Rio's Lagoa. The result is a sexy, modern, loungelike restaurant with the best Chinese food in town, of course. Mr. Lam and his kitchen team from China (he quips, "You wouldn't put any Chinese players on your Brazilian soccer team?") serve up authentic cuisine. Start off with an order of dim sum, some spring rolls, or chicken satay. Main courses include various prawn dishes (sweet-and-sour, black bean, or garlic), crispy fried noodles, and stir-fries with beef, chicken, or pork. The *pièce de résistance* is Mr. Lam's signature Peking Duck: tender morsels of rich meat and crispy skin, served with pancakes, scallions, cucumber strips, and plum sauce (allow an hour for preparation). And although not a cheap meal, it will cost a lot less than a meal in New York (minus airfare).

Rua Maria Angelica 21, Lagoa. ✆ **021/2286-6661.** www.mrlam.com.br. Main courses R$45–R$99. AE, DC, MC, V. Mon–Thurs 7pm–midnight; Fri–Sat 7pm–1:30am; Sun 1–11:30pm. Bus: 170 or 571.

Olympe ★★★ FRENCH You can tell from the Web address that chef Claude Troisgros doesn't exactly lack for ego, but then his restaurant and his recipes do regularly win awards for the best French cooking in the city and the country. His recipes combine a French approach with ingredients drawn from Brazil. Thus for appetizers there are Burgundy escargots with oven-roasted palm hearts. Mains include roast quail stuffed with *farofa* mixed with raisins, served with a sweet-and-sour *jabuticaba* sauce. Other chefs have tried this approach of course; Troisgros just does it better. There are also more traditional French dishes: oven-roasted rabbit in red wine and chocolate sauce, coquilles St. Jacques with a caviar tapioca. The wine list is high end (nothing much under R$100) and drawn largely from France.

Rua Custódio Serrão 62, Jardim Botânico. ✆ **021/2539-4542.** www.claudetroisgros.com.br. Reservations recommended. Main courses R$55–R$95. MC, V. Mon–Thurs 7:30pm–12:30am; Fri noon–4pm and 7:30pm–12:30am. Bus: 572 (from Leblon or Copacabana) or 170 (from downtown).

Expensive

Capricciosa ★ PIZZA One of Rio's trendiest pizza restaurants, Capricciosa features beautiful people at the tables and a wood-burning oven at the back. This turns out great-tasting pizzas and calzones, including the signature Capricciosa, with tomato, ham, artichoke, mushrooms, bacon, and egg. There's also a delicious cold-cut and antipasto buffet, served with slices of homemade crusty bread, and a selection of pasta dishes. Those who prefer a more low-key and intimate setting can opt for the wine bar, to the left of the busy and bustling main dining room; the menus are the same. Note that a cheap meal this ain't . . . these prices would buy you a juicy steak elsewhere, but that is the price you pay to hobnob with the hip.

Rua Maria Angelica 37, Jardim Botânico. ✆ **021/2527-2656.** www.capricciosa.com.br. Main courses R$28–R$42. AE, DC, MC, V. Daily 6pm–1am (later if it's busy). Bus: 572 (from Leblon or Copacabana) or 170 (from downtown).

Lorenzo Bistrô ★ FRENCH/ITALIAN Cute little bistros are hard to find in Rio and this is a real gem, tucked away in a Jardim Botânico side street. Grab a table on the pleasant sidewalk patio or find a spot in the cozy upstairs dining room. The menu offers satisfying French and Italian "comfort food." No fussy, precious haute cuisine, but a decent steak *au poivre* or a traditional steak with *pommes frites* (make sure your fellow diners get a portion or they will steal yours!). Other dishes include boeuf bourguignon, a hearty coq au vin, or more Italian-inspired options such as risottos, fish, and pasta. Red wine drinkers will be pleased to find a number of good (and affordable) South American reds and whites.

Rua Visconde de Carandai 2, Jardim Botânico. ℂ **021/2294-7830.** Main courses R$38–R$52. AE, MC, V. Mon–Thurs noon–11:30pm; Fri–Sat noon–12:30am; Sun 1–7:30pm. Bus: 170 or 571.

Roberta Sudbrack ★★★ BRAZILIAN   Maybe it was Sudbrack's 7-year stint as chef at Brazil's presidential palace that inspired her to bring good food to the masses. Although she has no qualms of charging Rio's well-heeled diners R$160 to R$195 for a tasting menu, on Tuesday nights dinner will only set you back R$49 and Friday's lunch goes for R$89. Sudbrack prides herself on cooking only with fresh, seasonal ingredients, giving typical Brazilian products a serious makeover. Some examples include the smoked okra with shrimp, *dourado* fish with green corn compote, or beet ravioli. Her small, modern bistro only seats 62 people. Once a month, Roberta Sudbrack also hosts a cooking class. See the website for details.

Rua Lineu de Paula Machado 916, Jardim Botânico. ℂ **021/3874-0139.** www.robertasudbrack.com.br. Reservations recommended. Main courses R$49–R$89. MC. Tues–Thurs 7:30pm–midnight; Fri–Sat 8:30pm–1am; Fri noon–3pm. Bus: 170 or 571.

Moderate

Bar Lagoa BOTEQUIM · In business since 1934 (when it was known as Bar Berlin), this Lagoa institution features a graceful Art Deco interior, cold clear chopp, and a menu drawn from Germany. Favorites include smoked pork with sauerkraut, or bratwurst with a heaping side of potatoes. Since 1987, the bar has been a designated heritage site. Have another chopp, sit back, and toast history.

Av. Epitacio Pessoa 1674, Lagoa. ℂ **021/2523-1135.** www.barlagoa.com.br. Reservations not accepted. Main courses R$10–R$25. MC, V. Daily 6pm–2am. Bus: 119.

Couve Flor ★ KILO   The mother of all kilo restaurants, Couve Flor is where it all started in the mid-'80s. Even now that the system has been widely adopted, Couve Flor still goes the extra mile. The menu offers an astonishing range of dishes, including elaborate and interesting options such as rabbit stew, fish *moqueca*, fresh pasta, at least 20 different kinds of salads, and grilled meats. The buffet even offers vegetarian choices such as stroganoff made with soybean "meat." In the evenings Couve Flor also serves a selection of pizzas from a wood-burning oven, and the weekend lunch buffet is legendary with even more dishes and a choice of 15 desserts. The beauty of the kilo system is that you can have a bite of as many dishes as strike your fancy.

Rua Pacheco Leão 724, Jardim Botânico. ℂ **021/2239-2191.** www.couveflor.com.br. Price per kilo: R$34–R$42. AE, DC, MC, V. Mon–Fri noon–5pm and 7–11pm; Sat noon–11pm; Sun 11:30am–9pm. Bus: 572 (from Leblon or Copacabana) or 170 (from downtown).

Da Graça ★ CAFE   Half the fun of going to Da Graça is in seeing the decor. It's wonderfully kitsch, decorated top to bottom in colorful hippie junk. The menu consists of numerous small dishes that you can mix and match according to your appetite. The main dishes change daily, but can include a *namorado* fish with capers or salmon with herb crust. Remember, these are just small portions. You can add a side of rice, salad, a baked potato with curry, or a penne with lemon sauce. In the evenings there are a few more snack options such as sardines, samosas, or falafel. This is a great place to go for a drink or a snack, rather than a full meal.

Rua Pacheco Leão 780, Jardim Botânico. ℂ **021/2249-5484.** www.dagraca.com.br. Main courses R$15–R$32. AE, DC, MC, V. Tues–Sun noon–2am. Bus: 572 (from Leblon or Copacabana) or 170 (from downtown), get off at corner Rua Jardim Botânico with Pacheco Leão, 10-min. walk or take bus 406 from Flamengo.

Exploring Rio de Janeiro

Most visitors to Brazil start or end their visit in Rio de Janeiro. A wise choice. There may be wider beaches in the north, higher mountains in the south, and larger jungles in the Amazon, but nowhere else on earth is there that wonderful combination of white-hot sand and tall green peaks, with a blaze of urban humanity filling all the spaces in between. Most people stay in the beachfront neighborhoods of **Copacabana** and **Ipanema.** They're great places to soak up the sun and to people-watch. But even if your time is limited, it's worth making the effort to explore further. In the historic downtown neighborhoods of **Centro, Lapa,** and **Santa Teresa** you'll find narrow cobblestone streets, grand plazas, gold-covered churches, and buildings of the baroque, Beaux Arts, and Art Deco styles. Shoppers will be in heaven; browse the crafts markets for souvenirs or check out the small shops in downtown's pedestrian streets. Upscale shoppers will love the **Rio Sul** mall and the fancy boutiques in Rio's tony Ipanema. If you have the energy, Rio's stunning setting offers numerous recreational activities: Hiking, hang gliding, surfing, rock climbing, and kayaking are just a few options. Taking in a game of soccer is an adventure in itself. Nowhere are the crowds larger or livelier than at Rio's Maracanã stadium. The city's vibrant cultural scene comes to life in the evening and never disappoints: See some of the local samba bands in Lapa, or emerging talents at the city's many live music venues, or splurge to see a big national star such as Caetano Veloso.

SUGGESTED RIO DE JANEIRO ITINERARIES

If You Have ❶ Day

If you're like me—a pale-skinned gringo—it's an act of utter insanity on the first day to set foot on the beach during the peak afternoon sunshine. On your first day **hit the beach early.** Enjoy the clear air and an hour or so of tanning in the softer morning rays. Then head up to the **Corcovado** and see Rio laid out below you in all its glory. Stop in for a quick lunch at any of Rio's countless kilo restaurants, then in the afternoon head to **Centro** to explore what you've seen from on high. Wander **old Rio,** making sure to check out the Uruguaiana shopping district, and to poke your head into any one of countless baroque churches. Finish your walk with a nice cold chopp (beer) at a sidewalk cafe in Cinelândia, or in the countless patios in the **Arcos do Teles.** Have dinner back in the Zona Sul, at one of the top-notch restaurants in **Leblon.** If it's a Saturday in pre-**Carnaval** season, go see a **samba school rehearsal.** Or find a **botequim** or restaurant that plays music and enjoy Rio until the wee hours.

If You Have ❷ Days

On your second day get some culture. Go see the **Museu de Arte Moderna (MAM),** or if painting's not your thing see the **Museu Histórico Nacional,** the **Forte de Copacabana,** or **Ilha Fiscal.** Have lunch overlooking **Sugarloaf (Pão de Açúcar)** at the **Círculo Militar** in **Urca** (p. 88). Afterward, work off those calories by climbing up to the Pão de Açúcar's peak. Reward yourself for your efforts by having dinner at the **Porção** on **Flamengo** beach—all-you-can-eat Brazilian barbecue, with a view of the bay and the Sugarloaf thrown in (p. 88). In the evening, go for a drink, some dancing, and some live Brazilian music at any of a number of spots in **Lapa.**

If You Have ❸ Days

In the morning take the old streetcar across the **Arcos da Lapa** to the quirky hilltop neighborhood of **Santa Teresa.** See the **Museu Chácara do Céu.** Enjoy the view at the **Ruin Park,** or have lunch in an outdoor cafe. In the afternoon, go **hang gliding.** Soar above the beach, feeling the wind, admiring the mountains and the waves below. Or if that's a bit too much, take a hike in the rainforest in **Tijuca National Park,** or stroll amid the stately palm trees in the **Jardim Botânico.** In the evening, stroll the walkway round the edge

of the **Lagoa,** or people-watch in the nightlife area of Baixo Leblon. Have a snack, a beer, or dinner at one of the many restaurants.

If You Have ❹ Days or More

Take Marcelo Armstrong's **Favela Tour** through the huge and hidden neighborhood of **Rocinha.** Or check out the sights in **Niterói** across the bay. Try some extreme sports, like **rappelling** or **rafting.** Or take a gentle tour down the coast to the **Museu Casa do Pontal** and **Grumari beach.** If you've got several days to spare, go inland to the summer capital of **Petrópolis,** or the pretty historical cities of **Paraty** or **Ouro Preto** and **Mariana.** Or else head up the coast to **Búzios** and do some **scuba diving** or just hang out on the long white **ocean beaches.** Lord knows, you could even spend more time on the beach in Rio.

1 THE TOP ATTRACTIONS

CENTRO

Espaço Cultural da Marinha ★ (**Kids**) With a destroyer, a submarine, and some great ship models, the Navy Cultural Center is guaranteed to delight naval and maritime buffs. Inside are countless ship models, including a full-size replica of the royal barge, and smaller-scale models of everything from the *Golden Hind* to primitive Brazilian sailing rafts. Moored outside the museum are the ***Riachuelo,*** a 1970s-era submarine, and the ***Bauru,*** a small World War II destroyer. Self-guided tours of these ships run from noon until 5pm.

Av. Alfredo Agache s/n, Centro. ✆ **021/2104-6025.** Free admission. Tues–Sun noon–5pm. Bus: 119 or 415 (Praça XV). From Praça XV turn right and walk 100m (328 ft.) underneath the elevated freeway.

Ilha Fiscal ★ This little ceramic castle afloat on its own island in the bay off Praça XV looks like the dwelling of a fair elfin princess, but in fact was built as the headquarters for the Brazilian Custom Service. Initial plans for a rather prosaic edifice were shelved after Emperor Pedro II intervened, and the result was the tiny jewel box of a building, designed by Adolpho Del-Vecchio. On the inside, alas, this Gothic Revival palace is mostly a small and rather boring museum on the Brazilian navy, which owns the island. The tour lasts about 2½ hours. On weekdays, the trip to the island is by boat, whereas on weekends it's by bus along a causeway.

Av. Alfredo Agache s/n, Centro (behind Praça XV). ✆ **021/2104-6992.** Admission R$10, R$5 children 12 and under. Guided tours only. Departures Wed–Sun at 1pm, 2:30pm, and 4pm. Bus: 415 (Praça XV).

Biblioteca Nacional **4**
Centro Cultural
  do Banco do Brasil **12**
Espaço Cultural
  da Marinha **14**
Ilha Fiscal **15**

Metropolitan
  Cathedral **3**
Ministerio da
  Fazenda **8**
Museu de Arte
  Moderna (MAM) **6**
Museu Histórico
  Nacional **9**
Museu Nacional
  de Belas Artes **5**
Nossa Senhora
  de Candelaria **13**
Paço Imperial **10**
Palácio Gustavo
  Capanema **7**
Palácio Itamaraty **1**
Palácio Tiradentes **11**
Royal Portuguese
  Reading Room **2**

Sambódromo
(See "Samba Parade
Grounds" map)

Av. 31 de Março

Av. Presidente Vargas

R. Frei Caneca

R. Marqués de Pombal

R. de Santana

R. Moncorvo Filho

R. General Caldwell

Central Station
(Central do Brasil
Railway)

R. Barão de São Felix

R. Visc. de Gávea

Praça da
República
(Campo de
Santana)

CENTRAL

Itamaraty
Palace
1

PRESIDENTE
VARGAS

R. Carlos   Sampaio
Praça Cruz
Vermelha

R. 20
de Abril

R. Alexandre Mackenzie

R. Camerino

R. Senador Pompeu

Av. Presidente Vargas

R. dos Inválidos

Av. Gomes Freire

R. do Lavradio

Praça
Tiradentes
2

R. da Constituição

Av. Passos

R. do Conceição

R. dos Andradres

Morro da
Conceição

Lad. J. Homen

R. do Acre

Av. Rodrigues Alves

LAPA

San Sebastião
Cathedral **3**

Av. Rep. do Paraguai

Largo do
São Francisco

URUGUAIANA

CENTRO

R. Uruguaiana

R. Gonçalves Dias

CARIOCA

Av. Rio Branco

R. 7 de Setembro

R. da Quitanda

R. Teófilo Otoni

Candelaria

R. Dom Gerardo

R. 1 de Março

Passeio
Público

Praça
Mahatma
Ghandi

CINELÂNDIA

4 **5**

R. México

CASTELO

7

8

Av. Pres. Antônio Carlos

11 **10**

Praça
XV de
Novembro

13

12

Av. Pres. Kubitschek

14

Museu
de Arte
Moderna
(MAM)

Av. Beira Mar

Av. Infante Dom Henrique

Museu
Histórico
Nacional **9**

Av. General Justo

Ferry
Terminal

Guanabara
Bay

Cobras
Island

6

Fiscal Island
(Ilha Fiscal)
15

LEBLON
IPANEMA

JARDIM
BOTÂNICO

Corcovado

Maracanã
Stadium

Area of
detail

BOTAFOGO
COPACABANA

CATETE
FLAMENGO

Sambódromo

CENTRO

SANTOS
DUMONT
AIRPORT

ATLANTIC
OCEAN

URCA
Sugarloaf

Cobras
Island

Guanabara Bay

Airport
Subway Station
Street Car

0   1/4 mi
0   0.25 km

Take a Break

On the second floor of the Modern Art Museum, the **Laguiole Restaurant** (© **021/2517-3129**) offers modern decor and inventive cuisine—Brazilian, with a subtle touch of French. And if the prices at the Laguiole give you a turn, head back down the ramp to the museum's ground-floor cafe—operated by the same chef—which offers reasonably priced light snacks, coffee, and desserts.

Museu de Arte Moderna (MAM) ★★ Located in the waterfront Flamengo park, the MAM is a long, rectangular building lofted off the ground by an arcade of concrete struts, giving the museum the appearance of an airplane wing. Inside, the concrete struts do all the load-bearing work, allowing for walls of solid plate glass that welcome views of both city and sea. Displays change constantly, and include Brazilian art and international exhibitions—check the website to see what's on. Signage—a rare bonus—is in both English and Portuguese. The MAM also has a cafe, a bookstore, and a film archive containing over 20,000 Brazilian titles. Allow an hour to 90 minutes. *Tip:* Have a look at the garden from the second-floor patio: The lawn, wavy shapes included, is the work of Brazil's great landscape architect Roberto Burle Marx.

Av. Infante Dom Henrique 85, Parque do Flamengo (Aterro), Centro. © **021/2240-4944.** www.mamrio. com.br. Admission R$8 adults, R$4 students and seniors, free for children 12 and under. Tues–Fri noon–6pm; Sat–Sun noon–7pm. Metrô: Cinelândia. Bus: 472 or 125 (get off at Av. Beira Mar by the museum's footbridge).

Museu Histórico Nacional ★★ This is the place for anyone looking for a good overview of Brazilian history from Cabral's arrival in 1500 to the present. Housed in the former national armory, the National History Museum features seven permanent exhibits on themes such as early exploration, coffee plantations, and modernism, each illustrated with abundant maps and artifacts. Better still, much of the Portuguese signage comes with often very opinionated English translation. Allow 2 hours.

Praça Marechal Ancora s/n. © **021/2550-9224.** www.museuhistoriconacional.com.br. Admission R$6 adults, free for children 5 and under. Free on Sun. Wed–Fri 10am–5:30pm; Sat–Sun 2–6pm. Bus: 119 or 415 (10-min. walk from the Praça XV).

Museu Nacional de Belas Artes ★ The National Museum of Fine Art houses a vast collection of European and Brazilian art, with an emphasis on 18th- and 19th-century European work. However, a rather lengthy renovation has closed all but the Modern and Contemporary galleries. Allow an hour.

Av. Rio Branco 199, Centro. © **021/2240-0068.** www.mnba.gov.br. Admission R$4. Free Sun. Tues–Fri 10am–6pm; Sat–Sun noon–5pm. Metrô: Cinelândia.

Paço Imperial ★ For 2 centuries this was the nerve center of Brazil, serving as vice-regal palace and then as the seat of imperial power from 1808 until the fall of the monarchy in 1888. It's a pleasingly simple structure, long, low, and rectangular, its many high-ceilinged rooms arranged around a pair of cool interior courtyards. Nowadays it serves as an exhibition hall for traveling cultural exhibits. A room on the ground floor charts the history of the palace, with maps, paintings, and engravings. Allow about an hour. The Café do Paço cafe in the ground-floor courtyard is a great place to take refuge on hot afternoons in Rio (open the same hours as the museum).

Tips **While You're in the Neighborhood . . .**

One of the best spots for a free peekaboo is from the **Ruin Park** in Santa Teresa, next to the Museu Chácara do Céu. The park was once a sizable mansion belonging to Laurinda Santos Lobo, one of Rio's leading socialites. When the house burned down, the city cleverly reinforced the gutted shell and then installed all manner of ramps and catwalks. Visitors can now clamber this way and that gaining excellent views of the city in all directions; one lookout at the top provides a 270-degree view of Rio.

Praça XV 48, Centro. ✆ **021/2533-4407.** www.pacoimperial.com.br. Free admission. Wed–Sun noon–6pm. Bus: 119 or 415 (and many others).

SANTA TERESA

Museu Chácara do Céu ★★ A wealthy man with eclectic tastes, Raymundo Castro Maya had this ultramodern mansion built in the hills of Santa Teresa, then filled it with all manner of paintings, engravings, and drawings. The museum displays European painters (Monet, Matisse, Picasso, Dalí) and Brazilian art, particularly 19th-century landscapes. The house itself is a charmer, a stylish melding of hillside and structure that evokes Frank Lloyd Wright's work in the American West. The views from the garden are fabulous.

Rua Murtinho Nobre 93, Santa Teresa. ✆ **021/3970-1126.** www.museuscastromaya.com.br. Admission R$5 adults, free for children 11 and under. Free admission Wed. Wed–Mon noon–5pm. Tram: Curvelo.

CATETE, GLORIA & FLAMENGO

Museu Carmen Miranda ★ A concrete bunker in a postage stamp–size park surrounded by four lanes of traffic hardly seems a fitting tribute to the flamboyant '40s film star who created the worldwide mania for bananas and pineapples as headgear. Inside, however, the small collection does a fine job, showing life-size publicity photos and numerous photos illustrating her life and career in music and movies. There's also a large collection of video documentaries, plus all of her movies, and a compilation of her songs. The receptionist is delighted to play these for visitors.

Av. Rui Barbosa s/n (across the street from no. 560), Flamengo. ✆ **021/2334-4293.** Free admission. Wed–Fri 11am–5pm; Sat–Sun 1–5pm. Metrô: Flamengo.

Museu da República—Palácio do Catete ★★ This gorgeous baroque palace served as the official residence of Brazilian presidents from 1897 to 1960. The more boring traditional displays preserve the air of the palace in its administrative days. The better exhibits try to engage visitors with the history and politics of the Brazilian republic. The best exhibit is the three-room hagiography of President Getulio Vargas, a curious choice, given that Vargas overthrew the First Republic in a coup in 1930, and killed himself in 1954 while facing impeachment and a likely coup. The exhibit includes the pearl-handled Colt that Getulio used to blast a hole in his heart. The surrounding gardens include a small folklore museum, with free admission.

Rua do Catete 153, Catete. ✆ **021/3235-2650.** www.museudarepublica.org.br. Admission R$6 adults, free for children 10 and under. Free on Sun. Tues–Fri 10am–5pm; Sat–Sun 2–6pm. Metrô: Catete.

> **Tips   Take a Break**
>
> The perfect spot for a break in Santa Teresa is the **Jasmim Manga Café,** Largo dos Guimarães 143 (📞 **021/2242-2605**). This cute courtyard cafe serves outstanding coffees and desserts.

BOTAFOGO & URCA

**Museu do Indio ★★ **   The Indian Museum's collection is one of the most important in Latin America, with over 30,000 artifacts, papers, and books, and over half a million historical documents on Brazilian Indian tribes. While that sounds a little dry, the museum's exhibits are some of the most innovative and artistic I have seen in a Brazilian museum. In one room the hunt is symbolized by a dark room with just a ray of light illuminating the floor, casting an eerie glow on spears and animal skulls. Signage is in Portuguese, but the exhibits are so vivid they speak for themselves. For kids there is a gallery with (washable) body paint and a large selection of stamps so they can adorn themselves as warriors, hunters, chiefs, or shamans. Allow 2 hours.

Rua das Palmeiras 55, Botafogo. 📞 **021/3214-8702.** www.museudoindio.org.br. R$3 all ages. Free on Sun. Tues–Fri 9am–5:30pm; Sat–Sun 1–5pm. Metrô: Botafogo.

Sugarloaf (Pão de Açúcar) ★★★   Along with samba, beaches, and beautiful women, the Sugarloaf remains one of the original and enduring Rio attractions. Deservedly so. Standing on its peak, the entire cidade maravilhosa lays at your feet: the beaches of Ipanema and Copacabana, the favelas of Babylonia, the Tijuca Forest, Christ the Redeemer on His mountain, the Bay of Guanabara, and the fortresses at the edge of far-off Niterói. It's a truly beautiful sight. The cable car leaves every half-hour from 8am to 10pm daily, more frequently if there are enough people waiting. *Tip:* If you're feeling active, hike up. The trail is challenging, but the rewards! You start just above the crashing waves, and the views just keep getting better as you go. See "Hiking," under "Outdoor Activities" later in this chapter, for details.

Av. Pasteur 520, Urca. 📞 **021/2461-2700.** www.bondinho.com.br. Admission R$44 adults, R$22 children 6–12, free for children 5 and under. Daily 8am–9pm. Last ride up at 8pm. Metrô: Botafogo, then catch the *integração* bus marked Urca.

LAGOA

Jardim Botânico ★   In the 2 centuries since its founding by Emperor Dom João VI, the botanical garden has grown to 141 hectares (348 acres) and added 6,000 species of tropical plants and trees to its collection. Most visitors come to enjoy the peace and beauty, meandering along the many little paths and garden trails; the bromeliad and orchid greenhouses are especially nice. Those more scientifically minded may find themselves frustrated. The gardens are run as a research institute under Federal Environment Ministry, with the result that treatment of visitors is somewhat hit-and-miss. Many trees and shrubs are labeled with common and Latin names, but there's not much more species information. Free English-language guided tours are supposed to be available (call ahead or check in at the visitor center) but the service is sporadic and unreliable.

Rua Jardim Botânico 1008. 📞 **021/3874-1808.** www.jbrj.gov.br. Admission R$5 adults, free for children 7 and under. Daily 8am–5pm. Bus: Integração (Jardim Botânico) from Metrô Botafogo.

ZONA SUL

Forte de Copacabana ★★   This place is simply massive. Built on the eve of World War I, Copacabana Fort boasts walls of reinforced concrete 12m (39 ft.) thick, and a monstrous 305mm (1 ft.) cannon that could fire a deadly shell 23km (14 miles) out to sea. Inside, rooms contain then-state-of-the-art instruments for targeting and aiming the great guns. Best of all, the bored soldiers guarding the place never leave the gate, so you're free to touch, fiddle, and play as much as you want. Twirl the knobs on the great cannon until its muzzle points toward your hotel, trundle a shell over from the magazine and let fly. Allow an hour.

Skip the **Army History Museum,** also on the fort grounds, an amateurish and laughably biased tribute to the role of the army in Brazilian history. Coup? What coup?

Praça Coronel Eugênio Franco 1, Copacabana. ✆ **021/2521-1032.** www.fortedecopacabana.com. Admission R$4 adults, free for children 9 and under. Tues–Fri 10am–5pm; Sat–Sun 10am–8pm. Bus: 415 to far end of Copacabana Beach.

Forte do Leme ★★ (Finds)   This is one of Rio's best-kept secrets. On the top of the 183m (600-ft.) granite rock you get a 360-degree view of Copacabana and Guanabara Bay. The main gate is toward the back of the square at the end of Leme beach. Once inside, you make your way up a cobblestone road that winds around the back of the hill. It's a 20-minute walk through lush forest to the top where you'll be rewarded with a splendid view of Copacabana and beyond. *Tip:* Grab some snacks and drinks from the Zona Sul supermarket in Leme (Av. Atlântica 866) and have a picnic at the top.

Praça Almirante Julio de Noronha s/n, Copacabana. ✆ **021/2275-7696.** Admission R$3. Sat–Sun 8am–4pm. Metrô: Cardeal Arcoverde/*integração* bus to Leme or bus 472.

COSME VELHO

Corcovado ★★★ (Kids)   The Corcovado was recently chosen as one of the new Seven Wonders of the World. The view from the toes of Rio's mountaintop Christ is spectacular: the mountains, the bay, and the city all lay revealed beneath your (His?) feet. It's enough to give you a feeling of omniscience. The statue was intended to mark the 100th anniversary of Brazilian independence in 1922, but in true Carioca fashion it arrived a decade or so late in 1931. Access is via a steep narrow-gauge railway, followed by a pair of escalators that whisk you up to the base of the statue. Allow 2 hours round-trip.

(Train Station) Rua Cosme Velho 513, Cosme Velho. ✆ **021/2558-1329.** www.corcovado.com.br. Admission R$36, free for children 5 and under. Trains depart daily every 30 min. from 8:30am–8pm. Bus: Cosme Velho Intergração from Metrô Largo do Machado.

FARTHER AFIELD

Feira de São Cristóvão ★★   This entry could just as easily go in the nightlife section, as the Feira Nordestino is essentially one long weekend party, Friday to Sunday

---

(Tips) **Take a Break**

The **Café do Forte,** on the seaside ramparts of the Forte de Copacabana, offers some of the best views in town. Operated by the Confeitaria Colombo (p. 84), the cafe offers outstanding pastries, cakes, and sandwiches. Open Tuesday to Sunday 10am to 8pm (✆ **021/3201-4049**). To enter you must pay the R$4 fort entrance fee.

> ## (Tips) Exploring What's Beyond the Saucer
>
> From Niemeyer's saucer-shaped museum, it's only a short walk to Niterói's main beach, Icarai, which offers a pleasant stroll and fabulous views of Rio. Niterói's main shopping street, Rua Coronel Moreira Cesar, runs parallel to the beach, 1 block inland. The stretch between Rua Miguel Frias and Rua Otavio Carneiro is lined with boutiques and *galerias* (small shopping centers). Take a break at the bakery and restaurant **Confeitaria Beira Mar,** Rua Coronel Moreira Cesar 149, corner of Rua Pres. Backer (© **021/2711-1070**), or for an excellent kilo lunch try **Buzin,** Rua Pereira da Silva 169 (© **021/2711-5208**), just 2 blocks past Rua Coronel Moreira Cesar. To return to the ferryboats, catch any bus on the waterfront that says BARCAS. You can also catch a van straight to Ipanema via downtown and Copacabana (R$5).

featuring exclusively *forró,* the dance-happy accordion two-step of Brazil's Northeast. Two large stages at either end of this market complex feature alternating bands, while more *forró* bleats out from three or four smaller restaurants in the no man's land between. In addition to the music, there are lots of shops selling Nordestino arts and crafts, and stalls and restaurants offering Northeastern cuisine. Visitors wander the shops, sample the snacks, and let their feet hippity hop to the happy accordion beat. The intriguing fair building—you'll see its swooping walls as you come in from the airport—replaced a field full of shacks where Rio's Northeastern community used to do much the same thing every weekend, just without official permission. The *feira* is also open for lunch during the week, but really, there's not much point. *Note:* The inside of the fairgrounds are quite safe, but don't go wandering the surrounding neighborhood after dark. Take a taxi there, and another one home.

Pavilhão de São Cristóvão. © **021/2580-5335.** www.feiradesaocristovao.org.br. Admission R$1 adults, free for children 10 and under. Tues–Thurs 10am–6pm; continuously 10am Fri till 8pm Sun.

Island of Paquetá ★★ (Kids) For an old-fashioned day trip visit the island of Paquetá in Guanabara Bay, a favorite destination since the early 1800s, when the Emperor Dom João VI began spending his summers on the island. In some ways not much has changed. No cars are allowed on Paquetá. Visitors toodle about the island on rented bicycles (R$2 an hour) or relax in horse-drawn carriages (R$35 for an hour, including stops). The island's attraction lies not in any one spot, but rather in the conjunction of its quiet pace, cobblestone streets, tree-lined beaches, graceful old summer homes, and wonderful views of the bay. Many visitors stop for a fresh-cooked fish at one of numerous beachside kiosks, but there are a half-dozen restaurants scattered around the island, all acceptable, none outstanding. If you love Paquetá enough to stay overnight, there's the **Hotel Farol** (© **021/3397-0402;** www.hotelfaroldepaqueta.com.br) or the **Pousada Paraiso** (© **021/2438-5073**). Though locals swim in most Paquetá beaches, the only ones given a green light by the City of Rio are Praia da Imbuca, Praia de José Bonifacio, and the very pretty Praia da Moreninha. Including the 70-minute ferry ride (each way), allow 4 to 6 hours for the trip.

Island Info: www.ilhadepaqueta.com.br. Ferry (© **021/2533-7524**) departs from Praça XV, R$9 round-trip. Rio-Paquetá departs 5:15, 7:10, 10:30am, 1:30, 4, 5:45, 7, 9, and 11pm. Return ferry Paquetá-Rio

---

> (**Tips**) **Tour du Jour**
>
> Rio Hiking (📞 **021/2552-9204;** www.riohiking.com.br) offers an excellent day tour (R$200 per person) that includes a visit to Pedra Bonita for the views (with the option of taking a leap in a hang glider) followed by a visit to the Museu Casa do Pontal, Sitio Burle Marx, and time for a swim or a walk along Grumari, one of the city's loveliest beaches.

departs daily at 5:30, 7, 9am, noon, 3, 5:30, 7:15, 8:30, and 10:15pm. It's a good idea to confirm return times upon arrival in Paquetá.

Jardim Zoológico—Rio City Zoo ★ (**Kids**)

If you haven't got time to get to the Amazon, this may be the place to come. Though not huge, the zoo is green, leafy, and pleasant, and has about 2,000 different species on display, most of them Brazilian. It's particularly good for birds. There are toucans (of Fruit Loops cereal fame), macaws, and other colorful tropical species, some in an open aviary so you can walk among them while they fly around. The reptile house and primate displays are also quite good. Some displays are inevitably small and cramped, which may produce cries of pity from your budding environmental activist, but all in all, the zoo does a creditable job reproducing habitats while providing access to the public.

Quinta da Boa Vista s/n, São Cristóvão. 📞 **021/3878-4200.** Admission R$6, free for children less than 1m (39 in.) tall. Tues–Sun 9am–4:30pm. Metrô: São Cristóvão.

Museu Casa do Pontal ★★

The museum's a long way off: an hour's drive from Copacabana along the coastal road past Barra de Tijuca. However, it's a gorgeous location—ocean on one side and mountains on the other—featuring a quirky and intriguing collection of over 5,000 pieces collected by French designer Jacques van de Beuque. The collection's charm lies in the beauty of its naive portrayal of traditional rural Brazilian life. The thousands of small clay sculptures, woodcarvings, and metal tableaus depict religious and music festivals and farm and family routines. The most astonishing room houses a mechanical diorama representing an *escola de samba* (samba school)—complete with cheering audience—marching in the Carnaval parade.

Estrada do Pontal 3295, Recreio dos Bandeirantes. 📞 **021/2490-3270.** www.popular.art.br/museucasa dopontal. Admission R$8 adults, free for children 7 and under. Tues–Sun 9:30am–5pm. No public transit.

Museu de Arte Contemporânea—Niterói ★

Oscar Niemeyer's spaceship design for Niterói's new Contemporary Art Museum has done for this bedroom city what Gehry's Guggenheim did for Bilbao, Spain: put it on the map (at least in Brazil). Set atop a promontory with a stunning view of Rio, the all-white flying saucer says clearly yet elegantly that here is a landmark structure. As a gallery, however, the museum has serious drawbacks, not least that most of the construction funds were spent on the exterior. Curators bring in a constantly changing selection of Brazilian contemporary art (think abstract sculpture, textiles, and painting) but one can't help thinking the best piece of work on display is the building itself. Allow about an hour.

Mirante de Boa Viagem s/n, Niterói. 📞 **021/2620-2400.** www.macniteroi.com.br. Admission R$4, free for children 7 and under. Tues–Sun 10am–6pm. From Praça XV take the ferry to Niterói, then take a short taxi ride along Niterói's waterfront and up the hill to the museum.

Museu Nacional (Quinta da Boa Vista) ★★   This pretty pink palace that was once the home of Brazil's royal family is now home to a vast and varied collection—many items were originally acquired by the Emperor Pedro II and Empress Teresa—including mastodon trunks, a saber-tooth tiger skull, and a monster meteorite cut in cross section so visitors can run their hands across its polished iron-nickel surface. One vast wing devoted to the Brazilian culture contains regional costumes, weapons and masks of aboriginal tribes, whips and saddles from interior cowboys, and much more. The other wing attempts to present all of life, beginning with the smallest protozoa. Many displays are old, and somewhat dated (some have recently been closed for renovations) but what makes it worthwhile is the volume and quality of the specimens: pretty corals, tarantulas in abundance, stuffed specimens of most of the mammals found in Brazil, and a protozoa room chock-full of all the various parasites that feed on human flesh. Signage is in Portuguese. The extensive palace grounds are a popular weekend destination for families with children. Allow 2 hours.

Quinta da Boa Vista s/n, São Cristóvão. ☎ **021/2562-6901.** www.museunacional.ufrj.br. Admission R$3 adults, free for children 10 and under. Wed–Sun 10am–4pm; park daily 5am–6pm. Metrô: São Cristóvão.

2 CULTURAL CENTERS & EXHIBIT HALLS

Centro Cultural do Banco do Brasil ★   It's worth stepping inside this gorgeous neoclassical building just to gaze up at the soaring domed atrium. Once the HQ of Brazil's national bank, the building is now one of the city's premier cultural spaces. Inside there's a pleasant cafe, a small bookstore with an excellent selection of art and architecture books (many in English), several small galleries featuring changing art exhibits, and three theaters featuring film, theater, and music. For coin freaks there's also a small exhibit on Brazilian coinage. Allow 30 minutes.

Rua Primiero de Março 66, Centro. ☎ **021/3808-2020.** Free admission; theaters or events may charge a separate fee. Tues–Sun 10am–9pm. Metrô: Uruguaiana.

Real Gabinete Português (Royal Portuguese Reading Room) ★   This is a temple to books. The interior is four stories tall, capped with a stained-glass cupola and stuffed with over 350,000 volumes, many of them from the 17th and 18th centuries. By showing ID (and maybe filling out a form—it depends on who's working) visitors can request and peruse these books, for as long as the room is open.

Rua Luís de Camões 30, Centro. ☎ **021/2221-3138.** Free admission. Mon–Fri 9am–6pm. Metrô: Carioca or bus 125 to Praça Tiradentes.

3 ARCHITECTURAL HIGHLIGHTS

HISTORIC BUILDINGS & MONUMENTS

Rio's a great place for architecture buffs, and an even better place to watch what happens when overconfident urban designers set their hands to the task of urban renewal. For a city so blessed with mountains, ocean, and historical roots several centuries deep, Rio's movers and shakers have suffered from a striking sense of inferiority. As a result, various well-meaning Cariocas have since the early 1900s taken turns ripping out, blowing up, filling in, and generally reconfiguring huge swaths of their city in order to make Rio look more like Paris or Los Angeles or, lately, Miami Beach. The results of these various move- ments are—for better and worse—now and forever on permanent display.

Around Cinelândia

"Rio Civilizes Itself." Armed with this slogan and a deep envy of what Baron Haussman had done in Paris, engineer-mayor **Pereiro Passos** set to work in 1903, ripping a large swath through Rio's Centro district to create the first of the city's grand boulevards, the **Avenida Central.** So efficient was "Knock-it-down" Passos that the old colonial Rio he set out to demolish can now be found only in the few square blocks around the **Travessa do Comércio** to the north of **Praça XV.** Accessed via the **Arco do Teles**—an arch built in 1790 to allow passage through a commercial building facing the square—it's a charming area of narrow cobblestone streets and gaily painted colonial shops, now much missed by civilized Cariocas.

The boulevard Passos created in its stead, however, was also quite graceful. Now renamed the **Avenida Rio Branco,** it runs from **Praça Mauá** south past the grand neo-classical **Igreja de Nossa Senora da Candelária** to what was then the waterfront at the **Avenida Beira Mar.** The four-story Parisian structures that once lined the street are now found only in photographs, replaced by tall and modern office towers. (Rio Branco remains the heart of Rio's financial district.) The best place to witness the handiwork of these turn-of-the-20th-century Parisizers is on the **Praça Floriano,** referred to by most Cariocas by the name of its subway stop, **Cinelândia.** Anchored at the north end by the extravagant Beaux Arts **Teatro Municipal,** and flanked by the equally ornate **Museu de Belas Artes** and neoclassical **Biblioteca Nacional,** the praça beautifully emulates the proportions, the monumentality, and the glorious detail of a classic Parisian square. The Teatro Municipal was in fact explicitly modeled on the Paris Opera House and inaugurated on Bastille Day (July 14) 1909. (Visitors can poke their heads into all of these buildings, but the best place to appreciate the square may well be seated at an outdoor cafe enjoying a nice cold draft.)

Around Castelo

The next stage in urban reform came in the early '20s, when a group encouraged by public health advocate **Oswaldo Cruz,** backed by a development consortium, decreed that the hilltop castle south of Praça XV had to go; the 400-year-old castle was a breeding ground, they said, for pox, plague, and other infectious diseases. In 1922, the castle was blown up, the hill leveled and—starting in the early '30s—construction begun on a series of government office towers inspired by the modernist movement then sweeping Europe. The first of these—then the Ministry of Education and Health but now known as the **Palácio Gustavo Capanema** (Rua da Imprensa 16; see "Palaces," below)—listed among its architects nearly all the later greats of Brazilian architecture, including **Lucio Costa, Oscar Niemeyer,** and **Roberto Burle Marx,** with painter **Candido Portinari** thrown in for good measure. International architects sat up and took note; other less avant-garde government departments commissioned architects with different ideologies, resulting in a **War of the Styles** that raged through the remainder of the 1930s. Perhaps the most bombastic counter-volley was the overblown neoclassical **Ministerio da Fazenda** building (Av. Presidente Antônio Carlos at Av. Almirante Barroso). The resulting enclave of office towers, known as Castelo, lies on the patch centered on the **Avenida Presidente Antônio Carlos.** Chiefly of interest to architectural buffs, it should be toured only during office hours.

Knock-it-down Passos had nothing on **Getulio Vargas.** On the national scene the Brazilian dictator was creating a new quasi-fascist political structure called the Estado Novo; in his capital city, he set about creating a **Cidade Nova** to match. In 1940, on Vargas's personal order, a monster 12-lane boulevard was cut through the city fabric from the beautiful **N.S. de Candelária Church** out through the **Campo de Santana** park to the northern edges of downtown. Anchoring this new megaboulevard was the **Central Station** (known officially as the Estação Dom Pedro II, it's worth popping in to see the Art Deco interior), a graceful modern building with a 135m (443-ft.) clock tower that still stands overlooking the city, providing a much-needed reference point in the northern half of downtown. Vargas's plan called for the entire 4km (2½-mile) street to be lined with identical 22-story office blocks. Cariocas, however, seemed to have a limited appetite for Identi-cubes. Only a few were ever built; they can be seen on the block crossed by Rua Uruguaiana. Even 60 years later, much of the rest of this ultrawide boulevard remains effectively vacant. As a silver lining, however, there was lots of space left for architect Oscar Niemeyer to build the **Sambodromo,** the used-once-a-year permanent Samba Parade Ground. Designed in typically Niemeyer all-concrete style, it stands in the shadow of an elevated freeway, about 1km (½ mile) along Presidente Vargas.

Around Aterro

The next great reconfiguration of Rio came 2 years after the federal capital fled inland to Brasilia. City designers took the huge high hill—**Morro Santo Antônio**—that once dominated the Largo da Carioca, scooped away the earth and dumped it on the beach from Lapa to Flamengo, creating a vast new waterfront park. On the rather raw spot where the hill once stood there arose the innovative cone-shaped **Catedral Metropolitana,** and at the intersection of the new avenidas **República do Chile** and **República do Paraguai,** a trio of towering skyscrapers, the most interesting of which is the "hanging gardens" headquarters of Brazil's state oil company **Petrobras.** On the waterfront park—officially called Parque do Flamengo but most often referred to as Aterro, the Portuguese word for landfill—designers created new gardens and pathways, a new beach, and a pair of modernist monuments: the **MAM** (Modern Art Museum) and the impressive **Monument to the Dead of World War II.** Not incidentally, the park also bears two wide and fast roadways connecting Centro with the fashionable neighborhoods in the Zona Sul.

PALACES

There aren't a lot of true palaces in Rio, for the simple reason that the aristocracy wasn't around long enough to build many. But as if to make up for this lack of palaces, Brazilians have taken to granting any number of grand structures the appellation "palace." The **Palácio Tiradentes,** Av. Presidente Antônio Carlos s/n (© **021/2588-1411**), for example, was built in 1926, long after the aristocracy had departed. Located at the back edge of Praça XV, this rather overwrought neoclassical structure was built to serve as the Brazilian Federal Legislature, which up until then had been meeting in an old jailhouse. Four years after its inauguration, dictator Getulio Vargas overthrew the government and turned the palace into his ministry of propaganda. Nowadays the building serves as the legislature for the state of Rio de Janeiro. Visitors can tour the permanent display that runs down the outside corridor of the building, but since the text-heavy exhibit is exclusively in Portuguese, there's probably not much point.

Older and more graceful is the **Palácio Itamaraty** ★, Rua Marachel Floriano 196, near the Central Station (© **021/2253-7691**). Built in the 1850s for a coffee merchant with the rather grand title of Baron de Itamaraty, the charming neoclassical design—the front has pink walls pierced by granite arches—was sold to the new republican government in 1889 and long served as the ministry of foreign affairs. It has since been converted into the Museum of History and Diplomacy, but this is now closed indefinitely *(sem previsão)*. However, as one small museum display remains open (again in Portuguese only), you do have an excuse to get past the guard (you have to show ID) and wander back to the gorgeous interior courtyard where two ranks of imperial palms flank a long reflecting pond in which jet-black swans swim round.

The most impressive palace in Rio is actually the most modern. Or rather, capital-M Modern. Located in the city's office district, the **Palácio Gustavo Capanema ★**, Rua da Imprensa 16 (no phone), was designed and built from 1932 to 1936 by a team of Brazil's top architects, then the best practitioners of modernism in the world. On the team were Oscar Niemeyer and Lucio Costa (the pair who would later design Brasilia), landscape architect Roberto Burle Marx, and artist Candido Portinari, who did much of the tile work that covers the buildings. Supervising as design consultant was Swiss über-modernist Le Corbusier. The result can be underwhelming at first, but that's because 70 years later we've seen a lot of things similar. But when this was built, no one had ever done anything like it. The entire structure has been raised on pilings 40 feet off the ground, creating an open, airy plaza beneath. And unlike later modernists, this team paid attention to the details: The support columns are covered in beautiful marble, the few ground-level walls in intriguing blue-and-white tile—many designed by Portinari. Ordinary people enjoy the open space thus created. Architectural fans can stand and admire this building for hours.

CHURCHES & TEMPLES

Rio is awash with churches, with some 20 in Centro alone. Likely the most impressive church in Rio is **Nossa Senhora de Candelária ★★**, set on a traffic island of its own at the head of Avenida Presidente Vargas (© 021/2233-2324). Although a church has stood on the spot since the 1680s, the current clean and simple neoclassical design dates from a renovation begun in 1775. Particularly worth noting are the huge and ornate cast-bronze doors, the ceiling panels telling the story of the church, and the two large Art Nouveau lamps on either side of the pulpit; they look like cast-iron Christmas trees. Open Monday through Friday from 8am to 4pm, and Saturday and Sunday from 9am to noon.

Worth a visit and much more centrally located is the **Igreja da Ordem Terceira de São Francisco da Penitencia ★**, Largo da Carioca 5 (© 021/2262-0197). Set on a hilltop overlooking Largo da Carioca, this and the Church of Santo Antônio next door form part of the large Franciscan complex in the city center. The São Francisco church is simply outstanding: Interior surfaces are filled with golden carvings and hung with censors of ornate silver. Open Tuesday through Friday 9am to noon and 1 to 4pm.

On a hilltop all its own is the **N.S. de Glória do Outeiro ★**, which can be accessed via the stairway located next to Rua da Russel 300 (© 021/2557-4600). It's unique among churches in Rio, thanks to its octagonal ground plan and domed roof. The hill on which it stands was the strategic point taken from an invading French force by the city's founder, Estácio de Sá, paving the way for the settlement of Rio on March 1, 1565. Open Tuesday through Friday from 9am to noon and 1 to 5pm, and Saturday and Sunday from 9am to noon.

Last and most innovative of Rio's significant churches is the **Catedral Metropolitana ★★**, Av. República de Chile 245 (© 021/2240-2669). Some dislike this building, finding its

> ## (Overrated) The Church That's Not Worth the Hike
>
> Still impressive, if not quite worth the hype or the long trek, is the **Mosteiro São Bento,** on a hill on the far-north corner of downtown. Access is via an elevator on Rua Dom Gerardo 40; open daily from 8 to 11am and 2:30 to 6pm. The church itself is a shining example of the Golden Church, the high baroque practice of plastering every inch of a church's richly carved interior in gold leaf. We find it disappointing the way the church forecourt has been transformed into a car park. And the monastery's strategic hilltop has no view whatsoever. Sunday morning Mass features Gregorian chanting by the monks. Service begins at 10am, but arrive early if you want a seat.

shape disconcerting and its interior dark. I love it. At each of the four cardinal compass points a rectilinear latticework of concrete and stained glass soars upward, tilting inward as it rises. Where they meet at the ceiling there's another stained-glass latticework—a cross—shining softly with light filtered in from the sky. The form is modern; the feeling is soaring High Gothic. Open daily from 7am to 6pm; Mass is held Monday through Friday at 11am and Sunday at 10am.

Note: The neighborhood around the cathedral is best visited on weekdays. The area can be unsafe on weekends when the streets are deserted.

4 NEIGHBORHOODS TO EXPLORE

Rio is normally divided into three zones: **North (Zona Norte)** from a few blocks north of Avenida Presidente Vargas all the way to the city limits; **Center (Centro),** defined narrowly as the old downtown and business section, or known in a broader sense to include older residential neighborhoods like Santa Teresa, Catete, and Glória; and **South (Zona Sul),** the beach neighborhoods of Copacabana, Ipanema, Leme, Lagoa, and São Conrado.

CENTRO ★★

The place where it all began, Rio's **Centro** contains most of the city's notable churches, squares, monuments, and museums, as well as the modern office towers where Rio's white-collar elite earn their daily bread. Roughly speaking, Centro stretches from the **Morro de São Bento** in the north to the seaside **Monument to the Dead of World War II** in the south, and from **Praça XV** on the waterfront east more or less to the **Sambo-dromo.** It's a compact, pleasantly walkable area; crossing from one side of downtown to the other on foot takes no more than 45 minutes.

Rio (and Centro's) first and most important square is **Praça XV,** located in the center of the city's old waterfront. This is the place where governors and emperors resided, and the site where the Brazilian republic was proclaimed on November 15, 1889. Notable sights around the square include the **Paço Imperial,** and on the north side of the square, the **Arco do Teles.** Walk through this unobtrusive old archway, and you come to a tiny remnant of old colonial Rio, complete with narrow shop fronts and cobblestone streets. The area's main street, the **Travessa do Comércio,** transforms into a lively outdoor patio/pub in the evenings.

Forming the back edge of Praça XV is **Rua Primeiro de Março,** a busy commercial street with a number of churches, including the **Ordem Terceiro do Carmo,** the **Santa Cruz dos Militares,** and near the far end of the street the massive yet lovely **Nossa Senhora de Candelária.** Continue along Primeiro de Março to the end, and you come to the foot of the hill upon which rests the **São Bento Monastery.** Southward, the Premeiro de Março transforms into **Avenida Presidente Antônio Carlos,** the main street of a not-very-interesting area of government office towers known as **Castelo.**

Continuing west from Praça XV along either the **Rua Ouvidor** or the **Rua Sete de Setembro** takes you to Centro's prime upscale shopping enclave. Its far border is marked (more or less) by the **Avenida Rio Branco.** Created in 1905 as an answer to Paris's Champs-Elysées, Rio Branco is still the city's most desirable commercial address. It runs from the cruise-ship terminal on the **Praça Mauá** southward to the pretty Parisian square known as **Cinelândia.** About halfway along, a block to the east of Rio Branco, lies the large irregular **Largo da Carioca.**

Though not very interesting in itself, the square is useful as a landmark. Above it on a hilltop stands the glorious golden **Igreja de Santo Antônio.** To the north of the square, from **Rua da Carioca** to the vast, traffic-choked wasteland known on maps as the **Avenida Presidente Vargas,** and from **Avenida Rio Branco** in the east to the **Campo de Santana** park in the west, lies one of Rio's prime walking, shopping, and sightseeing areas. It's an area of narrow, irregular streets, two-story shops, little squares, and charming small churches. Among the chief sights are the **Largo de São Francisco de Paula,** the **Real Gabinete Português (Royal Portuguese Reading Room),** and an old-style tearoom called the **Confeitaria Colombo.** Shopaholics will enjoy the **informal market** centered on the **Uruguaiana** Metrô stop and the bargains to be had elsewhere in the neighborhood.

Looking south, the Largo da Carioca marks the transition from old Rio to new, and from low-rise to high-rise. Toward the east, **Avenida República de Chile** has many of the city's most important commercial skyscrapers, including the landmark **Petrobras** building and the distinctive conical ziggurat that is the **Catedral Metropolitana.** Just south of the modern concrete cathedral, the past makes a token resurgence in the form of the **Arcos da Lapa,** a Roman-style aqueduct that now carries trams south from the city center up to the hilltop neighborhood of **Santa Teresa.**

South and west of Largo da Carioca lies **Cinelândia** (officially called **Praça Floriano**), a Parisian city square faithfully reproduced all the way down to the opera house (or **Teatro Municipal,** as its called) and the many sidewalk cafes. Many of the high-rises surrounding the square show the Art Deco and modern touches of buildings from the '30s and '40s. Across from the Teatro stands the lovely neoclassical Biblioteca Nacional. It's worth poking your head in just to see the grand entrance hall with staircases extending up through a lofty atrium five floors high.

South again from Cinelândia, making use of a pedestrian overpass to cross a pair of wide and busy roads, you come to the man-made **Parque do Flamengo;** the chief sights in the park are the **Museu de Arte Moderna (MAM)** and the soaring concrete **Monument to the Dead of World War II.**

LAPA

A tiny, funky little neighborhood once known as the "Montmartre of the Tropics," Lapa is easy to find. It's centered at the **Largo da Lapa** at the foot an old picturesque aqueduct known as the **Arcos da Lapa.** In addition to those two sights, Lapa offers some lovely old colonial buildings and—in recent years—an active nightlife scene.

SANTA TERESA ★★

Most hilltop neighborhoods in Rio are favelas—unsanctioned shantytowns. Santa Teresa is anything but—it's a respectable, slightly bohemian neighborhood with a number of sights to lure visitors. Chief among these is the *bonde,* the old-fashioned streetcar that whisks passengers from downtown over the **Arcos da Lapa** into Santa Teresa. The attractions in the **Museu Chácara do Céu** (p. 105) are worth a visit, and when you're done, wander the neighborhood enjoying the fabulous views, and the mix of modern, colonial, and Art Deco architecture.

Note: The Santa Teresa tram station is not easy to find. It's behind the big "hanging gardens" Petrobras building, on Rua Prof. Lélio Gama, a little street that runs off Rua Senador Dantas. A less charming but certainly more efficient connection is the Metrô/bus *integração;* take the Santa Teresa bus from the Cinelândia Metrô station (make sure you purchase the Metrô-*integração* ticket and save the stub to present to the bus driver).

GLORIA/CATETE/FLAMENGO ★

Extending south from the Glória Metrô stop to the top end of Botafogo bay, these three neighborhoods once comprised Rio's toniest residential area—that is, until the tunnel to Copacabana opened in 1922. Recently, however, the area's made a comeback as Carioca yuppies and other urban pioneers have discovered the advantages (high ceilings, huge windows, and so on) of the old 19th-century houses, while residents and visitors alike have realized that thanks to the Metrô, the area is but minutes from both Centro and Copacabana. The main north-south street—known variously as the **Rua da Glória,** the **Rua do Catete,** and the **Rua Marques de Abrantes**—is well worth an afternoon or evening stroll. Particularly pretty is the **Largo do Machado,** at the Metrô stop of the same name. For visitors, the chief attractions in this area include the lovely hilltop **Church of Our Lady of Glória** and the **Catete Park and Palace,** home to the **Museum of the Republic.**

BOTAFOGO

The neighborhood Botafogo reacted to the rise of Copacabana and Ipanema by reinventing itself as a secondary commercial center. Its broad streets contain a number of office high-rises and big retail shopping malls, including the **Shopping Rio Sul,** the first mall to open in the city. The neighborhood is experiencing quite the revival with many new apartments going up and the opening of a several new movie theaters and restaurants. Botafogo has a couple of worthwhile sights of its own, including the **Villa-Lobos** and **Indian museums** and the bustling food fair and nighttime music-jam in the **Cobal Public Market.**

URCA

Urca is the pretty little neighborhood nestled round the foot of the Pão de Açúcar. Partly residential, partly home to a naval training college, the area was built on a landfill during the 1920s, thus accounting for the Art Deco and modern style of many of the neighborhood's buildings. Architecture aside, for nonresidents the only reason to visit Urca is for the views. The first is from the peak of **Sugarloaf (Pão de Açúcar),** reached by cable car from Urca's Avenida Pasteur. The second view can be enjoyed while strolling the sea wall on **Avenida Portugal.** A jutting peninsula, Urca provides an excellent vantage point from which to gaze back at the Rio skyline; its relative isolation makes it safe to stroll blithely along even late at night. And for those who think views go best with something cold, the third and final view spot is from a table at the **Circulo Militar** (p. 88), on the edge of **Praia Vermelha.** The view of the Sugarloaf is without a doubt the best in town.

COPACABANA ★★

Beach! The one word comprises everything there is to say about Copacabana, but then it's a word that contains within it an endless variety of human behavior. Four kilometers (2½ miles) long and bright white, Copacabana beach is the stage upon which people swim, surf, jog, preen, make sand castles, sunbathe, and play volleyball. The broad and beautifully landscaped **Avenida Atlântica** runs along the beach's entire length. Running parallel two streets inland, **Nossa Senhora de Copacabana** is the main shopping and commercial street. These two avenues and their many cross streets contain numerous hotels, restaurants, and bars. For more on Rio's beaches, see "Beaches, Parks & Plazas," below.

IPANEMA ★★

The famous stretch of beach immortalized in Tom Jobim's song "The Girl from Ipanema" nestles in between Copacabana, Leblon, and Lagoa. No more than 8 blocks wide in some areas, it is one of the most coveted residential neighborhoods in all of Rio. Built mostly after Rio's Art Deco boom, there are very few landmark buildings to speak of; most apartment buildings are nondescript, some downright ugly. What Ipanema does offer is great shopping on **Rua Visconde de Pirajá** and its side streets, an excellent nightlife scene, some terrific restaurants, and of course, the beach, the major recreation area for residents and visitors alike. Joggers and walkers cruise the black-and-white patterned sidewalk every day of the week, but Sunday is the day to see and be seen when the beachside **Avenida Vieira Souto** is closed for traffic and people cycle, inline skate, and scooter along, at all times showing tans and tight form to advantage.

LEBLON ★★

A smaller and, if anything, trendier version of Ipanema, Leblon sits directly to the east of Ipanema; the dividing line is the drainage canal for the Lagoa, now landscaped into a park called the **Jardim de Ala.** The most significant difference between the two neighborhoods is the street names. The beachside avenue in Leblon is known as **Avenida Delfim Moreira,** while the main shopping street is **Avenida General Martin.** Most of the best restaurants cluster around the end of **Avenida Ataulfo de Paiva** where it meets **Rua Dias Ferreira.**

LAGOA

Lagoa is an odd neighborhood, as the focus is the big lagoon (**Lagoa Rodrigo de Freitas**) that drains into the ocean between Ipanema and Leblon. For the majority of Cariocas, this is primarily a recreation area. They come to walk, cycle, inline skate, or run the 8.5km (5¼-mile) pathway that circles the lagoon. In the afternoon and evening, the neighborhood's pleasures become more hedonistic as people come to the many waterside kiosks to grab a drink, have some food, or listen to live music.

BARRA DE TIJUCA

The Brazilian envy of things American has finally expressed itself in architecture. Though ostensibly part of Rio de Janeiro, Barra (as it's usually called) looks and feels much like an American beach city, like L.A. or Miami Beach. Streets are wide and filled with 4×4s because in Barra—as in L.A.—only somebody who's a nobody walks. Instead, folks here drive—to the beach, to their penthouse apartment, or to the full-size replica of Studio 54 at the **American Center** mall.

TIJUCA NATIONAL PARK

Backstopping all of these Zona Sul neighborhoods is the massive **Tijuca National Park.** Mostly mountainous, the 3,300-hectare (8,151-acre) forest was begun in the 1800s as a personal project of the Emperor Dom Pedro II. It's invariably shown on maps as one big swatch of green, but in fact any number of shantytowns (favelas in Portuguese) have taken over parkland, usually in areas adjacent to official city neighborhoods. The park that's left—and there's lots of it—is cut through with excellent walking and hiking trails, many leading to peaks with fabulous views. Climb to the top of the Pico da Tijuca at 1,022m (3,352 ft.) on a sunny day, and beneath your feet you'll have a view of every neighborhood in Rio.

---

5 BEACHES, PARKS & PLAZAS

BEACHES

Beaches are to Rio what cafes are to Paris. And while each beach has its own particular traits, there are some general rules to help you take the waters like a true Carioca.

BE PREPARED   First and foremost: **Get a Brazilian bikini** (though perhaps not if you're male). No matter how funky or fashionably teeny your swimsuit looked up north, on a Rio beach it's guaranteed to scream *gringo.* And if you're thinking your figure's not quite bikini-ready, relax. In Brazil everybody and their grandma wears a two-piece. (Note, however, that no matter how small they may shrink that top, Brazilian women *never* go topless—that's for the heathen French.)

Second: **Don't be a pack rat.** If you observe your fellow beachgoers you'll note that Brazilians bring neither picnic basket nor backpack full of stuff and gadgets. Why bring

---

Frommer's Moment: Baywatch Rio-Style

On hot summer days, Cariocas take to the ocean like fish to water, except of course, that many Cariocas can't swim. On days when wind and waves get rough, this can lead to some exciting beach theater. One day on Leme beach a helicopter zoomed down along the surf line from the direction of Copacabana, stopping to hover over a spot some 15m (50 ft.) offshore. We could see a swimmer in the circle of water beat flat by the helicopter blades. A rescue jumper appeared in the open door of the chopper, then plunged into the ocean. The helicopter lowered a big net and scooped up swimmer and diver. It hovered over to the beach and plopped the swimmer unceremoniously on the sand. The rescuer was then raised on a line and the helicopter sped off; the swimmer skulked into the crowd. Five minutes after it began the beach was back to normal again. On a busy weekend, helicopters can perform up to 200 such rescues.

⓪ Tips Know About the Beach Entrance

Maybe it's to keep sand from tracking in the lobby, or maybe it's to avoid having the Speedo-clad squeezing into an elevator full of suits. For whatever reason, many beachfront hotels have a separate entrance and elevator for those going to the beach. Normally marked ENTRADA DE BANHISTAS or ENTRADA DE SERVIÇO, these elevators lead to the hotel service entrance where—as a bonus for following the local etiquette—you can pick up a beach towel, chair, and umbrella. Returning from the beach you enter the same side entrance and drop the stuff off again.

---

anything when everything you could possibly want is for sale on the beach? Blankets, inflatable mattresses, and quilts are likewise no-nos. A foldable beach chair is acceptable for women; Brazilian men stand or sit on the sand. All you really need is a towel, sunscreen, and a little bit of cash for beer, food, and other incidentals.

Third and most important: **Relax.** Go for a little swim, chat with the one that brung ya or the cutie on the towel next door, have a beer and some snacks, and soak up those rays.

For further discussion of the more subtle social beachgoing dynamics, see "Know the Beach Rules," below.

WATER CONDITIONS   The beaches facing Guanabara Bay (primarily **Flamengo** and **Botafogo**) are nearly always too polluted for swimming. Thanks to a substantial current, the ocean beaches (**Copacabana, Ipanema,** and **Barra**) are much cleaner, but even so, sometimes after a heavy rain the fecal coli form count rises beyond acceptable levels. The newspaper *Globo* prints a daily beach report listing all beach closings. Consult that or ask at your hotel.

SAFETY ISSUES   Another argument for traveling light to the beach is security. You're unlikely to get mugged on a Rio beach in the daytime, but leaving that iPod, wallet, or pocket camera on the sand while you head off for a swim *is* an open invitation to be relieved of your valuables. I would also advise against moonlit strolls by the waterline. At night the sand is dark and deserted; stick to the large sidewalk fronting the beach—it's well lit and patrolled often by the tourist police.

THE BEACHES   **Botafogo** and **Flamengo** are fine and picturesque for an afternoon stroll, but too polluted for swimming. Off by itself in Urca, **Praia Vermelha** ★ faces the ocean and is often fine. It offers a fabulous view of the Sugarloaf, and next to no tourists. On the other hand, it's completely lacking in waves.

The first of the ocean beaches, **Copacabana** ★★ remains a favorite. The wide and beautifully landscaped Avenida Atlântica is a great place for a stroll. (The wavy landscaped sidewalk mosaic is the work of landscape designer Roberto Burle Marx.) When the feet start to tire, pull up a chair at any of the countless beachside kiosks, grab a chilled coconut or a *cerveja,* and spend some time admiring the picture-perfect view. (The new kiosks also offer modern, clean bathroom facilities, at a cost of R$1.) The far end of the beach near the Forte de Copacabana is where fishermen beach their small craft; it's a good place to find freshly grilled shrimp or other seafood. For those with other fish to fry, the area in front of the Copacabana Palace around the Rainbow kiosk is a well-known gay area.

The *postos* (lifeguard stations) along Copacabana and Ipanema beaches are open daily from 8am to 8pm. They offer first aid (free if needed) and changing and toilet facilities

Tips **Know the Beach Rules**

Certain unspoken, gender-specific rules govern the public behavior of men and women on the beach at Ipanema—and by extension, on all Brazilian beaches. What follows is a tongue-in-cheek rundown of beachgoing do's and don'ts.

Sunbathing 101: The most important rule is that *nothing* shall come between a man and the raw, hot sand. A man who uses a beach chair, a towel, or a *kanga* is not a man but a gringo, and shall be shunned. A Brazilian man must plant his Lycra-covered butt down in hot white silicon, making sure his lower back and thighs are covered in sticky white grains.

There are certain exceptions. A man may sit on a sheet of folded newspaper. A man may sit on a *tiny* corner of a woman's *kanga*, provided the woman is beautiful and he occupies no more than 3% of the total *kanga* surface. A man may also stand, drinking a *cerveja* (beer), looking around manfully and sharing the company of other men.

A woman must sit on a *kanga*. Beach chairs are also acceptable. Women do not touch the sand, nor do women stand. Women do not join in beach sports such as soccer or foot volley, nor do they plod sweatily down the beach pretending to be joggers. The acceptable positions for women are lounging on their backs, lying dreamily on their bellies, or sitting cross-legged in a circle with at least three other women.

When rising from the sand—or newspaper, or corner of a woman's *kanga*—a man may not brush the sticky white sand from his butt. A man may not touch his butt. A man who touches his butt is not a man but a *bicha* (sissy) or a gringo.

A woman, when rising from the sand, must brush herself voluptuously, making sure both glutes are thoroughly massaged from waist down to lower thigh. Particular attention must be paid to readjusting the bikini bottom so that it rests comfortably between her butt cheeks.

for a charge of R$1. *Postos* are numbered 1 through 11 starting from Leme and ending in Leblon. Cariocas often use them as reference points.

Ipanema Beach ★★★ was famous among Brazilians even before Tom Jobim wrote his song about the tall and tan and young and lovely girl he saw and sighed over. Stretching almost 3km (2 miles) from the foot of the Pedra Dois Irmãos to the Ponta Arpoador, the beach at Ipanema is a strand like nowhere else. Part of the attraction does involve observing the self-confident sensuality with which the Ipanema *garotas* (girls) stroll the sands. (Equal-opportunity purists should note that there's an equivalent amount of male beefcake on hand—it just doesn't inspire songs or poetry.) But more than anything, Ipanema is a carnival. Watch the games of volleyball or *futvolei* (like volleyball, but no hands allowed), beach soccer, surfing, and wakeboarding. Forgot your bikini? Wait a moment and a vendor will stop by with one for sale—along with towels, sarongs (called *kangas* in Brazil), hats, shades, peanuts, beer, cookies, Walkmans, suntan lotion, Styrofoam airplanes, Winnie-the-Pooh books, sticks of grilled shrimp, shelled coconuts, even

Water Frolicking 101: Men *must* swim or at least pretend to swim (many Cariocas actually don't know how to swim but will fake it). A man who dibbles his toes or contemplates the waves with a far-off look in his eye is not a man but a gringo, and must be shunned. Men approach the sea in a series of angry stomps, stopping at the waterline to regard the surf with a steely glare before sprinting forward and diving into a breaking wave. Once immersed, a man may swim farther out, or he may bodysurf. A man may *not* play in the waves.

Women may play in the waves, turning their backs to the surf and giggling as the water breaks over them. This, however, is rare. Generally, a woman dips her toes, advances as deep as mid-calf, and then waits for a breaker, at which time she squats and allows the surf to immerse her bikini bottom. If this is found to be too traumatizing, a woman may also bring a cup to the beach, dip it in the frothy foam and pour the water over various parts of her body, thoroughly massaging each part for *at least* 30 seconds afterward.

Beach Flirting 101: Men and women do not enter the water together. This is not to say they do not interact. For instance, a man may approach a group of no more than three pretty women sitting cross-legged on their *kangas* and ask them to watch his shorts and sandals while he manfully attacks the ocean. Their agreement obtained, the man will then place his stuff on the sand near their *kangas* and stomp angrily toward the surf, which he will regard with a glare all the more steely for the fact that he knows three pretty women are admiring the manful way he's attacking the elements. The women will ignore him, missing the determined plunge into the roiling surf and the angry stomp back up the beach. But at least they will never call him a gringo!

deep-muscle massages. Claim a piece of sand on Ipanema, and all of life's essentials will come to you.

The section just around the point from Copacabana—called **Praia do Arpoador**—is a prime surf spot and a great location for watching the local dudes take to the waves. One of the surf schools also runs lessons for kids from the local favelas. The area around Posto 8 (opposite Rua Farme Amoedo) is Ipanema's gay section.

Farther down into **Leblon** (still the same beach, just a different name once you cross the canal) you will find the **Baixo Baby.** This play area, equipped by corporate sponsors with lots of playground equipment and beach toys, is a popular gathering place for nannies and parents to watch their kids run around and play with sand.

Off on its own surrounded by mountains, **São Conrado Beach** offers some fine scenery and a (relative) sense of isolation. Its other main claim to fame is as a landing strip for all the hang gliders (*asa delta* in Portuguese) who leap from nearby peaks.

Farther from the city is the beach at **Barra de Tijuca.** The main reason to go out here is if you're a surf-head desperate for a wave. The surfing is said to be the best in Rio, particularly around the Barraca de Pepê (Pepê's Shack) where surfers like to gather. The only reason to go even farther beyond Barra is to get to **Grumari,** a lovely small beach set in a nature reserve. Grumari has no high-rises or beachside restaurants, just lush vegetation and a few kiosks by the side of the road. However, don't expect to get away from the crowds even this far out; on weekends the place is packed.

PARKS & GARDENS

In addition to numerous beaches, Rio is also blessed with a variety of parks. On the waterfront near Centro there's **Flamengo Park,** a good place to stroll in the late afternoon if you're looking for a nice view of the Sugarloaf.

Just past the northern edge of downtown, the **Quinta da Boa Vista,** the royal family's former country residence, sits on Avenida Bartolomeu de Gusmã, just a short walk from the Sao Cristóvão Metrô stop. It's as delightful now as it was when the royal princesses scampered round the villa gardens. Designed in the Romantic style, the Quinta da Boa Vista has all the tricks of the gardener's trade: tree-lined dells, small ponds and waterfalls, a grotto, a lookout, even a temple of Apollo. The park is also home to the city zoo and the national museum (see "The Top Attractions," earlier in this chapter). Open daily from 7am to 6pm.

Closer to the city core lies the **Campo de Santana,** opposite the Central Metrô stop on Avenida Presidente Vargas. A pretty, formal park, its fence and four iron gates protect 50 species of trees, four ponds, and a grotto. The fence also encloses numerous *agoutis* (a bizarre-looking mini-capybara), ducks, peacocks, and marmosets, as well as a large collection of stray cats. Open daily from 7am to 7pm.

Last and best, the **Parque Nacional da Tijuca (Tijuca National Park)** ★★ is a wonder. At more than 3,360 hectares (8,300 acres) it's the biggest urban forest in the world and one of the last remnants of Atlantic rainforest on Brazil's southern coast. It's a great place to go for a hike, splash in a waterfall, or admire the view. Among its more special points are the Pico de Tijuca, the Vista Chinesa, and the Pedra da Gávea.

SQUARES & PLAZAS

What's the difference between a *largo* and a *praça?* Simple, although not really. A *praça* is a city square, and a *largo* is, well, also a city square except a *largo* is always bigger than a *praça,* except—like with the Largo de Boticario—when it isn't.

Tucked away just a few hundred meters uphill along Rua Cosme Velho from the Corcovado Train Station is one of Rio's prettiest squares, the **Largo de Boticario** ★★. It's a gem of a spot, with five gaily painted colonial houses encircling a fountain in the middle of a flagstone square. Mature fig trees overhead make for abundant shade, while traffic noise seems completely drowned out by the soft gurgling of the Rio Carioca (from which residents of Rio derive their nickname) taking its last few breaths of air before disappearing forever beneath the city streets. It's well worth the 5-minute detour if you're going to the Corcovado anyway.

The best way to arrive in **Praça XV de Novembro** is by sea—if not on a sailing ship from Portugal then a ferry from Niterói will do the trick. Rio's most important square, Praça XV is also its most abused. Earlier generations of city planners ran six lanes of traffic in front of it, a freeway over the top of it, then knocked down most of the old structures used to frame the space, and erected 20-story glass blocks. Still, some of the old charm shines through (and six lanes of traffic have been sunk in an underground tunnel, which helps). To your right as you arrive, beyond a statue of Dom João VI on a horse, is the **Chafariz do Mestre Valentim,** an ornate fountain that marks Rio's former coastline.

Moments **Spectacular—& Free—Views**

Rio's best two views—from the **Sugarloaf** and the **Corcovado**—are both ticket-charging attractions. But in a city with so much geography it's impossible to fence off everything. What follows are views you get for free.

Smack in the middle of Botafogo is the **Mirante do Pasmado.** It is walkable (enter off Rua General Severino, close to the Shopping Rio Plaza), although it would probably take you at least 30 minutes. A lot easier is to take a taxi up and then walk back down. The views of Sugarloaf, the bay, and the Christ are quite spectacular.

Just a short 3km (2-mile) drive uphill along Estrada da Canoa from the beach at Sao Conrado, the **Canoas Lookout (Mirante de Canoas)** provides a view of São Conrado, Rocinha, and the Pedra Dois Irmaos near Leblon, and looking back uphill, the 2,100-foot **Pedra Bonita** from whence the hang gliders launch. Carry on up the road for 2km (1¼ miles), then turn left on Caminho da Pedra Bonita, and you too can stand by the hang gliders as they launch.

The military fort in Leme (p. 107) offers the most spectacular views of Copacabana, the Bay of Guanabara, and Sugarloaf. At R$3, it's effectively free.

The **Largo de São Francisco de Paula** in Rio's old shopping district is well worth a visit. There's an outdoor market on one side of the square, and on the other the huge baroque-style **Igreja de São Francisco de Paula.**

For a further discussion on the city's best squares and plazas, see "Neighborhoods to Explore," earlier in this chapter.

6 ESPECIALLY FOR KIDS

There are few things in Rio that *aren't* for kids. Brazilians take their children everywhere—restaurants, bars, even dances—and voice no objection when others do the same. Still, a few places stand out as being especially kid-friendly. First and most obvious is the **beach.** Sun, surf, and sand castles have kind of an enduring kid appeal. For younger children the beach at **Leblon** features the **Baixo Baby,** a free play area equipped with all manner of toys and play stuff geared for toddlers. On Sundays and holidays, the waterfront avenues that line the beaches of Flamengo, Copacabana, Ipanema, and Leblon are closed for cars. With no traffic, the miles and miles of waterfront become the world's best playground. Both adults and children will enjoy the pleasant bustle of Carioca families going for a stroll and there's plenty of entertainment to boot. You'll find an array of buskers such as jugglers, magicians, musicians, stilt-walkers, and fire-eaters, as well as bike rentals and small electric toy-car rentals. For slightly older kids, the **city zoo (Jardim Zoológico;** p. 109) is guaranteed to delight and just possibly to educate. One of the few museums of interest to kids is the **Museu do Indio** (p. 106) in Botafogo. The museum offers kids stamps and (washable) body paints so they can practice adorning themselves like natives; the re-creations of Indian houses on the grounds are fun places to crawl in and out of. In Catete, the beautiful (if slightly formal) **Parque do Catete** has a

> ### (Tips) DIY When It Comes to Tours
>
> When booking a tour or outdoor adventure, it's best to make the call yourself. (Don't worry about a language barrier; most tour operators speak English.) If you let the concierge or desk staff make the booking it will cost you anything from 10% to 50% more, and you may not even get the tour you want. Rio concierges are notorious for informing guests that a tour is "full," then putting them on a tour with another company—one offering the concierge a bigger cut.

brinquedoteca, a kind of toy library from which you can loan out toys by the hour for a nominal fee (about R$7 per hour). Few kids can resist the fun of a train—or tram ride. The Santa Teresa tram zooms over a high aqueduct, then snakes through the narrow cobblestone streets.

7 ORGANIZED TOURS

BUS TOURS   Gray Line (© 021/2512-9919; www.grayline.com) offers a number of tour itineraries: the 4-hour US$43 walking tour of Rio's historic downtown is a quite reasonable value; the US$55 half-day tours of the Corcovado or Pão de Açúcar are really a bit of a racket; all they're providing is transfer to and from the train station or gondola, at a very hefty markup.

BOAT TOURS   Saveiros Tour ★ (© 021/2225-6064; www.saveiros.com.br) offers 2-hour tours of Guanabara Bay aboard an antique wooden fishing schooner. Cost is R$55, children 5 to 10 R$25, children 4 and under free, including snacks of fresh fruit. Departure is at noon Tuesday, Thursday, and Saturday from the Glória Marina (Metrô: Glória).

Take to the water for sundown. **Pink Fleet** (© 021/2555-4063; www.pinkfleet.com) offers evening dinner cruises on Guanabara Bay. Passengers begin boarding at 6pm; the boat departs at 9:15pm and returns at 11pm. Cost is R$80, not including dinner, which you order from an a la carte menu. On Saturdays, there's an additional afternoon tour, departing at 11:45am. The boats depart from the Enseada da Glória, just behind the Museum of Modern Art.

HELICOPTER TOURS   Rio is a town where taking the high ground is rewarded. **Helisight** (© 021/2511-2141, on weekends 2542-7895; www.helisight.com.br) offers helicopter sightseeing tours. They cost R$150 per person for a 6-minute circuit around the statue of Christ; R$300 per person for a 12-minute flight over the Christ, Botanical Gardens, Rocinha, Lagoa, Leblon, Ipanema, Copacabana, and the Sugarloaf. Minimum of three people per flight. Tours depart from Urca Hill (halfway up to the Sugarloaf) and the shore of Lagoa (opposite the rowing stadium in Leblon).

FAVELA TOURS   Rio's hillside favelas, or shantytowns, are huge, complex, and fascinating—a whole other world, in fact—but as an outsider it's difficult (and dangerous) to navigate your way through this world. Licensed guide Marcelo Armstrong of **Marcelo Armstrong's Favela Tour ★ (© 021/9989-0074** mobile; www.favelatour.com.br) knows the territory; he's been doing tours since 1993, longer than any of his competitors.

A 3-hour tour to the favelas of Rocinha and Vila Canoas costs R$85 if booked directly, including pickup and drop-off. A portion of the fee goes to fund a school that tourgoers get to visit. While some foreign visitors have qualms about the ethics of touring a poor community, the fact is most favela residents welcome such visits—not so much for the economic spinoffs (though these are welcome) but for the sense of validation that comes with having foreigners visit their neighborhood (just as they might visit Ipanema or Copacabana). They too are a part of Brazil, and the tours to their community show it.

COMMUNITY VISITS   For a very different tour, experience **Ikoporan's** community tours (© **021/3852-2916;** www.ikoporan.org). This local organization sets up volunteer projects for foreign visitors who would like to help a community organization. Those who don't have the time to dedicate to volunteering can spend a day visiting one or more community projects, getting to know some of the social projects that support some of Rio's most socially disadvantaged groups, learn more about social issues, and talk to staff, volunteers, and local residents. Tours start at R$150 and include transportation, an English-speaking guide, and lunch. Part of the proceeds are donated to the projects.

WALKING TOURS   Rio Hiking (© **021/9721-0594;** www.riohiking.com.br) offers a 3-hour guided walking tour of the historic, bohemian neighborhood of Santa Teresa. Tours depart daily at 9am and 2pm, and cost R$70.

8 OUTDOOR ACTIVITIES

Rio Hiking ★★ (© **021/9721-0594;** www.riohiking.com.br) is Rio's adventure-sport specialist, offering a range of exciting outdoor sports that take full advantage of Rio's extraordinary geography. Rio Hiking offers **hiking, rock climbing, rafting, ocean kayaking, cycling, hang gliding, horseback riding, scuba diving, surfing** (with lessons), and **rappelling.** Depending on the sport, half-day adventures cost from R$80 to R$150, full-day adventures from R$150 to R$250, guides and transfer to and from your hotel included. The **white water–rafting** trip takes you to a river about 2 hours north of Rio with Class III (and sometimes Class IV) rapids. The descent takes about 3 hours. Cost is R$190. The company also offers 3-day **trekking** trips (see "Trekking," below).

   Rio Adventures (© **021/2705-5747** or 8204-7559; www.rioadventures.com) offers a variety of tours and adventure-sport options, including hiking, rappelling, hang gliding, tree canopy tours, and more. On the **rappelling** trip, you drive past Barra de Tijuca to beautiful Guaratiba, hike for an hour to a cliff overlooking an undeveloped beach, then rappel down a 377m (115-ft.) rock face. Then you hang out, swim for bit, and head back. Minimum age is 12. The tree canopy tour involves zipping through the tops of the rainforest trees in lovely Tijuca Forest. Cost for either tour is R$250 per person for two people, including transportation and lunch. With a bigger group the price goes down significantly.

BICYCLING   **Rio Hiking** offers two half-day guided bike tours of the city. The first involves an easy ride along the beachfront of the Zona Sul. The second, more challenging tour rides through the gorgeous rainforest of the Floresta da Tijuca. The tour costs R$150 per person.

GOLFING   Rio's only public golf course is out in Barra da Tijuca. **Golden Green,** Av. Conde de Marapendi 2905 (© **021/2434-0696**), is a par-3, 6-hole course inside a private condominium but open to the public. The course is open Tuesday to Sunday from

7am to 10pm. The course is floodlighted for evening play. Greens fees are R$60 Tuesday to Friday and R$75 on weekends and holidays. One of the city's best courses (par-5, 18 hole) is the elegant **Gávea Golf Club,** Estrada da Gávea 800, São Conrado (☎ **021/3323-6050;** www.gaveagolf.com.br). However, the club—like virtually every golf course in Brazil—is private. The Copacabana Palace Hotel and the Sheraton Rio Hotel are a few of the hotels that have an arrangement allowing their guests to tee off. If you are a golf fiend, check first with your hotel of choice for privileges.

HANG GLIDING   For a bird's-eye view of Rio's beaches and mountains, check out **Just Fly Rio** ★★ (☎ **021/9985-7540** mobile, or 2268-0565; www.justfly.com.br). Flight instructor Paulo Celani used to be an agricultural engineer, until he decided he'd much prefer to fly for a living. That was more than 20 years ago. Since then Paulo has soared in tandem with hundreds of people ages 5 to 85. There's no experience or special skills necessary, aside from a willingness to run off a ramp into the open sky. It's one of the most exciting things you can do in Rio, well worth the R$240 per flight, pickup and drop-off included. *Tip:* There's a 10% discount on the price if you call and book with Paulo directly. Also, if you are keen on flying, it's a good idea to contact Paulo on the day you arrive. As the activity is weather dependent (and what may be a great day for the beach may not be the best flying weather), you can let Paulo contact you when flying conditions are best. **Rio Hiking** ★★ also offers a very similar hang gliding tour, for a comparable price.

HIKING   **Rio Hiking** ★★ offers guided hiking trips to most of Rio's peaks. The 4-hour Sugarloaf trip, which includes a short stretch of rock climbing, costs R$150. The 6-hour Pedra da Gávea hike offers terrific views, a waterfall in the middle, and an ocean dip at the end. Cost is R$200. Less strenuous is the Tijuca Forest tour, which involves a tour of the forest, stops at a waterfall and a couple of lookouts, and a 2-hour hike to Pico de Tijuca. Cost is R$150, with the option of returning via the fascinating hilltop neighborhood of Santa Teresa. Guides Denise Werneck and Gabriel Barrouin know Rio well, speak excellent English, and are a delight to be with.

JEEP TOURS   Although we always thought they looked kind of goofy, the open jeep tours are incredibly popular with visitors to Rio. The most popular tours visit the Tijuca Forest combined with a visit to the Corcovado—R$125. There are also tours to the hilltop neighborhood of Santa Teresa, and to the favela of Rocinha. For information and bookings call **Jeep Tour** (☎ **021/2108-5800;** www.jeeptour.com.br).

SEA KAYAKING   Get out onto Guanabara Bay. **Rio Hiking** organizes kayaking tours from Praia Vermelha at the foot of the Sugarloaf, traveling out to one of the small islands just off the coast for some snacks and snorkeling. Cost is R$160 for a half-day tour, including transfers, refreshments, and English-speaking guide.

SURFING   Rio has a number of good spots to catch the waves. And if the waves aren't as big as in Hawaii, the water's certainly warmer than Vancouver Island. The surfing beach closest to the main part of Rio is **Arpoador Beach** in Ipanema. Waves are between 1 and 3m (3–10 ft.). São Conrado Beach is off and on. Sometimes there are good 2m (6½-ft.) waves, sometimes it's dead. Out in Barra de Tijuca the main surf beach is **Barra-Meio,** a 1km-long (½-mile) stretch in the middle of the beach (around Av. Sernambetiba 3100). Waves average around 2m (6 ft.). Carry on down that same beach another 6.5 to 8km (4–5 miles), and you come to **Macumba-Pontal,** a 2.5km (1½-mile) beach with waves up to 3m (10 ft.). If you've brought your board and just need transport, there's a **surf bus** that departs the Largo do Machado at 7, 10am, 1, and 4pm and goes along

Copacabana, Arpoador, São Conrado, and Barra de Tijuca as far as Prainha, past Recreio. Call to confirm departure times (✆ **021/2539-7555** or 8702-2837; www.surfbus.com. br); tickets cost R$4 each way. If you need a board, **Hot Coast,** Galeria River, Rua Francisco Otaviano 67, loja 12, Ipanema (✆ **021/2287-9388**), rents short boards, fun boards, and long boards for R$40 a day. You need to book ahead if you want a board on the weekend.

If you're looking for **lessons,** a surf school is conveniently located in Ipanema. The **Escolinha de Surf Paulo Dolabella** (✆ **021/2259-2320** or 9814-9702 mobile) is in front of the Caesar Park Hotel. The regular lessons are Tuesday and Thursday from 8 to 10am and 3 to 5pm, but you can also arrange for a lesson on the weekends or other days. Drop-in rates are R$60 per hour, including the equipment. However, like true surf dudes, they rarely answer phones; it's best to go find them. **Rio Hiking** (✆ **021/9721-0594;** www.riohiking.com.br) offers the most hassle-free option, a half-day surf lesson with an English-speaking instructor, plus gear and transportation for R$200. In Recreio de Bandeirantes, **Surf Cades** (✆ **021/2490-3271;** www.surfecades.com) offers group and private lessons (R$60/hour). The **EBC** (**Escola Bodboarding de Copacabana;** ✆ **021/2236-6676;** www.escolabc.com.br) offers private bodyboarding lessons on Copacabana beach; each 90-minute lesson costs R$80. Contact **Flavio Brito** (✆ **021/ 8855-1774**) for more information.

TREKKING **Rio Hiking** ★★ offers a number of guided 2- to 3-day treks in the mountains or rugged coast around Rio. Particularly recommended is the 2-day trek in the **Serra dos Orgáos National Park** (R$440), where the Atlantic rainforest is pristine and the views extraordinary. Avid hikers will certainly enjoy the spectacular hikes in Itatiaia National Park. Located about 3 hours from Rio, on the border of the states of Minas Gerais and São Paulo, the park is home to the highest peak in the state, the 2,787m (8,000-ft.) Agulhas Negras. This 3-day trip takes you to some of the region's best scenery and includes a visit to the waterfalls in the lower part of the national park, a full-day hike to the highest peak in Rio state, and on the third day a 4-hour hike to the stunning rock formations of the Prateleiras (shelves), with an optional rappel. This 3-day package costs R$660 per person and includes accommodations, food, specialized guides, and transportation. All you have to bring are sunscreen, hiking boots, warm clothes, and a raincoat.

9 THE ONLY SPECTATOR SPORT IN RIO

FUTEBOL AT THE MARACANÃ ★★★

The best and only true way to experience the world's largest soccer stadium is to come during a big game. What an experience! Fans arrive at Maracanã, Rua Profesor Eurico Rabelo s/n (✆ **021/2569-4916;** www.suderj.rj.gov.br/maracana.asp; Metrô: Maracanã), hours beforehand, literally—for a 4pm game they arrive at 1pm *at the latest*—and the world's biggest party begins. Outside folks drink ice-cold beer. Inside the *torcedores* (fan club members) bring out the samba drums and pound away for a good half-hour, psyching themselves up before parading in the banners—huge flags in team colors—to the wild applause of their fellow fans. Then the other team parades in their flags, and your team boos. Then your side sings a song insulting their team. Then their team sings a song insulting your team. Then they unveil a massive *banderão* covering half the stadium.

Tips　　**Maybe Beware of Organized Soccer Fun**

We've always said that organized trips to the Maracanã are a scam. They charge R$80 to R$100 for a ticket (which costs R$20) and bus transport (to a stadium that's on the Metrô line). Even if you took a cab there and back, you'd still come out ahead. However, if Rio's big games do move to the Engenhão stadium in the Zona Norte, an organized tour with bus transport begins to look like much better value.

Then your side unveils your *banderão*. Samba drums beat all the while. Eventually after several hours of this silliness a soccer game breaks out. Tickets are quite affordable, ranging from R$10 to R$40.

Unfortunately, Rio's world-famous Maracanã stadium may well be set to close for an extended period of repairs, in preparation for the 2014 World Cup. Exact dates and plans have not yet been announced. Some reports suggest only brief and partial closures; others indicate full closure for a full 2 years, for a thorough-going renovation. In that case, the stadium would reopen only in 2012. In the interval, the big games may be transferred to the new Engenhão stadium, in the Rio suburbs, but again plans have not been finalized. The best places for information are the websites of Rio's four best teams: **Flamengo** (www.flamengo.com.br), **Fluminense** (www.fluminense.com.br), **Botafogo** (www.botafogo. com.br), and **Vasco de Gama** (www.crvascodagama.com). Any game pitting one of these teams against another is worth seeing. The websites list upcoming games and locations, though in Portuguese only. The sports section of the English-language Web paper **The Gringo Times** (www.thegringotimes.com) covers Rio's soccer teams.

Tip: While you can sit in the neutral stands in the middle, it's more fun if you choose sides. Violence at Brazilian football never came anywhere close to the problems seen in Europe; since they prohibited beer inside and reduced the stadium seating capacity, it's vanished almost altogether.

10 SHOPPING IN RIO

THE SHOPPING SCENE

If Cariocas had to list their primary joys in life, shopping certainly wouldn't come out at the top—there are, after all, beaches, music, and sex to consider—but it'd certainly be in the top five. Even on the beach, vendors peddle an enormous range of products. Elsewhere clothing, shoes, arts and crafts, musical instruments, and other souvenirs can all be had at good prices.

The old downtown neighborhood of Centro offers great deals for clothes and shoes. Fun to explore are the pedestrian streets around **Rua da Alfândega, Rua Uruguaiana,** and **Rua Buenos Aires,** jampacked with hundreds of merchants in small shops side by side. Back in the '70s the area was slated to be demolished to make room for a viaduct, but over 1,200 shopkeepers formed a merchant's association and banded together to put a halt to the development. The best days for shopping are Monday through Friday when downtown is full of office workers. More upscale clothing can be found around the **Rua Gonçalves Dias,** with many stores selling Brazilian brand names and local designers.

Botafogo has two interesting shopping centers, the **Botafogo Praia Shopping** and the older **Rio Sul.** Rio Sul was one of the first malls of Rio and is still a very popular shopping destination. Many Brazilian stores can be found in this mall, and it makes a convenient place to browse and get a sense for brands and prices.

Copacabana, Ipanema, and Leblon don't have any large malls, just boutique malls known as *galerias* in Brazil. The prominent shopping areas are the main streets of the neighborhood. In Copacabana, **Nossa Senhora de Copacabana** is the main shopping street, with the best stores concentrated around the Rua Santa Clara and Rua Figueiredo de Magalhães. The beachfront area also houses a street market on Saturdays and Sundays, selling souvenirs and arts and crafts from various regions of Brazil. For upscale and exclusive shopping in Ipanema, try **Rua Visconde de Piraja,** especially between the **Rua Anibal de Medonça** and **Rua Vinicius de Moraes.** Another popular destination for Rio's well-heeled shoppers is the classy São Conrado Fashion Mall, located in São Conrado, a neighborhood wedged in between Leblon and Barra. Those who prefer megamalls may want to head straight for Barra da Tijuca. This newly developed neighborhood is home to many malls, including the **Barra Shopping**—the largest mall in Latin America.

Hours for small stores and neighborhood shops are typically Monday through Friday from 10am to 7pm, and 9am to 1pm on Saturday. Malls are usually open from 10am to 10pm Monday through Saturday and limited hours on Sundays (2–8pm). In tourist areas shops will often be open on weekends.

While street vendors and markets take only cash, most shops accept one or more type of credit card. Often you can negotiate a discount for paying cash instead of with a credit card. Sometimes you will see two prices listed on items: *á vista* (always the lower price) refers to cash payments; *cheque ou cartão* is the price for payments made with a check or credit card. Please note that there is a difference between *Credicard* (a brand of credit card) and *cartão* or *cartão de credito* (the generic word for any kind of credit card).

SHOPPING FROM A TO Z

Antiques

Shopping Cassino Atlantico   Attached to the Sofitel Hotel, this 180-store mall specializes in antiques and art galleries. Every Saturday from 11am to 7pm the mall features an antiques fair. Av. Atlântica 4240, Copacabana. (*C*) **021/2523-8709.** www.shoppingcassino atlantico.com.br. Bus: 474.

Arts & Crafts

Brasil&Cia   This Ipanema store specializes in Brazilian arts and crafts, featuring quality artwork made from wood, ceramics, paper, and fibers. Look for the collection of ballerina dolls made from gourds and painted in delicate colors and patterns. Rua Maria Quitéria 27, Ipanema. (*C*) **021/2267-4603.** www.brasilecia.com.br. Bus: 472.

O Sol   O Sol is run by a nonprofit society dedicated to supporting and promoting the work of regional artists. The collection varies from beautiful but not very portable furniture pieces to portable miniature terra-cotta sculptures, chess sets, and textiles, including carpets and wall hangings. Rua Corcovado 213, Jardim Botânico. (*C*) **021/2294-5099.** www. artesanato-sol.com.br. Bus: 572.

Pé de Boi   In Laranjeiras, Pé de Boi's collection goes beyond just Brazilian arts and crafts to include work from popular Peruvian, Ecuadorian, and Guatemalan artists. It's also a great spot to browse for arts and crafts from other Brazilian regions such the Amazon,

Pernambuco, and Minas Gerais. Rua Ipiranga 55, Laranjeiras. © **021/2285-4395.** www.pede boi.com.br. Bus: 584.

Trilhos Urbanos   A great little store in Santa Teresa, Trilhos Urbanos sells a variety of Brazilian artwork, including paintings, photographs, and crafts made out of tile, paper, and other materials. Rua Almirante Alexandrino 402, Santa Teresa. © **021/2242-3632.** Tram stop: Largo dos Guimarães.

Beachwear

Blue Man   My favorite swimwear store. Blue Man is known for its original designs, offering bathing suits and bikinis in various styles, allowing you to mix and match tops and bottoms. Visconde de Pirajá 351, loja 308, Ipanema. © **021/2247-4905.** www.blueman.com. br. Bus: 474. Also in the Rio Sul shopping center.

Bum Bum   This is the place to shop for the infamous Rio bikini. Collections vary constantly, but one thing never changes—the smaller the better. The styles and colors on display will give you a quick feel for the current beach fashions for both men and women. Rua Vinicius de Morais 130, Ipanema. © **021/2521-1229.** www.bumbum.com.br. Bus: 415.

Lenny Niemeyer   Lenny Niemeyer, or simply Lenny, is quickly becoming one of Brazil's premier beachwear designers. Nicole Kidman ordered several of her pieces after seeing Lenny's collection in *Vanity Fair*. Her collection includes both bikinis and bathing suits, and she recently added bags and accessories. Rua Garcia d'Avila 149, Ipanema. © **021/ 2227-5537** and several other stores, including in the São Conrado Fashion Mall. www.lenny.com. br. Bus: 415.

Rosa Chá   Another Brazilian beachwear label that is now available internationally is Rosa Chá. Designs here are intricate and the materials go far beyond plain lycra. The collection also includes a good variety of one-piece suits. Note that this is not the place to come looking for bargains. São Conrado Fashion Mall, Estrada da Gávea 899, shop 221 F, Gávea. © **021/2422-3744.** www.rosacha.com.br. Bus: 593.

Books

Letras e Expressões   The Ipanaema store offers a wide selection of foreign magazines and newspapers, plus in the travel section a number of excellent books on Rio, including some beautiful coffee-table books. Internet terminals are available. The Leblon store also has a decent music collection and excellent coffee shop. Rua Visconde de Pirajá 276, Ipanema. © **021/2247-8737.** www.letraseexpressoes.com.br. Bus: 415. Also at Av. Ataúlfo de Paiva 1292 C, Leblon. © **021/2511-5085.**

Livraria da Travessa   With floor-to-ceiling shelves stuffed with books, this store positively invites hours-long browsing sessions. They have a good collection of English-language books, plus children's books and guidebooks. On the mezzanine there's a cafe that serves coffee, sweets, sandwiches, and wines. Av. Rio Branco 44, Centro. © **021/2519-9000.** www.travessa.com.br. Bus: 128. Also at Rua Visconde de Pirajá 462, Ipanema. © **021/3205-9002.** Bus: 474 or 128.

Carnaval Costumes

Casa Turuna   For those creative types who want to make their own Carnaval costume, Casa Turuna is the supplier of choice. Established in 1920, this store in Rio's downtown sells everything you can imagine: beads, feathers, sequins, fabric, headdresses, and so much more. Rua Senhor dos Passos 77, Centro. © **021/2509-3908.** www.casaturuna.com. Metrô: Central.

Fashion

For Men

Sandpiper Offering trendy casual wear that is a bit more upscale than Taco (see below) but still fun and hip, this is a great spot for shirts or informal jackets. Like most men's stores in Brazil, they add a few more splashes of color than you may be used to. Rua Santa Clara 75, Copacabana. ℃ 021/2236-7652. www.sandpiper.com.br. Metrô: Arcoverde.

Siberian For more dressy menswear, check out Siberian. The store sells its own label as well as several other Brazilian labels and focuses on quality clothing at an affordable price. Their fall and winter collection sales offer great bargains for those who live in colder climates and want to pick up some cords or long-sleeved shirts. Rua Lauro Muller 116, Shopping Rio Sul, Botafogo. ℃ 021/2543-2881. www.siberian.com.br. Bus: 119 or 415.

Taco Taco offers inexpensive, good-quality casual wear. A nice pair of jeans can be had for as little as R$40. It has good selections of casual dress shirts and T-shirts in lots of different colors. Most products are 100% Brazilian cotton. Rua Gonçalves Dias 56, Centro. ℃ 021/3970-6993. www.taco.com.br. Another branch at Av. Rio Branco 151, Centro. ℃ 021/2531-8162. Metrô: Carioca.

Toulon This is an excellent spot to pick up smart casual wear. Quality jeans, khakis, colorful long-sleeve cotton dress shirts, and T-shirts are available at reasonable prices. Rua Visconde de Piraja 135, Ipanema. ℃ 021/2239-2195. www.toulon.com.br. Bus: 474. Also at Av. N.S. de Copacabana 978, lojas B/C, Copacabana. ℃ 021/3201-1331. Bus: 474.

For Women

Folic Folic sells upscale clothing for women over 30. The clothes are sophisticated and elegant and fit beautifully. The collection ranges from casual, including jeans, to office wear and evening wear. The store will make any adjustments to your purchases for free to ensure the absolutely perfect fit. The March and August sales at Folic are legendary as prices drop up to 70%. N.S de Copacabana 690, Copacabana. ℃ 021/2548-4021. www.folic.com.br. Bus: 415.

Gang Jeans If you have always wanted to have a curvier behind, this is the store for you! *Vogue* magazine described Gang Jeans as "wonderbras for your buttocks." The jeans are incredibly tight but, thanks to a secret formula of fabrics, also very comfortable. Best of all, they are designed to enhance your best asset and boost your confidence. The collection always includes plain styles as well as some decorated with strass stones or embroidery. Shopping Rio Sul, Rua Lauro Muller 116, 2nd floor, shop 201, Botafogo. ℃ 021/2543-9264. www.gang-rio.com.br. Bus: 474.

Vertical Shopping Here you'll find 13 floors, umpteen stores, all of them for women. This downtown shopping mall features chic boutiques and ready-to-wear fashions, lingerie, swimwear, jewelry, and more, all of it shoehorned in to a tall, thin office high-rise. Elevators take you one floor to the next, and open directly into the shops. For men, nary a tobacconist or knickknack shop. Best to leave the better half at the entrance and head elsewhere. Open Monday to Saturday 9am to 8pm. Rua Sete Setembro 48, Centro. ℃ 021/2224-0697. www.verticalshopping.com.br. Metrô: Carioca.

Galleries

For many more galleries, see www.mapadasartes.com.br.

Atelier D-79 The hilltop neighborhood of Santa Teresa is a hotbed of artists and ateliers, many of whom hang their work in this gallery. The collective also organizes the

EXPLORING RIO DE JANEIRO

6

SHOPPING IN RIO

annual Open Doors days, in which Santa Teresa artists throw open their workshop doors to visitors (usually held in June). Open Wednesday to Sunday 2 to 7pm. Travessa do Oriente, 16A. © 021/2232-6572. www.chavemestra.com.br.

Ateliê Selaron   A local artist who works out of his atelier just behind the Sala Cecilia on Lapa Square, Selaron is known both for his paintings and for the interesting frames he creates. He is also the artist who created the mosaics on the famous Lapa steps. Escadaria do Convento 24 (enter off the Rua Joaquim Silva), Lapa. © 021/2242-0922. www.selaron.net. Metrô: Cinelândia.

Ateliê Tetê Cappel and Eduardo Fallero Studio   Smaller is better; this duo has made their fame creating tiny reproductions of well-known landmarks—famous tourist sites, but also small-scale versions of bars, houses, and heritage buildings. Rua Vinicius de Moraes 190, Ipanema. © 021/2522-1141. Bus: 415.

Gifts & Souvenirs

Gilson Martins   For fun, colorful, and practical souvenirs, check Gilson Martins' collection of bags. That is, bags in the broad sense, which includes purses, backpacks, wallets, and toiletry bags. His "Brasil" collection is decorated in yellow and green, often with designs of the Brazilian flag. Visconde de Piraja 462, Ipanema. © 021/2227-6178. www.gilsonmartins.com.br. Bus: 474. Also Rua Figueiredo de Magalhães 304A, Copacabana. © 021/3816-0552. Metrô: Siqueira Campos.

O Que Não Tem   The name here comes from an old Brazilian shopkeeper's expression *"So falta o que não tem"* which translates as "We only lack what we don't have." That's little enough, as this largest of souvenir stores stocks nearly everything: woodcarvings, Bahian dolls, T-shirts, mugs, and Brazilian bikinis, as well as somewhat tacky original paintings and craftsmanlike semiprecious jewelry, all at the slightly inflated prices tourists expect. There's a smaller, sister store, **Tem Mas Acabou,** Rua Cosme Velho 535A (© 021/2285-5436), near the Corcovado tram station. Av. N.S. de Copacabana 687A, loja C. © 021/2541-2587. Metrô: Cardeal Arcoverde.

Jewelry

Amsterdam Sauer   This Ipanema location of Brazil's best-known name for gems, jewelry, and semiprecious and precious stones houses both a store and a museum; it's worth a visit even if you don't plan to buy. The museum shows off many of Mr. Sauer's original finds when he first came to Brazil in 1940 and started working as a miner, gem-ologist, geologist, and finally as a jeweler. The store offers a wide range of jewelry and loose gemstones including emeralds, aquamarines, imperial topaz (mined only in Brazil), tourmalines, citrines, and Brazilian opals. The staff is friendly and low-pressure. Items can be delivered to your hotel. Rua Visconde de Piraja 484, Ipanema. © 021/2279-6237. www.amsterdamsauer.com. Bus: 474.

Arte Coletiva by Silvia Blumberg   This award-winning designer has various collections: One uses Brazilian stones, another combines precious metals with Amazon seeds and nuts. Her creations range from the loud, flamboyant, and fun to elegant and discreet. If Silvia's in, you'll get to hear the story behind each of her pieces. Visconde de Pirajá 300, store 214, Ipanema. © 021/2513-4181. www.silviablumberg.com.br. Bus: 474.

H. Stern   Come within sniffing distance of a Rio hotel and you'll receive an invitation to visit an H. Stern store, transportation complimentary. Or you can phone a store and they'll be pleased to come pick you up. (I once read a story about a man who saved on cab fare by calling the H. Stern store nearest his destination whenever he went out. He paid nothing for taxis, but wound up buying his girlfriend a very expensive ring.) The store in Ipanema is the world headquarters. Specializing in precious and semiprecious stones, the company also owns mines and polishing shops, guaranteeing the quality of their products from start to finish. Rua Visconde de Pirajá 490, Ipanema. © 021/2274-3447. www.hstern.com.br. Bus: 474.

Leather Goods

Mala Amada   Run out of space for all your souvenirs? Mala Amada has an excellent selection of handbags, purses, briefcases, and wallets. All are made with high-quality Brazilian leather and produced in the store's own factory. Rua Visconde de Piraja 550, Ipanema. © 021/2239-8648. www.malaamada.com.br. Bus: 474. Also Rua Sete de Setermbro 88, Centro. © 021/3852-1827. Metrô: Carioca.

Malls & Shopping Centers

Botafogo Praia Shopping   The mall's spread out over seven floors, which makes for a lot of escalator time, but that's the only drawback. There's an excellent selection of clothing stores, and the Kodak Express shop on the ground floor for your photo needs. The seventh-floor food court has a pair of excellent restaurants (Kotobuki [p. 90], Emporium Pax), with gorgeous views of Botafogo beach and the Pão de Açúcar. Praia de Botafogo 400, Botafogo. © 021/3171-9872. www.botafogopraiashopping.com.br. Metrô: Botafogo.

Rio Sul   One of the largest and most popular malls in the city, Rio Sul is very accessible, located in Botafogo just before the tunnel that goes to Copacabana. With over 450 stores, a movie theater, and an excellent food court, Rio Sul is always busy and a great place to get a feel for Brazilian fashion and prices. Rua Lauro Muller 116, Botafogo. © 021/2122-8070. www.riosul.com.br. Bus: 119 or 474.

São Conrado Fashion Mall   The favorite haunt for Rio's well-heeled and fashion-conscious shoppers. If you are up on Brazilian movie stars and models, this will be the place to spot them! Over 150 stores carry national and international designers. The mall's food court is the best in town with a number of high-end restaurants. Estrada da Gávea 899, São Conrado. © 021/2144-4444. www.scfashionmall.com.br. Bus: 178.

Shopping Leblon   Rio's newest mall sits right on the edge of Leblon and Ipanema and offers an elegant shopping experience. The mall offers a good selection of upscale stores and labels but certainly not as high-end as the São Conrado Fashion Mall. The excellent food court has views of the lagoon and the Corcovado. Rua Afrânio de Melo 290, Leblon. © 021/3138-8000. www.shoppingleblon.com.br. Bus: 415.

Markets

Feira Hippie Ipanema   In the '60s, this square was the hippie hangout in Rio, and it's still a fun place to browse for arts and crafts. Open every Sunday, rain or shine, 8am to 6pm. Praça General Osorio (intersection of Rua Teixeira de Melo and Rua Visconde de Pirajá). No phone. www.feirahippieipanema.com. Bus: 474.

Feira do Rio Antigo (Lapa Antique Market)   Every first Saturday of the month, the Rua do Lavradio becomes a large bustling outdoor antique market. Although not quite garage-sale prices, good bargains can still be had. Of course, an event in Lapa wouldn't be complete without samba; there are live music performances in the afternoon. Arrive early if you are serious about bargain hunting. Rua do Lavradio, Lapa. Bus: 464.

Feirarte   If you need to grab some last-minute souvenirs, the two Feirarte markets in Copacabana are ideal. The smaller market operates only on the weekends in front of the

Lido park (cross street Rua Rodolfo Dantas). The larger market runs every night from 6pm to 1am on the median, opposite Rua Djalma Ulrich. On offer is the standard array of souvenirs such as T-shirts, jewelry, leatherwork, ceramics, precious stones, bikinis, and paintings. Bus: 119 or 415.

Music

Modern Sound   Music buffs will think they have died and gone to heaven. This store houses an amazing collection of music. The staff is very knowledgeable and happy to help, but half the fun is browsing through the large wooden CD bins. In the evenings, the store is often used as a small concert venue. To check the programming go to their website and look under "Allegro Bistrô Musical" for details. Rua Barata Ribeiro 502, Copacabana. ✆ 021/2548-5005. www.modernsound.com.br. Bus: 415.

Toca de Vinicius (Finds)   In the heart of Ipanema, this small temple is dedicated to the god of bossa nova, poet and composer Vinicius de Moraes. The second floor even houses a tiny shrine with original manuscripts, photos, even a lock of hair from the great poet himself. Anything related to bossa nova can be found in this tiny store: an impressive collection of CDs and vinyl, songbooks, and (mostly Portuguese) books and magazines on the smooth and mellow sounds of Brazil. Rua Vinicius de Moraes 129, Ipanema. ✆ 021/2247-5227. www.tocadovinicius.com.br. Bus: 474.

Musical Instruments

The *berimbau,* that wooden string instrument from Bahia, is one of Brazil's most popular souvenirs, but for music lovers there are many more interesting instruments to choose from (most of which are far more portable). The Rua da Carioca has turned into Music Store Central with at least five shops grouped together on its short length. Look for rattles that fit in the palm of your hand, or else pick up a tambourine or small set of drums. The *agôgô* is an interesting-looking double bell used to keep a beat. Guitar players will love the *cavaquinho,* a Brazilian mandolin. It's what gives samba its distinctive twang. For these and more visit **Musical Carioca,** Rua da Carioca 89 (✆ 021/3814-3400; www.musicalcarioca.com.br); **Casa Oliveira Musicais,** Rua da Carioca 70 (✆ 021/2252-5636); or **Guitarra Prata,** Rua da Carioca 37 (✆ 021/2262-9659; www.aguitarradeprata.com.br). Metrô: Largo da Carioca.

Perfume

O Boticario   This Brazilian success story is known for its fragrances made with flowers and herbs. In recent years the store has branched out (à la the Body Shop) to include skin-care products and makeup, but the most popular items remain the lightly scented perfumes and soaps for men, women, and children. Various locations including Rua Buenos Aires 220, Centro. ✆ 021/3970-1232. www.boticario.com.br. Metrô: Uruguaiana.

Shoes

Arezzo   If Carioca women had to choose a favorite shoe store, it would undoubtedly be Arezzo. This company always seems to stay just a step ahead of the trends without being too avant-garde, and the prices are reasonable. It also sells a great selection of high-quality leather purses. Various locations, including Rio Sul and Rua Visconde de Pirajá 295, Ipanema. ✆ 021/2513-0783. www.arezzo.com.br. Bus: 415.

Constança Bastos   Consider yourself a real shoe connoisseur if you have already heard of Constança Bastos, the Manolo Blahnik of Brazil. This young designer's shoes are taking are perfect for elegant evening wear. Stars like Charlize Theron and Cameron Diaz

have recently worn her creations. Constança's latest project has been the creation of a **135**
more affordable, casual label called Peach. www.constancabasto.com.br. Various locations, including the São Conrado Fashion Mall, ✆ **021/2422-0355,** bus: 178; Shopping Leblon, ✆ **021/2511-8801,** bus: 415; the Peach label can be found at the Rio Sul, Av. Lauro Muller 116, ✆ **021/2295-5632,** bus: 119.

Mr. Cat Mr. Cat goes for classic designs, business as well as evening wear, for men and women. All shoes are made of high-quality Brazilian leather. Prices are very reasonable, ranging from R$80 to R$150 for a pair of top-quality leather men's dress shoes. Rua Visconde de Piraja 414, loja D, Ipanema. ✆ **021/2523-4645.** www.mrcat.com.br. Bus: 474. Another branch at Rua Gonçalves Dias 18, lojas D, E, Centro. ✆ **021/2509-1163.** Metrô: Carioca.

Sporting Goods
Galeria River Cool central; this is not just one shop but a minimall with at least a dozen sports and outdoor stores that sell skateboards, surf gear, inline skates, and climbing equipment as well as accessories such as clothing, sunglasses, and hiking boots. A great place to pick up tips on where to go, lessons, and local hangouts. Galeria River, Rua Francisco Otaviano, Ipanema. www.galeriariver.com.br. Bus: 128.

Surf Shops
Hot Coast One of the few surf stores that stocks rentals, Hot Coast is conveniently close to the best surf spot in Ipanema, Arpoador beach. It's open Monday through Saturday only, so you'll need to book ahead if you want to surf over the weekend. Rentals range from R$25 to R$60 for a short board, fun board, or long board. Galeria River, Rua Francisco Otaviano 67, loja 12, Ipanema. ✆ **021/2287-9388.** Bus: 128.

11 RIO AFTER DARK

It's an open question whether Cariocas possess some hidden nightlife gene or whether they've trained themselves for decadence through years and years of practice. Whatever the case, Rio has a lot to keep you busy at night. It starts early and continues very late. Cariocas themselves don't make a big deal about a night on the town: They're happy either heading out for beers or dancing to *forró* music or eating shrimp in some hole-in-the-wall botequim. However, if you as a visitor want to go for the quintessential Rio experience, you have to learn to pace yourself. Whether you spend the day seeking out sights or on the beach, head back to your hotel in the afternoon for a wee nap. Trust me, this will be the key to making it through the night. Once you're up again, head out in the cool early evening for a coconut juice on the beach. Sip it while watching the sunset (in summer around 8pm), then around 9pm stroll over to a patio for a predinner drink, or maybe walk along the pathway by the waterfront in Copa or Ipanema and find a table at one of the new beachfront kiosks. Plan to have dinner around 10pm, to be ready for your evening of dancing around midnight or 1am. (Most places don't even open until 11pm.) Your options at this point depend on the day and the time of year. If you're in Rio between September and Carnaval, attending one of the **samba school rehearsals** on Saturday night is a must. Otherwise, on a Thursday night see who's playing at some of the hip samba spots in Lapa like the **Rio Scenarium, Carioca da Gema,** or the **Centro Cultural Carioca.** Or just enjoy the scene by the Arcos de Lapa on a Friday night. Of course, there are a number of discos and bars to choose from, and then there are always the botequins, Rio's neighborhood bars. Wherever you wind up, after 3 or 4 hours dancing

> ### (Fun Facts) Words to Help You Through the Night
>
> Here's some vocabulary to help you decipher the listings in the newspapers.
>
> Under *Música* or *Show* you will find the listings for live music. Lovers of Brazilian music should look for anything under *Forró, MPB (música popular brasileira), Bossa Nova, Choro, Pagode,* or *Samba.* Listings under *Pista* refer to events at nightclubs or discos. Most listings will include the price of admission: *Couvert* is the cover charge and *consumação* states the drink minimum. It is quite common to have two rates, one for women *(mulher)* and one for men *(homem),* the latter usually paying more.
>
> Children's programs are listed under *Infantil* or *Para Crianças.* Many dance clubs offer a matinee program on Saturdays or Sundays for teenagers. The days of the week are given in abbreviations: *seg* or *2a* (Mon), *ter* or *3a* (Tues), *qua* or *4a* (Wed), *qui* or *5a* (Thurs), *sex* or *6a* (Fri), *sab* (Sat), and *dom* (Sun).

you may find yourself getting peckish. For a late-night or early-morning snack in Lapa, stop in for some pizza at the lovely upstairs **Pizzaria Carioca da Gema,** Av. Mem de Sá 77 (© **021/3970-1281;** www.barcariocadagema.com.br), open until at least 4am on weekends. In Leblon, **Pizzeria Guanabara** and **Jobi** are both open until at least 5am on weekends. By the time they throw you out, it'll just be time to wander down to the beach and watch the sunrise, ready for a new morning—and another night—in Rio.

To find out more about listings for arts and entertainment, check the Friday editions of the *O Globo* (www.oglobo.com.br), *O Dia* (www.odia.com.br), or *Jornal do Brasil* (http://jbonline.terra.com.br) newspapers. Available at all newsstands, all three publish a detailed weekly calendar of events, including nightlife, performing arts, concerts, and other events in the city. The Rio tourism agency **Riotur** also publishes a detailed booklet of events in English and Portuguese called *Guia do Rio* or *Rio Guide,* available at its main information center at Av. Princesa Isabel 183 in Copacabana, or call **Alô Rio** at © **021/ 2542-8080** or 0800/707-1888 for information on events around town; they keep an updated list and their staff speak English.

THE PERFORMING ARTS

The performing-arts season in Brazil runs from early April until early December. April is a particularly good time—the equivalent of the Northern Hemisphere's September—as theaters and companies unveil their programs and kick off their season premières.

Centro Cultural do Banco do Brasil   The two theaters in the center host regular recitals, concerts, dance performances, film, and Portuguese-language theater. There are also regular photography and art exhibits in the center's small exhibition rooms. Check the website for more information. Rua Primeiro de Março 66, Centro. © **021/3808-2007.** www. cultura-e.com.br. Admission varies from free–R$30. Exhibits are always free. Metrô: Uruguaiana.

Sala Cecelia Meireles   This lovely heritage building on the Largo da Lapa is a very popular venue for classical music, offering concerts and recitals. There's also often more

modern Brazilian rhythms such as bossa nova, jazz, and *choro*. Largo da Lapa 47, Centro.
📞 021/2224-3913. www.salaceciliameireles.com.br. Ticket prices R$20–R$80. Metrô: Cinelândia.

Teatro Municipal Brazil's prime venue for the performing arts, the elegant Parisian-style Teatro Municipal stages everything from opera to ballet to symphony concerts. The theater's ballet corps and symphony orchestra perform regularly throughout the year, and the theater also hosts many visiting companies. Besides the formal programming, the theater also offers an inexpensive noon-hour opera series *(opera do meio-dia)* and Sunday morning concerts starting at 11am for R$5. Praça Marechal Floriano s/n, Centro. 📞 021/2332-9195. www.theatromunicipal.rj.gov.br. Ticket prices range from R$15–R$70 on most performances. Metrô: Cinelândia.

Teatro Rival This small theater has just received a major overhaul and is a great venue for seeing local and popular national acts, mostly of MPB. Ticket prices are quite reasonable. You may be looking at the next Marisa Monte or other of Brazil's many talented performers who haven't made it big internationally. Rua Alvaro Alvim 33, Centro. 📞 021/2240-4469. www.rivalbr.com.br. Ticket prices R$10–R$60. Metrô: Cinelândia.

MUSIC & DANCE CLUBS

If you're a fan of samba, check out the website **www.samba-choro.com.br** for weekly listings of all the clubs in Rio (and São Paulo) offering live samba. Check out the **Rio Hiking** website (www.riohiking.com.br) for tips on where to catch live music or just grab a drink and meet people. (Click on "Rio Hints.") If you don't like going out by yourself, you can also book a Rio Hiking Nightlife Tour to some of the hippest places around for R$120 (📞 021/2552-9204), a great way to meet other travelers as well.

In most clubs and discos you can expect to pay a cover charge. Women usually pay less than men; you'll see the two prices listed at the door. Often there is also a drink minimum which can go up as high as R$120 at upscale Ipanema clubs. In most venues you are handed a paper card or electronic swipe card upon entry that is to be used to record all your purchases. The bill is then settled when you leave. A 10% service charge will be included, and a tip on top of that is not required. Hang on to your card for dear life. If you lose it you'll be charged an astronomical fee.

Many clubs have a restricted VIP area overlooking the dance floor, usually with comfortable couches or tables. The definition of VIP varies from club to club: Sometimes it's for members only, sometimes you can get in if you call and reserve ahead of time, and sometimes all that's required is paying a higher drink minimum. The advantage of being in the VIP area is you get a guaranteed seat in an area off-limits to most of the rest of the crowd, allowing you to leave your drinks, jackets, or purses at your table while you're dancing.

Traditional Brazilian Music

Club Democraticos This is an old-style dance hall with a vast wood floor and a long stage where a dozen or so musicians strum and pluck and sing the sounds of samba. It gets packed here, but couples on the dance floor still strut their stuff. For those not dancing there are lots of tables, and balcony windows that look out over the street. Friday and Saturday 9pm to 4am. Rua Riachuelo 91, Lapa. 📞 021/2292-5504. www.clubedosdemocraticos.com.br. Cover R$15–R$25. Bus: 464.

Elite One popular *gafieira,* or traditional dance hall, is the Elite, tucked in behind an arcade of Romanesque arches on the second floor of a little pink-and-plaster gem of a

> **Moments**   **The Gafieira of Days Gone By**
>
> The traditional ballroom dance halls known as *gafieiras* once defined the Carioca nightlife scene. Still worth a visit even if you can't dance, *gafieiras* are a legacy of the elegant days of old, when couples would dress for the occasion and everyone knew the steps. Most folks don't show up in suits or ball gowns anymore, but couples still dance with elegance and the tunes are unmistakably Brazilian: samba, *pagode*, a bit of rumba or foxtrot, and nowadays lots of *forró*.

colonial building in Centro. Recently, Elite has begun programming more live music—samba, *forró*, even salsa—attracting a younger crowd, but the old die-hard dancers still show, making for an intriguing mix. Only open Friday (after 7pm), Saturday (after 10pm), and Sunday (after 6pm). Rua Frei Caneca 4, Centro. ✆ 021/2232-3217. www.gafieira elite.com. Cover R$15. Taxi recommended.

Estudantina   Only open on Friday and Saturday, the *gafieira* Estudantina is another mainstay on the Carioca ballroom scene. Older couples in elegant white linen suits and billowing skirts strut their stuff with elegance and style. Students of the dance school come and show off, but newcomers and novices are made to feel equally welcome. A live samba band plays every weekend. Doors open at 7pm. Arrive early to grab a table. Praça Tiradentes 79, Centro. ✆ 021/2232-1149. Cover R$10–R$15. Bus: 125 to Praça Tiradentes.

Plataforma 1 **Overrated**   Ah, the tourist trap. Every city has one. Some are fun in a tacky kind of way. This one should be labeled with a radioactive sticker reading AVOID. What's offered is supposedly a song-and-dance showcase of Brazilian culture, but the reality is a mediocre supper served up with a glitzy Vegas-style show. The whole slick and packaged product has all the spontaneity and charm of a McDonald's Big Mac combo—and about as much connection to Brazilian culture. Rua Adalberto Ferreira 32, Leblon. ✆ 021/2274-4022. www.plataforma.com. Admission price depends on whom you book through. Minimum price R$120. Bus: 415.

Samba School Rehearsals   If you are in Rio in the period from September up to Carnaval, you can attend a samba school rehearsal to get a feel for the event and the rhythms. Although located in the poorer neighborhoods away from the Zona Sul, a number of the *quadras* (where the rehearsals are held) are very accessible and just a short taxi ride away (for more information see "Watching a Rehearsal," p. 152). Mangueira, Salgueiro, Vila Isabel, Viradouro, and Rocinha are easy to get to by taxi from the Zona Sul and are used to receiving foreign visitors.

Live Music

Aside from these listings, many small *chopperias* and botequins (see "Bars & Pubs," below) will often have a singer or small combo playing. Usually there's a small cover charge (*couvert* in Portuguese) for this entertainment. By sitting down and listening you're agreeing to foot the bill. The fee is automatically added to your tab. If you want to know what the *couvert* is before deciding to stay, simply ask the waiter. The key phrase is *"Quanto é o couvert?"* or "How much is the cover?"

Café Sacrilégio **Finds**   Located next door to Carioca da Gema, the Café Sacrilégio could be its twin. The venues look similar—both are renovated heritage homes—and

> ### (Finds) The New Lapa—Gamboa
>
> Just beyond the Praça Mauá, close to the port, lies one of Rio's older neighborhoods, Gamboa. It features lovely 19th-century buildings, pretty squares, and a fascinating history (it served as Rio's slave market and was also the likely birthplace of samba). It's also on the cusp of an urban revival similar to Lapa's 10 to 15 years ago. The pioneer was **Trapiche Gamboa,** Rua Sacadura Cabral 155 (𝄞 021/2516-0868; www.trapichegamboa.com.br; closed Sun–Mon). Taking up a gorgeous three-story building from 1856, it has been transformed into a fabulous live-music venue playing, what else, samba. More recent newcomers are the **Week,** Rua Sacadura Cabral 154 (𝄞 021/2253-1020; www.theweek.com.br), Rio's hottest new gay dance club, and **Sacadura,** Rua Sacadura Cabral 147 (𝄞 021/2233-0378; www.sacadura.com.br), an upscale live-music venue. Keep an eye on this area as new places seem to open up every couple of months.

both house excellent samba bands. It's hard to say which one is better. We usually poke our heads in, listen to the music, and pick the one that we like best. Either way it's hard to go wrong. Best of all, Café Sacrilégio is open every night of the week. Rua Mem de Sá 81, Lapa. 𝄞 021/3970-1461. www.sacrilegio.com.br. Cover usually R$15–R$20. Bus: 464.

Canecão   It's old and tattered but it's also got tradition. Everyone who's anyone in Brazilian music has played this aging 3,000-person auditorium, from Djavan to Milton Nascimento to Gal Costa. The best sections in the house are the tables in Section A and the **balcão nobre.** These give you great views of the stage and a chance to have a drink or a snack. Avoid the *poltronas* (numbered seats) as these have horrible side views of the stage. The box office and theater are just across the street from the Rio Sul shopping center. Av. Venceslau Brás 215, Botafogo. 𝄞 021/2543-1241. www.canecao.com.br. Ticket prices range R$150–R$250 for front-row seats at the big-ticket shows. Bus: 474 to Rio Sul.

Carioca da Gema   One of the best little venues in town, Carioca da Gema offers all samba all the time. Even on weeknights when many other places are closed or slow, Carioca da Gema is often hopping. The busy nights are Friday and Saturday when latecomers will be left with standing room only. The show normally kicks off at 9pm, so come early if you want to grab a spot close to the stage and enjoy a bite to eat while waiting for things to heat up. Open Monday through Saturday. Rua Mem de Sá 79, Lapa. 𝄞 021/2221-0043. Cover varies but is rarely more than R$18. Bus: 464.

Centro Cultural Carioca ★★ (Finds)   This beautifully restored building from the 1920s (just off the Praça Tiradentes) makes a great live-music venue. Housed on the second floor, the Centro Cultural hosts local musicians and big names who specialize in samba, MPB, *choro,* and *gafieira.* The room is cozy and intimate, and guests sit at small tables to watch the shows. No shows on Sunday, usually. Rua do Teatro, Centro. 𝄞 021/2252-6468. www.centroculturalcarioca.com.br. Cover varies, usually R$15–R$20. Bus: 125 to Praça Tiradentes.

Cinemathèque JamClub   With Botafogo's revived nightlife scene it was only a matter of time before it would produce a decent live-music venue and the JamClub is all that. With room for only 150 patrons, it is intimate and small and still manages to draw big names on the local music scene. Both Preta Gil (Gilberto Gil's daughter) and Martinalia are regular performers here. The outside area has a lovely patio and bar, perfect for a pre- or postconcert bite or drink. Rua Voluntários da Pátria 53, Botafogo. ⓒ **021/2579-6736.** Cover R$15–R$30. Metrô: Botafogo.

Circo Voador   This large tentlike structure (the name translates as "flying circus") is located right beneath the aqueduct in Lapa. Modeled after the original '80s *Circo* that was the venue for avant-garde, up-and-coming artists, the new Circo Voador is one of the most eclectic venues in town, offering everything from samba and *pagode,* to house and funk. It's a great venue. The open structure is perfect for Rio's tropical climate and a large outdoor patio allows you plenty of space to take in the music under the stars, with the rambling of the streetcar on the arches overhead for company. Rua dos Arcos s/n, Lapa. ⓒ **021/2533-0354.** www.circovoador.com.br. Cover depends on event but ranges R$10–R$60. Bus: 464.

Espaço Rio Carioca ★★   The Casas Casadas, a row of meticulously restored 19th-century town houses, feature a bookstore, cafe, bar, bistro, and live-music venue. The small intimate concert room is perfect for taking in some local bossa nova, MPB, or jazz acts. Shows take place Wednesday to Saturday, starting around 8pm. Afterward, enjoy a drink or an excellent meal on the upstairs terrace. The cafe/bookstore is open Tuesday to Sunday noon to 10pm; the bistro is open Tuesday to Friday 6pm to midnight and Saturday and Sunday noon to midnight. Rua das Laranjeiras 307 (corner of Rua Leite Leal), Laranjeiras. ⓒ **021/2225-7332.** www.espacoriocarioca.com.br. Bus: 184.

Estrela da Lapa   Here is proof that Lapa's appeal extends beyond the young and bohemian. This elegant star in the neighborhood caters to the moneyed 35-and-older Zona Sul crowd. Music varies from jazz to salsa, samba, swing, and even instrumental. The venue—a restored Lapa mansion—is lovely, and though the stage is small, three levels of seating make for enough room even on busy nights. Rua Mem de Sá 69. ⓒ **021/ 2507-6686.** www.estreladalapa.com.br. Cover R$10–R$30. Bus: 464.

Mas Será o Benedito   Lapa's newest live samba venue takes up three floors of a big red renovated Lapa mansion: The first floor is a *pé sujo* bar, floor two is for pool, and on the third floor there's another bar, a dance floor, a stage, and live samba. It's a great space, good music, and an agreeable crowd. Plus there's cold chopp draft and a good menu of snacks and munchies. Av. Gomes Freire 599, Lapa. ⓒ **021/2232-9000.** www.seraobeneidto.com. Cover usually R$15–R$20. Bus: 464.

Rio Scenarium ★★★ Ⓞⓥⓔⓡⓡⓐⓣⓔⓓ   It may seem like a contradiction to give the Rio Scenarium both three stars and an overrated at the same time but let me explain. The Rio Scenarium is probably the most beautiful bar in Rio. Located in a renovated warehouse on the edge of Lapa, this antiques-store-turned-bar is one of the places that played a big role in reviving Lapa's nightlife several years ago when there were few classy options available. Now, however, I'd say the Rio Scenarium is a victim of its own success. Recommended by every single guidebook and travel article about Rio, the place is often packed with more gringos (and women who like gringos) than locals. Although still worth seeing, don't make this your only stop when exploring Lapa's music scene. Rua do Lavradio 20, Centro. ⓒ **021/2233-3239.** www.rioscenarium.com.br. Cover R$20–R$25. Taxi recommended.

Vivo Rio ★★★   One of Rio's newest concert venues, the Vivo Rio is located right next to the Museu de Arte Moderno on Rio's downtown waterfront. Similar in size to the Canecão, it has been specializing in big-name concerts, with both Brazilian and foreign artists, with people like B.B. King, Maria Bethania, and Gilberto Gil. The only drawback here is the high ticket prices—R$180 or more for a decent seat is not unheard of in this

Nightlife Zones: Lapa

Bars and clubs have their moments, and so do neighborhoods. Lapa is definitely on the up again. In the roaring '20s Lapa's vibrant nightlife earned it the nickname "Montmartre of the Tropics." It fell on hard times in the '50s and '60s, but in the last few years Lapa has undergone a major revival as even Cariocas from trendy Ipanema and Leblon come here to party. Things hop almost every night of the week, but the best days are Thursday, Friday, and Saturday. Lapa's nightlife consists of two different kinds of experiences. There are the carefully preserved heritage buildings turned music venues such as Carioca da Gema, Estrela da Lapa, Rio Scenarium, and Café Sacrilégio that offer some of the best samba in town. Then there is the much grittier street scene, revolving around the Rua da Lapa and the parallel running Rua Joaquim Silva. These two streets are a major *point* (definition of *point* on p. 146) where mostly young people come to drink, chat, flirt, and dance. The small music venues on the Rua Joaquim Silva are anything but nicely renovated (some are big-time sleazy), but half the fun is walking around and poking your head in (cover rarely exceeds R$5). In a 2-block range you will hear anything from reggae to samba to *brega*, hip-hop, funk, and salsa. The square in front of the arches is packed with food and drink stalls. As long as you stick to the main streets that have lots of people on them the area is quite safe at night.

venue. Rua Infante Dom Henrique, Centro, next to the Museu de Arte Moderna. ℰ 021/2272-2900. www.vivorio.com.br. Cover R$60–R$300. Taxi recommended.

Dance Clubs

Baronneti　One of the most happening dance clubs in Rio, Baronneti attracts a well-to-do and attractive crowd in their 20s to 40s. Part of their secret is the minimum drink requirement; at a stiff R$70 minimum for guys on Saturdays, there's no rubbing elbows with the riffraff here. What you get is a fine-looking classy upscale club, two floors of fabulous dance music to dance the night away, plenty of couches, and a chill-out space. Rua Barão da Torre 354, Ipanema. ℰ 021/2247-9100. www.baronneti.com.br. Drink minimum women R$20–R$50, men R$50–R$80. Bus: 474.

Bunker　Not everyone swoons to bossa nova or the upbeat sounds of samba and *forró*. At Bunker 94, Rio's young and pierced move to the pounding sounds of techno, hip-hop, trance, and house as spun by three different DJs on three different dance floors. This is a gay-friendly club. Open Thursday through Saturday after 11pm. Rua Raul Pompeia 94, Copacabana. ℰ 021/2247-8724. Cover R$15–R$25. Bus: 415.

Fosfobox　Fosfobox is Copacabana's trendy *club du jour*, or rather *de nuit*. Located in a small basement off Rua Siqueira Campos, the club only has room for about 150, who hear discs spun by a variety of DJs. On Thursday it's rock, Friday and Saturday are house and techno. Open Wednesday through Sunday. Rua Siqueira Campos 143, 22A basement, Copacabana. ℰ 021/2548-7498. www.fosfobox.com.br. Cover R$20. Metrô: Siqueira Campos.

Ladies of the Night . . . & Day

They've been an integral part of the neighborhood since the '40s, the working girls and their customers who occupy selected slices of the Copacabana waterfront. The good news is that these places are not dangerous or even overly sleazy. Indeed, it can be interesting observing the hustle and bustle and to and fro, though the atmosphere is not exactly family entertainment (unless you come from a very odd family). Regular hangouts for sex tourists and working women include the Balcony Bar and the Lido square, which is also home to a number of strip clubs. This area is between the Copacabana Palace and the Avenida Prado Junior, Copa's main drive-by thoroughfare for street prostitutes. Farther down the waterfront by the Help disco, the Terraço Atlantico is where johns and hookers hook up in the afternoon and early evening. For those who like people-watching it can make for a fascinating scene. The area around the Rio Othon Hotel is another popular meeting place. Daytime contacts are made at the Meia Petaca patio or else out on the beach while working on that tan line.

Help (Overrated) Often recommended by hotel concierges to (sometimes unsuspecting) male visitors, Help is where gringo travelers and Brazilian working girls meet. No self-respecting Carioca woman would be seen in the place, which means that beautiful dark-eyed lovely with whom you're getting on so well with is definitely expecting payment. Most negotiate their rates at the start of the evening, just to keep everything upfront. Recently the city announced it would be closing Help and replacing it with a museum, but so far the club remains open. Av. Atlântica 3432, Copacabana. © 021/2522-1296. www. discoteca-help.com. Cover R$25–R$50. Metrô: Cardeal Arcoverde.

Melt Melt is a great unpretentious club that has been making quite a name for itself with excellent live music by a variety of interesting artists. Open daily, the small club offers a range of music, varying from hip-hop to salsa, dance, or samba-rock, and in the summer months samba on Sunday. Rua Rita Ludolf 47, Leblon. © 021/2249-9309. www.melt bar.com.br. Cover R$15–R$40. Bus: 415.

Nuth A lovely, very upscale club in Lagoa, Nuth has a small restaurant upstairs, an outdoor patio section, and an indoor dance floor featuring lounge music early on and dance beats as the night goes on. Arrive early (before 10pm) if you want to make it past the doormen—VIPs and beautiful women get preference, and if you're not one of these, you may find yourself exiled to a long wait in the outside line. Open Tuesday through Saturday after 7pm to 4am. Av. Epitacio Pessoa 1244, Lagoa. © 021/3575-6850. www.nuth. com.br. Cover R$30–R$50. Bus: 415.

00 Pronounced *zero-zero,* this nightclub is located right next to the Planetarium in Gávea. The club has a large outdoor deck with wooden benches and comfortable recliners, perfect for those warm summer evenings. The inside space is divided into a restaurant area and a small bar and dance floor. The dance floor, alas, is not only small but also located in front of the bathroom doors. However, the fabulous outside space and beautiful

(Moments) The Culture of Botequins

Botequins are to Rio what pubs are to London and cafes are to Paris: the spot where locals gather, be it for end-of-day drinks or impassioned late-night philosophizing. Brazilians refer to botequins as *pé sujos*—literally "dirty feet"—meaning they're nothing fancy, often just plastic tables and fluorescent lights (though rich in character and local flavor). Some botequins have developed into popular nightlife attractions, offering live music and excellent food, and drawing crowds from all over the city. But most botequins remain small, not very fancy watering holes where one can kick back with a cold beer, have some snacks, and catch up with the latest gossip.

people make up for that. Still, 00 is better as a bar than a club. Rua Padre Leonel France 240, Gávea. ✆ 021/2540-8041. www.00site.com.br. Cover R$20–R$30. Taxi recommended.

Bars & Pubs

There are various ways that bar and restaurant owners can extract money from guests: One of them is the *couvert*. The *couvert* in restaurants used to refer to the small appetizer plate that is served when you first arrive—olives, bread and butter, pâté, and the like. Nowadays it's also the name given to a live-music fee. If the bar has a musician playing, chances are something between R$2 and R$10 per person or per table will be added to your bill. Always ask when going into a restaurant or bar with live music if there is a cover or *"couvert para a música,"* to avoid any surprises when your bill comes.

Botequins

Arco do Teles Tucked away in an alley just off Praça XV, the Arco do Teles, which looks like a movie set of old Rio, is an area with dozens of bars. Perfectly preserved colonial two-stories are set on narrow cobblestone streets lined with restaurants and cafes. Though it's a good place for a quick lunch, prime time is after work hours, especially on Thursday and Friday. Office workers flock here to grab a few cold chopps and catch some music before heading home. Often they forget to go home. As the evening wears on, tables and chairs take over the alley, creating a large impromptu patio—it's one of the best people-watching spots in town. With over 15 bars and botequins it doesn't matter which one you pick. If you get there after 10pm you'll be lucky to find a seat at all. Travessa do Comércio, Arco do Teles (from the Praça XV, facing toward the bay, you will see the arch that marks the entrance to the alley on your left). Bus: 110 or 415.

Belmonte An old-fashioned botequim with the bright lights, dark-wood furniture and tile floors, the Belmonte serves up great beer, sandwiches, and snacks at almost any time of the day, but in the evenings and on weekend afternoons things get really hopping: Patrons spill out on the sidewalk, making do with improvised tables made out of barrels. It's now a local chain with brand-new old-fashioned Belmontes in Lagoa, Ipanema, and Copacabana, but the Flamengo Belmonte remains the best. Praia do Flamengo 300, Flamengo. ✆ 021/2552-3349. www.botecobelmonte.com.br. Bus: 464.

Bip Bip Another internationally acclaimed botequim—the Parisian daily *Le Monde* featured this tiny bar on its front page—Bip Bip owes its fame to an outstanding musical program. Tuesday and Sunday nights are the best evenings to catch some great samba or

Finds   The Kiosks of Lagoa

They began as lowly concession stands, but the kiosks around the Lagoa Rodrigo de Freitas have evolved into a fun, casual nightlife scene. Known in Portuguese as *quiosques da Lagoa,* they're the perfect place to stroll, munch, drink, and people-watch. Set at regular intervals along the pleasant green path that girdles the Lagoa, the kiosks range in size and quality from simple snack stands to full-fledged restaurants and entertainment centers. The cuisine ranges from Brazilian basic to Lebanese, Japanese, or Italian, while the entertainment ranges from a boombox on volume "11" to excellent live bands (some of which charge a small cover). The thickest concentration of kiosks begins opposite the Jockey Club. Another grouping clusters close to the Parque da Catacumba at the Ipanema and back end of Copacabana of the Lagoa. They're open year-round, but they're especially popular in summer; weekday hours are from 6pm onward—they get busy around 10pm—and on weekends from noon onward. A full loop around the Lagoa is 7.5km (4^1/$_2$ miles), making for a pleasant 2-hour walk. For an interactive map of all the kiosks, showing opening hours, types of cuisine and music, and opening hours, see **www.lagoarodrigodefreitas.com.br**.

pagode (a more mellow kind of samba); it's not unusual to see some Brazilian greats such as Beth Carvalho, Nelson Sargento, Walter Alfaiate, and others come out to sing and play. Owner Alfredo Melo—Alfredinho to most everyone—tries to keep his neighbors happy, so on Sunday the live music winds down early at 10pm. The bar stays open daily until 1am. Rua Almirante Gonçalves 50, Copacabana. (✆) **021/2267-9696.** Bus: 432.

Bracarense   Once voted the best botequim in town—the *New York Times* even proclaimed it the best in Brazil—Bracarense may be suffering a bit from its own success. On Saturday when the botequim is packed, service often slows to a crawl. Still, Bracarense's beer remains top-shelf. Food quality is another key part of the botequim experience, particularly the little munchy appetizers that go so well with beer. At Bracarense these are in the expert hands of the Minas Gerais native Alaíde, who works miracles in the small kitchen. Rua José Linhares 85, Leblon (corner of Ataulfo de Paiva). (✆) **021/2294-3549.** Bus: 464.

Jobi   Jobi is busy any day of the week, but on Friday and Saturday a line is guaranteed. You may as well make friends with others in the line, as chances are you'll be seated closely together in this cozy bar. Jobi has excellent beer, tasty snacks, and a great atmosphere. On top of that, Jobi stays open until 4:30am, making it a favorite postparty haunt to wind down from an evening out. Av. Ataulfo de Paiva 1166, Leblon. (✆) **021/2274-0547.** Bus: 434.

Other Bars & Pubs

Academia da Cachaça   A field trip to the Academia da Cachaça puts the concept of advanced education in a whole new light. Here you can dispute and discuss the finer points of the fiery white cane liquor that is Brazil's national drink. For though all *cachaça* comes from cane juice, not all *cachaças* are created equal. The selection at the Academia is overwhelming. Ask the bartenders for advice, and begin that lifelong intellectual quest for the perfect "white one." Just don't down them on an empty stomach. The menu here offers a variety of Brazilian snacks to munch on while trying yet one more shot. Or two

(Finds) Waterfront Upgrade

In 2006, Rio began a major overhaul of the sidewalk kiosks along the waterfront, replacing the old ones with modern glass kiosks with spacious decks, a full bar and kitchen, and underground washrooms and showers. Leme and Copacabana have all new kiosks. Ipanema and Leblon are slated for upgrades in the coming years. The new beachfront spots are often run by popular bars or restaurants. Standouts include the **Siri Mole** kiosk (✆ **021/3684-6671;** www.sirimolepraia. com.br), opposite Rua Bolivar, which serves Bahian seafood dishes; **Bar Luiz** kiosk (✆ **021/7819-1258;** www.barluiz.com.br), opposite the Copacabana Hotel; the **Nescafé** kiosk (✆ **021/3684-0624**), near Posto 4, for 20 different type of crepes; or the **Rainbow Pizzaria** kiosk (✆ **021/3185-0162**), opposite Rudolfo Dantas Street.

more shots. Or three. Or . . . Rua Conde de Bernadotte 26, loja G, Leblon. ✆ **021/2529-2680.** www.academiadacachaca.com.br. Bus: 415.

Bar dos Descasados ★★★ Rio's most romantic patio bar sits tucked away inside the recently restored Hotel Santa Teresa. Spend a lazy afternoon or evening (or both, once you get comfortable you may not want to leave) lounging in a big comfy chair on the terrace of a 19th-century mansion. Order a caipirinha and enjoy the fabulous views of Santa Teresa and downtown. *Tip:* This is a prime sunset spot. Rua Almirante Alexandrino 660, Santa Teresa. ✆ **021/2222-2755.** Bus: 206

Devassa What started as a cute neighborhood bar in Leblon is slowly spreading around the city. The original location on the Rua General San Martin still packs them in on most nights but patrons now have the option of heading out to the Jardim Botânico location and enjoying the large patio. The Devassa microbrews can now be purchased at many other bars around the city. The most popular Devassa brews are the blond *(loura),* redhead *(ruiva),* and brunette *(morena).* Rua General San Martin 1241, Leblon. ✆ **021/2540-6087.** www.devassa.com.br. Bus: 415. Also at Av. Lineu de Paula Machado 696, Jardim Botânico. ✆ **021/2294-2915.** Bus: 572 (get off at Rua Jardim Botânico, corner Rua J.J. Seabra).

Garota de Ipanema (Overrated) The bossa nova tune "The Girl from Ipanema" (*"Garota de Ipanema"* in Portuguese) is indeed a thing of sublime beauty, composed in one afternoon by poet Vinicius de Moraes and singer Tom Jobim while the two sat drinking chopp and watching the Brazilian beach beauties go by in a little bar then called the Veloso. Though still there, the bar is now somewhat less than beautiful and anything but sublime. After the tune became a world hit the bar changed its name and plastered the song's lyrics and score on the wall in a blatant attempt to cash in. Jobim and Moraes themselves shunned the place in short order, driven out by the hordes and attendant crass commercialism. Nowadays, the beer is cold and the food okay (both come at a premium), and the people walking by are still tall, tan, young, and lovely, but the Garota itself is neither a musical nor cultural hot spot. Rua Vinicius de Moraes 49 A, Ipanema. ✆ **021/2523-3787.** www.garotaipanema.com.br. Bus: 434.

Mercado Cobal de Humaitá (Finds) Is it a bar? Is it a restaurant? Or is it a great seething mass of people at plastic patio tables quaffing chopp, munching food, and listening to tunes from one or more live bands? That last is probably the best description

(Moments) Making Your Point

Rio is full of *points*. Pronounced poin-*chee* in Portuguese, a point is a location on the street that attracts people who attract other people who attract people who provide food, drinks, sometimes music, and all the other ingredients of a party. Complicated? Here's an example: One night we were headed over to Galeria Café with some friends. Just as we got there we met up with some other friends, and when we saw there was a bit of a line we got to chatting outside and bought some beers from a street vendor. Some other friends came, and other people whom we didn't know but who were there to meet some of their friends. We ordered more beers, and later some munchies from another vendor; before we noticed it was time to go home. We never did set foot in the bar we intended to patronize. That evening was a classic *point*—a fun, impromptu street party. No one can say for sure when one will emerge, or why they show up where they do. Points just . . . *are*.

of the nighttime scene at the Mercado Cobal. Seven or eight different restaurants and *chopperias* (*chopperias* sell draft beer and very basic snacks) all meld into one large bustling patio, with busy waiters racing up and down the aisles trying to keep their tables straight. **Galeto Mania** serves up a tasty grilled chicken, **Pizzapark** offers a full range of pizzas, and **Manekineko** whips up tray after tray of fresh sushi, while **Espirito Chopp** serves the best cold draft beer. The beauty of this place is that you don't have to commit to one specific restaurant. Once you've found a table, just order from any of them. With superhero skill, the waiters somehow manage to keep track of it all. Cobal de Humaitá, Rua Voluntários da Patria 446, Botafogo. Galeto Mania, (*C*) **021/2527-0616.** Manekineko, (*C*) **021/2537-1510.** Bus: 178.

Venga Rio's first tapas bar forwent the trendy fusion route and opted for a classic Spanish approach. The bustling bar has a casual atmosphere, popular with Rio's 30-plus crowd. The kitchen serves some interesting minidishes, which most people accompany with a glass of sangria or Spanish wine. Smack in the middle of Leblon's nightlife district, the people-watching is superb! Monday to Friday 6pm to 1am, Saturday and Sunday 1pm to 1am. Rua Dias Ferreira 113, Leblon. (*C*) **021/2512-9826.** Bus: 474.

GAY & LESBIAN NIGHTLIFE

Rio's gay community is smaller than one would expect from a city of 10 million people. For all Rio's reputation for sexual hedonism, the macho culture still predominates. As lasciviously as heterosexual couples may behave in public, open displays of affection between same-sex couples are still not accepted in Brazil. This is changing, though only slowly. Rio's mayor and governor have only just begun attending Rio's gay pride parade. The big exception, of course, is Carnaval, when many straight and gay men dress as women (Carmen Miranda is always a popular costume), and parades with drag queens are cheered by everyone. But this spirit of openness lasts only until the samba drums fade away at the dawn of Ash Wednesday.

Currently, the most popular nightspot is in Ipanema around the Galeria Café on the Rua Teixeira de Melo. During the day the stretch of sand close to Posto 8 (opposite the Rua Farme de Amoedo) is also popular. Copacabana has a number of gay clubs and bars as well as a popular meeting place on the beach at Rainbow's, in front of the Copacabana Palace Hotel. A good resource to pick up is the latest edition of the *Gay Guide Brazil*, a small booklet available at some of the clubs and bookstores in Ipanema, or check http://riogayguide.com. The Brazilian term for gay friendly is GLS, which stands for gay, lesbian, and sympathizers. Often you will see this abbreviation used in listings or restaurant and bar reviews.

After a day at the beach, go to **Bar Bofetada,** Rua Farme de Amoeda 87 (© 021/2227-6992). Located just a few blocks from Ipanema's prime gay beach, this botequim is perfect for a beer, snack, and flirt with local guys.

Set in a small gallery stunningly decorated with a changing display of work by local artists, the **Galeria Café,** Rua Teixeira de Melo 31E, Ipanema (© 021/2523-8250; www.galeriacafe.com.br), packs a gorgeous collection of men, shoulder to shoulder, bicep to bicep, into its combo art space, dance club, and bar. Those that can't fit—and there are many—just hang out in front. The Galeria really gets hopping, inside and out, after 1am. The cover charge is R$10 to R$25; open from Wednesday through Sunday.

Also popular is **Dama de Ferro** (the **Iron Lady**), Rua Vinicius de Moraes 288, Ipanema (© 021/2247-2330; www.damadeferro.com.br). Decorated by artist Adriana Lima, who also did the amazing decor at Galeria Café, Dama de Ferro is the it-spot at the moment, popular with gays and straights; high tolerance for electronic music is a must. Cover is R$10 to R$25; open Wednesday through Sunday.

Le Boy, Rua Raul Pompeia 102, Copacabana (© 021/2513-4993; www.leboy.com. br), is the largest and best-known gay club in Rio. It's glamorous, funky, and extremely spacious with a soaring four-story ceiling hovering somewhere above the dance floor. A range of special events attracts national and international celebrities and assorted (beautiful) hangers-on. Go after midnight, when things really start to hop. The club is open Tuesday through Sunday; cover ranges from R$5 to R$15 for men. This may be the only club in town where women pay more than men; any night of the week the cover for women is set at a hefty R$60. All for equal opportunity, Le Boy's owner recently inaugurated **La Girl** next door, Rua Raul Pompeia 102 (© 021/2247-8342; www.lagirl.com. br), Rio's first truly upscale nightclub for gay women with excellent DJs and go-go girl shows. La Girl is open on Monday and Wednesday to Sunday (men allowed only on Mon and Sun). Cover ranges from R$5 to R$15.

The **Week,** Rua Sacadura Cabral 154, Saude (© 021/2253-1020; www.theweek. com.br), is the new hottest gay dance club in town. This huge mega dance club can hold 2,000 people and is packed every Saturday night. Famous national and international guest DJs and go-go boys keep the crowd going. Open Saturdays at midnight. Often open for events on Fridays and Wednesdays; check listings.

In Centro, **Cine Ideal** (© 021/2221-1984; www.cineideal.com.br) is a gay-friendly outpost of house music, open every Friday and Saturday 11am to 6am. Cover R$40.

12 EVERYTHING YOU NEED TO KNOW ABOUT CARNAVAL

Ah, Carnaval. The name evokes explosive images of colorful costumes, lavish floats, swarming masses, and last-minute debauchery before the sober Lenten season begins. Though it may look like sheer entertainment, Carnaval means hard work and dedication for many Cariocas; to some, it's a full-time job.

WHAT'S IT ALL ABOUT?

The religious aspect of the celebration faded some time ago, but Carnaval's date is still determined by the ecclesiastical calendar, officially occupying only the 4 days immediately preceding Ash Wednesday. With typical ingenuity and panache, however, Cariocas have managed to stretch the party into an event lasting several months, culminating in the all-night feast of color and sound that is the **Samba School Parade,** where tens of thousands of costumed dancers, thousands of percussionists, and hundreds of gorgeous performers atop dozens of floats all move in choreographed harmony to the nonstop rhythm of samba.

If you're not able to attend Carnaval itself, **rehearsals**—which usually start in mid-September or early October—are an absolute must, and the closest you'll get to the real thing. Even if you are in town for Carnaval, attending a rehearsal will give you a great appreciation of the logistics involved in putting together the parade, plus you'll learn all the words and dance moves.

In the 2 weeks leading up to the big event, you'll begin to see the **blocos.** These are community groups—usually associated with a particular neighborhood or sometimes with a bar—who go around the neighborhood, playing music and singing and dancing through the streets. Their instruments and costumes easily identify the official bloco members, but everyone is welcome and encouraged to follow along and add to the merriment. A number of blocos are so well known that they draw throngs of followers in the tens of thousands. The **Banda de Carmen Miranda** in Ipanema with its extravagant drag queens is a hoot.

Carnaval finally kicks off on the Friday before Ash Wednesday with an explosion of lavish **balls** *(bailes).* Originally the *bailes* were reserved for the elite, while the masses partied it up with vulgar splendor in the streets. Today, they're still a pricey affair and the **Copacabana Palace Ball** remains *the* society event in Rio. The **blocos** also kick into high gear once Carnaval arrives with several groups parading every day from Saturday through Tuesday.

WATCHING THE SAMBA PARADE

Then, there is the *pièce de résistance:* the **Samba School Parade,** the event that the samba schools work, plan, and sweat over for an entire year. Starting Sunday and continuing through Monday night, the 14 top-ranked samba schools (really community groups whose sole focus is the parade) compete for the honor of putting on the best show. The competition takes place in the **Sambodromo,** a 1.5km-long (1-mile) concrete parade ground built in the center of Rio for this once-a-year event. Each night over 60,000 spectators watch the contest live, while millions more tune in on TV to catch this feast for the senses.

Even before the parade starts, the streets surrounding the **Sambodromo** are closed to car traffic, while the grounds around this stadium are transformed into Carnaval Central. A main stage hosts a variety of acts and performances, and hundreds of vendors set up shop with food and drinks. This *terreirão do samba* (samba land), as Riotur calls it, is open the weekend prior to Carnaval, from Friday through Tuesday during Carnaval, and then again for the Saturday afterward for the Parade of Champions.

On the day of each parade, the schools arrive outside the parade grounds to assemble their floats, props, and other gear. The streets around the Sambodromo, including Avenida Presidente Vargas, are closed for traffic, and pedestrians can stroll watching the schools put finishing touches on a year's worth of work. A great opportunity to take a

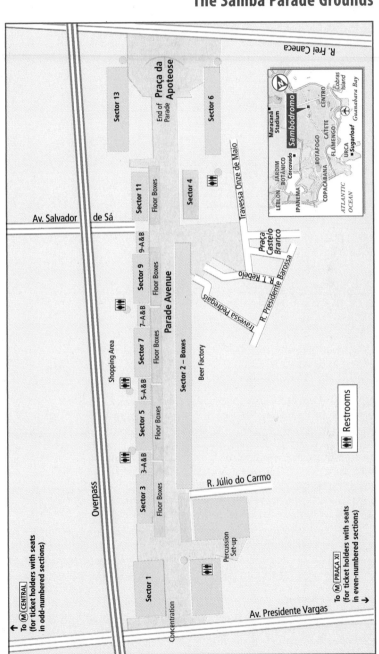

close-up look at the floats, take pictures, and meet some of the people who put it all together.

HOW & WHERE TO GET TICKETS

It is next to impossible to buy tickets directly from Liesa, the **Liga das Escolas de Samba** (© 021/3213-5151; www.liesa.com.br). The tickets go on sale a few months before Carnaval and always sell out in 20 minutes. The few tourist tickets that remain Liesa sells at an extraordinary markup. Most tourists are left buying from scalpers or travel agencies. Reputable travel agencies include **Blumar** (© 021/2142-9300; www.blumar.com.br), **Rio Services Carnaval** (© 877/559-0088 U.S. and Canada; www.rio-carnival.net), and **BIT** (© 021/3208-9000; www.bitourism.com), which sell good tickets at reasonable rates, but which often sell out early. If you've got your heart set on seeing the parade, buy your tickets by October or at the latest November preceding the year you want to go. As a next to last resort, try your hotel, but expect to pay a hefty premium for this service. As a last resort, you can try the scalpers outside the stadium. (The scalpers will find you as you come out any of the Metrô stops near the Sambódromo.) Be careful! Each ticket consists of a magnetic plastic card and an attached paper slip—you need both to enter. The best deals come after the first couple of schools have paraded (say 11pm) when the scalpers start to get a little desperate.

Depending on the agency, or the desperation of your scalper, tickets for the bleachers begin at around R$110 for section 4, and rise to R$300 for section 7. Chairs in a front row box *(frisa)* start at R$3,000 in section 4 and R$4,800 in section 7. These are base prices. Many agencies charge much more.

Note: Many tour agencies offer transportation to and from the Sambódromo, at a very hefty markup (the cheapest charges some US$80 for the bus ride). These transfers are not only unnecessary, they're actually a disadvantage. Getting to the parade, the easiest, safest quickest route is by Metrô. Due to street closures, buses will take much, much longer to reach the stadium. Coming home, there are plenty of taxis outside the Sambódromo, and you can leave whenever you want. If you've booked a package, you're expected to wait on the bus until 7am when the last school finishes before you can go home.

General seating is in concrete bleachers, with no space assigned. Your ticket gives you access to the section. After that it's up to you to find a spot and squeeze in. There are pillows for sale, or you can bring your own. The exception to the hard concrete rule is in section 9, the tourist section, where there are numbered assigned places. The advantages are obvious. The disadvantage is that you miss out on some of the *joie de vivre* that comes with being surrounded by hundreds of happy partying Brazilians.

In addition to the bleachers, there are front-row boxes, called *frisas* in Portuguese. These are comfortable chairs that sit in a strip of boxes located at ground level along the parade route. There are six seats to a box (three rows of two) and seating is assigned. The frisas have the advantage of closeness and assigned seating. The disadvantages are a higher price tag and—some say—being too close to really appreciate the whole of the spectacle (like sitting in the very front row at a musical or movie).

Besides frisas and bleachers, there are the exclusive VIP boxes. However, if you can wangle an invitation to one of those, you don't need any help from us.

Whether you choose bleacher or *frisa,* the best sections are 5, 7, and 9. These place you near the middle of the parade avenue, allowing you to see up and down as the schools come through. Avoid sitting at the start or the end of the Avenida (sections 1, 3, 4, 6, and 13).

> ### (Tips) Carnaval Redux
>
> If you miss the parade during Carnaval, attend the Parade of Champions on the Saturday after Carnaval. The five top schools give an encore to close the Sambodromo Carnaval season. Tickets go on sale the Thursday after Carnaval. At R$80 and up for a good spot, they're considerably less expensive than the original event. Contact the **Liga das Escolas de Samba** (© **021/3213-5151;** www.liesa. com.br), **Blumar** (© **021/2142-9300**; www.blumar.com.br), or **Rio Services Carnaval** (© **877/559-0088** U.S. and Canada; www.rio-carnival.net) for ticket sales.

If you have tickets you can head directly to the Sambodromo. The parade grounds are divided into sections (see map on p. 149): Even-numbered sections can be accessed from the Central Station side (Metrô: Central); odd-numbered sections can be accessed from the Praça XI side (Metrô: Praça XI). Don't worry, lots of police and staff are around to point you in the right direction.

The parade starts at 9pm, but unless you want to stake out a particular spot you may as well take your time arriving, because the event will continue nonstop until about 7 or 8am. We recommend leaving a bit early as well to avoid the big crunch at the end when the entire crowd tries to squeeze through a narrow set of revolving gates. Food and drinks are available inside the Sambodromo. Though prices aren't outrageous, it's a serious pain elbowing your way back and forth from your seat: Grab something at one of the many inexpensive kiosks outside the Sambodromo before you head in.

A Few Helpful Hints

Whether you are attending a rehearsal, following a bloco, or watching the parade, here are a few helpful hints to ensure you have a good time.

- Dress casually and comfortably. The weather is usually hot and humid so a tank top or bikini top and shorts are fine. Comfortable shoes are a must as you will be on your feet for hours, dancing and jumping to the music.
- Pack light. A purse or any extra accessories are not recommended, especially at the rehearsals and the blocos as you will be dancing and moving around. When watching the parade you can bring a small bag or knapsack and leave it at your feet, but the lighter you travel the better. Make sure you bring enough cash for the evening, some form of ID (driver's license or some other picture ID that is not your passport), and maybe a small camera you can tuck into your pocket. Leave jewelry and other valuables at home.
- The events themselves are very safe, but be aware of pickpockets in large crowds. At the end of the event, take a taxi or walk with the crowds, avoiding any deserted streets or unfamiliar neighborhoods.
- Keep in mind that prices will be slightly higher, cabs may add a premium, and drinks and food at the parade and some other venues may be higher than what you are used to in Brazil.
- Plan to have enough cash for the entire Carnaval period. All financial institutions close for the duration, and it's not unusual for bank machines to run out of money.

If you think watching the parade from up close sounds pretty amazing, imagine being in it. Every year, the samba schools open up positions for outsiders to participate in the parade. Putting on this extravaganza is an expensive proposition, and by selling the costumes and the right to parade, the school is able to recuperate some of its costs. But outside paraders are also needed for artistic and competitive reasons. To score high points the school needs to have enough people to fill the Avenida and make the parade look full and colorful. A low turnout can make the school lose critical points.

To parade (*desfilar* in Portuguese) you need to commit to a school and buy a costume (about R$500–R$1,200), which you can often do online. Some sites are in English as well as Portuguese; if not, look under *fantasia* (costume). Depending on the school, they may courier the costume or arrange for a pickup downtown just before the parade, or you may have to make the trek out to wherever they are.

For an added charge, a number of agencies in Rio will organize it all for you, getting you in with a school and arranging the costume. **Blumar** (✆ 021/2142-9300; www.blumar.com.br) or **Rio Services Carnaval** (✆ 877/559-0088 U.S. and Canada; www.rio-carnival.net) can organize the whole event for you for about R$1,000. For other organizations, contact **Alô Rio** (✆ 021/2542-8080 or 0800/707-1888).

As a participant in the parade you do not automatically get a ticket to watch the rest of the event. If you want to see the other schools you need to purchase a separate ticket. If your school finishes in the top five there will be a repeat performance in the Parade of Champions, held on the Saturday after Carnaval. If you are not able to parade again, consider donating your costume to a fellow traveler or keen Brazilian.

WATCHING A REHEARSAL

Every Saturday from September (or even as early as Aug) until Carnaval, each samba school holds a general samba rehearsal (*ensaio*) at its home base. The band and key people come out and practice their theme song over and over to perfection. It may sound a tad repetitious, but you'd be amazed how a good band playing the same song over and over can generate a *really* great party. People dance for hours, taking a break now and then for snacks and beer. The income generated goes toward the group's floats and costumes. By the end of the night (and these rehearsals go until the wee hours) everyone knows the words to the song and has—hopefully—turned into an ardent fan who will cheer this particular school on at the parade. (General rehearsals usually don't involve costumes or practicing dance routines.) In December and January, the schools also hold dress rehearsals and technical rehearsals at the Sambodromo. Check with Riotur for dates and times.

Most of the samba schools are based in the poorer and quite distant suburbs, but a number of schools such as **Mangueira, Salgueiro, Vila Isabel, and Rocinha** are very accessible and no more than an R$30 cab ride from Copacabana. Nor should you worry overly much about safety. Rehearsals take place in an open-air space called a *quadra* that looks like a large gymnasium. There is always security, and the rehearsals are very well attended. Plan to arrive anytime after 11pm. When you are ready to leave there'll be lots of taxis around. Just don't go wandering off into the neighborhood, unless you're familiar with the area. Many hotels will organize tours to the samba school rehearsals, but unless you prefer to go with a group it's not really necessary and certainly a lot cheaper to go on your own.

Tip: A number of the famous schools that are located on the outskirts of the city will hold special rehearsals in the Zona Sul. The ones organized by Beija Flor and Grande Rio

(Tips) Carnaval Behind the Scenes

In 2005 the **Cidade do Samba** (Samba city) was inaugurated in Rio's old port zone (Rua Rivadavia Correia 60, Gamboa, © **021/2213-2503**; http://cidade dosambarj.globo.com). This large warehouse-style construction provides the samba schools with a space to build their floats and work on their costumes. Visitors can have a look behind the scenes and see what it takes to put this event together. Twice a month, on Thursdays, the Cidade do Samba also hosts a musical performance giving viewers a taste of the parade. These shows are really designed for tourists and don't have anything of the authenticity that the rehearsals at the actual schools have, but if this is your only opportunity to get a taste of Carnaval it may be worth it. Open Tuesday through Saturday 10am to 5pm for visits (R$5). The evening musical performances are always held on a Thursday, starting at 9pm. Admission includes a buffet dinner, R$190 or R$95 for Rio residents (proof of residency required). For more information and to check on scheduling, please contact the **Liga das Escolas de Samba** (© **021/2253-7676**) or **Alô Rio** (© **021/2542-8080** or 0800/707-1888). There's also some good information at the private site, www.sambacity.info.

are the most popular, often attended by models, actors, and other VIPs. For an authentic experience, it's still better to go to the actual school.

To find out more about specific schools, rehearsals, or participating in the parade, contact the **Liga das Escolas de Samba** (© 021/3213-5151; www.liesa.com.br). If you can't find anyone there who speaks English, contact **Alô Rio** for assistance (© 021/2542-8080 or 0800/707-1888). Or you can try contacting one of the samba schools directly; below is a partial list:

- **Mangueira,** Rio's most favorite samba school and close to downtown, Rua Visconde de Niterói 1072, Mangueira (© **021/3872-6786;** www.mangueira.com.br).
- **Beija-flor,** far from downtown but a crowd favorite and winner in 2003, 2004, 2005, and 2007, Rua Pracinha Walace Paes Leme 1025, Nilópolis (© **021/2791-2866;** www.beija-flor.com.br).
- **Imperatriz,** the winner in 1999, 2000, and 2001, Rua Prof. Lacê 235, Ramos (© **021/2560-8037;** www.imperatrizleopoldinense.com.br).
- **Portela,** Rua Clara Nunes 81, Madureira (© **021/2489-6440;** www.gresportela.com.br).
- **Rocinha,** young school, located in the Zona Sul close to Ipanema and Leblon, Rua Bertha Lutz 80, São Conrado (© **021/3205-3318;** www.academicosdarocinha.com.br).
- **Salgueiro,** close to downtown, very popular, Rua Silva Telles 104, Andaraí (© **021/2238-0389;** www.salgueiro.com.br).
- **Vila Isabel,** close to downtown, mostly locals and very untouristy, winner in 2006, Bd. 28 de Setembro 382, Vila Isabel (© **021/2578-0077;** www.gresunidosdevila isabel.com.br).

HANGING WITH THE BLOCOS

To experience the real street Carnaval, don't miss the parading blocos. The key to the popularity of the blocos is the informality; everyone is welcome, and you don't need a costume, just comfortable clothes and shoes. (Bear in mind, however, that the informality

(Moments) Reveillon: New Year's Eve in Rio

Trust Brazilians to throw a party where everyone is welcome and admission is free. At Rio's annual New Year's Eve extravaganza, millions pack the beach for an all-night festival of music, food, and fun, punctuated by spectacular fireworks.

Arrive early and enjoy a New Year's buffet at one of the scores of restaurants or hotels along the beachfront Avenida Atlântica. Music kicks off at 8pm, as people make their way down to the beach until every square inch of sand is packed. By midnight, more than two million have joined the countdown. As the clock strikes midnight, the fireworks begin. Barges moored off Copacabana beach flood the sky with a shower of reds, greens, yellows, and golds. When the last whistling spark falls into the sea, bands fire up their instruments and welcome in the new year with a concert that goes on until wee hours. Many stay all night and grab a spot on the sand when they tire. The event is perfectly safe.

During the party, followers of the Afro-Brazilian religion Candomblé mark Reveillon in their own way. New Year's Eve is an important moment in Candomblé, a time when followers make offerings to the sea goddess Yemanjá. Along the beach circles of women dressed all in white light candles and prepare small boats loaded with flowers, mirrors, trinkets, and perfumes. They launch the boats into the surf in hopes of obtaining Yemanjá's favor for the year to come.

Cariocas traditionally wear white on New Year's Eve; it's the color of peace and the color worn by devotees of Candomblé to honor Yemanjá. Don a pair of white shorts and a T-shirt, but don't forget your swimsuit. The traditional New Year's Eve "polar bear swim" will be even more tempting when the temperature is a balmy 40°C (105°F). Many Cariocas will also buy flowers to take to the beach and offer these to Yemanjá by tossing them in the ocean.

The best way to get to the event is by subway (buy tickets in advance to avoid lines). Most streets in Copacabana are closed to traffic; parking anywhere near the beach is impossible. The Rio newspaper *O Globo* (www.oglobo.com) normally publishes a full schedule in early December. You can also contact **Alô Rio** at ✆ **021/2542-8080** or 0800/707-1888.

extends to scheduling. If your group doesn't start on time, grab a beer and chill—they'll show eventually.) Different blocos have certain styles or attract specific groups, so pick one that suits you and have fun. Riotur publishes an excellent brochure called *Bandas, Blocos and Ensaios,* available through Alô Rio (✆ **021/2542-8080** or 0800/707-1888). Also available from Riotur, Av. Princesa Isabel 183, Copacabana (✆ **021/2271-7000**), is the *Rio Incomparavel* brochure, which has a full listing of events. In Portuguese, the website www.samba-choro.com.br provides a comprehensive list of blocos, including parade routes and starting times. The *Globo* newspaper (www.oglobo.com.br) also provides a bloco listings page.

Some of the best blocos to look for are **Bloco Cacique de Ramos** and **Cordão do Bola Preta** in Centro; **Barbas** and **Bloco de Segunda** in Botafogo; **Bloco do Bip Bip**

BAILES

More formal than the blocos, the samba balls *(bailes)* are where you go to see and be seen. Traditionally reserved for Rio's elite, some—such as the Copacabana Palace ball—remain the height of elegance, while others have become raunchy and risqué bacchanals. Numerous clubs around town host Carnaval balls.

Among the most fabulous is the notorious **Baile Vermelho e Preto (Red and Black Costume Ball)** held every year on Carnaval Friday in honor of Rio's most popular soccer club, Flamengo. It's known for both the beauty of the female attendees and the skimpiness of their costumes. The **Baile do Preto Branco (Black and White Ball),** also on Carnaval Friday, takes place at the Clube Botafogo. For both events contact **Alô Rio** (✆ **021/2542-8080** or 0800/707-1888) for details and ticket information. The popular Copacabana nightclub **Le Boy** (p. 147) organizes a differently themed ball every night during Carnaval, Friday through Tuesday included. These balls are gay-friendly but not gay-only. Call ✆ **021/2240-3338.** The prime gay event—and one of Rio's most famous balls—is the Tuesday night **Gala Gay** at the Scala nightclub, Av. Afranio de Melo Franco 296, Leblon (✆ **021/2239-4448**). TV cameras vie for position by the red carpet, à la Oscar night. Google "Gala Gay" for video clips of the silliness.

The grand slam of all Carnaval balls is the Saturday night extravaganza at the Copacabana Palace Hotel, the **Grande Baile de Carnaval,** which plays host to the crème de la crème of Rio's high society. This is the ball of politicians, diplomats, models, business tycoons, and local and international movie stars. Tickets start at R$600 per person and sell out quickly. Call ✆ **021/2548-7070** for details.

Rio Services Carnaval (✆ **877/559-0088** U.S. and Canada; www.rio-carnival.net) offers tickets to many of the balls listed above. Tickets start at US$60 for the Red and Black ball (or US$467 for a table for four people) and rise to US$635 for the Copacabana party (US$3,300 for a table for four).

Side Trips from Rio de Janeiro

Two of the greatest joys of Rio are its mountains and its beaches. Side trips from the cidade maravilhosa explore these two features in greater detail. On weekends and holidays, many head north to the beach resorts dotting the warm Atlantic coast. First and most famous of these is the town of **Búzios,** "discovered" in the 1960s by a bikini-wearing Brigitte Bardot. Now it's a haven for Rio socialites, visiting Argentines, and anyone else who loves their beaches Brazilian-style—civilized, with a beachside table in sight, and a caipirinha in hand.

Heading inland, one finds the summer refuge of an earlier, prebeach generation, the mountain resort. The prettiest of these is also the closest: **Petrópolis,** the former summer capital of Emperor Pedro II. Just an hour from Rio, this green, graceful refuge is a place of peaceful strolls, great museums, and mountain hikes in the Atlantic rainforest.

Want your history served up with a splash of ocean? The perfect blend can be found in the former colonial port of **Paraty.** Situated almost halfway between Rio and São Paulo, this beautiful historic town had its heyday in the 18th and 19th centuries as a prime transshipment point for gold and later for coffee. Visitors can sail the bays and visit the surrounding sandy beaches and islands in the daytime, and at night wander the cobblestone streets of this UNESCO World Heritage Site, in search of architectural beauty or just some very fine dining.

Finally, there's **Ilha Grande,** a pristine island (and former political prison) to the south of Rio, where forest-clad tropical mountains splash their toes in a clear blue green tropical sea.

1 BUZIOS

134km (83 miles) E of Rio de Janeiro, 489km (303 miles) NE of São Paulo

It's anyone's guess how small or sleepy the fishing town of Búzios truly was when French starlet Brigitte Bardot stumbled onto its sandy beaches in 1964, but it's certain that in the years since the little town used the publicity to turn itself into Rio's premier beach resort. In the summer the town is packed; many Carioca celebrities own places here, and Argentines continue to invade with a gusto not seen since the Falklands. Despite the influx, the town has managed to retain a good deal of the charm of its fishing-village past.

Búzios (the town's full name is Armação de Búzios) sits on the tip of a long, beach-rich peninsula jutting out into the clear blue Atlantic. The sheer number of beaches close to town makes it easy to experience Brazilian beach culture firsthand. **Geribá Beach** is the place for surfing. Quiet and calm and very deep, **Ferradura Beach** is a perfect horseshoe-shaped bay ideal for a lazy afternoon snorkel. Far from town are more isolated spots to steal a quiet moment with a special beach friend, while right in town on **Ossos Beach** you can sip a caipirinha at a beachside cafe and pretend for a moment you're young, rich, and beautiful. In this South American Saint-Tropez, everyone else certainly is.

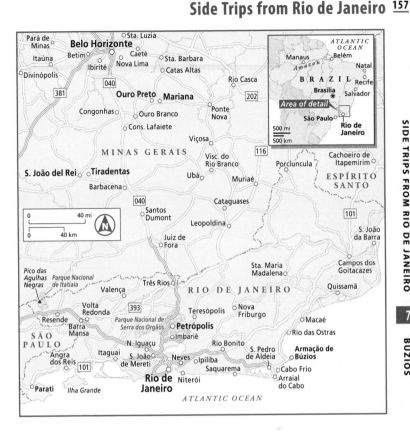

Finally, on top of serious inquisitions into beach culture, there are more trivial pursuits such as diving, sailing, windsurfing, fine cuisine, and endless opportunities to shop. And at night, everyone comes to the busy, bar- and cafe-lined **Rua das Pedras** to stroll, primp, drink, and party.

ESSENTIALS
Getting There
BY CAR   Búzios is about a 2-hour drive from Rio de Janeiro. Leaving Rio, follow the signs to Niterói to cross the 16km-long (10-mile) Rio-Niterói bridge. Remember to have R$4 handy to pay the toll. Across the bridge, stay in the left lane and take the Rio Bonito exit. Once close to Rio Bonito, take the Via Lagos to Araruama/Cabo Frio and follow the signs to the RJ-106 and Búzios. Note that the Via Lagos is also a toll road (R$9.40 on weekdays, R$14 on weekends).

BY VAN/TAXI   **Malizia Tours in Búzios** (© 022/2623-1226 or 2623-2022; www.maliziatour.com.br) offers transfers to/from Rio by van and taxi. Cost in a 15-person air-conditioned minibus is R$50 per person one-way. Pickup can be at your hotel or from the airport.

BY BUS **Auto Viação 1001** (© 021/4004-5001; www.autoviacao1001.com.br) has departures seven times a day from Rio's main bus station (**Novo Rio Rodoviaria;** Av. Francisco Bicalho 1, Santo Cristo; © 021/3849-5001). Cost of the 3-hour trip is R$28. In Búzios, buses arrive (and depart) at the Búzios Bus Station (© 022/2623-2050) on Estrada da Usina, corner of Rua Manoel de Carvalho, a 10-minute walk from the center of town.

Getting Around

BY WATER TAXI Water taxis are an efficient and fun way to get around, but they run only in the daytime and only on the protected side of the bay, from João Fernandes to Tartaruga. To catch a water taxi you can hail one from the beach or the pier in town, or phone © 022/2620-8018. When being dropped off by water taxi, you can set a time for pickup. From Centro to Azeda beach costs R$6 per person and from Centro to João Fernandes beach R$8 per person. Taxis carry up to seven people.

BY TAXI Taxis can be hailed at the *ponto* in Praça Santos Dumont (© 022/2623-2160) or by calling **Búzios Rádio Táxi** (© 022/2623-1911).

BY RENTAL CAR **Malizia,** Rua José Bento Ribeiro Dantas 16, Shopping do Canto, Búzios (© 022/2623-1226; www.maliziatour.com.br), has rental cars. Cost starts at R$75 per day for a Fiat Palio with air-conditioning. Includes 120km (74 miles) per day and insurance.

Visitor Information

The **Búzios Tourism Secretariat** operates an information kiosk on the downtown Praça Santos Dumont 111 (© 022/2633-6200; daily 8am–10pm). Two good websites on Búzios are **www.buziosonline.com.br** and **www.buziosturismo.com**.

FAST FACTS **Banco do Brasil,** Rua Manuel de Carvalho 73 (4 blocks from Rua das Pedras), is open Monday through Friday from 11am to 6pm. ATMs are open 24 hours. You will find most major **ATMs** in the Praça Santos Dumont. **Búzios Cybar,** Shopping de Búzios, loja 4, corner of Rua Turibe (© 022/2623-2969), has Internet for R$8 per 30 minutes. *Note:* Practically all hotels in Búzios have Wi-Fi.

EXPLORING BUZIOS

Hitting the Beaches

The charm of Búzios lies largely in its beaches, the 20 stretches of sand large and small within a few kilometers of the old town. Thanks to the irregular topography of this rugged little peninsula, each beach is set off from the other and has developed its own beach personality. Farthest from the old town is **Manguinhos** beach. Sheltered from the heavy surf, this gentle beach is where many learn to sail and windsurf. A short hop over the neck of the peninsula lies **Geribá** beach, a wonderful long stretch of sand facing out toward the open ocean. This is the beach for surfing, boogie boarding, and windsurfing. Closer to town is **Ferradura** or **Horseshoe** beach. Nestled between rocky headlands in a beautiful horseshoe bay, this beach offers calm, crystal-clear waters, making it the perfect place for a long, lazy afternoon's snorkel. Tiny and beautiful, **Olho de Boi** or **Bull's Eye** beach is tucked away on its own at the far end of a small ecological reserve. It can only be reached by a 20-minute walk from surfers' favorite **Brava** beach. Thanks to this isolation, Bull's Eye beach has been adopted by Búzios's clothing-optional crowd. Back on the calm inland side of the peninsula, **João Fernandes** and the pocket-size **João Fernandinho** beaches are busy, happening places lined with beachside cafes and full of people intent on getting and showing off their tans.

Outdoor Activities & Watersports

Most everything in the way of watersports equipment can be rented in Búzios, generally right on the beach.

On **Ferradura** beach, **Happy Surf** (© 022/2623-3389) rents **sailboards, lasers, Hobie Cats,** and **kayaks.** Happy Surf also gives courses. A 6-hour beginner's **sailboard** course costs R$150. More advanced students can choose from 1- and 2-hour courses costing from R$35 to R$60. Lasers rent for R$35 per half-hour, R$45 with instructor. Hobie Cats rent for R$25 per half-hour, R$40 with instructor. Kayaks rent for R$5 per half-hour.

The following equipment is available at **João Fernandes Beach: kayaks,** R$5 for 30 minutes; **mask and snorkel,** R$12 per hour; and **sailboard,** R$30 per hour.

On **Manguinhos** beach, **Búzios Vela Club,** Rua Maurício Dutra 303 (© 022/2623-0508), rents windsurf equipment. A full-day rental ranges from R$150 to R$210. Manguinhos is also a popular **kite-surfing** location. Intensive weekend courses are available for R$600, including gear and 6 hours of instruction. To book a lesson call **Búzios Kite Surfing School** (© 022/2633-0396; www.kitenews.com.br).

BIKING Hard-core mountain bikers would likely find it a little tame, but Búzios is an excellent place for gentle, recreational off-road cycling. There are lots of trails accessible only to pedestrians and cyclists. **Buzios Dacar,** Manoel José Carvalho 248 (© 022/2633-0419), rents bikes for R$45 per day.

BOATING **Schooner trips** are a great way to spend a day in Búzios. A small fleet of converted fishing schooners makes a circuit of about eight of Búzios's beaches plus three offshore islands. On board you trundle along in the sunshine eating complimentary fresh fruit and drinking free caipirinhas (or mineral water). At any of the beaches you're free to get off, hang out and swim for a bit, and then hop back on the next schooner (from your company) that comes along. There are enough boats that you usually don't have to wait long. One company is **Malizia Tour** (© 022/2623-1226), but there's really no need to seek them out. Just walk along Rua das Pedras anywhere near the pier, and you're guaranteed to be approached by a schooner tout. The exact price depends on how the time of year and how hard you negotiate, but competition between various schooner operators keeps things fairly competitive. Expect to pay from R$25 to R$45 for a half-day's cruise.

DIVING The islands just off Búzios are—along with Angra dos Reis and Arraial do Cabo—some of the best diving spots within a 1-day drive of Rio. Diving takes place at a number of islands about 45 minutes off the coast. Water temperature is normally around 22°C (72°F). Visibility ranges from 10 to 15m (30–50 ft.). Coral formations are fairly basic—mostly soft coral—but there are always lots of parrotfish, and there are often sea turtles (green and hawksbill) and stingrays of considerable size.

Casa Mar, Rua das Pedras 242 (© 022/9817-6234; www.casamar.com.br), offers a full range of services including cylinder refill and courses all the way from basic to nitrox. For a certified diver, a two-dive excursion costs R$110 or R$150 if you need to rent all the equipment such as a regulator, BCD (buoyancy control device), wet suit, and mask/fins/snorkel. For those wanting to get their diving license, a 5-day PADI open-water course costs R$850. If you just want to try diving, there are also introduction dives—you practice in the pool first and then the dive instructor takes you out for a controlled one-on-one dive in the open ocean—for R$180. Nondivers who come on the boat pay R$80.

FOR KIDS If your kids get bored with the beach you may want to bring them to **Radical Parque,** Estrada da Usina 1 (right next to the bus station; ✆ **022/2623-2904;** www.parqueradical.com.br; daily 9am–11pm). This oversize playground offers rappel, climbing walls, giant trampolines, paintball, and go-karts. Prices are per activity and range from R$10 for climbing or rappel to R$30 for half an hour of paintball or R$35 for 15 minutes of karting.

GOLF The **Búzios Golf Club & Resort** (✆ **022/2629-1240;** www.buziosgolf.com. br) is located just in from Manguinhos beach. Greens fees for this 18-hole course are R$165 per day for unlimited golf. Cart rental is R$100 for 18 holes and R$50 for 9 holes.

SURFING **Geribá** and **Tocuns** beaches are the best for surfing. They're located on the way in to Búzios, about 5km (3 miles) from downtown. Closer to town, **Brava** beach also often has good waves. Surfboard rentals and/or lessons are available at **Escolinha de Surfe do Rato** (✆ **022/9262-4756**) on Geribá beach.

WHERE TO STAY

Búzios is known for its pousadas, similar to North American B&Bs. These small, often owner-operated hotels provide excellent personalized service. By avoiding high season (Dec–Mar and July) and weekends throughout the year, you should be able to get a discount, although you will still expect to pay more at a pousada in Búzios than you would anywhere else in Brazil.

Very Expensive

Insólito Boutique Hotel ★★★ This exclusive luxury boutique hotel clings to the rocks overlooking Ferradura beach. With only 12 rooms set amid lush tropical gardens and spectacular terraces, guests practically have the place to themselves. All rooms face the ocean and are exquisitely decorated with tasteful modern Brazilian artwork, books, and furniture. King-size beds, 300-thread count sheets, LCD TVs, DVD players, and iPod docking stations are par for the course in each room. We are not sure why you would want to leave paradise and mingle with the crowds in downtown Búzios, but the hotel provides a free shuttle service just in case.

Praia da Ferradura, Armação de Búzios, 28950-000 RJ. ✆ **022/2623-2172.** Fax 022/2623-2923. www. insolitohotel.com.br. 12 units. High season R$1,000 double; low season R$860 double. AE, DC, MC, V. No children 13 and under. **Amenities:** Restaurant; bar; saltwater and freshwater outdoor pool; room service; sauna; spa. *In room:* A/C, TV/DVD, hair dryer, minibar, MP3 docking station, Wi-Fi.

Pousada Casas Brancas ★★ Tucked away on Orla Bardot, Casas Brancas sits on a hill overlooking the ocean, yet is only a 5-minute walk from the nightlife and restaurants of the busy Rua das Pedras. This sprawling Greek villa–like hotel offers spacious, comfortable rooms decorated in a clean, modern style. Only the best rooms face the ocean and feature a private terrace; the other rooms offer a partial ocean view or face the garden. Fortunately all guests have equal access to the hotel's gorgeous swimming pool and sun deck. Service is attentive and competent, and the well-equipped spa offers a wide range of professional beauty treatments.

Rua Alto do Humaitá 10, Praia da Armação, Armação de Búzios, 28925-000 RJ. ✆ **022/2623-1458.** Fax 022/2623-2147. 32 units. Dec–Mar R$550 standard room (garden view), R$750 deluxe room (ocean view); low season R$420–R$490 standard room (garden view), R$680 deluxe double. Extra person 30% extra.

AE, DC, MC, V. No children 4 and under. **Amenities:** Restaurant; bar; outdoor pool; room service; spa; Wi-Fi. *In room:* A/C, TV (upon request), hair dryer, minibar.

Expensive

La Boheme ★ (Kids) At the beginning of João Fernandes Beach, La Boheme overlooks the beach and the ocean from its hillside vantage point. The apartments all offer beautiful ocean views and are within walking distance of the main village and the beaches. All are very spacious and feature kitchenettes, perfect for groups or families traveling with children. A few are split-level suites and sleep up to seven people; the other apartments are on one level only, accommodating up to four people comfortably. The pool area includes a great children's pool, and the beach, about 90m (300 ft.) below the hotel, is safe enough even for the little ones, with almost no waves and perfect bathtublike temperatures.

Praia de João Fernandes, Armação de Búzios, 28950-000 RJ. ✆ **022/2623-1744.** www.labohemehotel. com. 40 units. R$420 1-bedroom apt that sleeps up to 4 people; R$680 double in an apt that sleeps up to 7 people. Children 4 and under stay free in parent's room, 5 and over R$50 extra. AE, DC, MC, V. Free parking. **Amenities:** Restaurant; 2 outdoor pools; room service; Wi-Fi. *In room:* A/C, TV, kitchen, minibar.

Pousada Abracadabra ★★ Right next door to Casas Brancas, Abracadabra has the same stunning location at a much more affordable price tag. But don't worry; you will hardly be slumming it (that is, as long as you avoid room no. 7, which feels like a glorified walk-in closet). The superior and deluxe rooms look out toward the ocean; the standard rooms have a garden view. The best part about this pousada is its privileged location on the top of a hill. Its swimming pool, sun deck, and bar offer a spectacular view of Búzios and the ocean. And when you have enjoyed all the quiet contemplation you can take, the hustle and bustle of the Rua das Pedras is only a 5-minute walk away.

Rua Alto do Humaitá 13, Praia da Armação, Armação de Búzios, 28925-000 RJ. ✆ **022/2623-1217.** Fax 022/2623-2147. 16 units. Dec–Mar R$270–R$340 standard room (garden view), R$450 deluxe room (ocean view); low season R$210–R$300 standard room (garden view), R$350 deluxe room (ocean view). Extra person 30% extra. Children 2 and under stay free in parent's room. AE, DC, MC, V. **Amenities:** Restaurant; bar; outdoor pool; Wi-Fi. *In room:* A/C, TV (upon request), hair dryer, minibar.

Moderate

Búzios Internacional Apart Hotel (Value) (Kids) One of the few relatively inexpensive options in town, this modern apart-hotel is just a few blocks from Rua das Pedras. Units are all self-contained flats equipped with a living room with foldout couch, kitchen, and either one or two bedrooms. These are an excellent option for a family traveling together. All units are pleasantly if simply furnished and come with a balcony and hammock looking out over a central garden. The complex also has a swimming pool, sauna, game room, and bar. Rentals are either calculated by day or by the week. Prices for two are comparable to the less expensive pousadas, but if there are more than three people (up to a maximum of six) savings can be significant. Discounts for 7-day stays available.

Estrada da Usina Velha 99, Armação de Búzios, 28980-000 RJ. ✆/fax **022/2537-3876.** www.buziosbeach. com.br. 44 units. High season (mid-Dec to Mar) R$260–R$300 for 2; low season (rest of year excluding holidays) R$160–R$200 for 2. Extra person R$40. AE, V. Free parking. **Amenities:** Restaurant; outdoor pool. *In room:* A/C, TV, hair dryer, kitchen, minibar.

WHERE TO DINE

Buzin KILO One of the better kilo restaurants, Buzin offers a large buffet of excellent salads, antipasto, and vegetables. The grill serves up a variety of cuts of steak, grilled to

Porto da Barra

The Rua das Pedras is no longer the only option for a fun night out in Búzios. A new dining area has developed on Manguinhos beach (Avenida José Bento Ribeiro Dantas 2900, Manguinhos; www.portodabarrabuzios.com.br; most restaurants closed for lunch on weekdays; 10–15 min. by taxi from downtown Búzios), overlooking the ocean and mangroves. Especially at night, this makes for a romantic outdoor dining destination when the restaurants and boardwalk through the mangrove are beautifully illuminated. Enjoy an Italian meal with a fabulous view at upscale **Quadrucci** (✆ **022/2623-6303**), or grab some fresh seafood at the **Bar dos Pescadores** (✆ **022/2623-6785**). Other options include delicious eclectic fusion dishes at **Zuza** (✆ **022/2623-0519**) and sushi at the **Captains Sushi Bar** (✆ **022/2623-9097**).

your preference. Of course, being right by the sea the restaurant also includes a daily selection of fresh seafood and fish in its offerings.

Rua Manoel Turibe de Farias 273. ✆ **022/2633-7051.** Reservations not accepted. Main courses R$44 per kilo. AE, V. Daily noon–midnight.

Estancia Don Juan ★★ STEAKHOUSE The Don loves only meat: the menu features *linguiça* (smoked sausage) and numerous exquisite beef cuts such as *picanha*, entrecôte, and *olho de bife*. Side dishes such as broccoli, baked potatoes, or carrots must be ordered separately. Fish flesh is also acceptable: The Don offers a toothsome catch of the day served with hollandaise sauce, capers, or balsamic vinaigrette. You can eat your meat on a lovely flowered patio, or in a multilevel hacienda dripping with atmosphere. The wine lists features a fine selection of South American reds (R$40–R$120 sold by the bottle). On Tuesday evenings at 9pm, there's a live tango show.

Rua das Pedras 178. ✆ **022/2623-2169.** Reservations accepted. Main courses R$34–R$52 for 2. AE, DC, MC, V. Mon–Tues 6pm–midnight; Wed–Sun noon–2am.

Sawasdee ★★★ THAI Over the last 10 years, chef Marcos Soudré and his wife Sandra have made Sawasdee into one of Brazil's finest Thai restaurants. The menu can be a bit overwhelming (it is huge), but everything is delicious so be adventurous. Don't just stick with the fragrant coconut soup, spicy red curry, or tangy pad Thai noodles. How about grilled fish with shiitake risotto and passion-fruit curry or grilled duck breast in tamarind sauce? The drink menu is equally creative and includes tasty tropical concoctions like the Koh Thao (vodka, lychee, and orange juice) or the Mai Tai (a vodka cocktail with mint, ginger, and lemon grass). Wine drinkers can choose from a variety of affordable options, either by the glass or by the bottle.

Av. José Bento Ribeiro Dantas 500 (Orla Bardot), Praia da Armação. ✆ **022/2623-4644.** www.sawasdee. com.br. Main courses R$32–R$58. AE, DC, MC, V. Sun–Tues and Thurs 6pm–midnight; Fri–Sat 6pm–1:30am. Closed Wed.

BUZIOS AFTER DARK

If you're looking for a night out, **Rua das Pedras** is the place to crawl. This 1,219m-long (4,000-ft.) street has pubs, bars, discos, and restaurants open on weekends until 5am.

To simply sit, sip a drink, and check out the action, the place to be is the **Anexo Bar and Lounge,** overlooking the happening waterfront. If you prefer your entertainment live, there's **Patio Havana,** which features a nightly selection of jazz, blues, and MPB. Thursdays is salsa night. Should you get bored of the band, you can wander out to the ocean-side patio and enjoy the nighttime view. For a late-night snack, locals and visitors gather at **Chez Michou**'s large outdoor patio for a crepe (open until 6am in high season). Popular Rio brewpub **Devassa** has set up shop in Porto da Barra (see above). To dance until you drop, Búzios boasts two mega-nightclubs on the Orla Bardot, **Privilege** and **Pacha** (one of Ibiza's hottest clubs). These only operate on Saturdays, with additional nights in high season. But remember, don't bother showing up until 1 or 2am.

2 PETROPOLIS ★

44km (27 miles) N of Rio de Janeiro, 371km (230 miles) NE of São Paulo

Known as *Cidade Imperial* (the Imperial City), Petrópolis is one of Rio de Janeiro's premier mountain resorts, located 720m (2,400 ft.) above sea level. Though only an hour from Rio, its quiet and calm put it light-years from the hectic pace of the city. The lovely tree-lined streets, the palaces, mansions, and museums can be comfortably explored on foot or by horse and buggy, and the mountain air ensures a pleasant climate year-round. Once just a stopover on the gold route between Minas Gerais (chapter 8) and Rio de Janeiro, its fine location and cool climate drew the attention of Emperor Dom Pedro II, who in 1843 founded the city of Petrópolis and built his summer palace (now the Imperial Museum) on a piece of land acquired by his father. Construction of the first railway in 1854 opened up easy access to the new city. Many of Brazil's merchant nobility—industrialists, coffee moguls, and politicians—built their summer residences here, turning Petrópolis into the de facto summer capital. Even after independence in 1889, Petrópolis maintained its prestige. In 1904 the former residence of the Baron of Rio Negro became the official summer residence of the president of the Republic.

Nowadays Petrópolis is a favorite weekend getaway for Cariocas: in the summer to escape the heat and humidity of the city, in the fall and winter for a chance to experience "really cold" weather, wear winter clothes, eat fondue, and sit by the fireplace. The historic part of the city, centered on the Imperial Museum and the Cathedral, contains the majority of the monuments and museums. Tree-lined canals and large squares give the small city a remarkably pleasant atmosphere; the side streets are worth exploring just to have a peek at the many mansions and villas. Particularly nice are Avenida Koeler and Avenida Ipiranga as far as the Casa Petrópolis.

In addition to the Cariocas's noble pursuit of culture and nature, they also flock here to visit the **Rua Teresa,** the best shopping street in Brazil. The area around Petrópolis has many textile factories, and the Rua Teresa has become the prime retail and wholesale outlet for cotton and knitwear at unbelievably low prices.

Petrópolis makes an easy day trip from Rio, but to experience the atmosphere of the city and take in some mountain air, it's better to spend the night. The region has a number of beautiful pousadas and excellent restaurants, and is close to a national park with excellent hiking trails.

ESSENTIALS
Getting There
Unica/Facil (© **021/2263-8792;** www.unica-facil.com.br) offers daily service between Rio's bus station, the Novo Rio Rodoviaria, and the main bus station in Petrópolis. The

trip takes 90 minutes. Buses traveling either direction leave daily every 90 minutes between 5:15am and midnight. Tickets cost R$15. In Petrópolis, buses arrive at the new bus station, **Terminal Rodoviaria Governador Leonel Brizola,** on the city outskirts, a short taxi ride from the historic center.

Getting Around

All the sites in the historic center are within walking distance of the bus station and each other. There is no need to drive or take a taxi.

BY RENTAL CAR   A rental car is useful if you're thinking of checking out some of the nearby national parks. Check out **Localiza,** Rua Coronel Veiga 746, Centro (© 024/2246-0100; www.localiza.com; Mon–Fri 9am–6pm, Sat 9am–2pm).

BY TAXI   For trips outside the city center, to pousadas or restaurants, call **Disk Taxi Imperial** (© 024/2242-9188) or just hail one of the many circulating taxis.

BY HORSE & BUGGY   This is a great way to see the city without doing all the walking. Buggies depart only from the main entrance of the Museu Imperial. (Buggies in front of other attractions are waiting for their clients to come back from their visit.) You have two options for sightseeing: The first tour, R$60 per buggy for up to six people, stops at the Cathedral, Palácio de Crystal, Casa de Santos Dumont, Palácio Rio Negro, and Palácio Barão de Mauá, allowing you to get off and visit each site while the buggy waits. It takes about an hour and a half. On the second, cheaper option you cover the same route, but the buggy never stops so you see the sights only from the outside. Cost is R$40 for up to six people, and it takes about 30 minutes. Tours run year-round, Tuesday through Sunday. *Note:* The tour price does not include admission to any of the museums along the way.

Visitor Information

The **Petrópolis Foundation of Culture and Tourism** maintains an English-language website (www.petropolis.rj.gov.br) and a toll-free information line **Disque Turismo** (© 0800/024-1516). There's also a number of tourist information centers around town. The main one is in the **Centro Histórico,** Praça Visconde de Mauá 305 (Mon–Sat 9am–6pm, Sun 9am–5pm); another is in the Governador Leonel Brizola **main bus terminal,** Rua Ministro Lucio Meira (daily 8am–6pm); and another is near the Rua Teresa shopping district, Rua Aureliano Coutinho s/n (Tues–Sun 9am–6pm). Ask for the English version of the excellent *Petrópolis Imperial Sightseeing* brochure. It comes with a map and opening hours of each of the attractions.

The Petrópolis Convention and Visitor's Bureau also has a website with information on Petrópolis attractions, accommodations, and restaurants: **www.pcvb.com.br**.

The **Banco do Brasil** branch is on the Rua do Imperador 940 (corner of Rua Alencar Lima; © 024/2243-6143).

Special Events

To honor the German immigrants who played an important role in the early days of Petrópolis, the city holds **Bauernfest,** an annual festival celebrating German music, culture, and food. It is held yearly on the last weekend of June and the first week of July. Contact Petrotur for more information (© 0800/024-1516).

Making the most of Petrópolis's reputation as a winter destination, the **Festival de Inverno (Winter Music Festival)** takes place in the last 2 weeks of July at the Palácio de

Tips **When Not to Go**

The absolute worst day to visit Petrópolis is Monday; most attractions are closed, and shops at the Rua Teresa open only at 2pm. Some attractions are also closed on Tuesday, and many restaurants are closed Monday through Wednesday. The best days to visit are Wednesday through Friday. Weekends can be busy, so book accommodations ahead of time. Avoid holidays as museum lines and traffic can be very bad.

Crystal, Palácio Rio Negro, Centro Cultural Raul de Leoni, and Praça da Liberdade. For information contact ℰ **0800/024-1516.**

EXPLORING PETROPOLIS

The historic heart of Petrópolis can easily be explored on foot: The city is fairly flat and extremely safe; even traffic is less hectic than in Rio. Following the directions below will take you to most points of interest.

Starting on the corners of Avenida Ipiranga and Tiradentes, the first thing you see is the **Cathedral São Pedro de Alcantara** (daily 8am–6pm), a neo-Gothic church named for both the patron saint of the Empire and—not coincidentally—the Emperor Dom Pedro II himself. Construction began in 1876, but the celebratory first Mass wasn't held until 1925. Just inside the main doors to the right is the Imperial Chapel containing the remains of the Emperor Dom Pedro II, the Empress Dona Teresa, their daughter Princess Isabel, and her husband (whose name no one remembers). The princess, who often ruled during her father's many trips abroad, lived in the beautiful mansion immediately across the street, now known as the **Casa da Princesa Isabel** (closed except for special exhibitions). Continuing along the Avenida Koeler as it follows the tree-lined canal, it's a 5-minute walk to the beautiful **Praça da Liberdade.** The bridge in front of this square offers the best view of the cathedral and the canal. Just behind the Praça da Liberdade is the **Museu Casa de Santos Dumont** (see below). From here follow Avenida Roberto Silveira, then turn right on Rua Alfredo Pachá to the **Palácio de Cristal,** Rua Alfredo Pachá s/n (ℰ **024/2247-3721;** admission R$5; Tues–Sun 9am–6:30pm). Commissioned by Princesa Isabel and built in France, the structure was inaugurated in 1894 as an agricultural exhibition hall. Nowadays, the palace is used for cultural events and exhibits (see "Special Events," above). The tourist information center inside the Palace has a great brochure in English featuring a map plus a listing of all the attractions with their opening hours.

Crossing the bridge to Avenida Piabanha, you come to the **Casa Barão de Mauá,** Praça da Confluencia s/n (ℰ **024/2246-9215**). Built in 1854 in neoclassical style by the industrial baron who constructed Brazil's first railway, the grounds of the house are open daily, from 9am to 6pm. The columns surrounding the winter garden are solid iron, made by the baron himself. Admission is free.

Continue by taking Rua 13 de Maio—right across the street from the Casa Barão de Mauá—toward the cathedral and then turning left on Avenida Ipiranga at the intersection just before the cathedral. Along this street are a number of interesting buildings as well as some gorgeous mansions and villas. Standing on the right side of the street at no. 346 is the 1816 **Igreja Luterana,** the oldest church in Petrópolis (open for visitation only during Sun morning service at 9am). On the left side of the street at no. 405 is the **Casa**

Rui Barbosa, the summer residence of the liberal journalist, politician, and positivist who helped found the First Republic. A bit farther along the Avenida Ipiranga at no. 716 is the lovely **Casa de Ipiranga,** a museum, cultural center, restaurant, and garden (see below). From here it's a simple matter to retrace your steps to the cathedral.

Casa de Ipiranga ★★   Guided tours of this beautifully preserved house will take you through numerous salons lavishly decorated with satin curtains and wallpaper, gold-leaf chandeliers, and ornate and beautiful furniture. The banquet room is a marvel of jacaranda wood—the room's generous palette of colors is the result of judicious use of variously colored jacaranda subspecies. The rest of the house is used for concerts and exhibits. Weekly concerts take place on Saturday night at 8pm; tickets cost R$15. The lovely garden is also well worth a look. Allow 1 hour.

Rua Ipiranga 716. ☎ **024/2231-8718.** www.casadaipiranga.blogspot.com. Admission R$5. Thurs–Mon noon–8pm.

Museu Casa de Santos Dumont ★   Who invented and flew the first airplane? Santos Dumont! Brazil's most famous aviator was the first in the world in 1906 to take off and land under his own power (unlike the Wright brothers, who used a catapult for takeoff on their first flight at Kitty Hawk). Dumont's creativity extended well beyond aviation. Among many other things, he also invented the wristwatch. Flying in balloons and blimps, he needed a watch at hand so he tied his pocket watch with a scarf to his wrist. Later he took the idea to his jeweler friend Cartier in Paris, who developed the first wrist strap. The Paris design house still comes out with a new watch design every year named "Santos." On display in this house are a number of bits of personal memorabilia: the medallions he earned for his many flight projects; his photos, books, and letters; and the Brazilian flag he carried with him on every flight. In the bathroom there's another Dumont original: the first hot shower in Brazil, heated by alcohol. Expect to spend 20 minutes. Helpful guides happily provide information in English.

Rua do Encanto 22. ☎ **024/2247-3158.** Admission R$5. Tues–Sun 9:30am–5pm.

Museu Imperial ★★   Built by Dom Pedro II in 1845 as his summer palace, this is now Petrópolis's premier museum. (On Sun and holidays the line can be fierce.) Visits take you through numerous salons decorated with period furniture, household items, and paintings and drawings depicting life and landscapes of 19th-century Rio. Best of all is Brazil's equivalent of the crown jewels: Dom Pedro II's crown, weighing almost 2 kilograms (4 lb.), encrusted with 639 diamonds and 77 pearls. Upstairs, visitors see the bedrooms, including lovely baby cribs made out of jacaranda wood and decorated with bronze and ivory—fit for a pair of princesses. In the garden, the palace's coach house has a beautiful collection of 18th- and 19th-century carriages. The highlight is the royal carriage, painted in gold and pulled by eight horses. Expect to spend 1½ hours.

Rua da Imperatriz 220. ☎ **024/2237-8000.** www.museuimperial.gov.br. Admission R$8 adults, R$4 children 7–14, free for children 6 and under. Tues–Sun 11am–5pm.

Palácio Rio Negro   Built by the coffee mogul Barão de Rio Negro in 1890, the palace has served as the summer residence of Brazilian presidents from 1903 onward. The rest of the year it functions as a cultural center. Most of the furniture inside is Portuguese baroque—dark, heavy, and beautifully carved. The hardwood floors are particularly ornate. Each room has a different pattern; the dining room floor is done in a coffee-bean pattern. Upstairs many of the rooms bear the decorative stamp of a particular president.

Av. Koeler 255. ☎ **024/2246-9380.** Free admission. Sat–Sun 10am–4pm.

HIKING   Petrópolis has great hiking in the hills surrounding the town. **Serra Trekking Ecoturismo** (🕾 **024/2242-2360;** www.serratrekking.com.br) offers everything from short day hikes to full overnight treks, ranging in price from R$25 to R$125. For do-it-yourselfers, the Petrópolis Convention and Visitor's Bureau **website** (www.pcvb.com.br) has a full page of information on local Petrópolis hikes. Click on "Trekking." To hook up with local hikers, try **Grupo de Ecoturismo Maverick** (🕾 **024/2291-3789;** www.grupo maverick.com.br). **Rio Hiking** (🕾 **021/2552-9204** or 9721-0594; www.riohiking.com. br) also organizes a variety of hiking trips in the Petrópolis region, with transportation to and from Rio included. A day trip can combine a short hike with some sightseeing of Petrópolis (R$200 per person) or you can opt for a 2-day hiking trip in the national park of Serra dos Orgãos close to Petrópolis (R$475).

HORSEBACK RIDING   Contact **Cavalgada Ecologica** (🕾 **024/2222-9666** or 8823-5528; www.cavalgadaecologica.com.br) for tours lasting from 2 to 4 hours.

WHERE TO STAY

Overnight visitors to Petrópolis can choose to stay at hotels or pousadas in the historic part of town, or head farther out and find a nice hotel in the hills and valleys close to town. The advantage of staying downtown is that all the attractions are easily accessible on foot. If you choose to stay farther out it's always a good idea to contact your pousada for instructions on how to get there; some can arrange for pickup or send a taxi. Petrópolis does not have a pronounced low or high season.

Casablanca Hotel Imperial ★ (Value)   More central would be almost impossible. Located next door to the Museu Imperial on one of Petrópolis's fine canals, Casablanca is within easy walking distance of all the city's historic sights. The hotel consists of the original mansion and a modern annex. The nicest rooms are the deluxe ones on the second floor of the original building. These have sky-high ceilings, air-conditioning, bathtubs, and antique dark-wood furniture. On the same floor there is also a lovely reading lounge with a fireplace looking out over the canal. The standard rooms with showers only—in the annex and on the ground floor of the main house—are pleasant but lack the same level of character. The only drawback to this hotel's central location is the neighboring school; it gets very noisy during recess.

Rua da Imperatriz 286, Petrópolis, 25610-320 RJ. 🕾 **024/2242-6662.** www.casablancahotel.com.br. 50 units, 7 with bathtub. R$190 standard; R$220 deluxe. Extra bed R$60. Children 6 and older R$35. AE, DC, MC, V. Free parking. **Amenities:** Outdoor pool; limited room service; sauna. *In room:* A/C (in *luxo* rooms only—standard rooms w/fans), TV, minibar.

Fazenda das Videiras ★★★ (Value)   The perfect romantic getaway spot in the mountains close to Rio. The chalets here feature king-size four-poster beds and fireplace, plus in the ample bathrooms a Jacuzzi for two with a skylight or peekaboo view of creek or woods. For more relaxation there's a little private deck with a view of babbling creek and mountains. The rooms in the main building are nice, but not really worth the price or effort of getting here. The French restaurant attached to the pousada is one of Petrópolis's best. Note that chalets usually rent for a 2-night minimum.

Estrada Araras 6000, Vale das Videiras, Petrópolis, 25610-320 RJ. 🕾 **024/2225-8090.** www.videiras.com. br. 5 chalets, 4 rooms. R$381–R$480 double; R$630–R$40 chalet (based on 2-night stay). AE, DC, MC, V. Free parking. Children 14 and under not permitted. **Amenities:** Excellent restaurant; outdoor pool; sauna. *In room:* A/C, TV/DVD, minibar.

Pousada Monte Imperial Koeller   This cute inn is located on one of the prettiest boulevards in Petrópolis, amid many of the historic buildings. Some of the rooms have a balcony and offer pleasant views of the gardens. Other rooms look out over the historic Casa da Princesa Isabel mansion next door. All rooms are nicely decorated and feature comfortable beds and Egyptian cotton sheets. Breakfast is included.

Av. Koeller 99, Petrópolis, 25620-000 RJ. © 024/2243-4330. www.pousadamonteimperial.com.br. 11 units. R$195–R$315 double. Extra person R$60. Children's rate negotiable. AE, DC, MC, V. Free parking. *In room:* TV, fridge, minibar.

Solar do Imperio ★★★   Fit for a king, or a princess to be more precise, the Solar do Imperio is a lovingly restored neoclassical palace built in 1875, and home to Brazil's Princess Isabela. Now, commoners can experience the regal elegance of this villa in the heart of Petrópolis. Upgraded, as much as possible to modern standards, the rooms have air-conditioning and heat, king-size beds with down comforters and pillows. Guests can choose between the *Real* suite or the Imperial suite. *Real* suites are much more spacious and have soaring high ceilings. Amenities, however, are the same in all rooms. The hotel also boasts a beautifully restored reading room, and an elegant veranda and garden—a royal experience indeed. (The hotel has recently added eight standard suites in the more modern spa building; though the quality is excellent they lack some of the historical charm.)

Av. Koeler 376, Petrópolis, 25610-220 RJ. © **024/2103-3000.** www.solardoimperio.com.br. 24 units. R$318–R$395 standard; R$365–R$450 Imperial; R$423–R$535 Real. AE, DC, MC, V. Free parking. **Amenities:** Restaurant; bar; outdoor pool; limited room service; sauna. *In room:* A/C, TV, hair dryer, minibar.

WHERE TO DINE

Petrópolis offers a range of dining opportunities, from schnitzel to sushi to *churrasco,* from cheap and cheerful to high-end (and expensive) fine dining. Check opening times carefully, though, as a number of restaurants are closed Monday through Wednesday or Monday through Thursday.

Expensive

Imperatriz Leopoldina ★★ BRAZILIAN   New in town and already winning awards, this elegant restaurant (in the Solar do Imperio hotel) features high ceilings, literally palatial windows, and walls decorated with creatures of the forest with knife and fork in hand, getting ready to tuck into dinner. As an appetizer, don't miss the *casuinha de bacalhau*—cod served with spices on a crab shell. For mains, the menu features succulent duck and lamb dishes, as well as regional favorites such as filet mignon with banana rice. Portions are generous, which may be why the wall animals always look so hungry.

Av. Koeller 376, Petrópolis (Centro) © **024/2103-3000.** www.solardoimperio.com.br. Main courses R$35–R$65. AE, DC, MC, V. Mon–Thurs noon–10pm; Fri–Sat noon–midnight; Sun noon–9pm.

Locanda della Mimosa ★★★ ITALIAN   The cuisine and wine list at this restaurant in the mountains have won plaudits and regular clients from Rio, Sao Paulo, and farther abroad. The dishes are Italian and contemporary, but the menu changes constantly to reflect seasonal ingredients and chef Dânio Braga's desire to create something new. Among the offerings is a four-course tasting menu, with wine pairings chosen from the Locanda's extensive cellars (awarded best wine list in Brazil in 2009 by the Guia Brasil). Decor is elegant and refined, and service is excellent. Note that the restaurant is only open on weekends.

Reservations required. Main courses R$65–R$125. DC, MC. Fri–Sat 12:30–3:30pm and 8–11:30pm; Sun 12:30–3:30pm.

Parrô de Valentim ★★ PORTUGUESE   Traditional Portuguese cuisine, which means simple ingredients—pork or cod, onions, olives, and potatoes—cooked with olive oil and seasonings, then served together in a large earthenware pan. Try the *bacalhau* (cod) *a Valentim,* or the *leitão a Portuguesa* (Portuguese suckling pig). You won't be sorry. Many dishes serve two. Save room for some of the traditional Portuguese sweets (mmm, *pastel de nata*).

Estrada União-Industria 10289, Itaipava (17km/27¹/₂ miles from Centro). ✆ **024/2222-1281.** www. parrodovalentim.com.br. Main courses R$35–R$65. DC, MC, V. Wed–Thurs 11:30am–10pm; Fri–Sat 11:30am–midnight; Sun 11:30am–9pm.

Inexpensive
Churrascaria Majoricá ★ CHURRASCO   A traditional-looking churrascaria with wood panels and booths, Majoricá is a local favorite when it comes to a good steak. Make your choice: T-bone, *picanha,* entrecôte. Most dishes serve two people.

Rua do Imperador 754. ✆ **024/2242-2498.** www.majorica.com.br. Main courses R$18–R$34. AE, MC, V. Sun–Thurs 11am–10pm; Fri–Sat 11am–11pm.

Luigi ITALIAN   This is a place for lovers of simple Italian food. Luigi's lists pasta and sauce separately, allowing guests to mix and match. There are also stuffed pastas such as cannelloni, ravioli, and lasagna. The large buffet includes cold cuts, cheeses, quiches, and sliced roast beef. In the evenings the restaurant serves excellent pizzas.

Praça Rui Barbosa 185, Centro. ✆ **024/2244-4444.** www.massasluigi.com.br. Main courses R$16–R$38. AE, DC, MC, V. Sun–Thurs 11am–midnight; Fri–Sat 11am–1am.

Paladar KILO   Just a block from the Santos Dumont Museum, the Paladar restaurant is great for a quick and inexpensive lunch. The restaurant puts out a great spread including salads, pasta, roast beef, chicken, beans, and other dishes. The selection varies from day to day.

Rua Barão do Amazonas 25. ✆ **024/2243-1143.** Main courses R$20 per kilo. AE, MC, V. Tues–Sun 11am–4pm.

Petit Palais Tea Room ★ (Finds) TEA/CAFE   Tucked away in the corner of the gardens surrounding the museum, this lovely tearoom is the perfect place for lunch. Head toward the coach house and follow the path downhill to the left. Full tea service is available, including cakes, pies, croissants, madeleines, toast, jam, cold cuts, and pâté. For something lighter the restaurant also serves a variety of quiches, omelets, soups, sandwiches, and pastas.

Rua da Imperatriz 220. ✆ **024/2244-7912.** Main lunch courses R$14–R$26; full tea R$39. No credit cards. Tues–Wed noon–7pm; Thurs noon–8pm; Fri–Sat noon–midnight; Sun noon–7pm.

3 ILHA GRANDE ★★★

Angra dos Reis: 114km (71 miles) SW of Rio de Janeiro, 246km (153 miles) NE of São Paulo

One man's paradise is another man's prison, quite literally in the case of Ilha Grande. During Brazil's long years of military dictatorship, the prison on the far side of the island was where the generals sequestered political prisoners, throwing them in the with the general population in the expectation that these effete intellectuals would get eaten alive. As it turned out, the political prisoners had solidarity and revolutionary theory on their side. Not only did they manage to dominate the general population, but they soon began to recruit among the other prisoners for the cause, imparting to these new cadres all their hard-won knowledge of revolutionary theory and urban guerilla warfare. With the return of democracy, the middle-class revolutionaries returned to politics, while the criminal cadres put their new skills to use revolutionizing the theory and practice of crime. The citywide drug syndicates that now control the favelas in Rio de Janeiro and São Paulo can be tracked back to lessons learned in the presidio of Ilha Grande. (A 2004 film version of this story, *Quase Dois Irmãos* [Almost Brothers] featured a screenplay by *City of God* author Paulo Lins.) The remains of the prison can still be seen on the island's windward shore, but that's not what draws people to Ilha Grande.

Instead, the reason most people sentence themselves to a stint on the Big Island has more to do with pristine beaches, turquoise ocean water, and green rainforest hills running from shoreline up to peaks over a thousand meters high. For the active, there's schooner tours and scuba diving, kayaking, rainforest hikes to hidden waterfalls, surfing and bodyboarding, and sailing. For the sedentary, there's quiet and calm and some of the prettiest beaches in Southern Brazil.

The main town on Ilha Grande—and the spot where the ferries and boats from the mainland arrive—is **Vila do Abraão** (often just Abraão), a not very big collection of pousadas and restaurants on the island's eastern end. Numerous other pousadas are tucked away on small bays and beaches around the rest of the island. Spend a few days here and you may find you've lost all will to escape.

ESSENTIALS
Getting There

To reach Ilha Grande you first travel by road, either to **Mangaratiba, Conceição de Jacareí,** or **Angra dos Reis,** and then by ferry, private schooner, or water taxi over to the island. Which point you depart from depends on where you're staying. If you're staying in or near the village of Abraão, then Conceição de Jacareí is probably the best bet, as the private schooner Saveiro Andéa offers four departures daily (six on Fri) and the trip is only 50 minutes. A large public ferry also travels from Mangaratiba and Angra dos Reis to Abraão on Ilha Grande. From Mangaratiba the ferry departs at 8am, while Angra dos Reis has an afternoon departure, either 3:30pm (weekdays) or 1:30pm (weekends). Angra is the larger town, the only one of three with banks and other services. Angra also has a number of private water taxis which offer transfers to pousadas spread out on the island. If you're staying in a pousada on the western half of the island, the water taxi likely departs from Angra.

BY BUS From Rio de Janeiro, **Costa Verde** (© 024/3371-1326; www.costaverde transportes.com.br) has approximately hourly departures to Mangaratiba, Conceição de Jacareí, and Angra dos Reis (it's the same bus) from Rio's main bus station (Novo Rio) starting at 4am and ending at 9pm. Cost is R$31. The trip takes to Angra takes about 2½ hours, to Mangaratiba and Conceição de Jacareí a little less. *Tip:* If you're planning to get off at Conceição de Jacareí, let the bus driver know when you board the bus. That way he'll stop and call out when you arrive. From São Paulo, **Reunidas Paulista** (© 0300/210-3000; www.reunidaspaulista.com.br) has four departures per day to Angra from the Tietê station, at 8am, 12:15pm, 4pm, and 10pm. The trip takes 7 hours and costs R$57.

BY PRIVATE TRANSFER   **Paraty Tours** (© 024/3371-2651; www.paratytours.com. br) offers private transfers from Rio de Janeiro with set times for a minimum of two people at 8:30am, 12:30pm, and 5pm. Airport pickups anytime between 8:30am and 5pm. Travel time is about 2½ hours. Rates per person are R$125. For three people or more you can set your own pickup time.

BY FERRY   From Angra dos Reis, **Barcas S.A.** (© 0800/704-4113; www.barcas-sa. com.br) has one departure a day, at 3:30pm on weekdays, and 1:30pm on weekends. The return trip from Ilha Grande to Angra departs at 10am. From Mangaratiba, the ferry departs at 8am daily (with one extra 10pm sailing on Fri). The return ferry to Mangaratiba departs at 5:30pm daily. For both routes, cost is R$14 one-way, R$25 return, and the trip takes about 80 minutes.

BY PRIVATE SCHOONER   The private schooner **Saveiro Andréa** (© 021/9744-0732 or 024/8826-3809) makes four trips daily between **Conceição de Jacareí** on the mainland and **Vila do Abraão** on Ilha Grande. From Conceição de Jacareí, the boat departs at 9, 11:30am, 3pm, and 6:15pm, with two extra sailings on Fridays at 6:45 and 9pm.

From Vila do Abraão, the ship departs at 7:30, 10am, 1, and 5pm. Cost is R$15 each way, travel time is 50 minutes.

From **Angra dos Reis,** the schooner **Saveiro Resta 1** (© 024/3365-6436) departs for **Abraão** at 8am weekdays, 7:30, 11am, and 4pm weekends. Going the other way, the boat departs at 5pm weekdays, 9:30am, 1, and 5pm weekends. Also from Angra dos Reis, the schooner **Saveiro Samurai** (© 024/3361-5920) departs for Abraão daily at 5pm. Journeys from Abraão to Angra take place in the morning, daily at 10am. Cost is R$10 to R$15 depending on the departure time, and the trip takes 90 minutes.

A new service, the **Catamaran IGT** (© 024/3365-6426 or 3361-5500), departs Angra dos Reis for the island daily at 8, 10:45am, and 4pm, and departs Vila do Abraão for Angra at 9am, 12:30, and 5pm. Cost is R$25. Time is 45 minutes.

Note: This being Brazil, schooner departure times, locations, and fares are subject to change at unpredictable intervals. Always call to confirm (or ask your pousada for the latest information).

BY WATER TAXI   Numerous smaller boats make the trip to Ilha Grande, either to ferry passengers to pousadas on more isolated beaches or to take visitors on day trips. Transfers on these smaller boats is normally R$50 per person, with a minimum of four people. To find a skipper, ask at your pousada, or try the **Associação dos Barqueiros de Angra (Boat Captains' Association of Angra;** © 024/3365-3165) or the **Associação dos Barqueiros da Ilha Grande** (© 024/3361-5920).

Getting Around

The town of Abraão is easily walkable, and there are numerous trails on the island.

FAST FACTS   There are no banks on Ilha Grande. Some pousadas and restaurants accept credit cards, but its best to check beforehand, and bring enough cash to cover your stay. The police are located in Vila do Abraão (© 024/3365-1635).

Visitor Information

Though there is no official Ilha Grande tourism bureau, a number of websites have useful information about Ilha Grande. These include **www.ilhagrande.org**; **www.ilhagrande. com**; and **www.ilhagrande.com.br**. They provide general tourist information as well as suggestions on hotels, tours, and excursions.

EXPLORING ILHA GRANDE
The Beaches

Though nearly all the beaches on Ilha Grande are beautiful, a few are simply spectacular. One of these is **Lopes Mendes,** facing the ocean on the eastern tip of the island. Considered the prettiest beach in the island, this long stretch of strand is unspoiled by any development, and features fine soft sand, clear clean water, and excellent surfing waves. You can walk to Lopes Mendes from Abraão (about 2½ hr.) but most people catch a boat (see "Boating," below) to the anchorage at Pouso, from which it's an easy 20-minute walk up and over a low ridge.

Dois Rios beach also lies on the open ocean side of the island. The ruins of Ilha Grande's **Candido Mendes Prison,** deactivated and destroyed in 1994, still stand at the southern end of the beach. Beach and prison are reached via a broad trail (a former road, in fact) from Abraão. The hike takes about 2½ hours, and is of medium level difficulty.

On the island's western end, the beaches of **Aventureiro, Praia Sul,** and **Praia Leste** slope gently out to sea, making for lots of shallows with only gentle surf. The beaches are

reached via schooner to Aventureiro, after which you walk along the shoreline to Praia
Sul and Praia Lest. Aventureiro has a small restaurant where you can relax and have lunch.

Though not strictly a beach, **Lagoa Azul** is a delightful area of shallows and small islands near the north (landward) tip of the island. Its calm waters and extreme visibility make it a great place to snorkel. The Blue Lagoon is reached via boat, a 40-minute trip from Abraão.

The Hiking Trails

The classic Ilha Grande hike goes from Abraão up to **Pico de Papagaio (Parrot Peak),** so-called because the mountain supposedly looks like a parrot's head. The trail is rough but reasonably well-marked, and covers 11km (7 miles) and gains 1,080m (3,543 ft.) in altitude. If you know how to hike, there's no need for a guide, but services are available (see "Hiking," below). Round-trip takes about 10 hours. There are several excellent lookout spots on the way up. The view from the peak is marvelous. Less intense hikes go from Abraão to **Lopes Mendes beach** (about 2 hr. one-way, easy), from Abraão to **Dois Rios beach** and the old prison (about 2 hr. one-way, medium). From Praia Vermelha on the island's western end you can also hike to **Provetá beach** (2 hr., medium) and from there to **Aventureiro** beach on the seaward coast (1½ hr., medium). Easiest and arguably best of all, the hike from Abraão to the 15m-high (49-ft.) **Cachoeira da Feiticeira** waterfall requires no great effort, and provides a tremendous reward (1½ hr., easy).

Outdoor Activities

BOATING   Numerous boats large and small transport visitors to various beaches and other spots around the island. In Abraão, the boats or their agents have ticket booths on the piers. If you're staying at a pousada out of town, odds are your pousada owner will know where and when to catch a boat, or you can call the **Associação de Barqueiros do Abraão** (© 024/3361-5920). The standard boat trip destinations include **Lopes Mendes** (R$25), **Lagoa Azul** (R$35), and (if staying near the western part of the island) **Aventureiro** (R$25). Trips to **Dois Rios** (R$35) often don't travel when waves and sea are rougher. Another excellent option is the full-day 8-hour trip by fast launch of the island's aquatic high points, including Cachandaço, Dois Rios, Lagoa Azul. These small boats take a maximum of 10 people, and you stop along the way to snorkel, swim, and enjoy the sights. The cost is R$150 per person. For details contact **Phoenix Turismo** (© 024/3361-5822).

DIVING   Excellent dive spots are all around the island. Located in the mini-shopping Buganville in Abraão, **Elite Dive Center** (© 024/3361-5501 or 9991-9292; www. elitedivecenter.com.br) offers day trips including two dives and all equipment for R$150. Four-day PADI course for beginners cost R$800.

HIKING   For guiding services on Ilha Grande hikes, contact **Phoenix Turismo** (© 024/ 3361-5822).

WHERE TO STAY

Vila do Abraão is the most settled part of the island. Staying here offers the chance to stroll out of an evening and have an ice cream, or sample a few different restaurants. Day trips are also easy to arrange from here. On the downside, the beach at Abraão is not as nice as elsewhere on the island, and the campers and backpackers can detract from the idyllic calm.

In Vila do Abraão

Pousada Manaca ★   On the beach, the Manaca offers the best compromise between being close to things while maintaining tranquillity and quiet. Rooms are airy and comfortable, featuring queen-size beds, verandas, and hammocks. The two best rooms are the upstairs suites with a view of the ocean. A lovely garden—where breakfast is served—adds to the atmosphere, as does the tasteful indigenous art displayed throughout the pousada. For cooler evenings, there's a sauna.

Praia do Abraão 133, Ilha Grande, 23970-000 RJ. ✆ **024/3361-5742.** www.ilhagrandemanaca.com.br. 7 units. Dec–Mar R$190–R$230 double; Apr–Nov R$150–R$170 double. Extra person R$50. Children 6 and under stay free in parent's room. MC, V. **Amenities:** Restaurant. *In room:* A/C, minibar, no phone, Wi-Fi.

Sagu Mini Resort ★★   The most luxurious spot within walking distance of Abraão, the Sagu sits on a rocky headland with a small micro-beach just a 2-minute walk to one side. Rooms are airy and elegant, with tile floors, wood accents and furnishings, and comfortable queen-size beds. All but two have a sizable private veranda with a hammock and a view of the sea (price is the same, so make sure to ask when reserving). The common grounds are lovely, with walkways, trees, and ocean views. The hotel restaurant, **Toscanelli Brasil** (see below), is one of the best on the island, offering innovative seafood dishes in a romantic setting (not included in the room rates). The resort also offers other services such as massage, kayak rental, dive trips, and hiking tours, at an extra cost. Free transfer to Abraão on check-in and checkout.

Praia da Bica, Ilha Grande, 23970-000 RJ. ✆/fax **024/3361-5660.** www.saguresort.com. 9 units. Nov–Apr R$360 double; May–Oct R$290 double. Extra person R$80. Children 4 and under stay free in parent's room. MC, V. **Amenities:** Restaurant. *In room:* A/C, minibar, Wi-Fi.

On Beaches Elsewhere

Estrela da Ilha ★★   What a spot. This place is set on a small cliff top overlooking the ocean, a 1-minute walk from a long and mostly deserted stretch of sand. Rooms are set in a long row, each looking out over a small veranda with hammock to the blue sea beyond. Beds are comfortable queens. The pleasant common area features a small selection of books and games and some comfy couches for relaxing. On the beach, there are free chairs and umbrellas and sunshine. And when that palls, the pousada offers a wide variety of extra activities (at an extra cost), including kayaking, guided hikes, snorkeling, and massages. Meals are delicious and included (ask beforehand if you want a vegetarian menu), as is transfer from the mainland.

Enseada das Estrelas, Ilha Grande, 23970-000 RJ. ✆ **021/9925-9756** or 024/9831-0020. www.estrelada ilha.com. 11 units. R$400 double. Rates include all meals and mainland transfer. Extra person R$80. Children 6 and under stay free in parent's room. DC, MC, V. **Amenities:** Restaurant; bar. *In room:* A/C, fan, no phone.

Pousada Lagamar ★   What makes this pousada special is its location, nestled on a hillside above a pocket beach, amid the trees of the Atlantic rainforest. There's verdant foliage all around, hummingbirds buzz beside you on the restaurant deck, while the view is of turquoise ocean and unspoiled sand. Praia Itaguaçú, a 2-minute walk from the pousada, features boulders, sand and blue-green water, and very little else. Praia Vermelha, the "busier" beach a 10-minute walk away, features a pier, some fishermen's homes, and all of two restaurants. Accommodations are comfortable but not luxurious. The chalet offers a double bed downstairs and a pair of singles in an upstairs loft. The suites feature comfortable doubles. Both suites and chalets offer a veranda and hammock, and the wood construction gives the place a pleasant rustic air. Breakfast and delicious seafood dinners are part of the package, as is the hospitality of Mel, the host and owner.

Praia Vermelha, Ilha Grande, 23970-000 RJ. (✆ **024/9221-8180** or 9218-9191. www.pousadalagamar. com.br. 4 suites, 1 chalet. Low season R$130 standard, R$175 suite; high season R$150 suite, R$210 chalet. Extra person add R$80. Rates include breakfast and dinner. MC, V. **Amenities:** Restaurant. *In room:* Fan, fridge, no phone.

WHERE TO DINE

Downtown Vila do Abraão offers a number of simple eateries, many of them acceptable, though none outstanding. The **Pizzaria Dom Pepe,** Rua Amancio de Souza 4 (✆ **024/ 3361-5910**), offers cheap and cheerful pizza and other dishes, daily from noon to 9pm. The **Bossa Nova Restaurant,** Rua Santana 145 (✆ **024/3361-5668;** daily noon–11pm), has a house specialty—grilled shrimp and fish served on a piping hot griddle—that's served in a pleasant candlelit room. **Mix de Sabores,** Rua Getulio Vargas 161 (✆ **024/3361-5727;** daily 4pm–midnight), offers a wide range of pastas, including a delicious seafood pasta.

Lua e Mar SEAFOOD   The nicest restaurant in all Abraão sits on the beach just on the outskirts of town. Dine inside in the small candlelit dining room or outside on plastic tables by the shoreline. The menu includes meat and pasta dishes, but ordering these is a waste of time. The specialty is seafood—rich stews of fish or shrimp or octopus—or fresh filets of fish served steamed or fried. Drinks include beer and a variety of fruity cocktails.

Rua da Praia 297. (✆ **024/3361-5113.** Main courses R$15–R$35. AE, DC, MC, V. Daily 11am–11pm.

Toscanelli Brasil BRAZILIAN   Innovative cuisine made with fresh seafood ingredients, along with traditional Brazilian seafood dishes, including an excellent fish *moqueca* and a delicious Bahian *bobó de camarão.* There are also meat and pasta dishes. The wine list is certainly the best on the island. The walk from Abraão takes only about 15 minutes, but bring a flashlight and watch for rocks and tree roots.

Sagu Mini Resort (see above), Praia da Bica. (✆ **024/3361-5114.** www.saguresort.com. Main courses R$25–R$45. AE, DC, MC, V. Daily 7–10pm.

ILHA GRANDE AFTER DARK

If you came looking for nightlife, then you made a wrong turn at Albuquerque. Evening excitement on the Ilha consists of watching newcomers troop off the ferry. That said, you don't have to stay cooped up in your pousada. **Espaco Café Tropical,** Rua Santana s/n (✆ **024/3361-5577;** Tues–Sun 9am–midnight), offers coffee and *cachaça,* and a vantage point in the thrumming heart of the downtown Abraão. Also in Vila do Abraão, the **Bar Biergarten,** Rua Getulio Vargas 161 (✆ **024/3361-5583;** Mon–Fri 6:30pm–midnight), features patio tables, a reasonable wine list, some fancy cocktails, and a tapas bar of snacks.

4 PARATY ★★★

156km (97 miles) SW of Rio de Janeiro, 200km (124 miles) NE of São Paulo

Paraty has a gorgeous colonial center, surrounded by turquoise blue waters and flanked by the soaring rainforest-covered mountains of Rio de Janeiro's Costa Verde. The historic core, a UNESCO World Heritage Site, features beautifully preserved colonial architecture. In contrast to the ornate baroque opulence of Ouro Preto, Paraty was a port, a working-class kind of town. The architecture is simple and colonial. Even the churches and municipal buildings seemed to have been built more for daily use than as a statement of wealth.

Paraty (also spelled Parati; if you want to start a long conversation, ask a local why there are two spellings) first grew in importance in the 1800s when it became the main shipping port for the gold from the mines of Minas Gerais (chapter 8). The gold was transported down windy trails and cobblestone roads from Ouro Preto to the coast, where it was loaded on ships sailing for Portugal. Once gold became scarce, Paraty switched to coffee, but with the abolishment of slavery in 1888, that too dried up and Paraty faded to near oblivion; the population fell from 16,000 in its glory days to 600 in the early 1900s. From a heritage perspective it was the city's saving grace.

In 1966 the historic colonial center of Paraty was declared a UNESCO World Heritage Site. To preserve its premodern character, cars were banished from the old colonial core. Radical as that may sound, it actually works rather well. Boat tours of the surrounding islands leave from the dock in the city center. Day trips into the surrounding hills include transportation.

The region surrounding the city adds much to Paraty's quiet beauty. The hills are still mostly covered in lush green coastal rainforest, and the waters around Paraty, dotted with 65 islands, are tropical turquoise, warm, and crystal clear, perfect for snorkeling, swimming, or scuba diving. If you only have time to visit one of the historic towns, Paraty makes a fine (long) 1-day or easy overnight destination from either Rio or São Paulo.

ESSENTIALS

Getting There

BY BUS   From Rio de Janeiro, **Costa Verde** (© 024/3371-1326; www.costaverde transportes.com.br) has eight departures per day, from Rio's main bus station (Novo Rio) the first at 6am, the last at 9pm. Cost is R$49. The trip takes approximately 4 hours. From São Paulo **Reunidas Paulista** (© 0300/210-3000; www.reunidaspaulista.com.br) has six departures per day from the Tietê station, beginning at 8am and finishing at 10pm. The trip takes about 6 hours and costs R$44.

BY PRIVATE TRANSFER   **Paraty Tours** (© 024/3371-2651; www.paratytours.com. br) offers private transfers from Rio de Janeiro with set times for a minimum of two people at 8:30am, 12:30, and 5pm; airport pickups are available anytime between 8:30am and 5pm. Rates per person R$145. For three people or more you can set your own pickup time.

Getting Around

ON FOOT   The historic center of Paraty is perfect for exploring on foot. The city center is closed to cars (parking is on the outskirts), making walking a traffic-free dream. Wear comfortable shoes as the big cobblestones make for a bumpy stroll.

BY TAXI   Taxis in Paraty can be hailed outside of the car-free historic city center, or call © 024/9999-9075 or 3371-2411.

BY RENTAL CAR   Car rentals are available from **Alugue Brasil Paraty,** Av. Roberto Silveira 99 (© 024/3371-0019; www.paratyturismo.tur.br).

Visitor Information

The official **Paraty Tourist Information,** Av. Roberto Silveira 1, on the corner of Rua Domingos Gonçalves de Abreu (© 024/3371-1897; www.paraty.com.br), is open daily

from the historic center at Av. Roberto da Silveira 11 (© **024/3371-2651;** www.paraty
tours.com.br). They provide general tourist information as well as suggestions on hotels,
tours, and excursions.

FAST FACTS **Banco do Brasil,** Av. Roberto Silveira s/n (© **024/3371-1379**), is open
Monday through Friday 10am to 3pm. ATMs are open 24 hours. **Paraty Web Internet
Access** is located inside the Quero Mais Restaurant, Rua Marechal Deodoro 243
(© **024/3371-7375**). Connection cost is R$4 per hour. There's also Wi-Fi in much of
the old historic center, R$20 for 2 hours, with **www.paraty.com**.

EXPLORING PARATY
The Historic Center

Start your exploration of Paraty at the main pier at the bottom of **Rua da Lapa.** Fishing
boats come and go, as well as frequent schooner excursions. Turn and face the city and
you will see the postcard-perfect vista of Paraty: the **Santa Rita** church framed by a
background of lush green hills. The church was built by freed slaves in 1722 and despite
its plain exterior, displays some fine rococo artwork. The church also houses the small
Museum of Sacred Art (Wed–Sun 10am–noon and 2–5pm; admission R$4). It's worth
a quick peek, though it can't compare to some of the fine art on display in Ouro Preto
or Mariana. The building just to the left of the church was once the town jail; now it's
home to the city library and historical institute. Paraty's biggest and most ornate church,
the **Igreja da Matriz,** stands on the Praça da Matriz, close to the River Perequê-Açu.
What started with a small chapel in 1646 became a bigger church in 1712 and was finally
replaced with the current large neoclassical building, completed in 1873. The **Casa da
Cultura** (Rua Dona Geralda) was originally built in 1754 as a private residence and
warehouse. Later it housed the town's public school. In the 1990s, the city restored it to
serve as a cultural center and exhibit space.

Outdoor Activities

BIKING A mountain bike is the perfect way to reach some of the waterfalls in the surrounding hills or some of the beaches just a 10km (6½-mile) ride out of town. **Paraty
Tours,** Av. Roberto da Silveira 11 (© **024/3371-1327**), rents bikes by the hour for R$10
or by the day for R$40. Maps are provided.

BOATING Just beyond the muddy Paraty waterfront, the coast is dotted with more
than 60 islands, many lush and green, surrounded by turquoise water. It shouldn't be
surprising then that schooner trips are extremely popular. The pier in the city center is
the main departure point. Boats leave daily, weather permitting, and take you on a 5- to
6-hour tour, stopping several times for a swim or snorkel and a lunch break. **Paraty
Tours,** Roberto da Silveira 11 (© **024/3371-2651;** www.paratytours.com.br), and
Saveiro Porto Seguro (© **024/3371-1254**) are just two of several companies that have
daily departures at 11am (as well as 10am and noon in high season); the cost is R$35 for
adults, free for children under 5, R$15 for 5- to 10-year-olds. To explore the bay at a
more leisurely pace, Paraty tours offers a kayak tour. The 6-hour paddle provides plenty
of opportunity for checking out some of the islands and beaches. Cost is R$75 per per-
son, including a guide and all the equipment (minimum of two people).

DIVING The islands around Paraty have some decent diving and cater to a variety of
levels. Most operators take you to the many islands around Angra dos Reis (up the coast
from Paraty). Dive companies in town include **Adrenalina,** Marina Farol de Paraty

(© **024/3371-2991**; www.adrenalinamergulho.com.br), **Una Tour e Dive,** Rua da Lapa 213 (© **024/3371-6188**; www.unatouredive.com.br), and **Paraty Tours,** Roberto da Silveira 11 (© **024/3371-2651**; www.paratytours.com.br). All offer a full range of services, including cylinder refill and courses, and an introductory dive if you do not have a license. For a certified diver, a two-dive excursion costs approximately R$190. This rate includes all the equipment such as a regulator, BC (buoyancy control), wet suit, and mask/fins/snorkel.

HIKING   In the surrounding hills one can still find stretches of the old wagon trail that was used to bring the gold from Ouro Preto down to the coast. Parts of the old cobblestone trail have been restored and are accessible to hikers. **Paraty Tours,** Roberto da Silveira 11 (© **024/3371-2651**; www.paratytours.com.br), offers an easy trek along this historic route. The 3-hour tour leaves Thursday through Sunday at 11:30am and includes a guide (R$25 per person, children 4–10 half price). Paraty Tours also offers a number of guided day hikes to the isolated beaches at Trinidade and Praia do Sono (R$35–R$45 per person). Transportation is by jeep and includes several stops. If you want a more serious hike, consider a 2- or 3-day trip. **Rio Hiking** (© **021/9874-3698**; www.riohiking.com.br) offers excellent hiking trips along the beaches and through the coastal rainforest on the peninsula just south of Paraty, called Paraty-Mirim. Transportation from Rio de Janeiro and rustic accommodations included (2-day trip R$450 per person, and 3-day trip R$650).

WHERE TO STAY

Paraty's historic center is jampacked with pousadas. Of course, retrofitting modern accommodations into 18th-century buildings requires some adaptations. Don't expect fancy plumbing. Stairways are narrow and steep and there is no parking, as all cars have to remain outside the historic core. What you do get are charming bed-and-breakfasts in beautiful heritage buildings.

Pousada Arte Urquijo ★★★   Paraty's most unusual pousada, Art Urquijo is a true labor of love by the owner, artist Luz Urquijo. Her bold and colorful artwork is prominently displayed throughout the pousada. Guests are greeted with classical music and asked to take their shoes off and help themselves to comfortable slippers. Luz has paid a lot of attention to detail and each of her six rooms is unique. Our favorite is the Sofia, which looks out over the rooftops toward the ocean and has a small deck. Probably the most unique room is Xul: as the ceilings are a bit low, Luz has used a Japanese bed (low on the floor) and mats and pillows to decorate. All rooms come with a very tiny private bathroom. The pousada is not for people who have difficulty with stairs; the higher floors can only be reached via a narrow winding staircase.

Rua Dona Geralda 79, Paraty, 23970-000 RJ. ©/fax **024/3371-1362**. www.urquijo.com.br. 6 units. High season R$350–R$390; low season R$330–R$370. Rooms are doubles only. DC, MC, V. No children 11 and under. **Amenities:** Bar; small outdoor pool. *In room:* A/C, TV, minibar, no phone, Wi-Fi.

Pousada da Marquesa ★   A lovely sprawling colonial mansion, Pousada da Marquesa offers affordable accommodations with some great amenities. The pousada actually consists of two buildings, the original main building and an annex along the side overlooking the garden and swimming pool. These rooms are on ground level and perfect for those who don't want to climb the steep and narrow stairs. All rooms are simply and nicely furnished and the common rooms have beautiful antiques. A swimming pool and garden offer a perfect refuge on hot summer days.

Rua Dona Geralda 99, Paraty, 23970-000 RJ. *©* **024/3371-1263.** Fax 024/3371-1299. www.pousada marquesa.com.br. 21 units. Dec–Mar R$380 double; Apr–Nov R$330 double. Extra person 30%–50% extra. Children 6 and under stay free in parent's room. AE, DC, MC, V. **Amenities:** Bar; free Internet; outdoor pool. *In room:* A/C, TV, minibar.

Pousada Porto Imperial   One of the largest pousadas in the city center, Porto Imperial still feels like a small inn. The decorations throughout are quite impressive, blending antique furniture with modern folk art and tropical colors. In contrast, the rooms are very simply decorated with plain wooden furniture and bedding. The inner courtyard hides a lovely garden and swimming pool as well as a sauna.

Rua Tenente Francisco Antonio s/n (across from the Matriz church), Paraty, 23970-000 RJ. *©* **024/3371-2323.** Fax 024/3371-2111. www.portotel.com.br. 50 units. R$400 standard; R$530 superior. Off season and weekdays 30% discount. Children 2–12 R$60. AE, DC, MC, V. **Amenities:** Outdoor pool; limited room service; sauna. *In room:* A/C, TV, minibar.

WHERE TO DINE

Banana da Terra ★★ BRAZILIAN   This beautiful little restaurant on one of Paraty's side streets offers exotic combinations of seafood and tropical ingredients. *Ponta Negra* is a fabulous fish dish served in a coconut sauce with shrimp. Another dish stars the lowly squid dolled up with a banana-and-cheese stuffing and served in coconut milk. Another seafood favorite is the risotto with squid, crab, and prawns spiced with ginger and chutney. Desserts include banana sweets or baked banana.

Rua Dr. Samuel Costa 198. *©* **024/3371-1725.** Main courses R$28–R$65 for 2. AE, DC, MC. Mon and Wed–Thurs 7pm–midnight; Fri–Sun noon–4pm and 7pm–midnight.

Café Pingado COFFEE SHOP   For your morning shot of caffeine or a sweet snack try this pretty, tiny coffee shop. Great espressos and cappuccinos, and a good selection of sweet and savory snacks. Only four tables, though, so order that coffee to go and take it for a stroll.

Rua Samuel Costa 11. *©* **024/3371-8333.** Everything under R$15. No credit cards. Daily 10am–8pm.

Kontiki SEAFOOD   If you thought only millionaires got to go for lunch on a private island, you're missing out. Kontiki restaurant is only a 10-minute boat ride from Paraty, on the tiny Ilha Duas Irmãs (Two Sisters Island). In the daytime, the restaurant operates a shuttle service from the pier in Paraty. Just ask for the Kontiki transfer. In the evenings the restaurant will only open with a minimum of 10 people (in total) so call in your reservations and they will confirm if there's enough to open the restaurant. The menu is

---

(Moments   Cachaça Festival

The region around Paraty is very well known for its *cachaça* (also known as *pinga*), the Brazilian booze made from sugar cane. Several distilleries are nearby, and each year, on the third weekend of August, the city celebrates the **Festival da Pinga.** Events include live music and lots and lots of tastings. *Tip:* If you miss the festival, make sure to stop at the **Emporio da Cachaça,** Rua dr. Samuel Costa 22 (*©* **024/3371-6329**), a specialty store with over 300 types of *cachaça* from all over Brazil.

The FLIP Festival

Paraty's most important event is annual writer's festival, flippantly referred to as the **FLIP** (Festa Literária Internacional de Paraty). This event takes place in early July and includes numerous well-known foreign authors. Readings and presentations are often in English. For more details on upcoming FLIPs see www.flip.org. br. Book early if you plan to attend the FLIP. This event has quickly become the toast of the town, and it's even outselling New Year's or Carnaval. Contact the tourist information office (② **024/3371-1897**) or the FLIP festival office in Paraty (② **024/3371-7082**) for details.

Mediterranean seafood, including lots of fresh prawns, crab, and fish. Pastas with seafood are also a good option as well as the authentic Spanish paella, a saffron rice dish with meat and seafood. The restaurant's two large verandas look out over the bay and the mainland. The island has a tiny beach, and rents masks, snorkels, and kayaks; showers are available in case you want to rinse off after a swim.

Ilha Duas Irmãs. ② **022/3371-1666.** www.ilhakontiki.com.br. Main courses R$34–R$68. DC, MC, V. Low season Mon–Tues and Fri–Sun 10am–5:30pm; summer daily 10am–5:30pm.

Restaurante Refúgio BRAZILIAN   A refuge indeed, Restaurante Refúgio is tucked away from the busy streets and offers a large patio overlooking Paraty's harbor. The specialty here is seafood. As an appetizer, try the *camarão casadinho* (a large deep-fried prawn stuffed with a spicy *farofa* and dried shrimp filling), a regional specialty found only in Paraty. For a main course, try the fish or seafood *moquecas* (stews with coconut milk and palm oil).

Praça do Porto 1, on the waterfront. ② **022/3371-2447.** Main courses R$25–R$45. DC, MC, V. Daily noon–11pm.

PARATY AFTER DARK

Paraty is not a wild party town (that's Búzios). The crowd's a bit older, the nightlife more laid-back. Enjoy some live music, have some drinks, and chat with the other folks who are quite likely visiting as well.

One of the more popular live-music venues is the **Café Paraty,** Rua do Comércio 253 (② **024/3371-2600**). It bills itself as a restaurant—and the food is pretty decent—but the place really gets hopping later in the evening, after 10pm or so. The restaurant has a small stage and the excellent bands usually play covers of popular Brazilian music. Daily 9am to midnight.

Another popular spot in the evenings is **Porto da Pinga,** Rua da Matriz 12 (② **024/ 9907-4370**). This bistro specializes in local *cachaças.* Live music nightly; a great spot to go and try some of the regionally produced firewater. Should you find one you particularly like, you can pick up some extra to take home from their on-site *cachaçaria.* Another restaurant doing double duty as a bar is the **Margarida Café,** Praça do Chafariz (② **024/ 3371-2441**). On weekends, there is always live Brazilian music, a perfect spot to enjoy a nightcap after dinner.

Minas Gerais: Belo Horizonte & the Historical Cities

Minas Gerais is the original gold rush state. Sometime in the early 1700s, explorers from São Paulo pushed beyond a forbidding range of mountains and discovered gold in the high plains beyond. Tens and then hundreds of thousands of miners poured into the new territory, setting up camp in and around the new town of Vila Rica de Ouro Preto.

The Portuguese crown tried to stem the tide, even banning emigration from Portugal for a time, to no avail. In 1720, Portuguese authorities bowed to the inevitable and switched their focus to taxing the new wealth. A new captaincy of Minas Gerais (General Mines) was declared, with Vila Rica as its capital, and a small army of Customs agents and tax collectors was sent out from the mother country to collect the royal fifth, the 20% tax owed the crown.

The gold that poured out of Minas Gerais made king and mother country rich, while changing the dynamics of colonial Brazil. In 1763, the capital was shifted south from Salvador to Rio de Janeiro, the port that served as the embarkation point for Minas gold.

The boom lasted for over half a century, but by the 1780s production was slumping, even as Portuguese taxation demands increased. The situation came to a head in 1789 in the Inconfidência Mineira, a short-lived conspiracy in Ouro Preto lead by a dentist known as Tiradentes (the "tooth-puller"). Though it accomplished next to nothing, the Inconfidência is now seen as a forerunner of the Brazilian independence movement.

With the gold petering out, miners shifted to ranching cattle, and later to growing coffee. A distinctive Mineiro culture developed, the archetypical Mineiro simple but proud, practical and self-reliant, and hospitable to strangers. The history of mining and ranching lead to a unique Mineiro cuisine, with rich stews and sauces.

In the early 1900s, geology again came to the fore with the discovery of iron ore deposits. Minas soon developed into Brazil's leading steel producer, and one of its leading manufacturing states.

The capital was shifted to a new planned city dubbed **Belo Horizonte**—the Beautiful Horizon—or more often just BH. Belo Horizonte today is a pleasant and efficient business city with some good Mineiro restaurants and pleasant strollable neighborhoods.

The real reason for a visit to Minas Gerais, however, lies back in those old gold towns. Built during the gold boom of the 18th century, the cities of **Ouro Preto, Mariana,** and **Tiradentes** are gems of high baroque architecture; thanks to the later gold-mining bust, most have been preserved in their original condition. Together, the Historical Cities of Minas Gerais are an architectural wonderland.

Several of these cities have excellent hiking nearby, but the main joys here are quiet and largely visual. It's enough to simply contemplate the beauty of the surrounding mountains and the architectural creativity of man.

1 BELO HORIZONTE

343km (213 miles) N of Rio de Janeiro, 487km (303 miles) NE of São Paulo

A large and bustling city, Belo Horizonte serves as the capital of Minas Gerais and is home to nearly 2.5 million Mineiros, as the proud inhabitants of this inland state are known. Minas Gerais is Brazil's second most important industrial state after São Paulo, and Belo Horizonte is an important city for business. It makes an excellent jumping-off point for a visit to the Historical Cities of Ouro Preto, Mariana, and Tiradentes. In and of itself, Belo Horizonte (or just BH) features some pleasant strollable neighborhoods, hearty restaurants, lively clubs and cafes, and a few intriguing sights. If you have some time to spare either before or after visiting the historical cities, BH is worth an afternoon and evening. That said (and though Mineiros will almost certainly beat me for saying it), if your schedule doesn't permit a stopover, you shouldn't spend a lot of time regretting what you've missed.

GETTING THERE

BY PLANE   **Azul** (✆ 031/3003-2985; www.voeazul.com.br), **Gol** (✆ 0300/115-2121; www.voegol.com.br), **Ocean Air** (✆ 031/4004-4040; www.oceanair.com.br), **TAM** (✆ 031/4002-5700; www.tam.com.br), **TRIP** (✆ 031/3003-8747; www.voetrip.com. br), and **Webjet** (✆ 0300/210-1234; www.webjet.com.br) have daily flights to most major cities in Brazil.

Most flights arrive at **Aeroporto Internacional Tancredo Neves–Confins,** Rodovia MG-10 (✆ 031/3689-2700), a new airport inconveniently located some 40km (25 miles) from the city center. A taxi from here to the city center costs about R$80. A cheaper alternative, **Shuttle Minas** (✆ 031/2526-2857; www.shuttleminas.com.br), operates a minivan shuttle between Confins and the hotels in the Centro and Savassi/ Afonso Pena neighborhoods. You can also call to request a pickup. The shuttle departs at approximately hourly intervals, from 6am to 6pm. Cost is R$20, one bag free, R$5 for each extra bag. If you can, book a flight that lands at **Pampulha Airport,** Praça Bagatella 204 (✆ **031/3490-2001**), the older, smaller airport next to the artificial lake near the center of the city.

BY BUS   Long-distance buses arrive at the **Terminal Rodoviaria Gov. Israel Pinheiro da Silva,** Praça Rio Branco 100, Centro (✆ **031/3271-3000;** www.rodoviariabelo horizonte.com.br). To/from Rio de Janeiro, **Util** (✆ **021/3907-3900;** www.util.com.br) has seven daily departures, the first at 8am and the last at 12:30am. The trip takes 7 hours, and costs R$67 to R$95. To/from São Paulo, **Cometa** (✆ **031/4004-9600;** www. viacometa.com.br) has 11 daily departures, the first at 9am and the last at 11:45pm. Cost is R$75 to R$135, and the trip takes 7 hours.

GETTING AROUND

ON FOOT   Downtown BH is pleasant and walkable by day and into the evening. Later in the evening it may be advisable to take a taxi.

BY BUS   The three types of buses in BH are coded by color. **Yellow** buses, called *circulares,* stick to the Contorno, the ring road around BH's center, and cost R$1.65. Short-distance city buses are **blue,** and cost R$2.40. Longer-distance city buses, for travel from the city to far-off suburbs, are **red** and cost R$3.

BY TAXI Taxis can be hailed in the street almost anywhere. To order a taxi, call **Coomotaxi** (☎ **031/3419-2020**) or **Coopertaxi** (☎ **031/3421-2424**).

BY CAR Navigating Belo Horizonte's inner city is extraordinarily difficult, due to the complicated street pattern and the shortage of parking. However, to explore the country-side and reach the historical cities, a car is ideal.

CITY LAYOUT

Created as the new state capital in the 1890s, Belo Horizonte was Brazil's first planned city, and thus a direct precursor of Brasilia (Juscelino Kubitschek, founder of Brasilia, was mayor of BH is the '40s). One legacy of this urban planning is BH's urban core, which features an intriguing street pattern: A wider grid of broad ceremonial avenues has been set atop the regular street grid, offset at a 45-degree angle. At every intersection where two broad avenues and two regular streets come together, it forms a city square. It's an intriguing and beautiful design, but for those used to a simple grid it does make for confusing navigation. (When you turn right, you are not turning 90 degrees, but 135 degrees.) The pattern was discontinued outside the city center, but as it happens that is precisely the area of most interest for visitors. The most important neighborhoods are

Savassi (more or less btw. Av. Cristováo Colombo and Av. Alfonso Pena), and **Lourdes** (centered on Av. Alvares Cabral). **Av. Alfonso Pena** is home to BH's main office and business district.

VISITOR INFORMATION

The city's official tourism agency, **Belotur** (© 031/3277-9777; www.belohorizonte. mg.gov.br), has tourism information centers at **Confins airport** (© 031/3689-2557); at the **bus station** (© 031/3277-6907); and in Centro at the **Mercado das Flores,** Av. Afonso Pena 1055 (© 031/3277-7666). All are open daily 8am to 6pm. There's also a tourist hot line, **Alô Turismo** at © 031/3220-1310.

(Fast Facts) Belo Horizonte

Car Rental **Localiza** (© 0800/979-2000); **Avis** (© 0800/725-2847); **Unidas** (© 0800/121-121); and **Hertz** (© 0800/701-7300). Rates start at R$100 per day for a compact car with air-conditioning and unlimited mileage. Insurance adds R$30 per day.

Currency Exchange **Banco do Brasil,** Av. Amazonas 303, Centro (near Praça 7 de Setembro; © 031/3218-2300; Mon–Fri 10am–4pm) has an ATM. **Action S/A,** Confins Airport (© 031/3689-2861; daily 5am–10pm). **Minas Cambio Turismo,** Av. Amazonas 507, Centro (© 031/3201-4515; Mon–Fri 9am–6pm).

Hospital **Hospital da Clinicas,** Av. Prof. Alfreda Balena 110, Santa Efigênia (© 031/3248-9300).

Internet Access **Internet Club Café,** Rua Fernandes Tourinho 385, Savassi (© 031/3282-3132; www.internetclubcafe.com.br; daily 9am–10pm), charges R$4 per hour.

Weather Located on an interior plateau, Belo Horizonte is similar in climate to São Paulo. December through March is hot and humid. Temperatures rise to the mid-30s Celsius (high 90s Fahrenheit). June through August, it can cool off to a minimum of 15°C (59°F), but during the day temperatures can sometimes rise to the 20s Celsius (70s or mid-80s Fahrenheit). Between May and September it can be quite cool in the evenings; bring some cool-weather clothes. Most rain tends to fall in the summer (Dec–Feb); January is especially wet.

EXPLORING BELO HORIZONTE

Downtown Belo Horizonte is a sight in itself, as planned cities often are. It's worth strolling the center admiring the broad avenues and smaller streets branching off at odd angles. The city center is safe and pleasant, and there are often shops to browse and cafes at which to snack.

Start with a visit to the **Praça da Liberdade,** located where the two broad avenues—Avenida Brasil and Avenida Cristováo Colombo—intersect. This was BH's central square—deliberately modeled on Paris—with fountains and a green central garden surrounded by official government buildings. Initially, the buildings were neoclassical, but as time wore on a modern Niemeyer building was put up, and then a postmodern pastiche

ATLANTIC OCEAN

Amazon

BRAZIL

Brasília

Belo Horizonte · Rio de Janeiro

500 mi
500 km

ATTRACTIONS ●

Mercado Central **3**
Mineiro Museum **5**
Museu de Artes e Oficios **4**
Museum of Mineralogy **7**
Praça da Liberdade **8**

ACCOMMODATIONS ■

Ibis **6**
Promenade Lourdes **2**
Royal Savassi Boutique Hotel **9**

DINING ◆

A Favorita **1**
Dona Lucinha **11**
Splendido **10**

was added to the mix. The square still works, though. Recently, the state government relocated to a large government compound near Confins airport, and the government buildings on the square were repurposed as museums. These include the **Museum of Mineralogy,** Av. Bias Fortes 50 (✆ **031/3271-3415;** Wed–Sun 9am–5pm; admission R$3), and the **Mineiro Museum,** Av. João Pinheiro 342 (✆ **031/3269-1168;** Wed–Sat 10am–6pm, Sun till 4pm; admission R$5), a neoclassical building featuring art and antiques of Mineiro origin.

Also worth a visit is the **Mercado Central,** Av. Augusto de Lima 744 (✆ **031/3274-9434;** Mon–Sat 7am–6pm, Sun till 1pm), BH's huge covered produce and fresh meat market. There's local *cachaças,* cheeses, fresh fruit, and numerous little *botecos.* Stop by **Casa Cheia,** Mercado Central (✆ **031/3274-9585**), for a sandwich of smoked turkey and *quiabo,* or smoked pork, or some homemade sausage.

The **Praça de Estação** (officially called Praça Rui Barbosa, but no one does) is the site of the old railway station. A suburban Metrô still operates from here, but the attraction is the neoclassical grace of the square and train station, now repurposed as the **Museu de Artes e Oficios (Museum of Arts and Crafts),** Praça Rui Barbosa s/n (✆ **031/3248-8600;** www.mao.org.br; Wed–Fri noon–7pm, Sat–Sun 11am–5pm; admission R$4). The museum uses displays, actual tools, and photographs to demonstrate the ways in which craftsmen and artisans make things. It's an intriguing concept, and a lovely display space.

Farther out from the city center one finds **Lake Pampulha,** and the **Pampulha Architectural Complex.** The area took shape in the 1940s, when a progressive young mayor named Juscelino Kubitschek hired an ambitious young architect named Oscar Niemeyer to design a complex of ceremonial buildings to give some form to what was then a new neighborhood on the edge of the city. Niemeyer's curvy forms and raw concrete didn't please everyone. The wavy-topped **Church of St. Francis of Assisi** (closed for renovations) is now a city icon, but it took the Catholic diocese 16 years to resign itself to the design, and actually consecrate the building as a church. The vivid blue exterior tiles are by noted Brazilian artist Portinari. The other buildings in the complex are less interesting. The ex-casino is now the **Museu de Artes da Pampulha** (✆ **031/3443-4533;** Wed–Sun 9am–5pm), which features visiting exhibits and sculptures in its garden. The small **Casa de Baile,** or dance hall, is now mostly closed, and anyway best appreciated from the outside.

The complex was completed in 1943. The mayor was so pleased with the results that when he became president 13 years later, he hired the same architect to design an entirely new city: Brasilia.

One of the best new sights in Belo Horizonte is **Inhotim,** Hwy. BR-381, Km 490, Brumadinho (✆ **031/3227-0001;** www.inhotim.org.br; Wed and Fri 9:30am–4:30pm, Sat–Sun 9:30am–5:30pm; admission R$15, children 12 and under R$7.50), an hour's drive from the city center, but well worth the trip. Opened in 2008 by a wealthy Mineiro industrialist, Inhotim is at its heart a modern art museum, with some 500 works by Brazilian and international artists, dating from the 1960s onward. What makes Inhotim special is the setting: a vast and beautiful tropical landscape, much of it laid out by noted Brazilian landscape designer Roberto Burle Marx. The paintings, sculptures, drawings, photographs, video, and sound installations are integrated into this vast tropical arcadia in innovative and intriguing ways.

It is best to travel by car to the museum. On Saturdays and Sundays you can also reach the museum by bus, departing at 9am from platform F2 of the Belo Horizonte bus

station, returning at 4:30pm (R$10; 90 min.). Contact **Saritur** (© **031/3419-1800**) for
details.

SHOPPING

Minas Gerais is known for its crystals and semiprecious gemstones, as well as its arts and crafts (many of them kitchen or culinary focused). For a one-stop shop, try the **Central de Artesenato do SESC,** Rua Tupinambás 956, Centro (© **031/3279-1476;** Mon–Fri 9am–6pm, Sat 9am–1pm). Though a bit heavy, the soapstone cooking bowls make fine gifts and souvenirs.

On Sundays, a large crafts fair takes place on the **Avenida Alfonso Pena,** corner of Avenida Alvares Cabral, which is closed to traffic for the day (9am–4pm). Hundreds of small kiosks offer bags, belts, sandals, and other leather work; jewelry, semiprecious gems, and crystals; soapstone cookware; woodcarvings and larger pieces of wood furniture; and antiques.

The **Patio Savassi,** Av. Contorno 6061, Savassi (© **031/4003-4171;** www.patio savassi.com; Mon–Sat 10am–10pm, Sun 2–8pm), where Avenida Crisovão Colombo intersects with the Avenida Contorno ring road, is an upscale shopping mall with a movie theater, bookstore, fine dining and food court, and dozens of upscale women's boutiques.

WHERE TO STAY

As a business city, BH empties out on the weekends and prices drop 30% to 50%. It pays to time your visit for the weekend.

Expensive

Promenade Lourdes ★★   The Promenade offers the extra space and kitchenette of a flat hotel, with the price and location of a regular hotel. Rooms are spacious, with a king-size bed, glass-top writing desk (with a good reclining desk chair), plus a kitchenette with fridge and sink, dishes and microwave, coffeemaker, and small breakfast table. The rooms even come with iron and ironing board, a rarity in Brazil. Master rooms are on higher floors with better views.

Rua Bernardo Guimarães 2032, Lourdes, Belo Horizonte 32224-050. © **031/3290-0933.** www.promenade. com.br. 102 units. R$285 double. Extra person add 30%. Children 5 and under stay free in parent's room. AE, DC, MC, V. Parking R$15 daily. **Amenities:** Restaurant; bar; fitness center; outdoor small pool; room service; smoke-free rooms. *In room:* A/C, TV, minibar, Wi-Fi.

Royal Savassi Boutique Hotel ★★   The Royal Savassi offers good quality accommodations plus a full-service business center in the city's best neighborhood. Rooms feature either carpet or tile flooring, king-size beds and good linen, a good work desk with three phone lines and free Wi-Fi, and good-size bathrooms with high-end toiletries. Service is good, and the little extras like fluffy robes and turndown service are nice, though perhaps not enough to justify the (new) claim to boutique hotel-dom. Still, they're trying.

Rua Alagoas 699, Savassi, Belo Horizonte 32228-050. © **031/3247-6999.** www.royaltowers.com.br. 81 units. R$350 double. Extra person 30% extra. Children 5 and under stay free in parent's room. AE, DC, MC, V. Parking R$15 daily. **Amenities:** Restaurant; bar; fitness center; outdoor pool; room service; sauna; smoke-free rooms. *In room:* A/C, TV, hair dryer, minibar, Wi-Fi

Moderate

Ibis ⓥ **Value**   Located just a block from the central Praça da Liberdade, this is the best value in BH's business district. Like all Ibis hotels, the concept is basic: All rooms are identical and accommodations are comfortable but plain. Each room has a nice firm double bed, a desk, and closet space. Bathrooms are equally frills-free but are modern and spotless and come with showers only. The hotel amenities are kept to a minimum to reduce the operating costs. Breakfast is optional, for R$15.

Av. João Pinheiro 602, Lourdes, Belo Horizonte 32433-050. (© **0800/703-7000** or 031/2111-1500. Fax 031/2111-0000. www.accorhotels.com.br. 121 units. R$129 double. Extra person R$55. Children 5 and under stay free in parent's room. AE, DC, MC, V. Parking R$15. **Amenities:** Restaurant. *In room:* A/C, TV, fridge.

WHERE TO DINE

A Favorita ★ SEAFOOD   Come to A Favorita, see the world. While the emphasis is always on seafood, the menu offers a range of culinary styles, among them French, Italian, Thai, and Chinese. Start with the *couvert,* a basket of fresh-baked breads and five types of pâtés. Other starters include a mix of mushrooms (portobello, Shimeji, Paris) grilled in truffle butter. Main dishes include grilled Atlantic lobsters, or lemon-scented *cherne* filet in a cashew crust with grainy mustards sauce.

Rua Santa Catarina 1235, Lourdes. (© **031/3275-2352.** www.afavorita.com.br. Main courses R$30–R$75. AE, DC, MC, V. Mon–Sat noon–1am; Sun noon–midnight.

Dona Lucinha ★ MINEIRO   A BH fixture for going on 20 years, Dona Lucinha puts out a vast spread of traditional Mineiro dishes. It's self-serve, allowing you to pick and choose what you like from the extensive buffet—great for those who have never experienced Mineiro cooking. Save room for dessert. Dona Lucinha also puts out a huge buffet of typical desserts—dried fruit compotes, fig, guava, pumpkin, papaya, often mixed with cheese or sweet condensed cream.

Rua Padre Odorico 38, São Pedro. (© **031/3227-0562.** www.donalucinha.com.br. Main courses R$20–R$45. AE, DC, MC, V. Mon–Sat noon–3pm and 7–11pm; Sun noon–5pm.

Splendido ★ ITALIAN   This restaurant serves northern Italian cuisine and a range of inventive pastas with a touch of Brazilian flair. Signature dishes include breast of duck

---

Mineiro Food

The food in Minas Gerais is renowned in Brazil for its heartiness and simplicity. The favorite dishes are rich stews and bean dishes with pork. Two typical Minas dishes are *Tutu á Mineira* and *feijão tropeiro*. In *Tutu* the beans are cooked, mashed, cooked again (similar to Mexican refried beans), and served with roasted pork, sausages, bacon, collard greens, egg, and rice with side dishes. The *feijão tropeiro* is fairly similar except the beans are kept whole and mixed with cassava flour. Two other traditional dishes are made with chicken: *frango a molho pardo* and *frango com quiabo. Frango a molho pardo,* originally a Portuguese dish, is a stew made with fresh chicken blood—a little gruesome sounding but surprisingly tasty. The other chicken dish is a rich tomato stew with okra. There's also *vaca atolada,* a kind of beef rib stew, and *torresmo,* crunchy deep-fried pork rind. You'll find these in almost every Minas restaurant. The servings are always enough for two.

House of (Cheese) Bread

Among its culinary claims to fame, Minas is home to the *pão de quiejo,* the little round cheese bread ball now ubiquitous throughout Brazil. Mineiros claim there are no cheese breads like Mineiro cheese breads (they claim much the same about *cachaça* and women). The place to test their claim (about the cheese breads anyway, for booze and women you'll need to try elsewhere)? Any corner lunch counter should do, or you can try the **Armazem Dona Lucinha,** Rua Padre Odorico 38 (corner of Av. do Contorno; ☎ **031/3281-9526**).

in a merlot truffle sauce, accompanied with a passion-fruit purée and potato galette. For dessert, the tiramisu is famous citywide.

In the Flat Volpi Residence Hotel, Rua Levindo Lopes 251, Savassi. ☎ **031/3227-6446.** Main courses R$75–R$125. AE, DC, MC, V. Mon–Fri noon–3pm and 7pm–1am; Sat 7pm–2am; Sun noon–5pm.

Xapuri ★ MINEIRO   This is the place for a Mineiro dining experience. Located out near Pampulha, Xapuri features a palm-frond roof covering long wooden tables upon which waiters plonk down heaping platters of traditional Minas fare—pan-fried chicken with collard greens, leathery steak, stews of all description, griddles of sizzling sausage, dried beef in gravy—all accompanied by *feijão tropeiro* (beans mixed with manioc, eggs, bacon, and shredded kale). In the evenings, men with leather hats, accordions, and a lasting ache in their hearts wander the room serenading diners with traditional Mineiro music. There's also a small gift shop offering Mineiro arts and crafts. And while yes, this does all scream "tourist trap," it's actually a restaurant sought out and enjoyed by locals.

Rua Mandacaru 260, Pampulha. ☎ **031/3496-6198.** www.restaurantexapuri.com.br. Main courses R$18–R$42. MC, V. Wed–Thurs 11am–11pm; Fri–Sat 11am–2am; Sun 11am–6pm.

Botecos

In addition to hearty home-cooking, BH is known for its ***botecos,*** simple bars selling cold draft beer and hearty home-cooked snacks. *Botecos* are a great place to relax after a long day, or if you feel like a snack but aren't hungry enough for dinner. BH's *botecos* typically open Monday to Saturday noon to 3pm and then again from 7pm to midnight (or later). Sundays they're often closed. **Clube da Esquina,** Rua Sergipe 146, Funcionarios (☎ **031/3222-5712**), offers cold beer and snacks in a 1902 heritage house. **Petisqueira do Primo,** Rua Santa Catarina 656, Lourdes (☎ **031/3335-6654**), features Galician-style snacks (cod and potatoes, paella, and so on) and, of course, beer. In business since 1929, **Tip Top,** Rua Rio de Janeiro 1770, Lourdes (☎ **031/3275-1880**), features German bratwurst, pig knuckles, sauerkraut, and beer.

BELO HORIZONTE AFTER DARK

Belo Horizonte's nightlife centers on the **Savassi** and **Lourdes** neighborhoods. **Praça Savassi**—the square where Avenida Getulio Vargas meets Avenida Cristovão Colombo is a *point*—has dozens of bars and cafes, but young people and students also congregate on the wide sidewalks, drinking, flirting, and playing guitar.

Nearby, for jazz, DJs, books, and a cool atmosphere of students and bohemians, try **Café com Letras,** Rua Antonio de Albuquerque 781 (☎ **031/3225-9973;** www.cafe comletras.com.br; Mon–Thurs noon–midnight, Fri–Sat noon–1am, Sun 5–11pm).

In Lourdes, **Marilia Pizzeria,** Rua Marilia de Dirceu 189, Lourdes (✆ **031/3275-2027;** www.mariliapizzeria.com.br), serves up good pizzas and at night becomes a *point,* a spot for hanging out, flirting, and conversing.

Also in Lourdes, the **Art from Mars** restaurant, Rua Rio de Janeiro 1930, Lourdes (✆ **031/3337-9116;** Wed–Sat 7pm–2am; no cover), offers an Asian-flavored menu, sushi bar, and an upscale lounge with a small chic dance floor.

Farther from the center of town, the **Boate na Sala** (✆ **031/3286-4705;** www.nasala.com.br; Thurs–Sat 10pm–3am; R$25 cover) is an upscale disco frequented by BH's young and pampered. Located inside the Ponteio Lar Shopping Mall in Santa Lucia.

2 OURO PRETO ★★★

279km (173 miles) N of Rio de Janeiro, 475km (295 miles) NE of São Paulo, 78km (48 miles) S of Belo Horizonte

The inland state of Minas Gerais struck it rich on gold just about the time the baroque style reached its elaborate architectural height. Newly wealthy citizens needed something to blow their money on, and they turned to architecture. The result? Several small cities with cobblestone streets, soaring palaces, and elaborate churches that rival St. Petersburg or Prague.

The largest of these is the hilltop town of **Ouro Preto;** its cobblestone streets wander up and down hills crowned with more than a dozen ornately carved and elaborately decorated baroque churches. Each corner turns on new surprises: mansions, fountains, ruins, beautiful terraced gardens, and towers glowing with colored tiles. Once known as Vila Rica (the rich town), Ouro Preto begs to be explored on foot. Yes, the cobblestone streets can get quite steep, but only on foot can you appreciate the rich details of the perfectly preserved houses, gaze at the intricately carved fountains, and steal glimpses of courtyards and living rooms. The monuments and museums can be visited in 2 days, allowing plenty of time to stroll and explore.

The Inconfidência Mineira

Ouro Preto has a special place in Brazilian history for its role in the Inconfidência Mineira (1788–92), a failed rebellion against the Portuguese Crown. The movement started as a protest against the 20% royal tax on gold production. A group of intellectuals (doctors, writers, and poets) began meeting with the idea of taking some sort of action. The ringleader was a dentist named Joaquim José da Silva Xavier, also known as Tiradentes (literally, "the teeth puller"). Unfortunately, before the group formulated a plan, someone betrayed their existence, and in 1789, Tiradentes and 11 of his confederates were arrested. All were condemned to death. The vice-regal governor commuted the sentences of the other 11 and sent them into exile. Tiradentes was hanged as an example, his body cut in four pieces, and each piece put on display. Nowadays, the Inconfidência is interpreted as Brazil's first uprising against Portuguese rule, and Tiradentes as Brazil's first martyr in the struggle for independence.

ACCOMMODATIONS ■
Luxor Ouro Preto Pousada **4**
Pousada Classica **13**
Pousada do Mondego **7**

DINING ◆
Bar do Beco **10**
Bené da Flauta **5**
Booze Café Concerto **12**
Cafe Geraes **14**
Casa do Ouvidor **11**
Restaurante Chafariz **16**

ATTRACTIONS ●
Mina do Chico Rei **1**
Museu da Inconfidência **8**
Museu de Aleijadinho **3**
Museu de Minas **15**
Museu do Oratorio **9**
N.S. do Rosario **17**
São Francisco de Assis **6**

GETTING THERE

BY CAR   From Belo Horizonte take the BR-040 for some 30km (19 miles), then turn onto the BR-356 to Ouro Preto. From Rio de Janeiro take the BR-040 highway as far as Conselheiro Lafaiete, then follow the Estrada Real to Ouro Preto. From São Paulo follow the BR-381 to Lavras and then take the BR-265 to Barbacena. In Barbacena take the BR-040 in the direction of Belo Horizonte.

From Belo Horizonte's Pampulha or Confins airport (Pampulha is about 40km/25 miles closer to Ouro Preto than Confins airport), it's possible to negotiate with a taxi to take you straight to Ouro Preto for a set fee (expect to pay around R$150–R$200, depending on your bargaining skills), or you can take the bus.

BY BUS   Regular buses connect from Rio (7 hr.), São Paulo (11 hr.), and Belo Horizonte (2 hr.) to Ouro Preto. **Util** runs a nightly 11:30pm bus from Rio to Ouro Preto, arriving first thing in the morning (© **021/2518-1133** in Rio, or 031/3551-3166 in Ouro Preto); tickets cost R$71 for a regular seat and R$115 for a comfortable almost bedlike seat *(leito)*. **Cristo Rei** has three daily departures between São Paulo Bresser Station (© **011/3692-4073**) and Ouro Preto (© **031/3551-1777**). **Passaro Verde** runs at least 20 buses a day between Belo Horizonte and Ouro Preto (© 031/3073-7575). Tickets cost R$22. The Ouro Preto bus station is a R$10 taxi ride from the historic core.

CITY LAYOUT

Ouro Preto is a city of twisting, turning streets that seem to change names at every corner, but despite this it's remarkably hard to get lost. Thanks to the ever-present incline you can usually pick out your destination—be it church, museum, or square—either above or below you. The main square in the center of the city is the **Praça Tiradentes.** The **Museu da Inconfidência** stands on one side of the square and the **University of Ouro Preto** on the other. Running downhill out of the square are two parallel streets— **Rua Sen. Rocha Lagoa** and **Rua Conde de Bobadela** (aka Rua Direita)—packed with restaurants, pubs, and shops. Following those streets will lead via a number of twists and turns first to the **Praça Reinaldo Alves de Brito** with its lovely sculpted fountain, and below that to the **Igreja Matriz N.S. do Pilar.** Below that again—possibly on the Rua Antonio Albuquerque, though there are several other routes—stands the lovely **Igreja N.S. do Rosario.**

Head downhill on the other side of Praça Tiradentes, and you'll come to the Largo de Coimbra, site of the **Igreja São Francisco de Assis.** Continue following the street down the hillside to the next important church, the **Matriz N.S. da Conceição** and the next-door **Aleijadinho Museum.** Past this church, strolling along **Rua Bernardo Vasconcelos,** the street crosses a lovely stone bridge before it starts to climb very steeply. At the top—the view is worth the effort, but if you're feeling lazy you can always take a cab from the main square for R$6—stands the **Matriz Santa Efigenia dos Pretos,** built by communities of slaves who were not permitted to worship in other churches. Note the Afro-Brazilian motifs, such as shells and goat horns. Retracing your steps down the steep street, you will be rewarded with a beautiful view of the city.

Bring good walking shoes. All the streets are cobblestone, and the sidewalks and steps are often carved out of uneven stones.

TOURIST INFORMATION

Ouro Preto Tourist Information is at Rua Claudio Manuel 61 (© 031/3559-3544; daily 8am–6pm). For tour guides, contact the **Ouro Preto Tour Guide Association** at © 031/3551-2655. A 4-hour English-language tour of Ouro Preto (with up to 10 people) costs R$100.

FAST FACTS **Banco do Brasil,** Rua São José 189 (© 031/3551-2663), has a 24-hour ATM. This branch will also exchange U.S. dollars. Almost next door, the **HSBC,** Rua São José 201 (© 031/3551-2048), also has ATMs. **Cyber House,** Rua Conde Bobadela 109 (© 031/3552-2048), is open daily from 10am to 8pm.

(Tips) **When to Go to Ouro Preto & Mariana**

Avoid visiting Ouro Preto and Mariana on Monday, as the majority of churches, museums, and attractions are closed. To take advantage of lower room rates in either town, visit Tuesday through Friday. Everything is open but not as busy as on the weekends.

Tips   **A Taxi Tour**

Many of the city's taxi drivers will also agree to a full- or half-day sightseeing rate. This is an ideal option for visiting Mariana or getting out into the countryside.

TOP ATTRACTIONS

If you can only take museums in small dosages, save your energies for the Museu de Arte Sacra in Mariana, well worth a visit.

Matriz da N.S. do Pilar/Museu de Arte Sacra ★   You may want to shield your eyes from the glitter of the over 400 kilograms (882 lb.) of gold that were used to decorate this church. Completed in 1786, it was built at the height of Brazilian baroque, when the phrase "less is more" would have evoked only laughter. More is more! And more there is: angels and cherubim everywhere, all of them dripping in gold. Recently opened in the basement, the Museu de Arte Sacra is disappointingly small.

Praça Mons, Castilho Barbosa. ℂ 031/3551-4736. Admission R$4. Tues–Sun 9–11am and noon–5pm.

Mina do Chico Rei (Kids)   Touring this former mine in the heart of Ouro Preto gives you a visceral feel for what life as a miner was like. Not for the claustrophobic, this self-guided tour lets you wander some of the narrow underground tunnels, poking your nose into some of the wall cavities where miners would store their finds during the day. Deeper in the mine, a mineral room shows various types of stone from this area, including the reddish-brown mineral that held Ouro Preto's gold. Allow 45 minutes.

Rua D. Silverio 108. ℂ 031/3551-1749. Admission R$10 adults, free for children 7 and under. Daily 8am–5pm.

Museu da Inconfidência (Overrated)   As interesting as the building is—it was the jail where the conspirators were imprisoned—the museum itself is seriously lacking in content: nothing but a mumbo jumbo of locks, keys, lamps, and other artifacts from the time of the Inconfidência. Given that there is little explanation, none of it in English, you may want to give this one a miss. Allow 30 minutes.

Praça Tiradentes s/n. ℂ 031/3551-1121. Admission R$6 adults, R$3 youth 10–18, free for children 9 and under. Tues–Sun noon–5:30pm.

Museu de Aleijadinho   Those hoping to find out more about the artist himself will be disappointed. Many of Aleijadinho's best works are in the churches around the city, leaving this museum with odds and ends and smaller pieces, often oratories and statues of saints. Not much is known beyond his work, and the museum hasn't really bothered to delve into the artist as a person. However, the displays do provide the opportunity to take a close-up look at the master sculptor's work. The faces of the statues seem almost alive, and the creases and folds of their clothes resemble soft flowing fabric instead of wood. On your way out, have a peek inside the church; Aleijadinho's father carved many of the angels, and both father and son are buried in the church. Aleijadinho's tomb is located on the right-hand side underneath the first altar. Allow 45 minutes. Your ticket is also good for the São Francisco de Assis church (see below).

Praça Antonio Dias s/n (entered through the Matriz N.S. da Conceição). ℂ 031/3551-4661. Admission R$5. Tues–Sat 8:30am–noon and 1:30–5pm; Sun noon–5pm.

The Incredible Aleijadinho

It's impossible to go anywhere in Ouro Preto (or any of the other historic cities, for that matter) and not hear the name or see the work of **Aleijadinho.** Brazil's finest baroque artist, he carved much of the soapstone decorating many of the finest churches both in Ouro Preto and in the other historical cities. (The church of São Francisco de Assis has some particularly fine examples of his work.) His signal achievements are all the more remarkable given that Aleijadinho worked without the use of his hands. The son of a Portuguese architect and a black slave woman, Antonio Francisco Lisboa was born in 1738, inheriting the name Aleijadinho in his 20s when a debilitating disease—probably leprosy— left his hands and legs crippled. Undaunted, Aleijadinho carried on working, even as his body degenerated to the point where his apprentices had to strap hammer and chisel to his wrists. He died in 1814, having completed his last sculpture just 2 years previously.

Museu de Minas ★ (Kids)   This place is part modern showroom, part old-fashioned museum, but well worth a visit. Unless you are into natural history, most people skip the ground-floor collection of stuffed animals and critters preserved in formaldehyde: The highlight of the museum is its mineral collection. The most valuable and interesting pieces are displayed on the ground floor in a flashy showroom, with perfect lighting and dramatic black backdrops. Opals, emeralds, topaz, quartz, and close to 2,000 lesser-known varieties can be seen. The remainder of the mineral collection is housed upstairs in an old-fashioned lab room with hundreds of small wooden cabinets containing 18,000 samples. To show how these samples were extracted, there's a collection of modern equipment and original tools from the past. Allow 1½ hours.

Praça Tiradentes 20. (✆ **031/3559-1597.** Admission R$5 adults, free for children 5 and under. Tues–Sun noon–5pm.

Museu do Oratorio ★★★   What is an oratory? Visit and ye shall see. One of the loveliest museums in Ouro Preto, the Museu do Oratorio displays a comprehensive collection of oratories, which are in fact little mini-altars, used by people so they could pray without having to go to church. The museum showcases home, travel, and work oratories. All are works of art; some are small enough to tuck into your pocket or bag for traveling. The Afro-Brazilian oratories are decorated with flowers and shells from the Candomblé religion and usually portray black saints such as Santa Efigenia. Allow 45 minutes.

Rua Brog. Musqueira s/n (next to the Igreja do Carmo). (✆ **031/3551-5369.** www.oratorio.com.br. Admission R$2. Daily 9:30am–5:30pm.

Nossa Senhora do Rosario ★★   The N.S. do Rosario was built by slaves who were forbidden to worship elsewhere. Rumor has it that they smuggled tiny bits of gold from the diggings to put toward the building of their church. Constructed over a period of 30 years, the church was finally completed in 1792. Strikingly elegant and very unusual in Brazilian baroque, the church was built in the shape of an ellipse, with beautiful soft curves. In lieu of gold, the altars are beautifully painted and dedicated to black saints such as Santo Elesbão and São Benedito. The Sunday Mass is held at 4pm. Visitors welcome.

Largo do Rosario s/n. © **031/3551-4736.** Free admission. Tues–Sat 12:30–5pm; Sun 1:30–5pm.

São Francisco de Assis ★★★   Completed in 1794, the São Francisco de Assis church is one of the top contenders for most beautiful church in Ouro Preto, if not the whole of Brazil. Most of the artwork was done by Aleijadinho, who designed and decorated the church. His elaborate soapstone carvings, including the pulpits and altars, are simply unbelievable. The baptismal font in the sacristy alone took him 3 years to make! The paintings are by Ataíde, who was also responsible for the ceiling mural of the Virgin Mary in heaven, surrounded by cherubs and musicians.

Largo de Coimbra s/n. © **031/3551-4661.** Admission R$6. Tues–Sun 8:30am–noon and 1:30–5pm. Your ticket is also good for the Aleijadinho Museum.

WHERE TO STAY

One of the busiest times of the year in Ouro Preto is Easter week (Semana Santa). The processions and concerts make it a worthwhile visit, but reserve accommodations at least a few weeks in advance. Carnaval is also a busy time of the year as many flock to take part in the lively street celebrations. Prices go up significantly.

Luxor Ouro Preto Pousada ★★   This lovely 200-year-old colonial mansion has been transformed into a fabulous cozy inn, decorated in authentic period antiques. The standard rooms come either with a double bed or two twin beds. Both the superior rooms and the suites look out over the Santa Efigenia and N.S. das Mercês churches. Many of the rooms feature bathtubs. The suites are much bigger and have a separate sitting room. The restaurant serves very decent Mineiro food.

Rua Dr. Alfredo Beata 16 (Praça Antônio Dias), Ouro Preto, 35400-000 MG. © **031/3551-2244.** www.luxorhoteis.com.br. 19 units. R$200 standard; R$300 suite. Extra person add R$50. Children 6 and under stay free in parent's room. AE, DC, MC, V. **Amenities:** Restaurant; bar. *In room:* A/C, TV, Internet, minibar.

Pousada Classica ★★   A fascinating blend of old and new, the Classica is in an old baroque mansion that's been gutted and completely renovated. The lobby is modern and spacious with large glass doors (in place of the original dark shutters). The rooms are very

MINAS GERAIS: BELO HORIZONTE & THE HISTORICAL CITIES

8

OURO PRETO

ⓘ Tips   Choose Your Guide Wisely

The square in front of the São Francisco de Assis church is particularly notorious for the guides that try to sell their services to visitors entering the church. Some are incredibly knowledgeable and will greatly add to your experience; others are trained only in spewing completely useless facts and can't answer any questions. If interested in a guide, check with the tourist information office on the Praça Tiradentes, or when negotiating with a freelancer be clear on the amount and the length of time (will he/she just give information on one church or visit a number of monuments with you?).

This quote was taken from one of the English-language guides for sale in Ouro Preto: "The constructive process of the temple began in 1733, reaching the decade of 80, when the frontispiece was concluded with base in Manoel Francisco's risk." In short, buyer beware!

pleasant with high ceilings, hardwood floors, and elegant furnishings, mixing modern amenities with the classic features of the building. The difference in price for a deluxe double and a super deluxe room or a suite is so small that you may as well go for the spacious suite with the whirlpool tub and the prime view. The standard and deluxe rooms don't have tubs, but the brand-new showers are spotlessly clean.

Rua Conde de Bobadela 96, Ouro Preto, 35400-010 MG. © **031/3551-3663.** Fax 031/3551-6593. www. pousadaclassica.com.br. 27 units. R$290–R$340 standard and deluxe double. 40% discount on weekdays and low season. Extra person add 25%. Children 5 and under stay free in parent's room. V. Free parking. **Amenities:** Restaurant; room service. *In room:* A/C, TV, Internet, minibar.

Pousada do Mondego ★★   Located in the heart of Ouro Preto, the Pousada do Mondego looks out over the Largo de Coimbra and the São Francisco de Assis church. The 24 units in this 250-year-old pousada are spread out over three floors. The prime rooms are the suites or deluxe units on the second floor overlooking the square and the city below. These rooms are spacious and elegant, with hardwood floors, a four-poster bed, a sofa, and large dressers. The superior rooms are also quite nice—the beamed ceilings give the rooms a cozy feel—but the view is of the internal courtyard. Avoid the standard rooms, as these have low ceilings and no view at all. Service is outstanding (the pousada belongs to the high-quality Roteiros de Charme association), so it's not surprising that rooms are often booked; call in advance.

Largo de Coimbra 38, Ouro Preto, 35400-000 MG. © **031/3551-2040.** Fax 031/3551-3094. www.mondego. com.br. 24 units. R$200 standard; R$270 superior; R$340–R$490 suite. Extra person R$40. Children 5 and under stay free in parent's room. AE, DC, MC, V. Free parking. **Amenities:** Room service. *In room:* TV, minibar.

WHERE TO DINE

The food in Minas Gerais is known throughout Brasil for its simple ingredients, country-style preparation, and large portions (see "Where to Dine" in "Belo Horizonte," earlier in this chapter). Ouro Preto abounds in Mineiro-style restaurants. Remember, in Minas Gerais, the servings are always enough for two.

Bené da Flauta ★★ BRAZILIAN   Although the chefs consider their menu Mineiro food with a contemporary twist, you will find plenty of other options. A great appetizer is the antipasto dish with roasted tomatoes and eggplant in olive oil, served with a basket of bread. Main courses are still far from being light cuisine but include options such as a veal *osso buco* with risotto or a grilled tournedos steak with creamy Piemontese rice. The 18th-century building itself has a lovely history; right next to Ouro Preto's monumental São Francisco de Assis church, it is here that painter Athayde had his atelier when he was working on the artwork for the church. The gorgeous dining room is decorated in beautiful antiques.

Rua São Francisco 32. © **031/3551-1036.** Reservations recommended on weekends. Main courses R$22–R$38. DC, MC, V. Daily noon–11pm.

Cafe Geraes ★ CAFE   Cafe Geraes is the perfect little cafe, and with only a dozen tables it is always busy. The best spot is on the mezzanine level overlooking the bar where you can still see part of the original clay and straw wall. Geraes serves delicious *caldos* (thick soups) together with a thick slice of home-baked potato bread. To nibble, you can order appetizers of salami, olives, and crackers. Or you can skip ahead and go straight for dessert. The strudels and pies are excellent and served with a generous dollop of fresh cream.

Rua Direita 122, Centro. © **031/3551-5097.** Main courses R$12–R$24. No credit cards. Sun–Thurs 11am–11pm; Fri–Sat 11am–1am.

Casa do Ouvidor ★★ MINEIRO   The Casa do Ouvidor is one of the best restaurants for trying out local cuisine. Located on the second floor above the Rua Direita, this elegant dining room basks in the warm glow cast from candles and numerous antique lamps. The menu includes the four typical Mineiro dishes. Some lighter items such as a grilled chicken breast and a beef brochette are offered, but I was on a mission and ordered the *Tutu á Mineira*. The dish was everything I expected and more; the beans were mashed to almost a paste, accompanied by a juicy grilled sausage, tender pork loin, and crispy roasted bacon bits. A side order of rice, a boiled egg, and thinly shredded, stir-fried greens completed my feast. Dessert, not a chance!

Rua Direita 42, Centro. (ℭ) **031/3551-2141.** Main courses R$22–R$36 for 2. AE, DC, MC, V. Daily 11am–3pm and 7–10pm.

Restaurante Chafariz ★ (Finds) BRAZILIAN   The dining room of the Chafariz does a great job blending old with new. Housed in the former residence of Ouro Preto's beloved poet Alphonsus de Guimaraens, the restaurant looks like an antiques shop with large armoires, wrought-iron chandeliers, and large wooden tables. In contrast, the heavy ceiling beams are painted in cheerful colors, and the glass art is positively funky. Open for lunch only, the restaurant serves an excellent buffet of the best of Minas food as well as a good selection of salads. Dessert is always included, and at the end of your meal, the waiter will bring a complimentary glass of liquor made from the tiny red *jabuticaba* fruit.

Rua São José 167. (ℭ) **031/3551-2828.** Main courses R$28 buffet. DC, MC, V. Daily 11:30am–4pm.

OURO PRETO AFTER DARK

Bar do Beco (Moments)   If I lived in Ouro Preto, I think I'd come to Bar do Beco every day and slowly work my way through the *cachaça* menu. With at least 65 varieties in stock at any given time, this bar is the perfect spot to embark on a taste trip. The bar special, the ice-cold Milagre de Minas, is made in-house with a secret 15-spice formula. The bartender also makes some wicked *cachaça* cocktails such as *da paixão* with Milagre de Minas, blue Curaçao, passion-fruit juice, and rose petals. With its smooth stone floors and low overhead beams, the bar has the feel of an old tavern. Opens at 6pm. Travessa do Arieira 15. (ℭ) **031/3551-1429.** No credit cards.

Booze Café Concerto (Finds)   A great spot to duck into after 9pm on a Friday or Saturday to catch some live music. Bands hail mostly from Minas Gerais and play MPB, blues, or jazz. The cafe itself is a large basement room with exposed brick walls, round windows that look out into the alley, and amazing glass art behind the bar. Daily 11am to midnight. Rua Direita 42, subsolo (basement). (ℭ) **031/3551-1482.** R$5 cover Fri–Sat. No credit cards.

---

3 MARIANA ★

18km (11 miles) E of Ouro Preto

Unlike Ouro Preto, Mariana is not a perfectly preserved historic town but rather a town with a perfectly preserved historic section. Unlike its larger neighbor, Mariana also still has active mining on the outskirts of the city. The historic part of Mariana makes a pleasant half-day trip from Ouro Preto. The monuments, museums, and churches can be seen in a few hours, and the trip by bus is only 30 minutes.

> ## ⓘ Tips   When to Go
>
> Time your visit to Mariana for the Friday (11am) or Sunday (12:15pm) concert, performed on the exquisite 18th-century organ at the Catedral da Sé.

GETTING THERE   Buses depart from Ouro Preto for Mariana daily every 30 minutes between 5:30am and 11:30pm from behind the Museu de Minas (Rua Barão Camargos). The trip costs R$2.20, takes approximately 30 minutes, and drops you in the center of Mariana. A much more scenic way to get to Mariana is by **steam train.** Originally built in 1883, the 18km (11 miles) of track that connect the two towns have recently been restored. The trip takes an hour; make sure you sit on the right-hand side as you leave Ouro Preto to get the best views of the landscape. Also, if you sit in the rear of the train you can take some great photos of the front carriages as the track curves. Departure Ouro Preto to Mariana Friday to Sunday at 11am and 4pm; return from Mariana to Ouro Preto only at 2pm. Visitors can return by bus or arrange a taxi. One-way fare: adults R$18, children 6 to 10 pay R$15; ✆ **031/3551-7705.**

VISITOR INFORMATION   Bring some information on Mariana from Ouro Preto's tourist information as the office here, at Praça Tancredo Neves s/n (✆ **031/3557-1158**), is notoriously unreliable. It's supposed to be open daily 8am to 5pm, but don't count on it.

EXPLORING MARIANA

From the bus stop, it is an easy stroll to all of Mariana's sights. Built according to a city plan in 1743, the old part of town has an easy-to-follow grid pattern. Following **Rua Josafia Macedo** out and then the parallel **Rua Dom Viçoso** back to the **Praça Cláudio Manuel** makes for a perfect loop. Starting off on **Rua Josafia Macedo,** the first stop of interest is Mariana's **Pelourinho** at the Praça Minas Gerais. This square is one of the few in Brazil that has kept the *pelourinho* (pillory) to attest to this bloody era of Brazilian history; the locals claim the square is haunted. Surrounding the pelourinho are the **Igreja São Francisco de Assis,** viewable upon request, the **Igreja N.S. do Carmo,** currently undergoing renovations after a recent fire, and the former jail and city council. Both churches were built in the late 18th century and are lovely examples of the local baroque architecture. Continuing up the street, now known as **Rua D. Silverio,** it is a pleasant 20-minute stroll to the top of the hill where the **Basilica de São Pedro dos Clerigos** overlooks the city from its vantage point. Coming back down, zigzagging through the side streets with beautifully preserved colonial houses, make your way to the **Praça Gomes Freire,** the main gathering place for locals. On the corner of the square you can still see one of the original drinking troughs used for watering the horses. After visiting the **Museu de Arte Sacra** and the **Catedral Basilica da Sé,** loop back to the bus station via the short **Rua Direita,** observing the colorful two-story houses.

Catedral Basilica da Sé ★★   Well worth a visit, this lovely cathedral is the oldest church in Mariana, completed in 1750. Some famous Brazilian baroque artists worked on the decorations: Aleijadinho's father carved many of the altars, Atayde painted a number of pieces, and the baptismal font in the sacristy was made by Aleijadinho himself. The stunning chandeliers in the center of the church are pure Bohemian crystal, imported from Germany. The organ, a gift from Dom. João V, has been fully restored

after a 70-year silence. Every Friday and Sunday the organist holds a 40-minute concert, followed by a detailed explanation of the organ itself.

Praça Claudio Manuel s/n. © **031/3557-1216.** Church visit R$2; concert R$12. Tues–Sun 8am–6pm. Concerts take place Fri 11am and Sun 12:15pm.

Museu de Arte Sacra ★★★ Although unassuming from the outside, the colonial mansion behind the cathedral houses one of the best collections of sacred art in Brazil. The vast collection is beautifully displayed and illuminated, and the stone floors and thick walls of the building create the appropriate stately ambience. On the ground floor you will find a large collection of silver and gold artifacts: crowns, diadems, crucifixes, and chalices. Also on display are intrinsically decorated *custodias*—a type of chalice used only for the host—as well as lanterns and processional crosses. Upstairs there's a collection of statues made by Aleijadinho, as well as a portrait of the artist done by Atayde. What makes the work of this baroque artist so vibrant is the painstaking effort he put in to preparing his canvases and paint. Often working on wood, he started with a white layer to bring out the luminosity in the paint, followed by an ocher layer, and then a white, almost transparent layer to increase the dark and light contrast. In his paints, Ataíde blended in gold dust, red dirt, coal dust, and metal shavings.

Rua Frei Durão 49. © **031/3557-2516.** Admission R$5 ages 5 and over, free for children 4 and under. Tues–Fri 9am–noon and 1:30–5pm; Sat–Sun 9am–2pm.

WHERE TO DINE

Most of Mariana's restaurants do not open for lunch except on weekends and holidays. A great lunch spot, open daily 11am to 3pm and popular with local families on Sunday, is the kilo **Lua Cheia,** Rua Dom Viçoso 26 (© **031/3557-3232**). Two more-upscale choices are **Tambaú,** Travessa São Francisco 26 (© **031/3557-1780**), serving tapas and great Brazilian finger foods, and **Bistrô,** Rua Salamão Ibrahim 61A (© **031/3557-4138**), for sushi, pasta, and pizzas. Both only open for lunch on the weekends.

4 TIRADENTES ★★★

217km (135 miles) N of Rio de Janeiro, 369km (229 miles) NE of São Paulo, 142km (88 miles) S of Belo Horizonte

Surely one of the loveliest little towns in all of Brazil, Tiradentes doesn't "wow" like Ouro Preto, doesn't seduce like Salvador or charm like Olinda, but it quietly wins you over and before you know it you, too, will be head over heels in love. Nestled at the foot of the Serra de São José, it's a place where time has stood still. When the last mine closed in 1830, people moved away and the town was left as if frozen in amber. A heritage designation early on in 1938 kept any further development at bay.

The town has only a few dozen streets and can easily be seen in a day, but why rush? See the sights, browse the fabulous antiques and jewelry stores, enjoy the fine dining, or just stroll the streets. Despite its size and isolation, Tiradentes has a well-developed tourism infrastructure. In high season and on weekends the town gets hopping; if you prefer peace and quiet, stick to weekdays for your visit.

GETTING THERE As there are no direct long-distance buses to Tiradentes, visitors must travel to São João del Rei first and from the *rodoviaria* connect with one of the 11 buses a day that cover the 14km (8½ miles) to Tiradentes in 20 minutes and cost R$4.

Moments   Mengooooooooo!

It was the day after Sunday's big game in Rio's Maracanã stadium: Flamengo won, making it a shoe-in (well, a cleat-in) for the Carioca cup. As I strolled through Tiradentes's sleepy streets I heard a car coming, the first one in 2 hours, and as it drove by I heard a loud "Mengooooooooo"—the drawn-out call of Flamengo fans—and turned to see three guys in Flamengo shirts, with the black-and-red flag proudly draped over the hood. Back in the main square, I was just in time to see residents put up a few tables, pull some *cervejas* from the trunk, and dance and sing to the boombox, belting out Flamengo tunes. Even 1 day later—and no matter where you are—a victory by Brazil's most beloved team is always a good excuse for a party.

Regular buses connect São João del Rei to Belo Horizonte, São Paulo, and Rio de Janeiro. The Viação Sandra line runs seven buses a day to Belo Horizonte. Paraibuna line runs at least three buses a day to Rio. The Vale do Ouro line has five buses a day to São Paulo, and one bus leaves for Ouro Preto every day at 5:30pm.

In a pinch one can always take a taxi from São João del Rei, for about R$50. For taxi service contact (✆ **032/3355-1466** or 3355-1100. The Tiradentes Rodoviaria is within walking distance of most pousadas.

To arrive in style, take the 115-year-old narrow-gauge steam train, called **Maria Fumaça (Smoking Mary)** ★★, from São João del Rei (✆ **032/3371-8485**). Following the Rio das Mortes, the train takes 35 minutes to reach Tiradentes's rail station. Trains depart São João del Rei Friday through Sunday and holidays at 10am and 3pm, and from Tiradentes at 1pm and 5pm. One-way tickets cost R$18 adults, R$9 children 6 to 10. The train station is a short taxi ride or a 10-minute walk from the historic center of town.

VISITOR INFORMATION   The **tourist office** is at Largo das Forras 71 (✆ **032/3355-1212**), open daily from 9am to 5:30pm.

EXPLORING THE TOWN

The list of attractions may seem small, but that's because the town itself is the main attraction. The only way to experience Tiradentes is on foot, getting lost in the little streets, absorbing the breathtaking architecture.

A Stroll Around Town

Start at the **Largo das Forras,** the large tree-lined square in the center of town. This is where the tourist office is located (daily 9am–5:30pm) and where, if you really don't want to hoof it, you can hire a buggy and horse to do the hoofing for you (R$15 for a 45-min. tour). Walk to the corner next to the tourism office, and you'll see the beautifully restored post office. Continuing up that street (Rua Resende Costas) you start to climb a bit, and soon to the right you will be able to catch breathtaking views of the Serra de São José. Stay on the street (now renamed Rua Direita) until you come to the **N.S. do Rosário dos Pretos** on your right. The oldest church in town, it was built entirely by Tiradentes's slave community. It's definitely worth a peek inside. The stars and moon painted on the ceiling refer to the fact that most of the construction had to be done at night, after the enslaved had completed their forced labor. The individually painted wooden panels on the ceiling represent the mysteries of the rosary. From here, instead of continuing up along Rua Direita, duck into the alley behind the church, and it will lead to the **Largo do Sol** and **Museu de Padre Toledo.** One of the *inconfidentes,* Padre Toledo lived in this house until he was arrested and exiled to Lisbon. The museum, unfortunately, doesn't tell much of the padre's story; instead, it's mostly a mishmash of furniture, paintings, oratories, and household objects. Stay on the Rua Padre Toledo as it leads up the hill to the **Matriz de Santo Antônio** church (see below). Take the street to the right of the Matriz and continue farther up the hill to the church of **Santissima Trinidade.** This church stands out for its simplicity: no fancy ornaments, no gold, not even a clock tower. But for an over-the-top display of faith, look no further than the room of miracles around the back of the church. The place where the faithful give thanks for cures and interventions is packed from top to bottom with letters, photos, wax and plastic body parts, and every piece of orthopedic equipment imaginable. Right next door is the holy shop of saints where you can purchase a statue of just about any saint in the calendar. Retrace your steps down the hill and continue past the Matriz to the charming little **Largo do O.** Beyond that, just across the bridge is the large **Chafariz de São José,** where residents used to obtain their water. Walking back toward the main Largo das Forras along the **Rua Direita** will take you through Tiradentes's gallery row. Many artists live and work here; painters, furniture makers, silversmiths, and craftspeople make high-quality pieces at reasonable prices. Typical souvenirs include locally made *cachaça,* sweets and preserves, silver jewelry, paintings, and quilts and rugs.

Matriz de Santo Antônio ★   One of the richest churches in Minas Gerais, the Matriz has recently been renovated and looks as good as new. Aleijadinho sculpted the front entrance, portraying a shield with the Lamb of God. The interior is completely plastered with gold; the main altar seems positively ablaze. The sacristy is worth a look for the paintings by Manuel Victor de Jesus representing scenes from the Old Testament. The steps of the church offer one of the best views in the city. On Friday, Saturday, and Sunday there is a sound-and-light show that tells the history of the church (R$10). The show begins at 8pm. On Fridays the sound-and-light show is followed by a baroque concert on the church's recently restored 18th-century Portuguese organ. Concert starts at 8:30pm (R$15).

Rua da Camara s/n. ℂ **032/3355-1238** for inquiries about concert. Admission R$2. Daily 9am–5pm.

Hiking

The hills around Tiradentes and São João del Rei offer some spectacular hiking and walking trails. Local company **Lazer e Aventura** (ℂ **032/3371-7956;** www.lazereaventura.com) specializes in trips in the region. One of the more popular hikes goes up to the top of the Serra de São José and offers fabulous views of the surrounding valleys. The company also runs a jeep tour, which follows a trail along the base of the hills through some stands of Atlantic forest and takes you through some small villages. More adventurous types can try out rappelling or caving as well. Most tours last about 4 hours and require just an average level of fitness. All transportation is included and prices range from R$40 to R$60 per person.

WHERE TO STAY

Pousada Pé da Serra   Run by a friendly family, this pousada sits only 150m (500 ft.) from the bus station directly behind the São Francisco de Paulo church. Thanks to the boost provided by a small ridge, five of the nine rooms offer sweeping views of the mountains and the town itself. The rooms are very basic and simple, no phones and no fancy furnishings, but the location makes up for a lot: Guests have use of a cozy sitting room with a fireplace and bar, and on sunny days can enjoy the large garden with a swimming pool and a complimentary afternoon tea.

Rua Nicolau Panzera 51, Tiradentes, 36325-000 MG. (✆) **032/3355-1107.** www.pedaserra.com.br. 9 units, shower only. R$130–R$180 double. Extra person add R$30. Children 6 and under stay free in parent's room. V. Free parking. **Amenities:** Bar; outdoor pool. *In room:* TV, fridge, minibar, no phone.

Pousada Tres Portas   Named after the three double doors forming the entryway, this lovely pousada is located within the historic town. Just off the main square, the views of the Serra São Jose are quite beautiful. The best room has a full view of the Serra and is furnished with a beautiful four-poster bed. The other rooms have partial views and are also very pleasant, featuring lovely antiques, hardwood floors, and colorful bedspreads on comfortable beds. All guests have the use of the lounge, a great spot to relax by the crackling fire.

Rua Direita 280A, Tiradentes, 36325-000 MG. (✆) **032/3355-1444.** Fax 032/3355-1184. www.pousadatres portas.com.br. 9 units, shower only. Mon–Fri R$195–R$230 double; Sat–Sun R$260–R$310 double. Extra person over 12, add 50%. Children 2 and under stay free in parent's room, ages 3–12 add 10%. MC, V. Free parking. **Amenities:** Restaurant; bar; small indoor heated pool; sauna. *In room:* TV, fridge, minibar, no phone.

Solar da Ponte ★★★   Though for very different reasons, the Solar da Ponte is much like the Eagles' Hotel California—you may never leave. Located in the heart of Tiradentes, this member of the Roteiro de Charme group of pousadas is the perfect home base for exploring this historic town. The rooms are all uniquely furnished with antiques, harmonious color schemes, fresh flowers, and comfortable couches and chairs. The standard rooms overlook the street and the stone bridge that the pousada is named after, while the superior rooms face out over the garden. The pousada also has a comfortable reading room with ample literature in English and a large fireplace for chilly evenings. The restaurant in the garden room serves a scrumptious breakfast with fresh warm rolls, eggs, cold cuts, cake, and fresh fruit, all on beautiful dishes made by a local artist. In the afternoon, the restaurant offers complimentary tea.

Praça das Mercês s/n, Tiradentes, 36325-000 MG. (✆) **032/3355-1255.** www.solardaponte.com.br or www.roteirosdecharme.com.br. 18 units, shower only. High season R$500 standard; R$610 superior. Extra person R$70. In low season 20%–30% discount. AE, DC, MC, V. Free parking. No children 7 years old and under. **Amenities:** Outdoor pool; sauna. *In room:* TV, hair dryer, Internet, minibar.

WHERE TO DINE

Tiradentes is quite sophisticated when it comes to restaurants. Most specialize in traditional Mineiro cuisine (p. 188). Every year, at the end of August, the city hosts a culinary festival and provides a wonderful opportunity for local chefs to show off their skills. During the off season check ahead for opening hours, particularly Sunday through Tuesday.

Many interesting restaurants can be found just by strolling along Tiradentes's streets. The top restaurants in town all specialize in local cuisine. **Estalagem do Sabor,** Rua Min. Gabriel Passos 280 (✆ **032/3355-1144**), is well known for its hearty regional fare. In addition to basic chicken and meat stews, try the *Mané sem Jaleco,* a dish that combines rice with beans, sliced kale, bacon, eggs, and pork tenderloin; lean cuisine it ain't. **Viradas do Largo,** Rua do Moinho 11 (✆ **032/3355-1111**), is another local favorite that has made a name for itself with outstanding Mineiro dishes. Many of the dishes are made with herbs and vegetables from the restaurant's own garden. Keep in mind that portions are generous, more so than in other restaurants; often a dish will feed two or three people. Appetizers include handmade pork or chicken sausages. For Mineiro cuisine with a modern twist, check out the restaurant **Tragaluz,** Rua Direita 52 (© **032/3355-1424**). Here you will also find some of the meat stews but with shiitake instead of cabbage and served with a side of mashed *inhame* (a Brazilian root vegetable) instead of rice. Desserts are creative; for example, the staple *goiabada* (guava paste) is served fried with a sprinkling of cashew nuts and cream cheese. Not open for lunch. For that special night out there is no restaurant more romantic than **Santissima Gula,** Rua Padre Gaspar 343 (© **032/3355-1162**). The cozy candlelit dining room only has a few tables and guests choose from a number of tasting menus with at least four or five courses. The cuisine is refreshingly modern and usually includes several seafood and meat options.

Minas is almost as famous for its food as it is for the outstanding *cachaça* (hard liquor made from sugar-cane juice) it produces. **Confidências Mineira** ★★, Rua Ministro Gabriel Passos 26 (© **032/3355-2770**), offers an extensive *cachaça* menu; many of the brands have florid and poetic names. For example, try Minha Deusa (My Goddess), a fruit-flavored variety of *cachaça.* One of the best *cachaças* around is Havana. Aged in balsamic barrels and made in small quantities, it is considered the champagne of *cachaças.* And, yes, it is possible to enjoy cuisines other than Mineiro cooking in Tiradentes. Overlooking the Ponte do Solar, **Sapore d'Italia** ★, Rua Francisco de Paula 13 (© **032/3355-1846**), cooks up some excellent Italian dishes. The menu offers a good selection of pasta dishes such as cannelloni with ham. The wine list includes mostly Portuguese, French, and Italian reds, all reasonably priced.

Settling into São Paulo

Look out the window as your plane descends toward São Paulo, and you'll see nothing but high-rises as far as the eye can see. It's a truly awesome sight.

Now the largest metropolis in South America—and, with 17 million people spread over 7,770 sq. km (3,000 sq. miles), the third-largest city in the world—São Paulo nevertheless sprang from humble beginnings. In 1554, Jesuit priests founded a mission on a small hill, strategically close to the River Tietê. The mission developed into a small trading post and then, in the 17th and early 18th century, into a jumping-off point for Bandeirante expeditions traveling into the interior. In 1711 the little market town was incorporated as the city of São Paulo. The seeds of its future prosperity showed up just 12 years later with the arrival of the first coffee plants in Brazil.

The climate and soil surrounding São Paulo turned out to be perfect for coffee. With the arrival of the railway in 1867, large-scale cultivation exploded. São Paulo became one of the largest coffee exporters in the world.

When slavery was abolished in Brazil in 1888, coffee growers started looking toward immigrant labor. Italians and Japanese, and later, eastern Europeans, Spanish, Portuguese, and Germans, made the trek to São Paulo. To this day São Paulo remains the most culturally diverse city in Brazil.

In the mid-1950s São Paulo surpassed Rio in population and kept growing. Foreign investment by car companies such as Ford, GM, and Volkswagen transformed the city into South America's largest car manufacturer.

Unfortunately, little foresight and only rudimentary planning were devoted to the growth of the city. So although wages are the highest in the country, São Paulo's traffic regularly snarls into nearly endless traffic jams.

Prospective visitors often hear of this chaos and shy away from Brazil's big city, which is a shame. Visitors to São Paulo get all the benefits of a sophisticated, cosmopolitan city—they can eat at the finest restaurants in Brazil, shop at boutiques that even New York doesn't have, browse high-end art galleries, check out top-name Brazilian bands almost any night of the week, and take advantage of one of Brazil's most dynamic nightlife scenes to party until the wee-est of hours. And they can do all this without ever experiencing the big drawback to this city, which is traffic.

The challenge to living in São is the commute. Visitors get a free pass. Stay in the Jardins, Higienópolis, or Centro, and all the sights and shops and galleries and restaurants are within easy reach. The word *commute* need never enter your consciousness.

Best of all, time in São Paulo is a chance to get to know that subspecies of Brazilian known as the Paulista. They're proud of their work ethic and their "un-Brazilian" efficiency. Lacking beaches and mountains, Paulistas have devoted themselves entirely to urban pursuits. They dominate Brazilian politics. They run Brazilian business. Dining out is an almost religious observance. And in São Paulo, the music and nightlife never end.

1 SÃO PAULO ESSENTIALS

359km (223 miles) SW of Rio de Janeiro

ARRIVING

BY PLANE Most international airlines fly through São Paulo. Even those heading for Rio often change planes or stop in São Paulo first. There are two main airports. International flights arrive at **Guarulhos Airport** (℃ **011/2445-2945**), 30km (19 miles) northeast of the city. Paulistas will also refer to this airport as Cumbica. São Paulo has a duty-free shop upon arrival **before clearing Customs,** where you can purchase up to US$500 of goods. Once you have cleared Customs you can change money or traveler's checks or use an ATM to obtain cash in Reais. The **American Express** office is open daily from 7am to 10pm and is located in Terminal 1 arrivals. The **Banco do Brasil** charges a US$20 flat rate for traveler's check transactions and US$5 flat rate for cash transactions. ATMs compatible with Visa/PLUS are in Terminal 1 arrivals.

From **Guarulhos Airport** to the city, travelers can either take a taxi or a bus. Prepaid taxi fares are available with **Taxi Guarucoop** (℃ **011/2440-7070;** www.guarucoop.com.br). Sample fares: Congonhas Airport R$92, São Paulo Centro and Tietê R$75, and Jardins and Avenida Paulista R$85. There are regular metered taxis, which are cheaper when traffic is good. When traffic backs up the prepaid ride turns out to be a much better deal. The **Airport Bus Service** (℃ **011/3775-3861**) operates six different shuttle bus routes to Congonhas Airport, to Praça da República, to Avenida Paulista (stopping at major hotels along the street), to Itaim Bibi, to the Rodoviario Tietê (bus station), and the Rodoviario Barra Funda. Cost is R$30, and each route takes about 50 minutes (if traffic is good). Shuttles depart daily every 30 minutes from 6am to 11pm, and then hourly overnight.

Congonhas Airport (℃ **011/5090-9000**), São Paulo's domestic airport, is within the city limits south of Centro. It is used by seven national airlines for their domestic flights. From Congonhas it is a 15- to 25-minute taxi ride to Jardins or Avenida Paulista. There are two prepaid taxi services with booths near the exit doors at arrivals. Unlike in Rio de Janeiro, prepaid here is a reasonable deal. The cheaper, white **Taxi Commun** (ordinary taxi) charges from R$33 to R$38 for the trip to Avenida Paulista or Jardins. The **Rádio Táxi Vermelho e Branco** (the Red and White Taxi Company; ℃ **011/3146-4000;** www.radiotaxivermelhoebranco.com.br) charges about 15% more—R$38 to R$45—but has slightly larger, slightly nicer cars. Regular metered taxis are also available, and will cost as little as R$24 or as much as R$40, depending on traffic.

BY BUS São Paulo has three bus terminals *(rodoviaria).* All are connected to the Metrô system. **Barra Funda** (℃ **011/3392-2110**), near the Barra Funda Metrô, serves buses to the interior of São Paulo, northern Paraná, Mato Grosso, and Minas Gerais. **Jabaquara** (℃ **011/3235-0322**), next to the Jabaquara Metrô, provides transportation to Santos and the south coast. The **Rodoviaria Tietê** (℃ **011/3235-0322**), for buses to Rio and connections to Paraguay, Uruguay, and Argentina, is by far the largest and most important bus station, located on the Tietê Metrô stop.

SÃO PAULO'S NEIGHBORHOODS AT A GLANCE

Some 17 million people make their home in and around São Paulo. It's a daunting number. But for all its ridiculous sprawl there's a charm to South America's biggest city, and getting around the areas of interest is neither difficult nor especially stressful. For a more detailed description of São Paulo's neighborhoods, see "Neighborhoods to Explore," in chapter 10.

CENTRO   The old heart of the city stands around **Praça da Sé,** atop what was once a small hill circled by a pair of small rivers. Little remains of that original city; Paulistas take a manic joy in knocking buildings down almost as soon as they go up. The neo-Gothic **Catedral da Sé** dates to only 1912. Evidence of the city's age can be seen only in downtown's narrow and irregular streets. **Rua Direita,** São Paulo's original main street, leads through this maze to a viaduct crossing over a busy freeway that now occupies the Anhangabaú valley and goes into the "newer" section of the old town. This area, centered on leafy green **Praça República,** contains government buildings plus office buildings from the '20s to the '40s (and later). Back at the edge of the Anhangabaú valley stands the ornate **Teatro Municipal,** a Parisian-style opera house still used for concerts and theater. The Anhangabaú River, which once separated the two halves of downtown, was long ago filled and covered with a freeway, which in turn has been covered over by a broad and open city plaza—the **Parque Anhangabaú**—which effectively rejoins the two halves of downtown. Together, these two halves of the old inner city are known as **Centro.**

HIGIENÓPOLIS   Immediately west of Centro is one of São Paulo's original upscale suburbs, **Higienópolis.** Though long since swallowed up in the city, Higienópolis remains a green and leafy enclave with some good restaurants and the city's **Museum of Brazilian Art,** also known as **FAAP.**

LIBERDADE & BIXIGA   To the south of Centro are two turn-of-the-20th-century working-class neighborhoods long adopted by immigrants. Due south of Centro is **Liberdade,** said to have the largest Japanese population of any city outside Japan. In addition to great food and interesting shopping, Liberdade is also home to the **Museum of Japanese Immigration.** Southwest of Centro lies **Bela Vista,** more often referred to as **Bixiga.** This is São Paulo's **Little Italy.** Bela Vista in turn butts up against São Paulo's proudest street, the **Avenida Paulista.**

AVENIDA PAULISTA   Long and straight and set on a ridge above surrounding neighborhoods, the **Avenida Paulista** has rank upon rank of skyscrapers, the headquarters of the city's banking and financial interests. On the adjacent side streets are numerous hotels catering to business travelers. Halfway along the street is São Paulo's top-notch **Museum of Art,** known by its Portuguese acronym as **MASP.** Avenida Paulista marks the border between the old working-class areas and the new middle-class neighborhoods.

JARDINS   Extending southwest from Avenida Paulista are a series of upscale neighborhoods developed in the '20s according to the best Garden City principles and accordingly named gardens (*jardins*) to emphasize their green and leafy separation from the gritty urban core. Though each area has a particular name—**Jardim Paulista, Jardim America, Cerqueira Cesar, Jardim Europa**—Paulistas tend to refer to them as a group as **Jardins.**

What these areas offer is a bit of calm, some terrific restaurants, and the best shopping in São Paulo. Particularly noteworthy is the **Rua Augusta,** which intersects the Avenida Paulista at the Consolação Metrô stop and continues southwest through the heart of the Jardins. The few square blocks where **Rua Augusta** is intersected by **Alameda Lorena** and **Rua Oscar Freire** is the apex of the city's upscale shopping scene, São Paulo's Rodeo Drive.

Rua Augusta continues on straight through the Jardins, changing names as it goes to **Avenida Columbia** and then **Avenida Europa** and finally **Avenida Cidade Jardim.** At this point it intersects with **Avenida Brigadeiro Faria Lima.** Though a much less fashionable street, Avenida Brig. Faria Lima is home to a number of large shopping malls;

the most important is Shopping Iguatemi. Following Avenida Brig. Faria Lima northwest leads to another Jardim-like area called **Pinheiros;** going the opposite direction leads to **Itaim Bibi** and then to a fun and slightly funky area of restaurants, clubs, and cafes called **Vila Olímpia.**

THE PARK   The last key element to São Paulo is a green space—**Ibirapuera Park.** Located immediately south of Jardim Paulista, Ibirapuera is to São Paulo what Central Park is to New York. It's a place for strolling, lazy sun-tanning, outdoor concerts, and the view to a couple of the city's top cultural facilities, including the **Modern Art Museum** and the **São Paulo Bienal.**

GETTING AROUND

São Paulo has a convenient public transportation system, and many of its tourist-oriented neighborhoods are compact enough for a stroll. However, at night it's safest to take a taxi to and from your destination.

ON FOOT   Though São Paulo itself is huge, many of the neighborhoods that make up the city are compact enough to be easily explored on foot. This is especially true of the more pleasant neighborhoods such as Centro, Higienópolis, Jardins, Vila Madalena, and Ibirapuera. During the day the city is quite safe; in the evening the safest neighborhoods are Jardins, Higienópolis, and the residential areas of the city. Best avoided are the quiet side streets of Centro, particularly the empty shopping streets around Praça Sé, Bexiga, and around Luz station.

BY METRÔ   The Metrô is the easiest way to get around São Paulo. There are four lines: the North-South line, the East-West line, and the line that travels underneath the Avenida Paulista. The fourth line sits isolated in the southwest of the city, and does not connect to the other three. The two main lines converge at Sé station, the busiest station of all. These two lines run daily from 5am until midnight. The line under Avenida Paulista meets the North-South line at Paraiso and Ana Rosa stations and runs daily from 6am to 10pm. It is usually a lot quicker to take the Metrô as close as possible to your destination—even if it means a bit more of a walk or a short taxi ride—than taking the bus all the way. Metrô tickets cost R$2.55. For more information contact ✆ **011/3291-7800** or see the very useful website: **www.metro.sp.gov.br**. Note that the Single Fare (Tarifa Unica) program which allows riders to pay one fare and make use of Metrô, bus, and commuter rail is available only to São Paulo residents.

BY BUS   Good as Sao Paulo's Metrô is, there are some places you can only get to by bus. São Paulo buses are plentiful and frequent, but the city's sprawling layout and lack of landmarks can make the system hard to navigate. The routing information on the front and sides of the buses works the same as in Rio (see "By Bus" under "Getting Around" in chapter 5 for details). A few useful routes are listed below (more are given with particular attractions and restaurants), but there will be many others running along

---

(Tips)   Watch Out for Rogue Motorcyclists

São Paulo has the highest number of motorcycles in the country, most of them used by couriers. Be careful; even when traffic is backed up motorcycles will ride at high speeds weaving in between stopped cars.

similar routes. Buses cost R$2.55, and you pay as you board through the front of the bus. Bus drivers generally won't stop unless you wave your hand to flag them down. Some useful routes are:

- **No. 702P, Belém-Pinheiros:** From Praça da República along Rua Augusta, then north on Avenida Brigadeiro Faria Lima into Pinheiros.
- **No. 701U, Jaçanã-Butantã-USP:** From Praça República along Avenida Ipiranga, Rua da Consolação, and Avenida Rebouças to Buntantã and the University of São Paulo.
- **No. 5100, 5131:** From Brigadeiro Metrô station, along Avenida Brig. Luis Antonio to Ibirapuera Park.
- **No. 5175, 5178:** From Ibirapuera Park (opposite main gate) along Avenida Pedro Alvares Cabral to Brigadeiro Metrô station.

The bottom line? If possible, we recommend going by Metrô, combined where necessary with taxis.

BY TAXI Taxis are a great way to get around São Paulo, and an absolute must late at night. You can hail one anywhere on the street, and taxi stands are usually found on main intersections, next to malls, squares, and parks. To order a taxi at a specific time, call a radio taxi. **Rádio Táxi Vermelho e Branco** ("Red and White") can be reached at © 011/3146-4000 (www.radiotaxivermelhoebranco.com.br). Cost depends on traffic, so the following prices are only guidelines: From Centro to Avenida Paulista, R$20; from Avenida Paulista to Vila Olímpia, R$25 to R$35; from Avenida Paulista to Higienópolis, R$20.

BY CAR Driving in São Paulo is for the daring, the foolish, or the infinitely patient; traffic is always chaotic and frequently snarled and slow, particularly during rainstorms when the streets flood. Oh, and parking is expensive and difficult to find. São Paulo's appalling traffic has given rise to the world's largest fleet of civilian helicopters that ferry commuting executives in from their suburban homes.

VISITOR INFORMATION

The single worthwhile service for visitors is produced not by Sao Paulo's state or city government, but by an association of the city's art galleries, which produces the excellent *Mapa das Artes São Paulo,* a clear and detailed city map showing the city's main attractions, its subway lines, and, of course, its art galleries (**www.mapadasartes.com.br**). The map is available, free of charge, at many city hotels, and at the government tourist information booths, if you can find one open.

The state of São Paulo provides a tourist information service, **SELT** (© 011/6445-2380), at Guarulhos airport in both Terminal 1 and 2, supposedly open daily from 7am to 9pm (but don't be surprised if there's no one there).

The city government tourism information center at Rua XV de Novembro 347, Centro (© 011/3231-4455; daily 9am–6pm), offers maps and pamphlets and not much else; the English that is supposedly spoken sounds much like Portuguese.

> **Fast Facts** **São Paulo**
>
> **Area Code** The area code for São Paulo is **011.**
>
> **Banks & Currency Exchange** Most banks are located on the Avenida Paulista. **Banco do Brasil** has branches at Av. Paulista 2163 (© **011/3066-9322**); Rua São

Bento 483, Centro (☏ **011/3491-4008**); and Guarulhos International Airport, daily 6am to 10pm (☏ **011/6445-2223**). Other options include **Bank Boston,** Av. Paulista 800 (☏ **011/3171-0423;** Mon–Fri 11am–3pm), and **Citibank,** Av. Paulista 1111 (☏ **011/4009-2563;** Mon–Fri 11am–3pm).

Car Rentals At Guarulhos airport are **Hertz** (☏ 011/2445-2801), **Localiza** (☏ 021/3398-5445), and **Unidas** (☏ 011/2445-2113). At Congonhas airport are **Avis** (☏ 011/5090-9300), **Hertz** (☏ 011/5542-7244), and **Unidas** (☏ 011/3155-5710). In the city are **Hertz,** Rua da Consolação 431 (☏ 011/3258-9384), **Avis,** Rua da Consolação 382 (☏ 011/3259-6868), and **Unidas,** Rua da Consolação 345 (☏ 011/3155-5710). Rates start at R$90 per day for a small (Fiat Palio, Ford Ka) car with air-conditioning and unlimited mileage. Insurance adds R$30 per day.

Consulates **Australia,** Al. Santos 700, ninth floor (☏ **011/3171-2889**); **Canada,** Av. das Nações Unidas 12901, 19th floor (☏ **011/5509-4321**); **United States,** Rua Henri Dunant 500, Chácara Santo Antonio (☏ **011/5186-7000**); **Great Britain,** Rua Ferreira de Araujo 741 (☏ **011/3094-2700**); **New Zealand,** Al. Campinas 579, 15th floor (☏ **011/3148-0870**).

Dentists **Portal do Sorriso** (www.portaldosorriso.com; Mon–Sat 7am–9pm) has offices in Pinheiros (☏ **011/2626-0889**) and Morumbi (☏ **011/3772-5941**). **Dr. Marcelo Erlich,** Rua Sergipe 401, suite 403, Higienópolis (☏ **011/3214-1332** or 9935-8666). Both services offer English-speaking service.

Electricity Generally 110V; some hotels have both 110 and 220 volts.

Emergencies Police ☏ **190;** fire brigade and ambulance ☏ **193.**

Hospitals **Albert Einstein Hospital,** Av. Albert Einstein 627, Morumbi (☏ **011/2151-1233**); and **Hospital das Clinicas,** Av. Doutor Eneias de Carvalho Aguiar 255 (☏ **011/3069-6000**).

Internet Access Internet access in São Paulo is easy to find in bookstores and Internet cafes. The **FNAC** chain has stores in Pinheiros, Praça dos Omaguás 34 (☏ **011/3579-2000**), and on Av. Paulista 901 (☏ **011/2123-2000**). Both open daily 10am to 9pm, with Internet for R$12 per hour. Just off the Avenida Paulista there's the **Monkey Lan House,** Al. Santos 1217, corner of Pamplona (☏ **011/3253-8627;** www.monkey.com.br; 24 hr.), for R$4 per hour.

Mail Downtown: Rua Florencio de Abreu 591, Centro (☏ **011/3229-0084**), and Rua Haddock Lobo 566, Cerqueira Cesar (☏ **011/3088-1610**). The branch at the international airport of Guarulhos is open 24 hours.

Pharmacies Pharmacies are called *farmacia* or *drogaria* in Portuguese. The following are open 24 hours: **Drogaria São Paulo,** Rua Augusta 2699, Cerqueira Cesar (☏ **011/3083-0319**), and Av. São Luis 34, Centro (☏ **011/3258-8872**); **Drogasil,** Rua Pamplona 1792, Jardim Europa (☏ **011/3887-9508**). Most pharmacies will deliver 24 hours a day, usually for a small surcharge (R$4–R$10); contact your hotel's front desk to place an order at the nearest one.

Police Emergency number ☏ **190. Tourist Police,** Av. São Luis 92 (1 block from Praça da República), Centro (☏ **011/3214-0209**), and Rua São Bento 380, fifth floor, Centro (☏ **011/3107-5642**).

Safety During the day, the tourist areas are generally safe for walking; in the evening the safest neighborhoods are Jardins, Higienópolis, and the residential areas of the city. At night, it's best to avoid the quiet side streets of Centro, particularly the empty shopping streets around Praça da Sé and Bixiga. The area around the Praça da Luz is definitely to be avoided after dark. At night, traveling by taxi is strongly recommended—don't rely on public transportation. The U.S. State Department has reported incidences of armed robbery and widespread pickpocketing in São Paulo, though this has not been our experience. As in any large metropolitan area with great disparities between rich and poor, it's wise to observe common-sense precautions: Don't flash jewelry or cash, and stick to well-lit and well-traveled thoroughfares.

Taxes The city of São Paulo charges a 5% accommodations tax, collected by the hotel operators. This amount will be added to your bill. There are no other taxes on retail items or goods.

Time Zone São Paulo is 3 hours behind GMT (as is Rio de Janeiro).

Visa Renewal Policia Federal, Superintendência Regional de São Paulo, Rua Hugo D'Antola 95, Lapa de Baixo (© **011/3538-5000;** Mon–Fri 10am–4pm). The fee is R$69, and you may need to show evidence of sufficient funds to cover your stay as well as a return ticket.

Weather São Paulo's summers, December through March, are hot and humid. Temperatures rise to the mid-30s Celsius (high 90s Fahrenheit). In the spring and fall, the temperatures stay between the mid-20s to mid-30s Celsius (high 70s and 90s Fahrenheit). In the winter, June through August, it can cool off to a minimum of 15°C (59°F), but during the day temperatures can sometimes rise to the 20s Celsius (70s or mid-80s Fahrenheit). Those traveling to São Paulo between May and September should bring some cold-weather clothes, the equivalent of what someone would wear in New York or London in the fall. Most rain tends to fall in the summer (Dec–Feb); January is especially wet. When it rains heavily the city is prone to flooding, particularly the area around the Tietê River.

2 WHERE TO STAY

As the financial and business hub of Brazil, São Paulo has many excellent hotels at very affordable rates. Hotels tend to cluster around the financial district of the Avenida Paulista, and in the upscale shopping and restaurant district Jardins. Jardins is one of the safest areas of the city, and even at night one can comfortably go for a stroll. Women traveling alone will feel completely comfortable in this part of town.

São Paulo attracts business travelers Monday through Friday and then sits empty from Friday afternoon to Monday morning. Hotels try to lure weekend travelers with museum or shopping packages, but capacity still far exceeds demand and prices drop up to 50% or even more. Hotels will often throw in free breakfasts and dinners, and checkout can be as late as 6pm on a Sunday evening.

Many visitors to São Paulo prefer to stay in an apart-hotel. These hotels usually offer suites: one- or two-bedroom apartments with fully furnished kitchens. The benefit is much lower prices; even the most expensive apart-hotels are still significantly cheaper than a luxury hotel, and the units are much larger than a standard hotel room. You do give up a few of the amenities that you would get in a top-notch hotel, but the majority of apart-hotels still offer breakfast, parking, a small gym, sauna, and swimming pool as well as limited room service.

CENTRO

Staying in Centro you're close to the fun and movement of downtown; many of the attractions are within walking distance, and public transit to other regions is very accessible. The drawback is that at night, Centro empties out. Dining and nightlife options are limited, and parts of downtown transform into red-light districts, particularly around the Rua Augusta and Praça da República. However, the savings can be significant, especially on weekends when hotels often slash their prices in half.

Expensive

Bourbon São Paulo Business Hotel ★ (Value) An elegant, slightly Parisian-style building on the outside, on the inside the Bourbon has been kept thoroughly up-to-date and comfortable. Superior rooms come in two types. Those with a queen-size bed are of a good size, with a small breakfast table and full-length mirror. Bathrooms are large and bright. Superior rooms with two single beds are similar but a little smaller. Both room types unfortunately lack any kind of desk. Junior suites are quite spacious, with a queen-size bed and an anteroom set up as a small office, plus a sizable bathroom with bathtubs and showers. The Bourbon often reduces listed rates by up to 50%.

Av. Vieira de Carvalho 99, Centro, 01210-010 SP. ℂ **0800/118-181** or 011/3337-2000. Fax 011/3337-1414. www.bourbon.com.br. 129 units. R$200 double; R$250 junior suite. 50% discount weekends and slow periods. Extra person add about 25%. Children 6 and under stay free in parent's room. AE, DC, MC, V. Parking 1 block away, R$15 per day. Metrô: República. **Amenities:** Restaurant; bar; weight room; room service; sauna; smoke-free floors. *In room:* A/C, TV, fridge, hair dryer, Internet, minibar.

AVENIDA PAULISTA

The hotels around Avenida Paulista cater to business travelers and executives who spend most of their time in the city's financial district. They're high-end and expense account–friendly. However, on weekends the rates drop almost in half; visitors can treat themselves to a great hotel at a bargain price. Metrô connections make it easy to travel back and forth from this area. From Paulista it is only a short walk or quick cab ride to the upscale neighborhood of Jardins.

Very Expensive

L'Hotel Porto Bay São Paulo ★★★ Just off the Avenida Paulista, L'Hotel is one of São Paulo's most elegant boutique hotels, offering luxury and friendly, attentive service. Rooms are luxuriously furnished with antique furniture, a queen- or king-size bed with top-quality linen, goose down pillows, and a pleasant well-lit work space. Bathrooms feature bathtubs and l'Occitane amenities. The suites feature a separate sitting room with a comfortable couch and armchair, a stereo, and a cordless phone. There's a small but well-designed fitness center, spa, small indoor pool, and business center. The prices listed are the high-season rack rates. Call or e-mail for discounts. Weekend packages can often be booked for as low as R$600 for 2 nights.

Al. Campinas 266, Jardim Paulista, 01404-000 SP. ℂ **0800/130-080** or 011/2183-0500. Fax 011/2183-0505. www.lhotel.com.br. 75 units. R$750 double; R$1,100 suite. Children 12 and under stay free in parent's room. Extra person add 25%. AE, DC, MC, V. Valet parking. Metrô: Brigadeiro. **Amenities:** Restaurant; bar; fitness center; small indoor pool; room service; smoke-free floors. *In room:* A/C, TV, hair dryer, minibar, MP3 docking station, Wi-Fi.

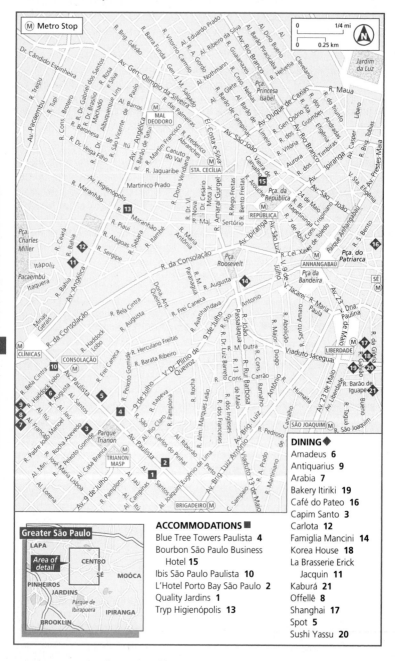

(M) Metro Stop

DINING ◆
Amadeus 6
Antiquarius 9
Arabia 7
Bakery Itiriki 19
Café do Pateo 16
Capim Santo 3
Carlota 12
Famiglia Mancini 14
Korea House 18
La Brasserie Erick
Jacquin 11
Kaburá 21
Offellê 8
Shanghai 17
Spot 5
Sushi Yassu 20

ACCOMMODATIONS ■
Blue Tree Towers Paulista 4
Bourbon São Paulo Business
Hotel 15
Ibis São Paulo Paulista 10
L'Hotel Porto Bay São Paulo 2
Quality Jardins 1
Tryp Higienópolis 13

Greater São Paulo
LAPA
Area of detail
CENTRO
SÉ MOÓCA
PINHEIROS
JARDINS
Parque de Ibirapuera
BROOKLIN
IPIRANGA

SETTLING INTO SÃO PAULO

9

WHERE TO STAY

Expensive

Blue Tree Towers Paulista ★★   This place offers a great location, friendly English-speaking staff, and comfortable rooms at a reasonable price. Rooms are clean and modern looking, with queen-size beds, high-quality linen, bright bathrooms with marble touches, and a good-size writing desk. Some floors feature carpeting, others tile flooring. The hotel is located just a few steps from the Avenida Paulista, the MASP, and the Metrô stop. On weekends, prices drop by 50% or more.

Rua Peixoto Gomide 707, Cerqueira César, 01409-001 SP. ✆ **011/3147-7000.** Fax 011/3147-7001. www.bluetree.com.br. 232 units. R$300 standard; R$375 superior; R$410 luxo. Children 12 and under stay free in parent's room. Extra person add 25%. AE, DC, MC, V. Valet parking. Metrô: Trianon-MASP. **Amenities:** Restaurant; bar; fitness center; indoor pool; room service; sauna; smoke-free floors. *In room:* A/C, TV, minibar, Wi-Fi.

Quality Jardins ★   The Quality Jardins offers some of the best affordable accommodations just off the Avenida Paulista. Rooms are a cross between a studio and a regular hotel room, featuring a desk and TV on a swivel in order to separate the sitting area from the sleeping area. The furnishings are modern and pleasant with light colors, blond wood, and comfortable lighting. The hotel offers three categories of rooms: superior, deluxe, and premium. The difference is mainly in the improved bathroom amenities and the turndown service and bathrobe that come with the premium rooms. Unless you get a free upgrade, it's not worth the money. The hotel has a good-size fitness room with saunas and an outdoor pool.

Al. Campinas 540, São Paulo, 01404-000 SP. ✆ **0800/555-855** or 011/2182-0400. Fax 011/2182-0401. www.atlanticahotels.com.br. 222 units. R$190–R$220 superior; R$210–R$250 deluxe; R$250–R$320 premium. Extra person add R$50. Children 5 and under stay free in parent's room. AE, DC, MC, V. Free parking. Metrô: Trianon-MASP. **Amenities:** Restaurant; concierge; health club; indoor pool; room service; sauna; smoke-free floors; Wi-Fi. *In room:* A/C, TV, hair dryer, Internet, minibar.

Moderate

Ibis São Paulo Paulista (Value)   The Accor group's budget Ibis brand offers predictable but quality accommodations in the heart of the business district. All rooms are identically furnished with good, firm double or twin beds, a desk, and a shower. Breakfast can be ordered for an extra R$9. This hotel is nonsmoking.

Av. Paulista 2355, Cerqueira Cesar, 01420-002 SP. ✆ **011/3523-3000.** Fax 011/3523-3030. www.accorhotels.com.br. 236 units. R$139 double. Children 12 and under stay free in parent's room. AE, DC, MC, V. Free parking. Metrô: Consolação. **Amenities:** Restaurant; limited room service; smoke-free hotel. *In room:* A/C, TV, minibar, Wi-Fi.

JARDINS

One of the most pleasant hotel neighborhoods in São Paulo, Jardins offers less traffic and streets lined with some of the city's best restaurants, shops, and cafes. The only disadvantage is that you're not on a Metrô line. A bus to Avenida Paulista (and the Metrô) along Rua Augusta will take 15 to 25 minutes; a bus into Centro will take 20 to 45 minutes. A cab to either will take 10 to 15 minutes. The area is safe and pleasant at night.

Very Expensive

Emiliano ★★★   The Emiliano offers the kind of five-star service that would cost far more in a place like New York or Paris. It's pampering all the way, from the welcome massage to the minibar stocked according to your preference, to the personalized selection of pillows, carefully fluffed and placed on your Egyptian cotton sheets. The hotel offers deluxe studios and suites. The fabulous, spacious suites come with designer furniture and feature original artwork and the latest home entertainment electronics. The bed is king-size and the bathroom is a minispa in itself; toiletries are customized to your skin type and you can sit back and relax in the claw-foot tub, maybe watch a little TV, or contemplate life on your heated toilet seat. The studios (really just a large room) are equally high design, half the size, and 40% cheaper—but really, is this any time to skimp?

Rua Oscar Freire 384, Cerqueira César, 01426-000 SP. ✆ **011/3069-4399.** Fax 011/3728-2000. www.emiliano.com.br. 57 units. R$925 double; R$1,600 suite. Check the website for special packages. Extra person add 30%. Children 10 and under stay free in parent's room. AE, DC, MC, V. Free parking. **Amenities:** Restaurant; upscale lobby bar; babysitting; concierge; small exercise room; room service; smoke-free floors; outstanding spa. *In room:* A/C, TV/DVD, hair dryer, Internet, minibar.

Fasano ★★★   Successful São Paulo restaurateurs, the Fasano family decided several years ago to apply their hospitality experience to the hotel industry. The hotel is decorated with elegant 1930s period furniture, combined with clean modern design elements. Rooms and suites are beautifully appointed with sober, modern furniture, hardwood floors, Persian rugs, and king-size beds with 500-thread Egyptian cotton sheets and goose down pillows. Moving up the categories, the rooms get progressively bigger and more luxurious. One up from superior, the deluxe room has a sitting area and a bathtub in addition to the shower. The suite is more than twice the size of the superior room and features a separate living room with a plasma TV and Bang & Olufsen sound system; the spacious bathroom has a Jacuzzi tub. The hotel's signature restaurant, Fasano, is one of the top Italian restaurants in South America.

Rua Vitório Fasano 88, Cerqueira César, 01426-000 SP. ✆ **011/3896-4000.** Fax 011/3896-4155. www.fasano.com.br. 57 units. R$850 superior; R$1,050 deluxe; R$1,450 suite. Extra person add 30%. Children 6 and under stay free in parent's room. AE, DC, MC, V. Free parking. **Amenities:** 2 restaurants; upscale jazz bar; babysitting; concierge; small exercise room; room service; smoke-free floors; small spa. *In room:* A/C, TV, hair dryer, minibar, Wi-Fi.

Expensive

Mercure São Paulo Jardins ★   At this pleasant, modern hotel, everything is crisp and clean, the decoration Scandinavian modern with blond wood, simple design, and lots of light. Rooms are spacious with king-size beds, a couple of small sitting chairs, and a good-size maple-wood desk with desk lamp and phone and power jacks for laptops. Bathrooms have nice fixtures but are functionally compact. More than half the hotel rooms are nonsmoking. The leisure area is small, offering only an indoor pool and sauna, but the Mercure's location is excellent, only a hop and a skip to the Avenida Paulista and a 15-minute walk downhill to the best shopping and dining in Jardins. Breakfast costs an additional R$25.

Al. Itu 1151, Cerqueira César, 01421-001 SP. ✆ **0800/703-7000** or 011/3089-7555. Fax 011/3089-7550. www.accorhotels.com.br. 126 units. R$260 double. Children 10 and under stay free in parent's room. AE, DC, MC, V. Free parking. Metrô: Consolação. **Amenities:** Restaurant; laptop-friendly bar; small indoor pool; room service; smoke-free floors. *In room:* A/C, TV, hair dryer, Internet, minibar.

Moderate

Quality Suites Imperial Hall ★★   The Imperial Hall sits in the heart of São Paulo's toniest neighborhood, surrounded by restaurants, designer boutiques, and trendy shops. The building is new, and the rooms are modern and pleasantly furnished. Built with the business traveler in mind, the hotel offers firm beds, large closets, a small kitchen, in-room Internet, and a large desk with easy access to lots of plugs. The master rooms on the 13th to 19th floors feature balconies and perks like fluffy bathrobes. As they cost only 30% more, they're worth reserving. There's also a floor exclusively for women travelers.

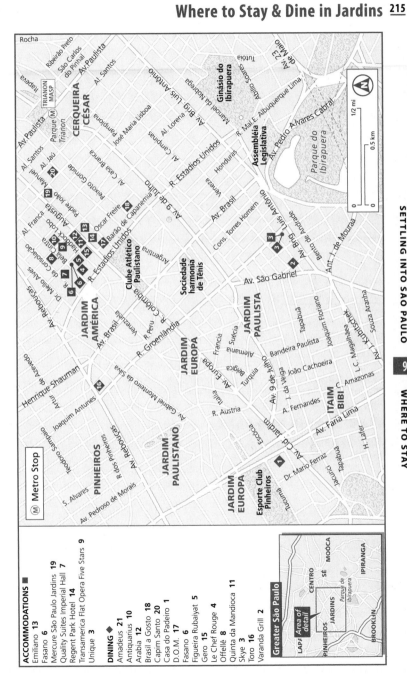

(M) Metro Stop

ACCOMMODATIONS ■
Emiliano **13**
Fasano **6**
Mercure São Paulo Jardins **19**
Quality Suites Imperial Hall **7**
Regent Park Hotel **14**
Transamerica Flat Opera Five Stars **9**
Unique **3**

DINING ◆
Amadeus **21**
Antiquarius **10**
Arabia **12**
Brasil a Gosto **18**
Capim Santo **20**
Casa do Padeiro **1**
D.O.M. **17**
Fasano **6**
Figueira Rubaiyat **5**
Gero **15**
Le Chef Rouge **4**
Offellè **8**
Quinta da Mandioca **11**
Skye **3**
Toro **16**
Varanda Grill **2**

Greater São Paulo

Area of detail

LAPA
PINHEIROS
JARDINS
BROOKLIN
CENTRO
SÉ
MOOCA
Parque de Ibirapuera
IPIRANGA

Rua da Consolação 3555, Jardins, 01416-001 SP. ℂ **011/2137-4555.** Fax 011/2137-4560. www.atlantica hotels.com.br. 150 units. R$250 standard; R$350 master. Extra person add 25%. Children 6 and under stay free in parent's room. AE, DC, MC, V. Free parking. **Amenities:** Restaurant; small weight room; rooftop pool; room service; sauna; smoke-free rooms; spa. *In room:* A/C, TV, kitchen, Wi-Fi.

Regent Park Hotel ★   This small apart-hotel is on one of the best-known streets in Jardins. The neighborhood is safe and packed with shops, cafes, and restaurants. The majority of units are one-bedroom suites, but two-bedroom suites are available as well. The furnishings are a little dated, with '80s rustic wood, but everything is very well maintained and clean, and all the suites have a full kitchen. The staff is exceptionally friendly and helpful, and business travelers will appreciate the small and efficient business center.

Rua Oscar Freire 533, Jardins, 01426-001 SP. ℂ **011/3065-5555.** www.regent.com.br. 70 units. R$270 1-bedroom; R$385 2-bedroom. Weekend discounts available. Extra person add R$40. Children 4 and under stay free in parent's room. AE, MC, V. Free parking. Bus: 702P. **Amenities:** Restaurant; concierge; small weight room; outdoor rooftop pool; limited room service; sauna; smoke-free rooms. *In room:* A/C, TV, fridge, Internet, kitchen, minibar.

Transamerica Flat Opera Five Stars ★ ⟨**Value**⟩   The bargain of the century happens to be in the heart of the city's best neighborhood. The Opera offers spacious flats, featuring a separate sitting room with comfy couch and TV and small dinette table, plus a good-size work desk with lamp and lots of plugs, plus a bedroom with firm queen-size bed and vast closets and full-length mirror, plus a kitchenette with stove and fridge, all for less than many hotels charge for just a bed. True, the furnishings are a tad dated (though nice, the rooms get nowhere near the five stars claimed in the name), but on the plus side, step out the door and you're in the heart of the Jardins shopping district.

Al. Lorena 1748, Cerqueira César, 04003-010 SP. ℂ **011/3062-2666.** Fax 011/3062-2662. www.trans americaflats.com.br. 96 units. R$240 double. Discounts available on weekends. Children 10 and under stay free in parent's room. AE, DC, MC, V. Free parking. Metrô: Consolação. **Amenities:** Restaurant; bar; small gym; small indoor pool; room service; sauna; smoke-free floors. *In room:* A/C, TV, Internet, kitchenette, minibar.

NEAR IBIRAPEURA PARK
Very Expensive

Unique ★★★   Unique truly is. In form, this latest São Paulo design hotel is a teetering verdigris-colored disk, chopped off at the top to make a roof deck, and propped up at either end by pillars hanging down like unfurled banners. Paulistas call it the *melancia,* or watermelon. Inside it's all high design, from the lobby bar the Wall to the rooms and suites that feature white-on-white decor, queen-size beds with luscious bedding, sparkling bathrooms with Jacuzzi tubs, clever desk space, and a plethora of room gadgets including electric blinds, 48-inch TVs, lots of light options, and a console to control it all. Suites are all located on the rim of the disk so their outer walls rise in one seamless curve from floor to ceiling. Views are excellent, but the ultimate view is from the rooftop pool and lounge where you see both Ibirapuera Park and the ridgeline run of skyscrapers on Avenida Paulista.

Av. Brigadeiro Luis Antônio 4700, Jardim Paulista, 01402-002 SP. ℂ **011/3055-4700.** Fax 011/3889-8100. www.hotelunique.com.br. 95 units. R$850 double; R$1,800–R$2,000 suite. AE, DC, MC, V. Parking R$20 daily. Metrô: Brigadeiro. **Amenities:** Rooftop restaurant, Skye (see review, p. 224); bar; concierge; fitness center; rooftop pool and indoor pool; room service. *In room:* A/C, TV/DVD, stereo, fridge, Internet, minibar.

Often overlooked by visitors, Higienópolis is a quiet, green, and pretty residential neighborhood with some excellent restaurants and shops located just a hop and a skip from Centro; a 20-minute walk from the Tryp Higienópolis takes you to the Praça da República. Better yet, prices are much lower than in Jardins.

Moderate

Tryp Higienópolis ★★★ (Value) Elegant and luxurious, the Tryp Higienópolis looks more like a high-end condominium than a hotel. The rooms are amazing. Much bigger than your average hotel rooms, these are bright and beautifully furnished with modern decor and colors. Rooms come in standard and superior. The only difference is that superior rooms have a balcony. Otherwise, both are the same spacious size, and come with a king-size bed and a large desk and comfy chair. Unusual for São Paulo, the hotel offers a partially covered pool as well as a large sun deck. As if all of that weren't enough, prices are a steal; Internet rates often go as low as R$160!

Rua Maranhão 371, Higienópolis, São Paulo, 01404-002 SP. (℅) **011/3665-8200.** www.solmelia.com. 252 units. R$220 standard; R$264 superior. Extra person add R$40. Children 6 and under stay free in parent's room. AE, DC, MC, V. Free parking. Metrô: Marechal Deodoro. **Amenities:** Restaurant; bar; concierge; exercise room; outdoor pool; limited room service; sauna; smoke-free floors. *In room:* A/C, TV, hair dryer, Internet, minibar.

---

3 WHERE TO DINE

São Paulo is the gourmet capital of Brazil. It's the city with the money to attract the country's best chefs, with the clientele to pay the tab at the most outstanding restaurants. Plus, with no beaches or mountains to play on, Paulistas amuse themselves by eating out. People dress up for dinner here (or more than they would elsewhere in the country) and usually go out around 9 or 10pm *at the earliest.* Though it's becoming more common for restaurants to accept reservations, many will do so only up to 9pm. After that, you have to take your chances. If waiting for a table drives you to distraction, better to arrive unfashionably early at 8pm.

The variety of cuisine is larger than anywhere else in the country. Like New York or Toronto, São Paulo is a city of immigrants. Many of the city's best restaurants are Italian. However, the city has a number of top Middle Eastern restaurants, as well as the best Japanese food in the country, plus Spanish, Portuguese, Bahian, and even Thai cuisine. Churrascarias are always a favorite, as are lunchtime kilo spots, which mad-for-work Paulistas see as the perfect way to fuel up for long hours at the office.

The *Guia São Paulo,* the entertainment listing published in the Friday *Folha de São Paulo* newspaper, contains a detailed restaurant section, handy for confirming hours and phone numbers. Also note that the long street names are often abbreviated by Paulistas; for example, the Rua José Maria Lisboa may also be known as Rua Lisboa.

CENTRO

For a map of restaurants in this area, see the map "Where to Stay & Dine in São Paulo Centro," p. 212.

Famiglia Mancini ★★ ITALIAN   A São Paulo institution, you'll find a line outside this traditional Italian trattoria almost any night of the week. Fortunately they pack in a lot of tables, all covered in little red-and-white checkered tablecloths, so the wait is never too long. Once inside, you're first stop should be the antipasto buffet, an impressive spread of olives, cold cuts, marinated vegetables, cheeses, quail's eggs, and salads. With that on your plate you'll have the energy to tackle the enormous pasta menu. There's every type and pasta kind imaginable, and more than 30 different sauces to match. Portions are huge, enough for two, or often three. Desserts are uninspiring, but by meal's end you should be too stuffed to even contemplate eating more.

Rua Avanhandava 81, Centro. ✆ **011/3256-4320.** www.famigliamancini.com.br. Reservations not accepted. Main courses R$34–R$68 for 2. AE, DC, MC, V. Sun–Wed 11:30am–1am; Thurs 11:30am–2am; Fri–Sat 11:30am–3am. Metrô: Anhagabau.

Inexpensive

Café do Pateo ★★ (Value) CAFE   Tired of the hustle and bustle of São Paulo? Tuck away into this great cafe inside the Pátio do Colégio, the place where the city was founded, for some outstanding coffees, sweets, quiches, sandwiches, and pasta.

Pátio do Colégio 2, Centro. ✆ **011/3106-4303.** Main courses R$18–R$35. No credit cards. Tues–Sun 9am–5pm. Metrô: Sé.

AVENIDA PAULISTA

Very Expensive

Antiquarius ★★★ PORTUGUESE   The Portuguese cuisine here is served up with flair and tradition, in the perfect elegant setting. The menu offers dishes hard to find outside Portugal, such as the *cataplana de peixes e frutos do mar,* a rich seafood and fish stew, with bacon and sausage thrown in for seasoning. Another traditional seafood favorite is *açorda*—crab, shrimp, and mussels baked together in a clay dish, served with a decorative egg on top. Then there's cod *(bacalhau),* a staple of Portuguese cooking since before Columbus set sail. The wine list leans to higher-end reds, drawn mostly from Portugal and France.

Al. Lorena 1884, Cerqueira César. ✆ **011/3064-8686.** www.antiquarius.com.br. Main courses R$65–R$125. DC, MC, V. Mon 7pm–1am; Tues–Fri noon–3pm and 7pm–2am; Sat noon–2am; Sun noon–6pm. Metrô: Trianon-MASP.

Expensive

Amadeus ★★ SEAFOOD   For 20 years and counting, this elegant spot off the Avenida Paulista has served up traditional top-quality seafood dishes—the shrimp couscous is locally renowned—as well as innovative plates that vary with the seasons, such as Norwegian haddock in a cashew nut crust with a side of garlic-kissed palm heart purée. The wine list leans heavily to expensive whites.

Rua Haddock Lobo 807, Cerqueira César. ✆ **011/3061-2859.** www.restauranteamadeus.com.br. Main courses R$55–R$95. AE, V. Mon–Fri noon–3pm and 6pm–midnight; Sat noon–4:30pm and 7pm–1am; Sun noon–4:30pm and 7–11pm. Metrô: Consolação.

Baby Beef Rubaiyat ★★ STEAK   One of the city's signature steakhouses, the Rubaiyat serves prime cuts of beef, many drawn from the owner's own cattle ranch in the state of Mato Grosso. Prime Brazilian cuts include *picanha,* master beef, and baby beef (a type of tender, very young calf). For those who prefer a thicker steak, there are cuts imported from Argentina. For those with a bit of patience or foresight, there's tender

3-week-old roast baby boar (2-hr. advance order). Wednesdays and Saturdays there's a full *feijoada*, served buffet style so you can pick and choose which bits of pork to add to your heaping plate of black beans. For the less carnivorous, the salad bar is well provisioned.

Al. Santos 86, Cerqueira César. ℂ **011/3141-1188.** www.rubaiyat.com.br. Main courses R$45–R$95. AE, DC, MC, V. Mon–Fri noon–3pm and 7pm–midnight; Sat noon–midnight; Sun noon–6pm. Metrô: Brigadeiro.

Capim Santo ★★ BRAZILIAN   Modeled after a famous Bahian restaurant, the Capim Santo in São Paulo is set in a lovely garden with lush mango trees and plenty of outside tables. The specialty is seafood. Try the *robalo* fish with a crust of cashew nuts and a side of *vatapá* shrimp stew, or the tender grilled tuna, or the stew of prawns in coconut milk, served in a hollowed-out pumpkin. For a vegetarian option try the mini-cannelloni stuffed with asparagus, ricotta, and tomato confit. Desserts often feature a tropical twist, such as the guava crème brûlée or the tarte tatin with banana. The lunchtime buffet offers 15 salads and more than 10 hot dishes, including seafood, chicken, and pasta, only R$36 (R$51 weekends) with dessert included.

Rua Ministro Rocha Azevedo 471, Cerqueira César. ℂ **011/3068-8486.** www.restaurantecapimsanto. com.br. Main courses R$26–R$49. AE. Tues–Sat noon–3pm and 7pm–midnight; Sun 12:30–4:30pm. Metrô: MASP.

Spot ★ BRAZILIAN   More than 10 years old and still trendy, Spot seems to be the exception to the rule that all that is hip soon melts into air. The daytime crowd consists of well-dressed office workers and businesspeople on expense-account lunches. In the evenings, Spot buzzes with musicians, designers, models, and other trendy types who crowd in to this glass-enclosed cocoon to flirt, schmooze, and preen. The food is decent; pasta dishes, such as a penne with melon, salads (try the Spot Salad—lettuce, Gorgonzola, dried pears, and nuts), grilled salmon, and tuna with vegetables. Spot's owners have seemingly created a perpetual motion machine: The young and beautiful flock to see the young and beautiful, who flock to see the young and beautiful, and so on . . .

Rua Min. Rocha Azevedo 72, Cerqueira Cesar. ℂ **011/3283-0946.** http://basilico.uol.com.br/spot. Reservations accepted. Main courses R$35–R$65. AE, DC, MC, V. Mon–Fri noon–3pm and 8pm–1am; Sat–Sun 1–4:30pm and 8pm–1am. Metrô: Trianon-MASP.

Inexpensive

Alaska (Finds) DESSERT   One of the city's favorite ice-cream parlors, Alaska has been serving over 30 homemade flavors for over 95 years. Flavor-wise it's fairly traditional: lots of chocolates, vanilla, and fruit, as well as excellent ice-cream desserts such as a banana split, peach melba, or the signature Alaska, served with a choice of two toppings, *farofa*, peach slices, and cookies.

Rua Doutor Rafael de Barros 70, Paraiso. ℂ **011/3889-8676.** Everything under R$15. No credit cards. Sun–Thurs 9am–midnight; Fri–Sat 9am–2am. Metrô: Brigadeiro.

LIBERDADE
Expensive
Sushi Yassu ★★ JAPANESE   The second-generation owners of this traditional Liberdade standard-bearer have begun introducing some new dishes to the Paulista palate. Try the grilled white tuna or anchovy, in salt or with a sweetened soy sauce, or a steaming bowl of udon noodle soup with seafood or tempura vegetables. For traditionalists there's a large variety of sushi and sashimi, plus stir-fried teppanyaki and yakisoba noodles with meat and vegetables. On Sundays there can be a line.

Rua Tomas Gonzaga 98, Liberdade. ✆ 011/3209-6622. Main courses R$20–R$66. AE, DC, MC, V. Tues–Fri 11:30am–3pm and 6–11pm; Sat noon–4pm and 6pm–midnight; Sun noon–10pm. Metrô: Liberdade.

Moderate

Kaburá JAPANESE   Twenty years and still going strong, Kaburá offers late-night dining in the heart of São Paulo's little Japan. The restaurant serves up the usual Japanese faves—sushi, sashimi, *donburi,* and tempura—in generous portions at a reasonable price. For interesting appetizers try the sashimi made from Brazilian *picanha* beef, or the breaded and crunchy deep-fried oysters.

Rua Galvão Bueno 346, Liberdade. ✆ 011/3277-2918. Reservations accepted. Main courses R$18–R$45. No credit cards. Mon–Sat 7pm–2am. Metrô: Liberdade.

Korea House KOREAN   It's some of the best Korean food in the city, but finding it involves a journey—head down a long hallway, up the stairs, and into a windowless room lit by fluorescent lights, with only the small BBQs built into every table to entice you into eating. The cuisine is a mix of Chinese and Korean, with both spicy dishes from the kitchen or Korean BBQ done in front of you at your table.

Rua Galvão Bueno 43, Liberdade. ✆ 011/3208-3052. Reservations not accepted. Main courses R$15–R$45. MC, V. Mon–Sat 11am–10pm; Sun 11am–3pm and 6–10pm. Metrô: Liberdade.

Shanghai CHINESE   Shanghai offers cheap and cheerful Chinese, in a busy room in the heart of São Paulo's Japantown. Order beef, chicken, vegetables, or splurge on one of the fish fresh from the entryway aquarium.

Rua Galvão Bueno 16, Liberdade. ✆ 011/3208-7914. Reservations accepted. Main courses R$18–R$42. MC, V. Mon–Sat 11am–9pm; Sun 11am–3pm and 6–9pm. Metrô: Liberdade.

Inexpensive

Bakery Itiriki BAKERY   This is the place for a delicious inexpensive break in Liberdade. There are quiches, sandwiches, rolls, coffee, and an extensive collection of desserts, including cakes of chocolate, *aipim,* and banana, plus a rich assortment of truffles.

Rua dos Estudantes 24, Liberdade. ✆ 011/3277-4939. Reservations not accepted. Main courses R$10–R$25. MC, V. Daily 8am–7pm. Metrô: Liberdade.

JARDINS

For a map of restaurants in this area, see the map "Where to Stay & Dine in Jardins," p. 215.

Very Expensive

D.O.M. ★★★ CONTEMPORARY   São Paulo's restaurant of the moment actually opened in 1999, when chef Alex Atala returned from years in Europe with a plan to showcase the best Brazilian ingredients, employing the most careful and innovative preparations in a custom-designed dining room. In the decade since, D.O.M. has racked up every significant restaurant award in Brazil, culminating with its inscription in *Restaurant Magazine*'s list of the top 50 restaurants in the world. The menu changes constantly—ask about the specials—but may include favorites such as *robalo* with *tucupi* and manioc, or duck in red-wine and golden-banana sauce. Diners can also opt for a four- or eight-course tasting menu including fish, meat, and cheese course. The wine list is extensive and expensive, but if you're dining here you expected that. Reserve at least a couple days in advance, or come prepared to wait. D.O.M. is popular.

Fasano ★★★ ITALIAN   Long considered the best Italian restaurant in the country, the Fasano continues to live up to expectations. The dining room combines black marble and dark furniture with exquisite lighting to create a warm and intimate ambience. The mainstay of the menu remains dishes from the Lombardy region from whence the Fasano family originally hailed. Start off with the traditional tomato soup with prawns and Italian bread. Pasta favorites include the delicate pumpkin tortelli or a hearty duck ravioli in orange sauce. Risottos feature Tuscan sausage and white beans or tender marinated tuna. Meat and seafood options include classic veal cutlets, roasted lamb, *filetto alla Rossini* with foie gras and truffles, or for a lighter choice, grilled tuna steak with Sicilian lemon. If you're feeling decision shy, opt for the five-course tasting menu and let the chef take you on a gastronomic journey around Italy.

Rua Vittorio Fasano 88, Cerqueira Cesar. ℂ **011/3062-4000.** www.fasano.com.br. Main courses R$98–R$160; 5-course tasting menu R$275. AE, DC, MC, V. Mon–Sat 7:30pm–1am. Bus: 206E.

Figueira Rubaiyat ★★★ BRAZILIAN/STEAK   The most beautiful restaurant in the city, Figueira (fig tree) Rubaiyat is built around the spreading limbs of a magnificent old fig tree. Seating can either be "outside" in the gazebo around the tree boughs or inside in the lovely restaurant. Rubaiyat's specialty is beef. Indeed, it serves the best prime beef in São Paulo, all of it raised with care at the owner's private cattle ranch. For the noncarnivorous, the Figueira also offers a wide variety of top-notch Mediterranean seafood dishes, such as paella, codfish, and grilled prawns.

Rua Haddock Lobo 1738, Cerqueira Cesar. ℂ **011/3063-3888.** www.rubaiyat.com.br. Main courses R$45–R$95. V. Daily noon–12:30am. Bus: 206E.

Expensive

Arabia ★★ MIDDLE EASTERN   This spacious and modern restaurant serves up a range of favorites from Lebanon, including a regularly changing tasting menu. At R$38 it's a great way to sample some of the chef's best. The main menu includes Moroccan rice with roasted almonds and chicken, or the signature stuffed artichoke with ground beef. For a lighter meal, try the *mezze*, the Lebanese equivalent of tapas. Each tray comes with at least half a dozen tasters of the most popular dishes, including hummus, falafel, tabbouleh, and a generous serving of pita.

Rua Haddock Lobo 1397, Cerqueira Cesar. ℂ **011/3061-2203.** www.arabia.com.br. Main courses R$25–R$65. AE, DC, MC. Mon–Thurs noon–3:30pm and 7pm–midnight; Fri noon–3:30pm and 7pm–1am; Sat-Sun noon–midnight. Bus: 206E.

Brasil a Gosto ★★ BRAZILIAN   Chef Ana Luiza Trajano made an extended culinary research tour through Brazil's vast hinterlands to come up with homegrown ingredients and recipes many Brazilians had never heard of. The result was a successful book and even more successful restaurant, which makes use of native ingredients—cane, cashew, *guarana, açaí,* sugar cane, manioc—to create innovative and delightful dishes: appetizers like *pirarucu* (Amazon fish) pastry, an entree of pork cutlets with *jabuticaba*-berry sauce with a side of grilled plantain, desserts of banana sweets with crushed Brazil nut and coconut covering, served with ice cream. For drinks, there's an extensive menu of homemade *cachaças.*

Rua Prof. Azevedo de Amaral 70, Jardim Paulista. ℰ **011/3086-3565.** www.brasilagosto.com.br. Main courses R$30–R$65. AE, DC, MC. Wed–Sat noon–4pm and 7pm–12:30am; Sun noon–6pm. Bus: 206E.

Gero ★★ ITALIAN   This modern, masculine room in the heart of Jardins is distinguished from the surrounding boutiques by discreet doormen, valet parking, and a lineup of clients waiting patiently for entry to this most successful of Italian establishments. Appetizers can be inventive, like the sliced and spiced fried pumpkin slivers, but the house forte is pasta, made fresh and served in intriguing combinations like the signature duck-filled ravioli in orange sauce. Nonpasta options include some excellent risottos—including one made with red wine, white beans, and hearty Tuscan sausage. Steaks and poultry are on the menu, but if that's what you're hankering for you should really go elsewhere.

Rua Haddock Lobo 1629, Cerqueira Cesar. ℰ **011/3064-0005.** www.fasano.com.br. Main courses R$40–R$75. AE, DC, MC. Mon–Thurs noon–3pm and 7pm–1am; Fri–Sat noon–4pm and 7pm–1am; Sun noon–4:30pm and 7–11:30pm. Bus: 206E.

Le Chef Rouge ★★ FRENCH   Listening to the *chansons* in Chef Rouge's cozy dining room, you could easily believe that you were somewhere on the Left Bank (although waiters here are friendly, attentive, and speak English). The menu includes hearty French fare such as the *trois filets aux trois sauces,* a trio of juicy grilled steaks each served with a different sauce and the *canard à l'orange,* thin slices of duck served in a sweet-savory orange sauce on a bed of wafer-thin potato chips. The wine list includes far too many expensive French bottles, but a small selection of Chilean cabernet sauvignon and Shiraz makes an affordable evening possible. For dessert, the cheese plate makes a wonderful change from Brazilian sweets.

Rua Bela Cintra 2238, Cerqueira César. ℰ **011/3081-7539.** www.chefrouge.com.br. Main courses R$32–R$75. AE, DC, MC, V. Tues–Sat noon–3:30pm and 7pm–midnight; Sun noon–5pm and 7pm–midnight.

Moderate

Quinta da Mandioca ★ BRAZILIAN   Come to this rustic-looking restaurant for some typically Brazilian "home cooking," including dishes such as *picadinho,* a spicy beef stew topped with a poached egg and served with baked banana, *farofa,* and rice. On Saturday, there's an excellent *feijoada* buffet with all the trimmings including rice, baked bananas, *farofa,* sliced oranges, and sautéed green cabbage. If you just want a quick snack or lunch, there's also a great sandwich menu.

Rua Oscar Freire 726, Cerqueira Cesar. ℰ **011/3064-4999.** Main courses R$20–R$45. AE, DC, MC, V. Sun–Thurs noon–11pm; Fri–Sat noon–1am.

Toro ★★ TAPAS   Somewhat late, but very good, tapas have finally arrived in Brazil. This warm terra-cotta restaurant, rich with the look and scents of the owners native Andalusia, offers a wide variety of Spanish-style small plates—perfect for snacking and sharing over a glass of red from the substantial wine list. For those less inclined to sharing, there's excellent paella and lamb. All dishes, big and small, are served on hand-painted plates brought directly from Spain.

Rua Joaquim Antunes 224, Jardin Paulista. ℰ **011/3085-8485.** Reservations recommended. Small plates R$15–R$45. AE, MC, V. Daily 8am–7pm.

Inexpensive

Casa do Padeiro CAFE   Open 24 hours a day, the Casa do Padeiro (Baker's House) dishes up way more than just bread. It's the perfect spot to grab a light meal any time of

the day. There are salads; sandwiches; pasta; desserts; excellent coffee including fresh
espresso, café au lait, and cappuccinos; and other hot beverages.

Av. Brigadeiro Faria Lima 2776, Jardim Paulistano. ℭ **011/3812-1233.** Everything under R$15. AE, MC, V. Daily 24 hr. Bus: 5100 or 5119.

Offellê ICE CREAM   Offellê's display case shows a dazzling rainbow of Italian gelato-style ice cream. Try the chocolate and mint or the chocolate with hazelnut. Exceptionally yummy. The fruit flavors are made with fresh fruit and range from the tropical passion fruit to more "foreign and exotic" raspberry and blackberry.

Al. Lorena 1784, Cerqueira Cesar. ℭ **011/3088-8127.** Everything under R$12. V. Daily 1–11pm. Bus: 206E.

VILA MADALENA
Expensive
Kabuki ★★ JAPANESE   Romantic, chic, Japanese. Not adjectives that usually go together (at least not in Brazil), but Kabuki's candlelit dining room, exposed brick, and wood accents make it an exception. For those who want to nibble, there's a large menu of appetizers including sautéed shiitake or *shimeji* mushrooms, deep-fried prawn, and grilled skewers with meat, seafood, or vegetables. Main courses include a large variety of sushi and sashimi combos, tempuras, yakisoba noodles, and grilled meats. Interesting dessert options include the flambéed mango and banana or tempura ice cream, a wonderful sensation of a hot, crunchy crust and a soft, cold, creamy center.

Rua Girassol 384, Vila Madalena. ℭ **011/3814-5131.** www.kabuki.com.br. Reservations accepted. Main courses R$22–R$70. AE, DC, MC, V. Mon 7–11pm; Tues–Sat noon–3pm and 7pm–1am; Sun noon–11pm. Metrô: Vila Madalena.

Santa Gula ★★ ⟨Finds⟩ ITALIAN   One of the quaintest restaurants in São Paulo, Santa Gula is reached via a fairy-tale lane lush with tropical plants, banana trees, and flickering candlelight. The lane leads to a dining room with the handmade furniture and rustic decor of a simple Tuscan villa. The kitchen serves up a mix of Italian and Brazilian flavors—think risotto with palm hearts or pasta stuffed with *carne seca* (a flavorful dried meat) and pumpkin purée. For meat lovers, the steaks arrive grilled to perfection. For dessert, don't pass up on the Brazil nut pie or the sweet coconut with tapioca mousse and tangerine sorbet.

Rua Fidalga 340, Vila Madalena. ℭ **011/3812-7815.** www.stagula.com.br. Reservations recommended. Main courses R$26–R$40. AE, DC, MC, V. Mon 8pm–midnight; Tues–Thurs noon–3pm and 8pm–1am; Fri–Sat noon–4pm and 8pm–2am; Sun noon–5pm. Metrô: Vila Madalena.

Moderate
Oficina das Pizzas ★ ⟨Value⟩ PIZZA   With over 40 varieties of pie to choose from at the Oficina das Pizzas, it may take you an eternity to make up your mind. There are traditional combinations such as tomato, ham, basil, cheese, and onion. Brazilians, however, have a real thing for sweet and savory pizzas—witness the Gorgonzola cheese with pineapple pizza, or the smoked bacon, tomato, and mango chutney combo. For something truly unique, try the banana with mozzarella, sugar, and cinnamon.

Rua Harmonia 117, Vila Madalena. ℭ **011/3816-7848.** Main courses R$26–R$37. AE, DC, MC, V. Mon–Wed 7pm–midnight; Thurs–Sun 7pm–1am. Metrô: Vila Madalena.

Inexpensive
Deliparis CAFE   A combination of cafe and bakery, Deliparis has an excellent selection of freshly baked breads, including loaves made with olives, nuts, or multigrain.

Clients linger in the cafe with a tea or cappuccino and some of the delicious fruit tarts, quiches, or brioches. Deliparis also bakes excellent pies and divine cakes: Think banana cake with almonds or creamy chocolate ganache.

Rua Harmonia 484, Vila Madalena. ✆ 011/3816-5911. Everything under R$12. No credit cards. Daily 7am–10pm. Bus: 473T.

HIGIENOPOLIS
Expensive

Carlota ★★ BRAZILIAN Owner and chef Carla Pernambuco blends the flavors of cosmopolitan New York (where she got her training) and her own Italian heritage together with fresh Brazilian ingredients to create dishes such as the *camarão pacifico:* shrimp grilled with sesame seeds and Thai chili sauce on a bed of vegetable-fried rice. She pulls off a great grilled duck with Dijon mustard on mashed mandioc, and the beef with balsamic port sauce and a fig risotto is also outstanding. For a lighter meal try the several pasta options, including the ravioli stuffed with brie or codfish.

Rua Sergipe 753, Higienópolis. ✆ 011/3661-8670. Main courses R$65–R$95. AE, DC, MC, V. Mon 7pm–midnight; Tues–Thurs noon–4pm and 7pm–midnight; Fri–Sat noon–1am; Sun noon–6pm. Bus: 8107.

La Brasserie Erick Jacquin ★★ FRENCH Celebrity chefs have begun putting their names on their eateries in São Paulo, as this new high-end spot in Higienópolis bears witness. The decor is warm, clean, and modern, with lots of leather and wood grain put to tasteful effect in both the airy front bar and the restaurant area. The cuisine offers both traditional French—duck confit in peppercorn sauce—and French with a Brazilian touch—prawns Provençal, sliced duck in a passion-fruit sauce. The wine list intelligently avoids overpriced French bottles for better value (and equivalent quality) from Chile and Argentina. Desserts feature lots of Belgian chocolate. Enjoy!

Rua Bahia 683, Higienópolis. ✆ 011/3826-5409. www.brasserie.com.br. Main courses R$65–R$125. AE, DC, MC, V. Sun–Thurs noon–midnight; Fri–Sat noon–1am; Sun noon–5pm. Bus: 8107.

Moderate

The Higienópolis Dining Triangle Smack in the middle of Higienópolis just behind the FAAP sits the delightful **Praça Vila Boim.** A lovely three-sided square with beautiful trees, the *praça* offers great casual dining options covering most of the world's cuisines. Sushi lovers will be pleased to find **Sushi Papaia** ★ (✆ 011/3666-2086; www.sushipapaia.com.br). For pizza lovers there's **Piola** ★ (✆ 011/3663-6539; www.piola.it), famous almost as much for its edgy, industrial-chic decor as it is for its 30 pizza combinations. Favorites include the Rimini (smoked salmon and ricotta) and the Mantova (mozzarella, brie, fresh tomatoes, and arugula). For a great burger and a heavy helping of nostalgia try the **Fifties** (✆ 011/5094-5454; www.thefifties.com.br), an old-style diner offering burgers, chili dogs, shakes, and fries. If steak is on your mind, look no further than the **Empório Natan** (✆ 011/3828-1402), which specializes in Argentine and Angus cuts. For Mexican lovers, there's **SiSenor** (✆ 011/3476-2538; www.sisenor.com.br), with an excellent selection of tacos, enchiladas, and burritos.

NEAR IBIRAPEURA PARK
Expensive

Skye ★★ (Finds) BRAZILIAN Even if you aren't staying at the Unique, it's worth coming to Skye, both to experience the architecture and to enjoy the rooftop restaurant. The views of the São Paulo skyline are spectacular. This modern lounge/restaurant serves

If This Is Higienópolis, It Must Be French

Deprived of their sought-after Brazilian colony in the 1500s, the French appear to have decided to take over Higienópolis, or at least a goodly portion of its restaurants. In addition to the **La Brasserie Erick Jacquin,** there's a pair of side-by-side Parisian bistros just around the corner on the Rua Pará. The **Ici Bistro,** Rua Pará 36 (✆ **011/3257-4064;** www.icibistro.com.br; Mon–Fri noon–3pm and 7pm–midnight, Sat noon–4pm and 7:30pm–12:30am, Sun noon–5pm), offers top-quality cuisine by a *cordon bleu* trained chef, plus a rooftop terrace with lighter quicker fare. The **Mercearia do Francês,** Rua Itacolomi 636 (✆ **011/ 3214-1295;** www.merceariadofrances.com.br; Mon–Fri noon–3:30pm and 7pm–midnight, Sat noon–5pm and 7pm–1am, Sun noon–5pm), offers more casual French fare, plus a replica of the Eiffel Tower on its patio. And if that wasn't enough, over at the Praça Vila Boim (in the Higienópolis Dining Triangle), where the rest of the world also has a foothold, there's **Le Vin Bistro,** Rua Armando Penteado 25 (✆ **011/3668-7400;** www.levin.com.br; Mon–Sat noon–midnight, Sun noon–11pm).

up creative and innovative Brazilian cuisine. The menu constantly changes but a few of the recent dishes have included duck confit with a Malbec and *rucula* risotto, or grilled salmon with yakisoba. Plus there's a full sushi bar that serves up excellent sushi and sashimi. In the evenings the lounge is a city hot spot and popular celebrity hangout. Reservations accepted only for hotel guests.

In the Unique (p. 216), Av. Brigadeiro Luis Antonio 4700, Jardim Paulista. ✆ **011/3055-4702.** Main courses R$42–R$69. AE, DC, MC, V. Daily noon–4pm and 7pm–1am.

Varanda Grill ★★ STEAK   In a country that values prime beef above everything but perhaps soccer and sex, the Varanda Grill stands out. Every type and kind of beef is available: porterhouse, rib-eye, and prime rib from the United States, *bife de chorizo* from Argentina, *picanha* and baby beef from Brazil, and the house signature dish, Kobe-style beef from Japan, known for its marbled texture and melt-in-your-mouth flavor (the latter available with a 24-hr. advance reservation). Decor is spare, perhaps even a tad too minimalist, though given the quality of the beef you may not even notice. The wine list contains over 400 bottles in a range of prices and nationalities (though higher end South Americans predominate), each with a helpful short description.

Rua Gen. Mena Bareto 793, Jardim Paulista. ✆ **011/3887-8870.** www.varandagrill.com.br. Main courses R$65–R$105. AE, DC, MC, V. Mon–Thurs noon–3pm and 7pm–midnight; Fri noon–5pm and 7pm–midnight; Sun noon–5:30pm.

Exploring São Paulo

Rio is a beauty. But São Paulo—São Paulo is a city.
—Marlene Dietrich

What was once a little market town in the cool high plateau has jumped its bounds and sprawled for the hills in all directions. São Paulo is now not only the largest city in Brazil, but it's also the largest in South America and the third or fourth largest in the world. What assembles and drives this vast collection of people is commerce. The city and surrounding municipalities account for an incredible 65% of Brazil's GDP. When Paulistas do take a break from work, they devote much the same energy to leisure. The city has some of the best galleries and museums in the country. It has by far the best cuisine and some of the best nightlife. And despite the seeming chaos, remain for a few days and you'll discover, as Paulistas have, that the city could not be otherwise; somehow São Paulo makes sense.

SUGGESTED SÃO PAULO ITINERARIES

If You Have ❶ Day

Get to know South America's largest city. Wander the busy pedestrian streets of the old downtown neighborhood of **Centro.** In the constant commercial chatter you'll feel, see, and hear Paulistas at their best: buying, selling, and trading. Drop down the busy **Rua 25 de Março** to the **Mercado Municipal,** to sample the exotic fruit or bite into a monster mortadella and Swiss. Ascend to the top of the **Banespa building** for a 360-degree view of the city. Have a coffee at the **Pátio do Colégio.** In the afternoon, take the Metrô out to the **Avenida Paulista.** Bask in the wealth and power a bit, then go see some fine art at the **MASP.** In the evening, take advantage of your presence in Brazil's culinary capital and go out for dinner at a truly fine restaurant like the **D.O.M.** or **Figueira Rubaiyat.**

If You Have ❷ Days

Get some culture. Anyone interested in modern Brazilian architecture should see the **Monument to Latin America.** Those interested in seeing Brazilian art should check out the **Pinacoteca do Estado,** or for older work the **Museu de Arte Sacra.** Reward yourself with an afternoon shopping in the green and leafy **Jardins** neighborhood. The intersection of **Rua Augusta** and **Oscar Freire** is perhaps the most exclusive shopping enclave in all Brazil. The neighborhood is also one of São Paulo's culinary hot spots. For a taste of the diversity in this most cosmopolitan of cities, seek out a Bahian dinner at **Capim Santo,** a French meal at **Le Brasserie Erick Jacquine,** or something Middle Eastern at **Arabia.** In the evening, head out to **Vila Madalena,** have a cold chopp and enjoy the people-watching, or a fine whiskey and light jazz at the **Piratininga Bar.**

If You Have ❸ Days

Set off to explore the Japanese neighborhood of **Liberdade,** topped off with a fine Japanese lunch. Walk off those calories with an afternoon in **Ibirapuera Park.** Stroll the pathways, rent a bicycle, and enjoy the people-watching. Don't pass up the **Afro-Brazilian Museum.** That night, check out some of the clubs or bars in **Vila Olímpia.** And if you're engine is still revving come midnight, head downtown to the newly renovated **Rua Augusta** to hear some music or dance the night away. Try to make it home by dawn.

1 THE TOP ATTRACTIONS

Pinacoteca do Estado ★★★   The Pinacoteca is a sunlit joy to be in, and one of the best-curated art collections in the country. It's the perfect place for anyone wanting to see and understand Brazilian art. Renovated in 1997, the roof and many interior walls were removed, replaced with a latticework of glass and open spaces, and connected by a series of catwalks. Though none of the signs are in English, the Pinacoteca does an excellent job of displaying some of the best Brazilian artists from the 19th and 20th centuries. The 20th-century work starts to break free of European influence and includes interesting examples of colorful Brazilian pieces bursting with energy. The Pinacoteca's sculpture collection includes a lovely statue by Raphael Galvez entitled *O Brasileiro,* as well as works by Alfredo Ceschiatti, the artist who designed many of the sculptures in Brasilia. Allow 2 hours.

Praça da Luz 2, Luz. © 011/3324-1000. www.pinacoteca.org.br. Admission R$6, free for children 10 and under. Free Sat. Tues–Sun 10am–6pm. Metrô: Luz.

Mercado Municipal ★★   Built in the 1930s, this gorgeous market hall with its skylights and stained-glass windows is a fabulous setting for the city's largest food and produce market. Stand and gawp at fruit stands piled high with exotic tropical offerings, many available only in Brazil. Better yet, buy a few and sample. Or peruse the herbal remedies stalls for that rare rainforest bark that will cure what ails ya. Or hang out by a deli stand sniffing the salamis and fondling the full round cheeses. Or bite into a monster mortadella sandwich at Bar do Mané (© **011/3228-2141**). Allow an hour, plus time for lunch. *Tip:* If you don't mind crowds and a bit of mess and confusion, it's a fun walk downhill to the market along the very busy Rua 25 de Março, starting from just behind the Pateo do Colegio. Hundreds of small shops sell inexpensive goods in bulk, with lingerie a specialty. The street is safe during business hours, though keep an eye for pickpockets and don't flaunt your camera gear.

Rua da Cantareira 306, Centro. © **011/3326-3401.** Free admission. Mon–Sat 5am–4pm. Metrô: São Bento.

Ibirapuera Park ★★   Blessed with over 2 million sq. m (22 million sq. ft.) of green space, São Paulo's version of Central Park offers quite a bit to see and do. You can wander the paths beside pleasant lagoons or rent a bicycle (R$6 per hour) and cycle the pathways. Every Sunday morning there's a **free outdoor concert** in the park's Praça da Paz. Sunday from 10am to 4pm you can take advantage of the **Bosque de Leitura,** a kind of free outdoor lending library that lets you borrow magazines or books (including many in English) to read in the park for the duration of day. In the corner near Gate 3 there's the **Museum of Modern Art** (see below). Just nearby there's the excellent **Afro-Brazil Museum** (see below) and the **OCA Auditorium,** a flying saucer–shaped building that often hosts traveling art exhibits. Allow half a day.

Administration © **011/5574-5177.** www.parquedoibirapuera.com. Free admission. Daily 5am–midnight. Bus: 5185-10 (or taxi from Metrô Brigadeiro).

Liberdade ★★ São Paulo's Japantown got its name (which means "Liberty") after the 1888 abolition of slavery when the neighborhood's main square, which once held the official city whipping post, was renamed **Praça da Liberdade.** Adopted shortly thereafter by Japanese immigrants, Liberdade is now the center of the largest Japanese community outside of Japan. The best way to experience the area is to get off at the **Liberdade** Metrô stop and take a stroll down **Rua Galvão Bueno.** In addition to pretty Japanese lamp standards, the street has some great sushi restaurants (plus Chinese and Korean cuisine as an added bonus), mineral and knickknack shops, Asian grocery stores, and Japanese faces everywhere. The small but excellent **Museum of Japanese Immigration** (see below) tells the story of the Japanese diaspora in Brazil. On Sundays, the square surrounding the Metrô stop becomes the giant outdoor **Sunday market.** The enthusiastic staff at the **Museu Historico da Imigração Japonesa** ★, Rua São Joaquim 381 (✆ **011/3209-5465;** www.nihonsite.com/muse; R$5 adults, R$1.50 children 8 and over; Tues–Sun 1:30–5:30pm; Metrô: Liberdade), is eager to show off three floors of photographs, artifacts, and film loops telling the 100-year history of the Japanese experience in Brazil.

Daily 9am–6pm. Metrô: Liberdade.

Museu Afro Brasil ★★ Dedicated to showing the cultural achievements of Africans in Brazil, both those brought as slaves and their descendants, this museum is thankfully neither boring nor earnest nor prone to guilt-inducing lectures. Instead, what's on offer is a celebration of the art and accomplishments of the African diaspora. Displays show short biographies of writers or painters or politicians who were black, including lots of their artwork and artifacts. Displays are gorgeous—particularly the art and photography—and the museum has wonderful natural light. Even the website is good. Allow an hour.

Parque do Ibirapuera. ✆ **011/5579-0593.** www.museuafrobrasil.com.br. Free admission. Tues–Sun 10am–5pm. Bus: 5185-10 from Metrô Brigadeiro.

Museu Arte São Paulo (MASP) ★★ São Paulo's flagship art museum is not actually the best place in town to see Brazilian art—that honor belongs to the lovely Pinocoteca do Estado. But this big, long box on the Avenida Paulista did recently reorganize its galleries to give much more space to homegrown talent. The top floor contains the permanent collection, an excellent selection of Western art—Dutch Rembrandts, English Turners, Spanish El Grecos, French everythings (Rodin, Renoir, Degas, and Monet). However, several rooms on this floor are now dedicated to the Brazilian greats, among them Di Cavalcanti and Portinari. Even better, the entire second floor is now a temporary gallery, dedicated to changing exhibitions of mostly Brazilian artists. The display space still has a bit of that big box warehouse feel, but the art is now worth the trip. Allow 2 hours.

Av. Paulista 1578, Cerqueira César. ✆ **011/3251-5644.** www.masp.art.br. Admission R$15 adults, free for seniors and children 10 and under. Tues and Thurs–Sun 11am–6pm; Wed 11am–8pm. Metrô: Trianon-MASP.

(i) **Tips** **Check Out the Antiques Market**

Every Sunday from 10am to 5pm an antiques fair springs up in the courtyard beneath the MASP building. Dealers are registered, and the quality is often good. Plus, it's the only time you'll ever find anybody voluntarily occupying that open space.

Tips **Take a Break near the FAAP**

Across the street and up the small rise from the FAAP you'll find the Praça Vila Boim, a small square dotted with dozens of casual restaurants, from pizza and sushi to Mexican and a '50s diner. It's a great spot to take a break.

Monument to Latin America ★ Shy of a visit to Brasilia, this is the best place to see Brazilian modernism in all its concrete austerity. Designed by famed Brazilian architect Oscar Niemeyer, the monument consists of a vast field of concrete dotted about the edges with perfectly geometrical concrete pavilions originally painted blinding white, but long since streaked by the rain. If architecture doesn't turn your crank, you probably shouldn't come here. That said, the two pavilions of most interest to non–architecture buffs are the Art Gallery—home to ever-changing fine art exhibits—and the Hall of Creativity, home to a fun and fascinating display of folk art from across the length and breadth of Latin America. Allow 2 hours.

Av. Auro Soares de Moura Andrade 664, Barra Funda (next to the Barra Funda Metrô stop). (© **011/3823-4600.** www.memorial.org.br. Free admission. Tues–Sun 9am–6pm. Metrô: Barra Funda.

Museu Arte Brasileira/FAAP ★ This majestic and slightly pompous building (think Mussolini monumental) in quiet Higienópolis plays host to an ever-changing parade of international exhibits. Check the website before you go. If the exhibit interests you, the FAAP is a lovely space. Supposedly, the museum is also home to a number of works by Brazil's great painters—Portinari, Di Cavalcanti, and others—but in repeated visits over the years I've never seen these actually make it to the display floor. (You're more likely to see the museum referred to as FAAP, which is the acronym for the cultural institute where it's located.) Allow 2 hours.

Rua Alagoas 903, Higienópolis. (© **011/3662-7200.** www.faap.br/museu. Admission varies from free to R$20 depending on exhibit. Tues–Fri 10am–8pm; Sat–Sun 1–5pm. Bus: 137T or taxi from Metrô Consolação.

Museu da Imagem e do Som ★ **Finds** Recently reopened under new direction, the Museum of Image and Sound showcases the best Brazilian contemporary image-makers. Photographs in the changing exhibits are always compelling, beautifully displayed, and intelligently curated. The video lab offers installations and presentations of and about video art. Information on current, future, and past exhibits is available on the website. Allow 1 hour.

Av. Europa 158, Jardim Europa. (© **011/2117-4777.** www.mis-sp.org.br. Admission R$4. Tues–Sat noon–10pm; Sun 11am–9pm. Bus: 373T.

Museu de Arte Moderna (MAM) ★★ Small but intriguing, the MAM in Ibirapuera Park has two galleries devoted to ever-changing exhibits of modern work, be it painting, sculpture, video, textile, or some other medium. At any one time, each of the main building's two spacious and well-lit galleries is given over to a particular artist. Check the website for upcoming exhibits. Surrounding the museum is a **sculpture garden** featuring 28 works by different Brazilian artists. When not on display, much of the gallery's permanent collection is online. Allow an hour.

Parque do Ibirapuera, Gate 3. (© **011/5085-1300.** www.mam.org.br. Admission R$5.50 adults, free for seniors 60 and over and children 10 and under. Tues–Sun 10am–6pm. Bus: 5185-10 from Metrô Brigadeiro.

Museu de Arte Sacra ★★ Sacred art refers to objects—chalices, crosses, statues, sculptures—created to adorn churches or for use in Catholic services. Built in 1774, the Mosteiro da Luz (which still functions as a monastery on the upper levels) provides the perfect setting to view these works; piped-in choral music echoes through the stone corridors as light pours in from the cloister, casting a warm glow on the beautiful collection. Many of the silver objects sparkle in ostentatious testimony to the wealth of the Church. Older pieces include woodcarvings and clay statues of angels and saints. Portuguese and English texts explain the origins and name of each piece.

Outside in the garden of the Luz convent is the **Presepio Napolitano,** a lovely miniature village composed of over 1,600 hand-painted figurines depicting life in an 18th-century Neapolitan village. Admission is included with the museum ticket.

Av. Tiradentes 676, Luz. ℂ **011/3326-1373.** www.museuartesacra.org.br. Admission R$6 adults, free for seniors and children 5 and under. Wed–Sun 11am–7pm. Metrô: Luz.

Museum of the Portuguese Language ★ This fun little museum tells the story of the Portuguese language in a way that's creative, interesting, interactive, and fun. The big drawback? No English signage. However, with a basic understanding of Portuguese, or an interest in the language, you should enjoy the experience. In addition to the displays, interactive terminals encourage you to punch up a word, see its origin and history, and hear it pronounced. All-time favorite? The X-burger (X in Portuguese is pronounced "Zhees"—think about it). On one wall, a giant 100m-long (328-ft.) screen shows images and clips relating to unique Portuguese words. Allow 1 hour.

The museum is inside the **Estação de Luz,** a beautifully renovated high Victorian railway station: Wander around and have a look at the Romanesque red-brick arches and cast-iron pillars that vault across the tracks and platforms.

Praça Luz s/n. Administration ℂ **011/3326-0775.** www.museudalinguaportuguesa.org.br. Admission R$6. Tues–Sun 10am–6pm. Metrô: Estação Luz.

2 ARCHITECTURAL HIGHLIGHTS

One of the few remaining relics of old São Paulo, the **Pátio do Colégio** complex sits a hop and a skip north from Praça da Sé on Rua Boa Vista, on the exact site where the original Jesuit mission was founded in 1554. Though built in 1896, the simple **Anchieta Chapel** (daily 9am–5pm) is an accurate reproduction of the original. Next door to the chapel, the **Museu Padre Anchieta** (Tues–Sat 9am–5pm; admission R$5) features a number of maps of São Paulo through the years, plus a large diorama of the original settlement. Better yet, at the back of the complex there's the green and quiet **Café do Páteo** (see "Take a Break," below).

Located at the birthplace of Brazilian independence—it was here that D. Pedro I in 1822 declared Brazil's independence from Portugal—the **Museu do Paulista do Ipiranga,** Praça da Independencia s/n, Ipiranga (ℂ **011/2065-8000;** www.mp.usp.br; admission R$4; Tues–Sun 9am–5pm), is a classic European palace with a Versailles-like garden out front and a "wilder" botanical garden out back. Inside are some gems of Brazilian art, photo exhibits showing 19th-century São Paulo as it developed, period furniture, and household objects.

São Paulo's Ellis Island, otherwise known as **Memorial do Imigrante,** Rua Visconde de Parnaiba 1316 (ℂ **011/6692-1866;** www.memorialdoimigrante.org.br; admission

Art & Cultural Exhibit Halls

São Paulo is blessed with a number of beautiful old buildings that have been converted to cultural centers. They play host to a cavalcade of interesting and ever-changing art exhibits. Even better, they're (almost) all free.

On the Avenida Paulista, the pretty mansion **Casa das Rosas,** Av. Paulista 37 (℃ **011/3285-6986;** www.casadasrosas.sp.gov.br; Tues–Sun 10am–6pm), plays host to art exhibits and author readings, while the rose garden—complete with small cafe—makes for the perfect escape from the Avenida Paulista. The Casa was built in 1928 by Ramos de Azevedo, the same architect who designed the Teatro Municipal and the Pinacoteca.

In the old downtown or Centro, the former headquarters of the **Banco do Brasil,** Rua Alvares Penteado 112 (℃ **011/3113-3651**), is now a three-floor cultural center, featuring art exhibits, plays, and screenings of experimental films.

On the far southern edge of the Jardins, the **Museu Casa Brasileira,** Av. Brig. Faria Lima 2705 (℃ **011/3032-3727;** www.mcb.sp.gov.br; admission R$4; Tues–Sun 10am–6pm), was built in 1945 for one of São Paulo's leading families. Inside the yellow Palladian villa, the museum displays an assortment of haute-bourgeois artifacts from the 17th to 19th centuries: jacaranda-wood furniture, porcelain, silver plates, the token oil painting by Portinari. Even better, a new curator has begun hosting changing exhibits and workshops focused primarily on modern Brazilian design.

R$4; Tues–Sun 10am–5pm; Metrô: Estação Bresser), saw about three million immigrants pass through during the 19th and 20th centuries on their way to a new life in Brazil. For today's visitors, the admission hall, office, hospital, and dormitories are shown in their original condition. On Sundays and holidays, a historic train takes visitors on a short ride around the museum area.

The 30-story **Edifício Martinelli,** at Av. São João 33, was the city's first skyscraper, inaugurated in 1929. Stylistically it's an interesting mixture—Italian palazzo with a mansard roof—and it remains an important landmark.

More daring and more interesting from an architectural perspective is Oscar Niemeyer's **Copan Building,** erected in 1951 at the corner of Avenida Ipiranga and Avenida Araújo. Its scale, its celebration of raw concrete, and its curvilinear shape were all quite advanced for the time. Photos of its curvy brise-soleil sides show up frequently in São Paulo postcards.

Churches & Temples

A Benedictine monastery has been on this site by the edge of the Anhangabaú Valley since 1600, just a few decades after São Paulo was founded. The current **Basilica de São Bento** dates to 1910 and is worth a look if you're passing by, though to tell the truth, despite all the marble, wood, and stained glass that went into the construction, the net effect is far from beautiful. Visitors may be most impressed by the German organ with

6,000 pipes. Come for High Mass on Sunday at 10am, and the service is accompanied by Gregorian chants. Open Saturday to Thursday 6am to noon and 2 to 6pm, and Friday from 2 to 6pm. Gregorian chanting is Monday and Friday at 7am, Saturday at 6am, and Sunday at 10am.

São Paulo's **Metropolitan Cathedral** is a curious structure, a blend of Byzantine and High German Gothic. Construction began in 1911, but wasn't completed until 1954. Its best feature may be the Praça da Sé out front, which is lined with stately imperial palms and occupied during the daylight hours by street preachers, some of them quite good. It's open Monday to Friday 8am to 7pm, Saturday 8am to 5pm, and Sunday 8am to 1pm and 3 to 6pm.

3 NEIGHBORHOODS TO EXPLORE

Though Paulistas do love their cars, most São Paulo neighborhoods can still easily be explored on foot. Just be very careful when crossing the street. São Paulo has the highest number of motorcycle couriers in the country, and motorcycles are responsible for the highest number of pedestrian deaths. Be particularly careful when crossing in between stopped cars; motorcycles often ride at high speed between lanes.

CENTRO

The original city of São Paulo was founded in 1554 on a hilltop between two rivers, the **Tamanduatei** and the **Anhangabaú.** The original site is now occupied by a partial reproduction of the old mission called the **Pátio do Colégio.** Close by, the **Cathedral da Sé** (also called the **Metropolitan Cathedral**) was completed only in 1954, though the square it occupies—the **Praça da Sé**—has had a church on it since the city's founding. Throughout the city center, streets veer off from and intersect with each other in odd and intriguing ways.

Key architectural sights in this area include the all-white **Banespa Tower** ★★ and the 1920s **Martinelli Building.** Two of the key pedestrian streets are **Rua Direita** and **Rua São Bento,** which leads northward to the **São Bento Monastery.** This, too, dates from the 20th century, but the site, high on the banks of what was once the Anhangabaú River, dates back to 1600.

The river itself was long ago filled and turned into a freeway, an act of ecological madness for which the city has paid ever since with flooded roadways. Where the freeway enters downtown (opposite the monastery), it's been sunk beneath a huge civic plaza called the **Parque Anhangabaú.** At either end, the park is crossed by two high viaducts, the pedestrian-only **Santa Ifigênia Viaduct** in the north and the **Viaduto do Chá** in the south.

Going across the middle of the Parque Anhangabaú you come out on the far side in the **Praça Ramos de Azevedo,** upon which stands the pretty Beaux Arts **Teatro Municipal.** This bank of the Anhangabaú is often called **Nova Centro** or New Centro, to

---

Take a Break

While strolling the historic part of downtown, duck into the **Pátio do Colégio.** The **Café do Páteo** (✆ **011/3105-6899;** Tues–Sun 9am–5pm), has a lovely garden and terrace where you can rest your legs over a coffee and slice of cake.

distinguish it from the old center, **Centro Velho,** across the way. The buildings are newer, and apartments and hotels are mixed in with the office towers. From the Teatro Municipal a number of crowded pedestrian streets—**avenidas 7 de Abril, Baron de Itapetininga,** and **24 de Maio**—lead west through downtown to the large and green **Praça República.**

Going northward from here leads through the run-down **Luz** neighborhood to the high Victorian **Luz Station** and adjacent **Luz Park.** Nearby one also finds the **Pinocoteca do Estado** and the **Sacred Art Museum.**

LIBERDADE
São Paulo's Japantown is interesting enough to merit its own entry in "The Top Attractions," p. 230.

HIGIENOPOLIS
Higienópolis (Healthy City) owes its name to a blatant bit of developer marketing. At the beginning of the 20th century wealthier Paulistas were starting to move out of Centro to get away from the mosquito-infested swamps around the banks of the Anhangabaú River. Green and leafy Higienópolis was one of most sought-after destinations. Even today some of the elegant mansions from 80 years ago still remain. It lies on a slight rise west of Centro, centered around **Rua Higienópolis** and **Avenida Angélica.** It's here you'll find the small but restaurant-packed **Praça Vila Boim** and the **Museu Arte Brasileira** (**FAAP;** p. 231), as well as one of the city's nicest malls, the **Shopping Pátio Higienópolis.**

JARDINS
What is currently called Jardins (gardens) is a combination of a number of neighborhoods such as **Jardim Europa, Jardim Paulista,** and **Jardim America** that extend southwest in a regular grid pattern (mostly) from the towers and offices of the Avenida Paulista. Built after the Avenida Paulista developed at the end of the 19th century, these neighborhoods were carefully planned according to the principles of the British Garden City movement, including rules on lot sizes and restrictions on apartment buildings. Some of these regulations have fallen by the wayside, though Jardim Europa is still home to mostly villas and mansions. The **Rua Augusta,** which runs through the heart of the Jardins, now has many hotels and some of the best restaurants in the city. Where Rua Augusta meets **Rua Oscar Freire** is now the prime shopping area in São Paulo.

AVENIDA PAULISTA
What was once a track along a ridgeline through virgin Atlantic rainforest has come quite a way in just over 100 years. Over one million people and 100,000 cars make their way along the **Avenida Paulista** on any given business day. Laid out back in 1891, the street was designed as a grand ceremonial boulevard, a place for São Paulo coffee barons and factory owners to build their magnificent villas. One of these grand mansions still remains, the **Casa das Rosas** near the Brigadeiro Metrô stop. Beginning in the '30s, however, the old mansions gave way to office buildings and then ever-higher commercial skyscrapers. Collectively, they make for an impressive statement of wealth and prestige, though individually the architecture is pretty mediocre. There are two worthwhile attractions near the north end of the Avenida: the **Museu Arte São Paulo** (**MASP;** p. 230) and, just opposite, **Siqueira Campos Park,** also called by its old name, **Trianon Park.** For shoppers, the south end of the avenue is anchored by a large upscale mall, the **Shopping Pátio Paulista.**

(Moments) ## Some Spectacular Views

The pedestrian-only **Santa Ifigênia Viaduct** runs from one side of Centro to the other, high above the Parque do Anhangabaú. At the midpoint you get a wonderful view of São Paulo's old downtown.

The best view of São Paulo is from atop the **Banespa Tower** ★★, Rua João Brícola 24 (*©* **011/3249-7428**). Ascending to its 35th-floor observation deck, you get an incredible view—high-rise towers, 360 degrees of them, filling every inch of land for as far as the eye can see. It's open Monday through Friday from 10am to 5pm, and better yet, it's free. Bring ID to show the door guards.

Built in 1965, the 42-story **Edifício Itália**, at Av. Ipiranga 344 near Praça da República, features a 41st-floor restaurant and piano bar, the **Terraço Itália** (*©* **011/2189-2929;** www.terracoitalia.com.br), which offers a great vantage point from which to view the city. (The food's not great—stick to drinks or tea.) Cover is R$10, and there's a R$15 drink minimum. It's open Monday through Saturday from 3pm to midnight, Sunday from noon to 11pm.

PINHEIROS/ITAIM BIBI

Linked by a single large arterial, **Avenida Brig. Faria Lima, Pinheiros** and **Itaim Bibi** flank the Jardins to the north and south respectively. Pinheiros lies sandwiched between Jardim Paulista and the nightlife-rich Vila Madalena. Itaim Bibi flanks the southeast side of Ibirapuera park. Both are prime residential neighborhoods, with good hotels and dining options. Itaim Bibi is particularly blessed with restaurants. **Avenida Brig. Faria Lima** also has the **Museu Casa Brasileira** (p. 233), and the upscale **Shopping Iguatemi** mall.

VILA MADALENA

Tucked away behind Pinheiros, Vila Madalena became popular in the '60s and '70s among University of São Paulo staff and students looking for affordable housing. The neighborhood still has a slightly bohemian feel, and many artists and designers have both homes and galleries here. The Vila is also one of the city's most popular dining spots, and pulses with bars and nightlife most evenings until the wee hours. The neighborhood centers around the **Rua Aspicuelta,** from **Rua Harmonia** to **Rua Murato Coelho.**

4 PLAZAS & PARKS

MARKETS

Saturday and Sunday on the **Praça Dom Orione** in the Italian **Bixiga** neighborhood is a small antiques/flea market. On Sunday on the **Praça da Liberdade** (next to the Liberdade Metrô stop) São Paulo's Japanese residents celebrate their heritage with an outdoor market featuring excellent and inexpensive Japanese cuisine, plus Japanese crafts and knickknacks.

PARKS & GARDENS

Adjacent to the Pinacoteca, the **Parque da Luz** is well worth a look. Inaugurated in 1825 as the city's botanical garden, the garden was then outside of the city limits, and locals at

the time wondered whether it was wise to set aside such a large piece of land. Nowadays
the park's lovely old trees contrast with the modern sculptures from the archives of the Pinacoteca that dot the park's walkways. Note that the large numbers of solitary ladies admiring the statuary are actually working girls; they're so discreetly dressed and nonaggressive they're easy to overlook. The park is heavily policed and safe during the day. It's open Tuesday through Sunday from 9am to 6pm.

Opposite the MASP is the green refuge of the **Parque Tenente Siqueira Campos,** often known by its old name of **Trianon Park.** The park is thickly planted with Atlantic rainforest vegetation, laced with walking trails, and dotted here and there with children's play areas. It's a wonderful green refuge from the bustle on Avenida Paulista and is open daily 6am to 6pm.

So much is there to see and do in the vast green space known as **Ibirapuera Park** that we've covered it under "The Top Attractions," earlier in this chapter.

OUTDOOR PLAZAS

The **Praça da Sé,** in front of the Metropolitan Cathedral, has recently been lovingly restored. Two files of imperial palms enclose a flagstone-covered courtyard with a sundial at the center. People stroll through this area, slowing or stopping to give an ear to the ever-present street preachers. Keep an eye for pickpockets.

Between the Praça da República and the Praça da Sé lies the city's newest and most interesting square, the **Parque Anhangabaú.** Running an eight-lane freeway over the top of the Anhangabaú River that once flowed through Centro was probably not one of São Paulo's better planning moves, but the city recently made amends by covering a 1km (½-mile) stretch of the freeway with this beautifully landscaped urban plaza. In the daytime it's occupied by pedestrians, sun-tanners, lunch-break idlers, and clusters of folks listening to street musicians.

In Centro, **Praça da República** is suffering from a renovation that has turned the top third of the park into a construction site. The remainder appears to have been occupied by camps of squatting homeless. The whole scene is best avoided.

5 ESPECIALLY FOR KIDS

Parque da Monica ★ (**Kids**) Young Brazilian kids love the Parque da Monica, an amusement park based on a popular Brazilian cartoon character. Will it translate for those not yet inculcated in the Cult of Monica? Take your kids to the Shopping Eldorado to find out. The park includes games, activities, rides, and shows geared toward kids in the 2-to-10 age range.

Shopping Eldorado, Av. Rebouças 3970. ② **011/3093-7766.** www.parquemonica.com.br. Admission R$21 adults and children 15 and over, R$30 children 2–14. Thurs–Fri 10am–5pm; Sat–Sun 11am–8pm. Bus: 6251.

(**Kids**) Take a Break at Siqueira Campos

Just opposite the MASP on Avenida Paulista, the lush Siqueira Campos Park has several small play areas featuring swings, teeter-totters, and slides. It's a fun and quiet refuge from the bustle of the city.

Taking an Organized Tour

Easygoing Brazil (☎ 011/3801-9540; www.easygoing.com.br) specializes in private tours for foreign visitors. They work with excellent English-speaking guides. The company offers a 1-day tour of São Paulo for R$150 that includes the city's "must-sees" and leaves room for your interests, whether it's art, museums, fashion, parks—anything. Easygoing also runs several tours that will take you out of São Paulo—to a coffee plantation, or to the mountain resort of Campos do Jordão, or on a hike along the Cantarareira hills that look over the city (R$250–R$350). Prices are for a private tour for two people; with three or more the price goes down significantly. Easygoing even has a 1-day tour of Rio (though we don't recommend it unless you have absolutely no alternative). They fly you to Rio on the early flight, show you the sights, and return you to São Paulo in time for a late dinner. The tour is popular with high-powered execs who only have a day to get away (R$425 not including airfare).

Playcenter ★ (Kids) Brazil's biggest roller coaster plus a huge variety of other rides and games are all at this large amusement park, about a 20-minute walk from the Barra Funda Metrô stop.

Rua José Gomes Falcão 20, Barra Funda. ☎ 011/3350-0199. Admission (with unlimited rides on most attractions) R$45 adults, R$22 children 3–10, free for children 2 and under. Sat–Sun noon–9pm. Metrô: Barra Funda. Playcenter runs a free shuttle from Barra Funda every 30 min. during open hours. To catch the shuttle follow signs to Terminal Rodoviaria.

Zoológico ★ (Kids) This large and impressive zoo has more than 3,000 species, most in large enclosures that resemble the animals' native habitats. There are also lunch and picnic areas, and a petting zoo for smaller children. It's about 45 minutes southeast of the city. Allow 3 hours.

Av. Migual Estéfano 4241, Agua Funda. ☎ 011/5073-0811. www.zoologico.com.br. Admission R$14 adults and children 13 and over, R$4 children 7–12, free for seniors and children 6 and under. Tues–Sun 9am–5pm. Metrô: Jabaquara; catch microbus to Jardim Zoológico from Jabaquara station (R$3.80).

6 OUTDOOR ACTIVITIES & SPECTATOR SPORTS

GOLF In the western suburb of Osasco, **São Francisco Golf Club,** Av. Martin Luther King 1527, Osasco (☎ 011/3681-8752; www.golfsaofrancisco.com.br), offers a 9-hole, par-71 course open to the public Tuesday through Sunday from 7am to 6pm. Greens fees are R$125 weekdays, R$265 weekends and holidays. The club also rents clubs and shoes.

HORSE RACING Races run Monday, Saturday, and Sunday at the **Jockey Clube de São Paulo,** Av. Lineu Paula Machado 1263, Cidade Jardim (☎ 011/2161-8300; www.jockeysp.com.br). On Monday races start at 6pm; on Saturday and Sunday the races start at 1:30pm. Minimum bet is R$2. The club has a restaurant open for dinner Monday through Friday and for lunch on weekends; the bar Cantér is popular even with those who don't watch the races.

MOTOR RACING   Important races such as the **Brazil Formula 1 Grand-Prix** take place at the Autódromo de Interlagos, Av. Senador Toetônia Vilela 259 (✆ **011/5521-9911**). Tickets start at R$525, run as high as R$1,650, and often sell out up to 6 months in advance; try www.gpbrasil.com.br for tickets and information on upcoming dates.

SOCCER   The big clubs in town are **São Paulo** (www.saopaulofc.net), **Corinthians** (www.corinthians.com.br), **Palmeiras** (www.palmeiras.com.br), and **Portuguesa** (www.portuguesa.com.br). Any match between these teams is likely worth seeing. So are all the state championships. Though the team websites provide details on upcoming games, deciphering soccer schedules is the stuff of serious scholarship; better to just ask your hotel clerk or bellboy if there are any big games coming up. The city's big stadium is the **Morumbi,** located in the Morumbi neighborhood at Praça Roberto Gomes Pedrosa 1 (✆ **011/3749-8071**).

7 SHOPPING IN SÃO PAULO

THE SHOPPING SCENE

Paulistas brag—correctly—that if you can't buy it in São Paulo, you can't buy it in Brazil. São Paulo has it all, from international boutiques to local crafts markets.

In terms of shopping areas, **Jardins** is known for its high-end fashion boutiques. The main shopping street is the **Rua Oscar Freire** and the parallel **Alameda Lorena,** and their cross streets the **Rua Augusta** and parallel **Rua Haddock Lobo.** This area is chic enough to have its own website—www.ruaoscarfreire.com.br—and comes packed with national and international brands, expensive clothing and jewelry, gourmet foods, and luxurious gift shops.

In **Centro** (downtown São Paulo), **Rua 25 de Março** is the place where Paulistas rich and poor browse the market stalls and small shops for inexpensive items such as belts, buttons, small toys, gadgets, towels, textiles, and socks. Inexpensive lingerie is a specialty. Keep an eye on your purse, though, as the streets are chaotic with vendors and stalls vying for space, and throngs of people making their way through.

Then there are the malls, which in São Paulo have been elevated to a whole other shopping experience: elegant, upscale, and refined. Sophisticated brands, boutiques, and fine dining can be found in a number of malls; the best-known ones are **Shopping Morumbi** (www.morumbishopping.com.br), **Shopping Iguatemi** (www.iguatemisao paulo.com.br), and **Shopping Pátio Higienópolis** (www.patiohigienopolis.com.br), located in upscale neighborhoods close to the city center, and the **Shopping Pátio Paulista** (www.shoppingpaulista.com.br) on the Avenida Paulista. And then there's **Daslu,** the one-stop ultimate luxury shopping spot. See "Malls & Department Stores," below.

HOURS   Most stores are open from 9am to 6pm Monday through Friday and 9am to 1pm on Saturday. Malls are open from 10am to 10pm, Monday through Saturday.

MONEY   Most stores will accept credit cards, though you can often get a discount if you pay cash. Traveler's checks are not normally accepted.

Books

Haddock Lobo Books and Magazines   Open every day until midnight, this bookstore has an excellent selection of international magazines and books, including some guidebooks. And if you can't find something, ask. Chances are the owner can dig it out for you. Rua Haddock 1503. ✆ **011/3082-9449.** http://haddocklobo.com.br. Bus: 7392.

Livraria Cultura   The flagship of one of Brazil's major booksellers has three floors of quality books plus a pleasant little cafe with free Wi-Fi. There's even a large selection of English-language novels and guidebooks. A number of smaller bookstores are in the same Conjunto Nacional mall. Av. Paulista 2073, Cerqueira Cesar. ✆ **011/3170-4033.** www.livraria cultura.com.br. Metrô: Consolação.

Mille Foglie   Everything you ever wanted to read on cuisine is here. This bookstore/cooking school stocks over 3,000 titles on culinary topics, many in English. There's also a section on Brazilian cooking. Open Monday through Friday 11am to 8pm, and Saturday 10am to 2pm. Rua da Consolação 3542 (corner Oscar Freire), Cerqueira Cesar. ✆ **011/3083-6777.** www.millefoglie.com.br. Bus: 7392.

Fashions

Huis Clos   Huis Clos offers high-end women's fashions, in the heart of the city's most fashionable shopping district. Just don't look at the price tags. Rua Oscar Freire 1105, Jardins. ✆ **011/3088-7370.** Bus: 7110.

Mr. Kitsch   Name aside, there's nothing tacky in Mr. Kitsch's excellent collection of fashionable menswear. The collection ranges from suits to trendy casual wear. Shopping Morumbi, Av. Roque Petroni Junior 1089, Morumbi. ✆ **011/5181-9304.** Bus: 5121 or 5154.

Rock Lilly   Just 2 years out of the gate, Rock Lilly mixes a classic vintage look with casual material (denim's a favorite) to create classy, kicky casual wear for women. Shopping Iguatemi, 3rd floor, Av. Brigadeiro Faria Lima 2232, Jardins. ✆ **011/3814-0920.** Bus: 7492.

Sinhá   Those looking for elegant and fashionable clothing in plus sizes will have a hard time in Brazil. Most stores only stock up to size 42 (the equivalent of a North American size 12 or 14). Sinhá offers a beautifully designed collection, including evening wear, for sizes up to 52 (North American size 20). Shopping Pátio Higienópolis, Av. Higienópolis 618. ✆ **011/3823-2519.** Bus: 508.

Food

Casa Santa Luzia   The size of a grocery store, Santa Luzia is stuffed with luxury food products that can be impossible to find anywhere else in Brazil, including cold cuts, pastas, sauces, and cheeses, as well as sweets and desserts; the mango-and-passion-fruit-flavored

---

Brazilian Fashion

The Jardins neighborhood is the place to find excellent Brazilian labels, including **Guaraná Brasil,** Al. Lorena 1599 ((✆ **011/3061-0182)**; **Maria Bonita,** Rua Oscar Freire 705 ((✆ **011/3063-3609)**; and **Forum,** Rua Oscar Freire 916 ((✆ **011/3085-6269)**. For the latest beach styles check out **Rosa Chá,** Rua Oscar Freire 977 ((✆ **011/3081-2793)**.

Tips **Your Gallery Guide**

For information on the city's galleries, pick up a copy of the *Mapa das Artes São Paulo* at the tourist office or check www.mapadasartes.com.br.

mini gâteaus are to die for! Al. Lorena 1471 (corner with Rua Augusta), Jardins. ✆ **011/3897-5000.** Bus: 7392.

Galleries

Galeria Estação This large and innovative gallery in the bohemian neighborhood of Pinheiros shows sculpture, woodcarvings, oils, and aquarelles, in a lovely warm display space. Rua Ferreira Arauko 625, Pinheiros. ✆ **011/3813-72653.** Bus: 2496.

Galeria Fortes Vilaça This gallery represents over 20 Brazilian and international Brazil-based artists. Exhibits range from paintings to installation art, sculpture, and mixed media. Rua Fradique Coutinho 1500, Vila Madalena. ✆ **011/3032-7066.** www.fortesvilaca.com.br. Metrô: Vila Madalena.

Galeria Luisa Strina One of the city's most venerable contemporary art galleries, Luisa Strina showcases work from young national and international artists, working in a variety of mediums: oils, bronze, glass, or photo art. The location is in the heart of the upscale Jardins shopping district. Rua Oscar Freire 502, Jardins. ✆ **011/3088-2471.**

Gifts & Souvenirs

Arte Tribal Now just a block off the trendy Rua Oscar Freire, this little store is a great place for a different kind of souvenir: Brazilian native art, including necklaces, pottery, baskets, bags, and woodcarvings. The rear of the store showcases crafts from native peoples all over the world. Brazilian shirts, baseball caps, and other knickknacks are also for sale. Rua Augusta 2795. ✆ **011/3081-8170.** Bus: 7392.

Casa do Amazonas Opened 30 years ago in Moema, this gallery/store offers art and craftwork from dozens of Amazonian tribes, among them the Karajá, Kaiapó, Tapirapé, Xavante, and Bororo. Offerings include furniture, hammocks, baskets, musical instruments, masks, and other products in wood, cloth, and terra cotta. Al. dos Jurupis 460, Moema. ✆ **011/5051-3098.**

Jewelry

Antonio Bernardo The clean, modern, and inventive designs here are done mostly in gold, silver, and diamonds. Rua Bela Cintra 2063. ✆ **011/3083-5622.** Bus: 7392.

Sara Joias The high-end design at this store often uses Brazilian gemstones to create a unique collection of rings, bracelets, pendants, earrings, and more. Rua Haddock Lobo 1576. ✆ **011/3081-8125.** Bus: 7392.

Malls & Department Stores

Shopping Iguatemi One of the more elegant malls in town, Iguatemi features high-end international and Brazilian brand names. On the top floor are a movie theater, a food court, and several full-service restaurants. Av. Brigadeiro Faria Lima 2232, Jardim Paulistano. ✆ **011/3816-6116.** www.iguatemisaopaulo.com.br. Bus: 775 or 637G.

EXPLORING SÃO PAULO

10

SHOPPING IN SÃO PAULO

Shopping Pátio Higienópolis   A favorite mall even among shopping-mad Paulistas. Built in 1999, the entrance resembles a Victorian crystal palace, with large glass and wrought-iron doors and awnings. No department stores or large chains are in this mall; the shops are mostly high-end boutiques. There's also a children's play area. Av. Higienópolis 618. ✆ 011/3823-2300. www.patiohigienopolis.com.br. Bus: 508 (from Paulista or Liberdade).

Shopping Pátio Paulista   An elegant mall on Avenida Paulista, featuring clothing, books, a cinema, cafes, and several restaurants. Av. Paulista 52. ✆ 011/3145-8200. www.shoppingpaulista.com.br. Metrô: Brigadeiro.

Villa Daslu   This is shopping taken to the nth degree, shopping with a capital "S." Daslu offers 17,000 sq. m (182,986 sq. ft.) of luxurious upscale shopping. Uniformed staff guide you through the maze, while strategically placed espresso bars keep you energized with complimentary hits of caffeine. A large part of the women's department is off-limits to men. Daslu offers some of the best-known international designers such as Prada, Dolce & Gabbana, Dior, Armani, and Gucci as well as an array of Brazilian names. Daslu also sells home decorating items, jewelry, sporting goods, audio and video equipment, even cars. Av. Chedid Jafet 131, Vila Olímpia. ✆ 011/3841-4000. www.daslu.com.br. Taxi recommended, though Daslu also offers a helicopter pad.

Music

The city's mega-bookstores, ironically enough, are the best place to find a wide variety of Brazilian music. **Livraria Cultura** (www.livrariacultura.com.br) has an extensive collection of CDs in its two São Paulo megastores: one in the Conjunto Nacional (✆ 011/3170-4033), the other in the Villa Daslu mall (✆ 011/3170-4058). The **FNAC** flagship store (Av. Paulista 901; ✆ 011/2123-2000; www.fnac.com.br) offers a whole floor of Brazilian and international CDs. Finally, in the Pátio Paulista mall on the Avenida Paulista is the **Saraiva Megastore** (Av. 13 de Maio 1947; ✆ 011/3171-3050; www.livrariasaraiva.com.br).

Casa Amadeus   This place has a great selection of Brazilian sheet music and very helpful staff. There's also a good variety of musical instruments: *cavaquinhos* (a Brazilian mandolin), percussion instruments, and hand-held rattles and shakers. Rua Quintino Bocaiuva 22, Centro. ✆ 011/3101-6790. Metrô: Republica.

Perfumes

O Boticario   Long before aromatherapy became a household term, O Boticario was already using fresh flowers and herbs to create its light fragrances. It now has a line of body products and makeup, but the bestsellers are still the perfumes. Look for several locations throughout the city. Rua Augusta 2887, Cerqueira Cesar. ✆ 011/3898-2973. Bus: 7392.

Shoes

Banana Price   Banana Price offers a huge collection of national and international designers at low prices, including heavily discounted collections from Nine West, Red's, Massimo, and Dilly. Other leather products available include bags, purses, and belts. Al. Lorena 1604. ✆ 011/3081-3460. Bus: 7392.

Melissa   Here you'll find high-end shoe designs, sold from a funky '60s *Barbarella*-style showroom where actual shoes actually don't appear. Instead, you scroll through the designs on offer on a video terminal, the pretty young clerks then bring you whatever catches your fancy. Rua Oscar Freire 867, Jardins. ✆ 011/3083-3613. Bus: 7392.

If Sinatra had known about São Paulo, he would never have given the "city that never sleeps" title to New York. Most Paulistas won't even *set foot* in a club until midnight. Take a cab into Vila Olímpia around the witching hour, and you'll find yourself in a traffic jam formed by everyone just heading out for the evening.

Less casual than Cariocas, Paulistas love to dress up when going out. Women are partial to black or other dark colors. Men are less formal. Good casual is fine, but jeans and running shoes likely won't make it past the door at many clubs.

To catch the big names in Brazilian music, São Paulo is the place. The city gets more of the stars, playing more often, than any other city in Brazil. São Paulo also offers a variety of theater, dance, opera, and classical music.

An excellent source of arts and entertainment information is the ***Guia da Folha,*** an entertainment guide published in the Friday *Folha de São Paulo* newspaper. In addition to theater and concert listings, it includes bars and restaurants (with updated hours and phone numbers) as well as exhibits and special events. On the first page is a useful overview of all the free events that week, titled in Portuguese *é gratis.* The guide also includes details on upcoming concerts (*shows* in Portuguese) and events at nightclubs *(casas noturnas).* ***Veja*** magazine (Brazil's equivalent of *Newsweek*) comes out every week on Sunday and includes a separate entertainment guide called *Veja São Paulo;* many hotels provide this insert for free. For vultures of high culture, the cultural department of the state government puts out a listing magazine every month, ***Revista Cultural,*** with details on classical music, dance, theater, and exhibits.

THE PERFORMING ARTS

São Paulo is considered—both by Paulistas and grudgingly by Cariocas—to be the cultural capital of Brazil. The classical music scene is excellent, and the theater scene positively thriving.

Theater

Estação Julio Prestes/Sala São Paulo The setting is glorious, in the soaring main hall of a grand railway station that's found a second life as a cultural center. Acoustical engineers did a brilliant job on the adaptation; the acoustics are said to be near perfect. The São Paulo Symphony Orchestra (www.osesp.art.br) now makes its home here. The inexpensive Saturday afternoon concerts often sell out. For concert information, check the website under *"programmação e ingressos."* Praça Julio Prestes s/n. ℂ **011/3367-9500.** www.salasaopaulo.art.br. Tickets R$25–R$100. Metrô: Luz.

Teatro Municipal This elegant 19th-century building provides the perfect backdrop for any performance. São Paulo's city opera company, ballet company, and city symphonic orchestra all make their homes here. The theater is also home to a pair of choral companies, an experimental orchestra, and a music school. Check the website listings (look under *"programmação"*) for lunchtime concerts, the perfect way to break up a day

 In São Paulo, Know Your Club Lingo!

The word *boate* or *boite* used in Rio for a nightclub or dance club refers in São Paulo almost exclusively to a strip or sex club.

of sightseeing or shopping. Praça Ramos de Azevedo s/n. ⓒ **011/3397-0327.** www.teatro municipal.sp.gov.br. Metrô: Anhangabaú.

MUSIC & DANCE CLUBS

Large and varied, São Paulo's nightlife scene is also quite spread out, with little entertainment clusters in neighborhoods all over town; barhopping is really more like car hopping. Best to pick a neighborhood, enjoy dinner, and then grab a drink or catch a show at a club nearby so you don't waste time and cab dollars stuck in one of São Paulo's late-night traffic jams. **Vila Olímpia** is where the 18- to 30-year-olds go for nightlife, with a number of large dance clubs and some of the city's best bars. **Vila Madalena** is more in vogue with the 25- to 45-year-olds who enjoy bars and restaurants more than dance clubs.

Many bars and clubs charge a drink minimum instead of or in addition to a cover charge. Patrons receive a slip of paper on arrival. All your expenses are recorded on the card and tallied up when you leave. Lose the card and you get charged a steep maximum fee (the assumption being that you've been on a bender all night).

Live Music

Bar Camará   This new bar-and-restaurant establishment offers three spaces in one—a large indoor atrium graced with tall tropical trees, one of the most graceful spots in the city to quaff a draft, plus an upstairs terrace with a fine view of the city, and a second floor bar with live music 7 nights a week. Clientele are upscale and in their late 20s to mid-30s. Open Tuesday to Friday 6pm to 1am, Saturday 1pm to 2am, Sunday 3pm to 1am. Rua Luís Murat 306, Vila Madalena. ⓒ 011/3816-6765. www.barcamara.com.br. Cover R$7–R$18.

Black Bom Bom   Now in a new location, this venerable São Paulo venue specializes in rap, hip-hop, and Rio de Janeiro–style funk, sometimes with a DJ, but more often live. Open Tuesday to Sunday 8pm to 3am. Rua Luis Murat 370, Vila Madalena. ⓒ 011/3813-3365. www.blackbombom.com.br. Cover R$20–R$30.

Bourbon Street Music Club   In the land of samba and *forró* it can be hard to find a club with blues and jazz on the menu. Such is Bourbon Street. This midsize venue with the signature piano-shaped bar is the place for a well-mixed drink and the sounds of jazz or blues, with a smattering of bossa nova or salsa. Doors open at 9pm; the show starts at 10:30pm (11:30pm on Fri–Sat). Rua dos Chanes 127, Moema. ⓒ 011/5095-6100. www.bourbon street.com.br. Cover R$15–R$35. Bus: 5154.

Grazie a Dio!   For 10 years and counting, this combo bar and restaurant has been one of the best places in the city for live music almost any day of the week. Expect anything from pop to samba-rock to salsa or merengue. Shows start at 10pm and cover rarely exceeds R$20. Open Sunday through Thursday 8pm to 1am, Friday through Saturday 8pm to 3am. Rua Girassol 67, Vila Madalena. ⓒ 011/3031-6568. www.grazieadio.com.br. Metrô: Vila Madalena.

HSBC Brasil   This is one of the city's best midsize venues, dedicated to Brazilian MPB. The new custom-built complex hosts big names such as Lulu Santos and Jorge Ben. Ticket prices range from R$50 to R$150. Rua Bragançao Paulista 1281, Chácara Santo Antonio. ⓒ 011/4003-1212. www.hsbcbrasil.com.br. Bus: 675N.

Morrison Rock Bar   Downstairs at Morrison it's all rock all the time, be it covers of Brazilian and international bands or original local acts. Upstairs it's the Morrison Hotel, a cozy bar with sofas where you can listen to the music from below, albeit at a lower volume. Open Wednesday to Saturday 8pm to 2am. Rua Inácio Pereira da Rocha 362, Vila Madalena, ⓒ 011/3814-1022. Cover R$15–R$25.

Return of the Rua Augusta

A streetwalker's stroll for much of the '90s, the stretch of Rua Augusta close to Centro has made a comeback as the locale for the city's hottest dance and music venues. **Club Outs,** Rua Augusta 486 ((℃ **011/3237-4940;** www.clubeouts.com; cover R$10), began the trend when it opened a couple of years back at number 486 (corner of Rua Marques de Paranagua). Open Thursday to Sunday, Outs offers live alternative rock, starting at midnight and continuing until 5am. For the GLS crowd there's **Studio SP,** Rua Augusta 591 ((℃ **011/3129-7040;** www.studiosp. org; Wed–Sat doors at 11pm, shows at midnight; cover R$20–R$30), all about live music and shows, with just about everything on offer, and **Studio Roxy,** Rua Augusta 430 ((℃ **011/7676-0622;** www.studioroxy.com.br; cover R$25), for dancing with two dance floors, two DJs, 2 nights only, Friday and Saturday, starting at 11pm and going until everyone finds a friend for the evening or just gets tired and goes home. Down below at **Inferno,** Rua Augusta 501 ((℃ **011/3120-4140;** www.infernoclub.com.br; Wed–Sun midnight–6am; cover R$10–R$50), it's live music—rock, funk, rap—in a venue with diabolically good acoustics. And then there's **Vegas,** Rua Augusta 765 ((℃ **0911/3231-3705;** www.vegasclub. com.br; Wed–Sat 11:30pm–7am; cover R$15–R$40), where some of the city's best DJs are invited to spin their stuff, often for over-the-top theme nights.

Piu Piu Now in its second decade, this downtown venue still hops with a range of Brazilian contemporary artists, from rock to samba to jazz. Tickets run from R$10 to R$20. Check www.cafepiupiu.com.br for listings. Rua Treze de Maio 134, Bela Vista. (℃ **011/3258-8066.** Metrô: Brigadeiro.

Samba The interior of this Vila Madalena hot spot features a 16m-long (52-ft.) collage of photos of famous sambistas of yore. Wednesdays onward the house moves to the sound of live samba. Open Wednesday to Sunday 7pm to 2am. Rua Fidalga 308, Vila Madalena. (℃ **011/3819-4619.** Cover R$10–R$20. Bus: 109P.

Dance Clubs

Azucar Azucar offers salsa and merengue most nights of the week, with free lessons Tuesday to Thursday. Doors open at 7pm daily, but things don't really get moving until after midnight. The relatively steep cover attracts a more mature (30- to 45-year-old) and upscale crowd. Rua Mario Feraz 423, Itaim Bibi. (℃ **011/3074-3737.** www.azucar.com.br. Cover R$15–R$40. Bus: 107P.

D-Edge São Paulo's hottest dance club features wall-long monster woofers, a *Saturday Night Fever* flashing disco floor, and some of the hottest heaviest funk beats this side of Birmingham. The crowd possesses youth, money, and ecstasy in abundance. Open Wednesday through Friday midnight to 6am and Saturday midnight to 10am. Al. Olga 170, Barra Funda. (℃ **011/3667-8334.** www.d-edge.com.br. Drink minimum R$50–R$60. Bus: 115P.

LOUNGES, BARS & PUBS
Lounges
Bar des Arts This is the place to go when you're trying to convince that would-be partner that, appearances to the contrary, you really do have a sweet and sensitive side.

Set in a large garden beneath mature trees, the tables surround an Italian marble fountain whose soft gurgling combines with the flickering candlelight to create a feeling of magic. Open Tuesday through Sunday noon to 1am. Rua Pedro Humberto 9, Chacara Itaim (behind the gas station). ℰ 011/3074-6363. www.bardesarts.com.br. Bus: 106A.

Piratininga Bar　Open since 1982, this small bar features a wonderful warm atmosphere, composed equally of cozy decor, piano on the mezzanine tinkling out jazz and MPB, and a selection of whiskeys and liquors from the bar. Come for a drink after dinner, or come earlier, sip whiskey, and graze from the extensive menu of snacks. Open Monday through Saturday 6pm to 3am, Sunday 3pm to 1am. Rua Wisard 149, Vila Madalena. ℰ 011/3032-9775. Cover R$10. Metrô: Vila Madalena

Bars & Pubs

Bar Brahma　Since 1948, Bar Brahma has been the meeting place for intellectuals, musicians, politicians, and businessmen. Renovations have restored the original wooden and bronze furnishings, and the chandeliers once again illuminate the crowds that gather to chat and drink beer. Open daily 11am to 2am. Av. São João 677, Centro. ℰ 011/3333-0855. www.barbrahmasp.com. Cover R$8–R$30. Metrô: República.

Bar Municipal　In the bubbling locale around the Rua Aspicuelta, this little bar is the favorite of the beautiful 25-to-35s, who quaff chopp and sip delicately from long-neck Stella Artois, while munching panini, admiring the giant photos of the Teatro Municipal and the beauty of their fellow patrons. Weekends from 6 to 11pm there's live MPB and samba. Rua Aspicuelta 578 Fiandeiras, Vila Madalena. ℰ 011/3812-0492. www.barmunicipal. com.br. Cover R$10–R$20. Bus: 6401.

Filial　A great place for a drink and a talk, Filial features a vast collection of bottles lining the walls, intermingled with sports photos from the 1950s. Tables are occupied by youngish clientele quaffing draft beer and nibbling from the snacks menu. Open daily noon to 1am. Rua Fidalga 254, Vila Madalena. ℰ 011/3813-9336. Metrô: Vila Madalena.

Jacaré Grill　There's an extensive menu of grilled meats on offer here, but the real reason locals flock here is to see and be seen, flirt, talk, and meet friends. The two large patios on opposite street corners offer maximum exposure to your fellow patio mates. Open Tuesday through Saturday noon to midnight, Sunday noon to 8pm. Rua Harmonia 321–337, Vila Madalena. ℰ 011/3816-0400. www.jacaregrill.com.br. Cover R$15–R$35. Metrô: Vila Madalena.

Madelaine　This cozy, small bar/restaurant features exposed red-brick walls, warm candlelight, and the syncopated bop-bebop of bossa nova and jazz, the perfect accompaniment to a meal or snack of wood-fired pizza washed down with a chopp or red wine by the glass. Open Tuesday to Sunday 7pm to 1am. Rua Aspicuelta 201, Vila Madalena. ℰ 011/2936-0616. www.madelaine.com.br. Cover R$10. Metrô: Vila Madalena.

Pirajá　It's all so very Rio de Janeiro. Lots of tables on the sidewalk, lots of people out for a beer and a chat with friends, while eternally surly waiters serve up a never-ending stream

Tips　**Late-Night Bite**

If you find yourself with an appetite at 4am, try the **Paris 6 Bistro,** Rua Haddock Lobo 1240 (ℰ 011/3085-1595; www.paris6.com.br), a French brasserie in the Jardins neighborhood open 24 hours a day, 7 days a week.

On the Radar: Vila Olímpia

In addition to Vila Madalena, São Paulo's other happening nighttime neighborhood is currently Vila Olímpia. Packed with clubs and bars, it's always busy, even on weeknights. Many of the more popular bars are concentrated on the **Rua Prof. Atilio Innocenti.** At Atilio Innocenti 780 is the **Buena Vista Club** (✆ **012/3045-5245;** www.buenavistaclub.com.br). Despite the name, the music is only a little Cuban and a lot Brazilian, live from Wednesday to Saturday. **Bar Favela,** Prof. Atilio Innocenti 419 (✆ **011/3848-6988;** www.barfavela.com.br), is anything but downscale. This hip bar attracts a happening crowd who come to see and be seen. **Athilio Music,** Rua Prof. Atilio Innocenti 618 (✆ **011/3044-0206;** www.athiliobar.com.br), is a split-personality kind of place, with an Irish/sports bar in the front and a dance club in back. The cover is R$10 to R$25. Also on the Atilio Innocenti is **Pennélope,** Rua Prof. Atilio Innocenti 380 (✆ **011/3842-3802**). Larger than some of the other bars, Pennélope has a small stage for live music and a couple of DJs who keep the crowd happy.

of chopp. Undeniably Paulista, however, are the fashion sense of the crowd and the high quality of the food. Nibbles include an outstanding cold-cut buffet with a huge variety of cheeses, olives, sun-dried tomatoes, and marinated mushrooms. Open Monday through Wednesday noon to 1am, Thursday to Saturday noon to 2am, and Sunday noon to 7pm. Av. Brigadeiro Faria Lima 64, Pinheiros. ✆ 011/3815-6881. www.piraja.com.br. No cover. Bus: 7214.

Rabo do Peixe This is a Brazilian pub at its most typical and beguiling. The patio fans out on all sides, and tables are packed every day. The food that'll put all pub food to shame is the grilled *picanha* (beef) served on a sizzling cast-iron skillet (R$36). Open Monday to Friday 5pm to 2am, Saturday and Sunday noon to 3am. Rua Riberão Claro 426, Vila Olímpia. ✆ 011/3842-8666. Bus: 6404.

GAY & LESBIAN BARS

Farol Madalena Although GLS, the emphasis in this busy little club is definitely on the "L" for lesbian. The bar has live Brazilian music most evenings. Open Wednesday through Saturday 7pm to 1am, Sunday 4pm to midnight. Rua Jericó 179, Vila Madalena. ✆ 011/3032-6470. www.farolmadalena.com.br. Cover R$8 plus R$12 consumption minimum. Metrô: Vila Madalena.

Studio Roxy Two dance floors, two DJs, 2 nights only, Friday and Saturday, starting at 11pm and going until 6am. The crowd is GLS, and the dancing doesn't really even begin until after midnight. Rua Augusta 430. ✆ 011/7676-0622. www.studioroxy.com.br. Cover R$25. Metrô: Consolação.

Vermont Itaim On the ground floor of a commercial building, the Vermont offers live music and a young crowd most nights—MPB on Wednesday, danceable pop Thursday though Saturday. The boys predominate through the week and on Saturday, but Sunday the girls take over with a nine-woman samba band. Open Monday to Thursday 6:30pm to 2am, Friday to Saturday 8pm to 4am, Sunday 4:30pm to midnight. Rua Pedroso Alvarenga 1192, Itaim Bibi. ✆ 011/3071-1320. Cover R$15.

Salvador & the Best of Bahia

A visit to Salvador is a chance to step back in time, to stroll through a perfectly preserved city from the 16th and 17th centuries. It's a chance to experience Brazil's close connection to Africa—to taste this connection in the food, hear it in the music, see it in the faces of the people. All of these elements—architecture, food, and music—mix together in Pelourinho, the restored colonial heart of the city of Salvador.

Beyond Salvador, a trip to Bahia is a chance to stock up on two of Brazil's greatest nonexportable products—sand and sunshine. The beaches of Bahia are some of Brazil's most varied and beautiful. They come blessed by sunshine, lapped by a warm southern ocean, and infused with a laid-back spirit that is uniquely Bahian.

The Italian navigator Amerigo Vespucci—the one who later gave his name to a pair of continents—was the first European to set eyes on the Baía de Todos os Santos, the beautiful bay around which Salvador now stands. He arrived in the service of the king of Portugal on November 1, 1501. By 1549, the new colony of Salvador was important enough that the Portuguese king had a royal governor and a small army to protect it from the French and Dutch.

The wealth of the new colony was not in silver or gold, but something almost as lucrative: sugar. Sugar cane thrived in the Northeast. As plantations grew, the Portuguese planters found themselves starved for labor, and so plunged headfirst into the slave trade. By the mid–19th century close to five million slaves had been taken from Africa to Brazil.

The wealth earned by that trade is evident in the grand mansions and golden churches in Pelourinho. The legacy of the slave trade is also reflected in the population. Modern Salvador is a city of two million, and approximately 80% of its people are of Afro-Brazilian descent.

This heritage has had an enormous influence on Salvador's culture, food, religion, and especially its music. Even in a country as musical as Brazil, Bahia stands out. A new term has been coined to describe Bahia's Afro-Brazilian blend of upbeat dance music: *axé,* from the Yorubá word for energy. Over the past 2 decades, groups such as Olodum and Timbalada have blended complex African drumming rhythms with reggae melodies, while adding some social activism to the mix.

Capoeira, the balletic mix of martial arts and dance, is now seen on almost every Salvador street corner. The African religious practice of Candomblé is also emerging from generations in the shadows.

This past 20 years has seen the resurrection of Salvador's Pelourinho neighborhood. Derelict until as recently as the '80s, Pelourinho—the 16th-century heart of what was once the richest city on the Atlantic coast—has been painstakingly brought back to its former glory.

And then there's Carnaval. Over a million people now come out to dance and revel their way through the city's streets. Salvador may soon claim to hold the biggest street party in the world.

1 ESSENTIALS

1,206km (749 miles) NE of Rio de Janeiro, 1,437km (893 miles) NE of São Paulo

ARRIVING

BY PLANE **Gol** (© 0300/115-2121), **TAM** (© 071/4002-5700), and **TRIP** (© 071/3003-8747) all fly from Rio, São Paulo, Recife, Brasilia, and other places with connections.

The modern **Aeroporto Deputado Luis Eduardo Magalhães** (© 071/3204-1010), Salvador's international airport, is 32km (20 miles) from downtown. The bank machines are all in the arrivals hall area, to the right at the end of the corridor (past the office for Costa do Sauípe). Cambio Gradual offers 24-hour money-changing services.

To reach your hotel, **Coometas** taxi (© 071/3244-4500) offers prepaid fares. The trip to **Pelourinho** costs R$100, to **Ondina/Rio Vermelho** R$89, and to the northern beaches (such as **Itapuá**), R$50. Regular taxis are cheaper; on the meter a taxi from the airport to Pelourinho costs around R$65 to R$70.

If you have very little luggage, an inexpensive airport-to-Pelourinho bus runs along the coast, stopping close to (though not at) most of the hotels located along the beach road. Its final stop is Praça da Sé on the edge of Pelourinho. The bus runs daily from 7am to 8pm; cost is R$6.

BY BUS Bus travelers go through the **Terminal Rodoviaria de Salvador Armando Viana de Castro,** usually simply known as **Rodoviaria.** It's located at Av. ACM (Antônio Carlos Magalhães) 4362, Iguatemi (© 071/3460-8300). For ticket information and schedules, travelers need to contact the specific bus company directly. However, the general bus station number will tell you which company to phone. **Itapemirim** (© 071/3392-3944) travels to Recife and Rio de Janeiro; **Real Expresso** (© 071/3246-8355) has scheduled service to Lençóis for people traveling to the Chapada Diamantina (see "Side Trips from Salvador," later in this chapter); **São Geraldo** travels to destinations like Natal and São Paulo (© 071/3244-0366).

CITY LAYOUT

The coastal part of Salvador is quite easy to navigate. Picture a wedge thrusting out into the ocean. One side of the wedge borders the Atlantic Ocean, the other side borders the bay (the **Baía de Todos os Santos**). The two sides meet at **Farol da Barra,** the skinny point of the wedge.

Perched on a high cliff on the bay side of the wedge one finds **Pelourinho,** the historic old downtown. This area is also sometimes referred to as the **centro histórico,** or as the **Cidade Alta,** the upper town. This is Salvador's chief area of interest. At the foot of the cliff lies **Comércio,** a modern area of commercial office towers. This area is also sometimes known as the **Cidade Baixa,** or lower town. Upper town and lower town are connected via a cliff-side elevator, the **Elevator Lacerda.** Except for the fun of riding the elevator, and visiting a large crafts market called the **Mercado Modelo,** there's little reason to visit Comércio (the downtown business neighborhood).

About 8km (5 miles) north of Pelourinho, the **Bonfim** peninsula juts out into the bay. Located on a headland on this peninsula is one of Salvador's most famous landmarks, the **Church of Our Lord of Bonfim,** source of many reputed miracles. The area between the church and Pelourinho is occupied by port, rail yards, and working-class housing.

Tips **Be Kind to Your Feet in Salvador**

Wear comfortable shoes in Salvador; high heels are both imprudent and uncomfortable on the large, uneven cobblestones and steep streets.

The photogenic point where All Saints Bay meets the Atlantic is marked by a tall white lighthouse, called the **Farol de Barra.** The point is also home to the sizable **Forte Santo Antônio de Barra,** which also contains the **Naval Museum.** The strip of beach (**Praia da Barra**) that stretches beyond the lighthouse toward Ondina has seen better days but is still one of the most popular gathering places during Carnaval.

The road running from the lighthouse out along the oceanside is called **Avenida Oceanica.** (Well, officially it's called Av. Presidente Vargas, but that name is used only sparingly.) The road continues past a number of good hotels to the oceanside neighborhood of **Ondina.** From here, road names change frequently, and neighborhoods come thick and fast: **Rio Vermelho, Amaralina, Pituba, Costa Azul, Pituaçu, Piatã, Itapuã,** all the way to **Stella Maris** adjacent to the airport. There are pleasant **ocean beaches** all along this stretch. Particularly noteworthy is the beachside park named **Jardim de Alah.**

GETTING AROUND

ON FOOT The old historic center, Pelourinho, can only really be experienced on foot and is a stroller's dream. The narrow streets and cobblestone alleys open onto large squares with baroque churches; the stately mansions and homes now house shops, galleries, and wonderful little restaurants.

The Cidade Baixa, around the Mercado Modelo, and the commercial heart of Salvador in Comércio are also pedestrian-friendly neighborhoods, but less safe at night and on weekends, when they get quite deserted. All the beaches make great strolls; just grab a bus or taxi to get out there and then hit the pavement or sand.

BY BUS Salvador's neighborhoods of interest all hug the ocean and are connected by one main avenue that winds along the coast and then leads into downtown, ending just steps from the historic center. Once downtown all the attractions are within walking distance of each other. As long as you have a general idea of the order of the beaches, you should be able to find your destination, as a bus from downtown traveling to the far-off beach of Itapuá via Ondina will automatically stop at all the beaches in between. Buses are marked by name; the main buses for travelers going from any of the beach neighborhoods to downtown are marked PRAÇA DA SE for Pelourinho or COMERCIO for the lower town. To travel to the city's main bus station (or the large mall across from the bus station) take buses marked IGUATEMI. When leaving downtown for the beaches, take a bus that says VIA ORLA, which means along the coast, and make sure that the bus's final destination lies beyond the beach neighborhood you want to reach. Along the coast, you have the option of taking a regular bus, for R$1.80, or an air-conditioned bus, called a *frescão,* for R$4 to R$6. These are more comfortable, but then again if there are three or four of you, a *frescão* is almost the same price as a taxi.

BY TAXI Local taxis can be hailed on the street or from any taxi stand. To book a radio taxi contact **Radiotaxi** (✆ **071/3243-4333**) or **LigueTaxi** (✆ **071/3357-7777**). You usually pay a surcharge of R$3 to R$5, but these taxis have air-conditioning and are

ACCOMMODATIONS ■
Ibis Rio Vermelho **18**
Monte Pascoal Praia
    Hotel **11**
Pestana Bahia **16**
Pousada Noa Noa **8**
Vila Galé **13**
Zank Boutique Hotel **14**

DINING ◆
Amado **3**
Barravento **12**
Companhia da Pizza **16**
Dona Mariquita **15**
Fogo do Chão **17**
Lambreta Grill **19**
Pereira **9**
SOHO **5**

ATTRACTIONS ●
Dique do Tororó **7**
Farol da Barra/
    Museu Nautico **9**
Forte de São Marcelo **2**
Museu de Arte Sacra **4**
Nosso Senhor
    do Bonfim **1**
Solar do Unhão **6**

See "Salvador's
Centro Histórico" map

*ATLANTIC
OCEAN*

Manaus · Belém
Amazon Natal
Recife
B R A Z I L
Brasília
Salvador
São Paulo ○ Rio de
Janeiro

RIBEIRA

BONFIM

MASSARANDUBA

SÃO CAETANO

ROMA

FAZENDA
GRANDE

*Bahia de
Todos os Santos*

CAIX
D'ÁGUA
*Parque da
Embasa*

CIDADE
NOVA

324

CENTRO
HISTÓRICO

NAZARÉ

MATATU

TORORO

FEDERAÇÃO

CANDEAL

*Parque da
Cidade
J.Silva*

GRAÇA

ALTO DAS
POMBAS

*Parque
Zoobotánico*

ONDINA

BARRA

RIO
VERMELHO

ATLANTIC OCEAN

Tips **Know the Hours for Exchanging Money**

> Note that most banks will change money only during certain hours, often 11am to 2pm. ATMs will often not dispense more than R$200 after 10pm.

usually new vehicles. Also, these two companies accept credit cards and can be reserved ahead of time.

BY CAR There is no need to drive in Salvador; the historic center of Pelourinho has no parking, and many of the streets are closed for traffic. To get between the city and the beaches, buses are quick and convenient, and taxis are cheap and readily available. Outside of Salvador, a car can be useful; see "Car Rentals" under "Fast Facts: Salvador," below, for information.

VISITOR INFORMATION

Note: All telephone numbers in Salvador now have eight digits, but you will still find lots of pamphlets, flyers, and other printed materials showing numbers that have not been updated. To get the correct eight-digit number, just add a "3" to the beginning of the older seven-digit number.

Bahiatursa, the state's tourist information service, has booths and kiosks throughout the city. The staff is friendly, although as of press time they had no useful brochures and pamphlets because the new state government was going to redo all of the materials. However, they should be able to help you with general information. There are Bahiatursa booths at the following locations: **Salvador International Airport** in the arrivals hall (© 071/3204-1244), open daily from 7:30am to 11pm; **Rodoviaria** (© 071/3450-3871), open daily from 7:30am to 9pm; **Mercado Modelo,** Praça Cayru 250, Cidade Baixa (© 071/3241-0242), open Monday through Saturday 9am to 6pm and Sunday from 9am to 1:30pm; and **Pelourinho,** Rua das Laranjeiras 12 (© 071/3321-2463 or 3321-2133), open daily from 8:30am to 9pm. The office at Pelourinho has the best stock of information and pamphlets. The Bahiatursa website (www.bahia.com.br) offers loads of useful information in English. For quick questions and information, visitors can also call the 24-hour telephone service (in Portuguese, Spanish, and English), **Disque Bahia Turismo** (© 071/3103-3103).

 Fast Facts **Salvador**

Area Code The area code for Salvador is **071**.

Business Hours Stores are open 9am to 6pm Monday through Saturday, and closed on Sundays. Pelourinho's stores open Sunday afternoon. Shopping centers open Monday through Saturday from 10am to 8pm; on Sunday malls are closed except for the movie theater. Banks are open Monday through Friday from 9am to 3pm, but exchanging money may be restricted to 11am to 2pm.

Car Rentals **Avis,** Av. Presidente Vargas 3097, Ondina (© **071/3251-8500**); **Hertz,** Salvador International Airport (© **071/3377-3633**); **Localiza,** Av. Presidente

Vargas 3057, Rio Vermelho (© **071/3173-9292**); and **Unidas,** Salvador International Airport (© **071/3251-8500**).

Currency Exchange & Banks **Banco do Brasil** is at Praça Padre Anchieta 11, Pelourinho (© **071/3321-9334**), or Rua Miguel Bournier 4, Barra Avenida, parallel to the Avenida Oceanica (© **071/3264-5099**). **Citibank** is at Rua Miguel Calmon 555, Comércio, close to the Mercado Modelo (© **071/3241-4745**), or Av. Almirante Marques Leão 71, Barra (© **071/4009-6310**). All have ATMs.

Dentist **Salvadent** is a 24-hour dental clinic, Rua Conde Filho 87, Graça (© **071/3332-9393;** emergency number © **071/8818-9603**).

Emergencies For police dial © **190;** fire and ambulance dial © **193.**

Hospitals **Hospital Portugues,** Av. Princesa Isabel 2, Barra (© **071/3203-5700**), or **Hospital Aliança,** Av. Juracy Magalhães 2096, Rio Vermelho (© **071/3350-5600**).

Internet Access Options include **Bahia Café.com,** Praça da Sé 20, Centro (© **071/3322-1266**); **Internet Café.com,** Rua João de Deus 2, Pelourinho (© **071/3331-2147**), and Av. Sete de Setembro 3713, Barra (© **071/3264-3941**); and **Pelourinho Virtual,** Largo do Pelourinho 2 (© **071/3323-0427**). Most are open daily, and rates range from R$6 to R$10 per hour.

Mail Downtown: Rua Visconde de Cairu 250, by the Mercado Modelo (© **071/3346-9518**); Pelourinho, Largo do Cruzeiro de São Francisco (© **071/3321-8787**). There is also a post office at the international airport.

Maps The tourist office has an excellent Salvador map for R$5 and free booklets with small maps of the main tourist areas.

Pharmacies Try **Farmacia do Farol,** Av. Sete de Setembro 4347, Barra (© **071/3264-7355**); or **Farmacia Santana,** Av. Antônio Carlos Magalhães 4362, at the bus station (© **071/3450-3599**), open 24 hours. Most pharmacies will also deliver 24 hours a day. Call © **136** to find the nearest pharmacy.

Restrooms Public washrooms are scarce, except during big events like Carnaval when the city provides chemical toilets. Your best bet is to try a hotel or ask nicely at a restaurant.

Safety Salvador's main sightseeing areas are heavily policed and safe, even at night. Still, it pays to follow some common-sense precautions. Don't carry valuables or excessive amounts of cash, or display expensive camera equipment unnecessarily. At night, stick to the main streets where there is more foot traffic and surveillance. The Cidade Baixa around the Mercado Modelo and the commercial heart of Salvador in Comércio are less safe at night, and mostly deserted on the weekends.

Taxes The city of Salvador charges a 5% accommodations tax, collected by hotel operators. This amount will be added to your bill. There are no other taxes on retail items or goods.

Time Zone Salvador is on the same time zone as Rio de Janeiro and São Paulo, 3 hours behind GMT. Due to out-of-sync daylight saving in the Northern and Southern Hemisphere, Salvador can be in the same time zone as New York (approx. May–Sept) or 2 hours ahead of New York (Oct–Apr).

Visa Renewal For visa extensions, go to the **Policia Federal,** Av. Oscar Pontes 339, lower city (℡ **071/3319-6082**). The fee is R$69. You may need to show a return ticket and proof of sufficient funds to cover your stay.

Weather Salvador has a tropical climate, with an average temperature of 26°C (78°F) year-round. With over 2,220 hours of sunshine a year, there is little precipitation; most of it falls between April and August when brief heavy showers are common. Summer clothes can be worn year-round, and fashions are very casual. But even in summer there is often a cool breeze coming in off the ocean. If you plan to go to the interior (Chapada Diamantina) or do a lot of boating, bring a few pieces of warm clothing.

2 WHERE TO STAY

For visitors, it's really a choice of staying either in the heart of historic Pelourinho or in modern Rio Vermelho, close to the city's prime beaches. Pelourinho offers a number of comfortable pousadas, most of them located in restored historic buildings. Rio Vermelho, on the other hand, offers modern, comfortable hotels, beaches, and plenty of great restaurants and bars. Once Salvador's prime beach area, Barra (near the Farol da Barra lighthouse) has lost much of its former glory. We recommend staying here only for Carnaval as it still is party central during Salvador's biggest street party.

Salvador's peak season ranges from mid-December to early March and maxes out during Carnaval. Hotels make big bucks during this time of year by jacking up their prices to insane heights, usually demanding payment in full upon reservation and requiring a minimum stay of 4 or 5 nights. Most Carnaval packages start at R$1,500. Even at these prices, rooms often sell out by October or November. The most popular Carnaval hotels are in Barra, as they are right on the beach and the parade route.

Once Carnaval is out of the way, occupancy rates drop, and your bargaining powers increase enormously. In the off season (Apr–June and Aug–Nov) some hotels give as much as a 50% discount, especially if you are staying a couple of nights.

PELOURINHO

The advantage to staying in Pelourinho is that you get to stay in restored 18th-century buildings, and you're minutes from the bustle and fun of the old city. The disadvantages? Rooms are older and quirkier, parking is difficult, and you're just minutes from the bustle and noise of the old city.

Very Expensive

Convento do Carmo ★★★   Finally Pelourinho has the boutique hotel it deserves. At the top of a steep cobblestone street leading up from Largo Pelourinho itself, the Convento has the perfect location on the outside, and luxurious accommodations inside. All rooms come with a large comfy queen fitted out with the softest of linens and piled high with a cornucopia of pillows. (For those tempted into working, there's also a big wooden desk, free high-speed Internet, and a flatscreen TV). Bathrooms—converted monks' cells, still with massive walls and thick wooden shutters—feature delightful rainfall showers, l'Occitane beauty products, plus a frosted window looking onto the cloister, where at night the fountain gushes quietly. The conversion respected the original architecture as much as possible, and for that reason there is no standard room layout. That said, the deluxe rooms are certainly all larger—the deluxe rooms on the third floor are a particular bargain; at no extra charge you get more space for a small sitting lounge plus a higher ceiling raftered with ancient wood beams. The hotel's common areas are a delight; at night, subtle lighting is used to show off the convent to lovely effect.

Rua do Carmo 1, centro histórico, Salvador, 40030-170 BA. ℰ/fax **0800/266-332** or 071/3327-8400. www.pousadas.pt. 79 units. R$450 double; R$650 luxury double. Extra person add R$50. Children 9 and under stay free in parent's room. AE, DC, MC, V. Parking R$25 daily. Bus: Praça de Sé. **Amenities:** Restaurant; bar; concierge; small health club; outdoor pool; room service; smoke-free rooms; spa. *In room:* A/C, TV, hair dryer, high-speed Internet, minibar.

Pousada Redfish ★★   Located in a gorgeous renovated colonial home, the Redfish features spacious rooms with high ceilings and tall windows. Standard rooms have two queen-size beds with firm mattresses, high ceilings, plus spacious bathrooms and a small balcony. (Avoid the two "garden" standard rooms that are just outside the breakfast area.) Room no. 6 is the largest standard room. No. 5 is the smallest. The luxury rooms have a vast king-size bed plus a second single bed, leather armchair, armoire, and vaulted ceiling, plus a large veranda with fresh ocean breezes and a view of the city. On the ground floor a gallery features the artwork of the owner.

Ladeira do Boqueirão 1, centro histórico, Salvador, 40030-170 BA. ℰ/fax **071/3241-0639.** www.hotel redfish.com. 8 units. R$240 standard double; R$300 luxury double. Extra person add R$45–R$60. Children 5 and under stay free in parent's room. MC, V. No parking. Bus: Praça de Sé. *In room:* A/C, minibar.

Solar dos Deuses ★★   Truly in the heart of Pelourinho, the Solar dos Deuses overlooks the square in front of the São Francisco church. Each of the seven lovely rooms is decorated in honor of an Orixá, the African deities of Candomblé. All rooms are elegantly furnished with period furniture and feature high ceilings, hardwood floors, and large windows looking out over the square or side street just off the square. Most rooms have king-size beds. Breakfast is served in the privacy of your own room at the time of your choice. The biggest room, Oxalá, can accommodate three or four people comfortably. Due to its central location this pousada is not for early sleepers.

Largo Cruzeiro de São Francisco 12, centro histórico, Salvador, 40020-280 BA. ℰ **071/3320-3251.** www. solardosdeuses.com.br. 7 units. R$260 standard double; R$300 luxury double. Children 6 and under stay free in parent's room. MC, V. No parking. Bus: Praça de Sé. *In room:* A/C, TV, minibar.

Expensive

Pousada do Pilar ★★   This beautiful heritage building has been completely gutted and renovated, giving rooms a modern feel and bringing them up to modern standards. All 12 rooms are huge; seven have a veranda and face out over the port and ocean. The remaining five rooms have a small balcony (standing room only) and look onto the street.

 Tips   **Prices Skyrocket for Carnaval**

Note that none of the prices listed below, even those for high season, remotely reflect the room cost during Carnaval. Most of the hotels have websites with information on special Carnaval packages that you can check out as early as September. Consult with the hotels directly, or contact a tour company like **Brazil Nuts** (www.brazilnuts.com).

A wonderful breakfast with regional cakes is served on the rooftop patio overlooking Salvador's waterfront. The location is perfect for exploring Pelourinho; the main square is only a 10-minute walk downhill. Unlike most Pelourinho hotels, the Pousada do Pilar has an elevator.

Rua Direita de Santo Antônio 24, centro histórico, Salvador, 40301-280 BA. © **071/3241-2033.** Fax 071/3241-3844. www.pousadadopilar.com. 12 units. City view R$230; ocean view and veranda R$270. Children 5 and under stay free in parent's room. Extra bed R$60. AE, DC, MC, V. Bus: Praça de Sé. **Amenities:** Room service. *In room:* A/C, TV, minibar, Wi-Fi.

Studio do Carmo   This place is as close as you can get to Pelourinho without sleeping on the square. Located on the Ladeira do Carmo just steps past the Largo Pelourinho, this pousada offers four bright rooms with double beds and hardwood floors, plus a breakfast table and small kitchen. The decor includes original artwork, much of it on loan from the gallery downstairs. Showers are clean and small, but functional. Thanks to a recent renovation, rooms now have air-conditioning. Room nos. 1 and 3 have a view out over the steps in front of the N.S. do Passo church. Room nos. 2 and 4 look back over the rooftops of Pelourinho; the view's not as nice, but these rooms get a better breeze. Breakfast is brought to your room on a tray each morning.

Ladeira do Carmo 17, centro histórico, Salvador, 40301-410 BA. © **071/3326-2426.** www.studiodocarmo.com.br. 4 units. R$180–R$250 double. Children 5 and under stay free in parent's room. V. No parking. Bus: Praça de Sé. *In room:* A/C, fan, TV, kitchen, Wi-Fi.

BARRA

Barra offers sea and sun, but the area seems to have lost much of its previous charm. Several empty buildings line the waterfront and Salvador's better restaurants and bars have moved to Rio Vermelho. We recommend staying in Barra only during Carnaval when the beachside boulevard transforms into one of the prime parade venues.

Expensive

Monte Pascoal Praia Hotel ★ (Value)   Fabulously located across from Barra beach, the Monte Pascoal Praia offers great value. All rooms come with a king-size bed or two double beds—great for families traveling with young children. Every room has a balcony and at least a partial view of the ocean. However, it's worth spending the extra money for a full ocean view. The one room that has been fully adapted for travelers with disabilities has wide doorways, handrails, an adapted toilet, and a chair for use in the shower. This hotel is incredibly popular during Carnaval, as its pool deck overlooks the main parade route and the beach is just 45m (150 ft.) across the street.

Av. Oceanica 591, Barra, Salvador, 40170-010 BA. © **071/2103-4000.** Fax 071/3245-4436. www.montepascoal.com.br. 83 units. R$185–R$235 double standard; R$250–R$300 double ocean view. Extra person R$60. Seasonal discounts available. Children 5 and under stay free in parent's room. AE, DC, MC, V. Parking R$12 per day. **Amenities:** Restaurant; bar; fitness room; outdoor pool; sauna. *In room:* A/C, TV, hair dryer, Internet, minibar.

Moderate

Pousada Noa Noa ★ (Value)   The bright red colonial house sits just around the corner from the lighthouse in Barra. Noa Noa will appeal to those who enjoy the bustle of a hostel and like to mingle with other travelers in the common lounge or kitchen, but still want a comfortable, nicely decorated private room. We recommend booking the Matisse, Margritte, or Degas room with ocean view (only R$30 more than the other rooms). Note that two of the 12 rooms (Gauguin and Cezanne) have a shared bathroom. The Pousada Noa Noa is located right on the Carnaval route so book early.

Av. Sete de Setembro 4295, Farol da Barra, Salvador, 40140-110 BA. (℃ **071/3264-1148.** www.pousada **257**
noanoa.com. 12 units, 2 units with shared bathroom. R$140–R$170 double. Extra person R$40. Children
5 and under stay free in parent's room. AE, MC, V. Street parking. *In room:* A/C, TV.

ONDINA/RIO VERMELHO

Ondina begins just around the bend from Barra on the open Atlantic coast. A number
of good hotels are located right on the waterfront; some even have private beaches. However the rocky shore doesn't make for great swimming. **Rio Vermelho,** just beyond
Ondina, is quickly emerging as Salvador's most happening neighborhood. It has a lively
restaurant and nightlife scene, centered around its main square, with hotels set far
enough away from the nightlife to guarantee a good night's sleep.

Very Expensive

Vila Galé ★★ **(Kids)** Located on a point just between Barra and Ondina, the Vila Galé
offers luxury and elegance. Rooms are very spacious and fit two queen-size beds or a
king-size bed, a comfortable chair, and a big desk. All rooms on the first floor have a
veranda. Standard rooms look out over the street behind the hotel; superior rooms have
gorgeous ocean views. The hotel also has a number of suites, the best of which is the
Oceano, which consists of a large L-shaped room with curved windows that look out
over the ocean. The Vila Galé's beachside location is great for families traveling with small
children; the spacious grounds include a play area and large swimming pool.

Rua Morro Escravo Miguel 320, Ondina, Salvador, 40140-610 BA. (℃ **0800/284-8818** or 071/3263-8888.
Fax 071/3263-8800. www.vilagale.com.br. 224 units. High season R$300 standard double; R$400 superior
double; R$580 suite double. Low season discounts 25%. Special rates for Carnaval and New Year's. Chil-
dren 6 and under stay free in parent's room. AE, DC, MC, V. Parking R$5. **Amenities:** Restaurant; bar; fit-
ness center; outdoor pool; room service; smoke-free rooms. *In room:* A/C, TV, hair dryer, minibar, Wi-Fi.

Zank Boutique Hotel ★★★ **(Finds)** This is just what the (travel) doctor ordered, a
stunningly beautiful, hip boutique hotel in the heart of Rio Vermelho. Zank is the pet
project of three enterprising sisters who started by renovating a lovely heritage building
and then added a modern, minimalist Miami-chic annex. With only 20 rooms, Zank is
an exclusive oasis on a hillside overlooking Rio Vermelho. To get the full experience
reserve one of the modern design rooms and let yourself be spoiled. The only "drawback"
is that it will take a concerted effort to tear yourself away from your room, the rooftop
lounge, or the tropical garden patio. Fortunately Rio Vermelho's restaurant scene is just
a short walk away.

Rua Almirante Barroso 161, Rio Vermelho, Salvador, 41950-350 BA. (℃/fax **071/3083-4000.** www.zank
hotel.com.br. 20 units. R$530–R$700 double; R$630–R$850 deluxe double. AE, DC, MC, V. No parking. Bus:
Rio Vermelho (short walk up steep hill). No children 13 and under. **Amenities:** Restaurant; bar; concierge;
outdoor pool; room service; smoke-free room; spa. *In room:* A/C, TV, hair dryer, minibar, Wi-Fi.

Expensive

Pestana Bahia ★★★ Set on an outcrop overlooking Rio Vermelho, the hotel's
privileged location guarantees all 430 units an ocean view. Rooms on the 2nd through
the 17th floors are superior; the ones on the 18th to the 22nd floors are deluxe. The
difference is really in the small details; the deluxe rooms have bathtubs, 29-inch TVs, and
a couch. Other than that the rooms are identical, very spacious with modern and funky
decorations. The outdoor pool and sun deck overlook the beach; the Pestana's beach
service includes towels, chairs, umbrellas, and drinks. A l'Occitane spa was inaugurated
in 2009. The hotel is about a R$25 cab ride from Pelourinho and just a 10-minute walk
from Rio Vermelho's happening nightlife scene.

Rua Fonte do Boi, Rio Vermelho, Salvador, 41940-360 BA. © **071/3453-8005.** Fax 071/3453-8066. www. pestanahotels.com.br. 430 units. R$240 superior double; R$320 deluxe double. Extra person add 30%. Children 12 and under stay free in parent's room. AE, DC, MC, V. Free parking. Bus: Rio Vermelho. **Amenities:** 3 restaurants; bar; concierge; small health club; large outdoor pool; smoke-free floors; spa. *In room:* A/C, TV, minibar, Wi-Fi.

Inexpensive

Ibis Rio Vermelho ★   The Ibis provides inexpensive accommodations without giving up too much comfort. This no-frills brand specializes in clean and plain rooms with quality basics such as firm beds with good linens, a desk or work table, and a hot shower. The hotel doesn't offer many services—no dry cleaning, gift shop, business center, buffet breakfast, or valet parking—but, you do have the possibility of an ocean view at bargain rates. There is no price increase for rooms facing the ocean so request one when you reserve or check in. Breakfast, not included, costs R$11. The Mercure hotel next door (owned by the same Accor group) offers pricier rooms with somewhat better amenities, but doesn't quite compare to the nearby Pestana.

Rua Fonte do Boi 215, Salvador, 41940-360 BA. © **071/3330-8300.** Fax 071/3330-8301. www.accorhotels.com.br. 252 units. R$115 double. Extra person add 30%. Children 12 and under stay free in parent's room. AE, DC, MC, V. Bus: Rio Vermelho. **Amenities:** Restaurant; bar; room service; smoke-free floors. *In room:* A/C, TV, minibar, Wi-Fi.

---

3 WHERE TO DINE

Bahian cuisine is truly regional, with ingredients and flavors not seen elsewhere in Brazil. The coastal version of Bahian cooking is rich in seafood and the distinct African flavors of dendê oil, dried shrimp, and coconut milk. These ingredients are combined into fragrant stews loaded with prawns, oysters, crab, or fish and finished with a handful of fresh cilantro and tangy lime juice. You can't say you have been to Bahia without trying a *moqueca de siri-mole* (stew with soft-shell crab), a *vatapá,* the famous *bobó de camarão,* and the popular *acarajé.*

PELOURINHO

Pelô, as the locals call Pelourinho, is not the place for fine dining, but does offer decent Bahian food and plenty of atmosphere. Located in historic colonial houses, restaurants in Pelô provide the perfect backdrop for Salvador's exotic flavors. Tuesday and weekends are the most bustling evenings, but any night is good. For a map of restaurants in this area, see the map "Salvador's Centro Histórico," later in this chapter.

Expensive

Pelô Bistrô ★★ BAHIAN   This cute bistro goes far beyond the standard Bahian fare. The kitchen combines delicious local ingredients with a French flair, bringing a touch of

---

> **(Tips) A Meal Built for Two**
>
> Remember that, except in fine-dining establishments, the portions are very generous; one main course is usually enough for two people. When in doubt, ask the waiter, *"Dá para dois?"* (Does it serve two?)

A Glossary of Bahian Dishes

Rich with African influences, Bahian cuisine comes with its own ingredients and terminology. Here is a list of the most common dishes and ingredients:

Abará (ah-bah-*rah*): Usually made by Baianas on the street, this is a tamale-like wrap made with bean paste, onions, and dendê oil, cooked in a banana leaf, and served with ginger and dried shrimp sauce.

Acarajé (ah-kah-rah-*zhey*): Similar to the *abará* in that the dough is made with mashed beans, but the *acarajé* is deep-fried in dendê oil and stuffed with a shrimp sauce, hot peppers, and onion-tomato vinaigrette.

Bobó de camarão (boh-*boh* dje cah-mah-*roun*): A stew made with shrimp, cassava paste, onion, tomato, cilantro, coconut milk, and dendê oil.

Dendê oil (den-*de*): The key ingredient for Bahian food, this oil comes from the dendê palm tree and has a characteristic red color.

Ensopado (en-so-*pah*-do): A lighter version of a *moqueca* made without the dendê oil.

Moqueca (moo-*keck*-ah): Bahia's most popular dish, the ingredients include any kind of seafood stewed with coconut milk, lime juice, cilantro, onion, and tomato. Though the taste is similar, this stew is much thinner than a *bobó*.

Pirão (pee-*roun*): As popular as *farofa* in the rest of Brazil, this dish looks more like porridge (or papier-mâché paste). Cassava flour is added to a seafood broth and cooked until it thickens.

Vatapá (vah-tah-*pah*): One of the richest dishes, the *vatapá* is a stew made with fish, onion, tomato, cilantro, lime juice, dried shrimp, ground-up cashew nuts, peanuts, ginger, and coconut milk. The sauce is thickened with bread.

sophistication to Pelourinho dining. Start with the grilled chicken satay with cashew sauce. Meat lovers may want to try the filet mignon with bacon and grainy mustard in an *açaí* reduction. Lighter fare includes a prawn stir-fry with pineapple rice or a grilled fish with banana and Bahian *vatapá* stew.

Rua das portas do Carmo 6, Pelourinho. ℂ **071/3266-8550.** Main courses R$39–R$48. AE, DC, MC, V. Daily noon–10:30pm. Bus: Praça da Sé.

Sorriso da Dadá ⓞ**verrated** BAHIAN   Dadá has made quite a name for herself and contributed to a renewed appreciation of Bahian cuisine. Brazilians and foreigners come from far and wide to taste her food, journalists write articles about her, and gourmet magazines rave about her restaurant. Her food certainly showcases the best of Bahian cuisine, specializing in seafood *moquecas*, *vatapá*, and *bobó de camarão*. However, Dadá may be coasting a little bit on her success. We found service uninspired and the prices higher than at other restaurants—typically 25% more than elsewhere. The food, however, was still as delicious as ever.

Rua Frei Vicente 5, Pelourinho. ℂ **071/3321-9642.** Main courses R$36–R$75 for 2. AE, DC, MC, V. Daily 11:30am–midnight. Bus: Praça da Sé.

Jardim das Delicias ★ (Finds) BRAZILIAN/CAFE   The Jardim das Delicias (Garden of Delights) is appropriately named. Tucked away inside an antiques store on the ground floor of a colonial house in Pelourinho, this lovely courtyard restaurant is the perfect getaway from the bustle and crowds of Pelourinho. The restaurant serves a full Bahian menu, including *moquecas, bobô de camarão,* and even foods from the interior such as beans with smoked meat and sausage. In the evenings there is live music. However, the Jardim is also very nice for just a drink (the caipirinha made with cashew fruit is delicious) or a coffee and some sweets while you rest your feet.

Rua João de Deus 12, Pelourinho. (℗) **071/3321-1449.** Main courses R$40–R$70; the more expensive dishes serve 2. Sweets and desserts are all under R$15. AE, DC, MC, V. Daily noon–midnight. Bus: Praça da Sé.

Inexpensive

A Cubana ★ (Finds) DESSERT   It's only right that a city with an abundance of tropical fruit and a year-round warm climate would have great ice cream. One of the oldest *sorveterias* (ice-cream parlors) in town, A Cubana can be found in the heart of Pelourinho. The menu is not huge, only 28 homemade flavors at any given time; the owners say they prefer quality to quantity. Try the unusual fruit flavors such as *jáca* (jack fruit) or *cupuaçu,* a fruit only found in the Northeast and the Amazon.

Rua das Portas do Carmo 12 (formerly known as Rua Alfredo de Brito), Pelourinho. A second A Cubana store is right next to the upper exit of the Lacerda elevator. (℗) **071/3321-6162.** Everything under R$12. No credit cards. Daily 8am–10pm. Bus: Praça da Sé.

(Finds)   Acarajés & Abarás

Everywhere you go in Salvador you'll see Baianas—women dressed in the traditional white hoop skirt, lace blouse, and turban—sitting behind big cooking pots serving up *acarajés* and *abarás,* falafel-like snacks made with beans, onions, and dendê oil, either deep-fried *(acarajés)* or cooked in a banana leaf and served with ginger and dried shrimp sauce *(abarás).*

Although the costume is always the same, there are Baianas, and there are Baianas. Each has her regular spot, sometimes inherited from a mother or aunt. **Abará de Dona Olga** in Pelourinho on Travessa Agostinho Gomes—in front of the Moderna Funeral Home—has been serving up *abará* for over 50 years, daily from 5pm to 3am. Outside of Pelourinho, by the lighthouse Farol da Barra, look for **Acarajé do Farol Celia.** This lady also sells excellent coconut sweets, daily from 1 to 11pm. At the end of Barra beach, next to Barravento restaurant, is **Acarajé de Dona Jó,** open Tuesday through Friday from 4 to 10pm and Saturday and Sunday from 9am to 6pm. The queen of all *acarajés* is **Dinha,** who runs the **Casa da Dinha** ★★, Rua João Gomes 25, Rio Vermelho (℗ **071/3334-0525**); she has traded in her metal tray for a little restaurant but still sells the best *acarajés* in town. Also worth trying are the *moquecas*—25 combinations of fish and seafood. Open Tuesday through Saturday from noon to 4pm and 6pm to midnight, and Sunday from noon to 6pm.

Located at the foot of a cliff directly below Pelourinho, the business and marina district of Comércio is fine for wandering in the daytime during office hours, but come evening the workers head home and the streets become quiet and empty. We recommend taking a taxi instead of walking.

Very Expensive

Amado ★★ CONTEMPORARY Ultimately cool waterfront dining—the room is vast and gorgeous, mixing wood and stone and glass with open views over the harbor and bay beyond. The cuisine takes traditional Bahian ingredients—manioc and seafood principally—and puts them to use in innovate ways, always with lovely presentations. We threw ourselves completely into the ocean, trying the giant squid stuffed with shrimp and leek in a Provençal sauce, the shrimp in a Gorgonzola and pistachio sauce, and a broiled *badejo* filet in a crust of cashews with an okra tapenade. For those not into fish, the menu has an equally intriguing array of chicken and beef creations. The wine list is on the pricey side—nothing good for under R$100, though they do eminently acceptable sparkling wine in the R$50 range. Service is young, pretty, and efficient.

Av. do Contorno 660, Comércio. ✆ **071/3322-3520.** www.amadobahia.com.br. Reservations recommended on weekends and in high season. Main courses R$36–R$54. AE, DC, MC, V. Mon–Sat noon–3pm and 7pm–midnight; Sun noon–4pm. Take a taxi. Even though it's not too far from the Mercado Modelo, the street is dark and very quiet at night.

Expensive

SOHO ★★★ JAPANESE Judging from the crowds, trendy Soteropolitanos (as residents of Salvador are called) have taken to sushi like fish to water. Located inside the Bahia Marina, SOHO sits at the waterline, offering great outdoor seating and excellent dining. The large menu offers most of the usual Japanese suspects—sushi, sashimi, tempura, yakisoba, and grilled meat teriyaki. But what earns this restaurant an above-average rating are intriguing local dishes such as the *shake lounge* (salmon sashimi with orange sauce, lime, and balsamic vinegar) and the *uramaki shake* (salmon with green onion and sesame seeds). Also worth trying are the *marina maki* (a salmon and prawn roll flambéed in *cachaça*) and the *kyo* (a lightly grilled tuna and *nira* in a thick soya sauce). Many of the hot dishes such as the yakisoba noodles are large enough to share, especially after a couple of the sashimi and sushi appetizers.

Av. do Contorno s/n, inside the Bahia Marina, Comércio. ✆ **071/3322-4554.** Reservations recommended. Main courses R$22–R$48. AE, DC, MC, V. Mon 7pm–midnight; Tues–Sun noon–3pm and 7pm–midnight. Take a taxi. Even though it is not too far from the Mercado Modelo, the street is dark and very quiet at night.

Moderate

Camafeu de Oxossi ★ BAHIAN Most self-respecting travelers would probably steer clear of a restaurant inside a huge crafts market, staffed by women in traditional costume. But this restaurant on the top floor of the Mercado Modelo offers surprisingly decent food, including nine types of seafood *moquecas*, and the views over the bay and the São Marcelo Fort are worth the price of admission.

Praça Visc. De Cayru 250, Mercado Modelo, Comércio. ✆ **071/3242-9751.** Main courses R$24–R$48 for 2. AE, DC, MC, V. Mon and Wed 9:30am–7:30pm; Tues and Thurs–Sat 11am–7pm; Sun 11am–4pm. Bus: Praça da Sé, then take the Elevator Lacerda to the lower city.

(Fun Facts   How Sweet It Is: Bahian Desserts

To say that Brazilians have a sweet tooth is like saying Italians are fond of pasta. Most Brazilian desserts are just a few ingredients shy of pure sugar—not surprising, given that Brazil was once the world's largest sugar producer. Nowhere is this truer than in the sugar capital of Bahia. From the Portuguese, Bahians inherited the habit of making sweets with egg yolks; they combined this with coconuts imported from Africa and the perfect dessert was born.

Most traditional sweets are just variations on those three ingredients: *Cocada,* the ubiquitous little clusters of coconut, are grated coconut with white or burned sugar; *quindim,* something between a pudding and a pie, is made with coconut, an incredible number of egg yolks (at least 10 per tiny serving!), and sugar; *manjar,* a soft pudding often served with plum sauce, combines sugar, coconut milk, and milk. My personal favorite is *Baba de Moça*—coconut milk, egg yolks, and sugar syrup. The name translates as "girl drool."

BARRA

This beach neighborhood is a popular evening destination as people gather around the lighthouse to watch the sunset. For the best views, you can't beat the patio of **Barravento** (see below).

Expensive

Pereira ★★ BRAZILIAN   This beautiful faux-rustic restaurant with exposed brick and expansive glass walls opens up to a lovely patio overlooking the ocean and sea wall in Barra. It's an excellent destination, be it for lunch, dinner, or just a drink and some tapas. In addition to the typical Brazilian snacks such as deep-fried cod or prawn dumplings (*bolinho de bacalhau* and *pastel de camarão*), you'll find bruschetta with ham and goat cheese or grilled squid in teriyaki sauce. Main courses range from pastas, pizzas, and risottos to grilled seafood and steak. Pereira is especially busy on weekends when Salvador's young and beautiful gather to preen and be seen. *Tip:* Don't bother with the Japanese eatery Sato next door. If you want Japanese go to SOHO (see above).

Av. Sete de Setembro 3959, Porto da Barra. (C) **071/3264-6464.** Main courses R$32–R$48. AE, DC, MC, V. Mon–Wed 6pm–midnight; Thurs–Sun noon–3pm and 6pm–midnight. Bus: Barra or via Orla.

Moderate

Barravento ★ BAHIAN   Underneath a large sail-shaped roof, Barravento offers alfresco dining on a beach patio overlooking all of the beach as far as the Farol da Barra. The menu includes a large selection of Bahian dishes such as *moquecas, marriscadas* (seafood stews), and grilled fish. One dish that every Baiano will recommend is the *moqueca de siri-mole* (soft-shell crab). If you're not in the mood for a full meal, Barravento serves a variety of appetizers such as *casquinha de siri* (spiced crabmeat) and fish pastries. The view is complimentary.

Av. Getulio Vargas 814 (aka Av. Oceanica), Barra. (C) **071/3247-2577.** Main courses R$21–R$45; all dishes for 2. DC, MC, V. Daily noon–midnight (if busy, open later on weekends and in high season). Bus: Barra or via Orla.

Over the last few years, Rio Vermelho has grown into a bustling, lively restaurant destination. There are several excellent options, most centered around the main square, Praça Brigadeiro Farias Rocha. Stroll around and see what strikes your fancy. We have included reviews of a few worthwhile restaurants that might otherwise get overlooked.

Expensive

Fogo do Chão ★★ STEAK   Even seafood lovers may crave a delicious piece of beef. This elegant all-you-can-eat steak restaurant serves up the finest beef in town. Cuts include all the Brazilian classics, such as *picanha, alcatra,* and *maminha,* as well as prime Argentine and Uruguayan beef. Unlike many other steak restaurants, the buffet is meant to enhance the meat and doesn't include sushi or seafood, but specializes in a delicious array of salads and vegetables. Make sure you try the dessert of grilled mango and pineapple with a hint of brown sugar and a serving of fresh coconut ice cream.

Praça Colombo 4, Rio Vermelho. ℂ **071/3555-9292.** www.fogedochao.com.br. Main course R$73 (doesn't include drinks or dessert; children 2 and under free, ages 3–7 R$24, and ages 8–11 R$48). AE, DC, MC, V. Mon–Fri noon–4pm and 6pm–midnight; Sat noon–midnight; Sun noon–10pm. Bus: Rio Vermelho.

Moderate

Companhia da Pizza PIZZA   This is one of the best pizzerias in town, and also one of the most happening restaurants in Rio Vermelho. In the evenings you may have to wait for a table, but it is worth snagging one on the patio so you have a prime people-watching spot. The menu includes more than 50 pizzas, from sweet to savory. Note that unless you ask for a filled crust you get a thin-crusted "São Paulo–style" pizza. Flavors to try include chicken with palm heart, *rucula* with sun-dried tomato and mozzarella, or the spicy Baiana, with pepperoni, *calabresa* pepper, and ground beef.

Praça Brigadeiro Farias Rocha s/n, Rio Vermelho. ℂ **071/3334-6276.** Main courses R$20–R$42. AE, V. Sun–Thurs 5:30pm–1am; Fri–Sat 5:30pm–2am. Bus: Rio Vermelho.

Dona Mariquita BRAZILIAN   Tucked away in a little laneway opposite the main square, this small restaurant is full of surprises. First up, all of Dona Mariquita, pleasant patio included, is beautifully decorated with high-quality Northeastern crafts and artwork. Then there are the delicious *caipiroscas.* We highly recommend the *umbu-caja,* combining two typical Northeastern fruit into one outstanding cocktail. And last but not least there is the food. Start off with the pastel, puffy fried savory meat dumpling served with a hot pepper jam. Main courses include specialties from the coast (seafood and fish *moquecas* and *bobó*) as well as interior dishes such as a bean stew and *carne seca* (sun-dried beef). On Friday evenings there is live music.

Rua do Meio 178, Rio Vermelho. ℂ **071/3334-6947.** Main courses R$28–R$36 for 2. AE, V. Tues noon–3pm; Wed–Sat noon–3pm and 6pm–midnight. Bus: Rio Vermelho.

Lambreta Grill BRAZILIAN/SEAFOOD   Japanese chef Fukino runs one of the most popular yet laid-back seafood restaurants in town. The decor is ultra-basic, but wait until you taste the food! Lambretas are small oysters, and the best way to try them is on the appetizer plate where you get a dozen of the little mollusks with toppings including sun-dried tomato, curry sauce, garlic, or *calabresa* pepper. For the main course try the grilled seafood served on a piping hot steel griddle, piled high with juicy and tender morsels of squid, prawns, mussels, and octopus, served with a side of potatoes and palm heart. *Note:* This small street can be hard to find. It runs uphill off the main waterfront street beyond a popular bar called Extudo (give that as a reference to your taxi driver). It is also just up the street from the Zank Hotel.

Rua Alexandre Gusmão 70, Rio Vermelho. © **071/3335-0107.** Main courses R$35–R$50 for 2. AE, MC, V. Mon–Sat 6pm–2am. Bus: Rio Vermelho.

4 EXPLORING SALVADOR

Brazil's first capital city, Salvador serves simultaneously as the repository of the country's historical heritage and the source of much that is new and vibrant in its culture. Nothing symbolizes this dual role better than Pelourinho. The historic core of Salvador, Pelourinho is a perfectly preserved urban gem from the 16th and 17th centuries, the capital of one of the grandest and richest colonial dominions in the Americas. Pelourinho today has a wealth of richly decorated baroque churches, tiny squares, and fine old colonial mansions. By day, one could wander its cobblestone streets for hours.

At night, Pelourinho assumes its cultural role. Bahia has long been the cultural wellspring of Brazil, the source of what's new in music. Since its revitalization in the '80s, Pelourinho has established itself as one of Salvador's main stages. Unfortunately, the new state government has cut much of the funding for cultural events, and the wonderful programming that kept Pelourinho hopping almost any night of the week has disappeared. Individual bars and restaurants have stepped in to fill the gap, however, and now schedule their own entertainment and events. Check with the Bahiatursa office in Pelourinho for upcoming concerts or shows.

Outside the old city are several good museums, great arts and crafts, and the glittering Baía de Todos os Santos, the bay that attracted the Portuguese to Salvador in the first place. Beyond the bay, warm Atlantic Ocean beaches stretch unbroken from the Farol de Barra lighthouse some 80km (50 miles) up the coast to Praia do Forte.

SUGGESTED SIGHTSEEING ITINERARIES

If You Have ❶ Day

If 1 day is all you've got, you better get moving! Exploring the historic center of Pelourinho is a must. You could spend hours here admiring the colorful colonial mansions and impressive baroque churches. Wander down and marvel at the gilded splendor of the Igreja São Francisco. See Nossa Senhora do Rosario dos Pretos, then take the Lacerda to the Cidade Baixa. Bargain hard at the Mercado Modelo. In the evening go munch on a *moqueca* or some other Bahian delicacy. Then wander the old town, enjoying the music and energy of Pelourinho by night.

If You Have ❷ Days

Begin day 2 by viewing some of Brazil's best Catholic art at the Museu de Arte Sacra. Then for a taste of the faith that produced such splendor, visit the most famous church in Salvador, Nosso Senhor do Bonfim. Afterward go for a stroll along Boa Viagem Beach and Forte Monte Serrat for the best views of the city and—if it's a weekend—some great people-watching as well. Be at the Farol de Barra around about 5pm in time to grab a drink and admire what will almost surely be a spectacular sunset. Have dinner in one of Barra's many restaurants, or splurge on a waterfront dinner at SOHO or Trapiche Adelaide, or else wander down the shore a bit and have dinner on the beach.

DINING ◆

A Cubana **3**
Jardim das Delicias **10**
Pelô Bistrô **14**
Sorriso da Dadá **9**

ACCOMMODATIONS ■

Convento do Carmo **18**
Pousada do Pilar **19**
Pousada Redfish **20**
Solar dos Deuses **7**
Studio do Carmo **17**

ATTRACTIONS ●

Casa de Jorge Amado **13**
Catedral Basílica **5**
Elevator Lacerda **4**
Forte São Marcelo **1**
Igreja de São Francisco **8**

Largo Pelourinho **15**
Mercado Modelo **2**
Museu Afro-Brasileiro **6**
Museu da Cidade **12**
Museu Tempostal **11**
Nossa Senhora do Rosário dos Pretos **16**

If You Have ❸ Days

Get some R & R by spending the day at one of Salvador's beaches enjoying the sunshine and fresh seafood at the *barracas.* On weekends, Flamengo and Stella Maris are the prime locations. Or take a schooner tour and enjoy the view of Salvador from the water, exploring the islands and beaches in the Bay of All Saints at the same time. In the evening head to the newly trendy Rio Vermelho neighborhood for a fine seafood dinner or casual pizza, then join the people-watching on Praca Brigadeiro arias Rocha, or if it's Tuesday night head to Pelourinho for the weekly Terça da Benção (Blessed Tuesday) party.

If You Have ❹ Days or More

Catch a catamaran to the small beach community of Morro de São Paulo, where life is simple and the beaches are fabulous. Or to really get away, go one island farther down to the tiny, quiet, gorgeous beach at Boi Peba. For a more mountainous experience, head inland to the hills and trails of the Chapada Diamantina, which has great hiking and exploring.

Tips **Take It Easy on Sundays**

Sundays are pretty slow in Salvador. Everyone's been up partying until 5 in the morning, so next to nobody is on the street. The Cidade Baixa and the Mercado Modelo are deserted, and even Pelourinho isn't much fun until the evening. In short, it's a good day to do as the locals do and head to the beach.

THE TOP ATTRACTIONS
A Visit to Pelourinho ★★★

Make your first stop the Bahiatursa office, located at Rua das Laranjeiras (© 071/3321-2133) to pick up maps.

In 1985 the historic core of colonial Salvador was designated a UNESCO World Heritage Site by the United Nations. It's well merited. One could spend years getting to know the history of the churches, squares, and colorful colonial mansions in this old part of the city. What follows is but a brief introduction.

Start a tour of Pelourinho in the main square, called the **Terreiro de Jesus.** Dominating the west end of the square is the 17th-century **Catedral Basílica** (see listing below). Flanking the cathedral is the neoclassical **Antiga Faculdade de Medicina** (see listing for Museu Afro-Brasileiro/Faculdade de Medicina, below), now home to the excellent Afro-Brazilian Museum. Also on the north side of the square is the smaller baroque **Igreja São Pedro dos Clerigos** (Mon–Fri 1–5pm). Facing the cathedral at the far end of the *terreiro* is the **Igreja de Ordem Terceiro de São Domingos de Gusmão.** Built between 1713 and 1734, this baroque church suffered through an 1870s renovation that destroyed most of its fine interior painting and tile work. On the south side of this church there's a wide cobblestone street with a tall cross in the middle. This is the **Praça Anchieta.** The saint on the cross is São Francisco de Xavier, patron saint of Salvador. At the far end of this little praça stand two of the most impressive churches in the city. The large two-towered one on the right is the **Igreja de São Francisco** (see listing below); the central element is the surrounding **Convento de São Francisco.** Next to it is the **Igreja de Ordem Terceira de São Francisco,** immediately recognizable by its ornately carved sandstone facade. Inside (open Mon–Fri 8am–noon and 1–5pm) is a small green cloister, around the outside of which is some fine blue Portuguese tile.

Back at the Terreiro de Jesus, the two streets on either side of the Church of São Pedro (Rua Joao de Deus and Rua Alfredo de Brito) both run downhill to the **Largo Pelourinho.** This small, steeply sloping triangular square gets its name from the whipping post that used to stand at the top end. This was where slaves and criminals were flogged. The smaller building at the top of the square, now the **Casa de Jorge Amado** (see listing below), used to serve as the city's slave market. Looking downhill, on the right-hand side of the largo you'll find the blue and creamy yellow **Nossa Senora do Rosário dos Pretos** (Mon–Fri 7:30am–6pm, Sat–Sun 7:30am–noon). Literally translated as Our Lady of the Rosary of the Blacks, the high baroque structure was erected over the course of the 18th century by and for the African slaves who represented the backbone of Salvador's sugar economy. Today, much of the congregation is still of African descent; new paintings inside show the Passion of Christ with an all-black Holy Family, and drums have largely taken the place of the organ in church services (the Tues 5:30pm

Mass is particularly well attended). At the far end of the square is the tiny **Praça de Reg-** **gae.** At the lowest point of the Largo Pelourinho a narrow street leads steeply uphill to a trio of old baroque churches, the **Igreja de Carmo,** the **Igreja de Ordem Terceiro de Carmo,** and the **Igreja do Santissimo Santo do Passo.** Only the Ordem Terceiro is open, and the views back over the city are only okay, so it's likely better to retrace your steps and explore one of the other delights of Pelourinho, its hidden interior courtyards. There are four of them: the **Praça de Arte, Cultura e Memoria;** the **Praça Tereza Batista;** the **Praça Pedro Arcanjo;** and the **Praça Quincas Berro d'Agua.** Their entrances branch off the little streets between the Largo Pelourinho and the Terreiro de Jesus. During the day they contain cafes and artisan booths and museums. At night, nearly every one features a band.

In Pelourinho

Casa de Jorge Amado   Though Jorge Amado was long one of Brazil's most beloved writers (he died in 2001 at the age of 93), there's not really much to see in his former house, now a museum dedicated to his memory. The ground-floor cafe has a collage of his book covers, showing the wide range of languages into which his dozens of works have been translated. On the upper floors, the text-heavy exhibits that tell the story of Amado's life are written exclusively in Portuguese. Better to just read one of his books. His most popular works are all set in Bahia. *Dona Flor and Her Two Husbands* is set in Pelourinho. *Gabriela, Clove and Cinnamon* (my personal favorite), and *Tieta do Agreste* take place in provincial towns farther south. *Gabriela, Tieta,* and *Dona Flor* have all been made into movies starring the luscious Sonia Braga.

Largo do Pelourinho 51. ℂ **071/3321-0122.** Free admission. Mon–Sat 10am–6pm. Bus: Praça da Sé.

Catedral Basílica ★   Thoroughly restored in 1996, the 17th-century basilica that dominates Terreiro de Jesus square now looks as good as it did when it was first erected by the Jesuits in 1672. The craftsmanship inside is impressive. Beautifully ornate, the many altars are made from cedar and covered with a thin layer of gold; the high altar alone consists of 18 gold-covered pillars. The image of Christ the Savior above the transept

---

ⓘ Tips   Consider a Freelance Guide

In Pelourinho freelance tour guides armed with ID badges will approach you and try to sell you on a tour of the old town. Some are indeed accredited tour guides; others just have fake IDs. It's nearly impossible to distinguish one from the other, nor is it really that critical; many of the independent guides are excellent. Prices are negotiable, depending on the size of the group, length of tour, time of year, time of the day, and your interests (churches, culture, architecture, museums, and so on). Typically you can expect to pay R$50 to R$75 for a 4-hour tour with two people. It's not a bad idea to test your prospective guide before engaging him. Ask him to give you a quick spiel on whatever sight is close at hand. If he seems to know his stuff and you can understand his English, go ahead and hire him. If you want to make sure you're hiring an accredited guide, stop by the **Singtur (guide association)** office, Praça José Anchieta 12, second floor, Pelourinho (ℂ **071/3322-1017**).

is the largest wood sculpture in Brazil. Like much of the carving work in the church, it was likely the work of trained slaves; look closely at some of the altars and you'll notice symbols of the Candomblé religion such as small fishtails, a tribute to Yemanjá, the goddess of the sea. The Basilica hosts "Barroco na Bahia," baroque chamber concerts on Sunday at 11am.

Terreiro de Jesus s/n. ☎ **071/3321-4573.** Admission R$2. Daily 8–11:30am and 2–5:30pm. Bus: Praça da Sé.

Igreja de São Francisco ★★★   At a time when Salvador was the biggest port in South America and Portugal still vied with Spain and Holland for the title of world's richest empire, the sugar barons of Salvador decided to splurge a little and let folks know that their colony had *arrived.* Beginning in 1708 and continuing until 1723, they took more than 100 kilograms of gold and slathered it over every available knob and curlicue in the richly carved interior of this high-baroque church. The result could hardly be called beautiful—works of the nouveaux riches seldom are—but by God, it's impressive. The inside fairly gleams; on nights when the doors are open it casts a yellow sheen all the way up to Terreiro de Jesus. If you can, time your visit on a Tuesday toward dusk (5:30pm-ish). The church will be packed with parishioners coming for a blessing, while outside wealthy matrons seeking the special favor of Saint Francis will be passing out little loaves of bread to a veritable mosh pit of Salvador's poor. On Monday, Wednesday, and Saturday, at 11:30am and 4pm, is an impressive sound-and-light show in the church.

Next door, the **Ordem Terceira de São Francisco church** (Mon–Fri 8am–noon and 1–5pm) has a gorgeous sandstone facade on the outside, and on the inside some fine blue tile and a rather silly hall of saints. Allow an hour for both churches.

Largo Cruzeiro de S. Francisco s/n (off Terreiro de Jesus). ☎ **071/3322-6430.** Admission R$3. Mon–Sat 8am–5:30pm; Sun 7am–5pm. Bus: Praça de Sé.

Museu Afro-Brasileiro/Faculdade de Medicina ★   This fine old building (built in 1808) is now home to the Museu Afro-Brasileiro, which attempts to show the development of the Afro-Brazilian culture that arose as African slaves settled in Brazil. Particularly good is the large portion of the exhibit space dedicated to the Candomblé religion, explaining the meaning and characteristics of each god (Orixá) and the role the god plays in the community. Make sure to ask for one of the English-language binders at the entrance—they contain translations of all of the displays. In the back room, 27 huge carved wood panels—the work of noted Bahian artist Carybé—portray the Orixás and the animal and symbol that goes with each. The museum staff can also provide information on Candomblé celebrations. Allow 30 to 45 minutes.

Two other small museums that were once located in this building, the **Memorial de Medicina** and the **Museu de Arqueologia e Etnologia,** have been closed with no reopening date foreseen.

Antiga Faculdade de Medicina, Terreiro de Jesus s/n (just to the right of the basilica). ☎ **071/3321-2013.** Admission R$5. Mon–Fri 9am–6pm; Sat–Sun 10am–5pm. Bus: Praça da Sé.

Museu da Cidade ⓘ **Overrated**   I love city museums. Pouring over old maps and photographs to see how a city grew and what people were wearing at a particular time fascinates me. In this case, however, curators have done such an uninspired job it's hardly worth the effort. The museum has some old photos and a few maps, but there's not much in the way of signage and what little there is certainly is not in English.

Largo do Pelourinho 3. ☎ **071/3321-1967.** Free admission. Mon and Wed–Sat 9:30am–6:30pm; Sun 9am–1pm. Bus: Praça de Sé.

> **(Tips) Ups & Downs**
>
> The quickest way to move between Pelourinho and the Cidade Baixa (lower city) is via the **Lacerda elevator,** which takes you from the Praça Tomé de Sousa to the Praça Visconde de Cairu, across from the Mercado Modelo. You can also use the **Plano Inclinado do Pilar,** a funicular railway farther down the Rua Direita de Santo Antônio, past the Carmo convent. Restored in 2006, the *plano inclinado* drops you at the Mercado do Ouro. And at R$.10 a ride you don't have to worry about blowing your transportation budget.

Museu Tempostal ★ Did you know the postcard was invented by Emmanuel Hermann? The Austrian professor first put a paper backing on a photograph and tossed it in the mail in 1869. By 1880, they were legal post in Brazil. This fun little museum has a large collection of postcards dating from the 1880s to the 1990s. Most are of Salvador itself; viewing the collection is a wonderful way to see how the city grew and changed. Indeed, it's much better than the city museum.

Rua Gregório dos Matos 33. (✆ **071/3117-6383.** Free admission. Tues–Fri 10am–6pm; Sat–Sun 1–7pm. Closed Mon. Bus: Praça de Sé.

In Centro

Museu de Arte Sacra ★★★ This small but splendid museum displays one of Brazil's best collections of Catholic art. The artifacts are shown in the former Convent of Saint Teresa of Avila, a simple, beautiful building that is a work of art in itself. The collection includes oil paintings, oratorios (a cabinet containing a crucifix), metalwork, and lots of wooden statues of saints. In general the cabinetry is better than the carving: The jacaranda-wood oratorios are things of beauty, while the wooden saints seemed to have kept the same look of stunned piety through more than 2 centuries. If you're pressed for time, head for the two rooms of silver at the back. Walk through these rooms and you can see how Brazilian silversmiths refined their technique, as the rather crude—but massive—works of the 18th century changed and developed until by the early 19th century, Brazilian artists were producing reliquaries, processional crosses, and crucifixes of astonishing refinement. Allow 1½ hours.

Rua do Sodré 276. (✆ **071/3243-6310.** www.mas.ufba.br. Admission R$5 adults, R$3 students with valid ID, free for children 6 and under. Mon–Fri 11:30am–5pm. Located just south of Pelourinho. From Praça de Sé walk 10 min. south on Av. Carlos Gomes, turn right and walk downhill on Ladeira Santa Teresa for 45m (150 ft.). Bus: Praça de Sé.

In Cidade Baixa

Forte São Marcelo ★ For years we have admired this perfectly round fort (Jorge Amado referred to it as "the belly button of Bahia") at the entrance of the lower city, thinking how cool it would be to visit. Now that it has been restored and we have visited, we have learned that some things look better from a distance. Originally built in 1650 and modified to its current configuration in 1812, it is still pretty cool to be able to set foot in the fort and have a look around, but it is not worth more than a 30-minute visit. There are a few exhibits on the history of the forts of Salvador (there used to be over 30; 17 now remain). For those who want to stretch their visit, a good restaurant called Buccaneros is inside the ramparts. Boats ferry visitors from shore regularly, leaving from inside the Centro Nautico (across from the Mercado Modelo, where the catamarans to Morro de São Paulo also leave from). If you are eating at the restaurant you are not required to pay the museum fee. Please inform the ticket office.

Access from the Terminal Maritimo da Bahia (across from the Mercado Modelo). ℂ 071/3495-8359. R$12, R$6 children 7 and older, free for children 6 and under. Tues–Sun 9am–6pm. Bus: Comércio.

Mercado Modelo ★   There's no sense pretending you're not a tourist in the Mercado Modelo. If you're here, you are. Still, it's a fun place to wander. This former Customs building and slave warehouse burned to the ground in 1984 and was then rebuilt in its original 19th-century style. It houses just about everything Bahia has to offer in terms of arts, crafts, and souvenirs. Merchants in the little stalls certainly want your business, but they're not annoying about it. Instead, in the best Brazilian tradition, they invite you in to look around, press you if you seem interested, drop their prices if you hesitate (bargain hard in here!), and concede gracefully if you decline.

Praça Cayru (just across from the elevator). ℂ 071/3243-6543. Mon–Sat 8am–7pm; Sun 8am–noon. Bus: Comércio.

Solar do Unhão ★★   An old sugar mill, the Solar consists of a number of beautifully preserved heritage buildings centered around a lovely stone courtyard that dates back to the 18th century. Half the fun is just to wander around and explore the various buildings set on the waterfront (the views are fabulous). The main building houses a small modern art museum; you'll find some works of Portinari and Di Cavalcanti on display. The path to the right of the main building leads above the rocks to the sculpture garden with works by Caribé and Mario Cravo. Allow an hour.

Tip: On Saturdays at 6pm there is a live jazz performance, a great way to spend happy hour (R$4).

Av. do Contorno 8. ℂ 071/3329-0660. Free admission. Tues–Sun 1–7pm. It is best to take a taxi from the Mercado Modelo or Pelourinho.

In Barra

Museu Nautico da Bahia/Farol da Barra/Forte de Santo Antônio ★   The lighthouse, fort, and museum are mostly worth a visit for the views over the Bay of All Saints. Erected in 1534, the Forte de Santo Antônio da Barra was the first and most important Portuguese fortress protecting Salvador. It thus had the honor of being taken by the invading Dutch in 1624, and retaken the following year by a combined Portuguese and Spanish fleet. You can wander the halls and admire the military architecture, but there's no signage on the history of the fort. The museum inside the lighthouse contains a small collection of maps and charts, navigational instruments, and a number

---

(Moments)   Catch the Sunset at Barra

Barra Point is the prime sunset spot in all of Salvador; 30 minutes before sunset the crowds start to gather and stake out their spots at the foot of the lighthouse. Even better, though, is the cafe on the fort's upper ramparts, where from the comfort of your patio table you can watch the sun sink slowly behind the island of Itaparica.

(Moments) **The Spectacle of Lavagem do Bonfim**

One of the most impressive demonstrations of faith (Catholic and Candomblé) takes place every year on the third Thursday of January on the steps of N.S. do Bonfim. Beloved because he offers protection even to non-Catholics, N.S. do Bonfim is associated by Candomblé followers with Oxalá, the supreme ruler and one of the most important Orixás (deities). On the day of the Lavagem, hundreds of women in their best Bahian outfits (hoop skirts, white turbans, lovely white lace blouses, and colorful jewelry) parade 8km (5 miles) from the N.S. Conceção de Praia church in the lower city out to the N.S. do Bonfim. They carry jugs of perfumed water, and are serenaded on the way by the music of the Sons of Gandhi bloco. Vendors sell food and drinks, and thousands of spectators follow along. At the church, the barefoot Baianas go about scrubbing the steps with brooms. The Catholic Church does not approve of this event and keeps its doors shut on this day. Once the actual washing is completed, the party in front of the church lasts well into the night with music, *capoeira,* and plenty of food and drink.

of archaeological finds from wrecks that the lighthouse obviously didn't help. Signage here is in English and Portuguese.

Farol da Barra, Praia da Barra s/n. © **071/3264-3296.** Admission R$6. Mon 8:30am–noon; Tues–Sun 9am–7pm museum, 9am–10pm cafe. Bus: Barra or Via Orla.

In Bonfim

Nosso Senhor do Bonfim ★★   Salvador's most famous church has a reputation for granting miracles. Tourists and faithful alike thus flock to this relatively plain 18th-century church on a small peninsula just north of downtown. (You'll be swamped on arrival by kids selling *fitas,* the colorful ribbons that people tie around their wrists for good luck; you may as well buy a dozen and get it over with.) Don't miss the Room of Miracles at the back where people give thanks for miracles by donating valuable or important objects. Definitely eye-catching are the numerous hanging body parts—models made of wood, plastic, even gold. This church also plays a very important role in the Candomblé religion and is dedicated to Oxalá, one of the highest deities. In January one of Salvador's most significant syncretist religious events takes place here, the famous washing of the steps.

Largo do Bonfim. © **071/3312-0196.** Free admission. Tues–Sun 6:30am–noon and 2–6pm. Located about 8km (5 miles)—or a R$20 taxi ride—north of Pelourinho on the Bonfim Peninsula. Bus: Catch a Bonfim bus at Praça de Sé or at the bottom of the Elevator Lacerda in Comércio.

ARCHITECTURAL HIGHLIGHTS
Historic Buildings & Monuments

The old town of **Pelourinho** was recognized in 1985 as a UNESCO World Heritage Site. See "A Visit to Pelourinho," earlier in this chapter, for descriptions of some of the hundreds of interesting structures in this neighborhood.

At the top of the cliff at the edge of Pelourinho one finds the **Praça Tomé de Souza,** flanked on one side by a glass-cube-on-stilts that houses the city hall, on the other side

Understanding Candomblé & the Terreiros

The religion of Candomblé is practiced throughout Brazil, but its roots are deepest in Salvador, where it forms an important part of community life. The practice originated with slaves brought to Brazil from West Africa; they believed in a pantheon of gods and goddesses (Orixás) who embodied natural forces such as wind, storm, ocean, and fire. Each Orixá had its own rituals, colors, habits, and even a day of the week associated with his or her worship. A believer who is prepared and trained can become possessed by a certain Orixá and form a link between humankind and the gods.

In Catholic Brazil, the practice of Candomblé was prohibited. Willing or no, Brazilian slaves were converted to Catholicism. Though they weren't allowed inside white churches, the slaves watching from without soon recognized aspects of their Orixás in various Catholic saints. By translating each of their gods into an equivalent saint, Candomblé followers found they could continue their native worship under the very noses of their Catholic priests and masters.

Oxalá, the creator and supreme ruler, thus became the Senhor do Bonfim; Iansã, the Orixá of wind and storms, resembled Santa Barbara; Yemanjá, the queen of the ocean and fresh water, seemed to have the same privileged position as Our Lady of Conception. Unlike the saints, Orixás are far from perfect; Yemanjá, for example, is notoriously vain and jealous. However, in the process of syncretizing Roman and West African practice, much that was Catholic was adopted, and the result is that Candomblé is now something uniquely Brazilian.

Actual Candomblé ceremonies are fun and fascinating—singing, chanting, and drumming, plus wonderful foods and perfumes are all used in order to please the Orixás and encourage them to come and possess some of the believers present. When a person goes into a trance and receives an Orixá, his or her movements, gestures, and voice change to reflect those of the Orixá. The

by the neoclassical **Palácio Rio Branco** ★, and on the cliff face by the Art Deco **Elevator Lacerda** ★. The original 80m-tall (236-ft.) elevator was built in 1872 to whisk people between the upper and lower city. The present Art Deco look was added in 1930, when the old mechanism was replaced with hydraulics. The elevator was also then rechristened "Lacerda" in honor of the original engineer. Open daily from 5am to midnight. Admission is R$.10, the cheapest ride in town.

Forts

After taking Salvador back from the Dutch in 1625, the Portuguese went on a bit of a fort-building binge. Fortresses small and large were built or strengthened all along the Bay of All Saints. Perhaps the city's most famous fort is the perfectly round **Forte São Marcelo** (see above), built in 1625 in the Bay of All Saints directly opposite the lower town. The current low, thick walls were built in 1738. Jorge Amado called the fort "the belly button of Bahia." It was recently restored and is now open for visits (Tues–Sun language used in Candomblé is Yoruba, a West African language spoken in parts of Nigeria.

There are many *terreiros* (areas of worship) in Salvador, though most are located in poorer neighborhoods far from downtown. Many accept visitors provided they follow a few basic rules: no revealing clothing (shorts and mini-skirts are out); white clothing is preferred; no video or picture taking; visitors cannot participate but only observe. This last is especially important. As inviting as the food or dancing may look, these practices are part of a religious ceremony for believers only. Real *terreiros* will not quote an admission price, but may ask for and will definitely appreciate a donation, to be given to the Mãe or Pai de Santo, the spiritual leader of the *terreiro*.

To attend a Candomblé session check with the Afro Brazilian Federation: **Federação Baiana de Culto Afro Brasileiro,** Rua Alfredo de Brito 39, second floor, Pelourinho (✆ **071/3321-1444**). Another good resource is the Afro-Brazilian museum in Pelourinho (✆ **071/3321-0383**).

Many tour guides and hotel concierges can arrange for you to attend a Candomblé session, although some services will be more touristy than others. If you only have a few days, this may be your only option. If you have more time and want to try harder to find an authentic ceremony, contact the *terreiros* listed below or get in touch with **Tatur Turismo** (✆ **071/3450-7216;** www. tatur.com.br) to find out on which dates ceremonies take place.

Terreiros that accept visitors include **Menininha do Gantois,** Alto do Gantois 23, Federação (✆ **071/3331-9231;** service led by Mãe Carmem); popular with artists and visiting celebrities is **Ilê Axé Opô Afonjá,** Rua Direita de São Gonçalo do Retiro 245, Cabula (✆ **071/3384-6800**); and **Casa Branca,** Av. Vasco da Gama 463, Vasco da Gama (close to Rio Vermelho; ✆ **071/3334-2900;** the oldest *terreiro* still in use, dating back to 1836). Always take a taxi to the *terreiro;* some are in less safe neighborhoods, and addresses can be hard to find.

9am–6pm). South of Pelourinho stand two forts fairly close to each other. The **Forte de São Diogo** saw a great deal of action during the second Dutch invasion of 1638. Inside, there's a small model of the system of forts protecting the city. Open Tuesday through Sunday from 9:30am to noon and 1:30 to 5:30pm. The **Forte de Santa Maria** is located on Avenida Sete de Setembro just a bit north of the Farol de Barra point. Its complement of large guns is still in position. Open Tuesday through Friday from 8am to 6pm, and Saturday from 8am to noon. The city's most important fortress, the **Forte de Santo Antônio** ★ (see above), was built in 1583, taken by the Dutch in 1624, retaken by the Portuguese in 1625, and rebuilt into its current form in 1702. Open Tuesday through Sunday from 9am to 7pm (to 9pm in summer).

Churches & Temples

Salvador has a wealth of beautiful old churches, so many in fact that a couple in the centro histórico stand abandoned, sizable trees growing from their ornate baroque bell towers. Some of the best churches are discussed above in the sections Pelourinho or Bonfim. One not covered but that's still worth mentioning is **Nossa Senhora da Conceição da Praia,** Largo de Conceição de Praia (✆ **071/3242-0545**). Open Tuesday through Friday from 6:30 to 11:30am and 3 to 5:30pm, and Saturday through Monday from 6:30 to 11:30am. Located in the lower city a couple hundred feet south (left) of the Elevator Lacerda, the building was prefabricated in Portugal, shipped in parts to Salvador, and erected in 1736. On the third Thursday in January a huge procession of white-clad Baianas sets off from this church—water jars on their heads—on their 8km (5-mile) trek to the Church of **N.S. do Bonfim,** where with great ceremony they wash the church steps (p. 271).

NEIGHBORHOODS TO EXPLORE
Pelourinho ★★★
The historic heart of the city, Pelourinho is a delight to explore. Indeed, it's so worthwhile, it's covered under "The Top Attractions," earlier in this chapter.

Comércio
The Cidade Baixa (lower city) was always the commercial center of Salvador. In the 16th century people preferred to live in the cooler heights of Pelourinho and keep their offices and warehouses on the waterfront below. The concept is the same today, but Comércio, as the area is known, is now planted thick with stubby commercial high-rises. The Elevator Lacerda is the easiest way to access this area—though there's really little of interest down here except the ferry docks and the crafts fair in the **Mercado Modelo.** A number of steep, shabby alleys also connect the lower city to the upper city, but it's safer to take the elevator.

Vitória
This quiet and green neighborhood lies immediately south of Pelourinho. It has some lesser city landmarks such as the **Castro Alves Theatre** and **Campo Grande Square.**

Barra ★★
One of the nicest beaches close to downtown, Barra is a residential neighborhood with some restaurants and shops located south of the city center just where the coastline makes a sharp turn to the east. Many hotels are located here but the area has lost a bit of its former bustle and seems a bit run-down. Sights in the area include the **Farol da Barra (Barra Lighthouse)** and the smaller **Forte Santa Maria.** The prime attraction, however, is the sunset; small crowds gather to watch the show.

Bonfim/Monte Serrat ★
Located on a small peninsula that juts out into the bay, Bonfim is home to the **Church of Nosso Senhor do Bonfim,** one of the most important religious sites in the city. Beloved by both Catholics and Candomblé worshipers (who revere their equivalent deity of Oxalá), the hilltop church draws huge crowds who come to pray or ask for miracles. The **washing of the steps** (p. 271), which takes place on the third Thursday in January, is one of the year's most colorful religious events. The neighborhoods of Bonfim, Ribeira, and Monte Serrat are now mostly home to the lower middle class and working poor, but they started out originally as summer destinations with cottages and summer homes. The other worthwhile sight is the **Forte de Monte Serrat,** which offers fabulous views of Salvador. On Sunday the sea wall is packed with families and teenagers out for a stroll.

ⓘ Moments   Spend an Easy Sunday at Boa Viagem Beach

Salvador, we discovered, is deserted on Sunday. No one in Pelourinho. No one at N.S. do Bonfim church. It wasn't until we wandered down the hill through the equally deserted Boa Viagem neighborhood that we discovered where everyone was. At the beach. The place was packed with flirting teens and moms with lawn chairs and little kids with beach balls and inflatable orca whales. We snagged a couple of beers from a passing vendor and watched a pickup soccer game for a while, waving now and again at the folks a little surprised to see a couple of pale-skinned gringos on an unfashionable working-class beach. Then we continued along the shoreline to an old fort where a cafe with tables sat on a tiny bit of sand below a tall stone sea wall. While the tide rolled slowly in we watched a dad and young son make sand breasts (it started out as a sand castle but evolved into a Lara Croft–size bosom), flinching now and again when neighborhood kids would take a run along the top of the sea wall, plant both feet, and do double forward somersaults into the sea.

Ondina, Rio Vermelho & Beaches ★

Once past Ondina, the coast is an almost uninterrupted string of beaches. Most neighborhoods are very modern and new, with little attraction beyond the beach itself. Popular beaches include Rio Vermelho, Praia dos Artistas, Praia de Piatã, Praia de Itapuã, Praia de Stella Maris, and Praia do Flamengo. **Rio Vermelho** is home to some of the city's best waterfront hotels, and has recently evolved into one of Salvador's prime nightlife enclaves. The area around the Praça Brigadeiro Farias Rocha is great for evening people-watching.

BEACHES

With over 48km (30 miles) of beaches within the city limits, finding a beach is much less trouble than deciding which one to go to. Here follows a short description of the main beaches: The beaches on the bay side of town (**Boa Viagem** and **Monte Serrat**) are not recommended for sunbathing but can be fun places to walk, watch a pickup soccer game, or have a beer. On weekends the **Forte de Monte Serrat** is crowded with working-class families having a day out.

Barra is the closest clean beach area to downtown. **Porto da Barra** is the beach on the bay side of the lighthouse, whereas **Farol da Barra** is on the ocean side. Both beaches have calm and protected waters and are great for swimming. Just around the bend you will come to **Praia de Ondina,** the first of the true ocean beaches. It's popular with the many visitors who stay in the Ondina hotels, but only because of its proximity; the beach itself is narrow and cut off from Avenida Atlântica by shade-throwing hotel towers. **Praia de Amaralina** is as much known for the excellent food stalls as for the excellent surf and windsurfing conditions; the strong seas make it less ideal for swimming. **Praia dos Artistas** is highly recommended for swimmers and has waves gentle enough for children. **Praia do Corsario** is very popular with the fit crowd; lots of people come to jog and play volleyball or soccer. At low tide the reefs form natural swimming pools. **Praia de Piatã** has that tropical paradise look with lots of palm trees and kiosks offering cold drinks and perfect seafood snacks. One of the prettier beaches, **Itapuã,** has inspired many a song, including one by Vinicius de Moraes. Fishermen still bring their rafts in at the end of the day. The most recently trendy beaches are the ones the farthest from downtown; **Praia de Stella Maris** and **Flamengo** are where the young and beautiful gather on the weekends. **Stella Maris** combines calm stretches that are perfect for swimming with some rougher spots where the surfers can do their thing. *Barracas* are springing up fast and furious to keep up with the crowds. The buses from downtown that are marked VIA ORLA will follow the coastal road connecting all the beaches until their final destination. Sit on the right-hand side, check it out, and get off when you see the beach you like. Keep in mind that on weekdays, especially in the low season, the beaches that are farther out can be quite deserted. On those days it's better to stick to beaches close to town, such as Barra or Porto da Barra.

SPECTACULAR VIEWS

The classic viewpoint in Salvador is from the **Farol de Barra,** the lighthouse at the point where the Atlantic Ocean meets the Bay of All Saints. The view here, of course, is not of the city but of the sunset. People start gathering in the park around the lighthouse about a half-hour beforehand.

The best place to see the city itself is from the **Forte de Monte Serrat (Forte São Felipe),** located at the foot of the tall headland upon which the Bonfim church stands. From here you can look back across a small stretch of bay at the lower town, the old city on the cliffs above, and behind that the high-rises of modern Salvador.

There are also a couple of good places on the cliff tops to look out over the bay. One is in **Praça Tomé de Souza,** next to the modern city hall and the **Elevator Lacerda.** To have a view with a fine lunch to go with it, go to either of the two restaurants on the top-floor balcony of the **Mercado Modelo.** Both have decent Bahian food and killer views of the bay.

ESPECIALLY FOR KIDS

A number of the city parks provide plenty of recreational opportunities for kids and adults alike. In **Dique do Tororó Park,** Av. Marechal Costa e Silva s/n (© **071/3382-0847**), kayaks and paddleboats are available for rent. This pleasant park is also known for the set of 6m-tall (20-ft.) sculptures of eight Orixás in the middle of the lake. In the evening these are beautifully illuminated.

Pituaçu Park, Av. Otávio Mangabeira s/n, Pituaçu, across from Pituaçu beach (© **071/3231-2829**), contains a 2,500-hectare (1,000-acre-plus) reserve of Atlantic rainforest. In addition to the native species there are lots of palms, cashews, mangoes, and *dendezeiros* (the small dendê palm tree). This popular recreational park has 18km (11 miles) of cycle trails (plus bikes for rent) and a children's playground.

ORGANIZED TOURS

Tour operators around town operate a fairly standard package of tours. A reliable company is **Tatur** (© **071/3450-7216;** www.tatur.com.br). The half-day city tours include either a visit to Pelourinho or a more panoramic tour to the lighthouse and the beaches. They range from R$40 to R$60. Full-day schooner tours in the Bay of All Saints usually stop at Ilha dos Frades and Itaparica. Cost is about R$50 to R$70. A number of evening tours include dinner and a folklore show, or a visit to a Candomblé ceremony. Prices range from R$60 to R$120. Farther afield, full-day tours to Praia do Forte or Morro de São Paulo depart Salvador almost every day. Praia do Forte costs R$60 to R$120, whereas

(Moments) The Ever-Present Capoeira

In Salvador, it is physically impossible not to witness the Brazilian martial art known as *capoeira*. Particularly around Pelourinho, you're bound to hear the sounds of the drums and the metallic drone of the *berimbau* (a banjolike instrument) as you walk around and catch a glimpse of two opponents spinning and kicking in a graceful half-fight, half-dance.

Though its origins are somewhat murky, most agree that *capoeira* evolved from rituals brought to Brazil by slaves from what is now Angola. The story goes that the slave owners were intimidated by the martial-arts rituals practiced by these tribes, and so tried to ban *capoeira* outright. The Africans then came up with a less-threatening form of the martial art, with a lot of moves that are more dance and acrobatics than martial arts. *Capoeira* was eventually outlawed anyway and its practitioners forced underground.

The practice never really went away, however, and with the changing times the public became more tolerant of *capoeira*. Finally in the '50s, *capoeira* received the establishment seal of approval when President Getulio Vargas referred to it as the only "true Brazilian sport."

a day trip to Morro de São Paulo starts at R$120 for the catamaran option or up to R$350 for the plane option. This company also offers a number of interesting multiday customized excursions such as African-heritage tours, folklore, history, or even archaeological tours to Bahia's interior.

TOUR GUIDES Salvador's attractions are so easily accessible that it's not really necessary to take an organized city tour. For Pelourinho it is a much better deal to book a tour guide through **Singtur,** the guiding association, Praça José Anchieta 12, second floor, Pelourinho (© 071/3322-1017). Two people can hire a guide for a few hours starting at R$30, depending on your negotiation skills, for a tour customized to your interests. Just let the guides know what you would like to see before you book.

BOAT TOURS ★ Definitely worth the money, the schooner trips in the Bay of All Saints depart daily from the dock in Comércio. The city views from the water are fabulous, and the beaches at Ilha do Frade and Itaparica are quite refreshing. Plus, if you've been wandering around the city for a day or two, it's a great feeling to be out on the water. To book a schooner trip contact **Tatur** (© 071/3114-7900) or **Prive Tur** (© 071/3338-1320). Prices range from R$50 to R$85 including pickup and drop-off at your hotel.

OUTDOOR ACTIVITIES

DIVING The coast and bay around Salvador have some interesting dive spots, including reefs and shipwrecks. Trips and times vary according to the tides and weather conditions. The prices are pretty competitive; expect to pay around R$100 for a dive trip excluding equipment, and R$160 for a dive trip including full equipment rental. The trip includes two dives. Contact **Dive Bahia,** Av. Sete de Setembro 3809, Barra (© 071/3264-3820; www.divebahia.com.br), for more information.

GOLF The closest golf course open to the general public can be found at the **Deville Salvador Hotel (formerly the Sofitel).** The 18-hole course is in Itapuá and subject to availability, as guests have preferred tee times. Greens fees are R$92 for 9 holes and R$145 to play the full 18-hole course; golf clubs rental R$40. Contact the hotel at ✆ **071/2106-8500** or the golf club directly at ✆ **071/2106-8522.** Other golf courses can be found farther north at the Iberostar hotel in Praia do Forte or at Costa do Sauipe. Contact Tatur for golf packages.

SPECTATOR SPORTS

CAPOEIRA There are a few good schools in Pelourinho where you can either watch or learn *capoeira* (see "The Ever-Present *Capoeira*," above). **Mestre Bimba's** academy, located on the Rua das Laranjeiras 1, Pelourinho (✆ **071/3492-3197;** www.capoeira mestrebimba.com.br), is the best known and is well set up to receive foreign students of all levels of experience, even those who want to try it for the first time. Visitors are welcome to have a look during lessons, but to see some good *capoeira* it is best to visit during the demonstrations Tuesday through Saturday, from 7 to 8pm. In high season there is a second demonstration at 8pm. The school asks for a small contribution to take pictures and to support the school, which offers free classes to children from low-income communities. For those interested in taking a lesson, the academy offers 1-hour lessons for R$15 per person, no experience required (wear long comfortable pants and a T-shirt or tank top). If you buy a package of 5 or 10 lessons the price drops to R$10 per lesson. The groups are very small, never more than three or four students per teacher. Contact the academy to schedule a lesson.

Another popular school is the **Associação Brasileira de Capoeira Angola,** Rua Gregorio de Matos 38, Pelourinho (✆ **071/3321-3087**). This school also holds lessons and regular demonstrations. Each class costs R$20, or you can purchase a package of six lessons for R$75. Contact the office for more details.

Many of the "spontaneous" *capoeira* demonstrations that take place around Pelourinho and the Mercado de Modelo are held for the benefit of tourists. They're fun to watch, but keep in mind that if you look on for a while and especially if you take pictures, you're expected to contribute some money to the group. Depending on how good the show is and how long I watch, I usually give between R$5 and R$10.

To watch a more authentic presentation, visit the **Forte de Santo Antonio Alem do Carmo,** aka the Capoeira Fort. Located at the very end of the Rua Direita de Santo Antonio, the fort is home to the *capoeira* academy of **Mestre João Pequeno de Pastinha** (✆ **071/3321-7587**). Events here take place on Tuesday, Thursday, and Saturday from 7:30 to 9:30pm and on Sunday from 5:30 to 7:30pm.

SOCCER The most popular spectator sport in town is soccer. The **Otavio Mangabeira Stadium,** built in the '50s, holds 80,000 people and hosts many important games. The big local teams are **Esporte Clube Bahia** and **Esporte Clube Vitória.** Contact the tourist information for details on upcoming games or contact the stadium at ✆ **071/3243-3322.**

5 SHOPPING

Salvador offers wonderful shopping and some of the best crafts in all of Brazil. The best buys include crafts made out of wood, ceramics, or leather; musical instruments; and CDs of *axé* music. Remember to always bargain.

ART

Pricey but unique pieces can be bought at the many galleries in Pelourinho. **Galeria 13,** Rua Santa Isabel 13 (© 071/3242-7783), has a large exhibit space with regular showings of work by local artists. **Galeria de Arte Bel Borba,** Rua Luis Viana 14 (© 071/3243-9370), specializes in the sculptures and paintings by Bel Borba; his work is colorful and fresh. For top-of-the-line names check out **Oxum Casa de Arte,** Rua Gregorio de Matos 18 (© 071/3321-0617). The large collection of art includes work by Mario Cravo and Carybé, who did the large wood panels of the Orixás in the Afro-Brazilian museum. The **Fundação Pierre Verger,** in honor of the French photographer and ethnologist who specialized in Afro-Brazilian culture, displays a fabulous collection of his works and sells Verger's amazing photo books; Rua da Misericordia 9, centro histórico (© 071/3321-2341).

ARTS & CRAFTS

Instituto de Artesanato Visconde de Mauá Founded by the government to promote and support regional artists, the institute is an excellent place to get a feel for Bahian arts and crafts. There are weavings, hammocks, furniture, woodcarvings, and ceramics. Prices are fixed. To see future artists at work take a peek at the third floor, where students learn the traditional arts through workshops and apprenticeships. Just as any American can grow up to be president, every Baiano has the potential to be an artist. As the saying goes, *"O baiano não nasce, estreia"*—a Baiano isn't born, he premiers. Institute and shop are open Monday and Wednesday through Friday 8am to 7pm, and Tuesday 8am to 6pm. The shop is also open Saturday and Sunday 10am to 4pm. Rua Gregorio de Matos s/n, Pelourinho. © 071/3321-5638. Bus: Praça da Sé.

BOOKS

Tom do Saber An odd pyramid-shaped building hides this beautiful bookstore and bistro. The bookstore has an excellent collection of arts, travel, and photo books of Salvador, Bahia, and Brazil as well as Brazilian literature (including translated versions), CDs, and DVDs. The complex also encompasses a small bistro, Tom do Sabor, that often hosts pocket shows. Check listings for schedule (www.piramidedoriovermelho.com.br). Rua João Gomes 249, Rio Vermelho. © 071/3334-5677. Bus: Praça da Sé.

MUSIC

Aurisom To pick up the latest *axé* or Afro-reggae tunes, stop in at Aurisom. The compilation CDs of *axé* music that come out every summer give you the best of a whole crop of Bahian artists. This store also has a fabulous selection of LPs of old Brazilian music. Praça da Sé 22, Pelourinho. © 071/3322-6893. Bus: Praça da Sé.

Midialouca This small music store in the heart of Rio Vermelho, near the Ibis hotel, has a huge collection of Bahian and Brazilian music. In addition to DVDs and CDs, you will also find books on music and arts and songbooks. Best of all, the store is open daily from 8am to midnight! Perfect for a browse before heading out for dinner. Rua da Fonte do Boi 81, Rio Vermelho. © 071/3334-2077. Bus: Rio Vermelho (or beaches beyond).

Oficina de Investigação Musical The *berimbau* must be the most purchased souvenir of all judging from the number of tourists I see leaving with these odd-shaped instruments under their arms. More portable and just as interesting are some of the drums, rattles, and tambourines used in Afro-Bahian rhythms. The shop is closed Sunday. Rua Alfredo Brito 24, Pelourinho. © 071/3322-2386. Bus: Praça da Sé.

SHOPPING MALLS

Salvador has a number of shopping malls outside of the downtown core. **Shopping Barra,** Av. Centenario 2992, Barra (✆ 071/3339-8222), is just a few blocks from the Farol da Barra; it's open Monday through Friday from 10am to 10pm and Saturday from 9am to 8pm. A bit farther out, next to the bus station, is one of the larger malls, **Shopping Iguatemi,** Av. Tancredo Neves 148, Pituba (✆ 071/3350-5060). It's open Monday through Friday from 10am to 10pm and Saturday from 9am to 9pm. Take buses marked RODOVIARIA. Here you'll find everything you need: clothing, souvenirs, books, and CDs, as well as movie theaters and an excellent food court.

SOUVENIRS

For above-average souvenir T-shirts, check out these stores: **Litoral Norte,** Rua Gregorio de Matos 30 (✆ 071/3322-3781), sells a beautiful collection of T-shirts and also has some lovely hand-painted hammocks; **Boutique Ilê Aiyê,** Rua Francisco Muniz Barreto 16 (✆ 071/3321-4193), sells CDs and T-shirts and other merchandise with the Ilê Aiyê band's logo, and part of the funds support the group's educational program; **Projeto Axé,** Rua das Laranjeiras 9 (✆ 071/3321-7869), is a nonprofit organization that sells great skirts, shorts, *kangas,* blouses, and other clothing to raise funds to support projects for street children.

Entre Dedos   This little shop sells every kind of Havaiana, as the Brazilians call the colorful flip-flops that are now popular around the world. Havaiana actually refers to the brand name that made this footwear popular many years ago. You'll find an amazing selection here, including special editions with images of endangered species and artwork. Rua Inácio Acioly 7, Pelourinho. ✆ 071/3321-1383. Bus: Praça da Sé.

Lembranças da Fé   For a different kind of souvenir try this store, which specializes in religious articles. Only in Bahia would you see saints sitting happily side by side with Orixás. Take time to browse the interesting herb mixes, shells, and cards used in Candomblé celebrations. Rua João de Deus 24, Pelourinho. ✆ 071/3321-0006. Bus: Praça da Sé.

SWEETS

Cafelier Santissimo   This lovely store fits into so many categories: cafe, bookstore, antiques shop, and souvenir store, but the great thing is that you can look at all the lovely objects, admire the view, and enjoy a delicious sweet or baked good. Rua do Carmo 50, Pelourinho. ✆ 071/3242-5151. Bus: Praça da Sé.

Delícias Bahia   Souvenirs bought here may not last until you get home. The shop has a large selection of coconut sweets, chocolates, jams, and candied fruit as well as over 100 different kinds of liquors flavored with fruit (try the banana or *cupuaçu* flavor), creamy condensed milk, or spices. Rua Inacio Accioli 9, Pelourinho. ✆ 071/3241-0775. Bus: Praça da Sé.

---

6 SALVADOR AFTER DARK

Night owls won't lack for options in Salvador. The old city center of Pelourinho hums with music, people, and a lively mix of activities that Brazilians call *movimento.* Farther out along the beaches music venues are bigger and more geared toward the club crowd, but it is still easy to find places with live music, particularly in the new nightlife enclave of Rio Vermelho. True, the "high arts" of theater, dance, and classical music do suffer a bit in Bahia, but with everything else going on, odds are you won't notice. The scene in

Bahia is very laid-back and casual; you won't find any upscale yuppie pretensions here,
unless you look really hard.

THE PERFORMING ARTS

Teatro Castro Alves   Home to the Bahian Symphony Orchestra and the Balé (ballet) de Castro Alves, this is your best bet for catching fine-arts performances. Occasionally this venue also serves as a concert hall for popular Brazilian musicians or local music acts. Check the schedule for upcoming events. Praça Dois de Julho s/n, Campo Grande. ✆ **071/3339-8000.** www.tca.ba.gov.br. Admission varies from R$10–R$60. Bus: Praça da Sé or Campo Grande.

Teatro Sesi Rio Vermelho   One of the best places to see contemporary bands is the beach neighborhood of Rio Vermelho. The Teatro Sesi Rio Vemelho is housed in a renovated heritage building and specializes in bringing in local and Brazilian acts. Music varies from jazz to blues to MPB (Musica Popular Brasileira) and even pop. Rua Borges dos Reis 9, Rio Vermelho. ✆ **071/3335-1529.** www.sesi.fieb.org.br/teatrosesi. Tickets range a fair bit from act to act, but you can expect usually to pay R$15–R$40. Bus: Praia Flamengo or Pituba.

Teatro Vila Velha   Much loved by locals, the Teatro Vila Velha has played an important role in the cultural life of Salvador. Caetano Veloso, Gal Costa, Maria Bethania, and Gilberto Gil all performed here in the early days of their careers. These days, it's home to two theater companies and one modern dance company—Viladança. For performances or other events such as MPB, *choro*, or *pagode* concerts, check the schedule. Tickets are inexpensive. Passeio Publico s/n, Gamboa de Cima. ✆ **071/3336-1384.** www.teatrovilavelha. com.br. Admission R$10–R$25. Bus: Campo Grande or Praça da Sé.

MUSIC & DANCE CLUBS
Pelourinho

In the evenings, Pelourinho often comes alive with music. Two of the most popular venues for concerts are the Praça Quincas Berro D'Agua and the Largo Pedro Archanjo. Check with the Bahiatursa office in Pelourinho or look in the newspaper for information on events (programming has become a bit spottier, alas, since a new state government cutback on cultural funding).

 Tips   **If It's Tuesday, It Must Be Terça da Benção**

Tuesday is known in Pelourinho as Terça da Benção (Blessed Tuesday). It's the day parishioners of the São Francisco de Assis Church give out bread and donations to the poor. Somehow, this simple act of charity has grown into a happening street party that kicks off every Tuesday after the 6pm Mass. The most interesting service takes place at N.S. do Rosário dos Pretos, an eclectic event held to the sound of African drums, attended by the church's black parishioners. At 7pm locals and tourists gather at the steps on the Ladeiro do Carmo to watch popular singer Geronimo perform. Afterward, take a walk through Pelourinho. Up and down the streets, music seems to pour from every corner as bands play in little largos or cafes crank their stereos. Inside Praça Teresa Batista, Olodum holds its traditional Tuesday show. Unlike the weekend street scene, this party ends relatively early. By midnight everyone heads home. Even Baianos have to get up early sometimes.

(Finds) The Mission of Olodum

Olodum is one of the best-known blocos in Salvador, maybe in all of Brazil. Founded in 1979, Olodum started as a recreational group for residents of Pelourinho who had few options during Carnaval. More than 20 years later, Olodum has grown into a cultural phenomenon with international fame, not to mention its own nifty logo, a peace sign filled with reggae colors. The group's mandate is to preserve and value black culture and heritage, and fight all forms of racism and violence. One of the ways they pursue this is through work with young children and teens in some of the poorer neighborhoods of Salvador. Over 150 kids are involved in Olodum-sponsored cultural activities. The money raised by international performances and recordings made with people like Paul Simon help fund the group's educational activities. Every Tuesday night the group performs at the Praça Teresa Batista starting at 8pm. Contact the Olodum office at (C) **071/3321-5010** or www.olodum.com.br for information on concerts and Carnaval rehearsals, or stop in at the gift shop located at Rua Gregorio de Matos 22, Pelourinho.

Live Music

Groove Bar Eighties Rock Rules! This live music venue is the best place in town for rock and blues. Thursdays and Fridays are reserved for excellent cover bands (think U-2, Pink Floyd), as well as original acts. Saturday's lineup is more pop and dance music, including classics from Michael Jackson and a range of Brazilian artists. Rua Almirante Marques de Leão 351, Barra. (C) **071/3267-5124.** www.groovebar.com.br. R$10–R$25. Bus: Barra.

Praça do Reggae In Pelourinho, reggae lives on. The Rasta flag flies proudly, dreadlocks are common, and Bob is still a hero, if not a full-on prophet. Reggae square is actually a combination of three bars—Negros Bar, Bar do Reggae, and Cravo Rastafari— but it doesn't really matter which of the three you pick; all put out Jamaican-laced tunes, and most of the action is outside anyway with live music every Friday and Saturday. Open Tuesday through Sunday 7pm to 1am. Ladeiro do Pelourinho, by the N.S. dos Rosarios dos Pretos Church, Pelourinho. No phone. R$5–R$12 cover for the band. Bus: Praça da Sé.

Dance Clubs

Boomerangue This place is a great combination of dance club and live-music venue, right in the heart of Rio Vermelho. This two-story club (decorated with boomerangs, hence the name) often features two different bands or may feature one band and a DJ. Usually open Thursday to Saturday, it sometimes hosts events on Wednesday and Sunday as well. Rua da Paciência 307, Rio Vermelho. (C) **071/3334-6640.** R$10–R$25. Bus: Rio Vermelho.

Madrre Madrre is Salvador's hottest dance club for lovers of house and electro. The beautifully designed space combines classic and modern elements and hosts a range of well-known national and international DJs. Av. Otávio Mangabeira 2471, Pituba. (C) **071/3346-0012.** R$15–R$35. Bus: Pituba.

BARS & PUBS

Bahia Café The Bahia Café is a popular bar/dance club close to Centro. The view is spectacular, overlooking the bay. Open Thursday to Sunday, the bar hosts popular local and regional bands, with DJs to keep the crowd going between sets. Die-hards who stay until the wee hours enjoy a plate of spaghetti or a bowl of hearty bean soup, courtesy of the house. Quartel dos Aflitos s/n (the entrance is at the very end of the square; walk toward the viewpoint). ℰ **071/3328-1332.** R$10–R$30. Bus: Praça da Sé.

Bar da Ponta ★★★ **Finds**   Built of glass and set at the very end of a long pier by the waterfront Trapiche Adelaide, this bar has a sweeping view of the Bay of All Saints, making it a prime sunset spot, particularly on Thursday and Friday afternoons during happy hour. The wine list and ultramodern decor attract a 30-something yuppie crowd who stay long after the sun goes down. Appetizers come from the kitchen of the excellent Trapiche restaurant next door. Open Monday through Saturday 6pm to 1am. Praça dos Tupinambas 2, Av. Contorno. ℰ **071/3326-2211.** Taxi recommended from the Mercado Modelo or Praça Castro Alves.

Café do Farol ★★ **Finds**   In all Salvador you can't find a better view. The Café do Farol is inside the lighthouse at Barra, and the patio has one of the most amazing views of the ocean and the city of Salvador. Come here for a drink, or snack on sweet or savory crepes. To access the cafe you must pay admission to the museum (R$6). Open Tuesday through Sunday 9am to 10pm. Praia da Barra s/n, Barra (inside the lighthouse). ℰ **071/3267-8881.**

Cantina da Lua ★   So what if you and every other tourist in town are on this patio? It happens to be one of the loveliest and largest patios on the Praça Terreiro de Jesus, offering the best view of all the activity on the square: the *capoeiristas* sweating in the sun, the hawkers selling souvenirs, and the dressed-up Baianas posing for pictures. In the evening it seems like all of Salvador strolls through this square. Open daily 11am until the last customer leaves. Praça Quinze de Novembro 2, Pelourinho. ℰ **071/3322-4041.** Bus: Praça da Sé.

Gay & Lesbian Bars

A great resource for gay travelers, the **Grupo Gay da Bahia,** Rua Frei Vicente 24, Pelourinho (ℰ **071/3321-1848;** www.ggb.org.br), has information on tourism and recreational opportunities in Salvador as well as on local social issues and community activism. Salvador has a small but growing Pride Parade that is usually held in October. Of course the parade includes lots of music and the *trio eletrico* sound trucks. Famous Bahian artists such as Daniela Mercury and Ivete Sangalo have taken part in previous years. Check the Grupo Gay da Bahia for details on the date. During Carnaval, don't miss the contest for Best Gay Costume, which takes place in front of Salvador city hall and includes drag queen performances and lots of music. One of the more popular Carnaval blocos that counts on a huge gay following is the **Bloco dos Mascarados** (ℰ **071/3237-0066**), led by Bahian singer Margaret Menezes. Rehearsals take place from November until Carnaval. Check with the tourist office for the dates and locations of these *ensaios.*

Salvador's gay scene is not as open as in Rio de Janeiro, but two popular hangouts are late Saturday afternoons at Porto da Barra beach and Sunday at the Barraca Aruba, a beach kiosk at Praia dos Artistas. In town, Avenida Sete de Setembro, from Praça da Sé to Campo Grande (particularly around the Praça da Piedade), as well as Pelourinho's Praça Pedro Arcanjo are known cruising areas.

The dance club at **Queens Clube,** Rua Teodoro Sampaio 160, just behind the Biblioteca Nacional (ℰ **071/328-6220**) is open Friday and Saturday midnight to 6am. The sex shop, DVD rentals, and movie screening rooms are open Monday through Saturday 3 to 10pm. Also popular, **Off Club,** Rua Dias d'Avilla 33, Barra (ℰ **071/3267-6215;** www.offclub.com.br), attracts a mixed crowd of both male and female clubbers. Open

Thursday through Sunday. On Friday the DJs play eclectic flashback hits, while Saturday is house and techno night; the other nights are a mishmash with go-go boys, drag queens, and other performers. Doors don't open until 11:30pm.

7 CARNAVAL IN SALVADOR

Carnaval is Salvador's biggest party. Over a million and a half people (locals and tourists) join in to celebrate. In contrast to Rio's more spectator-oriented celebration, the focus in Salvador is on participation. There are no samba schools with outlandish costumes and big floats—in fact, there is hardly any samba at all. The beat of choice is *axé* or Afro *axé,* the unique Bahian rhythm that combines African percussion with Caribbean reggae and Brazilian energy. The action is out on the streets with the blocos.

In Rio, blocos are groups of locals who gather up a few instruments for an impromptu parade. In Salvador, blocos started out years ago as flatbed trucks with bands and sound systems, leading people on an extended dance through the streets. The concept's still the same, but as the number of participants has grown, Salvador blocos have evolved into more highly organized affairs. All now follow set routes. Many have corporate sponsorship. Some even belong to production companies. Unavoidably, it also comes with a price tag.

The revelers that follow a bloco must buy a T-shirt *(abadá)* to identify themselves. In return they get to sing and dance behind the music truck in a large cordoned-off area, staffed by security guards who keep troublemakers out. Following the revelers is the support car with a first-aid attendant, bar, and washrooms (to which only *abadá* wearers have access). If you follow the entire route you can expect to be on your feet for at least 6 hours. Most blocos parade 3 days in a row, and your *abadá* gives you the right to come all 3 days, if you've got the stamina. It is also possible to purchase an *abadá* for just 1 day.

Carnaval officially begins at 8pm on the Thursday evening before Ash Wednesday, when the mayor of Salvador hands the keys of the city over to King Momo, who will rule for the next 5 days.

BLOCOS

Blocos all follow one of three set parade routes and start at designated times. Most blocos will take 4 to 6 hours to complete the course. The routes are **Osmar, Dodô,** and **Batatinha.** (Osmar and Dodô are named after the two musicians who first came up with the *trio eletrico* idea of mounting the band on a flatbed truck in the '50s.) The 7km-long (4¼-mile)

 Tips   Some Carnaval Do's and Don'ts

Do not bring any valuables with you; bring a photocopy of your passport or driver's license instead of the real thing. Buy a disposable camera that tucks into your pocket. Only bring as much money as you think you'll need and spread it out; put some in your pocket and a few bills in your shoe. Do not underestimate the heat, and drink sufficient water or coconut milk. Don't dress up: For blocos just wear your *abadá,* shorts, and running shoes; otherwise shorts and a tank top will do just fine.

> **(Tips) Carnaval Central**
>
> The most convenient **Central do Carnaval** location is in the heart of Pelourinho, Rua Gregorio de Matos 13 (corner of the Rua Laranjeiras; ℂ **071/3321-9365**). Other locations can be found at the Shopping Iguatemi and Shopping Barra. Book early as some of the popular blocos sell out by August!

Osmar route starts at Rua Araujo Pinha in Campo Grande, goes up Avenida Sete de Setembro as far as Praça Castro Alves, and returns to Campo Grande via Avenida Carlos Gomes. The **Dodô route** was designed in the '80s to accommodate the increased number of blocos. It follows the coastal road from Ponto da Barra to Ondina Beach. **Batatinha** is the preferred route for the percussion-heavy Afro *axé* blocos as well as the colorful drag queen blocos. Sticking close to the historic center, Batatinha runs from Praça da Sé to the Praça Municipal, then to Praça Castro Alves, and finishes up in Campo Grande. The blocos parade from Friday to Tuesday, some on 3 days, others on 4. Order and start times vary, so pick up an updated calendar just before Carnaval at one of the tourist offices.

The best resource for all Carnaval programming is the state tourism agency Bahiatursa (www.bahiatursa.ba.gov.br); they have information about all the parades and events taking place around town. In addition to the regular tourist information offices (see "Visitor Information," earlier in this chapter) they have booths with English-speaking staff along the three parade routes. Another great resource on sale at newsstands is the *Guia do Ocio,* a monthly arts-and-entertainment magazine that publishes an amazingly detailed Carnaval edition for R$5.

See the list below to help you decide which blocos to follow. To purchase an *abadá,* contact the bloco directly or else call the **Central do Carnaval** (ℂ **071/3372-6000;** www.centraldocarnaval.com.br); they represent at least a dozen of the most popular blocos. The prices for the *abadás* range from R$300 to R$900 for 2 or 3 days. The Central can also sell you an *abadá* for a day if you don't want to commit to the entire 3 days or want to try different blocos.

Ara Ketu Though it's getting more and more known across Brazil, Ara Ketu's roots remain in Salvador where the group works with community organizations and runs music and theater workshops for disadvantaged children and teens.

Blocos Axé Many of the blocos *axé* originated in the poorer and overwhelmingly black neighborhoods on the outskirts of Salvador. With the recent revival of black culture and pride, these blocos have become more and more popular and are now part of the mainstream events. The most popular ones are Ilê Aiyê, Olodum, Filhos de Ghandi, Ara Ketu, and Filhas de Oxum.

Camaleão Founded in 1978 by a group of university students, Camaleão parades Sunday through Tuesday along the Osmar route. Chiclete com Banana is the lead attraction, one of the most popular Bahian bands. This bloco was a recent winner of the best bloco and best band award. It also takes first prize for most expensive bloco. The 2010 *abadás* for all 3 days topped out at R$2,500 and still sold out!

Cerveja e Cia Given that Ivete Sangalo's producer owns this bloco, it only makes sense that Sangalo—Bahia's musical sensation—is the star attraction. The bloco parades Thursday through Saturday along the Dodô beach route.

Filhos de Ghandi   Popular during Carnaval for its symbolic message of peace, this bloco is instantly recognizable for the white Ghandi costumes worn by its 10,000 all-male followers. The bloco parades Sunday through Tuesday (along the Osmar route Sun and Mon and along the Dodô on Tues). To purchase an *abadá* (the Ghandi uniform) contact ✆ **071/3321-7073.**

Ilê Aiyê   One of the most traditional Afro blocos, Ilê lets only blacks parade, but everyone is welcome to watch and cheer. Its music is a wonderful blend of reggae and percussion; the drums are phenomenal. The group parades on Saturday, Sunday, and Tuesday along the Osmar route. For *abadás* contact ✆ **071/3388-4969.**

Olodum   Internationally known, Olodum's popularity draws huge crowds. The music is fun, some reggae, a little bit of samba, and lots of drums. Olodum always provides a great show. The group parades on 4 days, Friday and Sunday through Tuesday. *Abadás* can be purchased at the store in Pelourinho, Rua das Laranjeiras 30, or contact ✆ **071/3321-5010.**

Papa   One of the older blocos, Papa was founded in 1979, and has for the past few years been led by the wildly popular local group Babado Novo. The bloco attracts mostly young people, who come to see immensely popular lead singer Claudia Leite.

REHEARSALS

Though less organized and structured than the samba school rehearsals in Rio, a small number of blocos do meet regularly in the months leading up to Carnaval. For some this is also an important money generator, and admission can cost as much as R$60. If you won't be in Salvador during Carnaval, these rehearsals are highly recommended.

The most popular rehearsals are run by **Olodum.** On Tuesday nights the group meets at the Praça Teresa Batista s/n, Pelourinho (✆ **071/3321-3208**). Tickets are R$20. Unfortunately the ticket does not allow in-and-out privileges, and Olodum's rehearsal coincides with Terça da Benção, one of the most fun nights in Pelourinho when there are bands and events galore. It's a bit of a tossup over which is more fun. On Sundays Olodum holds a free rehearsal starting at 6pm at the Largo do Pelô. Several of Salvador's big names such as **Ara Ketu, Ivete Sangalo,** and **Vixe Mainha** hold regular rehearsals in the months leading up to Carnaval. If you are in Salvador between October and Carnaval, check with the tourist office for details.

ⓣ︎ips   Commitment Shy?

Instead of committing to one specific bloco and following along for hours, you can also get a seat in the stands that line the parade route and watch all the blocos go by. Tickets for box seats *(camarote)* or tables are expensive. The Central de Carnaval sells tickets to box seats at three different venues; prices range from R$150 to R$390 per person per day. The ticket often includes drinks, food, and entertainment. To reserve a seat in one of the much less pricey bleachers that line the parade route, contact Salvador city hall at ✆ **071/3450-2711** or the Central do Carnaval at ✆ **071/3372-6000.** Bleacher seats go for about R$80 to R$130 per day but don't include any of the fancy trappings. Some hotels, like the Monte Pascoal in Barra, set up their own bleachers for guests.

> **(Moments)** **The End of Carnaval: It Ain't Over 'til It's Over**
>
> In most cities, Carnaval comes to a quiet end as partygoers run out of steam in the early hours of Ash Wednesday and finally flop into bed. In Salvador, the party goes out with a bang. Although this event is an informal one, it takes place every year at the Praça Castro Alves. At the meeting of the trios *(encontro dos trio eletricos)*, a few of the blocos that have finished their parades meet to compete for the last bit of energy the crowd has to offer. Usually the party keeps going until the sun comes up. In recent years, Caetano Veloso and Carlinhos Brown were among the prominent musicians who came out for the grand finale and packed the square with tens of thousands of people.

Some great planning resources for Carnaval are available online. Though in Portuguese only, they certainly give you an idea of what things look like: The official city site, www.carnaval.salvador.ba.gov.br, has pictures, important phone numbers, programming details and maps; www.centraldocarnaval.com.br has *abadás* for sale and provides detailed scheduling and program information. For more information, contact the Central do Carnaval at 🕐 **071/3372-6000.**

8 SIDE TRIPS FROM SALVADOR

PRAIA DO FORTE
70km (43 miles) NE of Salvador

As recently as 10 years ago, Praia do Forte was a sleepy little fishing town with a handful of streets (none of them paved), no banks, no post office, no business hours, a couple of small pousadas, and a tiny seaside church. Then a firestorm of real estate speculation swept the coast, bringing massive new resorts, upscale hotels, chain restaurants, and expensive clothing boutiques. The main street was covered with interlocking paving stones, festooned with signs brought to you by Visa, and flanked by shop windows of brightly lit plate glass offering R$300 bikinis and the chance to act now and secure your place in the latest real estate opportunity on the coast.

Why anyone would come all this way to stroll a mall-ified street looking at the same chain stores found in any big shopping mall is beyond me. Indeed, what the people pushing all this development seem to have overlooked is that the attraction of Praia do Forte was never its beach—which is nice but not exceptional for Brazil—but rather the low-key laid-back charm of the place. Now that that's gone, there's hardly any reason to visit Praia do Forte at all. There are much prettier and still practically unspoiled beaches and small towns south of Salvador.

The Projeto Tamar sea turtle project is still there. If it's the right season and the turtles are hatching it may be worth making a short day trip to see the hatchlings make their mad dash for the sea. But if you're looking for a beach experience near Salvador, head south to Morro São Paulo or Boipeba or farther down to Barra Grande.

Projeto Tamar The sea turtle organization Tamar is Brazil's one big environmental success story. Starting out as a poor and unloved environment agency in the early '80s, Tamar has since come into the mainstream, forming alliances with the Brazilian environment agency IBAMA and with Petrobras, Brazil's national oil company, and making its SOS (Save Our Sea turtles) symbol a mainstay of posters, billboards, and bumper stickers across the country. Tamar now has numerous conservation outposts along the Brazilian coast, with one of the most important on the nursery beach at Praia de Forte. Most evenings, beginning in December and continuing until mid-March, three different species of sea turtles swim ashore, clamber up the beach, and dig a small pit into which they deposit anywhere from 50 to 200 eggs. Each night, teams of Tamar biologists sweep the beach looking for laying turtles. If the mother has chosen a suitable nest site, the biologists simply cover the eggs with a chicken-wire screen for added protection and mark the spot with a tall white stake. If the eggs are too close to the high-tide line or too near human habitation, Tamar collects the eggs and transfers them to its incubation site nearby. Fifty days later, more or less, the little turtlings hatch, dig their way up through the sand, and make a mad scramble to the sea. Nationwide, Tamar has to date released over three million hatchlings. Unfortunately, it's tough being a sea turtle. Only 1 out of 100 hatchlings will return 35 years later to the same beach to begin the cycle again. Visitors to the Tamar site in Praia do Forte see turtles from days-old hatchlings to 20-year-old adolescents. (There's also a kid-friendly video, a cafe, and a gift shop.) Better still, on certain nights during laying season, visitors are allowed to watch mother turtles lay. Best of all, from late January to the end of April, Tamar lets visitors witness the little turtles hatch out and make for the ocean. Exactly when depends on the turtles, of course, but during February there's a hatch-and-scramble nearly every evening, usually just before sunset.

Av. do Farol s/n, Praia de Forte, BA 48280-000. © **071/3676-1045.** www.projetotamar.org.br. Admission R$12 adults, free for children 4 and under. Daily 9am–6pm.

Getting There

BY CAR Praia do Forte is 50km (31 miles) north of Salvador on the Estrada do Coco highway, which starts just past Itapoã beach by the airport.

BY BUS The **Nossa Senhora das Graças** bus company provides regular service between Praia do Forte and Salvador, leaving from the Salvador Rodoviaria. Buses run almost every hour between 6am and 6pm. For exact times phone © **071/3676-1607.** Fares are R$8. The trip takes 2½ hours.

BY TAXI **Centro Turistico** (© **071/3676-1091** or 9989-9864; www.prdoforte.com. br) offers transfers to Praia do Forte from anywhere in the city of Salvador for R$65 per person or R$60 per person from Salvador airport.

Where to Stay

If for whatever reason you find yourself staying in Praia do Forte, **Pousada Ogum Marinho,** Alameida do Sol s/n (near Projeto Tamar) (© **071/3676-1165;** www.ogum marinho.com.br), has comfortable doubles with verandas and air-conditioning for R$180 to R$250, parking and breakfast included. Fancier and quieter but more expensive is **Rufugio da Vila,** Aldeia dos Pescadores Qd. 39 (© **071/3676-0114;** www.refugio davila.com.br). The Refugio offers a pool and pleasant garden area, plus king-size beds, parking, and breakfast for R$310 to R$400 double.

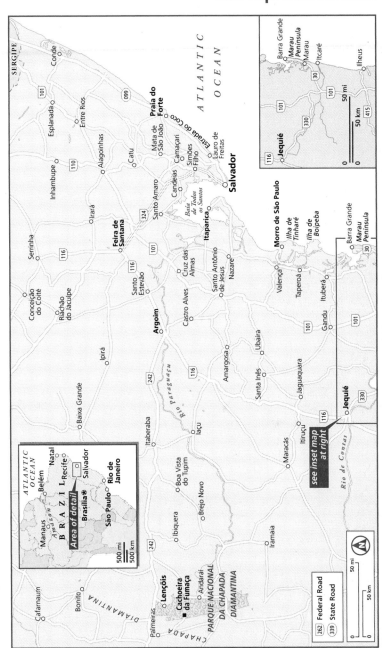

314km (195 miles) NW of Salvador

In the hinterland of Salvador, just outside of the town of Lençóis, lies the Chapada Diamantina, or Diamond Highlands. Valleys of lush green dotted with bright tropical flowers surround a mountain range of twisted red-rock formations reminiscent of the American Southwest. Numerous small rivers carve their way through the highlands, splashing over waterfalls and natural slides. There are also numerous caves, some many kilometers long. Many are quite popular, some just being discovered, some restricted yet to geologists who are trying to figure out just how they and the rock formations they contain were formed.

The gateway community of Lençóis is an old colonial town of stone streets and little churches, with cellphone towers the only real sign of the modern world. The attractions here are entirely natural. People walk the highlands, explore caves, mountain bike old miners' tracks, and swim in natural pools and waterfalls.

Essentials

BY CAR   The town of Lençóis is 395km (245 miles) from Salvador. Take BR-324 to Feira to Santana, turn onto BR-116 to Argoim and then BR-242 to Lençóis. The road is paved the entire way, but the asphalt breaks up in places on the BR-242.

BY BUS   **Real Expresso** (© 0800/617-325; www.realexpresso.com.br) makes the approximately 5-hour journey between Salvador and Lençóis at a cost of R$48. Buses depart the Salvador Rodoviaria for Lençóis daily at 7am, 4:30pm, and 11:30pm. From Lençóis, buses depart the bus station at Av. Senhor dos Passos s/n (© 075/3334-1112) for Salvador daily at 7:30am, 1:15pm, and 11:30pm.

BY PLANE   **TRIP** (© 0300/789-8747; www.voetrip.com.br) operates a weekly flight between Salvador and Lençóis. Flights depart Salvador on Saturday at 9:50am and arrive in Lençóis at 10:45am. From Lençóis, flights depart every Saturday at 11am, arriving in Salvador at noon. Flights cost as little as R$120 one way, if you book early.

GETTING AROUND   All parts of Lençóis can be reached by foot in less than 15 minutes. Excursions to the many caves and waterfalls in the area all include transport. Car rental is best done in Salvador.

VISITOR INFORMATION   In Lençóis, the local tourism agency **Sectur Lençóis,** Av. Sr. dos Passos s/n, opposite the Portal Lençóis Hotel on the far side of the river from the main square (© 075/3334-1327), has pamphlets on tours and attractions in the area. Staff speaks Portuguese only.

The official city tourism website is www.guialencois.com. In English, there's a reasonably good website with geology, trail maps, and more at www.gd.com.br/candomba/english.

Worthwhile books on the Chapada Diamantina include *A Visitor's Guide to the Chapada Diamantina Mountains* by Roy Funch and *Trilhas e Caminhos: Circuito do Diamante* by Roberto Bandeira, worth it just for the top-quality topographic map. Both books are published by the State Secretary of Tourism (SCTP) and usually available in Lençóis at Loja Dois Irmaos on the main square, or in bookstores in Salvador.

FAST FACTS   The **Banco do Brasil,** Praça Horario de Matos 56 (main square), is open Monday through Friday from 9am to 1pm. ATM is open 24 hours—PLUS/Visa only. There's Internet access at **Pede Trilha,** Rua Miguel Calmon s/n, opposite the market hall (© 075/3334-1124); it's open daily from 8am to 10pm. Connection costs R$6. For

first-aid and medical supplies there's **Pharmacia Maciel,** Av. 7 de Setembro 50 (© 075/
3334-1224), open daily from 8am to 8:30pm. The post office is at Av. Sete de Setembro
18. Open Monday through Friday from 9am to 5pm.

Exploring the Town & Beyond

The town of Lençóis is a tiny colonial gem, but it won't take more than an hour to see it
all. After that, it's out into the highlands to see what the natural world has to offer. A
number of excellent hikes in the area lead either to waterfalls or mountaintop viewpoints.
Some of these sights are far enough to require transportation, but quite a few you can
find with your own two feet.

From the bridge in Lençóis a trail leads up beside the Lençóis River to the **Serrano
swimming hole** and **Primavera Falls.** An hour's walk south of town will lead you to the
Riberão de Meio rock slide, a huge natural water slide flanked by many natural swimming holes. A long (8-hr.) hike up this same river leads to the **Sossego** canyon and
waterfall.

The most famous waterfall in the park is **Cachoeira de Fumaça (Waterfall of
Smoke),** so called because the thin stream of water slipping over the 335m (1,100-ft.)
precipice fades into a fine mist before it reaches the ground.

The park is also known for its mesalike mountain formations. The most famous are
Morro do Pai Inácio (located right next to BR-242 west of Lençóis), the 1,067m
(3,500-ft.) **Morro do Camelo,** and the 1,403m (4,600-ft.) **Monte Tabor** (also called
Marrão). All have trails to the top, and from the flat top of any one, you have the entire
Chapada spread at your feet.

Caves are a fascinating aspect of the Chapada Diamantina Park. Some of the best-
known ones in the area include **Gruta de Lapão,** a rare sandstone-and-quartzite cave
over 1km (½ mile) long from end to end. It's located about 5km (3 miles) from Lençóis.
Farther afield one finds a number of the more traditional limestone caves, with rock
flowers, stalagmites, and stalactites. The prettiest cavern may be **Gruta da Lapa Doce,**
which extends 850m (2,788 ft.) underground. In the same area is **Gruta da Pritinha,**
where an underground river emerges into the sun. Inside there's a large pool where you
can dive and swim. Nearby is the small **Gruta Azul.** Late in the afternoon when the sun
reaches into this cave, the water glows cobalt blue.

Outdoor Activities

When the weather gets hot (and it does), take to the natural swimming pools. Close to
Lençóis, and so popular that there are now beer and refreshment stands lining its banks,
is the **Mucugezinho River.** Below these stands on the same river is a deep cold pool
called the **Poço de Diablo.** South of Lençóis, near the town of Andaraí, is an underground pool with crystal-clear water and excellent limestone formations called the **Poço
Azul,** where swimming is allowed.

Swimming is not allowed at the **Poço Encantado,** and it's a long way from anywhere
down some pretty bad roads, but it's worth seeing anyway. It's a large underground cavern
with crystal-clear water. Between April and August light reaches down through a hole in
the cavern wall, and the water glows electric blue.

For wildlife watchers there's the **Marimbus** wetland. In addition to lots of caiman, it
is also home to capybaras and a wide variety of colorful bird life.

BIKING **Rony Bike** (© **075/3334-1700**) offers guided mountain-bike trips and
also rents bikes. Owner **Rony Oliveira** has lived in the area for over 10 years and biked
every possible trail. The cost for one person including a bike and guide is R$75 per day.

Itineraries can be customized to suit all interests and abilities. **Adilson Trilhas, Passeios e Bikes,** Praça Samuel Sales 32 (© 075/3334-1319), is another option for mountain-bike tours and rentals.

HIKING   Trails in the Chapada Diamantina are quite good—many are old miners' supply routes—but signage is nonexistent. Carry a map, compass, and some spare food and water (locals insist the water from the highlands is drinkable, but there are enough cattle still pastured up there that I have my doubts). If in doubt of your trail-finding skills, bring a guide along. To locate a guide, try the tour agencies below or contact the guide association directly: **ACVL** (Associação dos Conductores de Visitores no Lençóis), Av. General Viveiros 61, across the river by the Cantos dos Aguas Hotel (© 075/3334-1425). **Roy Fuchs Specialized and Personalized Guide Services** (© 075/3334-1305) is another source of guide information. Roy is American, but has lived in the area for years.

There are dozens of hikes in the Chapada Diamantina. The following are just suggestions. A short hike up the Lençóis River from the bridge will take you to the **Serrano** swimming holes, composed of little pools of pink conglomerate rock. About .5km (¼ mile) farther up the river, there's the larger **Hartley natural pool.** A short, pretty walk beyond that a small tributary comes in from the right, the **Grizante Creek.** Follow that up and you'll come to **Primavera Falls.**

An hour's walk south of town will lead you to the **Ribeirão de Meio** natural water slide. The water slide is also the trail head for a long (8-hr.) hike along the banks of the Ribeirão River to **Sossego Canyon** and **Sossego Falls.**

A good day hike that will take you through the heart of the Chapada is the 25km (16-mile) trek from the **Capão Valley to Lençóis** (or vice versa). Done from Lençóis, it's possible to get an 8am bus to Palmeiras (R$6) on the far side of the Chapada, then hire a cab to take you over the rough gravel road to the trail head (R$40). The hike takes about 8 hours and provides some excellent views.

HORSEBACK RIDING   For horseback riding, find one-armed **Taurino Sousa Alcantera** in his souvenir shop at Rua das Pedras s/n, about halfway up the street (© 075/3334-1403). Itineraries include a 5-hour ride to the **Rio Capivara** (R$60), a short 40-minute ride to **Ribeirão de Meio** (R$30 per person) where you can then play on the natural water slide, and an 18km (11-mile) daylong ride through several rivers to the **Rio Roncador** (R$90 per person).

RAPPELLING   A popular sport in Brazil, rappelling is the act of lowering yourself down a length of rope with a harness and a locking carabiner. You can rappel down a cliff face, a waterfall, into a cave, whatever. In Lençóis, the rappelling specialist is **Nativos da Chapada,** Rua Miguel Calmon 29 (© 075/3334-1314 shop, or 9960-0131 cellphone). The company offers a number of different rappel outings, including a 30m (98-ft.) drop down the **Alto da Primavera Cliff,** a 48m (157-ft.) descent into the **Gruta do Lapão Cave,** a 150m (492-ft.) descent from the **Pai Inácio Mesa,** or a soaking 50m (164-ft.) drop through the waters of **Mosquito Falls.** On most outings you get to make six descents. Cash only; prices range from R$80 to R$140 (for two–four people).

TOUR OPERATORS   **Lentur,** Avenida Sete de Setembro (© 075/3334-1271; www.lentur.com.br), offers seven different **guided minivan tours** to just about all of the local caves, springs, waterfalls, and mesas (Lapa Doce, Gruta Azul, Poço do Diable, Poço Encantado, and so on). Tours are in eight-passenger minivans. They begin at 8:30am and end at 6pm, and include a light lunch. Minimum group size is four. Cost for each tour is R$65, including the services of a Portuguese-speaking guide. An English-speaking guide costs R$90, with that cost divided by however many require his services.

Lentur also does **guided trail hikes** for groups of up to six people. Included is a guide and transportation to and from the trail head. The prices range from R$60 to R$120 per day for the trip (not per person). Trips include the 1-hour walk to Ribeirão de Meio, the 3-hour walk to Sossego Falls, the 4-hour walk to and through Lapão Cave (bring a flashlight), the 8-hour walk from Capão to Lençóis, and the 5-hour walk from Pai Inácio Mesa to Lençóis. There is also a 3-day hike to Cachoeira da Fumaça in the center of the Chapada. Cost is R$110 per person per day, including meals and guide. A sleeping bag is required.

On the main square, **Venturas & Aventuras,** Praça Horácio de Matos 16 (② 075/ 3334-1304; www.venturas.com.br), is run by English-speaking guides. Slightly less volume-oriented than the above two companies, they are also somewhat more expensive. In addition to 1-day trips, this company also offers a number of 2- and 5-day trekking packages.

Shopping

Dois Irmãos, Praça Horario de Matos 3, on the main square (② 075/3334-1405; daily 8am–10pm; V), sells high-quality trekking and hiking gear: boots, backpacks, sandals, sleeping bags, and so on. If you're looking for souvenirs, the Diamantina region is famous for semiprecious stones, which local craftsmen make into interesting jewelry. One good shop is **Casa das Pedras,** Rua das Pedras 129 (② 075/3334-1434). On the main square, photographer Calil Neto runs a small shop (**Calil Neto Fotografia;** Praça Horácio de Matos 82; ② 075/3334-1950; daily 7–10pm; no credit cards) displaying his beautiful Ansel Adams–like photographs of the Diamantina highlands.

Where to Stay

Lençóis has everything from the cheap and simple to wonderful pousadas to top-service resorts. Note that in the off season (Mar–June and Aug–Nov), all of the establishments below will cut prices from 10% to 40%.

Expensive

Canto das Aguas Hotel ★ Located just below the stone bridge leading to the town square, the Canto occupies a series of terraces cascading downward to a pool and patio that rest by the edge of the riverbank. The standard rooms (the old wing) are vaguely dark and dank, but the special rooms in the new wing are lovely, bright, and spacious; they each come with a queen-size bed and foldout sofa, a nook with a small sitting table, a good-size bathroom, and, overlooking the river, a veranda upon which to sling your hammock. The only special rooms to avoid are nos. 210 and 211, which lack a river view. The hotel is part of the Roteiros de Charme, an association of top-quality inns and pousadas.

Av. Senhor dos Passos s/n, Lençóis, 46960-000 BA. ②/fax **075/3334-1154.** www.lencois.com.br. 44 units. R$180 standard; R$250 special double; R$300–R$360 suite. Extra person add 20%. Children 6 and under stay free in parent's room. AE, DC, MC, V. Free parking. **Amenities:** Restaurant; bar; outdoor pool; room service. *In room:* A/C, TV, fridge, hair dryer, minibar, Wi-Fi.

Hotel de Lençóis ★★ (Kids Set in lush gardens in the upper part of the village, Hotel de Lençóis is run by American-born Rebecca and her family. All rooms are comfortably furnished with brand-new king-size beds, fine linens, and lovely regional artwork. Not all the rooms have air-conditioning but, considering Lençóis's cooler mountain climate, this is most often not a problem. The best rooms are the eight terrace hill apartments with private patios offering great views. The absolute top room is the romantic terrace room, a very spacious and cozy hideaway with breathtaking views, a lovely walk-in bathroom, and a large veranda. Families traveling with kids can enjoy the swimming pool, the playground, and walks on the beautiful grounds.

Rua Altina Alves 747, Lençóis, 46960-000 BA. ©/fax **075/3334-1102** (hotel); for reservations call **071/ 3369-5000.** www.hoteldelencois.com. 50 units. R$140–R$180 standard double (high season); R$200– R$250 terrace room double (high season). Low-season rates 20%–25% less. Extra person add R$45. Children 6 and under stay free in parent's room. AE, DC, MC, V. Free parking. **Amenities:** Restaurant; bar; outdoor pool; room service; free Wi-Fi in lobby and restaurant. *In room:* A/C, TV, hair dryer, minibar.

Moderate

Alcino Estalagem ★★ (Finds) Every town should have such a pousada. Housed in a replica of a 19th-century colonial house, there's antique furniture inside and comfortable nooks upstairs and down to hide out and peruse the sizable book collection. Out back, on the far side of a well-manicured pocket garden, is where the owner keeps his pottery workshop and kiln. The garden is where breakfast is served, and it is a tour de force; the cook brings out delicious local specialties until the table is covered with plates and platters. Next morning she does it all again, but no dish ever seems to appear twice. The only drawback is that three of the eight rooms have a shared bathroom. However, considering all the other advantages, it's a minor complaint.

Rua Tombe Surrão 139, Lençóis, 46960-000 BA. ©/fax **075/3334-1171.** 7 units, 3 with shared bathroom (showers only). R$90–R$150 double. Children 6 and under stay free in parent's room. DC, MC. Street parking. **Amenities:** Internet. *In room:* Fridge, no phone.

Where to Dine

Picanha na Praça, Praça Otaviano Alves 62, Lençóis (© **075/3334-1248**), serves up the best Brazilian steak sizzling hot and done to perfection. If you don't like steak, there's not much point in coming, and the side dishes are the usual forgettable assortment of Brazilian carbohydrates. But mmmmm, that *picanha* is good. The owner of **Cozinha Aberta Restaurant,** Rua da Baderna 111, Lençóis (© **075/3341-0066**), has traveled the world collecting recipes so you can choose from Italian pasta, pad Thai, goulash, or Indian curry. Dishes are made with fresh regional ingredients and served in a cozy, colorful dining room. Daily from 12:30pm until 11pm.

MORRO DE SÃO PAULO/ILHA DE BOIPEBA ★★
63km (39 miles) SW of Salvador

To really get away from it all (as if the rest of Bahia wasn't relaxed enough) consider the ultimate beach holiday in Morro de São Paulo or the even more remote little village of Boipeba. Built on an island only accessible by boat or plane, these small beachside villages are blissfully isolated—no cars, no lights, no motorcars, though luxuries abound. The main mode of transport is your feet; wheelbarrows double as taxis transporting everything from luggage to food and drinks for the evening beach party.

Tip: Plan your trip from April through June to take advantage of low-season rates and enjoy peace and quiet in destinations such as Morro de São Paulo, Boipeba, and Barra Grande. However, call ahead to check if your chosen hotel is open. Many owners schedule their own vacations during these quiet months.

By sea, the best approach is by catamaran, leaving from behind the Mercado Modelo in downtown Salvador. A 2½-hour boat ride brings you to Morro (as the locals refer to it), located on the island of Tinharé. As you approach, you'll notice the outline of a large hill (*morro* is "hill" in Portuguese) and the remnants of an old fort. Upon arrival locals with wheelbarrows vie for your business, offering to take your bags to your pousada for R$5 to R$10 per bag—bargain hard and you should be able to get it for R$10 per wheelbarrow. A steep uphill trail takes you from the docks to the main village, which consists of only a handful of sand-covered streets. The main (sand-covered) street, called Broadway, leads from the main square down to the beaches. The beach at the bottom of the main street is called First Beach (Primeira Praia), followed by Second Beach (Segunda Praia), Third Beach (Terceira Praia), and so on. Most of the pousadas are on Second and Third beaches. The island itself is still lush and green, and the beaches vary from busy and fun to almost deserted.

Essentials

None of the addresses in Morro de São Paulo have street numbers, but there are only a handful of streets and locals are very helpful with directions. For visitor information stop by the **CIT** (Central de Informações Turisticas), Praça Aureliano Lima s/n (© **075/3652-1083**). This office can assist you with accommodations and transportation as well as book excursions. It also has a number of Internet terminals and doubles as the post office. An excellent website on the area is www.morrodesaopaulo.com.br.

BY CAR   As no cars are allowed on the island, drivers will have to leave their vehicles in Valença, the nearest city to the island.

BY BUS   From Salvador, **Viação Camurujipe** (© 075/3642-3280) runs a daily service to Valença (approx. 4 hr.). From Valença there are at least two ferry options: The regular service, **Bio Tur** (© 075/3652-1062), takes about 2 hours and costs R$6. The fast ferry, **Atobás** (© 075/3641-3011), costs R$14 and takes 45 minutes. In high season you will find a number of other boats offering transportation.

BY CATAMARAN   The most direct route to Morro de São Paulo is via the catamaran departing from downtown Salvador; the Terminal Maritimo do Mercado Modelo is just across the street from the Mercado Modelo. There are several daily departures: 8:30am and 10:30am, Lancha Ilhabela (© **071/3326-7158** or 9195-6744); 1:30pm, Catamará Farol do Morro (© **075/3652-1083**); and at 9am and 2pm, Catamará Biotur (© **071/3326-7674**). Each way costs R$70 and takes about 2 hours. The boats return from Morro de São Paulo at 9am (Farol do Morro), 11:30am and 3pm (Biotur), and 2pm (Ilhabela). Note that the sea can get rough, and voyagers on this boat often get seasick. Always confirm departure times.

BY PLANE   The quickest way to get to Morro de São Paulo is to fly. Both **Addey** (© 071/3377-1993) and **Aerostar** (© 071/3377-4406) offer at least three flights a day, more on weekends and in high season; one-way fare is R$230, and flying time is 30 minutes. Flights depart and arrive at Salvador's international airport, making for convenient connections with onward flights.

SPECIAL EVENTS   For New Year's and Carnaval book a few months ahead. Most pousadas work with 5-night packages, and prices rise significantly. It's also when the island fills to capacity and even beyond.

FAST FACTS   There are no banks in Morro de São Paulo, but there is one Banco do Brasil ATM. It is a good idea to bring some extra cash just in case the ATM doesn't work. Most pousadas and restaurants accept credit cards. In a pinch, they will also exchange small-denomination U.S. dollars ($10s and $20s).

The main attraction of Morro de São Paulo is the beach, or better, the beaches. Each has a unique flavor. **First Beach** is mostly residential; **Second Beach** has lots of pousadas and people. This is where you'll find vendors, watersports, and restaurants and nightlife after sundown. **Third Beach** is quite narrow; at high tide it almost disappears. It is much quieter, perfect for a stroll. **Fourth Beach** is the (almost) deserted island tropical beach—wide, white sand, palm trees, and a few small restaurants. The town itself consists of just a few streets and the main square. During the day it's pretty quiet, as most people hang out at the beach. In the evening, a crafts market starts up, attracting both locals and tourists to the main square. The restaurants surrounding the main square fill up with diners feasting on local seafood dishes. More active pursuits include boating, horseback riding, and hiking.

Outdoor Activities

Marlins, Rua da Prainha s/n (© **075/3652-1242**), the island's main tour operator, offers a number of trips. The most popular is the **8-hour boat trip** around the island with plenty of stops for swimming or snorkeling. Another great boat tour goes out to **Ilha de Boibepa** (a small island off the main island). Tours cost R$50 per person, lunch not included. More active trips include **hikes** to waterfalls or a **walk** along the cliffs and beach to Gamboa for R$20 to R$30 per person.

Another operator that offers a number of interesting activities is Rota Tropical, Rua da Prainha 75 (along the trail that connects Second and First beach; © **075/3652-1151;** www.morrodesaopaulobrasil.com.br). The company covers practically every possible destination in the region. Full-day boat tours range from R$60 to R$80 per person (minimum of two people). Other tours include horseback riding, various hikes, and boat tours. This tour operator also offers excellent, inexpensive accommodations packages at the Anima Hotel (see review below under "Where to Stay").

Along Third and Fourth beaches you will find a number of local **horseback** tour operators; the common rate is R$15 per person per hour. The best time to go is early in the morning, around 9am or 10am when the horses are fresh.

For scuba diving contact **Companhia do Mergulho,** Pousada Farol do Morro, Primeira Praia (© **075/3652-1200**). Conditions are best in the summer months (Dec–Jan). In the winter (June–Sept), when the rains are heavy, visibility can be poor. A double dive with all equipment included costs R$150. The dive store also rents out masks and snorkels for R$10 to R$15.

Tip: Don't be late for the sunset: One of the best spots in Morro de São Paulo to watch the sunset is from the old fort next to the catamaran quay. From the docks take the path toward the left above the cliffs; it's an easy 15-minute walk. The fort, originally built in 1630 and expanded in 1728, is extremely photogenic; the red rocks glow in the rich light of the setting sun and keen spotters will often see dolphins or whales from their vantage point above the rocks.

Shopping

Bring enough toiletries, sunscreen, and personal items to last for your entire stay, as these tend to be pricey in Morro de São Paulo. Every evening in the main square there's a crafts market with some beautiful items for sale, well worth browsing.

Where to Stay

Morro de São Paulo is not a luxury destination; although there are many lovely pousadas, most tend to be small, simple, and casual. Amenities are minimal.

Anima Hotel ★★   The lovely Anima hotel sits in splendid isolation on the outer reaches of Fourth Beach on a still largely pristine stretch of sand. Everything has been built with taste and care. A small swimming pool faces the beach, and a comfortable lounge and sitting area was made from local palm and coco fibers. Accommodations are in self-contained bungalows. Some face the sea; others hide back in the coconut groves. All feature comfortable queen-size beds with top-quality linens, big windows, high ceilings, rattan chairs for relaxing, and hammocks on the balconies for relaxing even more. Two of the bungalows feature private outdoor Jacuzzis. The only disadvantage to staying here is the long hike back to the village.

Praia do Encanto (Quarta Praia), Morro de São Paulo, 45428-000 BA. (© **075/3652-2077.** Fax 075/3652-1397. www.animahotel.com. 9 units. High season R$250–R$330 double; low season R$200–R$240 double. Extra person add about 20%. Children 7 and under stay free in parent's room. AE, V. **Amenities:** Restaurant; bar; Jacuzzi; outdoor pool. *In room:* A/C, TV/DVD, CD, fridge, minibar, no phone.

Pousada o Casarão ★★   In the heart of the village overlooking the main square, this pousada can be deceptive. From the sandy street, it appears to be (just) a beautiful heritage building (though one with quite a pedigree—it was here that the Emperor D. Pedro II stayed when he visited in 1859). What you can't see from the street is the lush back garden with nine bungalows set against the sloping hillside. Each is decorated in a different style—Indonesian, Japanese, Indian, African—with rich furnishings and artwork. The best bungalows are nos. 15 and 16. Located at the top of the property, these look out over the gardens, the square, and the ocean.

Praça Aureliano Lima s/n, Morro de São Paulo, BA 45428-000. (©/fax **075/3652-1022.** www.ocasarao.net 16 units, 6 rooms and 10 bungalows. Units in the main building R$125–R$180 double; bungalows R$160–R$280 double (showers only). Extra person add 25%. Children 5 and under stay free in parent's room. AE, DC, MC, V. **Amenities:** Restaurant; bar; 2 outdoor pools; sauna. *In room:* A/C, TV, minibar, no phone.

Vila Guaiamú ★★★   Vila Guaiamú may just have the perfect location in Morro: far enough from the village for total peace and quiet, yet close enough that within 10 minutes you can be dancing the night away. This lovely pousada consists of 24 cabins set among the lush green gardens (through which skulk the cute little species of burrowing freshwater crab that gives the Vila its name). All have verandas with hammocks and are simply furnished. Cabins come in standard or deluxe, the only difference being the air-conditioning and television in the deluxe rooms. The pousada is located halfway down Terceira Praia, about a 20-minute walk from the village.

Terceira Praia, Morro de São Paulo, 45400-000 BA. (© **075/3652-1035.** Fax 075/3483-1073. www.vilaguaiamu.com.br. 24 units, showers only. High season R$240–R$340 double; low season R$160–R$195 double. Extra person add R$40. Children 5 and under stay free in parent's room. AE, V. Closed May–June. **Amenities:** Restaurant; bar. *In room:* A/C, TV (in 12 rooms only), minibar, no phone.

Where to Dine

For a small village in the middle of nowhere, Morro de São Paulo has a surprising number of excellent restaurants. The main street of the village, Broadway, is lined with eateries. Although most are open for lunch, it's in the evening that things really get hopping. **Sabor da Terra** (© 075/3652-1156) is famous for its generous portions of outstanding *moquecas* and *bobó de camarão* (prawn stew). Meat eaters can order the *picanha na chapa,* tender steak served at your own table grill. The tables on the veranda (if you can snag one) offer great views of the main street. One of the prettiest viewpoints in town is that of **O Casarão** (© 075/3652-1022; closed Sun), overlooking the main square. The menu offers a number of excellent fish and seafood dishes (portions serve two people) including *moquecas* and

Visiting Boipeba Island ★★★

Although most people visit Boipeba on a day trip from Morro de São Paulo, the island is worth a longer stay. A half-hour boat trip south of Morro de São Paulo, Boipeba is often described as "Morro 20 years ago." And indeed, after spending some time in Boipeba, Morro will come to seem "big" and "busy" in comparison. The advantage of spending the night is that, as soon as the day-trippers head back for Morro, you have the beach pretty much to yourself. The island offers enough to see that you can easily spend 2 or 3 days exploring. A variety of coastal hikes will lead you to other, more remote beaches. For a full day of hiking, you can traverse the length of the island to reach a fishing village on the southern tip. Instead of walking back you can arrange for a boat to bring you back to Boca da Barra. The Rio Inferno estuary is also worth exploring for its bird life and the beauty of its vegetation and sweeping vistas of ocean and river. For photos and information check www.boipeba.tur.br.

If you want to stay overnight it's a good idea to reserve ahead, particularly in high season. The few pousadas here are all quite small. We recommend staying at the lovely **Pousada Santa Clara ★★★**, Boca da Barra (© **075/3653-6085;** www.santaclaraboipeba.com). Rates range from R$120 to R$150, depending on size of room and time of year. Built and managed by two American brothers—Mark and Charles—the pousada combines Brazilian warmth and luxury with American customer service and amenities, and is only steps from the beach. The pousada has an outstanding restaurant, which serves a three-course gourmet breakfast (complimentary for guests). At night the restaurant is open to the public and serves creative and fresh regional dishes. A little farther up the hill, **Pousada Mangabeiras ★★**, Boca da Barra

grilled fish. Located on Fourth Beach (Quarta Praia), **Pimenta Rosa** (at Pousada Vila dos Corais; © **075/3652-1506;** daily 10am–6pm, closed May–June) is a great spot for a long leisurely lunch by the beach. Specialties include grilled fish and seafood stews.

Note: All restaurants mentioned above accept Visa or MasterCard. However, bring extra cash when dining out because the online authorization can be fickle and sometimes service is unavailable.

Nightlife

Surprise, surprise, Morro's nightlife is centered on the beach. If you do want to make a night of it, it's wise to take a nap before starting out—things get hopping only around 1am. While most people are having dinner in the main village, browsing the crafts market in the square, or sampling a dessert from the stalls on Broadway, locals are busy setting up their drinks stands on Second Beach. Around midnight, the village empties out and people head to the nightclubs at the end of Second Beach: **Ponta da Lua** or **Praia Clube Caitá.** These are pretty casual affairs—sand-covered dance floors and lots of open-air space right by the beach. The atmosphere is great, with locals and tourists mingling (there is, of course, nowhere else to go). The fruit-laden bar *barracas* specialize in caipirinhas or *batidas* made

(✆ **075/3653-6214;** www.pousadamangabeiras.com.br) offers a spectacular view of the bay. This exclusive retreat is nestled in a tropical oasis of fruit trees and lush green and makes for the perfect romantic getaway. Laze by the pool, enjoy a massage, or savor a delicious meal with organic local produce. Rates range from R$250 to R$375, in high season.

Getting There   The quickest way to reach Boipeba is by plane. **Addey** (✆ **071/3377-1993**) offers three flights a day from Salvador to Boipeba with a minimum of two passengers (R$340 per person). The landing strip is on Fazenda Pontal, just across the river from Boca da Barra. Transfer from the air-strip to the village (a 5-min. crossing) is included. Boipeba can easily be reached by boat from Morro de São Paulo (2 hr.). The cheapest transfer option is to go with a day tour that leaves Morro around 9:30am and reaches Boipeba in time for lunch. This is perfect in combination with a stay in Morro for a few days. Those who don't want to go through Morro and want to come or return directly to Salvador, can take the ferry from downtown Salvador to Itaparica (there are at least five ferries a day). Upon arrival, the buses to Valença meet the ferry passengers and it takes about 2 hours to reach Valença, and another 15 minutes to reach Graciosa. Two bus companies cover this route: **Cidade do Sol** and **Aguia Branca.** It is possible to catch a boat to Boipeba from either Valença (4¹/₂ hr.) or Graciosa (2¹/₂ hr.). Charles, of Pousada Santa Clara, can also arrange to have a private boat bring you over, or arrange a car and driver to meet you at the Itaparica ferry at quite reasonable rates, especially if three or four people divide the bill.

with the fresh fruit on display. Just point to your favorite fruit, pick your booze of choice (vodka, *cachaça,* or rum), and it all goes in the blender, coming out as a delicious cocktail.

BARRA GRANDE/MARAU PENINSULA

113km (70 miles) SW of Salvador

Once you get a taste for this part of Bahia you may want to explore farther south. The Marau Peninsula is a magical place where deserted beaches and unspoiled scenery are still easily found. The main village of Barra Grande sits at the very top of the peninsula that juts out into the Bay of Camamu, the third-largest bay in all Brazil. Part of what has helped preserve the beaches in this region is the limited access. Wedged in between the Atlantic on the east and the enormous bay and its many islands on the west there are no real roads to speak of (although Itacaré is only 50km/31 miles from Barra Grande, it is a 3-hr. drive in a 4×4) so most visitors arrive by boat from Camamu. What they come for are the miles and miles and miles (and miles!) of unspoiled beaches, the beautiful bay and islands, mangroves and lagoons, the Atlantic rainforest and bromeliads, and the excellent food and accommodations. Most visitors stay in or near Barra Grande. It offers a number of excellent bed-and-breakfasts and several great restaurants set amid lots of green in a sleepy village with streets made of sand. A must-see day trip, or even better as an overnight visit, is **Taipu de Fora,** listed as one of the most beautiful beaches in Brazil (p. 302).

Essentials

One of the best resources for planning your trip to Barra Grande and Taipu de Fora is **Turismo Taipu** (℗ **073/3258-9051** or 071/9962-6222). The owner, Tatiana Pugliese, speaks excellent English, has lived here for years, and knows the area like the back of her hand. She and her staff can set up transfers, accommodations, and sightseeing. For a great map of the region, see www.pousadapontadomuta.com.br/chegar.htm.

BY CAR   There is effectively no car access. Cars aren't allowed on the ferry (see below). From the south, the only road access is hard-core 4×4 territory.

BY BUS & FERRY   From Salvador, the best route is to take the ferry from Salvador to Bom Despacho on Itaparica island (approx. 1 hr.). From there you can connect with a bus that will take you to Camamu 180km (112 miles) away. Both **Viação Camurujipe** (℗ **073/3255-2508**) and **Aguia Branca** (℗ **073/3255-1823**) run a daily service to Camamu from Bom Despacho Valença (approx. 4 hr.; tickets cost R$20). Then from Camamu you catch another ferry to Barra Grande. You can either take the regular ferry (every hour, btw. 7am and 5:30pm, R$6 per person), which takes an hour and a half or a fast boat that will get you there in 35 minutes; departures at 7am, 9am, 1pm, and 4:30pm. Tickets are R$25 per person.

BY PLANE   Unfortunately, the direct flights to Barra Grande from Salvador or Morro de São Paulo have been canceled, due to a licensing issue with the Barra Grande airstrip. Only guests of the Kairoa resort can make use of their private air transfer from São Paulo. The other option is to fly to Ilheus. There are daily flights by **TAM** (℗ **071/4002-5700**) and **Gol** (℗ **0300/115-2121**). From Ilheus you need to travel to Camamu and take the ferry (see above).

SPECIAL EVENTS   Only during New Year's and Carnaval does this region get really full. To visit during this period book a few months ahead. Better to go in the off season, when you have the beaches practically to yourself.

FAST FACTS   There are no banks or bank machines in Barra Grande. Most pousadas and a number of restaurants accept credit cards (mostly MasterCard and Visa) but it is a good idea to bring plenty of cash. You will find the **Lan House Barra** Internet cafe in the main square, across from the church. Open daily from 8am to 10pm; R$8 per hour.

Hitting the Beach & Exploring the Town

The main attractions of Barra Grande are the beach and the glorious bay that bathes the peninsula. The beaches in Barra Grande proper are pretty enough and make for a great sunset spot. The pousadas listed below are right on the beach so you can just set out and explore. The town itself consists of three main streets and can be explored in an hour or so. However, this is best done at night when the cozy restaurants and charming patios add a warm glow to the sultry evening. In high season the town is livelier, with live music and a few more bars. The calm and quiet off-season atmosphere is also very attractive. In the daytime you are best off exploring some of the farther beaches such as Taipu de Fora, or setting off on a boat tour of the bay and the many islands.

Outdoor Activities

Taipu Turismo (℗ **073/3258-9051**), the island's main tour operator, offers a number of trips. The most popular is the 8-hour boat trip around the Bay of Camamu, the third-largest bay in Brazil, with several stops at some of the islands for swimming or snorkeling, and a visit to Cajaíba, the wooden boat center of the region. Other boat tours can be combined with a visit to Camamu, the region's main town, a hike to a waterfall, or a visit to a *quilombo* community, a settlement founded by runaway slaves. Another great tour goes out to **Taipu de Fora** ★★★ (one of the region's most beautiful beaches), where you can snorkel in the natural pools that form at low tide. The tour by 4×4 takes you across the peninsula's back roads to the Cassange lagoon and the Bromeliad trail. These are not just your boring run-of-the-mill bromeliads. These are humongous alien-looking bromeliad creatures perched high in the treetops that grow to the size of a family sedan. Tours range from R$45 per person, lunch not included, for a boat tour to R$120 for a full day tour, including a hike.

Shopping

Bring enough toiletries, sunscreen, and personal items to last for your entire stay, as there is very little available here. In the evening there is a small crafts market where local artisans make lovely lampshades and other decorative items of natural materials.

Where to Stay

Barra Grande has a surprising number of excellent pousadas and even a high-end resort.

Very Expensive

Kiaroa ★★ The Kiaroa offers the most luxurious accommodations in the region. This seaside resort is set on a gorgeous stretch of beach amid a lovely lush garden; all the bungalows are tastefully furnished in a tropical style, using lots of rustic natural materials and colorful artwork; perfect for a romantic getaway. The deluxe bungalows come with a private swimming pool and a separate sitting room, two bathrooms with Jacuzzi tub, and a large-screen plasma TV. The apartments are significantly smaller, somewhat noisy, and frankly not worth the money. Splurge or stay elsewhere. Breakfast and dinner are included. If you contact a travel operator like Brazil Nuts or Tatur in Salvador they may well find you a more affordable package.

Praia da Bombaça, Barra Grande, 45445-000 BA. ✆ **073/3258-6215.** For reservations contact ✆ 071/3272-1320. www.kiaroa.com.br. 10 bungalows and 14 apts. R$1,050 apt; R$1,600 bungalow; R$1,900–R$2,300 deluxe bungalow. AE, DC, MC, V. No children 13 and under. **Amenities:** Restaurant; bar; large outdoor pool; room service; spa; tennis court. *In room:* A/C, TV/DVD, CD, hair dryer, minibar, Wi-Fi.

Pousada Barra Bella ★★ **Kids** Barra Bella offers affordable and child-friendly accommodations, right on the beach and within walking distance of the village. The pousada features a large garden with plenty of play room and a swimming pool. All rooms are nicely furnished with colorful touches and local artwork. Many look out toward the ocean, and the duplex mezzanine room and the master room are each big enough to comfortably accommodate a family of four or five.

Rua Vasco Neto s/n, Barra Grande, 45428-000 BA. ✆ **073/3258-6298.** www.pousadabarrabella.com.br. 13 units, showers only. Low season R$140–R$160 standard, R$180–R$200 mezzanine or master; high season R$240 standard, R$290 mezzanine or master. Extra person add 25%. Children 5 and under stay free in parent's room. AE, V. Closed May–June. **Amenities:** Restaurant; bar; outdoor pool. *In room:* A/C, TV, hair dryer, minibar.

Pousada Ponta do Mutá ★★ An affordable and pleasant pousada, Ponta do Mutá is centrally located between the village and the beach. All rooms have a veranda with a hammock and look out either over the garden (the lower ones) or the ocean and garden (the top ones). The pousada is set in a lovely garden with several pleasant sitting (or snoozing) areas in the shade or overlooking the beach. Kayaks are available free of charge.

Visiting Taipu de Fora ★★★

Often sold as part of a day tour from Barra Grande, Taipu de Fora is well worth an overnight stay, particularly if you like your beaches endless, gorgeous, and empty. This vast wide strand is framed by thick groves of palm trees, dotted in just a few spots with pousadas. When the day-trippers leave you have the place to yourself. Time your visit during the full moon and you may very well believe you have found paradise. Go for a stroll, enjoy a swim (at low tide there are some impressive natural pools; a mask and snorkel can be rented on the beach for R$10), enjoy a delicious grilled seafood platter at the **Bar das Meninas** (✆ **073/3258-9051;** www.bardasmeninas.com.br), and try one of the many delicious fruit *roscas* (vodka and fruit juice cocktails).

There are two good options for an overnight stay. We recommend the **Village Taipu** (see the site of Bar das Meninas for pictures), a pleasant house with ocean view and only two rooms—a studio that sleeps two (R$120) and a one-bedroom suite that sleeps four people (R$240). Breakfast is served on the lovely beachside patio. Another good option is the **Pousada Taipu de Fora** (✆ **073/3258-6278;** www.taipudefora.com.br). This 28-room pousada also looks out over the ocean and provides more comfortable accommodations with some amenities such as room service, rooms for travelers with disabilities, and recreation for children. Rooms range from R$250 to R$315.

Rua do Anjo s/n, Barra Grande, 45428-000 BA. ✆ **073/3258-6028.** www.pousadapontadomuta.com.br. 10 units. Low season R$150–R$190; high season R$300 double (showers only). Extra person add 25%. Children 5 and under stay free in parent's room. AE, DC, MC, V. **Amenities:** Restaurant. *In room:* A/C, TV, hair dryer, minibar, Wi-Fi.

Where to Dine

Barra Grande has a number of excellent restaurants. In fact, if you are only staying for 1 or 2 nights, one of the challenges will be choosing which place to try!

Whatever you do, don't miss **Donanna**'s restaurant, Rua do Anjo s/n (✆ **073/3258-6109**), just past the pousada Ponta do Mutá. This simple restaurant serves up delicious local seafood. Make sure to order the *salada de polvo* (octopus salad), the best we ever had! Other dishes worth trying include the grilled lobster, fried fish, and *bobó*. A great place for dinner, **Café Latino,** Rua Dr. Chiquinho 19 (✆ **073/3258-6188**), is a cozy bistro/eatery run by a Brazilian-Argentine couple. They serve up excellent homemade pastas, have a decent wine list, and also make delicious specialty coffees and desserts. Even if you don't have dinner here it is worth going for a dessert coffee. For a local home-cooked meal visit **a Tapera,** Rua Dra. Lili s/n (✆ **073/3258-6119**). The only dish to order here is the *moqueca,* the house specialty. Portions are generous, so you can easily share a main course, especially if you have an appetizer such as the *casquinha de siri* made with shredded crabmeat baked in a clay dish. During the off season, restaurants will close for a few weeks in May or June, so please check for opening hours.

Note: All restaurants mentioned above accept Visa or MasterCard. However, bring extra cash when dining out because the online authorization can be fickle and sometimes service is unavailable.

159km (99 miles) SW of Salvador

The small town of Itacaré is nestled at the mouth of the Rio das Contas, the river that separates the mainland from the southern tip of Marau peninsula. Once a thriving export center of cacau, the town's economic activities now focus mostly on tourism, taking advantage of the exceptional natural beauty of this region. Unlike the coast north of here, where long beaches lined with groves of palm trees form the landscape, Itacaré is set in lush Atlantic rainforest and its small beaches are tucked away in bays protected by rocks and hills. Best of all, most beaches can only be reached on foot, on scenic trails through the forest, keeping most development (still) at bay. The ocean here is often quite rough with big waves, making it a surfer's paradise. For the nonsurfer, Itacaré offers lovely unspoiled beaches, great short hikes, and excellent accommodations and dining.

Essentials

BY CAR   Itacaré is a great place to have your wheels. The roads are in great shape and most of the beaches are a short drive outside of the city. You can either rent a car in Itacaré or at the airport in Ilheus and drive the 64km (40 miles) north on your own. The BR-001 has recently been repaired and the drive takes you along a windy road through the beautiful Atlantic rainforest.

BY BUS   Rota (© 073/3251-2181) offers regular bus service between Ilheus and Itacaré. Buses go every hour, between 7am and 7pm. Tickets are R$7.

BY PLANE   The nearest airport to Itacré is in Ilheus. There are daily flights by **TAM** (© 073/4002-5700) and **Gol** (© 0300/115-2121). From Ilheus it is 64km (40 miles) to Itacaré. Many pousadas can arrange transportation. **Eco Trip** (© 073/3251-2191; www.ecotrip.tur.br) also offers a private transfer service from the airport in Ilheus to Itacaré for R$120 for two people.

FAST FACTS   There is only a Bradesco bank machine in Itacaré in the Praça do Forum so it's wise to bring some extra cash in case it's down or doesn't accept your card. Most restaurants, hotels, and tour companies accept credit cards (MasterCard and Visa are most common). Internet cafes are everywhere, especially along the Rua Pedro Longo where you will find at least six cybercafes.

Hitting the Beach & Exploring the Town

The main attraction of Itacaré is the beach, or rather the beaches. In town, the most popular beach is **Praia da Concha,** which is also where a number of pousadas are concentrated. Especially in the summer this is a lively evening destination, as people meet at the beach bars to listen to music and dance. From there it is only a 5-minute drive or a 15- to 20-minute walk to the "city beaches" of **Resende, Tiririca, Costa,** and finally **Ribeira** where the road ends and the trail to the more isolated beaches starts. Starting here, just south of the main village there begins a string of lovely small beaches, each tucked away in its cove, separated from the next by steep hills and rocks. The only way to reach any one of these beaches is to hike from the trail head down to the ocean. Most trails are short (20–45 min.) and your reward is a practically unspoiled beach framed by stands of Atlantic rainforest. From the trail head past Ribeira beach, a 45-minute walk through the forest takes you to the first of the more rugged ocean beaches, **Prainha.** At the end of Prainha, you can pick up the trail again and continue to the next beach over, **São Jose.** Trail guides who hang out at the parking lot will try to frighten you into contracting their services with tales of multiple trails and confusing pathways, but it's really quite straightforward. To reach the more popular beaches farther south, such as **Engenhoca** (a surfers' and hippies' favorite), **Havaizinho** (with more gentle surf, better for swimming), and **Itacarézinho** (a 5km-long/3-mile sandy beach), you need to drive out on the main highway to the appropriate trail head (usually well marked), and then walk from there. From the Havaizinho trail head the walk to Havaizinho takes about 15 minutes, while the walk to Engenhoca takes about 25 minutes. The trail head for Itacarézinho is a little farther south on the highway. It too is well marked, but there's a R$10 parking fee. The walk to the beach takes about 20 minutes. Bring water, plenty of sunscreen, and anything else that you are likely to need, because you will find almost no services at these beaches.

Outdoor Activities

Besides surfing, Itacaré offers a number of other outdoor activities. The town is at the mouth of the Contas river and there are several excursions, either by kayak or by fast boat upriver to explore the estuary, the mangrove forests, the side channels, and the waterfalls upstream. Even farther upriver there is rafting, but don't expect serious wild water. The Atlantic rainforest also offers some interesting tours. Tree climbing has become very popular. Well, tree climbing with the help of walkways, as you make your way through the forest, overcoming obstacles, and challenging yourself in a fun climbing game. If you are not traveling to the Marau peninsula you can take a day tour by jeep to explore across the river (not recommended for people with back problems; the dirt road is in very poor shape and the trip is uncomfortable). Local eco-tourism operator **Eco Trip** (✆ **073/3251-2191;** www.ecotrip.tur.br) offers all these activities. Trips range from R$60 for a kayak trip to R$140 for the jeep tour or R$120 for the tree climbing (these prices are for two people).

Where to Stay

Despite all the surfers and younger travelers, Itacaré is not a cheap destination. The best accommodations within walking distance of the amenities and nightlife in the village are in Praia da Concha.

Very Expensive

Txai ★★★ For the ultimate in luxury accommodations check in at the Txai, a resort carefully built to make the most of a stunning location. Set on Jacarezinho beach (approx. 18km/11 miles from Itacaré), the bungalows and facilities are spread out to offer fabulous views and privacy. The most luxurious bungalow comes with a private pool, but even the standard ones are spacious and elegantly furnished. All rooms feature a king-size bed, sofa, CD player, outside shower, and veranda. The hotel's leisure area is beautiful

---

ⓘ Tips   Renting a Car

Car rental costs approximately R$100 per day for unlimited mileage. For insurance add another R$30. If you are arriving in Ilheus, your best plan is to rent a car at the airport. All the major companies (plus some really obscure local ones) are represented here. Some are in the arrivals hall (**Hertz** ✆ **073/3231-5042** and **Localiza** ✆ **073/3231-8007**) and a dozen more are out across the street from the airport. Prices are very similar so we recommend going with a well-known company that offers decent service.

The Perfect Resort ★★★

On a beach not so far away, in fact only a 50km (31-mile) drive south of Ilheus, there stands the perfect resort, **Fazenda da Lagoa**, Rodovia Una-Ilheus Km 18 (📞 **073/3236-6046;** www.fazendadalagoa.com.br). Set on what is, for all intents and purposes, an island, the resort has been carefully hidden away at the end of an unmarked dirt road, beyond which you come to a river that you have to cross by boat. A labor of love of a Rio designer and her husband, the Fazenda offers luxurious accommodations without being over-the-top. Staying at the Fazenda you feel like you're visiting a friend—albeit a friend with oodles of money and exquisite taste. What makes this place so special? First of all, it's the only pousada, and one of only a handful of buildings, on a beautiful 10km-long (6-mile) stretch of beach. Then there are the fabulous 140-sq.-m (460-sq.-ft.) bungalows with king-size beds, large decks, outside (and inside) showers, a beautiful swimming pool, and a lovely main lounge with an outstanding library. There is a small spa, an excellent restaurant, and only 14 bungalows, which means you never have to worry about the crowds. If you can tear yourself away from the lap of luxury (and nobody says that you have to) you can borrow bikes at low tide and ride out along the beach. Or you can take a short hike to the private lagoon with crystal-clear water and enjoy a swim, a paddle, or simply sunbathe or snooze on the wooden deck, then dig into a delicious picnic lunch that the staff will prepare for you in advance. And did I mention that you have the beach practically to yourself? At the Fazenda da Lagoa, the isolation is truly splendid. Low-season rates are R$880 to R$1,100; high season R$1,100 to R$1,450. Children 2 and under stay free, those 3 to 8 years are 50% off.

with several swimming pools and decks, an exclusive spa, and of course, the beach. Guests have the entire long strand all to themselves.

Rodovia Ilhéus-Itacaré BR 101, Km 48, BA. 📞 **073/2101-5000.** For reservations 📞 011/6858-777. www.txai.com.br. 40 units. R$800–R$1,100 apt; R$1,150–R$1,400 bungalow. Children 3 and under stay free in parent's room. AE, DC, MC, V. **Amenities:** 2 restaurants; 4 bars; concierge; health club; Jacuzzi; room service; 2 large pools; children's pool; sauna; spa; tennis. *In room:* A/C, TV/DVD, CD, fridge, minibar, no phone.

Expensive

Aldeia do Mar ★★　The Aldeia do Mar is fabulously located at the very end of Praia da Concha, the prime sunset spot! The hotel offers 16 brand-new apartments or chalets; all feature a veranda and new, firm mattresses, and are pleasantly furnished in bright colors. The hotel has a spacious lawn, a beach volleyball court, and a large swimming pool. Kayaks can be rented to explore the gentle waters of the inlet.

Praia da Concha, Itacaré, 45530-000 BA. 📞/fax **073/3251-2230.** www.aldeiadomar.tur.br. 29 units. R$400 apt; R$440 Master chalet; R$560 Aldeia chalet. Extra person add 20%. Children 5 and under stay free in parent's room. AE, DC, MC, V. **Amenities:** Restaurant; bar; outdoor pool. *In room:* A/C, TV, minibar.

Pousada Solar da Baronesa ★ ⓥ**alue**　Even in high season rooms in this lovely heritage building don't cost more than R$250 and for an expensive town such as this, that is a pretty good deal. The seven units are all uniquely furnished. The two loveliest ones are the Tropical Suite, with a small winter garden, and the Baronesa, with a four-poster bed and a view of the ocean. Afternoon tea is included. Set in the village, the pousada is a short walk from the beaches and close to the shops and restaurants.

Rua Plinio Soares 101, Centro, Itacaré, 45530-000 BA. ℂ **073/3251-2532.** www.solardabaronesa.com.br. 7 units. High season R$250 double; low season R$150–R$180 double. Children 5 and under stay free in parent's room. No credit cards. *In room:* A/C (2 rooms only), fan, minibar.

Where to Dine

Itacaré has a number of excellent restaurants that specialize in Bahian food. The village is small enough that you can go for a stroll and see what takes your fancy. **A Brasileira,** Rua Pedro Longo 175 ((ℂ **073/8825-3560**), proves that organic health food can also be delicious and hip. This lovely restaurant serves a range of contemporary seafood dishes in a beautiful and romantic setting. For excellent pizzas, try **Pizzaria Boca de Forno,** Rua Lodonio Almeida 108 ((ℂ **073/3251-2174**). The oven-baked pizzas are delicious, and the courtyard restaurant has a great atmosphere.

Along Rua Pedro Longo you will find probably a dozen restaurants that serve up Bahian food, sandwiches, crepes, and burgers. One that stands out for the quality of the food (and drinks too; the *caipiroscas* are delicious!) is **O Restaurante,** Rua Pedro Longo 170 ((ℂ **073/3251-2012**). This plain and unpretentious restaurant serves up some of the best *moquecas* and *bobós* in town. Portions are huge so order wisely. In addition to seafood, the restaurant serves pasta and outstanding Argentine steaks.

Note: All restaurants mentioned above accept Visa or MasterCard. However, bring extra cash when dining out because the online authorization can be fickle and sometimes service is unavailable.

Recife & Olinda

Recife and Olinda stand within sight of each other on Brazil's Northeast coast, one city on a hilltop, the other on a river mouth, one founded by the Portuguese, the other by the Dutch.

Recife, in keeping with the commercial character of its Dutch founders, is busy, flat, efficient. Modern. Recife is the second-largest city in Brazil's Northeast, and aside from a small but pretty historical core, it's not really worth a visit, at least not in comparison with Salvador or São Luis.

Then there's Olinda. Founded by the Portuguese in 1530 on a steep hill overlooking the harbor, Olinda grew rich and proud on sugar exports. The Dutch at the time were keen to move in on the sugar business, so after trying (and failing) to take Salvador in 1624, they arrived in Pernambuco in 1630, took its capital, Olinda, and with the exception of a few churches, utterly destroyed it. In need of a capital of their own, the Dutch abandoned the ruins of Olinda, and set to work draining and diking the islands at the mouth of the harbor.

Their new city of Mauritstad quickly turned into a bustling commercial center. When the Dutch were expelled in 1654, the Portuguese rebuilt Olinda as a matter of pride, but the center of the region had shifted. The former Dutch city was renamed Recife, after the long coral reefs that menace the harbor. By the 19th century, Recife had far outgrown Olinda; the older town was left blissfully free of development pressures, still in its largely pristine 17th-century condition.

Restoration work began on Olinda in the 1970s. In 1982 its lovingly preserved historic core was declared a UNESCO World Heritage Site. Unlike Salvador's Pelourinho, however, Olinda feels very much lived in. Walk its streets and you'll come across kids playing soccer on a patch of hard-packed dirt, women carrying groceries, perhaps artists in courtyards carving interesting-looking woodwork. The city is hilly but distances are short, and with so much to capture your attention, it's a joy to explore.

Recife has tried to follow Salvador's example by restoring its colonial downtown and promoting the area as a music and nightlife center, but its efforts haven't been as successful. Old Recife is worth a visit if you're here; it's not worth a trip in itself.

The same can be said for the beaches south of Recife. Most are beautiful—Porto de Galinhas is gorgeous, a laid-back town with long, wide beaches, and hotels that cost but a fraction of larger resorts.

1 ESSENTIALS

1,874km (1,164 miles) NE of Rio de Janeiro, 2,121km (1,318 miles) NE of São Paulo, 682km (424 miles) NE of Salvador

ARRIVING

BY PLANE **Azul** (© 085/3003-2985; www.voeazul.com.br), **Gol** (© 0300/115-2121; www.voegol.com.br), **Ocean Air** (© 0300/789-8160; www.oceanair.com.br), **TAM** (© 081/4002-5700; www.tam.com.br), **TRIP** (© 030/0789-8747; www.voetrip.com.br), and **Webjet** (© 0300/210-1234; www.webjet.com.br) all have flights to Recife. Visitors fly into Recife's **Aeroporto Internacional dos Guararapes,** Praça Ministro Salgado Filho s/n, Boa Viagem (© 081/3464-4188), about 12km (7½ miles) south of the city center and just a few kilometers from the beachside hotels in Boa Viagem. A taxi to Boa Viagem costs R$18 to R$26 and to Olinda, R$45 to R$60. You'll find a queue for **Taxi Coopseta Aeroporto** (© 081/3464-4153) on the arrivals level. For visitors staying in Boa Viagem, the regular **airport bus,** no. 33 or 42, leaves every 15 minutes and passes within 1 block of most hotels along the beach; the fare is R$1.80.

BY BUS Buses arrive at Recife's **Terminal Integrado de Passageiros (TIP),** Rodovia BR-232, Km 15, Curado (© 081/3452-1999), 14km (8½ miles) west of downtown. A Metrô connects the bus station to downtown Recife's station, Estação Central. *Note:* Buses from Recife to Olinda or to Porto de Galinhas leave from downtown and Boa Viagem, not from this station.

CITY LAYOUT

Recife's downtown layout can be a little confusing as it is made up of various islands that are connected by several bridges. Downtown Recife consists of three main areas: **Bairro do Recife** (often called Recife Antigo, or Old Recife), **Santo Antônio,** and **Boa Vista/ Santo Amaro.** Recife Antigo is the oldest part of the city, founded by the Dutch in the 1630s. Ongoing renovations are reviving and revitalizing this area, à la Pelourinho in Salvador (see chapter 11). An area of at least 15 city blocks centered on the **Rua da Bom Jesus** has been restored to its former glory. The best time to experience this area is during the weekends when it is at its liveliest.

Three bridges connect Old Recife with **Santo Antônio.** It's one of Recife's main commercial areas, and the home of many of its most interesting sights. Narrow streets packed with shops and vendors surround beautiful baroque churches and plazas. On weekdays this part of downtown just hops, particularly the narrow and twisting streets around the **Patio de São Pedro.** The principal street in Santo Antônio is **Avenida Dantas Barreto,** a wide boulevard that runs down the spine of the island. Buses to and from downtown leave from this street, either from **Praça da Independencia,** where Dantas Barreto meets Rua Primeiro de Março, or from farther up opposite **N.S. de Carmo Basilica.**

West of Santo Antônio on the mainland lie the modern and not very interesting office districts of **Boa Vista** and **Santo Amaro.**

 Tips **Stay Alert for Sharks**

BATHERS IN THIS AREA ARE AT A GREATER RISK OF SHARK ATTACK reads a sign on Boa Viagem beach. But greater than what, exactly? Those who don't go in the water? The first recorded shark attack occurred on Boa Viagem beach 14 years ago. Since then there have been numerous others, some of them fatal. Locals say the new port built just south of Recife forced the sharks out of their usual habitat and moved them up the coast. Attacks have decreased lately due to more public awareness, but caution is still required on Pina, Boa Viagem, and Piedade beaches. Follow the directions of lifeguards and don't go beyond the reefs.

The main beach and residential area of Recife starts just south of downtown and carries on uninterrupted for many miles. The first stretch, where **Avenida Boa Viagem** begins, is called **Pina.** The area around **Polo Pina** is a popular nightlife spot with some bars and restaurants. Farther along the beach the neighborhood name changes to **Boa Viagem.** This is the city's main hotel area. The beach itself is pleasant and clean but unfortunately the area has the highest number of shark attacks in all of Brazil. At low tide the reefs that lie just off the coast are easily visible in the perfectly clear blue water.

Olinda lies atop a hill, 7km (4¼ miles) north of downtown. Regular buses make the trip in about 30 minutes. You'll arrive at the **Praça do Carmo** bus station at the foot of Olinda. From there it's all uphill. The town is small enough that directions aren't really necessary. Keep strolling and you'll see everything.

GETTING AROUND

BY BUS　From Boa Viagem, regular buses run along Avenida Domingos Ferreira into downtown, about a 20-minute trip. Those marked CONDE DA BOA VISTA will loop through Boa Vista and into Santo Antônio via the Duarte Coelho Bridge, stopping at Praça da Independencia. Some of these buses continue across the Mauricio de Nassau bridge into Old Recife (ask the ticket seller). If not, it's only a 10-minute walk. Once downtown, all sights are easily reachable on foot.

From Boa Viagem, two regular buses travel directly to and from Olinda's Praça do Carmo bus station: SETUBAL-PRINCIPE and SETUBAL-CONDE DA BOA VISTA. The trip takes about 50 minutes.

From Olinda, all buses depart from the bus station on Praça do Carmo. Buses marked RIO DOCE go to Santo Antônio, stopping on Avenida Nossa Senhora do Carmo. Buses marked JARDIM ATLANTICO also go to Santo Antônio but stop in front of the post office on Rua Siqueira Campos. The trip takes 30 minutes. All buses cost R$2.30.

BY TAXI　Taxis are quick and reliable and can be hailed anywhere or booked by phone. Your hotel will usually hail a more expensive radio taxi; to catch a regular one just grab one on the street. **Coopseta Aeroporto** (© 081/3464-4153) specializes in airport service. Both **Ligue-taxi** (© 081/3428-6830) and **Tele-Taxi** (© 081/3429-4242) can be booked ahead of time.

BY METRÔ　There's a Metrô in Recife, but it's not useful to tourists. The stations are too far from Boa Viagem to walk, and given the time required to take a bus to the Metrô station, you might as well take the bus straight into downtown.

VISITOR INFORMATION

Recife's airport has a **tourist information booth** at the arrivals level that's open daily from 8am to 6pm (© 081/3462-4960). The best information booth is at Praça Boa Viagem, open daily from 8am to 8pm (© 081/3463-3621). The staff is helpful and will provide an excellent free map of Recife.

In Olinda, the tourist information office is located near the Largo do Amparo on Rua do Bonsucesso 183 (© 081/3439-9434), open daily from 9am to 6pm. There is also a kiosk at the Praça do Carmo, where the buses from Recife arrive. The tourist office website is not overly helpful, but being improved with English information (www.ipernambuco.com.br).

Fast Facts **Recife & Olinda**

Area Codes The area code for Recife and Olinda is **081.**

Banks **Banco do Brasil:** in Recife—Rua Barão De Souza Leão 440, Boa Viagem (*C* **081/3462-3777**); in Olinda—Av. Getulio Vargas 1470, Bairro Novo (*C* **081/3439-1344**).

Car Rentals **Avis** (*C* **081/3462-5069**); **Localiza** (*C* **081/3341-2082**); **Unidas** (*C* **081/3461-4661**).

Consulates **United States,** Rua Gonçalves Maia 163, Boa Vista (*C* **081/3416-3050**).

Currency Exchange Options include **Monaco Cambio,** Praça Joaquim Nabuco 19, Santo Antônio (*C* **081/3424-3727**); and **Colmeia Cambio,** Rua dos Navegantes 783, Boa Viagem (*C* **081/3465-3822**).

Dentist **Clinica Odontologica** is at Rua Ademar da Costa Almeida 130, Piedade (*C* **081/3341-3341**).

Emergencies Dial *C* **190** for police, *C* **193** for fire and ambulance. **Tourist Police,** Praça Min. Salgado Filho s/n (at the airport; *C* **081/3303-7217**).

Hospital **Centro Hospitalar Albert Sabin** is at Rua Senador José Henrique 141, Ilha do Leite (*C* **081/3421-5411**).

Internet Access **Olind@.com Cyber Café,** Praça João Pessoa 15, Carmo, Olinda (*C* **081/3429-4365**), charges R$6 per hour. **Recife Internet,** Shopping Guararapes, Av. Barreto de Menezes 800, Piedade (*C* **081/3464-2107**), charges R$8 per hour.

Pharmacies **Farmacia dos Pobres** is at Av. Conselheiro Aguiar 3595, Boa Viagem (*C* **081/3301-3117**). Open 24 hours.

Visa Renewal Go to the **Policia Federal,** Cais do Apolo 321, Bairro do Recife (*C* **081/3425-4026**). You may need to show both a return ticket and evidence of sufficient funds to cover the remainder of your stay.

Weather Recife, just below the Equator, has a pleasant, warm climate year-round, with average temperatures of 28°C (82°F). Most rain falls in winter (July–Sept). The most pleasant months are March through June; it's warm but not as hot as in December through February.

2 WHERE TO STAY

Just a 20-minute bus ride from downtown, the beach neighborhood of Boa Viagem offers a variety of hotels, some good restaurants, and a bit of nightlife, all with easy access to the beach. Unfortunately, none of the hotels in Recife really stand out. However, whatever Recife lacks in interesting hotels, Olinda more than makes up for with a number of gorgeous pousadas, most in buildings 200 years old or more. Olinda also has some of the best restaurants in the area, and there's great daytime sightseeing. We recommend staying in Olinda for at least 1 or 2 nights and exploring the city from there. A bus between Olinda and Recife takes about 30 minutes and taxis are affordable as well.

BOA VIAGEM/PIEDADE

Recife's main hotel neighborhood for tourists is Boa Viagem, as close as you can get to downtown and Olinda while still being in a safe neighborhood on a lovely, clean beach. Most of the hotels are located within 3 blocks of the water, if not directly on the beachside Avenida Boa Viagem. From late March to June and August through October, rates can drop 50%, sometimes even more.

Very Expensive

Atlante Plaza Hotel ★★   The Atlante Plaza is in a prime location across the street from Boa Viagem beach. Despite the rather plain exterior, the rooms have been recently renovated and pleasantly redecorated with modern and bright furnishings. All rooms are pretty much the same. The only advantage as you go higher (floorwise and pricewise) is the view. A nice touch is the extensive pillow menu, perfect for accessorizing your kingsize bed. The hotel offers rooms for travelers with disabilities. Unfortunately the rooftop leisure area can only be accessed by a set of stairs.

Av. Boa Viagem 5426, Recife, 51030-000 PE. ⓒ 081/3302-3333. Fax 081/3302-3344. www.atlanteplaza. com.br. 141 units. R$360 superior double; R$480 executive double. Check Internet for off-season discounts. Children 7 and under stay free in parent's room, 8 and over are charged 25% of room rate. AE, MC, V. Bus: Boa Viagem. **Amenities:** 2 restaurants; bar; babysitting; concierge; gym; outdoor pool; room service; sauna; smoke-free rooms. *In room:* A/C, TV, hair dryer, Internet, minibar.

Expensive

Beach Class Suites ★★★   The best option in Boa Viagem, the brand-new Beach Class Suites offers bright and spacious rooms at a lower rate than most five-star properties. All rooms are decorated with modern furniture, predominantly white with some splashes of colorful art. All rooms have balconies; some also have a small kitchen with a microwave and coffeemaker. A nice feature is the women-only floor, ideal for women traveling alone. Internet rates offer as much as 50% savings over the rack rate.

Av. Boa Viagem 1906, Boa Viagem, Recife, 51011-000 PE. ⓒ 0800/55-5855 or 081/2121-2626. www. beachclasssuites.com.br. 145 units. R$280–R$390 double. Internet special R$226–R$260. Extra person in room add 25%. Children 7 and under stay free in parent's room. AE, DC, MC, V. Free parking. Bus: Boa Viagem. **Amenities:** Restaurant; bar; exercise room; outdoor pool; room service; sauna; smoke-free rooms. *In room:* A/C, TV, hair dryer, Internet, minibar.

Moderate

Best Western Manibu ★ (Kids) (Value   The Best Western Manibu is one of the few hotels that easily accommodates three to four people in a room at a decent price, making it ideal for families or friends traveling together. The hotel offers affordable and comfortable rooms, pretty much what you would expect from a Best Western. Several floors, including all rooms in the green wing, have recently been renovated and are in tiptop shape. Being 2 blocks off the waterfront translates into significant savings. Senior travelers (56 and over) are entitled to an addition 10% off. The leisure facilities have also been renovated and include a pool, sauna, and small gym.

Av. Conselheiro Aguiar 919, Boa Viagem, Recife, 51011-031 PE. ⓒ 081/3084-2811. Fax 081/3084-2810. www.hotelmanibu.com.br. 156 units. R$175–R$220 double. Extra person in room add 20%. Children 12

Old Recife

DINING◆
Assucár **8**
Leite **3**

ATTRACTIONS●
Capela Dourada **4**
Casa da Cultura **2**
Estação Geral **1**
Forte das Cinco Pontas **7**
Kahal Zur Israel Synagogue **10**
Malakoff Tower **11**
Mercado de São José **6**
Paço Alfandega **8**
Patio de São Pedro **5**
Zero Marker **9**

Rua de Aurora
Ponte Boa Vista
Ponte Duarte Coelho
Ponte Princesa Isabel
Rua do Sol
R. F. Peixoto
Praça J. Nabuco
R. da Concórdia
R. F. Caneca
R. da Palma
R. T. Barreto
R. Nova
das Flores
Av. Guararapes
R. D. Barreto
Praça da Republica
Av. N.S. de Carmo
R. Dq. de Caxias
R. Imp. Dom. Pedro II
Av. Martins de Barros
Ponte Buarque de Macedo
Rua Direita
R. de Penha
R. da Praia
Ponte Maurício de Nassau
Rio Capibaribe
Cais de Sta. Rita
Cais de Sta. Rita
R. C. da Alfândega
R. Madre de Deus
Av. M. de Olinda
R. Barros
Av. Rio Branco
Av. Sul
Ponte 12 de Setembro
(Pte. Giratória)
Cais de Apolo
Rua do Brum
Tv. Tiradentes
R. B. de Veira Melo
R. de São Jorge
Av. B. Lima
R. do Apolo
R. do Bom Jesus
Av. Militar
Av. Alfredo Lisboa

0 — 2 mi
0 — 2 km
To Olinda
OLD RECIFE
SANTO ANTÔNIO
SÃO JOSÉ
Area of "Old Recife" detail, above
ATLANTIC OCEAN
PINA
Area of "Boa Viagem" detail, below
BOA VIAGEM

0 — 1/4 mi
0 — 0.25 km

Boa Viagem

Av. Dom João VI
R. Coelho
R. Carlos Anísio
R. Cel. Anísio
R. A. Freire
R. E. de Paula Santos
R. A. Lopes
Av. des João Paes
R. Ribeiro de Brito
Shopping Center Recife
Av. Fernando Simões Barbosa
R. J. Ferreira Melo
R. José Trajano
R. Bruno Veloso
R. Dália
R. de Carapuceiro
R. Félix de Brito e Meb
R. Mamanguape
R. Visc. de Jequitinhonha
Av. Hélio Falcão
R. Cel. Benedito Chaves
Av. Domingos Ferreira
R. F. B. B. Barreto
Av. des Sousa Leão
Av. Conselheiro Aguiar
R. dos Navegantes
R. dos Navegantes
Av. D. Ferreira
Av. Conselheiro Aguiar
Av. Boa Viagem
Av. Boa Viagem
ATLANTIC OCEAN

0 — 1/4 mi
0 — 0.25 km

DINING◆
Alphaiate **2**
Bargaço **5**
É **7**
Mingus **8**
Spettus **3**

ACCOMMODATIONS■
Atlante Plaza Hotel **30**
Beach Class Suites **7**
Best Western Manibu **4**
Hotel Jangadeiro **6**

RECIFE & OLINDA

12

WHERE TO STAY

and under stay free in parent's room. AE, DC, MC, V. Free parking. Bus: Boa Viagem. **Amenities:** Restaurant; bar; exercise room; small outdoor pool; room service; smoke-free rooms. *In room:* A/C, TV, fridge, hair dryer, Internet.

Hotel Jangadeiro ★★ (Value) Overlooking Boa Viagem beach, Hotel Jangadeiro offers the best value for money in this upscale neighborhood. This small, pleasant hotel has been recently renovated and the rooms are spacious and bright. It's worth paying a little bit extra for the oceanview rooms; all come with balconies and offer stunning views of Boa Viagem beach. The standard rooms look out onto the neighboring buildings, or have a partial ocean view but lack the balcony. Bathrooms come with showers only but are spotless and modern.

Av. Boa Viagem 3114, Boa Viagem, Recife, 51020-001 PE. © **081/3465-3544.** Fax 081/3466-5786. www.jangadeirohotel.com.br. 90 units. R$180 double; R$210–R$230 oceanview double. Children 7 and under stay free in parent's room, 8 and over extra bed add 25%. AE, MC, V. Free parking. **Amenities:** Restaurant; small rooftop pool; room service. *In room:* A/C, TV, minibar, Wi-Fi.

OLINDA

Olinda's pousadas, located in the city's historic center, provide charming and comfortable accommodations. Staying in a 200-year-old building does mean giving up a few modern conveniences (especially elevators), but in return these pousadas offer personalized, attentive service and beautifully furnished digs in a unique setting.

Note: No buses run within Olinda, as it is a small hillside neighborhood. However, all restaurants, accommodations, and attractions are within walking distance of the main bus station.

Expensive

Hotel 7 Colinas ★★★ (Kids) Set on the grounds of a former sugar plantation, the hotel has beautiful lush gardens and the best leisure area of any hotel in the region. Rooms are spread out over a few low-rise buildings, and all come with verandas that overlook the garden. Rustic room interiors feature tile floors and dark-wood furniture. Even the smaller standard rooms are still very pleasant. The hotel's large outdoor pool is set in the lovely garden, with lots of space for kids to run and play, and there's a pleasant bar and restaurant. It may be hard to tear yourself away to see the sights of Olinda just steps away.

Ladeira de São Francisco 307, Olinda, 53020-170 PE. ©/fax **081/3493-7766.** www.hotel7colinas.com.br. 45 units. R$270 double; R$350 deluxe double. Extra person add about 25%. Children 5 and under stay free in parent's room, children 6–12 pay 15%. AE, MC, V. Free parking. Bus: Rio Doce. **Amenities:** Restaurant; large outdoor pool; children's pool. *In room:* A/C, TV, minibar, Wi-Fi.

Pousada do Amparo ★★★ The most charming place to stay in all of greater Olinda is this concatenation of two 200-year-old colonial buildings in the heart of historic Olinda. Views down the hillside from the sumptuous back garden and pool deck are fabulous. Inside, tile floors, heavy ceiling beams, and lots of dark colonial furniture create a period feel. The addition of light wells and an internal courtyard space have given the building a wonderfully sunlit feel. Rooms come in several configurations; most are quite spacious, and several have verandas. All are furnished with a combination of antiques and modern artwork. The three rooms that face directly onto the street are a bit noisy and better avoided. *Tip:* The downstairs **Restaurante Flor de Coco** (Tues–Sun 6pm–1am) is one of the better ones in Olinda.

ACCOMMODATIONS ■
Hotel 7 Colinas **7**
Pousada do Amparo **3**
Pousada dos
   Quatro Cantos **9**

DINING ◆
Creperia **11**
Don Francesco **8**
Marim **2**
Oficina do Sabor **4**

HORTO D'EL REY
BONFIM
R. do Bonsucesso
R. S. Marinho
R. do Amparo
Ladeira de Misericordia
R. Bispo Coutinho
R. do Bonfim
R. C. Joaquim Cavalcante
R. Prudente de Morais
Av. Joaquim Nabuco
Av. Joaquim Cavalcante
R. 13 de Maio
R. São Bento
Tv. do São Francisco
R. São Francisco
Rua do Sol
R. do Farol
Av. de Liberdade
Praça da Abolição
Praça do Carmo
CARMO
ATLANTIC OCEAN
R. 15 de Novembro
Av. Sigismundo Gonçalves
Rua Manoel Borba
VARADOURO

0   1/4 mi
0   0.25 km

ATTRACTIONS ●
Convento de São Francisco **6**
Igreja da Sé **5**
Mamulengo Puppet Museum **10**
Mercado Eufrasio Barbosa **13**
Mosteiro de São Bento **12**
N.S. do Amparo **1**

RECIFE & OLINDA

12

WHERE TO STAY

Rua do Amparo 199, Olinda, 53020-170 PE. ☏ **081/3439-1749.** Fax 081/3419-6889. www.pousada doamparo.com.br. 18 units. R$260 double; R$360–R$520 deluxe double. Extra person add about 25%. Children 10 and under stay free in parent's room. V. Street parking. Bus: Rio Doce. **Amenities:** Restaurant; small pool; children's pool; sauna. *In room:* A/C, TV, minibar.

Moderate

Pousada dos Quatro Cantos ★   A lovely large colonial building, this pousada takes up the entire block, hence the name (*quatro cantos* means "four corners"). The best rooms are the three deluxe ones that offer a view of the pool or the city. Also very nice are the newly upgraded deluxe superior rooms that have a jetted tub. The best room is the Veranda Suite, a spacious chamber overlooking the garden. The two rooms on the ground floor lack air-conditioning and bathrooms, and they're next to the lobby. An annex across the garden contains five more rooms, which are comfortable but lack character.

Rua Prudente de Morais 441, Carmo, Olinda, PE. ☏ **081/3429-0220.** www.pousada4cantos.com.br. 17 units, showers only. R$95 annex room double, shared bathroom, no A/C, fan; R$140 double; R$170–R$230 deluxe and deluxe superior double. Seasonal discounts up to 20%. Extra bed add 25%. Children 5 and under stay free in parent's room. MC, V. Street parking. Bus: Boa Viagem. **Amenities:** Small outdoor pool. *In room:* A/C, TV, fridge.

3 WHERE TO DINE

CENTRO

Recife's historic downtown is a bustling and fascinating part of the city during business hours. Most of the restaurants in Centro cater to a business and office-lunch crowd and are closed at night and on weekends. The best spot in the evening is in Old Recife around the Rua do Bom Jesus, where most bars serve full meals or excellent appetizers. See "Recife & Olinda After Dark," later in this chapter, for more information.

Expensive

Leite ★★ BRAZILIAN Leite was founded in 1882 and is one of Brazil's oldest still-functioning restaurants. It is also consistently one of Recife's top downtown restaurants, an oasis of old-world elegance with mirrors, dark-wood paneling, and tables set with fine linen and china. It has a large menu with numerous steak dishes including *filet a Dijon*, a grilled steak with mustard sauce and rice with broccoli. Fish dishes include sole in almond sauce and prawns in coconut milk with onions and tomatoes. The kitchen also serves Portuguese dishes such as *bacalhau á moda*, a grilled cod filet with onions, potatoes, olives, and garlic. The most popular dessert is the *cartola*, a fried banana with cheese, sprinkled with sugar and cinnamon.

Praça Joaquim Nabuco 147, Santo Antônio. ☏ **081/3224-7977.** R$26–R$45. DC, MC, V. Sun–Fri lunch only, 11:30am–4pm.

Moderate

Assucár REGIONAL We don't often recommend restaurants in shopping malls, but then Paço Alfandega is not just any mall. The view from the top-floor dining room is fabulous, and the kitchen serves up modern, regional cuisine with plenty of seafood, grilled fish, and steak dishes. The delicious *couvert* (appetizer plate) features an inventive bean broth cooked with just a dash of *cachaça*. Main dishes include classic regional fare such as carne-de-sol, grilled fish with banana purée, as well as risottos and chicken. The best part of dinner is the panoramic view over the Capibaribe River. It's worth waiting at the bar to get a window table.

Cais da Alfandega 35, Recife Antigo (top floor of the mall). ☏ **081/3224-3920.** Reservations recommended on Fri–Sat evenings. Main courses R$24–R$39. AE, DC, MC, V. Mon–Tues noon–10pm; Wed–Sat noon–midnight; Sun noon–6:30pm.

BOA VIAGEM
Expensive

Bargaço ★★ SEAFOOD/FISH A Recife institution, the Bargaço restaurant is *the* place in town for seafood. The menu includes such offerings as grilled fish and garlic-fried shrimp, but we recommend ordering those as an appetizer in order to save room for a *moqueca*. The menu features eight varieties, including lobster, octopus, shrimp, fish, or crab, but it's the Bahian *moqueca* dish that made this restaurant famous. If you can't decide, try the seafood combination *moqueca mixta*. These main courses are big enough for two. Your best bet for dessert is the *cocada*, a typical Bahian sweet made with sugar, more sugar, and coconut.

Av. Eng. Antonio de Gois 62, Pina. ☏ **081/3465-1847.** Reservations recommended on weekends. R$39–R$68, most dishes serve 2 people. DC, MC, V. Sun–Thurs noon–midnight; Fri–Sat noon–1am.

(Finds) Try a Tapioca Pancake

Thursday through Sunday from 2 to 10pm, there's a small market at the Praça da Boa Viagem. Though the crafts are nothing special, the **tapioca pancakes** are worth writing home about. These small pancakes are made from scratch with tapioca flour; it's kind of fun to watch the women pour the tiny tapioca grains on the skillet and see a pancake slowly take form. Served either sweet (with coconut and condensed milk) or savory (with cheese), these are mighty addictive little treats.

E ★★ CONTEMPORARY Recife's best restaurant of the year takes you on a culinary tour of some interesting cuisines. Chef Douglas van der Ley loves to play with techniques and flavors from all across the world, and his dishes reveal touches of Vietnamese, Thai, Japanese, Italian, and French cuisine. Some interesting dishes you will find on the menu include *Fillet Ban Chá* (grilled beef medallions served on pasta with a Dijon, miso, and green tea sauce) and the Thai prawns (deep-fried and served with a sweet-and-sour honey sauce). The kitchen is open late, until 1:30am.

Rua do Atlântico 147, Boa Viagem. (C) **081/3325-9323.** www.egastronomia.com.br. Reservations recommended on weekends. R$36–R$52. AE, DC, MC. Tues–Sat 8pm–1:30am. Bus: Boa Viagem.

Mingus ★★ CONTEMPORARY Almost across the street from E is another popular Recife restaurant, Mingus, named in honor of jazz bassist and composer Charles Mingus. The kitchen serves up excellent contemporary cuisine, using Brazilian ingredients in creative combinations. Try the grilled lamb with shiitake mushrooms and baby potatoes, or the grilled partridge with linguine au poivre. Seafood lovers will also be pleased with dishes such as the grilled fish in cashew crust with leek risotto or the salmon with a ham and melon risotto. Desserts are deliciously decadent and worth lingering over . . . especially the warm apple compote with a cashew crust and vanilla ice cream or the warm chocolate biscuit with nuts and chocolate mousse topped with rich crème anglaise and red fruit.

Rua do Atlântico 102, Boa Viagem. (C) **081/3465-4000.** www.mingus.com.br. Reservations recommended in the evening. R$29–R$48. DC, MC, V. Sun–Mon noon–3:30pm; Tues–Sat noon–3:30pm and 7pm–midnight. Bus: Boa Viagem.

Spettus ★★ STEAK It may look more like a hip lounge, but this is one of Recife's most popular all-you-can-eat steak restaurants. The meat menu alone covers more than 20 different kinds of beef, chicken, lamb, and pork. However, seafood lovers and even vegetarians (if they can get over the constant parade of succulent meat) can feast on a variety of seafood, sushi, salads, vegetables, and antipasti. Dessert isn't included in the price, but chances are you will be too stuffed to want any.

Av. Eng. Domingos Ferreira 1500, Boa Viagem. (C) **081/3326-3070.** R$62 per person. AE, DC, MC, V. Daily 11:30am–midnight.

Moderate

Alphaiate ★★ STEAK The Alphaiate is the perfect spot to take a break from eating fish and seafood. Located in Boa Viagem, the restaurant faces the ocean and offers indoor as well as covered alfresco dining. Even if you don't feel like a full meal, the Alphaiate is great for just a beer and snack. The beer list includes over 20 options, and a variety of the steaks come in appetizer format. Also good for nibbling are the pork spareribs, served with *farofa* and vinaigrette sauce. Main courses will often feed two people. The most popular dish is the *picanha* steak for two, served with a side of *farofa,* rice, and beans.

Rua Artur Muniz 82, Boa Viagem. (©) 081/3465-7588. R$16–R$46, more expensive dishes serve 2 people. DC, MC, V. Sun–Wed 11:30am–1am; Thurs–Sat 11:30am–2am. Bus: Boa Viagem.

OLINDA

Who'd-a-thought artists could cook? Long known as an artistic center, Olinda has recently begun to establish itself as the best place for fine dining in Recife.

Expensive

Oficina do Sabor ★★★ BRAZILIAN   If you only have time for one meal in Olinda, make sure you reserve a table on the patio of Oficina do Sabor. The most popular dishes are the *Jerimums,* a local variety of pumpkin. Bestsellers include the *Jerimum recheado com camarão ao maracuja* (pumpkin filled with prawn and passion-fruit sauce). Another popular dish is the *Jerimum recheado com lagosta ao coco* (pumpkin filled with lobster in coconut milk). Inside, the Oficina is a beautifully decorated space in a lovely restored building—but that's just icing on the pumpkin. The patio offers gorgeous views of Olinda.

Rua do Amparo 335, Olinda. (©) 081/3429-3331. www.oficinadosabor.com. Reservations recommended on weekends. R$34–R$60, most dishes serve 2. AE, DC, MC, V. Tues–Fri noon–4pm and 6pm–midnight; Sat noon–1am; Sun noon–5pm.

Moderate

Don Francesco ★★★ (Finds ITALIAN   This little restaurant serves up some of the best Italian food in town. Owner and chef Francesco Carretta takes care of the kitchen, and his wife, Norma, looks after the dining room and welcomes guests into the cozy restaurant. Many of the herbs and vegetables come from their organic garden. The pastas are made from scratch by Francesco and served with simple sauces. You choose whether you prefer the tagliatelle, ravioli, or rondelle and pick one of the sauces such as the organic pesto, fungi mushrooms, Gorgonzola, or tomato with basil and ricotta. The menu always includes a traditional and a vegetarian lasagna. All desserts, except for the ice cream, are also made in Don Francesco's kitchen.

Rua Prudente de Moraes 358, Olinda. (©) 081/3429-3852. R$18–R$32. MC, V. Mon–Fri noon–3pm and 7–11pm; Sat 7pm–midnight.

Marim ★★ BRAZILIAN/SEAFOOD   Not too far from the Oficina do Sabor is another great cozy restaurant where the lovely decorations aren't the only works of art. The kitchen serves some beautiful dishes, specializing in regional seafood such as prawns with mango sauce, grilled fish in banana leaf, or fish stuffed with spicy crabmeat. The atmosphere is bustling and pleasant, and the service is knowledgeable and friendly.

Rua do Amparo 157, Olinda. (©) 081/3429-8762. Reservations accepted. Main courses R$18–R$41. AE, DC, MC, V. Daily 11am–11pm. Bus: Rio Doce.

Inexpensive

Creperia (Value CREPES   Set in a lovely house just across from the church on the Praça João Alfredo, the Creperia serves up—surprise, surprise—crepes. The menu offers a variety of savory and sweet crepes. Perfect for a quick lunch or snack, try the Ilha de Marajó, made with melted mozzarella cheese, arugula, and sun-dried tomatoes. The prawns with curry sauce are also tasty. In addition to crepes, the kitchen serves up salads and fruit juices. The restaurant has a great patio.

Praça João Alfredo 168, Carmo, Olinda. (©) 081/3429-2935. Everything under R$15. DC, MC, V. Tues–Sun 11am–11pm.

4 EXPLORING RECIFE & OLINDA

The allure of both Olinda and Recife lies not so much in particular sights as in the urban fabric. In Olinda, while no particular church merits a special trip, the ensemble of 300- and 400-year-old architecture makes for a memorable stroll. If your time is limited, head first for Olinda, making sure to go up to the Igreja da Sé for the best views.

Downtown Recife has a number of interesting monuments and buildings to see; the Zero Marker makes a fine starting point. From there it's a nice stroll through restored Old Recife (make sure to walk down Rua do Bom Jesus and take a peek from the Malakoff Tower). Then cross the bridge to Santo Antônio; the commercial heart of Recife is as packed with vendors and food stands as any Asian market. Staying in Boa Viagem makes it easy to fit in a morning swim and stroll on the beach. If you need more sand time than that, remember that small, laid-back Porto de Galinhas boasts one of the finest beaches in the Northeast (see "A Side Trip to Porto de Galinhas," later in this chapter).

HIGHLIGHTS OF OLINDA

The only way to truly explore Olinda is by hitting the cobblestones and setting off on foot. It's hard to get lost in the historic part of the city. The hilltop **Igreja da Sé** dominates the city to the west, while the ocean is always visible to the east; Recife's skyline stands out to the south. Most attractions are open daily; churches usually open from 8am to 5pm, with a 2-hour closure for lunch from noon to 2pm. Sunday and Monday are pretty quiet. If you like it more lively and bustling, visit on Friday and Saturday.

Buses from Recife will drop you off at the Praça do Carmo, dominated by the lovely **N.S. do Carmo church** ★. This more-than-400-year-old church has finally undergone a much-needed renovation. It's worth peeking in to see the huge ornate jacaranda-wood altar. The large leafy square on the front side of the church is known as **Praça da Abolição (abolition square)** because of the statues of Princess Isabel, who was responsible for abolishing slavery in 1888. Follow Avenida da Liberdade, and you'll pass by the 1590 Church of **São Pedro Apostolo** before turning right and walking up the steep **Ladeira da Sé** to the **Igreja da Sé** ★.

Alternatively, from N.S. do Carmo you can swing to your right on the Rua Sá Francisco, which leads to the **Convento de São Francisco** ★★ (R$2; closed Sat afternoon and all day Sun). Built in 1577, this was the first Franciscan monastery in Brazil. It's worth ducking in to see the life history of Jesus in the N.S. das Neves, done in Portuguese blue tile.

(Tips) **Give Your Guide a Test Drive**

In most of the squares, especially at the Praça do Carmo, young guides will offer their services for a fee (usually around R$25). Many are former street children trained by the city as tour guides. Some are good; some are hopeless. If you're interested, test out your prospective guide, if only to make sure you can understand his English. Hiring a tour guide protects you from being hassled by other guides and vendors. If you're lucky, they may also show you the city's nooks and crannies.

> **Moments** **The Passion Play at Nova Jerusalem**
>
> If you're in the Recife area in the 10 days leading up to Easter, don't miss the **passion play in Nova Jerusalem, Fazenda Nova ★★**. More than 500 actors and extras assemble on nine different stages to act out the last days in the life of Christ. The specially built theater is massive—the size of 12 football fields, with tall towers and thick walls resembling old Jerusalem. The play's been going since 1968, but in recent years it's become much more popular; well-known actors and actresses now take the coveted roles of Jesus, Mary, Pontius Pilate, and Judas. What makes it worth the trip to Fazenda Nova, 190km (118 miles) from Recife, is the street fair and festival that accompanies the play. Performances start on the Saturday of the week before Easter. Good Friday and Hallelujah Saturday (the day before Easter) are the most popular nights. Up to 8,000 people make the trip out to Nova Jerusalem each night. Tickets cost R$30 to R$40. Performances start at 6pm and finish at 9pm. For up-to-date info on actors and starts, see the play website: www.novajerusalem.com.br. For day tours, contact **Luck Viagens** (② 081/3302-6222; www.luckviagens.com.br; R$75 for tour and ticket), or **Caravana Turismo** (② 081/3221-1623; R$65 for day trip plus ticket).

From the Convento São Francisco, the Travessia São Francisco leads up to the Ladeira de Sé and the **Igreja da Sé.** Originally built in 1537, this now rather austere church is more interesting for what it's suffered over the years than anything else. A series of photographs and drawings just inside the main door shows the church's various incarnations.

The square in front of the Igreja da Sé provides the best view in town. You see the red-tiled roofs and church towers of Olinda, and thick stands of tropical trees set against the sparkling blue ocean below. Farther south you get great views of Recife's skyline all the way to Boa Viagem. It's a good place to ponder Recife, Olinda, and the nations that made them. The Portuguese, coming from cities like Lisbon, founded Olinda on a hilltop. The Dutch, with models like Amsterdam in mind, founded Recife on a bit of mudflat by the river mouth. The Dutch choice proved the more practical. But the Portuguese city is far more beautiful.

The square in front of the Igreja da Sé has a great crafts market and excellent food stalls selling fresh tapioca pancakes and shots of flavored *cachaça.* Nearby, at Rua Bispo Coutinho 726, you'll find the **Museu de Arte Sacra de Pernambuco** (Tues–Fri 9am–12:45pm). It's not one of the great ones; if you saw the sacred art museums in Salvador or São Paulo, skip this one.

The very steep **Ladeira da Misericordia** leads down toward the **Rua do Amparo ★★.** This is one of Olinda's prettiest streets, featuring small, brightly colored colonial houses packed with galleries, restaurants, and shops. **Largo do Amparo ★** has the feel of a little Mexican square. On the square itself, **N.S. do Amparo** (built 1613) features two bell towers (a sign they could afford to pay the bell-tower tax back in the old days) on the outside, and some nice tiles and gold work inside. Farther up the hillside, **N.S. do Rosario dos Pretos** and **São João Batista** have nothing inside worth hoofing it up the hill.

Leaving the square and following Rua Amparo until it becomes **Rua Treze de Maio,** you come to the **Mamulengo Puppet Museum** ★ (✆ **081/3429-6214;** Tues–Fri 10am–5pm, Sat–Sun 11am–5pm; free admission). The small three-floor museum assembles puppets used in Northeastern folk drama. Puppet characters come in a wide variety of shapes and sizes. Some have hidden levers that cause them to stick out their tongues (or other, ruder appendages). Almost next door, the **Museu de Arte Contemporânea de Pernambuco (Museum of Contemporary Art;** ✆ **081/3429-2587)** has next to nothing inside.

Farther down, following **Rua São Bento** leads to the **Mosteiro de São Bento.** Built in 1582, this monastery is still home to 27 Benedictine monks, and only the church is open to the public.

From the monastery, **Rua XV de Novembro** leads down to the **Largo do Varadouro;** the large crafts market **Mercado Eufrasio Barbosa** is worth a visit. Those returning to Recife can take a bus from this square instead of returning to the Praça do Carmo.

HIGHLIGHTS OF RECIFE

The place to start a tour of Recife is at the **Zero Marker** in the heart of Old Recife. Gaze out toward the ocean from here, and about 90m (300 ft.) offshore you'll see the long, low reef from which the city draws its name. On the reef sits a strange tall green pillar capped with something that could charitably be said to resemble a tulip. This more than slightly phallic monument is the work of an eccentric ceramics artist named **Francisco Brennand.** If you're interested in seeing more, he has a large estate on the far edge of town (**Oficina Cerâmica Francisco Brennand,** Av. Cachangá, Varzea; ✆ **081/3271-2466;** Mon–Thurs 8am–5pm, Fri 8am–4pm) brimming with weird and wonderful ceramic creations, many of them long, hard, and potent-looking (see attractions below).

A block back from the Zero Marker is the **Rua do Bom Jesus.** The street and this whole island are the oldest part of Recife, founded not by the Portuguese but by the Dutch. The reconstructed **Kahal Zur Synagogue,** rebuilt on the foundations of the first synagogue in the Americas, is worth a visit. On weekends this part of the city is a fun area to visit for free outdoor concerts. The center of the nocturnal activity is the **Praça Artur Oscar.** At the north end of the square the tall thing like a Norman castle is the **Malakoff Tower,** a former astrological observatory now open as a public viewing platform.

From here north all the way to Forte Brum, Old Recife reverts from antique to just plain old—run-down and a little slummy. The fort at the end of the 5-block walk isn't special enough to warrant the trip, so head back to **Avenida Rio Branco,** and cross the Buarge de Macedo bridge to **Santo Antônio.**

ⓘ Tips Olinda, City of Artists

Every year, Olinda hosts a large open house event, called **Olinda, Arte em Toda Parte** (Olinda, Art Everywhere). During the last 10 days of November, the city's artists open their studio doors to visitors and a number of special events, exhibits, and cultural presentations take place. For more information check the website www.olindaarteemtodaparte.com.br or stop by the tourist information center at the Largo do Amparo on Rua do Bonsucesso 183 (✆ **081/3439-9434**), open daily from 9am to 6pm.

This area, too, was the work of the Dutch. In the heyday of the Dutch colony, Santo Antônio was called Mauritsopolis, after the founder and ruler, Enlightenment prince Maurits van Nassau. The large green neoclassical square almost at the foot of the bridge was once Nassau's private estate, but is now the **Praça da República** ★. It's one of Recife's most graceful public areas.

Just behind the Beaux Arts **Palácio da Justiça** on Rua do Imperador Dom Pedro II, you pass by the **Capela Dourada** (see below). Then, turning right on Rua Primeiro do Março, you come to a big blue-and-white Beaux Arts confection of a building that has, since the 1880s, been home to the city's premier paper, the *Diário de Pernambuco.* Across the street is the **Praça da Independencia,** a good place to catch a bus, but of no interest otherwise.

Crossing Primeiro do Marco and sneaking south through the fun maze of narrow streets (parallel to but not on Av. Dantas Barreto) you will come—provided you find **Rua do Fogo** on the far side of **Avenida N.S. do Carmo**—to the **Pátio de São Pedro,** a popular outdoor music venue.

The **Concatedral de São Pedro de Clérigos** is a classic example of Portuguese colonial baroque. Nice as it is, however, it's the patio that makes the spot special. This broad cobblestone square is enclosed by dozens of small, restored shops, all gaily painted in bright pinks, blues, and greens.

Crossing Avenida Dantas Barreto from here you would come to the **N.S. do Carmo Basilica,** which would be worth a quick look before continuing for a few more blocks to the **Casa da Cultura** (see below) and the **Estação Geral.**

As it turns out, however, the little shops surrounding the patio are a great place to grab a chopp (cold Brazilian draft) and have a seat at—what else?—a patio table. Toward the end of the day the place fills up with the one-for-the-road crowd; there's often a band. This is a good place to cease exploring for a while.

Capela Dourada ★

The Golden Chapel is aptly named. The altar is a two-story arch of jacaranda and cedar, gilt with gold. Christ hangs on a golden cross with gold and silver rays shining out behind his head. The chapel is part of a Franciscan complex that includes a small sacred art museum with a few nice pieces of silver work. Also worth a look is the **Church of the Ordem Terceiro de São Francisco.** One wall of this church is decorated with a rather disturbing oil painting showing Franciscan monks getting crucified. Someone else obviously took a dislike to it; the face of every soldier has been scraped away. Don't miss the **church archives** behind the altar. The cabinets are 3m (12 ft.) high and made of solid jacaranda—gorgeous craftsmanship.

Rua do Imperador Dom Pedro II 206, Santo Antônio. ✆ **081/3224-0530.** Admission R$2 adults, free for children 7 and under. Mon–Fri 8–11:30am and 2–5pm; Sat 8–11am. Bus: Conde da Boa Vista.

Casa da Cultura ★

This former penitentiary has only barely changed since its prison days; the cells, still with their original numbers, are now occupied by souvenir shops. You'll find a good selection of local crafts: ceramics, woodcarvings, leather sandals, lace, and clothing. Prices are reasonable, but a bit of bargaining is expected. There's still more than frisson of dread as you climb the heavy iron catwalks and duck through a thick doorway into one of the old cells. Good thing there's nothing more frightening than handicrafts inside.

Rua Floriano Peixoto, Santo Antônio. ✆ **081/3224-2850.** Mon–Fri 9am–6pm; Sat 9am–5pm; Sun 10am–2pm. Bus: Conde de Boa Vista.

Centro Cultural Judaico de Pernambuco/Kahal Zur Israel Synagogue ★★

This reconstructed synagogue is built on the foundations of the original Kahal Zur Israel synagogue, founded in the 1640s when Recife was ruled by religiously tolerant Holland. With the end of Dutch rule in 1654 many of Recife's Jews fled to New Amsterdam (later New York), and the synagogue was confiscated and sold. Over the centuries, evidence of the temple all but disappeared. In the late 1990s, traces of the old synagogue were discovered in the form of a *mikve,* or ritual bath. The reconstructed building is not a replica of the original but more a monument that honors the Jewish community in Recife. The museum tells the history of Jews in Recife. On the ground floor you can see the remains of the 17th-century temple. The second floor houses the actual synagogue; and if you aren't familiar with Jewish traditions, a guide will show you around. The third floor has a TV lounge where staff will play an excellent documentary (with English subtitles) on the history of the Jews in Recife and the rebuilding of the synagogue. Expect to spend an hour.

Rua do Bom Jesus 197, Bairro do Recife. ☏ **081/3224-2128.** Admission R$4. Tues–Fri 9am–5pm; Sun 2–6pm. Bus: Conde de Boa Vista.

Forte das Cinco Pontas/City Museum ★★
Perhaps the most curious thing about the "Fort of Five Points" is that it has only four. The original Dutch fort built in 1630 had five, but the Portuguese leveled that fort and rebuilt in their traditional four-pointed style. The fort today has been wonderfully restored; you can wander the ramparts at will. Unfortunately, the city has crept out far past this once seaside installation, leaving the fort outflanked by a freeway. The excellent city museum, which takes up two wings of the fort, has two rooms devoted to the Dutch period, including a wealth of maps and drawings of the early colony.

Largo dos Cinco Pontas, Bairro de São José. ☏ **081/3224-2812.** Admission R$3. Tues–Fri 9am–5pm; Sat–Sun 1–5pm. Bus: São Jose.

Oficina Cerâmica Francisco Brennand ★★★
Although somewhat off the beaten track, this ceramics workshop/museum is more than worth the price of admission. The lifelong work of ceramic artist Francisco Brennand is on display at this sprawling estate/workshop. Although famous for some notorious giant phallic sculptures, his collection is so much more and includes thousands of sculptures, tiles, and pieces of ceramic art, as well as drawings. His work is beautifully displayed in several buildings as well as various outdoor settings. The Burle Marx garden was designed by the landscape artist himself and decorated with Brennand statues. *Tip:* The restaurant inside the gift shop serves excellent regional dishes and juices.

Propriedade Santos Cosme e Damião s/n, Várzea. ☏ **081/3271-2466.** www.brennand.com.br. Admission R$4. Mon–Thurs 8am–5pm; Fri 8am–4pm. Taxi recommended.

Note: All in the Family

Don't confuse the Oficina Cerâmica Francisco Brennand with the nearby Instituto Ricardo Brennand, Alameda Antônio Brennand, Várzea (☏ **084/2121-0352;** Tues–Sun 1–5pm; R$5)! This large museum contains mostly European art, such as a large collection of weapons and an exhibit on the 17th-century Dutch occupation of Recife. Out of the two, the ceramics museum is by far the most fascinating.

> **Tips** **Where to Find the Most Spectacular Views**
>
> No one should miss the view from the front steps of the **Igreja da Sé** in Olinda. Look out over the red-tile roofs and church towers of the old Portuguese city, the white sand, and bright blue of beach and sea. In Old Recife it's worth taking the elevator to the top of the restored **Malakoff Tower,** an old astronomical observatory on Praça Artur Oscar. It's only four stories high, but the view of the low-rise old city is still good. Open Tuesday through Sunday from 3 to 8pm; free admission.

ESPECIALLY FOR KIDS

Veneza Water Park (Kids)   Just 10km (6¼ miles) north of Olinda, the Veneza Water Park is a great place to frolic. There are slides, pools, a wave pool, water volleyball, Jacuzzis, and many other types of aquatic entertainment. Special family and group rates apply.

Praia Maria Farinha. ℂ **081/3436-6363** or 3436-8845. www.venezawaterpark.com.br. Individual ticket R$60 adult, child 1–1.4m (3–4½ ft.) tall R$46, free for children under 1m (3 ft.), family pass (2 adults and 2 children) R$140. Daily 10am–5pm. Bus: to Maria Farinha beach. Catch bus from Terminal Av. Dantas Barreto across from N.S. do Carmo church. A taxi from Olinda would cost approximately R$25–R$30.

ORGANIZED TOURS

BOAT TOURS   Recife's location on a series of islands makes a boat tour a good way to see the town. **Catamaran Tours** (ℂ **081/3424-2845;** www.catamarantours.com.br) offers sightseeing tours on broad, comfortable catamarans. Historical tours of 1½ hours show the old city. Full-day tours head up the coast to visit Fort Orange and the beaches of Itamaracá. The city tour costs R$25; the 6-hour Itamaracá tour costs R$35. Children ages 6 to 10 pay half price. Tours depart from Avenida Sul, 50m (164 ft.) past the Forte Cinco Pontas. Exact departure times depend on the tide. Call ahead to confirm.

BUS TOURS   **Luck Viagens** (ℂ **081/3366-6222;** www.luckviagens.com.br) offers a range of bus tours. There's a 4-hour city tour that shows the highlights of Recife and Olinda (R$30). There's also a full-day tour to Itamaracá island, R$75, where the Dutch built Fort Orange in 1631, and day trips to Porto de Galinhas for the best beaches and snorkeling in the area, R$65.

OUTDOOR ACTIVITIES

Wreck divers will be in heaven; at least 15 wrecks are diveable and within easy reach. For excursions contact **Projeto Mar,** Rua Bernardino Pessoa 410, Boa Viagem (ℂ **081/ 3326-0162;** www.projetomar.com.br). Two dives including all the gear cost R$130; a nondiving companion pays R$30.

5 SHOPPING

In Recife's downtown neighborhood of Santo Antônio, the streets around the **Pátio São Pedro** and in between **Avenida N.S. do Carmo** and **Rua Primeiro de Março** are all jampacked with little shops. Some of the alleys are so narrow that they resemble Asian street markets. The best time to explore is weekdays during office hours; in the evening this part of town is deserted. Larger, more fashionable stores are located just on the other side of the Duarte Coelho Bridge on **Avenida Conde da Boa Vista.** There are large modern malls located out in Boa Viagem as well as the new Paço Alfandega, the restored 18th-century Customs hall in Old Recife.

Olinda's historic downtown also offers prime shopping: Two markets sell excellent souvenirs (see below), and you will find many more galleries and interesting shops once you start to explore the winding streets.

GIFTS & SOUVENIRS   In Olinda there are two excellent markets for local handicrafts. **Mercado Eufrasio Barbosa** (also called Mercado Varadouro) is located in the former Customs house at Sigismundo Gonçalves s/n (✆ **081/3439-1415**). Open Monday through Saturday from 9am to 6pm, this market has great souvenirs at reasonable prices. Up the hill close to the Praça João Alfredo is the **Mercado Ribeira,** Bernardo Vieira de Melo s/n (✆ **081/3439-2964**), which is open daily from 9am to 6pm. The merchants there specialize in religious arts, paintings, woodcarvings, and regional crafts.

Olinda is jampacked with studios and ateliers that are open to the public. If you like colorful artwork, visit **Imaginário,** on the Rua Bispo Coutinho 814 ✆ **081/3439-4514**). This large store displays a comprehensive collection of high-quality local artwork. More expensive but worth checking out is the **Estação Quatro Cantos,** Rua Bernardo Vieira de Melo 134 (✆ **081/3429-7575**).

In Recife, a great shop with above-average souvenirs is **Paranambuco,** Rua do Bom Jesus 215 (✆ **081/3424-1689**). The best spot for picking up local crafts is in the **Casa da Cultura** (p. 322), Rua Floriano Peixoto s/n, next to the train station (✆ **081/3224-2850**). Those who are staying in Boa Viagem can visit the large crafts market on the Praça Boa Viagem; Monday through Friday 3 to 11pm and 8am to 11pm on weekends.

MALLS & SHOPPING CENTERS   **Shopping Center Recife,** Rua Padre Carapuceiro 777, Boa Viagem (✆ **081/3464-6123**), is a modern mall; all buses heading downtown stop here. Farther along the beach where Boa Viagem becomes Piedade there's another pleasant mall, **Shopping Center Guararapes,** Av. Barreto Menezes 800, Piedade (✆ **081/3464-2211;** www.shopping-guararapes.com.br). The most beautiful mall is the **Shopping Paço Alfandega,** Cais da Alfandega 35, Recife Antigo (✆ **081/3419-7500;** www.pacoalfandega.com.br). Housed in the restored 18th-century Customs building, this is one of the city's prime shopping destinations. The bookstore **Livraria da Cultura** has an above-average selection of English-language books. Malls are open Monday through Friday from 10am to 10pm and Saturday from 10am to 8pm.

MARKETS   A bustling fruit-and-vegetable market in a lovely old iron-and-glass building, the **Mercado de São José,** Praça Dom Vital s/n, Santo Antônio (no phone), is a great place to browse. Vendors sell locally made hammocks, baskets, ceramics, and lace. Hours are Monday through Saturday from 6am to 5:30pm and Sunday from 6am to noon.

---

6 RECIFE & OLINDA AFTER DARK

THE PERFORMING ARTS

Recife's prime theater venue is the elegant **Teatro Princesa Isabel,** Praça da República s/n (✆ **081/3224-1020**), built in 1850. Just reopened after years of renovations, it's worth checking local listings for events held at this lovely venue.

Recife's historic downtown has undergone a complete face-lift, becoming a cultural and entertainment district. Activities center on the **Rua do Bom Jesus;** lined with at least 15 bars and restaurants, this is one of the best places in town Thursday through Saturday and Sunday afternoons. Free concerts add to the entertainment, and on Sunday there's a street market.

One of Old Recife's nicest bars is the **Arsenal do Chopp,** Praça Artur Oscar 59, at the corner of Rua do Bom Jesus (© 081/3224-6259). Most tables are spread out over the sidewalk; for a quiet spot grab a table inside. Another great venue downtown is the **Patio de São Pedro.** Beautifully restored, this square now hosts a variety of free outdoor music events. On Tuesday, locals gather for the Terça Negra, an event with Afoxé music, a style with heavy African influences. On Saturday, a younger crowd gathers to dance to *maracatu, mangue beat,* and other regional tunes. Events start at 7 or 8pm.

In Boa Viagem the favorite nightspot is **Polo Pina,** a few square blocks around Pina beach and Avenida Herculano Bandeira de Melo. Recently named the best bar in Recife, **Biruta Bar,** Rua Bem-te-Vi, Pina (© 081/3326-5151; www.birutabar.com.br), features a large veranda looking out over the ocean, making it the perfect setting for a special date. On Thursday, Biruta presents blues bands and on Friday there's *forró.* **Tip:** This bar is not easy to find and the small detour cuts through a bit of a dark corner at the end of Pina. We recommend taking a taxi.

For more live music head out to the **Uk Pub,** Rua Francisco da Cunha 165, Boa Viagem (© 081/3465-1088; www.ukpub.com.br). Open Tuesday through Sunday, there is live music (samba, rock, pop) every night except Wednesday. It also has a great beer menu with more than 50 specialties. Cover ranges from R$5 to R$15. The best night for dancing at **Boratcho,** Av. Herculano Bandeira 513 (inside Galeria Joana d'Arc) (© 081/3327-1168; www.boratcho.com.br), is Thursday when DJs play a variety of music, including samba-rock and regional rhythms. **Boteco,** Av. Boa Viagem 1660, Boa Viagem (© 081/3325-1428), is a popular destination almost any night of the week. Serving the best beer in town, the bar is often packed with locals stopping by for an ice-cold chopp. Open daily.

Olinda is not known for its nightlife; most folks settle for wine and conversation over a late-night supper. One of the best spots for a drink or a stroll is the **Alto da Sé.** On weekends (Sun evening especially), locals flock to this prime view spot to grab a drink or some food from the many stalls and just hang out for an impromptu outdoor party. Olinda's cutest hole-in-the-wall spot is **Bodega de Veio,** Rua do Amparo 212 (© 081/3429-0185). It's just a small bar/old-fashioned convenience store where people put their drinks on the counter or sit on the sidewalk. Saturday features live *forró.* Note that this is not a late-night place; last round is at 11pm. Another laid-back fun spot is the **Casa Maloca,** Rua Amparo 183 (© 081/3429-7811), an art gallery and restaurant with, at the very back, the lovely **Bar Olindita.** Guests can sit at a long bar or funky tables scattered about the room. The best spots are on the patio, looking out toward Recife.

GAY & LESBIAN BARS   **Metropole,** Rua das Ninfas 125, Boa Vista (© 081/3423-0123; www.metropoledance.com.br), is a huge gay club for men with a bar, dance floor, and video room. Regular shows include go-go boys, strippers, and drag queen performances; it's open Friday and Saturday from 10pm until at least 5am. Another popular gay venue is the **SPTZ,** Rua Joaquim Nabuco 534, Graças (© 081/3223-9100). Open Tuesday through Sunday, from 6pm until at least 4am.

7 A SIDE TRIP TO PORTO DE GALINHAS ★★★

70km (43 miles) S of Recife

Porto de Galinhas is one of the nicest beach destinations in all the Northeast. Known for its crystal-clear water, its lovely beaches, and the tidal pools that form in the nearby reefs, the region is a perfect water playground for adults and children. Development has been kept resolutely small-scale. With no high-rises, the town is mostly small pousadas and low-rise hotels. The town has perhaps six streets: enough for a dozen restaurants, a bank, some surf shops, and some beachside bars. Colorful *jangadas* (one-sail fishing rafts) come and go all day, and the beachside restaurants and cafes are packed with people soaking up rays.

ESSENTIALS

Getting There

BY CAR   Porto de Galinhas is just 70km (43 miles) south of Recife, an hour by car. From Recife take BR-101 south until it connects with the PE-60, then look for the turnoff for the PE-38 that leads to Porto de Galinhas. Exits are well marked but the road has heavy traffic and is in very poor shape. If you are just driving to Porto de Galinhas it's not worth renting a car.

BY BUS   Buses to Porto de Galinhas leave daily from 6:30am to 6:30pm every hour on the half-hour from the Avenida Dantas Barreto bus terminal in downtown Recife (across from N.S. do Carmo). Tickets are R$8 and the drive takes 2 hours. A number of these buses go through Boa Viagem and all stop at the airport on the way. From Porto de Galinhas to Recife buses depart daily once an hour from 5:40am to 5:40pm.

BY TAXI   A taxi from Recife airport or downtown will cost from R$80 to R$120 for up to four people and luggage. The price will depend on your bargaining skills. Don't go on the meter, though. Agree on a price beforehand. Many hotels and pousadas can book a taxi service for you at a reasonable rate.

Getting Around

A minivan shuttle runs from the village to Pontal do Cupe and back, stopping by request at hotels and pousadas along the way. Departures are more or less half-hourly from the Petrobras station on Rua da Esperança (R$2).

There are taxi stands *(ponto de taxi)* for dune buggy taxis in the village and halfway down the beach in front of the Armação do Porto hotel. One-way fare is R$15 from the village to either Cupe or Maracaípi beach. If you're planning to spend time at Maracaípi beach, it's a good idea to set a pickup time with your driver as it can be difficult to find a buggy to return. A full-day rental, including driver and up to four passengers, costs R$120 to R$150. In the unlikely event you can't find a buggy, contact **APCI Buggy** (*©* **081/3552-1930**).

Visitor Information

The **tourist office** is at Rua da Esperança 188 (*©* **081/3552-1480;** www.porto degalinhas.com.br). Hours are Monday through Friday from 9am to 5pm, Saturday and Sunday from 9am to 3pm.

FAST FACTS **Banco do Brasil,** Via Porto de Galinhas s/n (℃ 081/3552-1855), has a 24-hour ATM. The bank is open Monday through Friday from 10am to 4pm. There is also a **Banco 24 Horas** ATM inside the Petrobras Gas Station, open from 7am to 10pm. Internet access is available at **Pé No Mangue,** Rua da Esperança 101, second floor; cost is R$9 per hour.

EXPLORING THE TOWN

The main attraction at Porto de Galinhas is the beach, whether you swim, surf, snorkel, or snooze. **Cupe** beach stretches 4km (2½ miles) north from town; it's wide and warm, punctuated at either end by small coral reefs full of fish. Around the point in the other direction, **Maracaípi** beach regularly hosts national and international surfing competitions. Even better, thanks to a nature reserve backing most of the beach, about the only development on Maracaípi is a few *barracas* selling fruit juice and fresh-steamed crab. And if the beach gets dull, you can take nature hikes, trips to nearby islands, or dive trips to offshore reefs.

BUGGY TOURS The best way to see the local beaches is to head out in a buggy. The most popular tour is the Ponta-a-Ponta, which takes you to four different beaches from the northern end of Porto de Galinhas to the southern end. A full-day trip costs R$120 to R$150, leaving from your hotel or from Avenida Beira Mar at the main square. Contact the buggy drivers at ℃ 081/9192-0280. You can fit four in a buggy, but you'll likely have more fun with just two or three so that one person doesn't have to sit in the boring passenger seat. Included in the tour is a stop at the mangroves of Pontal do Maracaípe. This protected nature reserve is home to several species of sea horses that live among the roots of the mangroves. Small rafts (R$8 per person) take up to 10 people on a gentle float through the mangroves. The guide will don a mask and dive into the water looking for sea horses, which he captures in a glass jar. You get a good look at the little critters before they are returned to their natural habitat.

Outdoor Activities & Adventure Sports

Porto de Galinhas is all about the sea and the best way to explore the region is by boat.

Tip: Inquire about the tides upon arrival as many tours are timed according to the tide tables.

BOAT TOURS One of the best ways to see the region is by boat, and **Cavalo Marinho** (℃ 081/3552-2180 or 8811-7393; www.catamaracavalomarinho.com.br) offers daily **catamaran tours** to offshore islands and isolated beaches such as Ilha de Santo Aleixo and Praia dos Carneiros. Both are to the south of Porto de Galinhas and offer plenty of nice scenery, swimming, and snorkeling (R$90 per person, children 11 and under, R$60).

DIVING Though most people opt for tide-pool snorkeling, a number of dive sites are in the surrounding area. Contact **Porto Point,** Praça Av. Beira Mar s/n (℃ 081/3552-1111), for charters. Expect to pay R$90 to R$150, including gear and two dives. Beginners can do an introductory lesson and dive for R$110. No credit cards.

SNORKELING The coast just off Porto de Galinhas is lined with coral reefs. At low tide they form natural pools that trap hundreds of tropical fish. With a mask and snorkel you just hop in and check out what's doing. The water is warm year-round (24°C–28°C/75°F–82°F) and the pools are never more than a few meters deep. Most pools are close enough that you could swim out, but another fun way of getting close is by taking a *jangada*. These one-sail fishing rafts are the boat of choice for local fishermen. For R$8 per person, local sailors will take you out to the best pools, and provide you with a mask, snorkel, and some bread to lure in the fish. Check the tide tables at your hotel for low tide; early morning is best if you want to avoid crowds.

If you want to play in the water by yourself, you can rent a **mask/snorkel** combo for R$15 per day at **Porto Point,** Av. Beira Mar s/n (*©* **081/3552-1111**). They also offer tours to the natural pools in the daytime (R$30) or at night (R$40), including equipment and guide.

WHERE TO STAY

Porto de Galinhas is gloriously free of sun-blocking high-rises. Accommodations are mostly in small family-run pousadas and a few larger cabana-style hotels. In recent years, a number of bigger resorts have sprung up, but even these have been kept to a reasonable scale and are located farther from the town. Prices are very reasonable, especially considering the high quality of the accommodations. In town, you'll be close to the action—too close perhaps in high season, when the streets are packed until the wee hours. Staying a bit farther out will ensure a peaceful night's sleep and access to a quiet stretch of beach. The disadvantage is that it's a R$10-to-R$15 taxi or buggy ride every time you come to town. However, most tours will provide pickup and drop-off at your hotel. In high season, particularly on the weekend, reservations for accommodations are required.

Very Expensive

Nannai Beach Resort ★★★   For those who like resort-style hotels, Porto de Galinhas has a wide variety, ranging from the loud and ostentatious (Enotel) to the generic (Beach Class) or bland (Summerville). The only one worth the splurge is the Polynesian-style luxury Nannai. This exclusive resort consists of 49 bungalows and 42 apartments set among lush tropical gardens. The apartments are not worth the money (small and somewhat noisy), but the bungalows are fantastic and perfect for a relaxing vacation. Each has a private swimming pool and beautiful rustic furnishings and decorations. The resort also offers a large, sprawling pool complex and a host of activities such as tennis, pitch and putt golf, beach soccer and beach volleyball, snorkeling, sailing, kayaking, and children's activities.

Muro Alto, Km 3, Ipojuca, Porto de Galinhas, PE. *©* **081/3552-0100.** Fax 081/3552-1474. www.nannai. com.br. 91 units. High season R$945 apt, R$1,585 bungalow; low season R$695 apt, R$1,170 bungalow. Rates include breakfast and dinner. Extra person add 25%. Children 2 and under stay free in parent's room; children 3–12 10%. AE, MC, V. Free parking. **Amenities:** Restaurant; bar; health club; large outdoor pool; room service. *In room:* A/C, TV/DVD, minibar.

Expensive

Tabapitanga ★★★ **(Kids)**   A member of the high-end Roteiros de Charme Association, the Tabapitanga offers gorgeous accommodations on the beach just 5km (3 miles) from the village. Rooms are in one- or two-story chalets. All rooms are spacious and decorated with colorful artwork. Furnishings are luxurious; the rooms have king-size beds, large flatscreen TVs, and big bathrooms. Each room also comes with a veranda or deck with patio furniture and a hammock. The least expensive rooms are set in the lovely garden. The newer two-story units offer a view of the ocean but the best units are the *frente mar* rooms with unobstructed views. The hotel has beach service as well as a great pool. A fabulous breakfast is included. Lunch and dinner are optional. The attentive staff is happy to book a variety of reasonably priced tours.

Praia Pontal do Cupe, Porto de Galinhas, PE. ✆ **081/3552-1037.** Fax 081/3552-1037. www.tabapitanga. com.br. 43 units. High season R$375–R$430 double ocean view, R$300–R$345 double garden or partial ocean view; low season R$360 double ocean view, R$260–R$290 double garden or partial ocean view. Children 10 and under stay free in parent's room. AE, DC, MC, V. Free parking. **Amenities:** Restaurant; bar; outdoor pool; smoke-free rooms. In room: A/C, TV, fridge, minibar.

Village Porto de Galinhas ★★ ⓚ︎ⁱᵈˢ   The Village Porto de Galinhas is right on the beach and offers good value for families traveling with kids. The facilities have recently been renovated and the swimming pools and leisure area have been expanded. All rooms are very spacious and, although not luxurious, pleasantly furnished with comfortable, firm beds and splashes of color. Every room has a balcony with a hammock, overlooking the garden and swimming pool, with a partial ocean view. Even though the hotel has almost 200 rooms, it has an intimate feel. The pool area can be a bit noisy in the daytime; not for couples seeking a romantic retreat.

Praia do Cupe 4.5 km, Porto de Galinhas, PE. ✆ **081/3552-2945.** Fax 081/3552-1673. www.villageporto degalinhas.com.br. 194 units. High season R$425 double garden or partial ocean view; low season R$320 double garden or partial ocean view. Extra person add R$80–R$100. Children 5 and under stay free in parent's room. AE, DC, MC, V. Free parking. **Amenities:** Restaurant; bar; outdoor pool. In room: A/C, TV, fridge, minibar.

Moderate

Pousada Canto do Porto ★★   Pousada Canto do Porto is a great option for those who want to stay close to the village without being smack in the middle of things. Only a 5-minute walk from the main square, the pousada is set right on the beach. The nicest room is the deluxe oceanview panorama suite, which offers primo views from its large wraparound veranda. The king-size bed and Jacuzzi are just icing on the cake. The more affordable master suites have a partial ocean view and a veranda. The only rooms to avoid are the small standard ones. These are set back behind the pousada in an annex and have no verandas or views.

Av. Beira Mar s/n, Porto de Galinhas, PE. ✆ **081/3552-2165.** www.pousadacantodoporto.com.br. 20 units. High season R$260–R$290 deluxe or master double, R$200 double; low season R$170–R$190 deluxe or master double, R$140 double. Children 6 and under stay free in parent's room, 7 and over R$30. AE, DC, MC, V. Free street parking. **Amenities:** Restaurant; bar. In room: A/C, TV, fridge, minibar, no phone.

WHERE TO DINE

Beijupirá ★★★ Ⓕⁱⁿᵈˢ SEAFOOD   One of the best restaurants in the region, Beiju-pirá is also one of the loveliest, set in a garden aglow with hundreds of candles and lan-terns. Everything about this restaurant is creative and fun; from the funky decorations to the phenomenally inventive kitchen. The dishes combine either seafood or chicken with a range of interesting spices that blend together sweet and savory. The *beijupitanga* com-bines grilled *beijupirá* fish with a sweet-tart *pitanga* sauce (a sour cherrylike fruit) and a side of rice with cashew nuts. The *camarulu* is a generous portion of grilled prawns with a glazing of cane molasses and rice with passion fruit. For non–seafood eaters there's the *Galinhatrololo,* grilled chicken breast with bacon and banana, served with cashews, rai-sins, and rice. Desserts are sweet and luscious; the all-time favorite (and we tried several) is the *cajuendy,* made with dried cashew fruit topped with cheese and honey, flambéed with cinnamon liquor.

Rua Beijupirá s/n, Porto de Galinhas. ✆ **081/3552-2354.** www.beijupira.com.br. Reservations required on weekends and holidays. Main courses R$26–R$38. AE, DC, MC, V. Daily noon–midnight.

Peixe na Telha ★★ SEAFOOD   Peixe na Telha offers one of the best patios in town, with a terrific view of the beach and fleet of *jangadas*. The menu offers regional fish and seafood dishes such as *moqueca* stews with coconut milk and red palm oil and *bobó de camarão,* a thick stew made with prawns and manioc. The house special is the *peixe na telha* (fish served on a red roof tile) accompanied with rice and *pirão,* a purée made of seafood broth, manioc flour, and spices. Bring your friends because this dish serves at least three people.

Av. Beira Mar s/n, Porto de Galinhas. © **081/3552-18323.** Main courses R$38–R$52. Most dishes serve 2–3 people. AE, DC, MC, V. Daily 11am–10pm.

Picanha Tio Dadá CHURRASCO   Turf on the surf. Tio Dadá serves up fine Brazilian *picanha* on a great patio, just steps from the beach. The meat comes to your table sizzling on its own grill. Vegetables include potatoes, french fries, and *farofa.* There are other cuts besides *picanha,* plus lamb, chicken, fish, and seafood. Forget the wine list—there isn't one—just order a cold Brazilian chopp.

Rua da Esperança 167, Porto de Galinhas. © **081/3552-1319.** Main courses R$27–R$38. MC, V. Daily 11:30am–midnight.

Natal

Natal is a city built on sand. It blows across the city streets and piles up in drifts like snow. It lines the city's beaches, landscapes the city's parks, and piles up in towering dunes that form the city's picture-postcard views. Outside Natal, the sand spreads in mountainous dune ranges that stretch for miles.

Perhaps because sand is not the most fertile of foundations, Natal has been an oft-overlooked sandlot of a city for much of its history, noticed by the powers that be only when some other power tried to take it away.

The Portuguese founded a town on the banks of the Potengi River to drive out the French. To hold the territory, the Portuguese built the Fort of the Three Kings in 1599. The fort's foundation was celebrated with a Mass on December 25, 1599, and so the city was named Natal (the Portuguese word for Christmas). After that, the Portuguese pretty much ignored the place. By 1757 there were a whopping 120 buildings in the area, among them a church and a prison.

Natal first came to American notice in the early 1940s. The U.S. had just entered the war against the Axis powers and sleepy little Natal—the closest land base to North Africa—was suddenly a place of world significance. Franklin Roosevelt paid a visit, meeting with Brazilian President Getulio Vargas to work out the details of Brazil's war effort. There's a famous picture of the two presidents, riding through the streets of Natal in an open limousine, sand barely visible beneath the wheels.

Natal became the "Trampoline of Victory," an air and communications base providing cover for the Allied invasion of North Africa. According to local folklore, one lasting legacy of that period was a new Brazilian dance step. Wanting to make the American airmen welcome, the Brazilians invited them to local dances, and developed a simplified two-step rhythm the rather club-footed Yanks could handle. They titled the dances "For All." The dance spread all over the Northeast, while the name got shortened to *forró*.

Only recently, as Europeans and Americans began to discover the true value of sand and endless sunshine, has Natal really begun to blossom.

Why visit? Natal offers endless beaches for surfing and tanning, and dunes, glorious dunes, hundreds of feet high and spilling down to within inches of the seashore. To the north of the city the dunes pile up so high that locals have begun to make use of them in a wide variety of peculiar and original sports. You can ski or toboggan down them, rope-slide from the top of them, camel ride across them, and buggy ride over, up, down, and all around them.

North and south of Natal the beaches stretch for hundreds of miles, dotted now and again with fishing villages and only lightly touched by tourism. The preferred method of transport in these regions is by dune buggy. Offshore—at places up the coast such as Maracajaú—wide coral reefs lie in shallow water, great places to spend a day snorkeling.

And everywhere you go, north and south and in the city, there's sand.

1 ESSENTIALS

2,068km (1,285 miles) NE of Rio de Janeiro, 2,312km (1,436 miles) NE of São Paulo, 873km (543 miles) NE of Salvador

ARRIVING

BY PLANE Azul (✆ 084/3003-2985; www.voeazul.com.br), **Gol** (✆ 0300/115-2121), **TAM** (✆ 084/4002-5700), and **Webjet** (✆ 0300/210-1234; www.webjet.com.br) offer flights from major cities in Brazil. Flights arrive at **Aeroporto Augusto Severo,** Rua Eduardo Gomes s/n (✆ 084/3087-1200), 15km (9¼ miles) from downtown and just a few miles from Ponta Negra beach. Taxis to Ponta Negra cost R$30 to R$35, and to downtown or Praia dos Artistas, about R$40.

BY BUS Long-distance buses arrive at the **Rodoviaria,** Av. Cap. Mor Gouveia 1237, Cidade Esperança (✆ 084/3232-7312), about 5km (3 miles) from downtown and Ponta Negra beach.

CITY LAYOUT

A small downtown aside, Natal is a postwar creation; in many ways it resembles the modern, sprawling cities of the southwestern United States. The original city was founded on a peninsula between the Potengi River and the Atlantic Ocean. Just off the tip of the peninsula, where ocean and river meet, the original **Forte de Reis Magos** still stands, a forgotten bit of the 17th century. Where the fort's causeway touches the mainland the 21st century begins—a modern ocean-side boulevard that under various names runs from here south through the length of the city and out into the dunes beyond. About 3km (1¾ miles) south of the fort the street is called **Avenida Presidente Café Filho,** and the surrounding neighborhood is **Praia dos Artistas.** From here the road climbs a bit, becoming **Avenida Governo Silvio Pedroso,** then **Via Costeira,** which runs for some 9km (5½ miles) between the ocean and a vast nature preserve called **Parque das Dunas.** There are a number of five-star resort hotels nestled in between the parkway and the ocean. Where the park ends, the road swings away from the beach a bit and becomes **Avenida Engenheiro Roberto Freire,** the backbone of the city's best beach neighborhood, **Ponta Negra.** Avenida Roberto Freire itself is a busy and rather ugly artery, but the streets leading off it down to the ocean are quiet and pleasant, lined with hotels and pousadas. The beach itself has no traffic at all along this stretch, just a pedestrian walkway and sea wall, punctuated by beachside kiosks or *barracas.* About two-thirds of the way along the lovely 3km (1¾-mile) beach, Avenida Roberto Freire drops downhill to the waterfront and becomes **Avenida Erivan França,** a busy beachside boulevard lined with pubs, restaurants, and nightclubs that runs all the way to **Morro do Careca,** the 117m (390-ft.) sand dune that overlooks the beach.

Going the other direction from the Forte dos Reis Magos, along the banks of the **Rio Potengi,** you pass the abutments of a bridge that leads across the river to **Genipabu.** The road then climbs and enters **Centro,** also called the **Cidade Alta,** the commercial heart of Natal. Centro has a few old squares—the **Praça André de Albuquerque** and **Praça Sete de Setembro.** The main street is **Avenida Rio Branco.**

North of Natal, the dunes and beaches begin as soon as you cross the river. This area is called the **Litoral Norte** (north coast). The first settlement is the former fishing village of **Genipabu,** about 25km (16 miles) north of downtown. Genipabu caters to tourists who swim at the beach and buggy and climb through the surrounding dunes.

South of Ponta Negra there's a long stretch of beaches known as the **Litoral Sul** (south coast), with something for everyone. **Búzios** beach is excellent for snorkelers, while **Barra de Tabatinga** is a surfer's hot spot. Capping off the string of south coast beaches is **Praia da Pipa,** a gorgeous stretch of sand and a destination in its own right.

GETTING AROUND

BY BUS   The bus is a quick way to travel from Ponta Negra to Centro and vice versa. In Ponta Negra, buses run along Estrada Ponta Negra. For downtown, look for buses marked CENTRO or CIDADE ALTA. There are two routes. Buses with signs saying VIA COSTEIRA follow the coast as far as Praia dos Artistas and then cut across to Centro. Other CENTRO buses use the inland route along Avenida Prudente de Morais or Avenida Hermes da Fonseca. To return to Ponta Negra, any bus that says PONTA NEGRA or VIA COSTEIRA will do. You enter buses through the front. Fare is R$2.20.

BY TAXI   You can hail a taxi anywhere. To reserve one, phone **Cidade Taxi–24 H** (✆ **084/3223-6488**) or **CoopTax** (✆ **0800/842-255** or 084/3205-4455). A taxi from Ponta Negra to downtown will cost about R$25 to R$30.

BY CAR   Natal is an easy city for driving; streets are wide, traffic is light, and parking not much of a problem. You can rent a car to explore up or down the coast, but you'll have more fun if you rent a buggy with a driver who can take you off-road.

VISITOR INFORMATION

Setur, the state tourism agency, has an English-language website at www.brasil-natal.com. br. Natal's **airport** has a tourist information center (✆ **084/3643-1811**) in the arrivals hall, open daily from 9am to 5pm. The **main tourist information center** is in Natal's Centro de Turismo (p. 342), Rua Aderbal de Figueiredo 980, Petrópolis (✆ **084/3211-6149**).

(*Fast Facts*)   **Natal**

Car Rental   Rental companies include **Localiza** (✆ **0800/979-2000**); **Avis** (✆ **0800/725-2847**); **Unidas** (✆ **084/3643-1222**); and **Hertz** (✆ **084/3087-1428**).

Currency Exchange   Near Centro are **Banco do Brasil,** Av. Rio Branco 510, Cidade Alta (✆ **084/3216-4500**), which also has a 24-hour ATM; and **Sunset Cambio,** Av. Hermes da Fonseca 628, Tirol (✆ **084/3212-2552**). In Ponta Negra is **Banco do Brasil,** Rua Dr. Ernani Hugo Gomes 2700 (✆ **084/3219-4443,** next to the Praia Shopping.

Hospital   In an emergency, go to **Monsenhor Walfredo Gurgel,** Av. Salgado Filho s/n, Tirol (✆ **084/3232-7500**).

Weather   Natal lies just 3 degrees from the Equator, so temperatures hover around 28°C to 34°C (82°F–93°F) year-round. In winter (June–Aug) it tends to rain a bit more. In summer you get 15 regular hours of sunshine a day.

2 WHERE TO STAY

High season in Natal is December through February, and then again in July during Brazil's winter holidays. Outside of this period there are substantial discounts.

PONTA NEGRA

Within Natal's city limits Ponta Negra beach is your best option. It's wide, clean, and busy, with good waves for surfing. On the waterfront, a pleasant walkway runs past a number of beachside restaurants and *barracas*. Many of the city's better restaurants are located in the area, and the cafes, bars, and nightclubs of Natal's Alto de Ponta Negra nightlife area are a 5-minute cab ride away.

Very Expensive

Manary Praia Hotel ★★★   The best and most romantic place to stay in Natal, the Manary is done up like a Spanish hacienda, with old dark beams, red-tile roofs, and large cool flagstones on the floor. The location is premium, with a large deck and two pools (one regular, one for children) facing out over the sea. In the rooms are king-size beds with top-notch linens, plus unique and tasteful furnishings. All rooms come with a balcony and ocean view. For the 15 standard rooms, the view is a bit oblique, but still lovely. The nine deluxe rooms have a straight-on view. The luxury suite has a broad veranda facing out over the water plus a Jacuzzi whirlpool. Breakfast here is memorable—fresh regional fruit, eggs, pancakes, and lots of regional delicacies. The restaurant here is one of the city's best.

Rua Francisco Gurgel 9067, Praia de Ponta Negra, Natal 59090-050 RN. *(€)*/fax **084/3204-2900.** www. manary.com.br. 24 units. High season Nov–Feb and July R$525–R$850 double; low season R$425–R$715 double. Extra person add 25%. Children 6 and under stay free in parent's room. AE, DC, MC, V. Free parking. Bus: Ponta Negra. **Amenities:** Restaurant; bar; 2 outdoor pools; room service. *In room:* A/C, TV, hair dryer, minibar, Wi-Fi.

Expensive

Visual Praia Hotel ★   Located right on the sea wall in Ponta Negra, the Visual Praia is kind of a mini–resort hotel, complete with a large pool deck, and waterside bar and children's play area. If it's really a full-service resort you want you'll be better off at the Ocean Palace (see below), but the advantage of the Visual Praia is its location on Ponta Negra beach and its cheaper price tag. Rooms are comfortable and beautifully furnished with blond wood and marble desktops. All but two have a view that ranges from partial to a full ocean view. Breakfast is served on the beachfront patio.

Rua Francisco Gurgel 9184, Praia Ponta Negra, Natal 59090-050 RN. *(€)* **084/3646-4646.** www.visualpraia hotel.com.br. 136 units. High season R$360–R$430 double. Extra person add R$75. 30% discount in low season. Children 5 and under stay free in parent's room. AE, DC, MC, V. Free parking. Bus: Ponta Negra. **Amenities:** Restaurant; bar; outdoor pool; children's pool and playground; sauna. *In room:* A/C, TV, fridge, minibar.

Moderate

Soleil Suite Hotel   The Soleil offers excellent value for the money, with generously sized rooms and a location that's just a 3-block walk from the beach. The least expensive room, the Suite Luxo, comes with tile floors, a firm queen-size bed, couch, and small kitchen table (no desk space, however); a kitchenette unit comes with fridge and hot plate and utensils, plus a balcony but with no view of the sea. The next step, the Suite Master, costs about 30% more and is identical except the balcony offers an ocean view. One step up again, the Suite Master Plus offers a couch that folds out to a double bed, plus French doors separating bedroom from sitting room. It's not a bad option if you have kids, but otherwise not worth the price. Another, more expensive family option is the top-floor Suite Executiva, which has two bedrooms plus a full kitchen and sitting/dining area and a sizable veranda. The hotel has a small pool and a children's wading pool, neither of which is nice enough to tempt anyone away from the beach.

Rua Elia Barros 70, Praia Ponta Negra, Natal 59090-140 RN. *(€)* **084/4005-5959.** www.soleilhotel.com.br. 31 units. High season Nov–Feb and July R$175–R$295 double. Low season 30% discount. Extra person add 25%. Children 5 and under stay free in parent's room. AE, DC, MC, V. Free parking. Bus: Ponta Negra. **Amenities:** Restaurant; outdoor pool and children's pool. *In room:* A/C, TV, fridge, minibar.

The Via Costeira parkway makes a lovely setting for a hotel but there are a couple of drawbacks. Though you get outstanding views and unmatched isolation, the ocean is rougher, the beach rockier, and there is nothing within walking distance, so you're looking at a cab ride any time you want to leave the hotel.

Expensive

Ocean Palace Beach Resort & Bungalows ★★   Rooms here are good but not outstanding (nowhere as nice as in the Manary Praia), but what makes the Ocean Palace stand out are its amenities: a vast multilevel pool complex featuring two large pools and another five wading or whirlpools, some with waterside bar, all on a lovely palm-shaded deck looking out over the crashing waves of the Atlantic. In addition, there's a children's playroom, saunas, spa, top-quality weight room, tennis court, squash court, and more. The basic room layout is long and narrow, with a pleasant modern decor, hardwood floors, firm queen-size beds, and smallish bathroom. Avoid the Superior rooms, which face back over the parking lot. The Luxo rooms face out over the ocean. Luxo rooms on floors one to three feature a balcony just large enough for a deck chair or hammock. On floors four and five, the balconies shrink to standing room only. Floor six houses the hotel's 20 suites, which aren't much bigger than the other rooms. The seaside bungalows are comfortable on the inside, but packed in trailer park–style in two rows along the waterfront. If you do opt for these, the *bungalôs suite* offers an unobstructed front-row view of the ocean.

Av. Via Costeira, Km 11, Praia de Ponta Negra, Natal 59090-001 RN. ℂ **0800/844-144** or 084/3220-4144. Fax 084/3219-3081. www.oceanpalace.com.br. 315 units. R$700–R$1,100 double; R$850–R$1,200 bungalow. Extra person add 25%. Children 6 and under stay free in parent's room. Off-season discounts (20%) Sept–Oct and Mar–May. AE, DC, MC, V. Free parking. Bus: Via Costeira. **Amenities:** 2 restaurants; 2 bars; exercise room; 2 Jacuzzis; 5 outdoor pools; room service; sauna; smoke-free floor; small spa; tennis court. *In room:* A/C, TV, hair dryer, minibar.

Serhs Natal Grand ★★★   The Natal Grand is the newest and most luxurious of the top-end resorts strung along the ocean-side Via Costeira. Rooms are bright and modern, with tile floors, clean bright bathrooms, and balconies facing out over the sea. Superior rooms feature firm double beds and a small writing desk. Family rooms feature two double beds but no extra space, making them a little squished. Junior suites are more spacious, with a separate sitting room and fold-out couch, making them a good option for those traveling with kids. A couple looking to splurge, however, should opt for a Senior or an Executive Suite, which feature an outdoor terrace with Jacuzzi built for two. Recreational facilities are top-notch. The entire front deck is one sprawling wavy pool, dotted here and there with little Jacuzzi islands. The sports center offers volleyball, soccer, and basketball, while the Japanese spa offers a full range of massage and beauty treatments. The Kid's Club features a kids' pool and indoor children's recreation area. On the beach, there's volleyball and soccer, plus beach chairs and a lifeguard service. The hotel's **Tapiro Grill** is excellent.

Av. Via Costeira 6045, Praia de Ponta Negra, Natal 59090-001 RN. ℂ **0800/702-2411** or 084/4005-2000. Fax 084/4005-2001. www.serhsnatalgrandhotel.com. 396 units. R$315–R$647 double; R$600–R$1,200 suite. Extra person add 25%. Children 6 and under stay free in parent's room. Off-season discounts (20%) Sept–Oct and Mar–May. AE, DC, MC, V. Free parking. Bus: Via Costeira. **Amenities:** 4 restaurants; 3 bars; exercise room; 3 Jacuzzis; 4 large outdoor pools and children's pool; room service; sauna; Japanese spa. *In room:* A/C, TV, hair dryer, Internet, minibar.

Natal's better restaurants have been steadily gravitating toward Ponta Negra. Better yet, quite a few have been moving off the busy and ugly Avenida Engenheiro Roberto Freire and into locations with more charm and better views. That said, there are still a couple of worthwhile places in other parts of the city.

PONTA NEGRA

Camarões BRAZILIAN/SEAFOOD   With a name that means "prawns," it's not hard to guess the house specialty. *Papa Jerimum* prawns are served in a pumpkin, while *Champagne* prawns are sautéed with butter in a champagne-and-apple sauce. The *Espaguete de Camarão* features spaghetti with sautéed prawns in a creamy cognac sauce. Portions are generous enough for two. The location offers a view over Ponta Negra beach.

Av. Engenheiro Roberto Freire 2610, Ponta Negra. ℂ **084/3209-2425.** www.camaroes.com.br. R$30–R$65 for 2. AE, DC, MC, V. Daily 11:30am–3:30pm and 6:30pm–midnight. Free parking. Bus: Ponta Negra.

Camarões Potiguar BRAZILIAN/SEAFOOD   Like its parent, this new hatchling of the long-established Camarões restaurant features a menu heavy on prawns and seafood, but while the mother ship is more international, here the emphasis is on local ingredients such as pumpkin, coconut, and cashews and traditional Brazilian recipes. The architecture of this smaller space matches the locally flavored menu—large, bright, and charmingly rustic, with flashes of sophistication.

Rua Pedro Fonseca 8887, Ponta Negra. ℂ **084/3209-2425.** www.camaroes.com.br. R$26–R$65 for 2. AE, DC, MC, V. Daily 11:30am–3:30pm and 6:30pm–midnight. Free parking. Bus: Ponta Negra.

Manary ★★ SEAFOOD/NORDESTINO   The best place in Natal for seafood, the Manary offers top-notch ingredients, good service, and a lovely setting—an outdoor patio overlooking the sea wall and beach of Ponta Negra. Among the most tempting menu items are the *misto fritti di mare* (a platter of grilled lobster, shrimp, octopus, mussels, fish, and grilled vegetables) and the *bobó de camarão*, a rich shrimp-and-pumpkin stew, flavored with dendê oil and coconut milk and served hot in a hollowed-out pumpkin shell. A memorable dish. The wine list is short but serviceable.

Rua Francisco Gurgel 9067, Praia de Ponta Negra. ℂ/fax **084/3204-2900.** www.manary.com.br. Main courses R$28–R$58. AE, DC, MC, V. Daily 11am–4pm and 7–11pm. Bus: Via Costeira.

VIA COSTEIRA

Tábua de Carne ★ (Value) BRAZILIAN   Perched on a cliff top overlooking the beach on the Via Costeira, Tabua offers carnivorous dining at its lip-smacking best. The menu includes treats such as lamb and pork chops and even fish (though for seafood you really should go elsewhere) as well as the traditional favorites of *carne de sol* (salted sun-dried beef, a specialty of Northeastern Brazil) and chicken and good old Brazilian *picanha* (sirloin steak). For the decision-shy, there's the Tábua, a wood platter containing *picanha*, sausage, chicken, and *carne de sol*. Dishes here are made for two and would easily feed three. The *picanha* melts delicately on the tongue. The wine list is of minimal length and questionable quality. Stick to beer or fruit juice by the half-liter earthenware jug. Tábua has a second location in Ponta Negra, Av. Engenheiro Roberto Freire 3241 (ℂ **084/3642-1236**), though on a viewless stretch of the road.

Av. Senador Dinarte Mariz 229. ℂ **084/3202-7353.** www.tabuadecarne.com.br. Main courses R$18–R$32 for 2. AE, DC, MC, V. Daily 11:30am–11pm. Bus: Via Costeira.

Mangai ★★ (Value) NORDESTINO   This is the ideal place to get a taste of Nordestino food, the cuisine of Brazil's dry, cattle-raising Northeast. Mangai offers a self-serve smorgasbord featuring over 40 different Nordestino dishes, some of them traditional favorites, others wonderful inventions made using traditional local ingredients such as *carne-de-sol* (sun-dried beef), *macaxeira* (sweet manioc root), *farofa* (ground, roasted manioc root), beans, and rice. The *carne-de-sol na nata* (butter-sautéed sun-dried beef) is a house specialty. Mangai is truly best for a long, leisurely lunch. After you indulge, take advantage of the hammocks slung on the patio and settle in for a snooze. Alcoholic beverages are not available, but there is an excellent array of fruit juices.

Av. Amintos Barros 3300 (on the inland road, about halfway btw. Ponta Negra and downtown). (C) **084/3206-3344.** www.mangai.com.br. Reservations not accepted. Main courses R$15–R$25. MC, V. Daily 11am–10pm. Bus: Centro.

---

4 EXPLORING

Natal isn't really the place to stroll around looking at pretty old buildings, but then odds are you're here for sun and surf and some time on those famous dunes. So enjoy the beach in **Ponta Negra** for a day, then rent a buggy and *bugreiro* (driver) and buggy up the beach and explore. Check out the monster dunes at **Genipabu.** Head farther north and snorkel the reefs off **Maracajaú.** Try *aerobunda* where you slap your behind into a rope-sling and slide *com emoção* into a rainwater lagoon. Or try sand boarding (see "Outdoor Activities," below), tobogganing, dune hiking, or camel riding. Finish the day watching a glorious sunset over the dune tops.

And don't forget the side trips. If buggying gets in your blood, do a second day trip south to the lovely, small beachside town of **Praia da Pipa.** Or for the ultimate in buggy adventure, do a 4- or 7-day expedition from Natal 800km (500 miles) north to Fortaleza. Or strike inland and see the otherworldly rock formations at **Cariri,** and 120-million-year-old footprints in the **Vale dos Dinossauros (Valley of the Dinosaurs).**

TOP ATTRACTIONS IN THE CITY

Forte de Reis Magos ★★   Every old fort should look like this, standing proud and alone on the reefs off the tip of the city, separated from the mainland by a sand spit that at high tide sinks below less than a meter (3 ft.) of water. Inside, the function of each room is carefully spelled out in Portuguese and English. The small museum in the officers' quarters has disappointingly little on the fort itself, which saw action when the Dutch occupied it between 1633 and 1654. From the ramparts, the view of the city's skyscrapers and the dunes to the north can't be beat.

Av. Pres. Café Filho s/n. (C) **084/3202-9006.** Admission R$3. Daily 8am–4:30pm. No public transit.

Museu Câmara Cascudo ★ (Kids)   The only noteworthy museum in Natal covers the natural history and anthropology of the state of Rio Grande do Norte. See the original *jangada* rafts made by local fishermen and walk through a fisherman's hut. Visit reproductions of Rio Grande do Norte's archaeological sites, and descend in a cave to see how these digs are carried out. Delve into a life-size salt mine. There are no English signs, but the displays are self-explanatory and great for kids. Allow 1 hour.

Av. Hermes da Fonseca 1398, Tirol. (C) **084/3215-4192.** www.mcc.ufrn.br. Admission R$3. Tues–Fri 8–11am and 2–5pm; Sat–Sun 1–5pm.

On the highlands above the port is the **Cidade Alta.** This commercial part of the city has a number of pretty squares that make for a fine stroll. There are actually four separate squares here, all melded together: **Praça João Maria, Praça Andrè de Albuquerque, Praça João Tibuco,** and **Praça Sete de Setembro.** The largest is the **Praça André de Albuquerque,** dominated by the **N.S. da Apresentação.** Just across from the church is the **Memorial Câmara Cascudo** ★, Praça Andre de Albuquerque 30 (ⓒ **084/3211-8404;** free admission; Tues–Sun 8am–5pm). One of Natal's most beloved sons, **Câmara Cascudo** (1898–1986), was a journalist, professor, founder of the federal university of Rio Grande do Norte, and author of the dictionary of Brazilian folklore; most Brazilian kids have read his stories of *jangadas,* fishing nets, and bumba-meu-boi (a peasant harvest festival involving the death and miraculous resurrection of a sainted bull). The memorial shows the life of Cascudo and artifacts portraying the folklore he wrote about. It also houses all of his works and his personal library. The museum is very small, but admission is free and the proud staff (one of them is Cascudo's grandson) love receiving foreign visitors.

PARKS

The 1,376-hectare (3,400-acre) **Parque das Dunas** ★ occupies a huge swath of Natal, from the edge of downtown all the way to Ponta Negra. There's a visitor center in the park headquarters, Av. Alexandrino de Alencar s/n (ⓒ **084/3201-3985;** www.parquedas dunas.rn.gov.br), from which you can set off on guided walks through the dunes. Entrance is R$2, which includes the trail fee. Walks depart at 8, 8:15, and 8:30am, and at 2, 2:15, and 2:30pm. Participants must sign up in advance.

TOP EXCURSIONS FROM NATAL

The best way to access the terrain north and south of Natal is by buggy, but if you'd prefer a more comfortable 4×4, contact **Cariri Ecotours** (ⓒ **084/9928-0198;** www. caririecotours.com.br). The company offers single and multiday 4×4 trips south to Praia da Pipa and north to Maracajaú. The 1-day trip to Praia de Pipa includes a trek through the Atlantic rainforest and dolphin spotting at Enseada do Madeiro.

BUGGY EXPEDITIONS ★★★ Untouched dunes, beaches, and lagoons stretch away north and south of Natal for hundreds of kilometers. The best way to see them in all their glory is to rent a dune buggy with a driver, and head out to explore. Prices average around R$200 for a full day for up to four people. If you're in a group of fewer than four, you can pay R$50 per person and the tour operator will make up a full group, but it's better to pay the full rental; if you have the buggy to yourself, it stops and goes at your command.

The classic north-coast day trip crosses the Potengi River and proceeds up to **Genipabu,** where you have the chance to ride camels or slide down the dunes on a sand board (see "Outdoor Activities," below). While here, make sure you don't miss the **Extreme Dune Park,** an enclosed area with monstrous dunes of shifting sands, some of them hundreds of feet high. Only licensed drivers are allowed in, and once inside they make use of buggy and terrain to provide a natural roller coaster ride. Among the stunts they'll treat you to are the Wall-of-Death and the Sheer Vertical Descent. Make sure your sun hat has a string. *Tip:* Make sure that your tour includes a stop in the Extreme Dune Park, and that your driver is licensed to enter.

From there you float your buggy across a small stream on a tiny raft and carry on up the beach to **Jucumã,** where you can try your bum at *aerobunda* (see "Outdoor Activities,"

below). From there, it's another 35km (22 miles) of wide, flat sand until you get to **Mara-**
cajaú, a magic spot where at low tide you can snorkel in the natural pools in the offshore
coral reef. (Buggy tours normally time their arrival to coincide with low tide.) At day's end,
the driver returns to Genipabu to see the sun set over the dunes.

The classic south-coast trip heads south along 55km (34 miles) of coast and sand to
Praia da Pipa (p. 344). Along the way, buggies pass along numerous gorgeous beaches,
among them **Búzios, Barra de Tabatinga, Barreta,** and **Tibau do Sul.** It's possible with
a full-day tour (about R$150 per buggy) to stop in at several and still enjoy time at Pipa
itself. Better still, head south and spend a few days in the Pipa, a pretty former fishing
village of small pousadas and cobblestone streets.

There are lots of buggy drivers in Natal. An excellent longtime *bugreiro* who speaks
English is **Kadmo Donato** of **Buggy & Cia** (*©* **084/9982-3162** or 9416-2222; www.
buggyecia.com.br). There is also **Buggy Tour** (*©* **084/3086-2258**) and the **APBCA,** the
buggy owners' association (*©* **084/3225-2077**).

SNORKELING THE POOLS AT MARACAJAU ★★ The coast north and south of
Natal is hemmed with shallow coral reefs that make for perfect snorkeling. Nowhere are
they more impressive than in Maracajaú, about 1 hour north of Natal. A stop here is often
included in a full-day buggy tour; if not, ask your buggy driver. You need to time your
arrival with low tide. From the beach a boat takes you about 7km (4¼ miles) offshore to a
moored diving platform. At low tide the honeycomb of reefs forms natural pools rich in
tropical fish and other marine life. As the maximum depth is about 4.8m (16 ft.), these
pools can be easily explored with just a mask and snorkel. The water is crystal clear and
warm. Expect to spend at least 2 hours. Contact **Maracajaú Diver,** Praia de Maracajaú
(*©* **084/3261-6200** or 9983-4264 mobile; www.maracajaudiver.com.br; snorkeling R$60
adults, R$35 children 6–12, free for children 5 and under; check the website for departure
times, which are tide related). *Note:* If you've never been scuba diving, Maracajaú Diver
offers a "baptism" dive. The water is never deeper than 4.8m (16 ft.), so there is no danger
of sinking or decompression. The cost is R$150 for 15 to 20 minutes.

OUTDOOR ACTIVITIES

AEROBUNDA JACUMÃ The perfect antidote to the high-tech world of the American
amusement park. At Lagoa Jacumã, Litoral Norte, Km 35, there's a dune about 60m
(200 ft.) high. At its foot is a big lake. At the top of the dune someone has hammered in
three telephone poles to make a scaffold, then attached a thick rope from there to another
peg on the far side of the lake. To execute the *aerobunda,* you slide your butt into a sling
hanging from a pulley attached to the line. The attendant then lets go. You scream down
toward the lake, gathering speed and momentum. Splash! Huge fun. Back on shore
you hop into a rickety iron cart, wave your arm at the guy on the donkey engine, and he
hauls you up the dune so you can go again. R$5 per ride; open daily from 8am to 5:30pm
(*©* **084/3228-2402**).

JANGADA RIDING A *jangada* is a narrow raft made of balsa wood (or Styrofoam)
equipped with a single triangular sail. The little boats are used by local fishermen, who
will also happily take you to the reefs or for a quick sail. You'll find them along Genipabu
beach. Cost is R$15 per person for an hour or so.

SAND BOARDING Sand boarding is worth doing as long as you believe that no sport
is too stupid to be tried at least once. As snowboarders, we felt obligated. Turns out that
sand doesn't glide nearly as well as snow. But then, I guess you can't snowboard in a

bikini. If you're interested, look for the entrepreneurs at the south end of Genipabu beach; cost is R$5 per trip (less, if you bargain).

SURFING   The beach at Ponta Negra is a great place to learn to surf. Waves vary from small and manageable to large and exciting. For instructors try the **Escola de Surf Ponta Negra** (✆ **084/8806-1087**), in a tent about halfway along Ponta Negra beach. Lessons cost R$25 per hour.

5 SHOPPING

GIFTS & SOUVENIRS   Natal has transformed its former prison complex into a crafts market, **Centro de Turismo de Natal,** Rua Aderbal de Figueiredo 980, Petrópolis (✆ **084/3211-6218**). About 40 crafts shops are now housed in the cells and provide easy one-stop shopping for local crafts. Look for the handmade white-linen tablecloths and the small painted clay figurines depicting characters from folk dances. There are also hammocks, woodwork, and sweets made with sugar cane and coconut. The market is a steep 15-minute walk from Praia dos Artistas. Open daily from 9am to 7pm. The **tourist information booth** at the entrance is open daily from 9am to 5pm.

In Praia dos Artistas is the large **Centro de Artesanato da Praia dos Artistas,** Av. Pres. Cafe Filho s/n (✆ **084/3202-4971**). Dozens of booths are packed with souvenir T-shirts and trinkets as well as some nice local handicrafts. Open daily 10am to 10pm. A **smaller evening crafts market** takes place Thursday to Sunday from 6 to 10pm, near the waterfront at Rua Conselheiro de Medeiros in Praia dos Artistas.

In Ponta Negra, the Shopping do Artesanato Potiguar, Av. Engenheiro Roberto Freire 8000 (✆ **084/3219-3207;** www.shoppingartesanatopotiguar.com.br), features more than 180 shops packed with souvenirs and local handicrafts.

Located in the nightlife area of Alto de Ponta Negra, **Alma Brasiliera,** Rua Dr. Manoel de Araújo 130 (✆ **084/3219-3174**), has a fine selection of local crafts, though prices are higher than at the downtown Centro de Turismo.

SHOPPING MALLS   The midsize **Praia Shopping,** Av. Engenheiro Roberto 8790 (✆ **084/3219-4323;** www.praiashopping.com.br), is at the edge of Ponta Negra, a short cab ride back in the direction of downtown. Shops are open Monday through Saturday 10am to 10pm, Sunday 3 to 9pm.

6 NATAL AFTER DARK

THE PERFORMING ARTS
Teatro Alberto Maranhão   This is Natal's main theater and concert stage. Check the calendar for upcoming events. During box-office hours you can have a peek inside this renovated colonial building. Open Tuesday to Sunday from 8am to 6pm. Praça Augusto Severo 251. ✆ **084/3222-3669.** www.teatroalbertomaranhao.rn.gov.br.

CLUBS & BARS
Natal's nightlife centers on the Ponta Negra neighborhood. The waterfront **Avenida Erivan França,** at the far end of **Ponta Negra beach,** is a busy and bustling area of restaurants and bars. Some years back much of the activity consisted of Brazilian women

looking to sell their services to male charter tourists from Europe, but the area has since been cleaned up substantially.

The prime nightlife scene, the **Alto de Ponta Negra,** is located on the heights on the far side of the busy Avenida Roberto Freire (near the corner of the Rua Dr. Manoel. A.B. de Araújo). It's a pleasant and strollable enclave of cafes and creperies, knickknack shops, bars, and discos.

Alto de Ponta Negra

If you're in the mood for a snack, **Casa de Taipa,** Rua Dr. Manoel A.P. de Araújo 130A (📞 **084/3219-5798**), offers tapioca pancakes with over 40 different types of filling, not to mention coffee and homemade ice cream. Open daily 5pm to midnight.

Rastapé   This place has a young and pretty crowd, a small stage pumping out live *forró,* and lots and lots of dancing. Open Wednesday to Saturday, 7pm to 2am. Rua Aristides Porpino Filho 2198. 📞 **084/3219-3164.** www.rastapenatal.com.br. R$15 cover.

Sgt. Pepper's Rock Bar   This is a comfortable bar offering casual dining and live rock 'n' roll. The menu offers burgers and pizza, while the small stage serves up covers and original local rockers. Open Tuesday through Saturday 7pm to 2am. Rua Manoel A. B. Araujo 130. 📞 **084/9113-6377.** www.sgtpeppers.com.br. No cover.

Taverna Pub   Natal's favorite bar is in the basement of an ersatz castle–cum–youth hostel. It's low and dark and cramped, with bad acoustics and terrible sightlines, and it's packed Thursday to Sunday with 20- to 30-year-olds who come for the DJs or local bands playing live on the tiny stage. Open daily 11pm to 4am. Rua Chile 25, Ribeira. 📞 **084/3236-3696.** www.tavernapub.com.br. Cover R$15.

Via Costeira

Cervejaria Via Costeira   This big, sprawling brewpub features tasty brews on tap and a credible cold-cut buffet. The crowd is a friendly mix of Brazilians and foreigners. Open daily 6pm to 1am. Via Costeira 4197A. 📞 **084/3202-1089.**

Downtown

Forró com Turista   If you want to dance *forró* but don't quite know the steps, this is the place to come. Held every Thursday night (10pm–2am) in the courtyard of the Centro de Turismo, it has numerous instructors on hand to show you how it's done. The dance is a simple fast two-step. Rua Aderbal Figueiredo 980, Petrópolis (Centro de Turismo). 📞 **084/3211-6218.** www.forrocomturista.com.br. R$15 cover.

7 SIDE TRIPS FROM NATAL

THE NATAL-TO-FORTALEZA BUGGY ADVENTURE ★★★

If you can't get enough of the coast, consider the 800km (500-mile) adventure trip from Natal north along the beach to Fortaleza. On the way you'll visit 85 beaches and countless dunes, some of them massive monsters seemingly transplanted from the Sahara. You'll pass through petrified forests and pocket deserts, float your buggy across dozens of little estuaries on rafts, and visit little fishing towns that rarely, if ever, see tourists.

Buggy & Cia, Rua Guilherme Tinoco 1274 (📞 **084/9982-3162;** www.buggyecia. com.br), specializes in this trip. The expedition takes 4 days, usually starting from Natal.

Cost is R$2,500 total for two people, including accommodations and breakfast plus buggy and driver. The owner, Kadmo Donato, speaks English. The website has a map of the route and some excellent photos showing what's in store on the trip. Note that with Buggy & Cia, a driver does the driving. Some find this a disappointment, but it actually allows you to spend your time drinking in the views from the prime buggy spot—above the roll-bars on the back of the buggy's chassis. The only company that allows guests to drive is the Paris-based firm **Brésil Aventure** (www.bresil-aventure.com). Brésil Aventure's Natal-to-Fortaleza trips take 2 weeks, and their guides speak French only.

HEADING INLAND

The hot, dry interior of the Northeast hides some outstanding natural beauty: indigenous petroglyphs, rock formations as odd and impressive as many in Utah, and fossilized dinosaur footprints 120 million years old. Based in Natal, **Cariri Ecotours** (✆ 084/9928-0198; www.caririecotours.com.br) specializes in trips into this Brazilian outback. The 4-day, 3-night Valley of the Dinosaurs package strikes inland for the far west of Paraiba state. Here, 120 million years ago, dozens of species of dinosaurs lived at the edge of a great shallow lake. The tracks they left in the mud of this lake filled with sediment and became fossilized; hundreds of tracks in this area remain clearly visible to this day. The tour then swings back toward the Cariri region, to the vast and magic rock formations at **Lajedo do Pai Mateus** and **Saca de Lã.** The expedition finishes up with a visit to one of Brazil's most significant archaeological sites, a stone wall inscribed with the symbols and artwork of a now-vanished prehistoric people. Trips can be made by either air-conditioned Land Rover or comfortable air-conditioned Fiat Duplo. Cost per person for groups of two to four people is R$2,600 by Fiat, R$2,955 by Land Rover. Meals are included, and accommodations are at some of the finer pousadas of the interior.

PRAIA DA PIPA

Located 80km (50 miles) south of Natal by road (or a mere 55km/34 miles if you go by beach buggy), **Praia da Pipa** is one of the most picturesque beaches in all of Brazil's Northeast. This former fishing village was discovered by surfers back in the 1970s, and developed in the decades since, without yet overdeveloping. Though the town does fill up on weekends and holidays, Pipa's pousadas and hotels remain manageable and small-scale. The village of Pipa is well known for its nighttime activity, and for the cafes and restaurants lining its cobblestone streets. Down on the long crescent beach are natural pools and reefs for snorkeling. Traveling south from Pipa one finds a string of beaches— **Praia do Amor, Praia do Moleque**—snuggling at the foot of tall coastal cliffs. The cliff-top drive from Pipa to **Praia do Cunhaú** is spectacular.

Pipa does not lack for places to stay. Two that stand out are **Toca de Coruja,** Av. Baía dos Golfinhos 464 (✆ 084/3246-2226; www.tocadacoruja.com.br), a Roteiro de Charme property that features luxurious self-contained chalets with private outdoor Jacuzzis, all in a large private garden; and **Sombra e Agua Fresca,** Rua Praia do Amor 1000 (✆ 084/3246-2144; www.sombraeaguafresca.com.br), located on the cliff overlooking the bay, which offers large rooms and two pools with terrific views.

Excellent restaurants in Pipa include the seafood-oriented **Cruzeiro do Pescador,** Rua da Gameleira s/n (✆ 084/3246-2026; www.cruzeirodopescador.com.br; daily 7–11:30pm), and for more varied fare, **Agua na Boca,** Av. Baía dos Golfinhos 687 (✆ 084/3246-2641; Mon–Sat 6pm–midnight).

Fortaleza

The capital of the state of Ceará is best known for its beaches: glorious long stretches of sand interrupted by impressive red cliffs, palm trees, dunes, and lagoons that offer a true tropical playground.

The most beautiful and isolated beach is the small settlement of Jericoacoara, a tiny coastal community with streets of sand, set by itself on the edge of its own tiny desert of Sahara-like dunes.

The first Portuguese settlers arrived in the area in 1603. The colony grew slowly, beset by attacks by Tabajara Indians, and later by the Dutch, who in 1637 drove out the Portuguese, only to be slaughtered in turn by the Tabajara. When the Portuguese regained control of the area in 1654, they gave the substantial five-pointed Dutch fort a new name: Fortaleza Nossa Senhora de Assunção.

Fortaleza remained a backwater until the 1820s, when Brazilian ports opened to foreign ships and the city began to grow into an important seaport, shipping cotton, cattle, and leather from the interior to England. In response to the resulting growth, city governors in 1875 commissioned a plan to transform Fortaleza into a tropical Paris, a city of broad boulevards overlaying a functional grid. Some of this early city planning can still be seen, but much was overwhelmed in the 1950s and 1960s as migrants from the state's dry and drought-stricken interior flocked into the city, practically doubling Fortaleza's population.

Now about two million strong, the city's major industries are cashews and tourism. The Dutch, Portuguese, and other foreigners land en masse on the beaches armed with cameras and bathing suits and a fierce will to enjoy the sun and ocean. What sets Fortaleza's beaches apart from Brazil's other 8,000km (4,960 miles) of coastline is the combination of colorful cliffs and huge sand dunes, best seen in nearby communities such as Morro Branco, Canoa Quebrada, and Jericoacoara.

For first-time visitors with limited amounts of time, the best plan of attack is to spend no more than a day in the city itself, then head out to explore the nearby beach communities, particularly the isolated Sahara-like dunes of Jericoacoara.

1 ESSENTIALS

2,169km (1,348 miles) NE of Rio de Janeiro, 2,358km (1,465 miles) NE of São Paulo, 1,019km (633 miles) N of Salvador.

ARRIVING

BY PLANE **Azul** (① 085/3003-2985; www.voeazul.com.br), **Gol** (① 0300/115-2121 or 0800/704-0465; www.voegol.com.br), **TAM** (① 0800/570-5700 or 085/4002-5700; www.tam.com.br), and **Webjet** (① 0300/210-1234; www.webjet.com.br) have daily flights to most major cities in Brazil. Flights arrive at **Aeroporto Internacional Pinto Martins,** Av. Senador Carlos Jereissati 3000 (① 085/3392-1030). Taxis cost about R$30 to the beaches or downtown.

BY BUS Long-distance buses arrive at the **Rodoviaria São Tomé,** Av. Borges de Melo 1630, Fatima (① 085/3256-2100).

Located just east of the Ceará River, the commercial heart of Fortaleza—called **Centro**—is small and quite walkable, though the traffic and sidewalk vendors can make the area seem a little hectic. Starting from the waterfront **Fortaleza N.S. de Assunção,** Centro stretches inland in a grid pattern. Following the **Avenida General Sampaio** or **Rua Barão do Rio Branco** will lead you straight into Fortaleza's main shopping area, centered on a large city square, the **Praça José de Alencar.** Smaller but lovelier is the **Praça dos Leões,** just 1 block east of the Rua Barão do Rio Branco at the corner of **Rua São Paulo.**

An easy stroll to the east of Centro leads to the ocean-side neighborhood **Praia de Iracema,** the first of a long string of beaches that line the waterfront, linked together by the **Avenida Beira Mar.** (Unfortunately, none of the urban beaches is recommended for bathing.) Iracema isn't so much a beach as an ocean-side party place. You'll find lots of restaurants and bars along the sea wall, and the **Rua Tabajaras** that runs parallel to the beach is packed with nightlife and restaurants. A kilometer (½ mile) or so east of Iracema you come to the next beach neighborhood, **Meireles.** From here onward, the beachside boulevard becomes a pleasure to walk. It's wide and shaded with plenty of kiosks for a drink or snack. The nightly **crafts market** (p. 354) always attracts large crowds. **Mucuripe** is the next neighborhood to the east of Meireles. At the end of Mucuripe beach there's a small colony of fishermen and a seafood market where the catch of the day is sold fresh off the boat. Farther east, the coastline curves south. The bend contains an industrial area of little interest to visitors, but once around the bend you come to **Praia do Futuro,** the only urban beach where the water is clean enough to swim. The beach becomes quite lively on Thursday evenings and on weekends but can be deserted during the week.

GETTING AROUND

BY BUS Most visitors use the bus to go between the beach neighborhoods and Centro. In Meireles or Mucuripe you catch the bus on the street parallel to the beach (Av. Abolição). Look for buses marked MEIRELES, CAÇA E PESCA, or GRANDE CIRCULAR. Fare is R$1.80.

BY TAXI Taxis can be hailed almost anywhere. To order a taxi, call **Disk Rádio Táxi Ceará (© 085/3243-8111), Taxi Fortaleza 24 Horas (© 085/3254-5744),** or **Rádio Táxi Cooperativa (© 085/3261-4181).** Fare from Meireles to Centro is about R$20, and from Mucuripe to Praia de Iracema about R$24.

BY CAR Within Fortaleza a car is more a nuisance than a pleasure: Traffic is chaotic and parking a challenge. However, to explore outlying beaches on your own, a car is ideal.

VISITOR INFORMATION

The state tourism agency **Setur** has a Portuguese-only website at www.setur.ce.gov.br. Fortaleza's **airport** has a tourist information center (© 085/3477-1667) in the arrivals hall, open daily 6am to 11pm, where you can pick up a good free map of the city. The **state tourist information center (Centro de Turismo do Ceará)** is downtown at Rua Senador Pompeu 350 (© 085/3101-5508), open Monday through Saturday from 9am to 6pm, Sunday 8am to noon.

ACCOMMODATIONS ■
Holiday Inn **6**
Hotel Luzeiros **8**
Ibis Hotel **7**
Othon Palace
Fortaleza **12**
Villa Mayor **9**

DINING ◆
Lautrec/Ryori
Sushi Lounge **15**
Moanna
Gastronomia
e Arte **13**
Piaf **14**
Pulcinella **10**

ATTRACTIONS ●
Centro Cultural
Dragão do Mar **5**
Centro de Turismo **2**
Fortaleza de Nossa
Senhora da Asunção **3**
Mercado Central **4**
Night Market **11**
Teatro José de Alencar **5**

(Fast Facts **Fortaleza**

Car Rental You can rent from **Localiza** (✆ **085/3477-5050**); **Avis** (✆ **0800/725-2847**); **Unidas** (✆ **085/3477-5038**); and **Hertz** (✆ **085/3477-5055**).

Currency Exchange **Banco do Brasil,** Rua Barão do Rio Branco 1515, Centro (✆ **085/3254-2122**), also has an ATM. Another option is **HSBC,** Av. Monsignor Tabosa 1200, Praia de Iracema (✆ **085/3219-2436**). Both open Monday to Friday 10am to 4pm.

Hospital For medical needs, go to **Hospital Batista Memorial,** Av. Padre Antônio Tomás 256, Aldeota (✆ **085/3224-5417**).

Internet Access **Cyber Café,** Av. Abolição 2655, Meireles (✆ **085/3242-5422**), charges R$4 per hour; daily 9am to 10pm. **Cyberoom Rent a Computer,** Av. Mons Tabosa 937, Centro (✆ **085/3219-6731**), also charges R$4 per hour; Monday to Saturday 10am to 8pm.

Weather Fortaleza has a pleasant sunny climate year-round, dry and tropical with an average temperature of 28°C (82°F); a cooling ocean breeze often takes the edge off the heat.

2 WHERE TO STAY

THE BEACHES

Most people stay within walking distance of the city beaches. The boulevards are pleasant and there are plenty of restaurants and activity along the oceanfront. The best of the beach neighborhoods is **Meireles,** which has a wide, well-trod boulevard by the sand, dotted with pleasant little kiosks where you can have a beer or fresh cool coconut. Meireles also has plenty of restaurants, vendors, and an excellent nightly crafts market. The beach neighborhood closest to downtown is **Praia de Iracema.** The beach here is wide and somewhat forlorn, but hotels in this neighborhood have the advantage of being within walking distance of Fortaleza's downtown attractions and the city's prime nightlife enclave. This is not the place for early sleepers. Farther east, **Mucuripe** is just a continuation of Meireles and runs all the way to a fishing colony at the eastern end of the beach.

Iracema
Expensive

Holiday Inn ★★ The Holiday Inn offers deluxe accommodations on the waterfront, just a few minutes' walk from the nightlife attractions in Praia de Iracema. The rooms are divided into deluxe, superior deluxe, and suites. All are spacious and have ocean views; even the most basic room is large with a queen-size bed, big desk, a pullout couch, and a separate vanity area next to the bedroom. The superior deluxe rooms are larger and come with a veranda and a king-size bed. The furnishings are in great shape and the amenities are top-notch—the pool is especially nice.

Av. Historiador Raimundo Girão 800, Praia de Iracema, Fortaleza 60165-050 CE. ✆ **085/3455-5000.** Fax 085/3455-5055. www.holidayfinn.com. 273 units. R$195–R$260 double. 20%–30% discounts in low season. Extra person add 30%. Children 5 and under stay free in parent's room. AE, DC, MC, V. Free parking. **Amenities:** Restaurant; bar; outdoor pool; room service; sauna; smoke-free rooms. *In room:* A/C, TV, hair dryer, Internet, minibar.

Moderate

Ibis Hotel (Value) Located a block off the water, the Ibis is the best value in Praia de Iracema. Like all Ibis hotels, the concept is basic: All rooms are identical and accommodations are comfortable but plain. Each room has a nice firm double bed, a desk, and closet space. Bathrooms are equally frills-free but are modern and spotless and come with showers only. The hotel amenities are kept to a minimum to reduce the operating costs. The optional breakfast is R$11.

Rua Dr. Atualpa Barbosa Lima 660, Praia de Iracema, Fortaleza 60060-370 CE. ℂ **0800/703-7000** or 085/3219-2121. Fax 085/3219-0000. www.accorhotels.com.br. 171 units. R$110 double. Extra person R$18. Children 5 and under stay free in parent's room. AE, DC, MC, V. Free parking. **Amenities:** Restaurant. *In room:* A/C, TV, fridge.

Meireles

Expensive

Hotel Luzeiros ★★★ This is as hip as Fortaleza gets. Nearly all rooms have balconies, all have king-size beds and are elegantly furnished. White tile floors, quality linens, and high-end finishes add an air of luxury to even the most basic rooms. The prime rooms have a full ocean view *(frente mar);* the standard rooms have partial views *(vista mar).* (**Tip:** Rooms ending in 5 do NOT have balconies; avoid these.) The swimming pool, business center, and fitness room are excellent.

Av. Beira Mar 2600, Meireles, Fortaleza 60165-121 CE. ℂ **085/3486-8585.** Fax 085/3486-8587. www.hotelluzeiros.com.br. 202 units. R$290 double, partial ocean view; R$360 double, full ocean view. Extra person add about 25%. Children 6 and under stay free in parent's room. AE, DC, MC, V. Free parking. **Amenities:** Restaurant; bar; outside pool; limited room service; smoke-free rooms. *In room:* A/C, TV, Internet, minibar.

Othon Palace Fortaleza ★★ (Value) This place has a great location and even better value. The hotel's rooms are all beautifully furnished in blue and yellow tones and come with king-size beds; the bathrooms are done in beautiful marble. The smaller, standard rooms do not have balconies but do look out over the ocean. The deluxe rooms all have balconies and are spacious—definitely worth the price difference. The executive suites are twice the size of a deluxe apartment, with two bathrooms, a separate sitting room, and balcony, perfect for families.

Av. Beira Mar 3470, Meireles 60165-121 CE. ℂ **0800/725-0505** or 085/3466-5500. Fax 085/3466-5501. www.othonhotels.com. 110 units. R$214 standard double; R$260 deluxe double; R$430 executive suite double. Extra person add about 25%. Children 4 and under stay free in parent's room. AE, DC, MC, V. Free parking. **Amenities:** Restaurant; bar; fitness center; large outdoor pool; room service; sauna; smoke-free rooms. *In room:* A/C, TV, fridge, hair dryer, Internet, minibar.

Moderate

Villa Mayor ★ (Kids) Just 2 blocks from the main beach and the nightly crafts market, this small hotel consists of several cute "heritage" low-rise buildings centered around a pleasant courtyard with a swimming pool and patio. The rooms are simply furnished but functional and clean; perfect for travelers who rather spend their money exploring the city but still want a central location. Families with small children will enjoy the children's pool and play area. **Note:** The three-story hotel has no elevators. Travelers with limited mobility or small children may wish to request a ground-floor or first-floor apartment.

Rua Visconde de Mauá 151, Meireles 60165-121 CE. ℂ **085/3466-1900.** Fax 085/3466-1920. www.villa mayor.com.br. 96 units. R$150–R$210 double. Extra person add about 25%. Children 7 and under stay free in parent's room. AE, DC, MC, V. Free parking. **Amenities:** Restaurant; outdoor pool; room service. *In room:* A/C, TV, hair dryer, Internet, minibar.

3 WHERE TO DINE

Fortaleza's restaurants are surprisingly excellent. There's fine dining, including outstanding seafood at surprisingly low prices. In the main tourist zone, **Praia de Iracema,** the **Rua das Tabajaras** and its cross streets are lined with restaurants and patios. Take care, however, as many of these touristy establishments sacrifice quality for high turnover. There are some real gems, however, so with a bit of discernment it's possible to dine well. Farther out, **Meireles** and **Mucuripe** beaches offer excellent options as well. For a fun dining scene frequented mostly by Fortalezans, head to the ever-more-vibrant restaurant enclave of **Aldeota.**

If you find yourself in desperate need of a high-end coffee, try **Santa Clara Café Organico,** Rua Dragão do Mar 81 (✆ **085/3219-6900**), located inside the Dragão do Mar cultural center. It features a range of excellent organically grown coffees and a range of chocolates and pastries. Open Tuesday through Sunday 3 to 10pm.

Piaf ★★ FRENCH This small cozy bistro just a couple blocks off Meireles serves creative French cuisine at reasonable prices. Start off with some fresh oysters flown in from the Brazilian island of Florianópolis. Main courses include more traditional dishes such as duck in orange sauce and exotic meats like ostrich served with risotto. For lunch the kitchen prepares excellent specials at R$19 a plate. Check the blackboard for the daily offerings. The wine list offers a decent selection from France, Italy, Portugal, Australia, and South America.

Rua Silva Jatahy 942, Aldeota. ✆ **085/3242-5079.** Main courses R$18–R$42. AE, DC, MC, V. Sun–Fri noon–4pm; Mon–Sat 6pm–midnight.

Moana Gastronomia e Arte ★★★ FRENCH Moanna has it all. Located on Mucuripe beach, the restaurant is absolutely gorgeous, decorated in a kind of gold-and-brown rustic chic, with a soothing waterfall against the back wall. And then there's the food. This is high-end dining with quality ingredients, creative cuisine, and excellent service, yet most dishes don't even crack the R$36 mark. Truly excellent is the *frango tropical,* succulent pieces of grilled chicken breast served in mango sauce with savory crepes stuffed with leek mousse. For desserts, there's a fruit carpaccio, thin slices of fruit served with a scoop of ice cream and a raspberry sauce. However, chocoholics may want to order the *último desejo* (the last wish), two slices of chocolate cookie stuffed with crème caramel served on a bed of crème anglaise with sliced strawberries and chocolate sauce. Who could ask for anything more?

Av. Beira Mar 4260, Mucuripe (inside the Golden Fortaleza Parthenon). ✆ **085/3263-4887.** R$12–R$48 for 2. AE, DC, MC, V. Sun–Thurs noon–1am; Fri–Sat noon–2am.

ⓘ Tips You Buy, We Fry

The fresh fish market in the fishing colony at the end of Mucuripe beach offers what may be the shortest distance anywhere between catch and cook. Buy fresh prawns or fish at one of the market stalls (about R$8 for a half-kilo of prawns) and the stall at the corner of the market will clean, cook, and serve your meal to you on plates with rice—all for R$6. Cold beer is extra. Open daily 2 to 10pm. No phone.

FORTALEZA

14

EXPLORING

> **Tips** **Good Eating at Aldeota**
>
> The restaurant neighborhood of Aldeota is becoming ever more popular with Fortalezan locals. Just a short taxi ride from the beach hotels, the area around the Shopping Buganvília mall off Rua Prof. Dias da Rocha has recently seen the opening of a number of outstanding restaurants. One of the most beautiful restaurants is **Lautrec,** Shopping Buganvília, Av. Dom Luis 1113 (☎ **085/3264-4020**), a small bistro offering outdoor dining and a menu of French and Italian seafood—think flambéed prawns with tarragon or grilled prawns with pesto and mozzarella. For sushi, there's **Ryori Sushi Lounge** (☎ **085/3224-9997;** www.ryori.com.br), inside the mall itself. For a more casual night out try **Zug Choperia,** Rua Prof. Dias da Rocha 579 (☎ **085/3224-4193;** www.zugchoperia.com.br), a lovely bar/restaurant with a large patio, live music, and fabulous appetizers, including a variety of *pasteis* or cold-cut-and-cheese platters.

Pulcinella ★ ITALIAN Voted Fortaleza's best Italian year after year, this eatery features a traditional pasta menu just ever so slightly tilted toward the sea. Antipastos include sautéed shrimp and squid or salmon carpaccio. Mains include risottos and pastas with mussels, shrimp, and octopus. Stuffed ravioli dishes are more land based, including regional specialties such as sun-dried beef and locally made *mussarella*, or chicken and catupiry cheese. The menu includes beef and chicken dishes for those not in the mood for pasta. The wine list includes a range of midpriced vintages from Brazil, South America, and Italy, with an added select few from Australia and France.

Rua Oswaldo Cruz 640, Aldeota. ☎ **085/3261-3411.** www.pulcinella.com.br. Main courses R$24–R$48. AE, DC, MC, V. Mon–Thurs noon–3pm and 6:30pm–1:30am; Sat noon–2am; Sun noon–1am.

4 EXPLORING

Fortaleza's main attractions are the beaches outside of the city, including **Morro Branco** with its multicolored cliffs, the sand dunes of **Canoa Quebrada,** and the idyllic and stunningly beautiful **Jericoacoara.** Fortaleza itself has a small **historic center** that's worth a visit if you have a day to spare, but it's certainly not worth the trip by itself. The **beaches** of Cumbuco, Canoa Quebrada, and Morro Branco make for a pleasant day tour. Only a short distance from Fortaleza, these beaches offer buggy tours, sand boarding, sand tobogganing, parasailing, boat rides—you name it and you can experience it, all under a hot tropical sun. But unless you are a kite surfer, these beaches also don't justify the trek to Fortaleza. What is worth the trip is Jericoacoara (see below), one of the jewels on the Brazilian coast. This isolated beach community features Sahara-like sand dunes, stunning white beaches, plus a steady wind that makes it Brazil's windsurf and kite-surf capital.

THE TOP ATTRACTIONS

CANOA QUEBRADA ★★ **(Kids)** Canoa Quebrada offers miles of soft white sand and green-blue waters framed by low red cliffs. The symbol of the town is a half-moon and star, representing fertility. Hippie heritage aside, locals have expanded their businesses to

Tour Operators in Fortaleza

Several good tour operators are in Fortaleza, including **Ernanitur,** Av. Barão de Studart 1165 (℃ **085/3533-7700;** www.ernanitur.com.br), **Girafatur,** Rua Tenente Benévolo 13 (℃ **085/3219-3255;** www.girafatur.com.br), and **Hard Tour Ecotourism,** Rua Francisco Holanda 843 ap. 203 (℃ **085/3224-9300;** www.hardtour.com.br). All three offer transfers to Jericoacoara (prices range from R$50–R$100 each way) and tours to Cumbuco, Canoa Quebrada, Morro Branco, and Beach Park. Prices at all three are around R$40 for a city tour, R$50 for Cumbuco, R$25 for Beach Park (not including admission), R$40 for Morro Branco, and R$50 for Canoa Quebrada.

include **horseback riding** for R$30 per hour, **sand boarding** for R$3 per trip, and especially **buggy rides** either along the beach or into the vast sand dunes piled up behind the city. The full 2½-hour buggy tour, which includes a passage along the beach and up into the dunes, costs R$180 per buggy (buggies seat two or three comfortably, four if you squish). Shorter tours ride along the cliff top overlooking the beach, usually with a stop at a rainwater lagoon that looks like an oasis in the desert, the perfect stop for a swim or a cold beer. On the beach, *barracas* (stalls) rent out chairs and umbrellas, and food and drink is always close at hand, while local women offer scalp and shoulder massages for R$10.

Canoa Quebrada is located 156km (97 miles) east of Fortaleza. For tourism information, see **www.canoa-quebrada.com**. To reach the community, take CE-040 east to Aracati. Just past Aracati there will be a turnoff for Canoa Quebrada. The easiest way to visit is to book a day trip from Fortaleza. See "Tour Operators in Fortaleza," below. By bus, the bus company **Viação São Benedito** (℃ 085/3272-1232 or 088/3421-2020) has departures from Fortaleza's central bus terminal at 8:30am, 1:40, and 3:40pm. Alternatively, there are six daily departures to the city of Aracati, located 9km (5½ miles) from Canoa. Either trip costs R$18. From Aracati it is possible to get a cab or local bus.

CUMBUCO ★★　Located just a 45-minute drive from the city (37km/23 miles east), Cumbuco is where many Fortalezans come to spend a day at the beach. The big attraction? Beach and dunes. The main activity? The dune buggy ride. Drivers are able to take you on a roller-coaster ride over the shifting sands, dropping down steep inclines, swerving over piles of sand as if they were minor speed bumps, and skidding and sliding at almost vertical angles off the face of the taller dunes. **Buggy rides** cost R$100 per hour for a buggy that fits two or three people comfortably. Gentler beach activities include **horseback riding** at R$20 for 30 minutes and **boat rides** on the *jangada* fishing rafts for R$10 per 30 minutes. Cumbuco is also one of the best places on the coast for **kite surfing.** Optimal kite-surfing conditions occur from late June throughout November (check conditions on www.windfinder.com/forecast/cumbuco). The Dutch owners of **Windtown,** Rua das Cavalas 6 (℃ 085/8819-7887; www.windtown.nl), have created a facility that offers top-notch windsurfing and kite-surfing lessons, plus a spa and resort that pampers and accommodates surfers and nonsurfers alike. Rooms cost R$160 to R$230. A 3-day basic kite-surfing course (9 hr. of instruction) costs R$650. If you want to come

out early and make a day of it at the beach, the **Aldea Brasil** restaurant (© 085/3318- **353**
7541) makes a good base. The restaurant has a pool, sun deck, beach chairs, and bar, all
of which are available to customers on the understanding that you'll order drinks and
snacks and likely lunch at the restaurant. Open daily 9am to 6pm.

To reach Cumbuco, follow the signs for CE-085. The turnoff for Cumbuco is 11km
(7 miles) past Coité. For transfers to Cumbuco see "Tour Operators in Fortaleza," below.

MORRO BRANCO ★   Most visitors come to see the maze of colored sand cliffs that
line the beach. Local guides (who work for a donation, anything from R$5–R$10) will
take you through the maze of cliffs, showing off the spots with the best colors. A close-up
look at the sand reveals incredible variations in color, ranging from almost pure white to
yellow, gold, pink, orange, red, and purple. At the top of the cliffs there are usually artisans working on the region's best-known souvenir, sand-filled glass bottles with intricate
designs of colored sands. The beach in itself is not significantly different from other
beaches in the region. Allow an hour for a tour of the sand cliffs.

Morro Branco is 85km (53 miles) east of Fortaleza. Take CE-040 to Beberibe, then
take the turnoff for Morro Branco (it's approx. 4km/2½ miles from the main junction to
the beach). For tours to Morro Branco see "Tour Operators in Fortaleza," above.

DOWNTOWN FORTALEZA

Downtown Fortaleza has some worthwhile sights if you want to take a day off from the
beach. Just a short stroll from the Praia de Iracema is the area that the locals call **Casario,**
a lovely collection of restored 19th-century colonial buildings, located primarily on the
Rua Dragão do Mar and **Rua Almirante Tamandaré.** The area really comes to life at
night, as most of the historic buildings house nightclubs or cafes. The new centerpiece
of this area—built in a contrasting but somehow complementary contemporary style—is
the **Centro Cultural Dragão do Mar,** Rua Dragão do Mar 81 (© 085/3488-8600;
Tues–Fri 8:30am–9:30pm, Sat–Sun from 2:30pm). This modern cultural center is built
in the shape of a mosque with a white spiraling walkway that rests on an arcade over the
historic buildings on the street below. At night, the structure glows with a faint blue light.
For the full range of programming at the cultural center, see www.dragaodomar.org.br.

On the waterfront, there's the **Fortaleza de Nossa Senhora da Assunção,** Avenida
Alberto Craveiro (© 085/3255-1600; daily 8–11am and 2–5pm). Built by the Dutch
in 1649 (as Fort Schoonenborch) in a five-point-star shape, the fort was rechristened
after the Dutch were driven from Brazil in 1654.

14

(Kids)   Splish Splash

Beach Park (© 088/4012-3000; www.beachpark.com.br) is located 29km (18
miles) outside the city on Praia do Porto das Dunas, and is the largest water park
on the Northeast coast. The park features four pools—including the earthquake
wave pool with 2.5m (8-ft.) waves—and a number of water slides. The largest, the
Insano, boasts a 41m (135-ft.) vertical drop. There are also restaurants and tennis
courts for adults. Open 11am to 5pm. Admission is R$95 adults, R$85 children 12
and under.

Shopping in Fortaleza

Ceará is known for its quality handicrafts. The most famous souvenirs are the sand-filled glass bottles. Though admittedly touristy, they are as wickedly complex as a boat-in-a-bottle. Other excellent souvenirs include handmade cotton hammocks and local craft *cachaças*. The **Mercado Central,** Rua Alberto Nepomuceno 199 (*©* **085/3454-8586;** Mon–Sat 9am–7pm, Sun 9am–noon), is one of the best crafts markets in the city. The large circular building houses over 500 stalls and small shops selling a variety of handicrafts, including hammocks, lace, T-shirts, leather products, and sweets. Another good place to browse for crafts is the **outdoor market** that takes place nightly from 5 to 10pm in **Meireles.** The other craft you will see everywhere is lace, a tradition brought to Ceará by the Portuguese. The lace-makers *(rendeiras)* create delicate and complicated patterns, requiring enormous amounts of work, which in Fortaleza can still be bought for relatively little. Look for tablecloths, bedspreads, blouses, place mats, and numerous other items with lace trims. Good-quality lace is available at the crafts markets mentioned above, as well as at the **Centro de Turismo,** Rua Pompeu 350 (*©* **085/3101-5508;** Mon–Sat 8am–6pm, Sun 8am–noon). Housed in the former city jail, it has over 100 crafts stalls (in addition to a tourist information booth that gives out a good free map).

If you are shopping for clothes, Fortaleza is one of the cheaper cities in Brazil. One main shopping area lies on **Avenida Monsenhor Tabosa.** From Avenida Dom Manuel 6 blocks down to Rua João Cordeiro, this street is devoted almost exclusively to locally made purses, shoes, and clothing. The other shopping area is on **Rua General Sampaio, Sen. Pompeu,** and **Barão do Rio Branco,** and particularly the side streets around the **Praça José de Alencar.**

The highlight of the square is the **Teatro José de Alencar,** Praça José de Alencar s/n (*©* **085/3101-2583**), open for visits Tuesday to Friday 8am to 5pm, Saturday 8 to 11:30am. At R$4, it's worth a peek. Built in 1908, the theater is a marvel of colorful high-Victorian cast-iron construction, shipped in from Scotland. The gardens, added in 1974, were designed by Burle Marx.

ORGANIZED TOURS & OUTDOOR ACTIVITIES

BOAT TOURS **Ceará Saveiros,** across the street from Av. Beira Mar 4293 (*©* **085/ 3263-1085**), runs two daily boat trips along Fortaleza's waterfront. The morning tour departs at 10am and takes in the city's main beaches. The 2-hour sunset tour leaves around 4pm.

WATERSPORTS The urban beaches of Fortaleza have relatively calm waters and are perfect for practicing watersports. **Brothers Wind School** offers a range of equipment rentals as well as lessons. Sailors can take out a laser or Hobie Cat for R$30 per hour. Windsurfers can rent a board for R$30. You can also purchase a package of 8 hours of instruction with 10 hours of free rentals for R$160. Kayaks rent for R$10 an hour. Brothers is located just across the street from the Parthenon Golden Fortaleza, Av. Beira Mar 4260 in Mucuripe (*©* **085/9984-1967;** daily 8am–5pm).

5 FORTALEZA AFTER DARK

THE PERFORMING ARTS

Teatro José de Alencar   This high Victorian theater is one of the loveliest venues in Fortaleza, with regular classical music performances by the Eleazar de Carvalho Chamber Orquestra. Call the box office or check out www.secult.ce.gov.br under *"programe-se"* for schedules. Praça José de Alencar s/n, Centro. (© **085/3101-2583.**

CLUBS & BARS

Fortaleza is well known for its nightlife, with something happening almost every night of the week. The two most happening areas are **Praia de Iracema** and the **Casario,** the historic buildings around the **Centro Cultural do Dragão,** located at **Rua Dragão do Mar** and **Rua Alm. Tamandaré.**

(*Note:* The four bars at the intersection of Rua dos Tabajaras and Tr. Iracema [Cafe del Mar, Europa, Bikini, and Kapital] are patronized exclusively by working girls and their customers. Bars in the rest of Iracema beach, and elsewhere in Fortaleza, try to prevent prostitutes from entering.)

On Monday night, everybody heads down to **Pirata,** Rua dos Tabajaras 325, Praia de Iracema (© **085/4011-6161;** www.pirata.com.br). Doors open at 8pm, the band comes on at 1am, and the party continues until the wee hours. Tuesdays, the crowds leave the beach and head out to Varjota, to **Arre Egua,** Rua Delmiro Gouveia 420 (© **085/3267-5610;** www.arreegua.com.br), where things catch fire with the *Nordeste* musical style known as *forró.*

Lupus Bier, Rua dos Tabajaras 340 (© **085/3219-2829**), is Fortaleza's biggest and most popular microbrewery. Tables come equipped with a tap-your-own beer installation; for R$50 you get 10 liters of ice-cold lager whenever you want it. On Wednesdays, Lupus Bier hosts an excellent and accessible regional folklore show by the group Txai. Tickets are R$20, and the performance starts at 8pm.

On Thursday night, locals head out to **Praia do Futuro,** southwest of Mucuripe, for a traditional evening of crab eating *(caranguejada).* The place to be is **Chico do Caranguejo,** Av. Zéze Diogo 4930 (© **085/3262-0108;** www.chicodocaranguejo.com. br). Things warm up after 7pm. The band starts around 8:30pm. Taxi recommended.

It's July, So It Must Be Carnaval?

Fortaleza's biggest event is **Fortal,** or Carnaval Out-of-Season. The event takes place beginning on the Thursday of the last weekend of July, and attracts over two million revelers. If you plan to be in town, book your accommodations well in advance. Most of the events take place in Meireles on the Avenida Beira Mar, which gets closed to traffic and covered in bleachers for spectators. The event is similar to Salvador's Carnaval. Each night there are blocos, often with the same well-known artists who perform in Salvador—Olodum, Chiclete com Banana, Timbalada, and Ivete Sangalo. You can either purchase a T-shirt and follow a bloco or buy a seat in the bleachers to watch all the blocos file past. For exact dates and a list of who's playing, see www.fortal.com.br or call (© **085/3261-4050.**

Friday through Sunday, the options abound. The historic downtown area around the **Centro Cultural do Dragão do Mar,** Rua Dragão do Mar 81 (© **085/3488-8600;** www.dragaodomar.org.br), features at least a dozen bars and nightclubs side by side. Many have live music and almost all have wonderful patios. **O Brasileirinho,** Rua Dragão do Mar, 441 (© **085/3219-3701**), has live music Thursday through Sunday. The house band plays samba from Thursday through Saturday, and on Sunday nights it's *forró.* The bar opens at 4pm, and the music usually starts around 10pm.

6 JERICOACOARA ★★★

233km (145 miles) NW of Fortaleza

The pearl on the Ceará coast, Jericoacoara's attraction is partially its isolation. Visitors can only arrive by 4WD, preferably driven by someone who knows what they're doing; the 18km (11-mile) drive from Jijoca through the constantly shifting sands is not for the uninitiated. The payoff for those who persevere? Miles and miles of gorgeous white-sand beaches, most completely unspoiled, many completely untouched, plus rock formations, lagoons, mangroves, palm trees, and a Sahara desert landscape of towering, beautiful sand dunes, some over 30m (100 ft.) tall.

In recent years this formerly sleepy fishing village has gotten, if not exactly crowded, certainly much more visited. The region is now an environmental protection zone, with laws forbidding the construction of new hotels and pousadas within the protected area and guidelines for garbage and recycling. These rules have preserved the laid-back charm of the area. Streets are still made of sand; local transportation is by foot or buggy. Still, in high season it can be busier than you'd expect in paradise, so plan your travel for the shoulder season (Aug–Nov and late Mar to June).

For visitors, Jeri (as locals call it) offers buggy tours, hikes, sand boarding, and visits to freshwater lagoons. Beyond that, there's the wind; Jeri is one of those places—like the Gorge in Oregon—with the kind of consistent near-gale beloved by top-notch windsurfers and kite surfers, especially from June until November. A useful tourism website is www.jericoacoara.com.br.

ESSENTIALS
Getting There

Jericoacoara is 300km (186 miles) west of Fortaleza. There are essentially two ways to get there—the cheaper and quicker way is by bus or minibus along the state highways, with the last short stretch across the sand. The trip takes 6 to 7 hours. The agencies listed in "Tour Operators in Fortaleza," above, all offer this kind of transfer. The other way is to travel by Land Rover, traversing the many beautiful beaches that lie between Fortaleza and Jeri. For this kind of tour, contact **Jeri Off Road** (© **088/3669-2268** or 9958-5457; www.jeri.tur.br), which offers both 1-day or 2-day transfers that include a lot of off-road driving and scenic beaches such as Cumbuco, Lagoinha, Mundaú, and Baleia (R$650 for three to four people). *Tip:* We don't recommend renting a car if you are going to Jeri. The road from Fortaleza is bad, and stops before reaching Jeri in any case. For those who do opt for this route, from Fortaleza take the CE-085 west to Barrento and then connect to the BR-402 to Jijoca. In Jijoca you will have to park and leave your car. The last 23km (14 miles) from Jijoca are completed by 4×4 as regular cars are not able to handle the sand dunes and poor road conditions.

but bring enough cash to pay local tour guides and cover small purchases. In high season, Jeri gets absolutely packed, which may well affect your experience. If you do come in high season make sure you reserve accommodations and transfers well ahead of time. Finally, allow plenty of time for your return transfer, especially if catching a flight from Fortaleza on the same day. The moving dunes, tides, and changing water levels may affect transfer times.

Getting Around

The village of Jeri only boasts a handful of sand-covered streets, and all hotels, restaurants and shops are within easy walking distance. Make sure you bring flat shoes.

EXPLORING JERICOACOARA

Jeri's attractions all involve the outdoors, be it on land, lagoon, or sea. Two of the top attractions, the Sunset Dune and Pedra Furada Rock, are within a short walk of the village. Every day, about half an hour before sunset, visitors and residents walk up the 30m-high (100-ft.) dune on the edge of town for a spectacular view of the setting sun. To reach the town's other landmark, Pedra Furada (a large rock with a hole in the center), requires a 30- to 45-minute walk (depending on the tide). Alternative modes of transportation include horseback or dune buggy (see below).

The two most popular day trips around Jericoacoara are Tatajuba and Lagoa Azul. Both destinations can be reached only by dune buggy as there are no roads. Make sure you bring plenty of sunscreen. The visit to Tatajuba takes you over some impressive large sand dunes, across river estuaries and long stretches of mangrove and beach, and it includes a stop at a small lagoon to observe sea horses in their natural habitat. The day trip to Lagoa Azul covers less terrain (or sand) but in compensation takes you to several beautiful lagoons where you can enjoy a swim and a delicious lunch. In some of the smaller dunes your driver will be able to show off his car-handling skills in the deep sand. You will also drive along Praia do Préa, one of Brazil's top beaches for kite surfing (high season for kite surfing is July–Nov). A day trip costs R$160 to R$200 for a buggy and driver. Each buggy can take up to four people, but you will have more fun with three people so that everybody can sit in the back. Contact **Jeri Off Road** (see below) or the **Buggy Association** (℡ **088/3669-2284**) to reserve.

Outdoor Activities

Jeri Off Road (℡ **088/3669-2268** or 9958-5457; www.jeri.tur.br) is one of the outdoor specialists offering a variety of sightseeing buggy tours and expeditions from Jeri to other destinations.

HORSEBACK RIDING   Jericoacoara's unpaved streets and dune trails are perfect for horseback riding. However, tours are best suited for more experienced riders. There are no organized tours, only local guides (who don't speak English) with a couple of horses. A perfect late afternoon tour takes you along a narrow trail above the steep cliffs to Pedra Furada and then across the village to the Sunset Dune. There is nothing more amazing than galloping at full speed through the deep sand to the top of this huge dune to be rewarded with a fabulous sunset. Guides and horses gather outside the Vila Kalango. A 2-hour ride costs R$40 per person.

KITE SURFING   **Clube dos Ventos** (℡ **088/3669-2288**; www.clubedosventos.com) is kite-surfing central in the heart of Jericoacoara. The facility has new, top-grade gear for rent. Price (with prebooking) is R$140 per day, R$725 per week. Their website has loads of details on gear and wind conditions (including a daily wind report). Private lessons start at R$125 for 1½ hours, including equipment. Staff are avid surfers themselves and can put together a customized package according to your level, interest, and time availability.

WHERE TO STAY

In many ways Jeri remains a rustic spot—no paved streets, no bank machines, but that doesn't mean you need to suffer. A number of excellent small hotels have set up shop recently. One of our favorite hotels in town is **Vila Kalango,** Rua das Dunas 30 (© 088/3669-2290; www.vilakalango.com.br; R$235–R$270 double, R$345–R$425 bungalow). This idyllic hotel is located on the beach, right on the edge of the village overlooking the sunset dune. The best accommodations are the rustic (but very comfortable) round bungalows on stilts that make the most of the breeze and the view. Those who prefer a more traditional hotel will enjoy the **Mosquito Blue,** Rua da Farmacia s/n (© 088/3669-2203; www.mosquitoblue.com.br; R$330 double). In addition to luxurious accommodations, the hotel also features an outstanding spa and restaurant. Less expensive but still comfortable is **Pousada do Capitão Thomáz,** Av. Beira Mar 202 (© 088/3669-2221; www.capitaothomaz.com.br; R$140–R$200 double). For the ultimate romantic getaway there is the brand-new **Chili Beach Hotel,** Rua da Igreja s/n (© 088/9909-9135; www.chilibeach.com; R$460–R$750). With only six rooms, this hip boutique hotel combines Miami chic with Brazilian hospitality. Rooms feature the latest gadgets and deluxe amenities, such as an iPod docking station, flatscreen TV, Wi-Fi, light dimmers, and 1,000-thread Egyptian cotton sheets. The restaurant is fabulous and the deck (which you will have practically all to yourself) overlooks an almost deserted stretch of beach.

WHERE TO DINE

Jeri is small enough that you can set out on foot (no heels please, the streets are made of sand) and explore the various restaurants. The variety and quality is surprisingly high. **Mosquito Blue's Oceano Restaurant,** Rua da Farmacia s/n (© 088/3669-2203), has one of the best locations right on the beach. The kitchen serves international cuisine with an emphasis on fresh fish and seafood. At night the candlelit tables by the beach make for pleasant outside dining. On Jeri's main street you will find **Leonardo Da Vinci,** Rua Principal 40 (© 088/3669-2222). The kitchen prepares excellent steak and fish dishes and the stuffed pastas are made from scratch. The scrumptious desserts come from the outstanding bakery next door. For a snack or a light meal try **Naturalmente Creperia,** Rua da Praia s/n (no phone). This small eatery on the beach, next to the Kite Center, prepares delicious sweet and savory crepes, as well as juices and salads.

São Luis & the Lençóis Maranhenses

It was the French, not the Portuguese, who founded the city of São Luis. In 1612 a French colony 500 strong under the command of Daniel de la Touche, Sieur de la Ravardiere, established a fortress and city that they named in honor of King Louis XIII.

Ironically enough, almost 400 years later, French and other visitors flock to São Luis because its historic center, better than almost any city in Brazil, preserves the look and feel of a traditional Portuguese city.

The northeast coast of Brazil was a void on explorers' maps when the French colonists arrived. Though Portuguese cities farther south such as Salvador and Olinda were already thriving, winds and currents conspired to isolate this part of the coastline. It was quicker to sail from Olinda to Lisbon than it was from Olinda up the coast to Belém. The French hoped to take advantage of this gap to establish a successful commercial and missionary settlement before the Portuguese even noticed.

It was not to be. The Portuguese rallied, and by 1615 succeeded in driving out the would-be French colonists. Portugal took over the colony, but kept the name bestowed by the French.

São Luis's heyday came in the 18th and 19th centuries, when the city grew rich on the export of sugar, cattle, and especially cotton. Sometime in the 1820s, the fashion spread among São Luis's rich middle classes of covering their houses with Portuguese ceramic tiles. Not only were the blue, yellow, and green tiles ornate and beautiful, but they also reflected the sun and kept houses cooler. São Luis became one of the richest, most beautiful cities in the Northeast.

But in the late 1800s the Maranhão economy went into a steep decline. The end of slavery spelled the end of cheap cotton and sugar, while the city's tidal port grew too shallow for the new large ships of the steam age.

Marooned in an economic backwater, the center of São Luis—tiles and all—survived the 20th century intact. Restoration work on the city's old center began in 1989, culminating with the recognition in 1997 of the historic center of São Luis as a World Heritage Site.

Though still one of Brazil's poorer states, Maranhão has lately seen an upswing. With a new deepwater port, São Luis now serves as the export point for iron ore mined in the interior. Brazil's satellite-launching facility is located across the bay from São Luis near the city of Alcântara. Tourism is also a growing force in the economy, but remains very much in its infancy.

Visitors to São Luis can wander the streets of a beautiful colonial city without the crowds now found in Salvador. They can also savor the strong musical culture of São Luis, expressed in its love of reggae and in the yearly celebration of bumba-meu-boi.

Farther afield, there is the chance to visit the Lençóis Maranhenses, a desert of snow-white sand dunes whose low points are full of water—truly one of the most intriguing natural landscapes in Brazil.

2,262km (1,405 miles) N of Rio de Janeiro, 2,340km (1,454 miles) N of São Paulo.

ARRIVING

BY PLANE   **Gol** (© 0300/115-2121; www.voegol.com.br) and **TAM** (© 0800/570-5700 or 098/4002-5700; www.tam.com.br) have flights to São Luis. The airport, **Marechal Cunha Machado,** Av. Dos Libaneses s/n, Tirirical (© **098/3217-6101**), is 13km (8 miles) from the city center. A taxi to the centro histórico costs R$40.

BY BUS   Buses arrive at the **Terminal Rodoviário de São Luis,** Av. Dos Franceses s/n, Santo Antonio (© **098/3249-2488**), 10km (6 miles) from the centro histórico.

BY FERRY   Ferries to Alcântara depart from the **Terminal Hidrovário** (© **098/3232-0692**), located opposite the Reviver area in the centro histórico. Ferries depart daily at 7am and 9:30am, and return at 8:30am and 4pm. Note that if the tide is out, ferries depart from the beach at Ponta D'Areia. Also, ferry departure times are only approximate. It's best to check at the ferry terminal the day before departure.

CITY LAYOUT

The city of **São Luís** sits on the **Ilha São Luis,** a vast low-lying alluvial island that floats between two large river estuaries, the **Baía São Marcos** (to the northwest) and the **Baía São José** (to the southeast). Small tidal inlets—called *igarapés*—divide the island into numerous smaller islands and peninsulas. The oldest part of the city—called the **centro histórico**—sits on one of these peninsulas, almost completely surrounded north and south by wide igarapés.

The old city's oldest section lies at the very tip of the peninsula. It is here (tide willing) that the ferries to Alcântara dock, and where in times past ships used to unload their cargos. On maps this area is often labeled **"Praia Grande."** In recent years, as the city has poured money into renovating old buildings and bringing the old city back to life, the area has been renamed the **"Reviver."**

Roughly speaking, the Reviver runs from the ferry dock east past the old Customs house and along the cobblestone streets up the steps to the **Praça João Lisboa,** and from the small rise in the north that holds the fort and governor's palace (**Palacio dos Leóes**) and south as far as the **Convento das Mercês.**

The city has long since spread beyond the original small peninsula. Two bridges lead from the north side of the original peninsula into the newer parts of São Luis. Closest to the mouth of the estuary, the **José Sarney bridge** (named for a former Brazilian president and Maranhão governor) turns into the **Avenida Castelo Branco** (named for a former president and dictator) which leads to the **São Francisco** neighborhood. This is São Luís's small central business district. It has a few banks and office towers, but is otherwise completely lacking in sights or restaurants or anything else of interest to tourists.

Beyond a roundabout at the top end of São Francisco, the road turns into **Avenida Ana Jansen,** which leads past the **Lagoa de Jansen** and then out to the first of the city's beach neighborhoods, **Ponta d'Areia.** The city recently installed a boardwalk and small park on the north side of Lagoa de Jansen, then encouraged bars and restaurants to move in, transforming the lake into one of São Luis's most popular dining and nightlife areas.

In Ponta d'Areia, the Avenida Jansen becomes **Avenida dos Holandeses,** a wide, busy highway that runs parallel to the coast forming the commercial backbone for the beach

ACCOMMODATIONS ■
Hotel Pousada Colonial **17**
Pestana São Luis **2**
Pousada Portas
 da Amazônia **13**
Rio Poty **1**

DINING ◆
Antigamente **15**
Cabana do Sol **5**
Kitaro Lagoa **3**
Maracangalha **6**
O Armazén da Estrela **16**
Por Acaso **4**
Restaurante Senac **9**

ATTRACTIONS ●
Casa das Tulhas **12**
Casa do Maranhão **10**
Centro de Cultura Popular **14**
Convento das Mercês **18**
Ferry Terminal **11**
Museu Historico e Artistico
 do Maranhão **7**
Palacio dos Leões **8**

neighborhoods of **Praia de São Marcos, Praia do Calhau, Praia do Caolho,** and **Praia Olho d'Agua.** Most of the hotels in these neighborhoods are located on the seaside Avenida Litorânea, which splits from Avenida dos Holandeses in Praia de São Marcos and travels out along the shoreline.

GETTING AROUND

BY BUS São Luis is a big spread-out city, not really ideal for bus travel. Buses to the old city are marked PRAIA GRANDE. Buses to the beach neighborhoods are marked PONTA D'AREIA or PRAIA CALHAU. Buses cost R$1.80. You board through the front.

BY TAXI Taxis are widely available. To reserve, phone **Cocoma** (☏ **098/3231-1010**) or **Coopertaxi** (☏ **098/3245-4404**). A taxi from Ponta D'Areia to the centro histórico costs about R$15 to R$25.

VISITOR INFORMATION

São Luís's airport has a tourist information booth in the arrivals hall that's open daily from 8am to 6pm (☏ **098/3244-4500**). In the city, there is a state tourist information office in the centro histórico on Praça Benedito Leite, Rua da Palma 53 (☏ **098/3212-6211**), open Monday to Friday 8am to 7pm, Saturday, Sunday, and holidays 9am to 2pm. Both give out an excellent free map of the old city.

ⒻastFacts   São Luís

Area Codes The area code for São Luís is **098**.

Banks In the centro histórico: **Banco do Brasil** (☏ **098/3215-4992**) on Av. Dom. Pedro II 78, in front of the Palácio dos Leões; also **Banco do Brasil** in the Reviver at Travessa Boa Ventura 26-B (☏ **098/3232-8507**).

Car Rentals In São Luís airport are **Avis** (☏ **098/3245-5957**); **Localiza,** also at Av. Dos Holandeses lotes 7 e 8 (☏ **098/3245-1566**); and **Unidas** (☏ **098/3217-6190**).

Dentist **Clínica Odontológica Maranhão** is at Rua Grande 1164, Centro (☏ **098/3232-7144**).

Emergencies Dial ☏ **190** for police, ☏ **193** for fire department, ☏ **192** for ambulance. The Tourist Police station is on Rua da Estrela 427 in the centro histórico (☏ **098/3214-8682**).

Hospital For medical attention, go to **Santa Casa de Misericórdia,** Rua do Norte 233, centro histórico (☏ **098/3221-0144** or 3232-0248).

Mail The main post office is on Praça João Lisboa 290 in the centro histórico. There is another post office in the airport terminal. Both are open Monday through Friday 9am to 4pm.

Pharmacies **Farmácia Gonçalves** is at Rua das Hortas 379A, centro histórico (☏ **098/3232-1072**); **Extrafone** delivers 24 hours daily (☏ **0800/983-000**).

Weather São Luís, just below the Equator, has a pleasant, warm climate year-round, with average temperatures of 28°C (82°F). Most rain falls in winter (July–Sept). The most pleasant months are March through June; it's warm but not as hot as in December through February.

---

2 WHERE TO STAY

There are essentially two options in São Luís, the centro histórico or the beach neighborhoods such as Praia d'Areia and Praia de Calhau. The centro histórico offers beautiful surroundings, some nice restaurants, and a busy nightlife scene in the Reviver area. However, there are no full-service hotels, and the few pousadas have only a limited number of rooms. The beaches have lovely resort-style hotels, but they are a 20-minute cab ride from the attractions of the old city.

Moderate

Pousada Portas da Amazônia ★★ The nicest place to stay in São Luis is this renovated colonial mansion in the heart of the old city. The best rooms, called Master Suites (nos. 1, 2, 15, 16, 17, 24, 25, and 26—the best of the best is no. 16), are vast and high ceilinged, with tall colonial windows looking out on the small cobblestone square. Master Suites also feature firm queen-size beds, often raised up on a small dais. Bathrooms feature electric showers and lots of counter space. Standard rooms are not as bright or spacious, with windows facing the courtyard. Bathrooms in the standard rooms are also a tad cramped. Breakfast is excellent.

Rua do Giz 129, Praia Grande, São Luis, 65080-680 MA. ⓒ **098/3222-9937.** Fax 098/3221-4193. www.portasdaamazonia.com.br. 35 units. High season R$130 standard; R$190–R$210 master. 20%–30% discount in low season. Extra person add about 20%. Children 7 and under stay free in parent's room. AE, DC, MC, V. No parking. Bus: Praia Grande. **Amenities:** Wi-Fi. *In room:* A/C, TV, fridge, minibar.

Inexpensive

Hotel Pousada Colonial The Colonial looks gorgeous from the outside—an old colonial mansion covered with intricate Portuguese tile—but inside the rooms can be a tad cramped, the walls and floors a bit scuffed up. All rooms feature either a firm queen-size bed or two single beds, plus small functional bathrooms with showers. The two best rooms—nos. 201 and 202—have large bright windows looking out on the street. These are definitely worth the price. The worst room—no. 105—is small, dark, and moldy and should be avoided at all costs. Between these extremes, the Colonial offers clean, functional accommodations in the heart of the centro histórico. If you can, stay at the Pousada Portas de Amazônia, but if that's unavailable the Colonial is a serviceable backup.

Rua Alfonso Pena (Rua Formosa) 112, centro histórico, São Luis, 65080-680 MA. ⓒ/fax **098/3232-2834.** www.clickcolonial.com.br. 27 units. R$125 double. Extra person add R$30. AE, DC, MC, V. Bus: Praia Grande. **Amenities:** Room service; Wi-Fi. *In room:* A/C, TV, fridge, minibar.

BEACHES

Expensive

Pestana São Luis ★★ Though a little far from the centro histórico, the full-service Pestana has the advantage of a lovely location on Praia do Calhau, the city's nicest beach. Formerly the Park, the hotel was recently bought and renovated by the Pestana group. Rooms feature tile floors, firm queen-size (or two twin) beds, and a private balcony. What really sets the hotel apart, however, are its amenities—a large outdoor pool and children's pool, tennis courts, a grass soccer field—and its location on the beach. The drawback, of course, is that the sights in the centro histórico are a R$25 cab ride away.

Av. Avicênia 10km, Praia do Calhau, São Luis, 65071-370 MA. ⓒ **098/2106-0505.** Fax 098/2106-0500. www.pestana.com. 111 units. R$300–R$390 double. Children 7 and under stay free in parent's room. AE, DC, MC, V. Free parking. Bus: Praia Calhau. **Amenities:** Restaurant; bar; weight room; outdoor pool and children's pool; room service; sauna; tennis courts. *In room:* A/C, TV, fridge, minibar, Wi-Fi.

Rio Poty ★ Located on the beach on Ponta D'Areia, the new Rio Poty is the best beach hotel closest to the centro histórico. The hotel's striking inverse ziggurat form means every room gets a view of the sea. Beds are queen-size (king-size in luxury rooms and suites), with tile floors, small granite desk and workspace with Internet, and clean, basic bathrooms with tub and shower. The large leaf-shaped pool—with little Jacuzzi islands—fans out over a vast sun deck looking out over the beach. There is little or nothing within walking distance, but the hotel itself offers a number of restaurants and bars (including a disco). The nightlife scene by the Lagoa Jansen is but a R$5 cab ride away; getting to the centro histórico will cost about R$20 by cab.

Av. dos Holandeses 4km, Praia da Ponta d"Areia, São Luis, 65077-310 MA. ✆ **098/3311-1500.** www. riopotysaoluis.com.br. 142 units. R$225–R$320 double. Children 7 and under stay free in parent's room. AE, DC, MC, V. Free parking. Bus: Lagoa Jansen. **Amenities:** Restaurant; bar; weight room; outdoor pool; room service; sauna. *In room:* A/C, TV, fridge, Internet, minibar.

3 WHERE TO DINE

CENTRO HISTÓRICO

Restaurants in the centro histórico cater mostly to tourists, and they usually look better than they taste. Expect mostly Brazilian food such as *carne seca* (lightly salted dried beef), seafood stews, grilled steak with fries and *farofa,* or deep-fried pastries *(empanadas)*. Farther out, there are a number of good restaurants by the edge of the Lagoa de Jansen.

Expensive

Restaurante Senac ★ BRAZILIAN   This lovely two-story historic building houses the restaurant of the regional hospitality industry training institute. Students have the opportunity to practice their skills and learn on the job. The lunch buffet is an excellent deal. For R$29 to R$35 (including dessert) you can feast on a variety of freshly prepared dishes. The most popular days of the week are Tuesday (Brazilian cuisine), Friday (seafood and fish), and Saturday (traditional *feijoada*). The restaurant also opens for dinner (Thurs–Sat only) with an a la carte menu of regional dishes.

Praça Benedito Leite s/n, centro histórico. ✆ **098/3198-1100.** Main courses R$24–R$43. AE, DC, MC, V. Mon–Sat noon–3pm; Thurs–Sat 7–11pm.

Moderate

Antigamente (Overrated) BRAZILIAN   Surely one of the prettiest restaurants, Antigamente is also lively and fun. The restaurant is located inside a renovated heritage building in the old city and has gorgeous mosaic floors and rustic furnishings. In the evenings it's one of the more happening restaurants with a great patio. The food, alas, is disappointing. Better to have a snack and just enjoy the atmosphere.

Rua da Estrela 220, centro histórico. ✆ **098/3232-3964.** Main courses R$12–R$39; the more expensive dishes are for 2. MC, V. Mon–Sat 10am–midnight.

O Armazém da Estrela ★ BRAZILIAN   This place is a mix of bar, restaurant, sandwich deli, and cybercafe, housed in a lovely two-floor mansion in the heart of the old city. Most nights, there's live music.

Rua da Estrela 401, centro histórico. ✆ **098/3254-1274.** Main courses R$12–R$44. AE, MC, V. Mon–Fri noon–midnight; Sat 6pm–1am.

PONTA D'AREIA/CALHAU

Cabana do Sol ★ BRAZILIAN   Cabana do Sol is one of São Luis's best known regional restaurants. People come in droves to try out the food here so it's a good thing the restaurant is large. The spacious open veranda-like structure can seat several hundred people, but thanks to a small army of waiters things go smoothly here. The dishes are huge, often enough for three people. Meat dishes, like *carne de sol*, suckling pig and roasted goat are the kitchen's forte. These are served on a large platter, hot off the grill, and come with a variety of the usual side dishes including rice and *farofa*. The menu also includes some fish and seafood options, but for more interesting dishes we recommend going to Maracangalha.

Rua João Damasceno 24, Ponta do Farol. © **098/3235-2586.** Main courses R$44–R$70 for 2 or 3. AE, DC, MC, V. Daily 11am–midnight. Bus: Ponta D'Areia or Culhau.

Maracangalha ★★ BRAZILIAN   One of the best restaurants in town for fresh seafood dishes is this tongue-twister, Maracangalha. Chef Dantas is developing quite a name for himself as a local celebrity chef and promoter of regional cuisine. Most dishes serve two people or more! One of our favorites is the grilled anchovy (nothing like those tiny salty slivers); this large fish is seasoned and grilled on a charcoal fire. The tender white meat is served with a number of side dishes, including the famous *cuxá* rice. Another popular dish is the *caldeirada,* the Northeast's version of a bouillabaisse, a delicious seafood stew. The restaurant doesn't close between lunch and dinner, making it a popular après-beach destination.

Rua Parnaiba 12 (off Av. dos Holandeses), Renascença. © **098/3235-9305.** Main courses R$52–R$70 for 2 or 3. DC, MC, V. Mon–Sat 11:30am–midnight; Sun till 5pm. Bus: Ponta D'Areia or Culhau.

LAGOA JANSEN

Kitaro Lagoa ★ JAPANESE/BRAZILIAN   Pretty much every self-respecting Brazilian town must have a trendy Japanese restaurant, and São Luis is no different. Overlooking the lagoon, Kitaro is a Zen oasis with soft lighting and modern furniture. The best tables are those that look out over the water, either inside or out on the patio. The menu covers the basics from sushi to tempura, teriyaki, and yakisoba noodles. Lately, the kitchen has been branching into regional Brazilian cuisines, including a delicious *moqueca* made with *jabiraca* (a local freshwater fish considered by some as tasty as cod). The restaurant has live music every night, usually starting around 9pm, and the kitchen is open late, until 3am on Friday and Saturday.

Av. Mario Meireles s/n, Lagoa de Jansen-Ponta D'Areia. © **098/3227-2416.** Main courses R$22–R$45. MC, V. Tues–Thurs and Sun 5pm–1am; Fri–Sat 5pm–3am. Bus: Ponta D'Areia.

Por Acaso ★ BRAZILIAN   Just down from Kitaro, also on the lagoon, is a great casual *chopperia*. This bar/restaurant is one of the more happening places at night. Even on a Wednesday evening it is packed with locals enjoying a beer and helping themselves to the outstanding antipasto buffet. The restaurant actually has a pretty decent menu with excellent steak and seafood dishes but the buffet is a meal in itself; a selection of cheeses, cold cuts, various salads, olives, marinated eggplant, sun-dried tomato, homemade dips, fresh bread, and more. There's nothing better than snagging a table by the window, ordering a few cold chopps, and making several trips to the buffet to try out the tasty nibbles. Live music daily at 8pm.

Av. Mario Meireles s/n, Lagoa de Jansen-Ponta D'Areia. © **098/3235-9881.** Main courses R$16–R$35. MC, V. Tues–Sat 5:30pm–1am. Bus: Ponta D'Areia.

4 EXPLORING SÃO LUIS

Perhaps for lack of other options, São Luis takes tourism seriously. The city does an excellent job in several small museums presenting the culture and history of the region. Many of the museums in the old city offer visually attractive and informative displays, professionally presented by engaging and informative museum guides. Even better, most of them are free.

"The Historic Center of São Luis do Maranhão is an outstanding example of a Portuguese colonial town that adapted successfully to the climatic conditions in equatorial South America and which has preserved its urban fabric, harmoniously integrated with its natural setting, to an exceptional degree." So read the UNESCO declaration, giving the center of São Luis a World Heritage designation in 1997.

The centro histórico formed the heart of São Luis through the 19th-century boom years, but went into decline in the 1920s. Restoration started only in 1989, under pressure from state governor Jose Sarney, and continues to today. The neighborhood still lacks modern water and sewer systems. There is also controversy over whether the historic center should be a tourist enclave or a real residential neighborhood. After fixing up buildings, the state government wants to turn them over to owners with the financial wherewithal to maintain them. That rules out the poor and working classes who for nearly a century have made the neighborhood their home. It's a problem that has not yet been resolved.

The centro histórico sits on a peninsula, almost completely surrounded north and south by wide igarapés. Twice every 24 hours the tide sucks the water from the estuary, leaving the city completely cut off from the ocean. If this seems an odd place to put a seaport, recall that the French expeditions that founded the city were interested mostly in defense. The old city is effectively an island, protected by the tides from large warships and their guns.

The **Reviver** area, the oldest part of the old city, lies at the very tip of the peninsula, to the east of the Jose Sarney bridge. This area contains most of the centro histórico's museums, and interesting streets and monuments.

The best plan is just to go for a stroll. Numerous antique buildings have been renovated into museums or tourist attractions of one kind or another. The best are given separate listings below. But just as rewarding is the fine-grained texture of the old city, and the serendipitous discovery of a lovely colonial building covered in brilliant blue or yellow tile.

The best place to start a walk is by the **Casa do Maranhão ★★**, just opposite the ferry terminal to Alcântara. Unfortunately at printing time this excellent small museum about the bumba-meu-boi folklore was closed for renovations. It should reopen again sometime in 2010, so it's worth checking to see if it has. The **Rua Portugal** is just around the corner. This narrow, cobblestone street features numerous restored colonial buildings from the 18th and 19th centuries, many covered in bright patterned tile. Close to the end of the street one comes to the **Casa das Tulhas ★**, Rua da Estrela 184 (Mon–Fri 6am–8pm, Sat 6am–6pm, Sun 6am–1pm).

Rua Portugal dead-ends at **Rua da Estrela.** This is the heart of the Reviver area. At night this wide, tree-shaded street is full of cafes and musicians. Parallel to Rua da Estrela 1 block farther in is **Rua da Giz.** This lovely colonial street serves as a kind of crossroads leading to many more of the old city's attractions.

Turn right on Rua da Giz and proceed uphill and you come to a small formal square, **Praça Benedito Leite.** The far side of the square is formed by the **Igreja da Sé** (© 098/3222-7380; Tues–Fri 8am–6:30pm, Sat 8am–noon, Sun 8am–noon and 4–7pm) and the **Bishop's Palace.** Just around the corner lies Avenida Pedro II, a broad ceremonial boulevard on which you find the **Palacio La Ravardiere,** which houses city hall, and the **Palacio dos Leões,** which was built on the foundations of the city's original

Bumba-Meu-Boi

It's a festival celebrated throughout Brazil under a host of names—boi-bumbá, boi calemba, boi surubim, boi zumbi—but locals insist that Maranhão is Brazil's leading stronghold of bumba-meu-boi. Through music, costume, and drumming, the festival tells the story of the life and death and rebirth of a magical Brazilian bull.

The bull belongs to a wealthy rancher. A peasant working for the rancher named Pai Chico steals the bull, kills it, and feeds its tongue to his pregnant girlfriend, Catirina, to satisfy her cravings. Discovering the deed, the rancher condemns Pai Chico and Catirina to death. It looks dark for the pair, but St. John warns the rancher in a dream not to kill the couple. Pai Chico and Catirina go to the *curandeiros,* the community's traditional healers, and with the help of everyone in the village, they magically drum the bull to life again.

In Maranhão, bumba-meu-boi has evolved into a kind of competition. Dozens of different groups—normally organized by neighborhood—hold their own bumba-meu-boi celebrations, competing with each other to see who can put together the best costumes and put on the best party. The music played by each group belongs to one of about five rhythms, or *sotaques* (accents), each of which has its own set of instruments. The *matraca sotaque* uses wooden blocks that musicians rap together to create complicated percussion rhythms. The *zabumba sotaque* uses only long wooden drums covered in snakeskin. Each *sotaque* also has its own elaborate costumes, and each group has its own magic bull.

Though made of a wire frame and papier-mâché (a dancer goes inside to act out the part of the bull) the bull is an important creature. A new bull is created each year, and the parties held by each bumba-meu-boi group mark the milestones in the magic bull's existence.

Rehearsals begin on the Saturday before Easter (these are open to the public). In early June, the bull is taken to the church to be baptized (after which there is a party). Different groups choose different dates for the christening. The most popular date is June 23, the day of São João (there is usually a party on this day). On June 29, all the bumba-meu-boi groups bring their bulls to the church of São Pedro in the Madre Deus neighborhood. And on June 30, all of São Luís comes to a halt as 200 or more bumba-meu-boi groups bring their bulls out to celebrate the feast of São Marçal, mostly in the João Paulo neighborhood.

The last step in the bull's life is the Morte do Boi, the Death of the Bull, which each group holds on a different day, anytime between June 30 and the end of December. For those who want to take part in the festivities, local papers publish the dates and locations where the different groups are celebrating the birth, blessing, life, and death of their bull.

SÃO LUÍS & THE LENÇÓIS MARANHENSES

15

EXPLORING SÃO LUÍS

fort, Fort Saint Louis. Guided visits through the upstairs salons of the Palacio dos Leões (© **098/3232-9789;** Mon, Wed, and Fri 2–5:30pm) show furniture and oil paintings from the 18th and 19th centuries, none especially distinguished.

Turn left on the Rua da Giz and you come first to the **Centro de Cultura Popular** ★★ (see below), and then at the far end of the street to the pretty **Convento das Mercês,** and the **Cafua das Mercês,** which is now home to the small **Museu do Negro** (no phone; Tues–Fri 9am–6pm). During the slave era, the courtyard inside the Cafua was used as an enclosure to keep slaves newly arrived from Africa penned up before they could be auctioned. A whipping post is still in evidence.

Go straight uphill from the Rua da Giz and you come to **Praça Joao Lisboa,** a rather ugly central square, with the **Teatro Arthur Azevedo** on one side. Built in 1817, the neoclassical Teatro reopened in 2006 after lengthy renovations (guided visits Tues–Fri 2–5pm; R$3; © **098/3218-9000**).

East of the Praça João Lisboa, the centro histórico becomes less touristed and more residential. Many of the buildings in this part of the centro histórico are just as historic and picturesque as down in the Reviver area, while the atmosphere is that of a working-class Brazilian neighborhood. In daylight hours it's a fine place to stroll and discover; however, at night it is best to be avoided. Highlights of this part of the old town include the **Museu Historico e Artistico do Maranhão** (see below) and the **Mercado Central** (daily 6am–5pm), the city's large public market, located at the far end of Avenida Magalhães de Almeida.

Centro de Cultura Popular ★★ The arid Northeast is one of the richest sources of folklore and folk festivals in Brazil. Located in a four-story mansion in the old city, this museum has dioramas and mannequins presenting many of these rich folk traditions. Included is bumba-meu-boi in all its various accents, as well as the rhythms such as the *tambor de crioula,* and more religious spiritual festivals such as the *Festa do Divino.* A highlight is the superb collection of photographs of folk festivals around the state, many showing the often aged matriarchs who rule these festivals decked out in all their sumptuous regalia. Guides should, but may not, speak English.

Rua do Giz 221, centro histórico. © **098/3218-9924.** Free admission. Tues–Sun 9am–6pm.

Museu Histórico e Artístico do Maranhão ★★ If you want to get a sense of how the elite of 19th-century São Luis lived, visit the Historical Museum of Maranhão. The museum is located in a mansion built in 1836, which has been restored and decorated with the heavy wood furniture, porcelain, crystal, and artwork favored by the commercial aristocracy of the time. Tours are guided, though in Portuguese only, and there is little explanatory signage. Allow 30 minutes (or more if you're an *Antiques Roadshow* person).

Rua do Sol 302, centro histórico. © **098/3218-9922.** Admission R$5. Tues–Sun 9am–5pm.

ALCANTARA ★★

A visit to Alcântara makes a great day trip. An hour's ferry ride north across Baía São Marcos, the village of Alcântara is a curious thing, a struggling small town living inside the ruins of a once-thriving colonial city. In the boom years of the 18th and 19th centuries, Alcântara was a regional capital, the place where the merchant and plantation elite kept their families and traded their sugar and cotton. With the end of slavery in 1888 the plantation economy crashed and the merchants and planters fled, leaving the half-empty city in the hands of newly freed slaves and their descendants.

In 1948, the city was declared a historic site, primarily for its lovely collection of colonial houses with ornately decorated doors and coverings of bright Portuguese tile. Called "Windows and Doors" (in Portuguese *Portas e Janelas*), the style is both functional (the tile reflects the heat) and extraordinarily pretty.

A visit to Alcântara involves strolling down the main cobblestone street that leads from the port up the hillside through a series of small squares to a beautiful ruined church on a hilltop. Along the way are hundreds of beautiful houses to admire, and at least six ruined churches to poke about.

There are also three fine, small museums. The best, the **Casa Historica do IPHAN Seculo XVIII (IPHAN 18th-Century Historical House;** Praça Gomes de Castro s/n; no phone; daily 9am–2pm) is a huge colonial mansion filled with paintings, porcelain, furniture, and all of the belongings of a rich merchant family, including the still-intact slave quarters in the interior courtyard. Guides do an excellent job telling the history of the house and the families that built it. Admission is R$1.

Everything in Alcântara is very laid-back. Local residents pretty much leave you to wander their city. There are a few gift shops and numerous small restaurants, which make good places to do as the locals seem to be doing—trying to keep cool in the blazing heat.

Brazil's satellite-launching center is just 5km (3 miles) away, but has been off-limits to visitors since a rocket blew up on the launchpad in 2003, killing 21 technicians. There's a visitor center in the town, but it's not worth visiting.

Lotus Turismo (✆ **098/3221-0942;** www.lotusturismo.com.br) has guided tours to Alcântara that cost R$60 per person.

The ferry to Alcântara departs daily at 7am and 9am. The trip takes about 1 hr. Tickets each way cost R$12. Call ✆ **098/3232-0692** for information. Tickets can be purchased on the ferry, or beforehand at the Terminal Hidrovário on the waterfront in the São Luis centro histórico. Ferries depart either from the terminal, or if the tide is out, from the sandbar by the yacht club in Ponto d'Areia. Check beforehand at the terminal. Departure subject to change and delay without notice. Returning from Alcântara, ferries depart from the Alcântara Terminal at 4pm.

5 SHOPPING

The best shopping in São Luis is in the **centro histórico.** The **Reviver** area features a number of good crafts and art shops, as well as the small but intriguing indoor market called the **Casa das Tulhas,** Rua da Estrela s/n (Mon–Fri 6am–8pm, Sat 6am–6pm, Sun 6am–1pm). Higher up in the old city, the principal shopping street **Rua Grande** features an intriguing mix of national chain stores and cheaper local stores selling clothing, hardware, refrigerators, and everything else. Rua Grande is pedestrian-only for much of its length, making it pleasant for strolling and people-watching.

The city's biggest shopping mall, the **São Luis Shopping,** Av. Euclides Figueiredo 1000, Jaracaty (✆ **098/3251-3621;** Mon–Fri 10am–10pm and Sat till 8pm), has a six-screen cinema, large food court, and hundreds of shops. It's located a little past the Bandeira Tribuzzi bridge leading out of the centro histórico.

GIFTS & SOUVENIRS In the Reviver area of the centro histórico are a number of shops selling products unique to the state of Maranhão. One of the best places to browse for lace, tiles, baskets, ceramics, and sweets is the **Ceprama** craft center, Rua S. Pantaleão 1332 (no phone; Mon–Sat 9am–6pm and Sun 9am–1pm). Local artisans gather here daily to display and sell their ware. If you like the tilework you've seen all over the old city, check out **Ateliê Mão na Massa,** Rua do Giz 117 (© 098/3232-5957; Mon–Sat 9am–6pm). In addition to tiles, the workshop also features beautiful pieces of glazed pottery, as well as cheaper souvenirs.

MARKETS In the Reviver area, there's the **Casa das Tulhas,** Rua da Estrela s/n (Mon– Fri 6am–8pm, Sat 6am–6pm, Sun 6am–1pm), also known as the Feira da Praia Grande, a small but bustling indoor market with staples such as *farinha* and dried shrimp and fish, as well as a selection of herbs, roots, and tree bark used for a variety of medicinal pur- poses. The market is open daily from 7am to 6pm. At night, the **Rua da Alfândega** in the Reviver fills up with stalls selling local sweets and pastries and handmade leatherwork and basketry. A little farther from the Reviver, the much larger **Mercado Central,** Rua do Mercado s/n (corner of Rua Jacinto Maia with Av. Guaxenduba), sells staples, fresh fish, and a wide assortment of local fruit and medicinal herbs. Open daily 6am to 4pm, but best early in the morning.

6 SÃO LUIS AFTER DARK

The best place to go for some music and fun after dark in São Luis in the **Reviver** area in centro histórico. Close to a dozen bars, cafes, and restaurants offer music in the eve- ning, most of it live. Most nights of the week, something's happening—with music usually starting around 8pm and ending around 1am. Thursday through Saturday it really hops, and the music continues past 3am. The **Roots Bar,** Rua da Palma 85 (© 098/3221-7580), and **Bar do Porto** on Rua Trapiche 49 (© 098/3221-3749), both offer reggae. Both charge a nominal cover of about R$5.

Outside of downtown, the Lagoa da Jansen has a number of more mellow music venues, often doubling as restaurants. **Kitaro Lagoa,** Av. Mario Meireles s/n (© 098/ 3268-6528), has live music—usually MPB—every night starting around 9pm. Farther along the lakeshore, **Por Acaso,** Av. Mario Meireles s/n (© 098/3233-5837), is a great casual *chopperia* offering live music daily at 8pm.

The **Observatório,** Rua da Estrela 370, Beco da Prensa (© 098/3222-5151; Fri–Sat 11pm–6am), is one of the oldest gay and lesbian clubs in São Luis and is a great place to dance the night away downtown.

7 A SIDE TRIP TO THE LENÇOIS MARANHENSES

The 155,000-hectare (383,000-acre) Parque Nacional Lençóis Maranhenses offers an intriguing and spectacular landscape seen nowhere else on earth—a vast desert formed of tall, snow-white sand dunes, interwoven with beautiful pools of turquoise rainwater. The dunes are formed by the region's strong coastal winds. During the December-to-May rainy season, over 1,500mm (60 in.) of rain falls and collects in the basins between dunes forming countless blue freshwater lagoons. In June, when the water levels are at their highest, the dunes look like a giant mosaic of white interspersed with sparkling dots of blue, turquoise, and green.

Visitors can enter the park only on foot. The town of Barreirinhas, just outside the park, is the jumping-off spot for exploring the park and the surrounding region. The best season is June through September, when the rainwater lagoons are deepest, most swimmable, and most spectacular, and the weather warm and dry. By December and January, the water has all but evaporated, leaving only desert.

ESSENTIALS
Getting There
BY CAR Barreirinhas is 250km (155 miles) from São Luis, along the BR-135 and MA-402 highways. Both highways were recently paved and are in good shape.

BY BUS **Santur** (✆ 098/3248-3072) offers daily service to and from Barreirinhas by comfortable air-conditioned minivan. The trip costs R$35 per person and takes 3 to 4 hours. Pickup is at your hotel. Vans depart São Luis anywhere from 5 to 9am (depending on demand). Vans depart Barreirinhas daily at 5pm. **Cisne Branco** (✆ 098/3243-2847) has regular non-air-conditioned buses four times daily in both directions, departing from either the São Luis *rodoviaria,* or the *rodoviaria* in Barreirinhas. The trip takes from 4 to 6 hours. Cost is R$29.

BY PLANE Unfortunately, there are no longer regularly scheduled flights between São Luís and Barreirinhas. Depending on demand and the time of year, flights may start up again, but we recommend checking availability before you go. Contact one of the Barreirinhas tour operators (see below), the Pousada Encantes do Nordeste, the Preguiças Resort, or confirm with your travel agency.

Getting Around
Taxi stands are in the city center. A taxi from the center to an outlying hotel costs R$12. A motorcycle taxi costs R$4 from center to the hotels. Call ✆ 098/3349-0687 or cell 9111-5609.

Visitor Information
There is no **tourist office** in Barreirinhas. A useful website for Lençóis Park is **www.parquelencois.com.br**. The tourism agency **Ecodunas,** Rua Inácio Lins 164, in the center of town (✆ 098/3349-0545; www.ecodunas.com.br; daily 9am–6pm), has a helpful staff. The state tourism website is **www.turismo.ma.gov.br/en/index.html**.

FAST FACTS **Banco do Brasil,** Av. Joaquim Soeiro De Carvalho s/n (✆ 098/3349-1172; Mon–Fri 9am–2pm), has a 24-hour ATM. Internet access is at **Sol e Lua Cybercafe,** Av. Beira Mar s/n (Mon–Sat 8am–noon and 1:30–11pm), R$4 an hour, but the connection is unreliable.

EXPLORING
Barreirinhas doesn't take long to see. The Rio Preguiças loops its way through town. There is a pleasant boulevard with numerous restaurants and cafes facing the river, and next to that a big dune where locals swim. Most pousadas are located on the banks of the river a little out of town.

Several companies specialize in multiday packages. These can be as simple as transportation to and excursions in Lençóis, or as complicated as multiday jeep excursions to the Lençóis and then through the Parnaiba delta all the way to Jericoacoara. For details contact **Ecodunas** (✆ 098/3349-0545; www.ecodunas.com.br) or **Rota das Trilhas** (✆ 098/3349-0372; www.rotadastrilhas.com.br).

Exploring the great shifting mass of glorious white dunes is the whole point of coming here. Contact **Ecodunas** (see above) or **Rota das Trilhas** (see above), both in Barreirinhas and offering similar tours at comparable prices.

There are several ways to explore the area:

- **Hikes:** The most popular is a **half-day trip** by 4×4 to **Lagoa Bonita.** The dirt road travels by increasingly rough sand trails to the park entrance, after which you climb into the dunes and hike for about 2 hours, allowing for plenty of time to swim in a couple of small rainwater lagoons. Cost is R$50. The half-day trip can be done in the morning, but in the afternoon it's cooler and you get to see the sunset. Variations on this trip go to other nearby lakes such as Lagoa Azul and Lagoa Paraiso. **Longer hikes** with customized itineraries can be arranged by consultation with Ecodunas. Guides are quite cheap at R$80 per day for up to three people. A 4×4 and driver—to drop you off or pick you up at a trail head—costs R$300 per day.

- **Four-Wheel ATV:** These full-day trips zoom up and down the dunes at the very fringes of the national park (ATVs aren't allowed inside the park boundaries), covering the roughly 30km (19 miles) between Barreirinhas and Atins on the coast. A full-day trip costs R$350 per ATV, which fits two people.

- **Scenic Flights:** The best way to admire the spectacular patchwork of crystal-clear lagoons amid the dazzling white sand dunes is from above. Cost of a 30-minute scenic flight is R$180 per person, with a minimum of three people. Flights are best in the morning.

Trips to Atins, Caburé & Mandacaru

At the mouth of the Rio Preguiças are two tiny villages sandwiched between the Lençóis dunes and the ocean. **Mandacaru** is a fishing village close to the mouth of the river; **Caburé** is a narrow neck of pure sand perhaps 200m (650 ft.) wide, with crashing surf on one side and the lazy Rio Preguiças on the other. What started as simple camps on this wind-swept piece of geography have since grown into a small collection of pousadas and restaurants.

One popular option for visiting these areas is to take a day trip by boat from Barreirinhas. The trip descends the river, stopping at the Smaller (Pequenos) Lençóis on the way. This sand dune area is still growing, and you can see where the advancing sand is eating away at the riverside forest. The trip stops in at Caburé for lunch, with time in **Mandacaru** to wander this tiny picturesque village and climb the 45m (150-ft.) lighthouse for a view of the national park, before returning to Barreirinhas. The tour can be arranged with **Ecodunas** or **Rota das Trilhas** (see above). Both charge R$60, lunch not included.

Many people opt to spend the night in Caburé or Atins. This allows time the next day to make a walking expedition into the Lençóis dunes along the coast beyond Atins. The route takes you through several beautiful and completely isolated small lakes before stopping at the **Restaurante de Luzia** (no phone), a tiny palm-frond covered shack at the ocean side that serves an orgiastic feast of giant prawns for R$15 per person. Cost of this coastal dune expedition is around R$100 for up to four people, prawn lunch not included, with departure from Caburé. You can arrange the entire trip (boat from Barreirinhas, coastal day trip, and boat back to Barreirinhas) with **Ecodunas** or **Rota das Trilhas** (see above).

If you decide to stay in Caburé, there are several rustic pousadas. The sandspit has no electricity, so it's generators only and at 10pm it's lights out, candles on. **Pousada Porto Buriti** (✆ **098/3349-1802** or cell 9984-0088) has the best infrastructure. It offers 10 small chalets at R$120 to R$160 a night. Make arrangements before staying overnight as accommodations are limited. An option in Atins is **Pousada Rancho do Buna** (✆ **098/3349-5005;** www.ranchodobuna.com.br), with basic but very clean and pleasant accommodations for R$110 double. The owners can also arrange horseback rides, bird-watching tours, or a variety of hikes and boat tours in the area.

Watersports
In other parts of the world, **Boia Cross** is called "floating down the river in an inner-tube." **Ecodunas** (see above) offers a half-day float. The trip there and back is 90 minutes each way, and you spend 2 hours floating downstream. Cost is R$50 per person.

WHERE TO STAY
Barreirinhas's two best pousadas are a little outside the town, a short ride by cab or moto-taxi. Though not nearly as nice, there are two options in town. The **Pousada Buriti** (✆ **098/3349-1800**) is a sort of motor-court motel. Rooms are quite large, but they're motel blocks surrounding a hot, treeless, courtyard parking lot. However, there is a pool and children's play area. The **Pousada Beira Rio** (✆ **098/3349-0579**) is a three-story hotel by the riverside. Rooms are simple and clean, with tile floors and small balconies overlooking the river.

Expensive
Porto Preguiças Resort ★★ (Kids)   The only luxury accommodations available in Barreirinhas, the Porto Preguiças Resort has 30 chalets set on a nicely landscaped piece of land by the river Preguiças. The leisure areas of the resort are nicely done. There's a gorgeous lagoon-shaped swimming pool with a sand-covered bottom, a hammock "central" for relaxing by the river, an authentic bocce game area, and a big beautiful restaurant and bar area. The chalets—which should be set by themselves off among the trees—are clumped together cheek by jowl. Inside, the chalets are spacious (many come with king-size beds) with large bathrooms with hot showers. Furnishings are rustic and simple. In short, the resort is very nice, though perhaps not worth what they're charging.

Carnaubal Velho 2km (1 mile) from town, Barreirinhas, 65590-000 MA. ✆ **098/3349-1220.** Fax 098/3349-0620. www.portopreguicas.com.br. 34 units, shower only. High season R$350–R$390 double; low season R$295 double. Extra person add 25%. Children 5 and under stay free in parent's room. AE, DC, MC, V. Free parking. **Amenities:** Restaurant (see below); bar; outdoor pool; sauna; kayaks. *In room:* A/C, TV, fridge, minibar.

Moderate
Pousada Encantes do Nordeste ★★ (Value)   Located just on the outskirts of town, the Pousada Encantes do Nordeste has a natural charm that makes it one of the nicest pousadas in the region. The chalets are set on a gently sloping hillside. The garden is beautiful and lush with a hammock for two to enjoy a lazy nap in the hot afternoon. A short trail leads to the river Preguiças. The rooms are very pleasant with nice, comfortable beds, air-conditioning, and television. There's even a closed-circuit DVD system that allows you to pick out a movie and watch it in your room. The staff at the pousada is very friendly and helpful in hooking you up with all the excursions. All tours include

Tips **Take the Long Way Home**

Just beyond the Lençóis Maranhenses lies one of Brazil's most beautiful and still unexplored regions, the **Parnaíba River Delta.** This magical landscape is composed of sand dunes, beaches, river estuaries, mangroves, islands, and remote villages. If you have a few extra days you can travel from Barreirinhas, by boat and/or 4×4, to Paulinho Neves, on the edge of the Pequenos Lençóis, another protected dune area, and then to Tutóia, the jumping-off point to a number of remote islands in the delta. One of the largest islands, Ilha do Caju, is a nature sanctuary with only one small rustic pousada (**www.ilhadocaju. com.br**), where guests can truly get away from it all. Instead of backtracking all the way to São Luis, you can continue overland to Jericoacoara and then to Fortaleza (chapter 14). Of course you can also start in Fortaleza/Jeri and make the trip in the other direction. There are several companies that organize this trip. In Barreirinhas contact **Ecodunas** (② **098/3349-0545;** www.ecodunas. com.br) or **Rota das Trilhas** (② **098/3349-0372;** www.rotadastrilhas.com.br). You may also contact adventure specialists **Jeri Off Road** (② **088/3669-2268;** www.jeri.tur.br) in Jericoacoara to help you plan your itinerary.

pickup and drop-off at the pousada. Brand-new bar/restaurant **Bambaê** (see below) on the edge of the river provides a great dining option within walking distance.

Rua Principal s/n Barreirinhas, 65590-000 MA. ② **098/3349-0288** or (São Paulo) 011/3331-3434. www. encantesdonordeste.com.br. 15 units, shower only. R$160–R$185 chalet. Extra person R$50. Children 6 and under stay free in parent's room. AE, V. Free parking. **Amenities:** Restaurant; bar. *In room:* A/C, TV, minibar, no phone.

WHERE TO DINE

For a town as small as Barreirinhas there are a surprising number of restaurants. Most of them have a fairly similar menu, involving grilled steak and seafood. The nicest restaurants are on the Avenida Beira Mar, the street that runs along the riverside. Next to and above the water—a number of tables are on the floating pier—is the **Tropical Marina Restaurant,** Av. Beira Mar s/n (② 098/3349-1143). The best dish here is prawn *moqueca* with coconut milk and palm oil. For R$25 you get a clay pot full of fragrant stew packed with shrimp that serves two people. The menu also includes steak dishes, pasta, and grilled fish. The Marina serves up an inexpensive and tasty kilo buffet, one of the few places where you can grab a quick hot lunch. Another nice waterfront restaurant is the **Barlavento,** Av. Beira Mar s/n (no phone), close to the Terraço Preguiças on the Avenida Beira Mar. The kitchen serves up grilled chicken and some steak dishes, as well as fish. Worth trying are the grilled fish with prawn sauce and the grilled fish in a passion-fruit sauce. Finally, for a more elegant night out try the restaurant at the **Porto Preguiças Resort,** Estrada do Carnaubal s/n (see above; ② 098/3349-1220). Start off with a drink or a cocktail from the best-stocked bar in Maranhão. If you are hungry, order the *peixada* seafood stew with sea bass; the generous portion will easily feed three people. To make it a special occasion, call ahead and order the lamb in coconut milk or the free-range chicken stew. These dishes require 4 hours notice as they are made from scratch but are worth the wait.

The new hip place in town is **Bambaê,** Estrada de São Domingos Km 4.5 (at Pousada Encantes do Nordeste, see above; ✆ **098/3349-0691**). This beautiful bar/restaurant on the shore of the Preguiças River is a perfect destination for a drink or a meal. The restaurant serves up snacks, sandwiches, and salads, as well as more sophisticated dishes such as the *robalo* fish with black olives. On Fridays and Saturdays there is live music. (Call ahead for opening hours in the low season.)

16

The Amazon:
Manaus & Belém

It was a lost Spanish conquistador who gave a name to the largest river and rainforest on earth. In 1541 Francisco de Orellana returned after a year's absence with a tale of a vast new river, and of attacks by hostile Indians, some led by bands of female warriors. In Europe, these women warriors were taken to be the last remaining members of the tribe whose queen Achilles slew at Troy. Land and river both were named for this likely mythical tribe—the Amazons.

Three centuries later, it was a British explorer, Alfred Russel Wallace, who first noted what is today very likely the Amazon's greatest claim to fame—its diversity. The Amazon rainforest has more biodiversity—more species of plants and animals per given patch of forest—than any ecosystem on earth. Being a naturalist, Wallace also proposed an explanation. It was due, he believed, to the Amazon's extraordinary number of rivers, streams, and channels, which effectively cut the forest up into millions of small islands. Marooned and isolated, a separated single species would evolve into many new species.

So logical did this seem that only in the past 10 years did scientists try to test it out. At which point they discovered it, too, was a myth. The reason for the Amazon's diversity has once again retreated into mystery.

The Brazilian Amazon today remains one of the most isolated, most sparsely populated regions on earth. Yet it is also home to more than four million people. Tarzan myths aside, most of them live not in the jungle, but in cities. Indeed, the state of Amazonas is one of the most urbanized in Brazil.

The Amazon's two principal cities are Manaus and Belém, capitals of the states of Amazonas and Pará, respectively. Belém sits at the mouth of the river, Manaus at the spot where the two principal tributaries—the Rio Negro and the Solimões—join to form the Amazon. Belém is the older, more civilized of the two, with colonial architecture, forts, stately churches, and a sense of itself as the natural senior partner, somehow left behind by a brash new upstart. The upstart, Manaus, has in the past 50 years grown from a city of a few hundred thousand to a metropolis of almost two million. There's an exciting, frontier feel to Manaus. Belém offers history, excellent food, and much better nightlife. Manaus offers a sense of its own future and an opportunity to step into the vastness of the tropical rainforest.

A visit to the Amazon is a chance to penetrate the mystery, to experience the tangle of myth and reality firsthand.

1 MANAUS

2,836km (1,762 miles) NW of Rio de Janeiro, 2,682km (1,666 miles) NW of São Paulo

On the surface, Manaus looks a lot like other Brazilian cities. The old downtown is shabby and bustling. Along the shoreline in the upscale Ponta Negra area you'll find the

DINING ◆
Bistrô Ananã 2
Glacial Sorveteria 5

ATTRACTIONS ●
Alfândega 9
Encontro das Águas 11
Hidroviaria do Amazonas
 (Riverboat Terminal) 8
Mercado Adolpho
 Lisboa 10
Museu do Indio 7
Palacio Rio Negro 6
Teatro Amazonas 4

ACCOMMODATIONS ■
Hotel Manaós 3
Saint Paul 1

16

THE AMAZON: MANAUS & BELÉM

MANAUS

familiar beachside high-rises, wide streets, and waterfront kiosks. But stop for a moment and contemplate: You're in the middle of nowhere with 1,610km (1,000 miles) of forest in every direction.

Inhabitants of the largest city in the Amazon, Manaus's 1.6 million people live on the shores of the Rio Negro, just upstream from where it joins the Rio Solimões to become the Amazon. Though first settled in the 1600s, there's a frontier feel to the place.

Near the end of the 19th century, when the Amazon was the world's only rubber supplier, there was a 30-year boom in rubber and Manaus got rich indeed. Some of the city's finest buildings date back to this time, among them the Customs house and the famous Teatro Amazonas. The boom ended around 1910, some years after an enterprising Brit stole some Amazon rubber seeds and planted them in new plantations in Malaya (modern-day Malaysia).

The city's next boom came in 1966, when Manaus was declared a free-trade zone. Electronics assembly plants sprouted across the city, and workers poured in to staff the factories. In the space of just a few years the city's population doubled to half a million. The retail traffic dried up in the early '90s when the government reduced import tariffs, but with the free-trade zone still in place, manufacturing carries on.

These days, the city's biggest employer is the Brazilian army, which has jungle-training schools, listening stations, and a substantial standing force stationed in the city—all to preserve Brazilian sovereignty over the Amazon. Tourism has also expanded, most of it focused on the rainforest. Manaus is the main departure point for trips into the Amazon.

ESSENTIALS
Getting There

BY PLANE Azul (② 092/3003-2985; www.voeazul.com.br), **Gol** (② 0300/115-2121; www.voegol.com.br), **TAM** (② 0800/570-5700; www.tam.com.br), and **TRIP** (② 092/3003-8747; www.voetrip.com.br) have flights from major cities in Brazil. Flights from Rio or São Paulo take about 5 hours. TAM also has regular direct flights to Manaus from Miami.

Manaus's international airport, **Eduardo Gomes,** Avenida Santos Dumont (② 092/3652-1212), is 17km (10 miles) from downtown. There's a **Tourist Information** desk in the arrivals hall (② 092/3652-1120; daily 7am–11pm) with free maps of the city and some information on hotels and tours. A taxi to Manaus Centro will cost about R$45. You also have the option of taking a **regular city bus,** no. 306 to Centro, for R$1.80. Guests of the Tropical can take the **Fontur shuttle,** for R$24 per person. There is a small currency exchange at the airport as well as Banco do Brasil and HSBC ATMs connected to the Visa/PLUS systems.

BY BOAT Boats dock at the new **Hidroviaria do Amazonas (Riverboat Terminal)** (② 092/3621-4310) in the middle of downtown at Rua Marquês de Santa Cruz 25. There is an information desk inside the front door where you can find out about arrival and departure times, and a ticket kiosk where you buy tickets. Boats for **Belém** normally depart Wednesday and Friday at noon. The trip downstream takes 4 days, upstream travel takes 5 days. Delays are not uncommon. For information on the 5-day journey from Belém to Manaus, see "By Riverboat," under "Essentials: Arriving," in the section on Belém (p. 405). Cost of a first-class hammock spot (on the upper deck) is R$245. Hammocks are not supplied. Buy one in Manaus (see "Shopping," later in this chapter). Cabins cost R$750 to R$900. Good, simple meals and filtered water are supplied on the boat at no extra cost. From the terminal it's a short walk or taxi ride, R$10 to R$15, to the downtown hotels. To the Tropical Manaus it's a 20-minute taxi ride R$50 or a 40-minute bus ride, no. 120 from Centro.

Tip: If you have some competence in Portuguese, you can negotiate a 10% to 20% cheaper fare by going directly to a riverboat, most of which dock downstream by the quay opposite the Mercado Municipal.

> ### ⓘ Tips Warning! Steer Clear of Aggressive Airport Touts
>
> The airport touts have (finally!) been banished from the baggage claim area of the Manaus airport, so now they accost newcomers in the arrivals hall, offering every type of city and jungle tour. *Do not book with these people!* Their standard MO is to ask what you're interested in doing. Surprise, surprise, whatever you want to do, they have that tour. Once you pay, they resell you to another operator doing the standard 50-people-on-the-boat Meeting of the Waters day tour. Complain all you like—you'll never get your money back.

There is now also a new fast catamaran to Santarem, which takes approximately 12 hours to make the journey downstream. The catamaran departs from the quay opposite the Mercado Municipal.

City Layout

The city is the river. Downtown, all activity gravitates toward the waterfront on the Rio Negro, and it's there that you really feel the heart of the city. The entire city is plotted in an easy-to-follow grid pattern; in the oldest part of town—which occupies a peninsula at the river's edge—the grid runs at a slight angle to that of the rest of the city. The **port** and the **municipal market (mercado municipal)** both face the river. The main attractions for visitors concentrate in a 20-block radius around the port and are easily accessible on foot. The downtown **bus terminal** is directly in front of the port; on the other side there's the busy and newly renovated **Praça da Matriz.** To the east of the square are a number of narrow parallel streets, centered on **Rua Guilherme Moreira,** that form Manaus's main downtown **shopping district.** The busy east-west **Avenida Sete de Setembro** marks the end of the oldest section of downtown. From here north, the grid angles slightly, and things get less interesting. The only real sight of interest is the **Teatro Amazonas,** 4 blocks farther north on **Rua Barroso.** The entire downtown area is safe during the day; just watch your purse and wallet in the crowds. In the evening stay on the main squares and avenues. Avoid the port area and the side streets along the *iguarapés* (river channels) at night; small slums have settled along the riverbed, particularly to the east and northeast of downtown. From the downtown core the city sprawls inland and along the river. **Ponta Negra Beach,** about 18km (11 miles) from downtown, is one of the more upscale neighborhoods where the beachfront has become a popular nightlife-and-entertainment area. This is also where you'll find the **Tropical Manaus.** A good part of the beach disappears in the wet season (Jan–Apr), but the food stands and entertainment stay. In the dry season the beach is a great place to swim and suntan on the shores of the Rio Negro.

Getting Around

BY BUS From the Tropical Manaus to downtown, take bus no. 120 (R$2); the trip takes 35 to 40 minutes. The bus stops at the **Praça da Matriz,** which is within easy walking distance of all downtown attractions. To get to the Ceasa Port from downtown, take the ceasa bus from Praça da Matriz.

BY TAXI Taxis can be hailed on the street or reserved for a specific time by phoning ahead. For the airport, contact **Coopertaxi** (© 092/3652-1544 or 3652-1568). In town, phone **Tele-Rádio Táxi** at © 092/3633-3211. You're most likely to use taxis if you are staying at the Tropical and going back and forth to downtown. For this trip taxis all quote the same price—currently R$52—and don't run the meter. You can knock R$10 off the price if you bargain before you get in the cab.

BY CAR Renting a car in Manaus makes little sense. In the city all the sights are within walking distance. Outside of the city it's, you know, a jungle.

Visitor information

The **Manaustur** tourism information desk at the airport is open daily from 7am to 11pm and located in the arrivals hall (© 092/3652-1120). They can provide city maps, brochures, hotel information, and telephone numbers of tour operators. The State of Amazonas tourism agency, **AmazonasTur** (www.visitamazonas.am.gov.br), has an info center at the airport (© **092/3182-9850**), open 24 hours. There is also a downtown location close to the opera house, at Av. Eduardo Ribeiro 666 (© **092/3182-6250**), open Monday to Friday 8am to 5pm and Saturday till noon.

Fast Facts   Manaus

Car Rentals Contact **Avis** (© **092/3652-1579**) or **Localiza** (© **092/3652-1176**).

Consulates **United States,** Rua Franco de Sá 310, sala 306 (© **092/3611-3333**); **Great Britain** (Honorary), Rua Poraquê 240, Distrito Industrial (© **092/4009-1819**).

Currency Exchange For your currency needs, go to **Banco do Brasil,** Rua Guilherme Moreira 315, Centro (© **092/3621-5500**); **Cortês Câmbio,** Av. Sete de Setembro 1199, Centro (© **092/3622-4222;** www.cortez.com.br); or **Amazonas Shopping** (© **092/3642-2525**).

Dentist **Clínica Odontológica Ortomax** is at Av. Joaquim Nabuco 2285 (© **092/ 3633-3121,** or cell 9964-5211).

Hospital For medical attention, go to **Pronto Socorro e Hospital dos Acidentados,** Av. Joaquim Nabuco 1755, Centro (© **092/3663-2200**).

Internet Access The **Tropical Manaus** has an Internet cafe open daily from 9am to 10pm; charge is R$18 per hour. In Centro, try **Amazon Cyber Café,** Av. Getulio Vargas 626 (© **092/3232-9068**). Open Monday through Friday 9am to 11pm, Saturday from 10am to 8pm, and Sunday from 1 to 8pm; R$4 per hour.

Time Zone Manaus is 1 hour behind São Paulo and Rio de Janeiro.

Weather It's hot year-round—hot and muggy and rainy from December through March (30°C–36°C/86°F–96°F) and just plain hot the rest of the year. The wet season (Dec–Mar) is the best time to experience the flooded forest; the river rises and brings boats and canoes up to eye level with the treetops. The dry season (Aug–Nov) is wonderful for exploring the forest and beaches that appear when the water recedes.

WHERE TO STAY
Centro
Expensive
Saint Paul ★   This hotel is convenient for those who are in town for a night before heading into the forest. The market, port, and opera house are all within walking distance. The area is not great at night when most of the businesses close, but a few restaurants are in the vicinity.

Rua Ramos Ferreira 1115, Centro, Manaus, 69020-080 AM. © **092/2101-3800.** Fax 092/2101-3838. www. manaushoteis.tur.br. 70 apts. R$280 double. Children 5 and under stay free in parent's room. AE, DC, MC, V. Free parking. **Amenities:** Restaurant; bar; small outdoor pool; room service; sauna. *In room:* A/C, TV, Internet, minibar.

Moderate
Hotel Manaós   Situated cater-cornered from the Opera House, the Manaós provides something rare in the Amazon—basic clean accommodations at a moderate price. Rooms come in two flavors: two singles, or a double and a single. The price is the same for both.

Bathrooms are extremely clean and bright (consider wearing your shades in the shower).
Best of all, for those in the know, room nos. 304 through 311 and 204 through 211
provide a fabulous view of the Opera House.

Av. Eduardo Ribeiro 881, Centro, Manaus, AM 69010-001. (*C* **092/3633-5744.** Fax 092/232-4443. www.
hotelmanaos.com.br. 39 units. R$190 double. 10% discount for stays of more than 1 night. Children 6 and
under stay free in parent's room. AE, DC, MC, V. Free parking. **Amenities:** Restaurant; room service. *In
room:* A/C, TV, Internet, minibar.

Ponta Negra

Located 20km (12 miles) from downtown, the Tropical Manaus is the best place to stay in
Manaus. Better yet, it's located on Ponta Negra Beach, a popular nightlife district on the
banks of the Rio Negro. Of all the hotels in Brazil, this one is definitely worth the splurge.

Very Expensive

Tropical Manaus ★★★   After the Copacabana Palace, this is the most famous hotel
in Brazil. Built on the shores of the Rio Negro, within its own little patch of rainforest, the
Tropical is a destination in itself. Outside there's a vast pool, zoo, children's play area, archery
range (lessons complimentary), a jogging trail, beach volleyball, soccer fields, horseback riding, and the list goes on. Inside, the original wing of the hotel is referred to as *ala colonial,* in
contrast to the more modern *ala moderna.* Where you stay is more a matter of preference than
quality. The colonial rooms have more character, with beautiful dark-wood furniture and
hardwood floors, but they can also be a bit musty. The modern wing is pleasantly furnished
with carpets and contemporary decor in light colors. All rooms are a good size with high ceilings and large windows, and the bathrooms are spacious and modern, with showers and
bathtubs. The deluxe rooms come with a balcony and more space. To really splurge, go for
the *suite nobre* (R$900, elegantly furnished with a large sitting room and Jacuzzi tub in the
bathroom). The junior suites are not a great deal, especially compared to the spacious deluxe
rooms. A travel agent may get better rates than those listed below.

Av. Coronel Teixeira 1320, Ponta Negra, Manaus, 69029-120 AM. (*C* **0800/701-2670** or 092/3659-5000.
Fax 092/3658-5026. www.tropicalhotel.com.br. 601 units. R$320–R$400 standard or superior double;
R$475 deluxe double. There is often a 10%–30% discount on these rates. Extra person add 25%. Children
10 and under stay free in parent's room. AE, DC, MC, V. Bus: 120. **Amenities:** 3 restaurants, including Karu
Grill (p. 383); 2 bars; disco; children's program; health club; large outdoor pool complex; room service;
sauna; smoke-free floors; spa; tennis courts; watersports. *In room:* A/C, TV, hair dryer, Internet, minibar.

Tropical Manaus Business ★★★   Located right on the shore of the Rio Negro,
the Tropical Business is the newest addition to the Tropical complex. Whereas the *old*
Tropical oozes elegance and conjures up visions of explorers ready to take off on a jungle
adventure, the new Tropical is all, well, business. Bright and sleek, the hotel offers modern and spacious rooms with king-size beds, high-speed Internet, efficient air-conditioning and phone system, 21st-century plumbing, electronic safes, and fabulous views of the
Rio Negro. The suite experience is identical to the regular rooms; the only added feature
is the veranda overlooking the river. As perks, the hotel offers a free shuttle service to the
airport and downtown and free 24-hour access to the business center. The hotel has a
large outdoor pool and sun deck overlooking the Rio Negro and a state-of-the-art fitness
center. Guests may also use all facilities of the old Tropical.

Av. Coronel Teixeira 1320, Ponta Negra, Manaus, 69037-000 AM. (*C* **0800/701-2670** or 092/2123-3000.
Fax 092/2123-3021. www.tropicalhotel.com.br. 184 units. R$290 standard; R$350 suite. Extra person add
25%. Children 10 and under stay free in parent's room. AE, DC, MC, V. Bus: 120. **Amenities:** Restaurant; 2
bars; concierge; health club; large outdoor pool; room service; sauna; smoke-free floors. *In room:* A/C, TV,
hair dryer, minibar, Wi-Fi.

Mango Guest House ★   The Mango is a nice small guesthouse, unfortunately located in a boring walled-off suburb about halfway between downtown and Ponta Negra. Rooms are simple, small, and pleasant, with tile floors, firm single or double beds, and clean, functional bathrooms with super-hot showers. All rooms have a small veranda that looks out on a grassy courtyard and small pool, and the guesthouse has several nice lounges and sitting rooms and free Internet access. The Mango is perfect for those who just need to spend a night in Manaus before or after a jungle stay. All tours pick up and drop off, and the guesthouse will happily store your excess luggage while you are off in the rainforest. Tell taxi drivers the guesthouse is in Kissia Dois, off Rua Jacira Reis, which runs off Rua Darcy Vargas.

Rua Flavio Espirito Santo 1, Kissia II, 69040-250 AM. ℭ 092/3656-6033. Fax 092/3656-6101. www. naturesafaris.com.br. 14 units. R$100–R$150 standard. Extra person add 25%. Credit cards only when booking online or via travel agency: AE, DC, MC, V. Bus: 121. **Amenities:** Restaurant; outdoor pool; Wi-Fi. *In room:* A/C, fridge.

Mercure Apartments Manaus ★   This is where the business travelers stay in Manaus. Located in Adrianópolis—fast becoming the city's restaurant hot spot—this new member of the well-respected Mercure chain offers comfortable clean rooms with tile floors and queen-size (or two twin) beds, plus a small functional work desk with plug-ins for laptops and high-speed Internet. As with all Mercure properties, the service is brisk and efficient. There's a small, pretty rooftop pool with a view of nothing much, and a good-quality fitness center with personal trainers in attendance, and a Jacuzzi for relaxing in afterward.

Av. da Recife 1000, Adrianópolis, 69040-250 AM. ℭ 092/2101-1100. Fax 092/2101-1101. www.accor hotels.com.br. 109 units. R$275 superior double. Extra person add 25%. AE, DC, MC, V. Bus: 118. **Amenities:** Restaurant; bar; fitness center; Jacuzzi; rooftop pool; room service. *In room:* A/C, TV, fridge, Internet, minibar.

WHERE TO DINE
Adrianópolis
Village BRAZILIAN   One of the city's best restaurants, the Village is a dining destination for the city's elite. The menu covers a vast range, with seafood and fish dishes, risottos and pastas, meat, chicken, and lamb dishes all on offer. The chef's approach has a slight Italian tinge, while the use of Brazilian ingredients (such as catupiry cheese with Bahian prawns) gives the dishes their local flavor. The wine list is likely the most extensive in Manaus.

Rua Mario Ypiranga Monteiro (formerly called Rua Recife) 948, Adrianópolis. ℭ 092/3234-3296. www. villagerestaurante.com.br. Main courses R$24–R$48. AE, DC, MC, V. Tues–Sat noon–3pm and 6pm–midnight.

Centro
Bistrô Ananã BRAZILIAN   This charming little bistro prepares dishes with Amazonian ingredients that you won't find anywhere else. The signature dish is rack of *tambaqui* (fish) ribs in a chutney of *tucupi*, with Bahian risotto and a *farofa* of local bananas. *Note:* They are only open on Friday and Saturday.

Travessa Padre Ghisland 38, Centro (near the Colégio Dom Bosco). ℭ 092/3234-0056. Main courses R$24–R$52. AE, MC, V. Fri–Sat 7:30pm–midnight.

Hot Spot in Adrianópolis

In the past few years, the upscale neighborhood of Adrianópolis has emerged as Manaus's culinary hot spot, with a number of fine restaurants in a relatively concentrated area. In addition to the **Village** (one of the city's best, reviewed above), there's top-quality (and top-dollar) Portuguese cuisine at **Casa do Bacalhau,** Rua Humberto Caldeirado Filho 1587-A (formerly called Rua Paraíba; ✆ **092/3642-1723;** Mon–Sat noon–4pm and 7:30pm–midnight, Sun 11:30am–4pm). For local—and more affordable—Amazonian dishes there's **Choupana,** Rua Mario Ypiranga Monteiro 790 (formerly called Rua Recife; ✆ **092/3635-3878;** Wed–Sat 11am–3pm and 6:30–11pm, Sun noon–4pm). Even cheaper, and arguably more fun, is **Açaí e Companhia,** Rua Acre (✆ **092/3653-3637;** daily noon–midnight), a kind of outdoor kiosk which specializes in local fish dishes such as *jambu* and *tambaqui.* On Friday and Saturday evening there's live music. Korean food is hard to find anywhere in Brazil, much less in the middle of the rainforest, and yet in Adrianópolis there's **Ara,** Rua Mario Ypiranga Monteiro 1005 (formerly called Rua Recife, casa 1; ✆ **092/3234-2650;** daily 11am–2pm and 6–10pm).

Glacial Sorveteria DESSERT   One of the best ways to try many of the exotic fruit of the Amazon is in the form of ice cream. Some suggested flavors are *cupuaçu, açai, jaca, bacaba,* and *graviola.* Grab a couple of flavors and taste away. Another shop is in Ponta Negra (✆ **092/3658-3980).**

Av. Getulio Vargas 161, Centro. ✆ **092/3233-7940.** www.glacial.com.br. R$4.50–R$9. No credit cards. Mon–Sat 10am–11:30pm; Sun 3–11:30pm.

Ponta Negra

Ponta Negra offers a number of nighttime dining options, none outstanding in terms of food, but most in very pleasant surroundings. On the waterfront, **Laranjinha** (✆ **092/ 3658-6666;** Mon–Sat 5pm–3am, Sun 5pm–5am) has a great patio and makes for fine people-watching. Most nights there's a slightly Vegas folklore show featuring beautiful young things (male and female) in skimpy "traditional" costumes. On a candlelit patio in the Tropical Manaus, the **Karu Grill** ★ (✆ **092/2123-5000)** offers a nightly buffet with excellent regional local fish, *macaxeira* (a local root that is often cooked like a potato), soups, or grilled steak and fresh salad.

EXPLORING MANAUS

You won't need more than 2 days to see Manaus. Start your exploration at the port. The new **Riverboat Terminal** is a little too air-conditioned and anodyne, but the **Mercado Adolpho Lisboa** is a great place to see local fish and produce, not to mention local folk remedies. Farther down, the **Feira do Produtor** has every Amazon product imaginable, and the waterfront out front where boats load up is a fascinating glimpse of Amazon frontier. The **Opera House** is an extravagant, impressive testament to the legacy of the rubber boom. A half-day trip out to the **Meeting of the Waters** is a worthwhile afternoon excursion. In the evening, head to the beach at **Ponta Negra,** and stop for a cold beer or an exotic ice cream as you watch the river. And then get thee out into the Amazon. There's wild stuff to see.

The Lowdown on Amazonian Cuisine

Amazonian dishes mix a dollop of Portuguese and a dash of African flavors with native traditions and lots of local ingredients. The star attraction in most dishes is fish, fresh from the Amazon's many tributaries. It's worth visiting the market in Manaus just to see what these creatures look like. Make sure you try at least the *tucunaré;* the meat is so tasty it's best served plainly grilled. *Pirarucú* is known as the codfish of the Amazon. It can be salted and used just like *bacalhau. Tambaqui* and *paçu* also have delicious firm flesh that works well in stews and broths. One popular stew is **caldeirada.** Often made with *tucanaré,* the rich broth is spiced with onion, tomato, peppers, and herbs. Very different is the **pato no tucupí,** a duck dish stewed with *tucupí,* the juice of fermented and spiced cassava. **Tacacá** is a delicious native soup, made with the yellow *tucupí* cassava, *murupí* peppers, and garlic, onion, and dried shrimp. You'll often see this for sale on the streets, traditionally served in a gourd cup. To add kick to your food, try some **murupí** pepper sauce.

The region is also rich in fruit, many of which can only be found in the Amazon, most of which do not even have English names. The citruslike **bacuri,** with its soft spongelike skin and white flesh, is addictive; like Christmas mandarins, you can't eat just one. The most commonly eaten fruit is **cupuaçu.** This large round fruit, like a small pale coconut, has an odd sweet-and-sour taste at first bite, like it's almost *too* ripe. But you'll learn to savor it in desserts and juices. **Tucumã** is a small, hard fruit similar to an unripe peach. Locals eat slices of it on bread. At lodges it's also a favorite of half-tame monkeys and parrots who will snag one whenever they get a chance. **Açai** is a popular fruit, but it can't be eaten raw; the berries are first soaked and then squashed to obtain the juice. You will find it in juices and ice cream. In the jungle you'll come across fruit that you don't even see in Manaus markets. My favorite is the **mari-mari,** a snakelike vine about as long as your arm; when opened with a quick twist it reveals a row of Lifesaver-looking fruit. Green, juicy, and full of vitamins.

The Top Attractions

CIGS Zoo (Kids) It's a strange place, this zoo. It's part of the army's jungle warfare–training center, and many of the animals were captured by soldiers on patrol. The animal enclosures range from the worst you've ever seen to quite sophisticated and humane habitats. One poor black jaguar is kept in a concrete-floored cage no more than two jaguar-lengths square, while the cougars are kept in sizable enclosures with grass and a small pond. The collection is tremendous: black and spotted jaguars, cougars and smaller cats, toucans, macaws, and more. You'll also see harpy eagles stuck in heartbreakingly small enclosures. Yet the monkey habitat is wide and well done—go figure. Allow an hour to 90 minutes.

Estrada do Ponta Negra, Km 13. (C) **092/3625-1966.** Admission R$2 adults, free for children 12 and under. Tues–Sun 9am–4:30pm. Bus: 120.

The Meeting of the Waters (Encontro das Aguas) ★★ For more than 200 years tourists have been venturing out to see this remarkable sight: The dark slow waters of the Rio Negro meet the faster muddy brown waters from the Rio Solimões, and because of differences in velocity, temperature, and salinity, the two rivers carry on side-by-side for miles, with progressively less distinct whorls and eddies marking the interface between these two rivers. It's a classic Manaus day trip, and a great excuse to get out on the Amazon. If you're booked at a lodge downstream of Manaus you'll pass through the Meeting of the Waters on the way there and back. If not, consider booking a day trip. This tour will usually include the main sights of Manaus, such as the public market, the port, the opera house, and a long stop at **Lago Janauary Ecological Park.** Located about an hour from Manaus, the Lago Janauary features some elevated boardwalks weaving through the trees and giant floating Vitoria Regia lily pads. *Note:* In the dry season (Aug–Dec), the trip through the Lago becomes impossible and tour operators take you to the Ilha da Terra Nova to see the rubber trees.

All Manaus agencies offer day tours for about R$110 per person. Try Viverde (☏ **092/3248-9988**).

Mercado Adolpho Lisboa ★ The Adolpho Lisboa is beautiful iron-and-glass copy of the now-demolished market hall in Les Halles, Paris. It's a great place to see some of the local fish, fruit, and vegetables. The variety of fish is overwhelming. Not for the squeamish, the vendors cut and clean the fish on the spot with complete disregard for the tender psyche; though chopped in half, some of the larger catfish still wriggle. The fruit and vegetable section is equally fascinating. Just in case you wanted to heal thyself, stop in at one of the herb stalls. A number of stalls have excellent indigenous handicrafts at reasonable prices.

Rua dos Barés 46, Centro. ☏ **092/3233-0469.** Daily 8am–6pm.

Museu do Indio Spread out over six rooms, this museum presents the culture and social structure of the indigenous peoples of the Upper Rio Negro. Artifacts and clothing give an overview of their hunting and fishing traditions, as well as showing the spiritual rituals of a funeral and healing ceremony. The displays contain photos, drawings, a large number of artifacts, and occasionally models and replicas. All descriptions are in Portuguese, English, and German. Allow 1 hour.

Rua Duque de Caxias 356, Centro. ☏ **092/3635-1922.** Admission R$5. Mon–Fri 8:30–11:30am and 2–4:30pm; Sat 8:30–11:30am.

Teatro Amazonas ★★ This is one "must-see" that is actually worth seeing. This remarkable landmark was erected in the midst of the Amazon jungle in 1896 at the peak of the rubber boom. The half-hour guided tour shows off the lobby of marble and inlaid tropical hardwoods, the fine concert hall, and the romantic mural in the upstairs ballroom. Even better is to see a concert (see "Manaus After Dark," below).

Praça São Sebastião. ☏ **092/3232-1768.** www.teatroamazonas.com.br. Guided 30-min. tours in English and Portuguese depart every 30 min. R$10. Mon–Sat 9am–5pm.

Architectural Highlights

The square and the buildings around the opera house—the **Largo de São Sebastião**—have been restored almost to their original condition. In the evenings, the city often programs free concerts here.

The pretty neoclassical **Public Library,** Rua Barroso 57 (Mon–Fri 8am–5pm), on the corner of Avenida Sete de Setembro, dates from 1870. It's worth climbing the grand central staircase to the top floor to see a large oil painting marking the end of slavery in the Amazon. Done in the best overwrought allegorical style, it positively overflows with bare-breasted Amazon princesses, each a symbolic representation of some aspect or another of the province. Farther east along Avenida Sete de Setembro (toward the Museu do Indo) stands the grand **Palacio Rio Negro,** Av. Sete de Setembro 1546. Built by a Manaus rubber baron in the early years of the 20th century, the main palace is wonderfully ornate, with rich tropical hardwoods used for floors and doors, and banisters and moldings. The building has been transformed into an excellent cultural center, but unfortunately it is closed for renovations (no foreseen opening date). The old Customs house, or **Alfândega,** on Rua Marquesa da Santa Cruz, was prefabricated in England, shipped to Manaus in 1912, and re-erected block by block. The tower on the water side of the building was once a lighthouse.

Neighborhoods to Explore

Downtown Manaus is a fun place to explore. Check out the waterfront behind the **Feira da Produtor** on **Avenida Lourenço da Silva Braga** to see riverboats discharging passengers or loading up with everything under the sun for the next trip up or down the river. Two blocks inland, **Rua dos Bares** is full of chandleries and hardware shops; it's also a good place to buy a hammock. Small and picturesque, **Praça Tenreiro Aranha** contains an informal outdoor crafts fair. The **Artindia** store in the center of the square is housed in a small iron-and-glass structure reminiscent of London's Crystal Palace, though on a tiny scale. The covered pedestrian mall **Rua Marechal Deodoro** is the center of Manaus's thriving downtown shopping bazaar. The triangular plaza at the corner of **Avenida Presidente Vargas** and **Avenida Sete de Setembro** is a pleasant place to relax in the shade for a spell. Like so many Brazilian squares, it goes by two names: either **Praça da Polícia** or **Praça Heliodoro Balbi.** The city's most famous sight, the **Opera House** or **Teatro Amazonas,** is but a short walk from here.

Plazas, Parks & Gardens

Mindu Park, Avenida Perimitral (© 092/3236-7702; Tues–Sun 8am–5pm; bus: 511), is a 33-sq.-km (20-sq.-mile) forest reserve that is also one of the last remaining habitats of the Sauim-de-Coleira monkey, a species found only in the Manaus area. The park has walking trails with interpretive signage, a suspended treetop walkway, and an interpretation center with a library.

The **Bosque de Ciência,** or Ecological Park, Rua Otávio Cabral (© 092/3643-3293; Tues–Sun 9am–3pm; bus: 511), was created by INPA, the National Institute for Amazon Research, to promote ecological awareness. There's a small aquarium on-site with river otters and manatees.

ORGANIZED TOURS

AIR TOURS To get an aerial view of the rainforest and the city, **Viverde,** Rua dos Cardeiros 26 (©/fax 092/3248-9988; www.viverde.com.br), offers sightseeing flights on a floatplane that takes off from the river in front of the Tropical Manaus. The best deal is the **30-minute flight** that gives you aerial views of the city, the flooded forest, and the Meeting of the Waters, an amazing sight from the air. It costs R$450 per person with a minimum of two people. For R$900 you get a **1-hour flight** that allows you to go as far as the Anavilhanas Archipelago (more than 300 islands in the Rio Negro) and buzz some of the beaches and forest on your way back.

BUS/BOAT TOURS The best Manaus tour operator is **Viverde,** Rua dos Cardeiros 26 (©/fax **092/3248-9988;** www.viverde.com.br). **Fontur,** located at the Tropical Manaus, Estrada da Ponta Negra (© **092/3658-3052;** www.fontur.com.br), also offers a variety of tours. Because of its location in the Tropical, Fontur tends to be a bit more expensive.

Both companies offer half-day **city tours,** with English-speaking guides and an air-conditioned vehicle, that cover the highlights: the Opera House, the port and the market, and one museum, either the Palaço Rio Negro or the Museu do Indio. Viverde offers a scientific city tour that includes a visit to the **Bosque de Ciência.** Cost is around R$150 per person. They also offer full-day tours that include a visit to the **Meeting of the Waters** and boat trips to the **Anavilhanas Archipelago.**

CITY TOURS Long the experts in deep Amazon exploration, **Amazon Mystery Tours** (© **092/3248-4258;** www.amazon-outdoor.com) has recently branched out into the city, offering innovative city tours. Canadian-born guide Jean Claude has developed a **Manaus by Night** series (R$90) which will take you out to a popular neighborhood to hang with locals, munch street food, and move to the sound of Manaus-based samba and *pagode.* The **Cultural Manaus** tours (R$90) offer visitors the chance to visit a kindergarten or spend a morning with Brazilian youth being shown their part of the city; there's also a tour that allows you to spend a night with a Brazilian family (R$150). And if all that's just too much culture, the company offers a day trip up to the waterfalls and caverns of **Presidente Figueiredo,** a beautiful highland area about 100km (62 miles) north of Manaus (R$250). Check the website for details on new tours being developed.

SHOPPING

Downtown Manaus is one big shopping area: Vendors hawk their wares, stalls clog up the sidewalks and squares, and the streets are jampacked with little stores. The main shopping streets run behind the **Praça Tenreiro Aranha, Rua Marcilio Dias, Rua Guilherme Moreira,** and **Rua Marechal Deodoro.** The streets around the market at **Rua dos Barés** sell more household goods and hammocks. The church square, **Praça da Matriz,** has a large market during weekdays selling everything from clothing to hair accessories and bags. The city's largest mall is **Shopping Amazonas,** Av. Djalma Batista 482, Parque 10 (© **092/3642-3555;** www.amazonasshopping.com.br). It's open Monday through Saturday from 10am to 10pm. Take bus no. 203, 209, or 214 from Praça da Matriz, Centro.

Arts & Crafts

Artindia The crafts market located on the Praça Tenreiro Aranha sells a wide variety of Indian crafts, including necklaces, bracelets, woodcarvings, baskets, and handbags. Open Monday through Saturday 8am to 6pm. Praça Tenreiro Aranha, Centro. © **092/3232-4890.**

 Tips **Stock Up to Put Your Feet Up**

Manaus is a great place to buy a hammock. They make great souvenirs, and if you're taking a riverboat, they're indispensable. The best stores are located on the Rua dos Barés, near the Mercado Municipal. Expect to pay R$45 to R$75.

Central de Artesanato Branco & Silva Located about a 15-minute cab ride north of downtown, Central de Artesanato is worth the trek. In one location you'll find 23 handicrafts shops specializing in regional crafts. A lot of the artisans work with wood, weavings, ceramics, bark, seeds, and other organic materials. The selection is amazing, and some of the crafts are of gallery quality. Open Tuesday through Friday 9am to 6pm, Saturday 9am to 4pm. Rua Mario Ypiranga Monteiro 1999 (formerly called Rua Recife), Parque 10. (✆ 092/3236-1241. By taxi only, no convenient bus route.

Native Original Products More high-end design than knickknack stand, this gift shop specializes in high-end crafts, artwork, and furniture made with local woods and seeds. The designs are often inspired by traditional native artifacts; one candle holder is made out of a stylized spearhead set in hardwood. Open Monday through Saturday 9am to 9pm and Sunday 9am to 5pm. Praça São Sebastião, inside the Teatro Amazonas. (✆ 092/ 8122-1354. www.nativeoriginal.com.br.

MANAUS AFTER DARK
The Performing Arts
Parque Cultural Ponta Negra Regular events and concerts take place in this large amphitheater on the Rio Negro, next to the Tropical Manaus. Contact Manaustur for information on programming (✆ 092/3622-4948), or just show up and wander around any evening Thursday to Saturday. Praia de Ponta Negra s/n, Ponta Negra. (✆ 092/3622-4948. Programming and prices vary. Check at your hotel for programming.

Teatro Amazons (The Opera House) The theater has a resident philharmonic orchestra, choir, and dance group (classic and popular dance) that perform regularly. Tickets are eminently affordable, usually around R$20 to R$40. The annual Opera Festival takes place in April and May. Praça São Sebastião s/n, Centro. (✆ 092/3232-1768. www.teatroamazonas.com.br.

Clubs & Bars
In downtown Manaus, the best spot for an evening drink is **Bar do Armando,** Rua 10 de Julho 593 (✆ 092/3232-1195). Located on the square in front of the Opera House, this venerable drinking spot is the nighttime home of Manaus's artists, intellectuals, journalists, and other ne'er-do-wells. The conversation is always interesting and the beer is served icy cold (closed on Sun). Farther down near the **Praça da Matriz,** Manaus's downtown nightlife scene degenerates into the sleazy mix of sailors and prostitutes traditional in a large port. Praça da Matriz itself remains reasonably safe, but it's best to stay off side streets like Rua Visconde de Mauá.

The city's best nightlife spot is out near the Tropical Manaus at **Ponta Negra Beach.** People stroll up and down the wide boulevard, there are regular concerts and events at the amphitheater, and a number of bars have live entertainment in the evening. The most popular is **Laranjinha** (✆ 092/3658-6666; Mon–Sat 5pm–3am, Sun 5pm–5am), which has a great patio and stays open until the wee hours of the morning. Lower down close to the river there's a bunch of *barracas* (beach kiosks) during the day when the beach is crowded and open at night for a causal beer or snack. Most places open at 5 or 6pm on weekdays and stay open until at least 1 or 2am. On weekends many venues open at 11am and stay open until 3 or 4am.

Centro has two popular Manaus gay bars: **Turbo Seven (TS),** Rua Vivaldo Lima 33, Centro (✆ 092/3232-6793; Sat and Sun 11pm), features drag shows and go-go boys; and **Planeta A2** (Rua Saldanha Marinho 780, Centro; ✆ 092/3673-0112; www. a2manaus.com.br), open Thursday to Saturday from 11pm to 6am.

2 INTRODUCING THE AMAZON

WHAT IS A RAINFOREST?

Rainforests are found throughout the world, wherever the annual rainfall is more than 2,000 millimeters (80 in.) and evenly spread throughout the year. Rainforests grow in temperate zones (such as the Pacific Northwest) as well as in tropical regions. Tropical rainforests are found in a thick belt extending around the earth on either side of the Equator. The constant heat and humidity in a tropical rainforest allow trees and plants to grow year-round. Vast columns of hot, humid air rise and then condense as rain, resulting in annual rainfall of between 2,000 to 10,160 millimeters (80–400 in.); annual temperatures average over 27°C (80°F).

What distinguishes the Amazon from other tropical rainforests is the sheer variety. Biologically, it is the richest and most diverse region in the world, containing about 20% of all higher plant species, roughly the same proportion of bird species, and around 10% of the world's mammals. Each type of tree may support more than 400 insect species. The Amazon is estimated to contain 2,000 species of fish—10 times the number found in European rivers—and countless varieties of reptiles. Why the Amazon should be so diverse is a question that mystifies scientists still.

Not only is it the most diverse, but the Amazon is also the largest tropical rainforest in the world, covering 3.7 million sq. km (2.3 million sq. miles) over nine countries, including Peru, Colombia, Venezuela, and Bolivia. The largest chunk, about 60%, falls within Brazil's borders.

The lifeline of the forest is the Amazon River, the second longest in the world and the largest in terms of water flow and drainage area. The river has over 1,000 tributaries, some of them sizable rivers in their own right. In March and April, the water levels in these rivers rise and flood the banks and the surrounding forest for months. A seasonally flooded forest is called *varzea* (on the Rio Solimões) or *igapó* (on the Rio Negro), while the upland forest that stays above water is called *terra firme.*

The annual flooding of the forest is one of the key factors in maintaining this ecosystem. As the river covers the forest floor, sometimes leaving just the treetops above water, the fish also expand their terrain. These fish play a vital role in the fertilization of the forest. Many Amazonian fish are fruit eaters that feast on the nuts and seeds of the trees in the wet season. The fish feces deposit the seeds in the fertile ground of the forest, and when the waters recede, new growth occurs.

The difference in water levels between wet and dry season can be as much as 12m (40 ft.). Many of the smaller side channels—called *igarapé*—and creeks that are perfectly navigable in March and April are completely dry by November.

The rainforest itself has a very defined structure. The **understory** is what you see when you hike through the forest. Shielded by the tall trees and overhead layers, the understory can be surprisingly dark. Plants, fungi, and animals found here thrive in the dark, humid conditions. The **canopy** is where a lot of the action is; birds, butterflies, and monkeys are usually up here, 18 to 27m (60–90 ft.) above the understory. With more sunlight and less humidity, the rainforest at this height is green and lush. The **emergent** layer refers to those trees, often upwards of 36m (120 ft.), that send their crowns above the canopy to find the sunlight. Being higher also means these trees are more exposed to storms and rain. Wide buttress roots support these trees. This layering of the forest contributes to the

Tips   Viewing Wildlife

Wildlife viewing in the Amazon is a subtle event. It's the occasional flutter of a giant blue butterfly, the glimpse of a startled bird, or the splash as a caiman swims away from your canoe. With a keen eye you may spy snoozing bats tucked away underneath the tree branches, or a large, perfectly camouflaged iguana draped over the branch of a tree. At night a flashlight reveals the many small frogs that dot the flooded forest; a searchlight shows the hiding places of the caiman as they lie in wait, only their eyes and snout above water. What isn't subtle is the noise. It's everywhere: the tortured squawks of macaws, the high-pitched screams of monkeys high in the trees. And in the "still" of the night, the decibel levels generated by chirping cicadas and "ribbiting" frogs rivals that of a construction site.

biodiversity; each layer has its own flora and fauna that thrive in those particular conditions. Cutting through the forest opens up the understory to bright, unexpected light. The dark, humid environment vanishes, other plants and trees take over the space, and the ecological balance is thrown out of whack.

EXPLORING THE AMAZON

There are many ways to explore the Amazon. What suits you depends on how much time you have and how comfortable you want to be. Most people choose to stay at a lodge. Most are land-based, located within a few hours by boat from Manaus, and make excursions to the surrounding area. Lodges vary in luxury but the programs offered are similar (see "Amazon Lodges," below).

Another comfortable way of seeing the Amazon is by riverboat. These range from basic to air-conditioned and luxurious. The vessel serves as your home base; you take excursions in canoes up the smaller channels. (See "Boat Trips," later in this chapter).

Regular boats that locals use to travel the river are another option. Although extremely inexpensive, these are *not* sightseeing tours; it's rare that you get close to shore, and no excursions are possible. You do meet locals traveling the river, and you'll have a front-row seat as you pull in to harbors along the way.

Specialized operators offer expedition-style trips where the emphasis is on truly experiencing the rainforest. You don't need to be in top shape for these; you just have to be able to hike or paddle a boat, and be willing to forego amenities like hot showers for a more hands-on jungle experience. One excellent outfitter is **Amazon Mystery Tours** (see "Deeper into the Amazon: Expedition Tours," later in this chapter).

THE AMAZON & ECO-TOURISM: QUESTIONS TO ASK

Some visitors come away from a visit to the Amazon energized and excited by what they've seen. Others come away pissed off: The forest was degraded, the animals impossible to see, the guide had no idea what he was talking about. Some of these complaints stem from expectations set too high, from mental pictures of animal encounters developed over too many years of nature documentaries. Other times the complaints are entirely legitimate.

Eco-tourism in the Amazon is far from perfect. The section that follows will give you a better idea of what to expect, and of what to do to make your experience the best it can

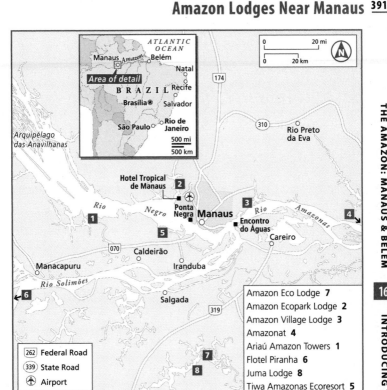

be. I'd also like to encourage you to use your power as a consumer to raise the level of eco-tourism as practiced in the Brazilian Amazon—for the benefit of the Amazon itself.

I love the Amazon. It's a dense, intricate, fascinating ecosystem. I also believe that eco-tourism, done right, can help endangered ecosystems throughout the world. At its best, eco-tourism teaches visitors about the ecosystem, while teaching locals that a functioning natural ecosystem is a thing of real economic value, to be guarded and preserved. Unfortunately, even after 20 years as a tourist destination, "eco-tourism" so defined has yet to develop around Manaus. Indeed, at its worst, Manaus-based eco-tourism seems to be teaching locals that you may as well chop it all down because you can show gringos any damn thing and they'll still ooh and aah, and pay the big bucks.

It's not all bad. Some of it is very good. But things seem to have fallen into a rut, and there's no local impetus for change. Only you, the consumer, can change things, and you can do it simply by demanding more. Below I give a checklist of things to ask, and things to verify before going.

What You Won't Get

First, though, let's dispel the unreasonable expectations. Most lodges, for logistical reasons (food, supplies, attracting staff, ferrying people back and forth to the airport), are located no more than a half-day journey from Manaus. This rules out the "never-before-seen primeval jungle" experience. You will see houses on the riverbank and lots of other boats. In recent years as cattle prices have soared, pastureland has begun replacing forest on accessible riversides close to Manaus.

Most lodges cater to foreign tourists. For Brazilians, the Amazon is quite expensive. The majority of your fellow travelers will be European, Japanese, or North American. Like it or not, you'll be lumped in with the gringos.

Animals are hard to spot in the rainforest. You will see caiman (you may yawn at caiman by trip's end) and more than likely little pink dolphins and some species of monkeys. You will see lots of birds—kingfishers and egrets (snowy, great, and cattle), herons (gray, green, tiger), cormorants, hummingbirds, parakeets, and vultures. Macaws and toucans are also common, though not guaranteed. You *may* see sloths (I've seen one in over 10 trips to the Amazon) and capybara and agoutis as well as other small nocturnal rodents. The odds of seeing a predatory feline of any species are astonishingly small. Amphibians are also tough—those famous photos of poison arrow frogs took a lot of work and a lot of time.

On the bright side, those worried about creepy-crawlies can rest easy. Insects in the Amazon are really not that bad. There are ants (some about the size of a bumblebee), butterflies, and flying beetles and mosquitoes. In all my visits to over a dozen different parts of the forest (including a 1-week kayak trip in the far-off depths of the Amazon) I've only ever seen one snake and it was tiny and harmless.

What You Should Get

What you can expect is an opportunity to see and experience the rainforest around Manaus. Much of it is in pristine condition, and the vegetation, the range of species, and the sheer oddness of the trees and plants are truly impressive and remarkable. You can expect to learn about life on the Amazon. As the river is the main means of transportation and a major source of food, most people live on or close to it. It can be fascinating watching children going to school by canoe, seeing 4-year-olds paddle themselves around, seeing women washing their dishes or catching dinner off the decks of houses built on stilts. You can expect to learn about the ecosystem. Many of the guides are quite knowledgeable and they speak foreign languages very well, making it easy to ask questions and learn about the Amazon environment. You should expect to eat well. The lodges put on a wonderful spread of Amazonian specialties, much better than in most restaurants in town. The river fish are delicious.

How to Get It (& Do Good Things at the Same Time)

The following is a checklist of questions to ask the travel agent (or better yet the lodge manager) when researching your stay in the Amazon. The list is by no means comprehensive, but it should help you find the best available option. As importantly, by putting these questions to the operators in the Amazon, you will be educating them on what matters to foreign, ecologically minded tourists. In the listings for the lodges I've created a lodge checklist with the answers to most of these questions.

1. **How far is the lodge from Manaus?** Farther is better. Although distance does increase travel time, it also lessens the "city effect" on the animals, trees, and people.
2. **Is the lodge surrounded by a private nature reserve? Of what size?** Obviously, larger is better. In recent years as cattle prices have soared there's been a second wave of deforestation on accessible rivers close to Manaus. There's not much lodge owners

can do about the Amazon as a whole, but they can work to preserve their little part. That's why we try to recommend not just lodges farther from Manaus, but lodges that are in some sort of private nature reserve that the lodge has set up and is trying to protect. I didn't include this information in the checklist simply because I have been unable to verify the legal status of various claimed reserves. You won't be able to either, but simply by asking you'll be emphasizing that this is important. Those lodges that haven't yet set up private reserves will hopefully move in that direction. Reserve sizes will likely be quoted to you in hectares. 1,000 hectares is a square about 2 miles long on a side.

3. **How big is the lodge?** Smaller is better. The more people there, the bigger the local environmental impact, the more the trails have been treaded and the animals spooked. Ten rooms is excellent, 20 acceptable, 35 pushing the limit, and 300 obscene.

4. **What is the group size?** Again, smaller is better. The larger the group, the less likely you will see animals or enjoy the forest peacefully. We have been to lodges where huge motorized canoes take 25 people out at a time. Lodges lie about group size, so I've found it more instructive to ask *"what is the maximum capacity of the boats used to take guests on outings?"* Generally, that's the group size.

5. **Are the guides trained naturalists?** Is there a biologist at the lodge? Is there a library or resource center at the lodge? Are there any nature talks? The answer to all these questions will be "no" (with the notable exception of the Mamiraua Reserve lodge). No one ever seems to have thought to hire university biology students to work as naturalists—both to train the regular guides and to give guests a deeper insight into the ecosystem. No one has ever considered hiring a full-time biologist, or even putting in a library with field guides and nature books. Hope springs eternal, however. I put in the questions because I'd like to see it happen. If enough people ask, maybe it will. And it's a good lead-in to the next question.

6. **What kind of training and education do the guides have?** Your guide can make or break your experience. Unfortunately, guides vary greatly in quality. Some are truly excellent. But the main qualification seems to be an ability to speak English (or French, Italian, or what have you). Nature training comes afterward. If you're lucky, the guide will have grown up in the forest, or have gone through the army's jungle-warfare program, or have an interest in biology. I wish I could recommend a lodge with particularly good guides, but in Manaus the guides are all freelance, contracted for periods of 3 or 4 days as guests come in. Turnover is high, because pay is not great. Ask about the qualifications of your guide beforehand. Demand one that has army-jungle training, specialized nature training (above the standard guide course), or at least grew up outside of Manaus. Ask questions of your guide when you meet him to see that he is as advertised. If he's not, complain. If he is, tip him well.

7. **When do trips go out?** Trips scheduled around breakfast and supper are almost guaranteed to show nothing but forest. If you want to see animals, you have to be on the water or in the forest at sunrise or sunset; ask about early morning or dusk excursions if you want to maximize your animal spotting odds.

8. **Are jungle-tour boats motorized or nonmotorized?** If motorized, what kind of engine? Nonmotorized canoes are the best, but only two lodges (the Mamiraua and the Ecopark) use these regularly. The noise of an outboard will scare off most wild creatures. However, they're justifiable if you're on the way somewhere farther off in the forest. But they should still be quiet outboards. Some lodges (the Ariaú is

especially bad) use so-called *rabete* engines, unmuffled high-revving two-strokes, with the engine mounted on the drive shaft. The smell and noise of these motors are enough to make you sick; never mind the animals that you'll never get to see.

9. **What kinds of excursions are there?** The standard package of outings includes a reconnaissance tour, a jungle walk, a visit to a *caboclo* house, and a nighttime caiman-spotting trip. These are fascinating, fun, and informative, but there could be so much more. They could set up a telescope and show you the stars (the Milky Way is incredible in the Amazon), they could take you out and show you insect life, or search for amphibians, but they don't because no one ever has, and operators in the Amazon are very conservative. So, ask the next question.

10. **Are there any excursions beyond the basic ones?** (And how much do they cost?) Maybe if enough people ask, they'll develop something.

11. **Are there canoes for guest use at the lodge?** There is inevitably a fair bit of downtime at a lodge. Tours go out early and late, leaving a big chunk of time in the middle of the day. Lodges could offer nature talks or presentations to fill this time, but they don't. Some people swim. Some snooze in their hammocks. I like to grab a small dugout canoe and go for a paddle. The water is flat and calm, and the scenery can be fascinating. Only the floating Amazon Eco Lodge keeps a fleet of canoes on hand. Other lodges can usually rustle one up if you make a fuss.

12. Finally, one question you should ask yourself. **How much do you want to rough it?** Can you live without air-conditioning, hot water, fridge, and TV? There is an Amazon trip for everyone. Picking the right one will greatly enhance your experience.

Forgive me if this all seems a tad didactic, but I assume that for people who have flown so far to see the Amazon, the important thing is to see the Amazon. I could be completely out to lunch on this. Certainly, the people who build and finance new lodges have concluded that what matters to people is not the quality of the nature experience but the quality of the bed. It's what has lead to the creation of places like the Tiwa, where the forest is poor and degraded but the swimming pool is excellent.

For the situation to improve, visitors will have to do one thing and one thing only—demand more. Whatever you do, don't let this explanation scare you off coming. The Amazon is a tremendous experience. But with a little effort it could be so much more. Make a pain of yourself. Ask operators if they have a biologist, if they have a library, if they have nature talks and canoes and highly trained guides. Tell them you'll go to the lodge that does. When you're there, ask for these things again. Maybe, slowly, the message will get through.

3 AMAZON LODGES

Lodges are a popular way to experience something of the Amazon while keeping comfort levels high. Most are within a 3-hour boat ride from Manaus. Some are more luxurious than others, but in all, your meals are taken care of—usually hearty and healthy fare made with local fish and fruit. You will have access to a shower and toilet, and guides are there to show you around. Nearly all the lodges include the same basic package of excursions: the introductory jungle tour, the sunset and/or sunrise tour, the forest hike, the visit to a native village, the evening of caiman hunting, and the afternoon of piranha fishing (yipes!). What distinguishes one lodge from another is the size of the lodge itself (smaller is better), the quality of the surrounding forest, and the quality of the guides.

Most lodges start off with a reconnaissance tour, taking you out in a motorized canoe to give you an idea what the area around the lodge looks like; this a good opportunity to check out some of the smaller channels. The **sunrise** or **sunset tour** is a great way to experience the forest at its most interesting times of the day, when animals are active and there are few disturbances around. All lodges will take guests on a **jungle hike.** This is where you really get a feel for the biodiversity of the forest; it's not the animals that make this jungle so overwhelming, it's the number of plants and trees and how these coexist. Another standard excursion is the **visit to a *caboclo* village.** *Caboclos* are river people. The visits provide a close-up look at how they build their homes, at the foods they grow, and the tools they use. Even their pets are neat; sloths and monkeys are the animals of choice. Finally there's the obligatory caiman spotting and piranha fishing. **Caiman spotting** is fun; you head out in a canoe on the river in the pitch-black night. Once you get to a good shallow area, the guide turns on the spotlight and starts looking for a caiman. The caiman should be big enough to impress the lodge-dwellers, but not *so* big that the guide can't leap into the water and wrestle it back into the boat. (That's exactly what he does.) Once it's in the boat the creature becomes the centerpiece of a short nature talk. Many enjoy **fishing for piranhas.** You put some beef on your hook and hold your rod in the water, pretty much like fishing anywhere. When you catch one, your guide will pull it off the hook—very carefully, those teeth really are razor sharp—and you'll see the little fish back at dinnertime when the kitchen serves it up grilled.

WHAT TO BRING: A CHECKLIST

Most hotels will let you store your luggage while you are away at a lodge so you don't have to carry it all with you. The smaller lodges often have a luggage limit. Whatever you leave behind, don't forget to bring the following:

- A small daypack.
- Binoculars.
- A light rain jacket.
- A few zip-lock bags to protect camera gear, notebook, and so on . . . in a sudden downpour, everything gets soaked.
- Good walking shoes.
- Sunglasses.
- Sunscreen. (The glare from the river can be quite strong.)
- Enough dry clothes; nothing dries once it's damp, so have a couple of changes of shirts and socks.
- Toiletries such as toothpaste, contact lens fluid, tampons. The lodges usually don't carry any such items.
- Medicinal items for personal use (aspirin, antacid, and so on; lodges and tour operators will have proper first-aid kits). Malaria is not an issue on the Rio Negro; the high acidity of the water prevents mosquitoes from laying their eggs.
- Anything you can't live without: chewing gum, dental floss, tissues, cookies, and the like.

BOOKING A LODGE

You can contact lodges directly or contact a tour operator who can assist you in choosing the right package. In the U.S. or Canada, your best option is to contact the experts at **Brazil Nuts** (© 800/553-9959; www.brazilnuts.com). In Manaus, contact **Viverde,** Rua dos Cardeiros 26 (© 092/3248-9988). They have an excellent English-language website (www.viverde.com.br) with detailed information on both tours and the Amazon in general.

Note: All prices are per person and include transportation, all meals, and basic excursions. Airport transfer is usually included in the price, but always check. The policies for children vary per lodge and per season; depending on occupancy you may have bargaining power. Most lodges offer up to a 50% discount for children 12 and under; ask when making reservations. All rates are given in U.S. dollars only; most lodges work directly with foreign currencies.

LODGES CLOSE TO MANAUS

Amazon Ecopark Lodge ★★

The Amazon Ecopark is one of the better lodges close to Manaus, as long as you arrive with the right expectations. The lodge itself is about a 2-hour boat trip from Manaus and sits on a private reserve. The igarapé is of exclusive use to the lodge, which gives it a secluded feel. In the dry season there are several beaches right across from the lodge, and the vegetation is lush and beautiful. The lodge also has some natural pools for swimming, particularly nice for people who are never quite comfortable swimming in the dark waters of the Rio Negro. Most of the excursions take place in proximity to the lodge and are done in nonmotorized canoes. Paddling into the flooded forest, you'll be able to get a good sense of the sights and sounds of the jungle. The lodge also houses a rehab for monkeys that are apprehended by Brazil's environmental agency, Ibama. Guests can see the daily feedings and observe and even interact with these monkeys. Most packages include a visit to an Indian village to observe a traditional ceremony. Although undoubtedly a touristy experience, it is well done as you actually visit a small community where a number of Indian families reside. You will be able to see their traditional houses and the little plots of land where they grow and process manioc and other fruit and vegetables. The ceremony itself is also quite authentic and gives you a much better impression of the native culture than the shows put on at a lodge or a hotel. All packages include airport transfers, all meals (the food is fabulous), deluxe accommodations, and well-trained guides who speak excellent English.

Lodge Checklist: Distance: 20km (12 miles); Biome: Igapó; Size: 60; Boat Capacity: 12; Boat Motors: Outboard; Canoes: Yes (canoes used for many excursions); Library: No; Biologist: No; Nature Talks: No; Other Excursions: "Jungle survival training."

Reservations office in Rio ✆ **021/2547-7742** or ✆/fax 021/2256-8083. www.amazonecopark.com.br. 64 units. A 3-day package costs R$1,030 per person; a 4-day package is R$1,190 per person (both these packages include a tour to the Meeting of the Waters). Children 6–12 pay 25% of rate, 13–16 pay 50% of rate. AE, DC, MC, V. **Amenities:** Restaurant; bar; outdoor pool. *In room:* A/C, fan, no phone.

Amazon Village Lodge ★

The Amazon Village is a well-run operation with its own small rainforest reserve, now alas being seriously encroached upon by ever-growing cattle operations and the beginnings of urban sprawl from the city. It's too bad, because the Amazon Village is a class act—owners treat guides well and do a good job presenting the rainforest. If at all possible, choose something farther from the city, but if you do for some reason have to be close, this would be a good option. The lodge buildings are attractively designed with local wood in the native *maloca* style, while rooms are small and clean with private toilets and showers. There is no hot water, and electricity is limited to the evening hours. There's the usual package of excursions. The lodge doesn't have a swimming pool, but you can swim in the river.

Lodge Checklist: Distance: 40km (25 miles); Biome: Igapó; Size: 36; Boat Capacity: 12; Boat Motors: Outboard; Canoes: Yes (1); Library: No; Biologist: No; Nature Talks: No; Other Excursions: No.

Rua Ramos Ferreira 1189, sala 403, Manaus, AM 69010-120. ✆ **092/3633-1444.** Fax 092/3633-3217. www.amazon-village.com.br. 45 units. 3-day packages start at US$440 per person. AE, DC, MC, V. **Amenities:** Restaurant; bar.

Tiwa Amazonas Ecoresort The Tiwa fills an odd ecological niche, neither jungle
lodge nor city hotel. It sits directly opposite the Tropical, on the far bank of the Rio
Negro. Access is via fast motor launch; the trip takes about 20 minutes, and there are
boats going back and forth every other hour. Each of the sizable rooms takes up half a
log cabin, which are set in circles around a small pond. The hotel pool is lovely. Theoretically, the Tiwa could serve as an alternative to the Tropical—a luxury resort, just a
little farther from the city. But what the Tiwa is selling itself as is a jungle lodge, with
2- and 3-day packages and the usual outings including caiman spotting and treetop walking. But the Tiwa is just simply too close to the city for that. The "forest" surrounding
the lodge is a small patch of barely regrown second-growth; walk too far and you stumble
onto roads and clear cuts. If you don't have time to go to a jungle lodge, and just want a
teensy-tiny taste of the Amazon, the Tiwa may be an option. Otherwise, go elsewhere.

Lodge Checklist: Distance: 8km (5 miles); Biome: Terra Firme; Size: 52; Boat Capacity: 50; Boat Motor:
Outboard; Canoes: No; Library: No; Biologist: No; Nature Talks: No; Other Excursions: Trips to Meeting of
the Waters, Lago Janauary.

Caixa Postal 2575, Manaus, AM 69005-970. ✆ **092/9995-7892.** www.tiwa.com.br. 52 units. 3-day packages with excursions and including transfers in and out cost R$850 per person. Policy for children nego-
tiable. AE, DC, MC, V. **Amenities:** Restaurant; bar; Internet; outdoor pool; Hobie Cat rentals. *In room:* A/C,
fridge, minibar, no phone.

LODGES FARTHER FROM MANAUS

Amazonat ★★ If you like space to move around, you will love the Amazonat, set on
its own 900-hectare (2,223-acre) reserve of *terra firme* 160km (98 miles) east of Manaus.
Amazonat is surrounded by extensive walking trails that you can roam at will. Though
the lodge is not on a river, there is a lake with a beach for swimming and an orchid park
with over 1,000 specimens to see and sniff and wonder at. The 3-day package includes a
number of guided walks and a river trip on the Urubu for bird-watching, as well as plenty
of time to explore on your own. The 4-day package includes all of the above plus a full
day on the Amazon River and a visit to the Opera House and the Meeting of the Waters.
The lodge itself is set in beautiful jungle gardens and the chalets are more than comfortable. There's also a variety of specialized programs for those who want to experience more
of the jungle: The Jungle Trekker package includes a variety of longer hikes and two
overnight stays at a jungle camp.

Lodge Checklist: Distance: 160km (98 miles); Biome: Terra Firme; Size: 20; Boat Capacity: 8; Boat Motors:
Outboard; Canoes: No; Library: Yes; Biologist: No; Nature Talks: No; Other Excursions: "Jungle survival"
excursions.

Caixa Postal 1273, Manaus, AM 69006-970. ✆ **092/3328-1183** (hotel), or ✆/fax 092/3652-1359 (reservations office). www.amazonat.com.br. 18 units. 4-day packages start at US$550 per person, 5-day pack-
ages US$660 per person. Children 6–12 pay 25% of rate, 13–16 pay 50% of rate. AE, DC, MC, V. **Amenities:**
Restaurant; bar; outdoor pool. *In room:* Fan, minibar, no phone.

Amazon Eco Lodge ★★ Located just a few kilometers from the Juma Lodge (see
below), the Amazon Eco Lodge has the same excellent forest surroundings, and the same
long trip from Manaus. The package of outings at both lodges is also essentially the same.
The one thing the Eco Lodge has over the Juma is its fleet of small canoes, always at the
ready should a guest feel like going off for a paddle. The Eco Lodge floats on the lake,
on top of huge log rafts, which is really quite charming. It's also a great place for river
swimming. The disadvantage is that accommodations are in fairly small rooms, built in
wings with wooden walls; it can get noisy. Also, toilets and showers are shared, in a

shower block near the center of the raft complex. Prices at the Juma and Eco Lodge are comparable, but for the money the Juma provides better value.

Lodge Checklist: Distance: 85km (53 miles); Biome: Igapó; Size: 18; Boat Capacity: 12; Boat Motor: Outboard; Canoes: Yes; Library: No; Biologist: No; Nature Talks: No; Other Excursions: No.

Rua Flavio Espirito Santo 1, Kissia II, Manaus AM 69040-250. (C) **092/3656-6033.** Fax 092/3656-6101. www.naturesafaris.com.br. 18 units, common bathrooms and showers. 4-day packages US$599 per person. Policy for children negotiable. AE, DC, MC, V. **Amenities:** Restaurant; bar; outdoor pool; Hobie Cat rentals. *In room:* A/C, fridge, minibar, no phone.

Ariaú Amazon Towers (Overrated)   Avoid this place. Just don't go. The Ariaú is all that is wrong with Amazon "eco-tourism"; it is the Disneyland Ford Factory of jungle lodges. Marketing photos of treehouses and boardwalks may suggest a Swiss Family Robinson adventure, but what the Ariaú delivers is mass-market tourism, with hundreds of guests getting trundled each day along a set tourist route that has already been treaded literally tens of thousands of times. Repetition is a factor at any lodge, but the Ariaú has a serious problem of scale—there are over 300 units in place—combined with a management fixation on minimum expense and maximum profit. Although the Ariaú charges top price and has economies of scale on its side, it has never seen fit to hire a lodge biologist or open an on-site interpretation center (though there is a gym and spa, a helipad, and a jewelry boutique). Excursions are the usual, but at the Ariaú, group size runs up to 25. Trips are always in motorized canoes, equipped with noisy, fume-spewing two-stroke *rabete* motors.

Lodge Checklist: Distance: 35km (22 miles); Biome: Igapó; Size: 300; Boat Capacity: 25; Boat Motors: Large rabete; Canoes: Yes (1); Library: No; Biologist: No; Nature Talks: No; Other Excursions: Yes, but at steep add-on prices.

Rua Leonardo Malcher 699, Manaus, AM 69010-040. (C) **092/2121-5050,** or in Rio de Janeiro **021/2254-4507.** Fax 092/3233-5615. www.ariautowers.com. 300 units. 3-day packages start at R$1,500, 4-day packages R$1,900 per person. Children 6 and younger are free, ages 7–11 pay 50% of rate. AE, DC, MC, V. **Amenities:** Restaurant; bar; gym; Internet (intermittent connection); outdoor pool; spa. *In room:* A/C, fridge, no phone.

Flotel Piranha ★★   The Flotel is unique among all the lodges in that it floats on *varzea*—flooded forest in the richer "white water" of the Solimões river system. Whitewater systems flow through younger, richer soils, and are thus richer in dissolved nutrients. Forests in the upland areas of white-water rivers have bigger, taller trees (though don't expect the trees close to the lodge to be huge—trees of the flooded forest, on both white and black rivers, don't grow to enormous sizes, simply due to the stress of getting covered for 4 months of the year in water). White-water rivers support richer, denser populations of aquatic life—more fish, and consequently, more birds. The catch in all this, of course, is that the base of the food chain is also more abundant; white-water rivers are much richer in insect life, including mosquitoes.

To avoid mosquitoes, all other lodges are on black-water rivers, but the Piranha decided that the benefit was worth the cost. And in truth, the mosquitoes aren't that bad. They're worse than on black-water lodges, certainly, but they're nowhere near as bad as they are, for example, in the hardwood forests of the eastern U.S. or Canada. You'll need repellent when you go for a walk in the forest, but out on the floating lodge it's only an issue for the 2 hours or so around sunset. The lodge has good screens on the rooms and dining areas. The benefit is you get to see and hear constant splashes from jumping fish, and see more and larger bird life, particularly wading birds.

Rooms on this floating hotel are small but tidy and pleasant—like cabins on a ship.
Beds have mosquito nets, though windows are screened. A generator powers air-conditioning in the evenings.

Lodge Checklist: Distance: 90km (56 miles); Biome: Varzea; Size: 20; Boat Capacity: 12; Boat Motor: Outboard; Canoes: Yes (1); Library: No; Biologist: No; Nature Talks: No, but planned for the near future; Other Excursions: Horseback riding (dry season only).

Rua Flavio Espirito Santo 1, Kissia II, Manaus AM 69040-250. ✆ **092/3656-6033.** Fax 092/3656-6101. www.naturesafaris.com.br. 20 units. 4-day, 3-night packages US$649 per person. Policy for children negotiable. AE, DC, MC, V. **Amenities:** Restaurant; bar. *In room:* A/C, no phone.

Juma Lodge ★★★   One of the best of the lodges in the area, the Juma gets jungle points for its small size and its distance from Manaus. Rooms are all in comfortable small cabins built on stilts. The best rooms are the charming self-contained doubles (room nos. 9, 10, and 11) with a view out over the lake. From your veranda you can often see dolphins and caiman. Cabins are connected to the dining hall by elevated boardwalks. The Juma is located in the middle of a sizable private nature reserve, so the forest surroundings are quite well preserved. The lodge offers the standard excursions. By prior arrangement, the more adventurous can also spend a night sleeping in a hammock in the jungle. The lodge also has one dugout canoe that guests can borrow to paddle on their own. Note that the trip to the lodge from Manaus often takes longer than 3½ hours. Though the lodge quotes this figure, it's a best-case scenario, possible only when the water is highest. At other times the trip is closer to 5 or 6 hours. It's not simply dead time, though. You see lots on the way out—from forest to birds to dolphins. On the trip back you have a chance to spend time—even swim—at the Meeting of the Waters.

Lodge Checklist: Distance: 90km (56 miles); Biome: Igapó; Size: 23; Boat Capacity: 8; Boat Motors: Rabete; Canoes: Yes (1); Library: No; Biologist: No; Nature Talks: No; Other Excursions: Will program night walks in forest and sleepovers in forest on request.

Lago do Juma (no mailing address). ✆ **092/3245-1177** (lodge) or 3232-2707 (reservations office). www.jumalodge.com.br. 23 units. 3-day, 2-night packages start at R$1,300 per person, 4-day packages R$1,600 per person. Children 6–12 pay 50% of rate. AE, MC, V. **Amenities:** Restaurant; bar. *In room:* Fan, fridge, no phone.

LODGES FAR, FAR, FAR FROM MANAUS

Pousada Uakarí in the Mamiraua ★★★   The only place in the Brazilian Amazon practicing real eco-tourism, the Uakarí pousada is the eco-tourism branch of the Mamiraua Sustainable Development Institute. The Mamiraua reserve was created on the upper Amazon in 1999 in order to preserve the prime habitat of the Ukarí monkey (a primate with a bright red face and pale white fur, often called the English monkey). Initiated by the Brazilian scientist who first studied the Ukairi, the institute fosters research, while working to preserve the area by helping local inhabitants develop alternate ways of exploiting the forest. The eco-tourism operation is part of that effort. Accommodations are in small but comfortable chalets, each with its own hot shower and veranda. Excursions completely break the pattern set in other lodges. In the wet season visitors get paddled through the forest in small canoes. In the dry season tours go on walking trails. Each trip goes to a different area, and the territory has very little human impact. Nighttime excursions aim not to capture a caiman, but to show off the nocturnal animals. A local guide is always present; normally there is a trained naturalist as well. Nature talks are a nightly occurrence. The researchers working in the area have dinner one evening with guests, and share their experience. For longer stays at certain times of year, guests can accompany researchers in the field. Good as all this sounds, there are disadvantages. Guides are local people being trained in tourism; they may not be as polished. It's a lot farther to go. The ecosystem is *varzea*, so there are more mosquitoes. And it's very nature-focused, which isn't for everyone.

Getting to Tefe: Tefe lies some 200km (125 miles) upriver of Manaus. **TRIP** (© **0300/789-4747**; www.voetrip.com.br) has flights 6 days a week. The cost of a one-way ticket starts at R$349. There is also a fast ferry departing Manaus for Tefe at 7am every Wednesday and Saturday. The journey takes about 12 hours. The cost is R$190.

Lodge Checklist: Distance: 200km (125 miles); Biome: Varzea; Size: 10; Boat Capacity: 12; Boat Motors: Outboard; Canoes: Yes, canoes used for most excursions, but no individual canoeing allowed; Library: Yes; Biologist: Yes; Nature Talks: Yes; Other Excursions: Yes.

Av. Santos Dumont 1350, loja 16 (Manaus Airport), Manaus, AM 69049-000. © **092/3652-1213** or (main eco-tourism line) 097/3343-4160. Fax 097/3343-2967. www.mamiraua.org.br. 10 units. 4-day packages cost R$1,000; 5-day packages are R$1,200 per person. Price does not include plane or boat fare to city of Tefe. AE, DC, MC, V. **Amenities:** Restaurant; bar.

4 BOAT TRIPS

On a boat-tour package, the experience is similar to that of a lodge; there are excursions on the small side channels, a sunset and sunrise tour, caiman spotting, piranha fishing, and a visit to a *caboclo* (river peasant) settlement. The difference is that in the time you're not on an excursion, you're moving on the river. There is always something to see, even if it's just the vastness of the river itself.

Viverde, Rua dos Cardeiros 26, Manaus (©/fax **092/3248-9988;** www.viverde.com. br), can arrange boat voyages or charters. Their website has photos and descriptions of the better Manaus-based touring boats.

Amazon Clipper Cruises (© **092/3656-1246**; www.amazonastravel.com.br/amazon_ clipper_i.html) has three old-style Amazon riverboats—the *Amazon Angler, Selly Clipper,* and *Selly Clipper II*—that make regular 3- and 4-day trips departing from the Tropical Manaus. The boats have cabins with bunk beds and private bathrooms, and in the evening the cabins have air-conditioning. The 3-day tour stays on the Amazonas River; the 4-day tour goes up the Rio Negro. Both tours include a visit to Janauary Park and the Meeting of the Waters. The price for the 3-day Amazonas tour is US$535, and the 4-day Rio Negro tour costs US$695. Children 12 and under receive a 20% discount. A newer and more luxurious boat has recently been launched, the *Amazon Clipper Premium.* The main differences are that the boat has a number of pleasant common rooms and the cabins come with real beds, not bunk beds. Rates, however, are at a premium; the 3-day Amazonas package costs US$750, and the 4-day Rio Negro tour US$950.

Swallows and Amazons ★, Rua Ramos Ferreira 922, Manaus (© **092/3622-1246;** www.swallowsandamazonstours.com), is run by New Englander Mark Aitchison and his Brazilian wife, Tania. The company's core trip is an 8-day adventure program that includes 2 nights in Manaus and then sets off up the Amazon and Rio Negro to explore the territory around the Anavilhanas Archipelago. Transportation is on company-owned traditional wooden riverboats, while exploration is done either on foot or by canoes. Accommodations are either on the riverboat (hammocks) or on a houseboat (with A/C and cabins). Prices range from US$1,350 to US$1,650 per person (includes all meals, transportation, and activities). These trips run year-round; check the website for timing and availability.

Cruising the Amazon in Style

For the ultimate Amazon river experience, travelers now have the option of taking a luxury cruise ship, the *Iberostar.* For those whose first reaction is *God no! Not a cruise!* think again. The *Iberostar* does an excellent job getting guests off the boat and out into nature (in addition, of course to pampering them silly). This 75-cabin pocket cruiser started operating in June 2005. The boat offers two programs, a 3-night Solimões cruise or a 4-night Rio Negro cruise. Both are worth taking; for most people it's just a matter of which one fits better into their travel plans. Cabins are beautifully appointed and feature king-size beds, large-screen TVs, a private veranda, and a luxurious bathroom.

All the luxury aside, however, the cruise is actually well set up (better than many of the lodges we have visited) for making the most out of your Amazon experience. There is a well-stocked library with interesting and rare books on the environment and the region, and staff are very knowledgeable (some even have bird books to help identify species, an unheard-of thing in Brazil) and give daily presentations on the fauna and flora of the region. Excursions are made in aluminum launches with twin 240-horsepower motors, allowing you to quickly get to any place of interest. As the boat is constantly moving, you move into far more diverse territory than at a lodge. A cruise is even a luxurious way of experiencing the mosquito-ridden Solimões. The increased presence of insect life on this white-water river (they don't bother you in the daytime when you are out exploring, only around dusk) also attracts more birds and other animals. We have seen some of our best wildlife on and around the Solimões. And it's a lot easier to put up with mosquitoes if you can do so from a fancy cabin, sipping a glass of complimentary champagne. *Tip:* Operators like Viverde or Brazil Nuts can often book a much better rate than listed on the Iberostar website.

Iberostar Grand Amazon   Rua Marquês de Santa Cruz 25, Hidroviária do Amazonas, AM 69005-050. © **092/2126-9900.** www.iberostar.com. 75 cabins. Packages start at US$848 per person for a 4-day package and US$1,160 per person for a 5-day package, including all meals, beverages (alcoholic and nonalcoholic), guides, excursions, and entertainment. AE, DC, MC, V. **Amenities:** 2 restaurants; 2 bars; 2 outdoor pools; room service; smoke-free rooms. *In room:* A/C, TV, fridge, hair dryer.

5 RIDING THE RIVERBOATS

The old-style wood or steel-hull riverboats that ply the Amazon basin are about transport, not seeing wildlife. They stick to deeper channels, taking passengers and goods up and down the Amazon. The most popular routes are Manaus-Belém and Manaus-Santarém. Most boats have small cabins, though it's more fun just to sling your hammock on deck. Good, simple meals and filtered water are supplied on the boat at no extra cost.

Boats depart from the new **Hidroviaria do Amazonas** (**Riverboat Terminal;** ✆ **092/3621-4310**) in the middle of downtown at Rua Marquês de Santa Cruz 25. An information desk inside the front door provides information about arrival and departure times, and numerous kiosks sell tickets. By purchasing here, you can be sure you will not be cheated. Boats for **Belém** normally depart Wednesday and Saturday at noon. The trip downstream takes 4 days. Delays are not uncommon. Cost of a first-class hammock spot (on the upper deck) is R$275. Hammocks are not supplied. Buy one in Manaus (see "Shopping," earlier in this chapter). Cabins cost R$750 to R$850. Boats for **Santarém** normally depart Tuesday and Thursday. The cost is R$125 for a first-class hammock, R$98 for a second-class hammock, and R$325 for a cabin. The trip takes about 40 hours.

6 DEEPER INTO THE AMAZON: EXPEDITION TOURS

Amazon Mystery Tours ★★★ (Value)   If you want to really explore the jungle, this is the company to go with. Amazon Mystery has the skills and experience to bring you deep into the rainforest; make your time there safe, fun, and informative; and then get you back to town again. The company has core adventures in either a kayak or speedboat of the Amazon tributary rivers upstream of Manaus. For the kayak adventures, a typical day includes a few hours of paddling, followed by a delicious lunch of fresh fish, followed by a hike to a waterfall or hidden cavern that few have ever seen. At night, you head out with a spotlight to search for caiman or other jungle creatures. The speedboating adventures cover much the same territory, but with less time on the river, and more time to explore the forest. The company's regular guide is a Tucano Indian with an extensive traditional knowledge of Amazon plants and animals. Participants need a basic level of physical ability—for example, you should be able to hike and paddle a small boat—but no special skills. The camping is very comfortable, the food is excellent (always important), and the company knows to bring along the little extras like folding chairs (not to mention caipirinha cocktails) that make camping civilized. You sleep in hammocks. At present, Amazon Mystery has 4- to 6-day descents on the Manacaparu river, 7-day descents of the Rio Urubu, and 10-day descents of the Jatapu river. However, the owner is always exploring new territory, so it's a good idea to check the website. The company also offers a 3-day adventure sports trip involving rappelling and white-water kayaking.

Av. Djalma Batista 385, sala 103, Manaus. ✆ **092/3248-4258**. www.amazon-outdoor.com. Prices average US$190–US$290 per person per day, which includes all airport transfers, accommodations in Manaus, equipment, drinks (alcoholic and non-), meals, guides, and excursions.

7 BELÉM

2,444km (1,519 miles) N of Rio de Janeiro, 2,468km (1,533 miles) N of São Paulo

Belém's an old city, founded in 1616 on the spot where the Amazon River reaches the sea. The first and most important building was the fort. Belém was not a commercial enterprise but a strategic investment. By controlling the mouth of the Amazon, Portugal could prevent other nations from penetrating into the vast interior, and not incidentally expand the borders of its own South American empire. Peasants and soldiers were required to feed and man the fort, along with a church and governor to keep peasants

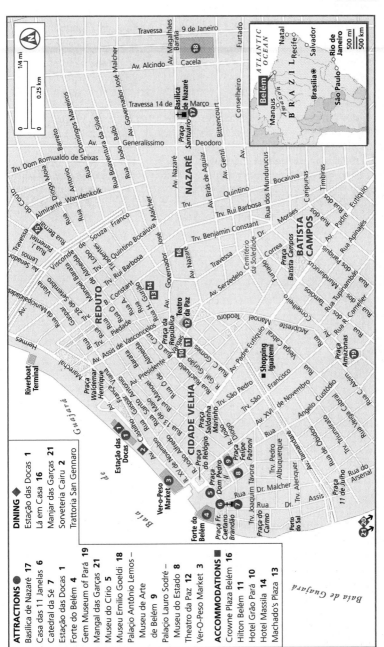

ATTRACTIONS ●

Basílica de Nazaré **17**
Casa das 11 Janelas **6**
Catedral da Sé **7**
Estação das Docas **1**
Forte do Belém **4**
Gem Museum of Pará **19**
Mangal das Garças **21**
Museu do Círio **5**
Museu Emílio Goeldi **18**
Palácio Antônio Lemos –
    Museu de Arte
    de Belém **9**
Palácio Lauro Sodré –
    Museu do Estado **8**
Theatro da Paz **12**
Ver-O-Peso Market **3**

ACCOMMODATIONS ■

Crowne Plaza Belém **16**
Hilton Belém **11**
Hotel Grão Pará **10**
Hotel Massia **14**
Machado's Plaza **13**

DINING ◆

Estação das Docas **1**
Lá em Casa **16**
Manjar das Garças **21**
Sorveteria Cairu **2**
Trattoria San Gennaro

and soldiers in line. And that, give or take a tiny merchant class, was pretty much Belém for some 200 years, until in the latter half of the 1800s a Scottish engineer named Dunlop discovered vulcanized rubber, and realized it would be the perfect thing to cushion the ride on that nifty new invention, the bicycle.

Demand for rubber latex, then grown exclusively in Amazonia, soared to unimagined heights. Awash in money from rubber, Belém's unimaginative elite began importing civilization wholesale from abroad: a cast-iron market hall from Scotland; streetlights and electric trams from England; dresses and lingerie from Paris. In the copied-from-England parade ground park (now Praça da República) they built a copied-from-Italy opera house, a nice counterpoint to the copied-from-Rome basilica in the suburb of Nazaré. Everything built and bought was of the finest materials: marble, jacaranda, ebony, iron, silk, lace. Then the price of rubber crashed, and Belém never quite figured out how to bounce back. Today the city of 1.5 million survives as an export point for Amazon products.

For visitors, the chief attraction remains that 19th-century legacy. The vast Ver-o-Peso Market on the banks of the Amazon has every rainforest product imaginable available for sale. The old downtown, with its fort and cathedral and decaying stock of 19th-century buildings, provides a decent day's strolling.

Belém's cuisine is remarkable, with a mix of Amazon and seafood ingredients found nowhere else in Brazil. No visit is complete without an evening at a good Belém restaurant, and a stop at a tropical fruit-juice stand or ice-cream shop.

In a long-ago world before deforestation, the other attraction to Belém might have been the rainforest, but Pará state has chopped its forest down with such enthusiasm there's very little original forest left within easy journey of Belém.

Instead, Belém's chief wildlife attraction is the island of Marajó, the world's largest freshwater island, which sits at the mouth of the world's largest river. Occupied by buffalo ranches and prone to periodic flooding, Marajó's landscape has vast flocks of colorful wading birds, caiman, and piranha.

For visitors with limited time to spend, I'd recommend no more than a day or two in Belém and then a 3- or 4-day journey to Marajó.

ESSENTIALS
Arriving
BY PLANE   Gol (© 0300/115-2121; www.voegol.com.br) and **TAM** (© 0800/570-5700 or 091/4002-5700; www.tam.com.br) fly to Belém's international airport, the **Aeroporto Internacional de Val-de-Cães** (© 091/3210-6039), 22km (13 miles) from downtown. **Coopertaxi** (© 091/3257-1720) operates all the taxis at the airport. The company can be reached 24/7 and accepts Visa and MasterCard. Fares to downtown (Praça da República area) average R$40.

BY BUS   The bus station, or **Terminal Rodoviario,** is located at Av. Almirante Barroso s/n on the corner of Avenida Gov. José Malcher (© 091/3266-2625); Bus 900, CIDADE NOVA IV—VER-O-PESO from in front of the Ver-o-Peso Market or on Av. Nazaré on the bottom tip of Praça da República). Companies that run popular routes include **Boa Esperança** (© 091/3266-0033) to Natal, Recife, São Luis, and Fortaleza; **Itapemirim** (© 091/3226-3458) to Salvador, São Paulo, and Rio de Janeiro; and **Transbrasiliana** (© 091/3226-1942) to Brasilia and São Luis. Brazilian long-distance buses are safe, air-conditioned, and comfortable, especially the overnight ones, which have fully reclining *(leito)* or mostly reclining *(semi-leito)* seats. Tickets can be purchased only at the station.

BY RIVERBOAT   Most people choose to make the 4-day riverboat journey downstream from Manaus to Belém, but you can make the 5-day journey upstream the other way. Tickets and information are available from the riverboat company kiosks located inside the **Rodoviaria Fluvial,** Av. Marechal Hermes s/n (© **091/3224-6885**), located on the waterfront a kilometer (½ mile) downstream of the Estação das Docas near the corner of Avenida Visconde de Sousa Franco. The terminal looks run-down and seedy, but it's safe enough during the day. Several boats make the journey, departing on different days of the week. **Macamazon,** Av. Boulevard Castilho França 744 (© **091/3222-5604**), has departures for Manaus Monday, Tuesday, Wednesday, and Friday at 6pm. Cost is R$350 for a hammock spot, R$600 for a cabin. You can often negotiate a 30% discount if you buy the day before sailing.

English-speaking agents at **Amazon Star** (© **091/3241-8624;** www.amazonstar.com. br) will gladly book you passage on board the NM *Santarem,* which departs every other Tuesday at 6pm, arriving in Manaus on Sunday. The boat stops for a day in Santarem en route, and passengers have the option of making a day trip to Altar do Chão, the beach resort on the Tapajos river.

City Layout

Belém was founded on a small headland where the Rio Guamá flows into Guajará Bay on the Amazon estuary. It was here in 1616 that the Portuguese erected the **Forte do Belém.** Defense taken care of, the Portuguese turned to religion, erecting both the **Catédral da Sé** and the **Igreja de Santo Alexandre** on the small square opposite the fort, **Praça Frei Caetano Brandão.** On a much larger adjacent square—**Praça Dom Pedro II**—the early city builders gave unto Caesar, erecting two palaces—the white **Palácio Lauro Sodré** and the blue **Palácio Antônio Lemos**—that would house the civil administration of the state and city, respectively. On the riverbank slightly downstream (north) is where they put the **Ver-o-Peso Market,** and next to that, the city's docklands, which have recently been renovated into a restaurant and shopping complex called the **Estação das Docas.** Running parallel to the river is the broad, busy **Avenida Castilhos França.** Inland from this street is the old commercial section of the city, an area of small shops and old colonial buildings called the **Cidade Velha** or **Old City.** It's a fun area to wander during business hours, but it should be avoided in the evening and on Sundays. The northern boundary of the old city is **Avenida Presidente Vargas,** which runs inland from the waterfront uphill out of the old city to a large green square—the **Praça da República**—upon which sits the **Theatro da Paz.** At the tip of the praça, **Avenida Nazaré** veers off at an oblique angle, leading into a more upscale residential district of **Nazaré,** home to the **Basilica of Nazaré,** as well as other attractions such as the **Museum of Emilio Goeldi.** This is also the street that leads to the city's bus station.

Getting Around

Most of Belém's main attractions are within easy walking distance of Praça da República. For destinations farther afield, Belém's buses are fast and efficient and the city's taxis are plentiful and affordable.

BY BUS   Bus fare is R$1.50 with no transfers. The buses' origin and destination are given on the front, while smaller signs on the front and sides give route information. Because of the many one-way streets in Belém, buses normally follow different routes going and coming, so the smaller signs list route information for the trip out—IDA—and for the return route—VOLTA. For visitors the two most useful routes are the ones that take you from either the Ver-o-Peso Market or Praça da República out past the Nazaré Basilica, the bus station *(rodoviario)*, and the Bosque Rodrigues Alves. The following will accomplish that, but as always there are others.

From in front of the Ver-o-Peso, the buses are BENGUI—VER-O-PESO; CIDADE NOVA IV—VER-O-PESO AF900; JIBÓIA BRANCA—VER-O-PESO AF 986.

From Avenida Presidente Vargas (Praça República), the buses are AGUAS BRANCAS—PRES. VARGAS AU 988; CASTANHEIRA—PRES. VARGAS AG 440; ICOARACI—A. BARROSO. (This bus will also take you out to Icoaraci.)

BY TAXI   Taxis are plentiful and inexpensive. They can be hailed on the street or at numerous taxi stands. Rides are always metered. Sample fares: from the airport to Praça da República, R$40; from the main bus station to Praça da República, R$20; from Praça da República to the Ver-o-Peso Market, R$10. **Coopertaxi (℃ 091/3257-1720** or 3257-1041) can be reached 24/7 and accepts Visa and MasterCard.

BY CAR   Belém drivers buckle up religiously and carefully observe posted speed limits; Belém's police enforce the rules ruthlessly. Roads and destinations are well-marked, making travel straightforward if you decide to rent a car.

Visitor Information

The city and state tourism agencies, **Belémtur** and **Paratur,** have side-by-side kiosks at the airport. Both have excellent free maps of Belém. The Belémtur kiosk is open Monday through Friday 8am to 11pm, Saturday and Sunday 9am to 9pm. The Paratur kiosk is open Monday through Friday 9am to 9pm, Saturday 9am to 1pm. Paratur also has a very good English-language website: www.paraturismo.pa.gov.br. In the city, **Paratur** (℃ **091/3212-0575**) has an office near the shipping port at Praça Maestro Waldemar Henrique s/n. If you're fluent in Portuguese it's possible to stop by and have a chat with the pretty girls who staff the office, though they have little information to impart, most of it wrong or out-of-date. **Belémtur** (℃ **091/3283-4850;** www.belem.pa.gov.br, Portuguese only) has an office at Av. Gov. José Malcher 257. The staff is equally friendly, equally unilingual, and equally less than totally useful. Both are open Monday through Friday 8am to noon and 1 to 6pm.

⎛Fast Facts⎞ Belém

Area Code The area code for Belém is **091.**

Banks & Currency Exchange Banco do Brasil, Av. Presidente Vargas 248, Comércio (℃ **021/2223-2537**) is open Monday to Friday 10am to 4pm (24-hour ATM on-site). **Turvicam** on Praça da República, Av. Presidente Vargas 640, loja 3 (℃ **091/9609-5539**), changes cash and traveler's checks. Open Monday to Friday 8am to 6pm, Saturday 8am to 1pm.

Car Rentals Avis is at the airport (℃ **091/3257-2257**) and Hotel Hilton (℃ **091/3225-1699**). Also at the airport is **Localiza** (℃ **091/3257-1541**).

Consulates Great Britain (Honorary), Av. Governador Magalhães Barata 651, Room 610 (℃ **091/4009-0050**).

Dentist Cliniodonto, Travessa Padre Eutiqiuio 1971 (℃ **091/3225-0413**).

Emergencies For police, dial ℃ **190;** fire and ambulance ℃ **192.**

Hospital For medical attention, go to **Hospital Ofir Loyola,** Av. Governador Magalhães Barata 992, Nazaré (℘ **091**/3249-9429).

Internet Access **TVTron Business Center** is in the basement of the Hotel Hilton on Praça da República (℘ **091/3225-0028**). Open Monday to Friday 7:30am to 10:30pm, Saturday and Sunday 7:30am to 6:30pm; R$10 per hour.

Pharmacies **Farmacia Big Ben,** Av. Serzedelo Correa 15, near Praça da República (℘ **091/3283-4145**), is open Monday to Friday 8am to 10pm and Saturday 8am to 4pm. Big Ben also has an order-by-phone service (℘ **091/3241-3000**) that is open 24/7.

Safety Pickpockets and purse snatchers are common in the Ver-o-Peso Market. They're especially fond of the two-man distract-and-snatch technique, so keep your wits about you and your bag or purse in front of you. Avoid the Old City completely on Sundays, and on weekdays after dark stick to main streets and squares (the Praça da República, Av. Pres. Vargas, and the Estação das Docas are well lit and policed in the evening).

Taxes Hotels add a 10% accommodations tax directly to your bill. There are no other taxes on retail items or goods.

Time Zones Belém is 3 hours behind GMT, the same as Rio.

Visa Renewal Go to the **Policia Federal,** Travessa Mariz Barros, Marco (℘ **091/ 3246-1800**), open Monday to Friday 8 to 11:30am and 2 to 5:30pm. The fee is R$67, and you may need to show a return ticket and proof of sufficient funds to cover your stay.

Weather Belém has two seasons: hot, humid, and rainy from December to May, and hot, humid, and less rainy from June to November. The daytime maximum temperature usually reaches 33°C (92°F) or slightly higher, and relative humidity is always above 90%. Rain comes in the form of short violent thundershowers, usually in the afternoon.

WHERE TO STAY

Accommodations aren't Belém's strong suit. Most of the hotels in the central part of the city are too old, run-down, or seedy to be worth considering—odd for a city that sees tourism as a serious part of its future. Those listed below are really all the hotels you should consider in Belém.

Expensive

Crowne Plaza Belém ★★   The Crowne Plaza is the only truly top-notch hotel in Belém. Better yet, it's located in Nazaré, a pleasant leafy neighborhood with shops and cafes and a nice safe feel, still just a pleasant 20-minute stroll from the sights in Centro. Rooms are spacious and modern, with tile floors and king-size or two twin beds, dressed up in top-quality Egyptian cotton, with bathrobes and slippers for an added touch of elegance.

Av. Nazaré 375, Belém, BR 66010-010. ℘ **0800/118-778** or 091/3202-2000. Fax 091/3202-2222. www. crownebelem.com.br. 174 units. R$400 superior double; R$500 deluxe double. Check the website for discounts and upgrades. AE, DC, MC, V. Parking R$20. **Amenities:** Restaurant; bar; exercise room; outdoor pool; room service; smoke-free rooms. *In room:* A/C, TV, fridge, hair dryer, minibar.

Hilton ★   A great location on the Praça República, plus a great pool and all the services that come with the Hilton brand. The standard rooms themselves—located on floors two through six—are pleasant if not outstanding, featuring a firm queen-size bed, work table, lounge chairs, a small balcony, and a bathroom with standard-size tub/shower combo, a good-size counter sink, and extras like a hair dryer and makeup mirror. Superior rooms are identical, except the superior rooms are located on floors 7 through 11. The deluxe rooms, on floors 12 to 14, have not only recently been renovated, but they include access to the 14th-floor executive business lounge. Junior suites aren't worth the cost premium, but the corner suites are. These—on floors 2 through 15—feature a furnished separate sitting room and sizable balcony with an excellent view of the Theatro da Paz.

Av. Presidente Vargas 882, Belém, BR 66017-000. ☏ **091/4006-7000.** Fax 091/3241-0844. www.hilton. com. 361 units. R$470 standard; R$490 superior; R$575 deluxe; R$615 corner suite. 30%–50% discount on weekends and low season. Children 8 and under stay free in parent's room. AE, DC, MC, V. Free parking. **Amenities:** Restaurant; bar; large gym; large outdoor pool; room service; smoke-free rooms. *In room:* A/C, TV, hair dryer, minibar.

Moderate

Hotel Massilia ★★ ⓥⓐⓛⓤⓔ   Considering price, quality, and location, this small hotel is the best place to stay in Belém. Unless you really need the four-star services of the Crowne Plaza or Hilton, this should be your first choice. The 10 standard rooms come with nice firm beds (either a queen-size or two singles), and are tastefully decorated with tile floors, exposed brick walls, and a writing desk made of tropical "cathedral" wood. Bathrooms are small but spotless, with showers that give lots of hot water. Upstairs the six suites, or *apartamentos,* spread out over two floors, with a small bed/couch and sitting area on the main floor, and a queen-size bed and desk in a small upstairs loft, all of it cooled by ultra-silent air-conditioning. A delicious breakfast, served outside on the patio, comes with an ever-changing variety of specialty breads.

Rua Henrique Gurjão 236, Belém, 66053-360 PA. ☏ **091/3222-2834.** Fax 091/3224-7147. www.massilia. com.br. 17 units. R$115 standard; R$130 apt. Extra person R$15. Children 6 and under stay free in parent's room. 10% discount with cash. MC, V. Free parking. **Amenities:** Restaurant; small outdoor pool. *In room:* A/C, TV, fridge, hair dryer, minibar.

Machado's Plaza ★ ⓥⓐⓛⓤⓔ   The Machado's Plaza stands literally next door to the Massilia. This small hotel was built in 2004 and offers pleasant and new accommodations. All 36 rooms come with lots of closet space and are nicely furnished with comfortable beds (doubles or two twins) with nice linens and firm mattresses. Every room also features a desk and complimentary high-speed Internet. There are no views to speak of; most rooms look out over Rua Henrique Gurjão, a narrow street a few blocks off the Praça da República. The advantage is that it's quiet at night and you're still within easy walking of some of the city's main sights. The hotel also features a small pool and restaurant.

Rua Henrique Gurjão 200, Belém, 66053-360 PA. ☏ **091/4008-9800** or 4008-9816. Fax 091/4008-9817. www.machadosplazahotel.com.br. 36 units. R$160–R$220 standard. Children 6 and under stay free in parent's room. Extra person add 25%. V. Free parking. **Amenities:** Restaurant; small outdoor pool. *In room:* A/C, TV, Internet, minibar.

Inexpensive

Hotel Grão Pará   This hotel has a fabulous location on the Praça República, two doors down from the Hilton. Guests come here for clean, fairly comfortable accommodations at a reasonable price. Rooms, with a firm queen-size mattress and good linens, aren't large—there is just space enough for a bed and a small breakfast table. Bathrooms are clean and functional. The staff here is friendly and professional. Given the small price difference and vast increase in quality, the Massilia is a better bet, but if it's full, the Grão Pará is an acceptable backup.

Av. Presidente Vargas 718, Belém, 66017-000 PA. ℂ **091/3321-2121.** www.hotelgraopara.com.br. 150 units. R$110 standard. Extra person R$30. Children 8 and under stay free in parent's room. AE, V. *In room:* A/C, TV, fridge, minibar.

WHERE TO DINE

Blessed by geography, Belém has one of the richest cuisines in Brazil. In addition to the whole range of Amazon freshwater fish, there are saltwater species, including shrimp and crab. Beef is plentiful, as is buffalo from the island of Marajó.

Tip: On the waterfront the **Estação das Docas** (ℂ **091/3212-5525**) has a half-dozen restaurants, waterfront incarnations of some of Belém's best restaurants with locations elsewhere. The specialist in regional cuisine is **Lá em Casa** (see below). The **Cappone** (ℂ **091/3212-5666**) Italian restaurant is a great spot for some pasta or risotto; sushi lovers can have a good meal on the patio at **Hatobá** (ℂ **091/3212-3143**); for a steak dinner, consider **Marujo Grill** (ℂ **091/3225-5723**). For a quicker regional snack, try the **As Mulatas** (ℂ **091/3212-5300**) kiosk for a bowl of *tacacá* soup, or the **Sorveteria Cairu** (ℂ **091/3212-5595**) for ice cream made with local Amazon fruit. You can dine on the waterfront overlooking the river, or inside in air-conditioned comfort. All six are open Monday to Friday noon to midnight, Saturday and Sunday 10am to 2am.

Lá em Casa ★ SEAFOOD/REGIONAL The longtime master of local Pará cuisine serves up creative dishes prepared with regional fruit and fish. For a sampling of local fish, try the *corridinho de peixe,* which includes fresh grilled *pirarucú,* skewers of *tambaqui,* local haddock, *filhote* in *tucupi* sauce, *pescada amarela,* and *farofa* flavored with *pirarucú.* Pará's signature dish of duck in *tucupi* sauce is particularly well done here. The lunchtime buffet is a perfect opportunity to try a variety of dishes. For dessert, try the tapioca balls with *cupuaçu* filling, served with *cupuaçu* ice cream.

Bd. Castilhos França (Estação das Docas). ℂ **091/3212-5588.** Main courses R$24–R$42. AE, DC, MC, V. Daily noon–midnight.

Manjar das Garças ★★ SEAFOOD/REGIONAL The excellent food at the restaurant in the Mangal das Garças park (p. 411) comes with complimentary views of the Guamá river. The lunch buffet is top-notch and includes a large salad bar and a variety of steak, fish, and seafood dishes such as the *filhote* in *tucupí* sauce or grilled calamari with onions. In the evenings, the restaurant serves an a la carte menu, specializing in fish and seafood. Dishes include local ingredients such as the grilled *tucanaré* with roasted palm heart in an orange sauce or the baked *pescada amarela* fish with a cashew-nut purée. Desserts include several wonderful pies with tropical ice cream; try the chocolate cake with *cupuaçu* coulis and tapioca ice cream. The restaurant has some outside tables and makes a wonderful sunset destination.

Praça Carneiro da Rocha (inside Mangal das Garças Park). ℂ **091/3242-1056.** R$38 lunch buffet; dinner main courses R$28–R$52. AE, MC, V. Tues–Thurs noon–4pm and 8pm–midnight; Fri–Sat noon–4pm and 8pm–2am; Sun 11am–6pm. Taxi recommended.

Sorveteria Cairu ★ ICE CREAM The specialized ice creams of the Amazon are one of Belém's treats. Made from a variety of Amazon fruit, they are delicious and exotic and not to be missed. There are numerous flavors, mostly made from fruit without English names. The best strategy is to go and sample.

Travessa 14 de Março 1570. ☎ **091/3267-2749.** Also at Estação das Docas. ☎ **091/3212-5595.** R$3–R$9. No credit cards. Daily 9am–11:30pm. Bus: Ver-o-Peso.

Trattoria San Gennaro ★★ ITALIAN   Trattoria San Gennaro offers trendy alfresco dining in the heart of Belém's nightlife district. The restaurant takes great pride in making all the pasta, bread, and sauces in-house. There's a choice of three pastas, spaghetti, gnocchi, and fettuccini, and sauces such as a creamy Gorgonzola, porcini mushrooms, or *romanesca* (cream, ham, mushrooms, and peas). The stuffed pastas are also excellent. We enjoyed the unusual duck ravioli in passion-fruit sauce and the prawn lasagna with Gruyère cheese. There are several excellent steak and seafood dishes. For dessert try the homemade ice creams. Flavors include pistachio, basil and papaya, white chocolate, and chocolate with hazelnut.

Av. Wandenkolk 666. ☎ **091/3241-0019.** Main courses R$18–R$38. MC, V. Tues–Sat 7pm–midnight; Sun noon–3:30pm and 7pm–midnight. Bus: Docas.

Other Options

The Umarizal neighborhood has a number of excellent dining options. In addition to **Trattoria San Gennaro** (see above), there's top-quality steak at Picanha e Cia (☎ **091/3224-3343**), Rua Bernal do Couto 260, on the corner of Avenida Almirante Wandenkolk. The city's best pizza restaurant is **Xícara da Silva** (☎ **092/3241-0167**), Av. Visconde de Souza Franco 978-A. It's a vast high-ceilinged room with a big pizza oven at the far end. In the evening, the **Boteco das Onze** (☎ **091/3224-8599**), Praça Frei Caetano Brandão s/n, located on the patio of the Casa das Onze Janelas, offers a lively atmosphere, good cold beer, and top-quality Brazilian fare.

EXPLORING BELEM

One day is likely enough to see all that Belém has to offer. *Tip:* On Tuesday, entrance is free to all Belém's museums at the fort.

The Top Attractions

Forte do Presépio ★   A wood-and-earth fort—constructed on the site of today's more substantial installation—was the very first thing built in Belém when the Portuguese arrived in 1616. The fort was variously abandoned, rebuilt, and renamed over the years (it's also known as the Forte do Castelo and the Forte do Belém). The last major military renovation occurred in the 1850s. In the 1980s the nearly ruined fort was again restored, this time by Brazil's federal caretaker of historic sites. From the ramparts you get a wonderful view of Ver-o-Peso Market, the Catédral da Sé, and the Praça Dom Pedro II. A small museum inside the fort tells the history of the area's indigenous tribes and the settlement of Belém. Allow 30 minutes.

Praça Frei Caetano Brandão 117. ☎ **091/4009-8828.** Admission R$2. Tues–Sun 10am–4pm. Bus: Ver-o-Peso.

Icoaraci ★   The central street of this seaside town close to Belém has evolved into a pottery and artisan's enclave. Belém pottery is fashioned in the style of either the **Marajóara** or **Tapajônica** tribes, Belém's indigenous inhabitants. The more ancient Marajóara tribe used angular geometric designs. **Tapajônica** pottery features countless rotund gods and animals, somewhat like Hindu sculpture. The better shops include **Anísio Artesanato,** Travessa Soledade 740 (☎ **091/3227-0127;** www.anisioartesanato.com.br), and **Cultura Indígena,** Travessia Soledade 790 (☎ **091/3233-4583**). Both are open business

The Círio of Nazaré

Every year in Belém on the second weekend of October more than one million of the faithful gather in the streets to watch and participate in the annual *Círio of Nazaré*, a procession of an image of the Virgin of Nazaré. The procession has been taking place for more than 200 years, ever since a Belém peasant discovered an image of the Holy Virgin in the forest on the spot where the Basilica of Nazaré now stands. According to legend, the holy nature of the image was revealed when the peasant brought the image back to his hut, only to have it disappear overnight and reappear back on that same spot in the jungle. That original image has now been permanently installed in the nave of the specially built Basilica of Nazaré. Each year a replica image heads a procession of hundreds of thousands of the faithful that travels from the Basilica to the Catédral da Sé and back again.

The procession begins on Saturday with a nautical journey, when the image departs from the beach in the village of Icoaraci and, along with a convoy of colorful floats, arrives around noon at the Estação das Docas. The image then travels to the Catédral da Sé. Sunday morning there's a Mass, and then around 7am the image departs the cathedral and begins its return journey to the Basilica of Nazaré. The 5km (3-mile) procession normally takes all day, with hundreds of thousands of the faithful following. At the end, the Virgin returns to her resting place in the square opposite the basilica, and the participants and onlookers throw themselves into a 3-week harvest festival party.

hours (Mon–Sat 8am–noon and 1–6pm). At the waterfront there are more pottery options at the **Paracuri Fair, Praça de São Sebastião. Amazon Star Turismo** (✆ 091/3241-8624; www.amazonstar.com.br) offers daily 3-hour tours to Icoaraci for R$90 per person, including transport and a guide to explain the pottery styles and introduce you to the potters. The public bus from Belém takes about 45 minutes.

Travessa Soledade (entire street). www.icoaraci.com.br. Daily 9am–6pm. Bus: Icoaraci, from Praça República.

Mangal das Garças ★★ Kids A birthday present from the navy (who donated the land) to the city of Belém, the park was inaugurated in January 2005. Located on the river Guamá, the Mangal does an excellent job representing Belém's regional culture, flora, and fauna. A series of lagoons portrays the Amazonian ecosystem, starting off with a narrow igarapé creek that opens up into a larger lagoon with white herons and scarlet ibises and finally empties into mangroves. There is a large viewing platform overlooking the river and the marsh along the shore. The park also has an excellent restaurant (p. 409), a gift shop, and a number of attractions. For R$9 you can see everything. This includes a 45m-tall (150-ft.) modern lighthouse that offers 360-degree views; a walk-through aviary that houses over 20 species of local birds; a butterfly world, a glass-enclosed space with hundreds of butterflies flying loose; and a small but interesting navigation museum that tells the story of many river craft used on the Amazon. Allow 2 hours. *Tip:* If you want to see the birds and butterflies at their best, avoid the heat of the day. Late afternoon is great as you can combine it with a sunset stroll on the deck or a drink at the restaurant.

Praça Carneiro da Rocha (behind the Navy Arsenal), Cidade Velha. ✆ **091/3242-5052.** www.mangal. com.br. Park is free, admission only for interior facilities R$9. Paid facilities Tues–Sun 9am–6pm. Park and restaurant open later. Closed on Mon. Taxi recommended.

Museu do Círio ★   Two air-conditioned rooms tell the story of the Círio of Nazaré— an incredible religious spectacle held each year beginning on the second Saturday of October, during which nearly a million participants either witness or participate in a 2-day procession behind an image of the Virgin Mary. The museum explains the origins and development of the procession, from the discovery of the Virgin's image by an 18th-century peasant to the huge festival today. Included are models of the parade, images of Círio's past, and examples of floats and costumes and models of the imitation body parts offered up by the faithful. Some of the tour guides speak limited English. Allow 30 minutes.

Praça Dom Pedro II (on the side closest to the river). ✆ **091/4009-8846.** Admission R$2. Tues–Sun 10am–6pm. Bus: Ver-o-Peso.

The Ver-o-Peso Market ★★★   The Ver-o-Peso Market is Belém's star postcard attraction. It's a vast waterside cornucopia, with just about every Amazon product available for purchase. Stroll into the original market hall—the one with the cute blue Gothic arches, imported prefab from England in 1899—and you're in an Amazon Fish World, with outrageously strange Amazon fish like the 100-kilogram (220-lb.) catfishlike *pirapema*, all laid out on ice or on the chopping table. Outside under the canopies there are hundreds of species of Amazon fruit; most of them for sale for R$3 per kilo or less. The love-starved can seek out the traditional medicine kiosks, where every potion and bark-derived infusion seems to heighten allure, potency, and fertility. There's also an arts-and-crafts fair with baskets, hats, spoons, and all manner of goods made from reeds and wood. When you tire of browsing, dozens of food counters sell cheap, quick eats and fresh-blended tropical fruit juices. Allow 2 hours.

Av. Castilhos França s/n. No phone. Daily 5am–2pm. Bus: Ver-o-Peso.

Other Attractions

Belém's **Theatro da Paz** (✆ **091/4009-8750;** tours every hour Tues–Fri 9am–1pm; admission R$4) is an ornate opera house modeled on Milan's La Scala theater. The inside is a rich assortment of Italian marble and tropical hardwoods, wrought iron, and gold gilt.

Located side by side on the Praça Dom Pedro II are two lovely colonial palaces. Both are worth a glance if you have time on your hands, but don't feel guilty if you miss them. The white neoclassical **Palaçio Lauro Sodré** used to house the Pará state government, but is now home to the **Museu do Estado,** Praça Dom Pedro II (✆ **091/3219-1138;** Tues–Sat 10am–6pm, Sun 10am–2pm; admission R$2), which displays the former state-rooms complete with lovely tropical furnishings. Each room is done in a different ornate style: Art Nouveau, rococo, neoclassical, and so on. Next to the Forte do Belém, the former Church of Santo Alexandre has been converted into a small and eminently missable **Sacred Art Museum (Arte Sacra;** ✆ **091/4009-8802;** Tues–Sun 10am–4pm). There's so little on display, in fact, that it's not really worth paying the R$4 admission.

Also located beside the Forte do Belém, the yellow 11-windowed **Casa das 11 Janelas,** Praça Frei Caetano Brandão s/n (✆ **091/4009-8823;** Tues–Sun 10am–6pm; admission R$2), has two floors of contemporary art by Belém painters and sculptors.

Housed in a former hellhole of a prison, the **Gem Museum of Pará (Museu de** **Gemas),** Praça Amazonas s/n (✆ **091/3230-4452;** admission R$4; Tues–Sat 10am–7pm, Sun 10am–7pm; bus: Igautemi [but take a cab back if you buy jewelry]), is definitely quirky enough to merit a visit. The museum showcases an extraordinary variety of Pará's crystals and gems. Geologists will be in heaven. Those less than rock-happy may find it a tad much. Other cells have been leased to private jewelry companies that show off their original designs.

Architectural Highlights

The **Cidade Velha,** or **Old City,** opposite the Ver-o-Peso Market is a wonderful mixture of Portuguese colonial, Art Nouveau, Art Deco, and concrete-and-glass '60s modernism. This promiscuous mixing of architectural styles is the reason Belém's downtown was denied UNESCO World Heritage Site status, though Belenenses protest that the mix of styles makes their historic core all the more intriguing. The most fascinating building is the **Paris n' America** shop at **Rua Gaspar Viana 136.** At the height of the rubber boom this was the boutique for haute couture in Belém, the place where wealthy rubber barons would dress their wives and daughters. Fashions were imported from Paris, along with models to show the rather provincial Belém baronesses how the clothes ought to be worn. It's worth traipsing up the sweeping iron staircase to have a look at the still-abandoned second floor.

Churches

The two most important churches in town are the **Catédral da Sé,** Praça Frei Caetano Brandão (✆ **091/3223-2362;** Mon 2–6pm, Tues–Fri 8am–noon and 2–6pm, Sat 5–8:30pm, Sun 7–11am and 5–8:30pm), and the **Basilica de Nazaré,** Praça Justo Chermont (✆ **091/4009-8400;** Mon–Fri 6am–7:30pm, Sat–Sun 6am–noon and 3–9pm). Located on the square opposite the fort, the Catédral da Sé is neglected and rather dilapidated but still gorgeous inside, a mix of baroque and neoclassical with soaring vaulted ceiling and lovely Art Nouveau candelabras. However, the church that Belenenses are most proud of is the Basilica in Nazaré, located on the spot where in the late 17th century a simple *caboclo* hunter supposedly tripped over an image of the Virgin. It's from here that a replica of that original image sets off on pilgrimage during the yearly Círio of Nazaré. The original image is now permanently ensconced in the wall above the altar. Modeled on St. Peter's Basilica in Rome, the church itself, like much of Belém, is a nouveau riche rehash of things done first and better elsewhere.

Plazas & Parks

The green anchor of Belém's downtown, **Praça República,** is a lovely three-sided traditional square with plentiful benches and many small patches of grass on which small children play with balls. The current classical configuration of this former military parade ground is the work of Belém's 19th-century rubber barons, who also erected the **Theatro da Paz** at the Praça's narrow end. Being snobby aristocrats, of course, they also put up a fence to keep the unwashed public out. The fence came down only after rubber prices crashed.

The gardens of the **Parque da Residencia,** Av. Magalhães Barata 830, corner of Travessa 3 de Maio, used to be part of the official residence of Pará's state governors. The park features fountains, a small orchid arbor, a display space with the governor's old Rolls-Royce, and a good if slightly pricey kilo restaurant, the **Restô do Parque** (✆ **091/3229-8000;** Tues–Sun noon–3:30pm).

The tour agency in Belém with the best and largest variety of tours is **Amazon Star Turismo,** Rua Henrique Gurjão 236 (© **091/3241-8624;** www.amazonstar.com.br). **Valeverde Turismo,** Estação das Docas, building 1 (© **091/3212-3388;** www.valeverde turismo.com.br), is another reputable agency, located at the upstream end of the Estação das Docas.

BOAT TOURS   The most unique tour in Belém is the early-morning **excursion to Parrot Island ★★,** a small semiflooded island a few kilometers offshore that is the bedroom of choice for hundreds of Amazonian parrots. Boats depart at 5am (4:30am hotel pickup) to arrive at the island in the gray predawn. As the sky lightens, the parrots awake. They squawk, circle around to find their mates, then fly away into the dawn. Afterward the tour explores the small side channels of islands in the estuary. **Amazon Star** does this tour particularly well. The price is R$100, hotel pickup and drop-off included (only Tues, Thurs, and Sat). For later risers, Amazon Star also has a half-day **River Trip** through the channels and creeks of Guamá River (a tributary of the Amazon), with a stop for a guided walk in the forest. Departures are 8:30am and 2:30pm; the R$90 fee includes pickup and drop-off.

A gorgeous evening option is **Valeverde's** 1½-hour **Sunset** tour that departs at 5:30pm or the 8pm **Lights of the City** cruise, which departs nightly from the Estação das Docas and circles offshore of Belém, allowing passengers to observe as the lights come on in the city's historic churches and monuments. The price is R$45; cruises depart Tuesday through Sunday.

BUS TOURS   The trip to Icoaraci (p. 410) is highly recommended. Both Amazon Star and Valeverde offer morning and afternoon tours; they cost about R$90 per person for a 3-hour tour.

HIKING   Highly recommended for those in reasonable physical condition are **Amazon Star's trekking tours.** The **1-day tour** departs before sunrise, crossing the Guamá River to a jungle-covered section of the Amazon estuary around Boa Vista. There follows a full-day trek in the jungle, observing wildlife and visiting *caboclo* communities who make a living growing cassava and fishing. At the far end of the Acará River there's time for a rest and some swimming, followed by a sunset cruise back to Belém. Cost is R$300 per person, guide and lunch included (July–Dec only; only Tues, Thurs, and Sat).

SHOPPING

The specialty of Belém is **pottery,** mostly fashioned in the style of either the **Marajóara** or **Tapajônica** tribes, the indigenous inhabitants of Belém. The Marajóara tribe used angular designs, somewhat like the Aztec or the tribes of the American Southwest. Marajóara pottery features countless rotund gods and animals, somewhat like Hindu sculpture. The best place to shop for pottery is in the village of **Icoaraci** (p. 410). The **Ver-o-Peso Market** (p. 412) is one vast shoppers' paradise. In Belém's historic downtown, the **Rua Gaspar Viana** is a pretty pedestrian street with cobblestones and countless small shops selling everything from hammocks to lingerie, clothing, appliances, and bootleg CDs. The **Largo das Mercês** is a good place to look for leather sandals, belts, and handbags. For jewelry and raw gemstones, go to the **Gem Museum of Pará** (p. 413). For anything else, there's the three-floor **Shopping Iguatemi** mall, Travessa Padre Eutíquio 1078, Batista Campos (© **091/3250-5353;** www.iguatemi.com.br; bus: Shopping Iguatemi), open Monday through Saturday 10am to 10pm, and Sunday 3 to 9pm.

The Performing Arts

Theatro da Paz This Escala-in-miniature offers symphonies, chamber concerts, and light operas most weekends throughout the fall and winter (May–Sept). Tickets are reasonable, and the acoustics are very good. Check the website under *"Agenda de espetaculos"* for programming. Av. de Paz s/n. ✆ **091/4009-8750.** www.theatrodapaz.com.br. Box office ✆ **091/4009-8758.** The box office is in the main lobby area.

Bars & Dance Clubs

The **Estação das Docas** features live music on Thursday through Sunday nights starting at 8pm. Belém's other nightlife area centers on the **Avenida Visconde de Sousa Franco** (usually known as **Docas Bd.**) and the surrounding small streets (notably the **Av. Almirante Wandenkolk**) located north of downtown. There are many clubs, bars, and discos in this area, close enough together that it's easy to stroll from one to the next. The better ones include the **Roxy Bar,** Av. Senador Lemos 231 (✆ **091/3224-4514**), and the popular **Ventura,** Rua Boaventura da Silva 727 (corner of Av. Wandenkolk; ✆ **091/3224-1053**).

One of the best places for live music is **Boêmio Cervejaria,** Av. Visconde de Souza Franco 555 (✆ **092/3224-0075**), on the corner of Avenida Senador Lemos in the Reduto neighborhood. Bands play MPB on Thursdays, rock on Fridays, and samba on weekends. R$5 cover.

If you're looking to hear local live music, try **A Pororoca,** Av. Senador Lemos 3316 (✆ **091/3233-7631;** www.apororoca.com.br). This traditional showplace has room for a 6,000 guests, and leans heavily toward *brega,* but also plays *forró,* MPB, and very occasionally samba. Cover is around R$10 and hours are Thursday to Saturday 10pm to 4am and Sunday 7pm to midnight.

Note that the outdoor **Bar do Parque,** located in the shadow of the Theatro da Paz, is exclusively patronized by prostitutes and their customers.

8 A SIDE TRIP TO MARAJO

Marajó holds the title for the world's largest river island, a vast land expanse in the mouth of the Amazon that is larger than many countries. The island has been settled for centuries so most of the original rainforest is gone. Instead, Marajó has low-lying, periodically flooded ranchland like that of the Pantanal. The ranches are lightly stocked with water buffalo and chock-full of incredible populations of large and colorful birds—egrets, herons, parrots, toucans, and startling scarlet ibis, not to mention caiman and the occasional troupe of monkeys. A number of these ranches *(fazendas)* have opened themselves up to tourism, allowing visitors to experience the island's nature and unique way of life.

GETTING THERE The only reason to go to Marajó is to stay at one of the hotel fazendas. Though there are two small towns—Selvaterra and Soure—close together on the eastern shore of the island, they are not in themselves worth a long ferry ride. (It's worth spending 1 night in Soure to get a feel for the local culture and community and enjoy a day at the beach, Marajó-style.) Most of the fazendas will include transportation in your package, which you should arrange ahead of time either with the hotel fazenda or through a tour agency such as **Amazon Star Turismo,** Rua Henrique Gurjão 236 (✆ **091/3241-8624;** www.amazonstar.com.br).

(Moments) Do Eat the Buffalo

One of the best things about Marajó is the food. Buffalo is the local specialty, and we were expecting to try a bite, but after a few days we lost track of all the dishes that were in some way or other derived from water buffalo. We tried buffalo roast beef for our first meal. The meat is delicious, very lean and tender, with a stronger taste than cow, though not as pronounced as lamb. For dessert we had caramel pudding made with buffalo milk. In the evening, with the cold beer and view of the sunset, our cook brought us slices of fresh Mozzarella di Buffalo. Only 24 hours old, the cheese had a light, creamy taste. Another dinner started off with a rich cheese and onion soup made with, you guessed it, buffalo cheese, followed by a buffalo meatloaf. Our breakfast buffet included buffalo butter, buffalo milk, buffalo cheese, and buffalo cream, in addition to waffles, omelets (no buffalo eggs), and other goodies. Had we stayed more than a few days it would have taken a buffalo to carry us out of there.

FERRIES There's a **Belém-Selvaterra passenger ferry,** run by **Araparí Navegação,** Rua Siquiera Mendes 120 (© **091/3242-1570**), departing from Portão 10 (downstream of the Estação das Docas). Departures are Monday through Saturday at 6:30am and 2:30pm, Sundays at 10am. The trip takes 3 to 4 hours and costs R$15. To reach Soure from the ferry dock in Camará is about a 30-minute bus ride (R$7) and then a 5-minute ferry ride (free for passengers). Competition for the public bus is fierce; better to have your transport arranged beforehand with a lodge or pousada.

LODGES

Most lodges offer similar activities. The most popular ones are horseback riding, the perfect way to explore the flooded fields; buffalo riding, which is much more comfortable than it sounds; fishing; and bird-watching.

Fazenda N.S. do Carmo ★★   Located on the banks of the Rio Camará, this lodge has a wonderful authentic feel. Accommodations are comfortable, clean, and basic. In the main ranch house there are six bedrooms with simple twin beds, and three shared bathrooms with not especially hot showers, plus a pair of sitting rooms and a shared phone and TV. Tours cover the ranch and the nearby forest. They include horse and buffalo riding, canoe and kayak tours on the river and smaller channels, fishing, bird-watching, and photo safaris, plus time to kayak the river or swim in the ranch's small freshwater lake.

Marajó. © **091/9161-1521** (lodge) or 3241-2202 (reservations). 8 units, showers only, shared bathrooms. Rate per day (including pickup from ferry, meals, and activities) R$230 per person. Children 5 and under stay free in their parent's room, children 6–10 R$100 per day. AE, DC, MC, V. *In room:* No phone.

Fazenda Sanjo ★★★ (Kids)   Talk about arriving in style. After a 50-minute boat ride from the ferry dock in Soure, horses await (nonriders can go by buffalo cart) for you to ride across the flooded field to the main house of Fazenda Sanjo. This ranch offers a wonderful rustic family experience. Ana, whose family has owned the ranch for generations, and her husband, Carlos, always look after their guests from the minute they pick them up in Belém or at the ferry. The ranch is not luxurious but quite comfortable. The six rooms are located on the ground floor of the ranch and have comfortable beds and screened windows. The common rooms and large decks are on the first floor, offering fabulous views of the surrounding landscape. Fazenda Sanjo still has a herd of 300 buffaloes that guests can help round up in the afternoon. It's quite the experience to chase after a bunch of large water buffaloes while on a horse. Guests are also welcome to observe the day-to-day activities on the ranch, such as the milking of the buffaloes and cheese making. The cheese, milk, and buffalo meat are used in a lot of the dishes; the food is excellent and portions are generous. The ranch also has a small spa specializing in treatments with local clay and mud.

Tip: For an additional R$180 per person, Ana and Carlos can take care of all transfers, door-to-door from your hotel to the ranch and back, including ferry tickets.

Marajó. ☎ 091/9145-4475 (lodge) or 3242-1385 (reservations). www.sanjo.tur.br. 6 units, showers only, shared bathrooms. 3-day packages R$650; 4-day packages R$790. Children 6 and under stay free in parent's room, children 7–12 50% discount. Daily departures. MC, V. *In room:* No phone.

SOURE

If you have an extra day, it's worth spending a night in Soure, a particularly charming small Brazilian town, wedged between the river and the bay. Streets are made of grass instead of dirt, and it is there that the buffalo roam. Indeed, buffalo play an important role in the life of the island and the town. Not only are they an economic resource for the farmers, but in Soure the buffalo are also put to work pulling the garbage carts, and used as transportation. There is even a squad of buffalo-mounted police. The best time to stay in Soure is on a Saturday night when locals gather in the main square, promenade along the river, eat ice cream, and as often as not enjoy cultural presentations put on in the city square. One evening we lucked out and saw a presentation of *carimbó,* the local dance, which is a mixture of Portuguese folk dancing with Caribbean rhythms and steps.

The beaches just outside of Soure are a unique experience. The water is mostly fresh, and the tides are thoroughly impressive. At low tide, so much of the beach lies exposed that locals ride bicycles to reach the far-off water's edge. At high tide, bathers retreat to the kiosks, nestled amid the vast spreading root systems of the coastal mangrove trees.

Pousada o Canto do Francês ★ This pleasant pousada offers inexpensive accommodations within walking distance of "downtown" Soure. The rooms are clean and comfortable; just keep your windows closed as there are no screens and the mosquitoes can be bad at night. The pousada rents bicycles (R$10). They're the perfect way to explore the area. It's only a 20-minute ride to the beach of Barra Velha, and within an hour you can ride all the way out to Pesqueiro beach. French owner Thierry can book you on a variety of local excursions.

Sexta Rua, esquina com travessa 8 (the 6th street, corner with the 8th cross street), Soure. ☎ 091/3741-1298 or 8822-8746. E-mail: thcarliez@ig.com.br or reserve through Amazon Star, www.amazonstar.com.br. 9 units. R$80–R$90 double. Children 5 and under stay free in parent's room, extra mattress or hammock R$20. V. **Amenities:** Bicycles. *In room:* A/C, no phone.

Brasilia

There are other planned cities in the world—Washington, D.C.; Chandigarh; Canberra—but none has the daring and sheer vision of Brasilia. In the 1950s, a country that had shucked off a failed monarchy, a corrupt republic, and a police-state dictatorship decided to make a clean break from the past by creating a brand-new space for politics.

In place of the pretentious Greek columns and stone facades that other political capitals used to engender awe, designers opted for modernism, a style of clean lines and honestly exposed structure, a style in love with technology and progress and the glorious possibilities inherent in the new materials of glass and steel and concrete.

The city plan was done by Lucio Costa. The buildings were designed by Oscar Niemeyer.

Costa's Master Plan was pure architectural modernism: Transit would be by road and car; activities would be strictly segregated; residential buildings were to be identical in size and shape and appearance. Worker and manager would live in the same neighborhoods, send their children to the same schools. In place of a grid, there were but two great intersecting streets, one straight, one curved. Viewed from on high, the city looked like an airplane in flight, or an arrow shooting forward into the future.

That the entire city was completed in just 4 years is thanks to the will of then-president Juscelino Kubitschek, elected in 1956 on a promise to move the capital inland from Rio de Janeiro. Few expected him to succeed.

The site, on Brazil's high interior plateau, was nothing but *cerrado*—short scrubby forest, stretching thousands of miles in every direction. It was nearly 644km (400 miles) from the nearest paved road, over 120km (75 miles) from the nearest railroad, 193km (120 miles) from the nearest airport.

Groundbreaking began in 1957. Thousands of workers poured in from around the country. By April 21, 1960, there was enough of a city for a grand inauguration. Politicians and civil servants began the long shift inland.

In years since, Brasilia has been a source of controversy. Even as ground was being broken, urbanists were beginning to doubt the rationality of rationalist planning. Cities, it was being discovered, were vital, growing entities, whose true complexity could never be encompassed in a single master plan. Costa's carefully designated zones for this and that now feels stifling, ill-equipped to address the vital, messy complexity of a living, growing city.

The social aspirations of the architecture also proved illusory—politicians were no less corrupt; rich and poor did not live in harmony. Instead, the rich banished the poor to a periphery beyond the greenbelt.

But if nothing else, Brasilia did succeed in shifting Brazil's focus from the coast to its vast interior.

For visitors, the attractions here are purely architectural. Brazil's best designers, architects, and artists were commissioned to create the monuments and buildings and make them beautiful. A visit to Brasilia is a chance to see and judge their success.

1 ESSENTIALS

924km (574 miles) NW of Rio de Janeiro, 870km (540 miles) N of São Pãulo

ARRIVING

BY PLANE Gol (📞 0300/115-2121; www.voegol.com.br), **TAM** (📞 061/4002-5700; www.tam.com.br), and **Webjet** (📞 0300/210-1234; www.webjet.com.br) have several flights a day to Brasilia from major Brazilian cities. Brasilia's airport, **Aeroporto Internacional de Brasilia—Presidente Juscelino Kubitschek** (📞 061/3364-9000), is about 10km (6¼ miles) west of the Eixo Monumental. Taxis from the airport to the hotel zones cost about R$35. Regular city buses aren't worth the trouble. They take you only to the main bus station, leaving you a painfully long walk (or taxi ride) from the hotels. *Note:* Brasilia's layout is so striking from the air that's it's worth getting a window seat on the flight in.

BY BUS Long-distance buses arrive at the **Rodoferroviario** (📞 061/3363-2281), located at the far western point of the Eixo Monumental. Keep in mind that Brasilia really *is* in the middle of nowhere: 1,000km (620 miles) from Salvador, 930km (577 miles) from Rio, and 870km (539 miles) from São Paulo.

CITY LAYOUT ★★★

What makes Brasilia unique—besides its amazing architecture—is its layout. Two main traffic arteries divide the city. **Eixo Monumental** runs dead straight east/west; **Eixo Rodoviario** runs north/south, curving as it goes. Seen from above, the city resembles an airplane or an arrow notched into a partially bent bow. Where these two axes intersect is the city's central bus station, the **Rodoviaria** (not the same as the long-distance bus station; see "Getting Around," below).

The other main distinguishing feature of the city plan is the strict separation of uses by zoning. All of the city's important government buildings are located at the "point" of the arrow—that is, on the eastern end of the Eixo Monumental. All of the city's hotels can be found in two hotel districts near the Rodoviaria. Similarly, the city's offices, shopping malls, theaters, and hospitals are in their individually designated clumps, usually close to where the "bow" meets the "arrow."

Because the plan is so simple, people mistakenly believe it's easy to find their way around. Figuring out how to navigate Brasilia requires delving back into the city structure in a bit more detail.

The Eixo Monumental (the east-west avenue with all the monuments and government buildings) divides the city into two perfectly symmetric wings, the **Asa Norte,** or N (north wing), and **Asa Sul,** or S (south wing). (Always check whether an address is in the south or north wing; otherwise, you could find yourself in the complete opposite part of town.) The various single-use zones (one in each wing) are designated on maps by letter codes. SHS for Setor Hoteleiro Sul (hotels), SBN for Setor Bancario Norte (banks), or SCS for Setor Comercial Sul (commercial business).

Addresses in Brasilia read like a futuristic code: "SQN 303, Bl. C, 101" or "SCS, Q. 7, Bl. A, loja 43" or "SHN, Q. 5, Bl. C." Here's how to do the decoding. The first three letters are the sector code (for example, SHS for Setor Hoteleiro Sul—hotels). Within each sector, a group of about 10 or so buildings is called a *Quadra.* Sometimes you can tell the buildings of a Quadra belong together either by appearance or spacing. Within each Quadra individual buildings are identified as *Conjunto* (conj.) or *Bloco* (B or Bl.).

An individual store or office can be identified by *loja* or *lote.* So an address that reads "SCS Q. 7, Bl. A, loja 43" means that the office is located in the Setor Commercial Sul (the commercial zone in the south wing), Quadra 7 and building A, and the shop number is 43. "SHN, Q. 5, Bl. C" would be Setor Hoteleiro Norte (the hotel zone in the north wing), Quadra 5, building C.

Residential addresses are given a three-letter prefix—SQN (Super Quadra Norte) or SQS (Super Quadra Sul). Within each wing, each Super Quadra is given a three-digit number (for example, 203, 404, or 508). Each Super Quadra then consists of 16 buildings or Blocos (Bl. or B) that are identified by a letter. Within each Bloco there are apartment numbers. So SQN 303, Bl. C, 101 refers to Super Quadra 303 in the north wing. Within that Super Quadra you look for building C and apartment 101.

One final note: When looking for restaurants or bars, it's important to note the following distinction. SCLN (or CLN) means Setor Commercial Local Norte and refers to the *local* block of retail and commerce that is found within each Super Quadra; CLN404 is the 1 block of small shops and restaurants found within the Super Quadra 404 in the north wing. Do not confuse this with SCN, Setor Commercial Norte, which is the large mall sector adjacent to the Eixo Monumental.

GETTING AROUND

The bus hub in the center of town, where the Eixo Monumental and Eixo Rodoviario intersect, is called the **Rodoviaria.** All city buses go through the Rodoviaria. It's where you transfer from an east-west to a north-south bus. Most of the city's malls and hotels are within walking distance of the Rodoviaria.

As long as you're on the Eixo Monumental looking at monuments or shopping, Brasilia is easy to understand. Stray into the residential sections, and confusion ensues. Costa's mass-production mentality means that every single Super Quadra looks identical. There are no landmarks whatsoever, so pay *close* attention to the street addresses. Get even one digit wrong, and you'll never find your destination. For visitors, it's often wiser to save yourself the hassle and just take taxis.

BY BUS   Buses run from the tip of the south wing to the tip of the north wing, along W1 and W3 on the west side of the Eixo Rodoviario (the bow) and on L1 and L3 on the east side of the Eixo Rodoviario. To travel across town you catch a bus traveling to the opposite part of the city: From Asa Sul catch a bus that says ASA NORTE, or vice versa. On the Eixo Monumental you can catch buses labeled PLANO PILOTO CIRCULAR that just circle up and down this main boulevard. Many buses will go via the Rodoviaria, located in the center of town. These will get you pretty close to the main monuments, hotels, and malls along the Eixo Monumental. Bus tickets are R$1.85.

BY TOURIST BUS   **Brasilia City Tour** (© 061/3356-1707 or 9298-9416; www. brasiliacitytour.com.br) offers a double-decker bus that covers the main tourist destinations along the Eixo Monumental. The bus operates Tuesday to Sunday, departing at 10, 11:30am, 2, 3:30, and 5pm from the Torre da TV (TV tower). It stops at 16 different attractions, including the City Park, the Memorial JK, the Cathedral, and main government buildings. For R$20 (children 6–12 pay half price), you can get on and off wherever you like. As the bus only comes by every 90 minutes you may want to plan your stops strategically around the more interesting museums and monuments.

BY METRÔ   Brasilia has a Metrô, but is unfortunately of little use to most visitors as it currently only runs from the bus station along the Asa Sul to the satellite cities and doesn't cover the hotel section or the Eixo Monumental.

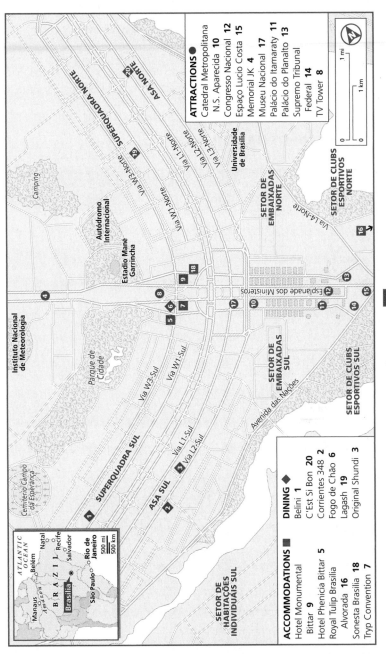

BRASILIA

17

ESSENTIALS

ATTRACTIONS ●

Catedral Metropolitana
N.S. Aparecida **10**
Congresso Nacional **12**
Espaço Lucio Costa **15**
Memorial JK **4**
Museu Nacional **17**
Palácio do Itamaraty **11**
Palácio do Planalto **13**
Supremo Tribunal
Federal **14**
TV-Tower **8**

ACCOMMODATIONS ■

Hotel Monumental
Bittar **9**
Hotel Phenicia Bittar **5**
Royal Tulip Brasilia
Alvorada **16**
Sonesta Brasilia **18**
Tryp Convention **7**

DINING ◆

Belini **1**
C'Est Si Bon **20**
Corrientes 348 **2**
Fogo de Chão **6**
Lagash **19**
Original Shundi **3**

ATLANTIC
OCEAN

Manaus
Belém
Natal
Recife
B R A Z I L
Salvador
Brasília ✱
Rio de
São Paulo
Janeiro

500 mi
500 km

BY TAXI Taxis are plentiful and my preferred transportation method, especially if I can't easily figure out where I'm going. Just hand the address to the driver and he'll figure it out. From the hotel sector to the tip of the Asa Sul costs approximately R$25. For taxis call **Brasilia** (⌀ 061/3344-1000) or **Rádio Táxi** (⌀ 061/3325-3030).

BY CAR Brasilia was designed specifically for cars. One of the big selling points of the original plan was that it made traffic lights unnecessary. All intersections were originally designed to be roundabouts (there are now traffic lights, but not that many). The rule for roundabouts: The car that's already in the roundabout (for example, going around on a curve) has the right of way. Traffic is relatively calm in Brasilia; residents even stop for pedestrians, but they're fierce if you break the roundabout rule.

VISITOR INFORMATION

The official government tourist agency **Setur** is reorganizing all of its information booths. The only information desk (Tues–Sun 9am–6pm) currently in operation is located on the ground floor of the Museu Nacional, the large white dome next to the cathedral. The site **www.infobrasilia.com.br** has short biographies of the city's founders, and some great photos.

(Fast Facts) Brasilia

Banks & Currency Exchange **Air Brazil Turismo** (⌀ 061/3321-2304), in the National Hotel. The **Banco de Brasil** (⌀ 061/3424-3000) on the second floor of the Conjunto Nacional and in Brasilia Airport (⌀ 061/3365-1183) has 24-hour ATMs. ATMs are in all of the malls.

Car Rental **Avis** (⌀ 061/3365-2344); **Localiza** (⌀ 061/3365-1288); and **Unidas** (⌀ 061/3364-2955).

Dentist For dental emergencies contact **Instituto Brasiliense de Odontologia,** SCLS406, Bl. A, loja 35, Asa Sul (⌀ 061/3244-5095).

Embassies **Australia,** SES, Q. 801, conj. K, lote 7 (⌀ 061/3226-3111; www.brazil.embassy.gov.au). **Canada,** SES Av. das Nações, Q. 803, lote 16 (⌀ 061/3424-5400; www.canada.org.br). **United States,** SES Av. das Nações, Q. 801, lote 3 (⌀ 061/3312-7000; www.embaixada-americana.org.br). **Great Britain,** SES Av. das Nações, Q. 801, lote 8 (⌀ 061/3229-2300; www.uk.org.br).

Emergencies Police dial ⌀ **190;** fire and ambulance dial ⌀ **193.**

Hospitals All hospitals are in the Hospital section (SHLS and SHLN). **Hospital Santa Lucia,** SHLS, Q. 76, conj. C (⌀ 061/3445-0000; www.santalucia.com.br).

Internet Access **Cyber Point,** on the bottom floor of the Conjunto Nacional mall (⌀ 061/3036-14955; R$6 per hour), is open Monday through Saturday from 8am to 10pm, Sunday noon to 6pm.

Pharmacies Try **Drogaria Distrital,** Shopping Conjunto Nacional, ground floor (⌀ 061/3328-0405).

Weather Brasilia is hot, hotter in the winter than in the summer. In the summer (Dec–Mar), cooling rains fall almost daily. In the winter, temperatures climb to 35°C (95°F), and rain holds off for weeks.

2 WHERE TO STAY

With few exceptions (see below) the vast majority of hotels in Brasilia are located in one of the two hotel sectors: SHN (Setor Hoteleiro Norte, north hotel sector) or the SHS (Setor Hoteleiro Sul, south hotel sector). The areas are within a 10-minute walk of each other, and of the city's two shopping sectors. The only variety is the level of luxury and size of the building.

The majority of hotel guests in Brasilia are politicians and businesspeople. Demand for hotel rooms is thus huge on weekdays and almost nonexistent on weekends. It pays to schedule your visit to Brasilia on the weekend as most hotels offer a decent discount. (Most monuments are open Sat and Sun and closed Mon). For the same reason, low season in Brasilia is during statutory holidays, January and February, and Carnaval. If you must visit Brasilia midweek, book well ahead of time (at least a month).

Hotels are concentrated in their own area with few services around, so amenities tend to be plentiful; many hotels offer fine dining, shopping, salons, car rental, and business centers. Even when not staying at a top luxury hotel, you can utilize the facilities in adjacent hotels.

LAKESIDE

The exception to the hotel-sector rule are the hotels situated on the shores of the lovely man-made lake surrounding the city. Staying here means a minimum R$20 cab ride whenever you want to visit any sites, shops, or restaurants. But then staying at the regular hotel sectors will still involve a cab for restaurants and nightlife. And the lake is lovely. It's a trade-off.

Expensive

Royal Tulip Brasilia Alvorada ★★★   Designed by Brazil's other hotshot contemporary architect, Ruy Ohtake, the Royal Tulip has quickly become one of Brasilia's top hotels. Set on the edge of the artificial lake that surrounds the city, the hotel encompasses a beautiful leisure area with a large outdoor pool complex, a spa, a fitness center, and a pier. The spacious rooms feature king-size beds and classy modern fixtures with desks big enough for two people. The hotel offers free shuttles into the city throughout the day.

Setor de Hoteis e Turismo Norte, Trecho 1, lt. 1-B, bl. C (Lago Norte), Brasilia, 70800-200 DF. ☏ **061/3424-7000.** Fax 061/3424-7001. www.brasiliaalvorada.com.br. 395 units. R$430 standard; R$500 superior. Off season and weekends 40%–50% discount. AE, DC, MC, V. Free parking. **Amenities:** 2 restaurants; bar; gym; outdoor pool; room service; smoke-free rooms; spa. In room: A/C, TV, hair dryer, Internet, minibar.

SETOR HOTELEIRO SUL

Expensive

Sonesta Brasilia ★★   This 4-year-old hotel offers comfortable and pleasant accommodations in the heart of the hotel sector. The decorations are modern and bright and the rooms feature queen-size beds, a comfortable work desk, and free Internet. The deluxe rooms include a small sitting area with a sofa, while premium rooms come with a small kitchen. There's also an outdoor swimming pool, sauna, and small fitness center. Check the website for discounts and early booking specials.

SHN, Q. 5, Bl. B, Brasilia, 70705-000 DF. ☏ **061/3424-2500.** www.sonesta.com/brasilia. 159 units. R$280 deluxe, R$340 premium double; weekends and off season R$140 deluxe. AE, DC, MC, V. Free parking. **Amenities:** 2 restaurants; bar; outdoor pool; room service; sauna; smoke-free rooms. In room: A/C, TV, hair dryer, Internet, minibar.

Tryp Convention ★★   Inaugurated in 2009, the Tryp offers top-quality accommodations and the little extras business travelers need. Rooms are spacious, with queen-size beds, nice lighting, comfortable chairs, and a sofa. Desk space is more than adequate; amenities are excellent and include the use of a heated outdoor pool and full business center.

SHS, Q. 6, Bl. B Brasilia, 70316-000 DF. ② **0800/703-3399** or 061/3218-4700. Fax 061/3218-4703. www.solmelia.com. 150 units. R$250 standard, R$280 superior; weekends and off season R$130 standard, R$175 superior. AE, DC, MC, V. Free parking. **Amenities:** Restaurant; bar; gym; outdoor pool; room service; sauna; smoke-free rooms. *In room:* A/C, TV, hair dryer, Internet, minibar.

Moderate

Hotel Phenicia Bittar ★   This small Setor Sul hotel recently renovated its floors and rooms as part of a transformation into a boutique hotel. Renovated rooms have lovely hardwood floors or new carpets, double or twin beds, wood furniture, a sitting area, and brand-new beds. Even better are the stylish renovated suites, which feature a living room with a dining table, large desk, and a spacious bedroom with a second desk. A third bed can easily be added for those with children.

SHS, Q. 5, Bl. J, Brasilia, 70322-911 DF. ② **061/3704-4000.** Fax 061/3225-1406. www.hoteisbittar.com.br. 130 units, shower only. R$240 double weekdays; R$150 double weekends and low season. AE, DC, MC, V. Free parking. **Amenities:** Restaurant; room service. *In room:* A/C, TV, Internet, minibar.

SETOR HOTELEIRO SUL

Hotel Monumental Bittar ★   The low-rise Monumental looks unassuming but it's actually a pleasant, moderately priced hotel. A recent spruce-up has meant new bedding and drapery. Rooms have either wall-to-wall carpeting or (a better choice) wood floors. Rooms with double beds are better than those with two twins—they have larger desks and closets and are larger overall. Avoid the east-facing rooms, which face the main street. A few rooms are adapted for travelers with disabilities.

SHN, Q. 3, Bl. B, Brasilia, 70710-300 DF. ② **061/3328-4144.** www.hoteisbittar.com.br. 111 units, shower only. R$175 double weekdays; R$120 double weekends and low season. AE, DC, MC, V. Free parking. **Amenities:** Restaurant; bar; room service; smoke-free rooms. *In room:* A/C, TV, Internet, minibar.

---

3 WHERE TO DINE

Brasilia has some outstanding restaurants; politicians and businesspeople prefer to eat well and having an expense account helps. Unfortunately the city's fine-dining establishments are scattered throughout the residential wings, the Asa Sul (south wing) and Asa Norte (north wing), or off in the Club Sectors. At night they can be particularly hard to find; taking a taxi is recommended. Some of the commercial strips in the Super Quadras have grown into small enclaves with a number of excellent dining options. The majority of top restaurants are concentrated in the Asa Sul.

ASA SUL

Belini ★ (Finds ITALIAN   This gourmet complex encompasses a deli, food store, restaurant, cafe, and cooking school. It's a great place to grab an espresso and some sweets, or buy some fresh bread and cold cuts for an impromptu picnic. The casual outdoor patio serves sandwiches (the pastrami, mortadella, and brie is good) for R$6 to R$14. For a more formal occasion, the restaurant upstairs serves fine Italian dishes such as lamb filet with mint sauce and risotto, or large prawns in an apple-and-ginger sauce. The restaurant also serves breakfast and afternoon tea.

SCLS 113, Bl. D, loja 36. ☏ **061/3345-0777.** www.belini-gastronomia.com.br. Main courses R$14–R$40. **425**
MC, V. Restaurant Tues–Sat noon–3pm and 7:30pm–midnight; Sun noon–4pm. Bakery daily 6:30am–midnight. Bus: W3 Asa Sul.

Corrientes 348 ★★ (Finds) ARGENTINE/STEAK   Corrientes 348 offers a large covered patio and some of the finest steaks in town. The menu offers classic Argentine appetizers, including grilled red peppers, stuffed empanadas, and grilled spicy sausage. Meat lovers will go gaga over the fine selection of prime Argentine steak, such as the *ojo de bife* (rib-eye) and *tapa de cuadril* (rump steak). Side dishes include salads, grilled vegetables, and rice. Note that all portions are extremely generous! Most plates come in half or whole portions, and for most people a half portion will be more than enough.

SCLS 411, Bl. D, loja 36. ☏ **061/3345-1348.** www.restaurante348.com.br. Main courses R$49–R$89 for 2.
AE, DC, MC, V. Mon–Thurs noon–3pm and 7pm–midnight; Fri–Sat 12:30pm–midnight; Sun noon–6pm.
Bus: W3 Asa Sul.

Fogo de Chão ★★ STEAK   One of the best all-you-can-eat steak restaurants in Brazil, the Fogo de Chão chain doesn't bother with a buffet and instead puts the focus on its high-quality cuts of meat. All dishes serve to enhance your steak-eating experience. Start off with some delicious antipasto, grilled vegetables, or a salad and then wait for the competent waiters to bring you cut after cut of fine beef, lamb, chicken, or pork. Feel free to request your favorite cut. The service is very attentive and friendly. As at most churrascarias, the drinks and desserts are not included in the price of the meal and tend to be on the pricey side, but the quality remains top-notch.

SHS, Quadra 5, Bl. E, Asa Sul. ☏ **061/3322-4666.** www.fogodechao.com.br. Main courses R$79. AE, DC,
MC, V. Mon–Fri noon–4pm and 6pm–midnight; Sat noon–midnight; Sun noon–10pm.

Original Shundi ★★ JAPANESE   This new Japanese restaurant makes a bold statement with its stunning red-and-black dining room, designed by Ruy Ohtake. Decoration aside, however, the food is the real star here. The best deal may be the all-you-can-eat lunch buffet (R$39), which includes creative sushi rolls, fresh sashimi, and several hot dishes. The a la carte menu goes way beyond the average list of sushi staples. Order one of the tasting menus and let the chef surprise you with dishes such as baby eel, mini octopus, or spring rolls with asparagus, mushrooms, and scallops.

SCLS 408, Bl. D, loja 35. ☏ **061/3244-5101.** Main courses R$36–R$64. AE, DC, MC, V. Mon–Fri noon–3pm
and 8pm–1am; Sat noon–5pm and 8pm–1am; Sun noon–5pm and 8–11pm.

ASA NORTE

C'Est Si Bon CREPES   The place for an inexpensive snack or light meal. Owner and chef Sergio Quintiliano has created more than 50 different savory and sweet crepes. One recent addition is the Crepe Almodovar, stuffed with tender beef, mushrooms, and creamy catupiry cheese. There are now two locations; the Asa Sul location also features a lovely patio and Thursday evening jazz music.

Asa Norte: SCLN 213, Bl. A, loja 13. ☏ **061/3272-1005.** www.cestsibon.com.br. Main courses R$12–R$20.
MC, V. Asa Sul: SCLS 408, Bl. A, loja 5, ☏ **061/3244-6353.** Both open daily noon–midnight.

Lagash ★★ MIDDLE EASTERN   The best Middle Eastern food in Brasilia. (Okay, there's not a lot of competition, but the quality here is excellent.) Appetizers include baba ghanouj, made with eggplant and tahini; hummus; and roasted *merguez* (lamb sausage). The most popular entree is the Moroccan lamb—tender pieces of boneless lamb cooked with nuts, scallions, onions, and rice. The wine list is heavy on the Italian and French reds to accompany the hearty and spicy dishes.

SCLN 308, Bl. B, loja 11. © **061/3273-0098.** Main courses R$20–R$60. AE, DC, MC, V. Mon–Sat noon–4pm and 7pm–midnight; Sun noon–6pm. Bus: W3 Asa Norte.

ELSEWHERE

Alice Brasserie ★★★ FRENCH   The best French restaurant in town began in Alice Mesquita's home and in 2007 moved into this lovely brasserie, where both food and service continue to garner rave reviews. The menu encompasses both classic French dishes—cassoulet maison, confit de canard, and beef bourguignon—and innovative Brazilian creations such as the grilled fish with spicy banana purée. The wine list features fine French vintages, as well as the usual suspects from Argentina and Chile. Tuesday to Saturday features an excellent lunch special, R$35 for a three-course meal.

SHIS QI 17, lojas 201-204, Edifício Fashion Park, Lago Sul. © **061/3248-7743.** Main courses R$48–R$72. AE, DC, MC, V. Tues–Sat noon–3pm and 7:30pm–midnight; Sun noon–4pm. No public transit.

---

4 EXPLORING BRASILIA

A day is enough to see all that Brasilia has to offer. The heat of Brasilia's sun makes it a good idea to get an early start. The eastern half of the Eixo Monumental is where you'll find some of the best modern architecture in the world. Time your visit to be at the TV Tower around sunset. The elevator ride to the lookout is free, and from the 72m-high (240-ft.) platform you have a 360-degree view of the city. On April 21, 2010, the city celebrated its 50th anniversary and several buildings (including the Presidential Palace and the Cathedral) underwent renovations to celebrate the occasion in style.

If it's sunny, bring a hat. There is little shade, and it gets *hot;* also bring a water bottle, because you won't find as many street vendors as elsewhere in Brazil. If you plan on visiting the cathedral, any monuments, or government buildings, do not wear shorts or a tank top. And perhaps most importantly, *be careful crossing the Eixo Monumental.* Cars go fast here and you must cross a lot of lanes.

THE TOP ATTRACTIONS

Catedral Metropolitana Nossa Senhora Aparecida ★★★   The cathedral is surprisingly small from the outside, but once you descend through the walkway, you emerge in the brightest and most spacious church you have ever seen. The floors and walls are made of white marble, with an expanse of glass overhead. The altar is surprisingly sparse, white marble decorated with a plain image of Christ on the cross. Sculptor Alfredo Ceschiatti designed the statues of the four apostles in front of the cathedral, as well as the angels suspended from the ceiling. You'll note his name on other sculptures, such as the figure of Justice in front of the Federal Supreme Court.

Esplanada dos Ministerios. © **061/3224-4073.** Free admission. Daily 8am–5pm. Mass Mon–Fri 6:15pm; Tues–Fri 12:15pm; Sat 5pm; Sun 8:30am, 10:30am, and 6pm. No touring of the cathedral during Mass. No shorts or Bermudas. Bus: Rodoviaria (short walk to the cathedral) or the Plano Piloto Circular.

Congresso Nacional   One of Brasilia's best-known images is the shot of the two towers on the Planalto Central, flanked by the two "bowls," one faceup and one face-down. It is quite beautiful in an abstract way. The inside is open for English-language tours (including a visit to the Chamber of Deputies), though it's really only of moderate interest to non-Brazilians. No shorts or tank tops allowed. If you don't take the tour, you're only allowed in the museum and the lobby.

Esplanada dos Ministerios. $\textcircled{C}$ **061/3216-1771.** Free admission. Daily 9:30am–5pm. Bus: Plano Piloto Circular.

Espaço Lucio Costa ★   Brasilia owes its shape and design to urban planner and architect Lucio Costa. This space, sunken beneath the surface of the square, contains a full-scale model of the city. Shy of a visit to the TV Tower it's the best way to get a bird's-eye view of his plan. Disappointingly, the Espaço has little information on Costa's life and career. On the back wall there are some photos of the city under construction and, best of all, reproduced and enlarged copies of Costa's original submission, the one that won him the competition.

Praça des Tres Poderes. $\textcircled{C}$ **061/3325-6163.** Free admission. Tues–Sun 9am–6pm. Bus: Plano Piloto Circular.

Memorial dos Povos Indigenas   Architect Oscar Niemeyer modeled the Monument to the Indigenous Peoples on the houses of the Bororó Indians. It was briefly redesignated as an arts museum, until the uproar caused it to be re-redesignated. However, it still seems underutilized. Exhibits highlight the art and daily life of Brazilian Indians. Headdresses of colorful feathers, pottery, baskets, hammocks, nets, spears, and paddles are on display. Unfortunately, there isn't any signage to indicate the origin or usage of the items. Museum staff come in varying degrees of helpfulness.

Praça do Buriti, Eixo Monumental Oeste. $\textcircled{C}$ **061/3344-1155.** Free admission. Mon–Fri 9am–noon and 1–6pm; Sat–Sun 10am–6pm. Bus: Plano Piloto Circular.

Memorial JK ★   This remarkable monument was built in 1980 by Oscar Niemeyer to honor the founder of Brasilia, Juscelino Kubitschek. Inside, the former president's remains rest beneath a skylight in a granite tomb, his only epitaph an inscription on the coffin reading O FUNDADOR. Aside from this slightly spooky scene, the memorial contains a lot of JK's junk that no one could care about (JK's ribbons and medals, JK's suits and tie clips). Upstairs, there's some interesting stuff on Brasilia, including photographs of the city being built, and copies of the designs that didn't get chosen.

Eixo Monumental Oeste. $\textcircled{C}$ **061/3225-9451.** Admission R$4. Tues–Sun 9am–6pm. Bus: Plano Piloto Circular.

Museu Nacional ★   You can't miss the large white dome of the Museu Nacional, rising like a giant igloo from the barren concrete tundra. Built in 2006, the museum's pleasant interior space houses free changing exhibits. Right next to the museum is the new national library, a large rectangular structure raised on short stumpy columns. Both are late Oscar Niemeyer designs, little more than austere geometric purity. Although open to the public, there are few books and not much to see. *Tip:* Tucked underneath the ramp of the Museu Nacional is a tourist information desk that gives out excellent maps and photo brochures of all the monuments in Brasilia.

Eixo Monumental Oeste. $\textcircled{C}$ **061/3325-5220.** Free admission. Tues–Sun 9am–6:30pm. Bus: Plano Piloto Circular.

Palácio do Itamaraty ★★★   One of the most beautiful modernist structures ever created (designed by Oscar Niemeyer with landscaping by Burle Marx and detailing by Milton Ramos), the Palácio do Itamaraty now serves as a ceremonial reception hall for the Department of Foreign Affairs. The interior is a match for the outside, so it's worth taking the tour. The ultramodern structure—mostly open space inside—is decorated with rich antique furnishings of Persian carpets, hand-carved jacaranda-wood furniture, and 18th- and 19th-century paintings. Somehow it really works. Guided tours only. Call ahead to request an English-speaking guide.

Esplanada dos Ministerios. ✆ **061/3411-8051.** Free admission. Mon–Fri 2 and 4:30pm; Sat–Sun 10am and 3:30pm. Guided tours only, call to confirm. No shorts or tank tops allowed. Bus: Plano Piloto Circular.

TV Tower ★★★ (Value) The best view in town is free! Take the elevator up to the 72m-high (240-ft.) lookout, and Brasilia is laid out at your feet. You'll get the best perspective of the Eixo Monumental with the ministry buildings lining the boulevard like dominoes waiting to be knocked over. Time your visit toward day end to take in the city with a fiery red Brasilia sunset. You can skip the gem museum without qualms.

Eixo Monumental (close to the bus station and malls). ✆ **061/3321-7944.** Free admission. Mon–Fri 9am–noon and 2–5:30pm; Sat–Sun 11am–5:30pm. Bus: Rodoviaria.

ARCHITECTURAL HIGHLIGHTS

The signature buildings in Brasilia were all designed by architect **Oscar Niemeyer.** The strength of this Brazilian über-modernist has always been with form; his structures are often brilliant. His weakness has always been detailing, materials, and landscaping. These bore Niemeyer, who prefers to work purely with bare concrete. Left to his own devices, Niemeyer creates austere, even boring, collections of pure geometry, like the new Museu Nacional or the Monument to Latin America in São Paulo. Fortunately, in Brasilia Niemeyer was teamed up with Brazil's best landscape designer, **Roberto Burle Marx,** and detailing- and materials-focused architects like **Milton Ramos,** and talented sculptors and artists like **Alfredo Ceschiatti.** Every building also had to conform to the overall plan of **Lucio Costa.** The result is a collection of buildings that has rightly been called the highest expression of architectural modernism on earth. Niemeyer's work is scattered far and wide throughout the city, but the best of the best is on the eastern portion of the Eixo Monumental, from the Rodoviario to the Praça dos Tres Poderes on the far side of the Congresso Nacional.

Several of these buildings are covered under "The Top Attractions," above: the **Congresso Nacional,** the **Catedral Metropolitana,** and the **Palácio do Itamaraty.** Also worth mentioning is a structure that no one would ever put in a top attraction, the standard ministry buildings, 17 of which flank the **Esplanada dos Ministerios** like big glass-and-concrete dominoes. The idea with these boring, repetitive buildings is that they be boring and repetitive. Costa and Niemeyer had notions that this rigidly enforced equality would cut back on bureaucratic infighting (as if) and, more importantly, provide an urban fabric against which the monumental buildings would stand out. That, at least, succeeded brilliantly.

Behind the Congresso Nacional stands the wide, austere Praça dos Tres Poderes (see below). On the north side of the square, the **Palácio do Planalto** is well worth a look. Visitors aren't allowed into this building, but can watch the not-very-exciting changing of the guard every 2 hours. Similar in form is the **Supremo Tribunal Federal,** the office of the Brazilian Supreme Court located on the other side of Three Power Plaza. The tribunal is open for guided visits, but only on weekends and holidays between 10am and 2pm.

PLAZAS & PARKS

Behind the Congress building, the **Praça dos Tres Poderes (Plaza of the Three Powers)** is immediately identifiable by the huge Brazilian flag flapping 99m (330 ft.) above the hot, wide-open space below. The plaza is named for the three branches of government that surround it: the legislative branch in the **Congresso Nacional** (see above), the judiciary in the **Supremo Tribunal Federal,** and the executive in the presidential **Palácio do Plan-alto** (see above). The praça itself is unrelieved Niemeyer, a vast expanse of pure white stone, with nowhere to hide from the blazing Brasilia sun. Don't visit on a hot afternoon, or you'll fry. Near the front of the square there's a long white marble box about the size and shape of a truck semitrailer, but cantilevered one floor off the ground. This is the **Museu de Cidade** (Tues–Sun 9am–6pm; free admission). Inside it's a bare marble room with eight inscriptions on each long wall telling the story of Brasilia. No maps, no photos, just words. Next to it, below the square, is the **Espaço Lucio Costa** (see above). Toward the southern side of the square is the awkward-looking **Panteão da Patria Tancredo Neves** (Tues–Sun 9am–6pm; free admission). The building's two interlocking rhomboids are supposed to suggest a dove, but it's hard to see. Inside the Homeland Pantheon it's dark as the tomb, with lighting only on a mural depicting the life and gruesome death of 18th-century rebel Tiradentes, and a book with brass pages, each inscribed with the name of a congressionally approved Brazilian hero. It's short reading so far—just four pages.

Brasilia's prime leisure space, the **Parque da Cidade,** was landscaped by Burle Marx. The park is mostly grass fields intersected by jogging and cycle paths. You'll also find playgrounds and a small fair.

ORGANIZED TOURS

BOAT TOURS ★   Tours take place on the lake, Lago Paranoá. Leaving from ASBAC (yacht club in the Asa Sul, close to Setor de Embaixadas Sul), the 2-hour tour passes the Palácio da Alvorada, the official residence of the Brazilian president (not open to the public) and continues around the lake. It's a great way to see the city from the water. Contact **Tôa Tôa** (✆ **061/9982-1161**). Departures are on Saturday and Sunday at 10am and 2pm and the cost is R$25 per person.

SPECIALTY TOURS   To make the most of your visit to Brasilia it pays to hire a tour guide. Not only will it save you all the time and hassle of getting around but you will also gain a greater appreciation of the city's architecture and structure. **Roberto Torres** (✆ **061/9963-4732;** carneirotorres@msn.com) is an experienced licensed tour guide with architectural knowledge who speaks excellent English. Book in advance. You can also contact **Prestheza Turismo,** Patio Brasil Shopping, Sala 917 (✆ **061/3226-6224;** www.prestheza.com.br). In addition to city tours, the company also offers a variety of other tours, such as a visit to the Vale do Amanhecer (Valley of the Dawn) spiritual community or to one of the national or regional parks in the area. Half-day tours start at R$80 per person.

5 SHOPPING

Shopping in Brasilia means malls. The granddaddy of Brasilia malls is the **Conjunto Nacional** (see below). Other shopping malls close to the hotel districts include the **Patio Brasil,** SCS Q.7 Bl. A (✆ **061/2107-7400;** www.patiobrasil.com.br), located in the South Wing not far from the Meliá hotel. Near the hotel sector in the north wing, the **Brasilia Shopping,** SCN, Q.5, lote 2 (✆ **061/3328-5259;** www.brasiliashopping.com.br), has a number of movie theaters and an excellent food court. Malls are open Monday through Saturday 10am to 10pm, Sunday 2 to 8pm.

For nonmall shopping, there is the **Feira de Artesanato da Torre de Televisão,** a large crafts fair that takes place every weekend underneath the TV Tower on Eixo Monumental, with crafts from the Northeast. It's open from 8am to 6pm.

Conjunto Nacional Built in 1971, the Conjunto Nacional was the first mall in Brasilia. Stores include two large drugstores, the Pão de Açucar supermarket, and a post office (Mon–Sat 9am–10pm). The large Siciliano bookstore has a CD department, English books, and a good variety of English magazines. Asa Norte, SCN. ℭ 061/3316-9733. www. cnbshopping.com.br. Bus: Rodoviaria.

6 BRASILIA AFTER DARK

There's a fair bit of stuff to do in Brasilia after dark, but there is no "scene" as such. Bars and cafes have sprung up in discrete, widely separate spots throughout the small commercial zones in the two residential wings. Best to decide what you're in the mood for, then choose your spot and stick with it.

Most classical concerts and dance and theater performances in Brasilia take place in one of the three concert halls at the **Teatro Nacional,** Setor Cultural Norte (ℭ 061/3325-6240). For program information, phone the events calendar hot line at ℭ 061/3325-6239. The box office (in the main lobby area) is open daily noon to 8pm.

Tip: During the season, the Teatro Nacional hosts free Tuesday night concerts of the Symphony Orchestra. Concerts start at 8pm and tickets can be picked up from the box office starting at noon on the day of the concert.

BARS & LIVE MUSIC

Armazém do Ferreira The Armazém resembles a bustling Rio de Janeiro botequim, decorated with lovely 1950s photos of Brazil's former capital. The bar is a very popular happy hour destination for Brasilienses, especially on Fridays. On Saturdays, the bar serves a delicous *feijoada* stew (R$29) for lunch, accompanied by live samba music. Open Monday to Thursday 5pm to 2am, Friday and Saturday noon to 2am. Closed on Sundays. CLN 202, Bl. A, loja 47, Asa Norte. ℭ 061/3327-8342. R$8–R$20.

Clube do Choro (Finds) This basement club on the Eixo Monumental specializes in *choro* and bossa nova. The crowd takes the music seriously so this is not the place to catch up with old friends. Shows from Wednesday to Sunday; starting times vary. Check the website for programming. SDC (Setor de Difusão Cultural), Eixo Monumental. ℭ 061/3224-0599. www.clubedochoro.com.br. R$20. No credit cards.

Feitiço Mineiro This restaurant in the Asa Norte has become one of the best places in town to catch well-known Brazilian acts, including samba, MPB, blues, and bossa nova. Shows usually take place Tuesdays through Saturdays and start around 10pm. The restaurant operates Monday to Saturday noon to 1am and Sunday noon to 5pm. 306 Norte, Bl. B, loja 45. ℭ 061/3272-3032. www.feiticomineiro.com.br. R$15–R$25.

Gate's Pub It looks like a British pub on the outside, but that's where the authenticity stops: The beer is cold, the crowd is beautiful, and the music hip. On Friday and Saturday jazz, blues, rock, and MPB bands take the stage. Programming often includes new, upcoming bands. The rest of the week, DJs take care of the sound and keep the crowd moving. Open Tuesday to Sunday 10pm to 3am. SCLS 403, Bl. B, loja 34. ℭ 061/3225-4576. www.gatespub.com.br. Cover R$5–R$20.

Iguaçu & the Falls

There are but three great water-falls in the world, and curiously they seem to all fall on borders: Niagara Falls, on the border between the United States and Canada; Victoria Falls, between Zimbabwe and Zambia; and Iguaçu Falls, between Brazil and Argentina.

I've seen them all. Iguaçu is without doubt the most beautiful of the three. Niagara is impressive, but marred by 2 centuries of industry and kitsch. Victoria Falls in Africa is higher, but also narrower, and the mist thrown up by all that water funneling into such a tiny gorge greatly obscures the view.

In Iguaçu, the water pours down over not one but some 275 different cataracts, spread over a precipice some 5km (3 miles) wide and 81m (266 ft.) high.

The fine mist tossed up by all that falling water precipitates down and creates a microclimate of lush rainforest, with tropical birds and an abundant population of glorious butterflies.

Iguaçu has been attracting visitors since the first European explorer stumbled across the area in the 1540s. In the 1930s more than 404,685 hectares (1 million acres) on the Brazilian side was made into a national park, and in 1985 the falls were designated a UNESCO World Heritage Site.

Iguaçu Falls never quite achieved the same iconic status as Niagara. The Iguaçu Falls did get one good breakout role, though, when they were cast almost as a supporting actor in the Robert DeNiro film, *The Mission* (worth renting for its story of the expulsion of the Jesuits, in addition to the great film footage of the falls).

Debate is endless as to whether the view from the Brazilian or Argentine side is better. You should really visit both sides to see for yourself.

Aside from the falls, there's not a lot to see in Iguaçu. Beyond the immediate zone of the falls, the national park is closed to visitors. The zodiac trips upstream toward the falls are highly recommended. There are also rubber raft trips through the rapids downstream, as well as an extraordinary 50m (164-ft.) rappel from the top of the gorge all the way down to the edge of the Iguaçu River.

The falls are remote enough that a 1-day trip is, well, insane. With a Brazilian air pass, Iguaçu makes a perfect 2-day stopover. Those with limited time, or money, should consider whether the falls—glorious though they certainly are—are worth the 1,000km (620-mile) trip from Rio or São Paulo.

1 ESSENTIALS

1,093km (679 miles) SW of Rio de Janeiro, 847km (527 miles) SW of São Paulo

GETTING THERE

BY PLANE Both **Gol** (© **0300/115-2121;** www.voegol.com.br) and **TAM** (© **045/ 4002-5700;** www.tam.com.br) have daily flights, connecting through São Paulo or Curitiba. Book ahead in peak season; flights fill up quickly.

The **Aeroporto Internacional Foz do Iguaçu** (© 045/3521-4200) is on BR-469 halfway between downtown and the national park. The 13km (8-mile) taxi ride to downtown Iguaçu costs about R$50. Many of Iguaçu's hotels are on the highway into town, making taxi fare considerably less. A bus connecting the airport to downtown takes 45 minutes; the fare is R$2.20. The airport's tourist information desk is open daily from 9am to midnight.

BY BUS Long-distance buses arrive at the **Terminal Rodoviario,** Av. Costa e Silva s/n (© 045/3522-3633). The station is 4km (2½ miles) northeast of downtown. The bus station has a tourist information office, open daily from 9am to 6pm. For buses to Rio de Janeiro, São Paulo, Curitiba, or Florianópolis, as well as long-distance buses to Argentina (Buenos Aires) and Paraguay (Asunción), contact **Pluma** bus company (© 045/3522-2515;** www.pluma.com.br). For buses across to Puerto Iguazú in Argentina, see review for Parque Nacional Iguazú (Argentine Falls), later in this chapter.

BY CAR Foz do Iguaçu is 1,200km (744 miles) from São Paulo and 620km (384 miles) from Curitiba on BR-277.

CITY LAYOUT

A small, modern city of 250,000 people, **Foz do Iguaçu** (normally just called Iguaçu) is effectively located on a peninsula. West of the city is the **Rio Paraná** and, beyond that, Paraguay. North of the city lies **Lago de Itaipu,** a great man-made lake created by putting up the world's largest hydroelectric dam across the Rio Paraná; the dam is well worth a visit. To the south of the city lies **Rio Iguaçu** and, beyond it, Argentina. The **falls** are upstream on this river, a 28km (18-mile) drive southeast from downtown. The city's downtown is small and easy to navigate, but offers few attractions. Just north of downtown, **BR-277** comes in from Curitiba and São Paulo and crosses the **Ponte da Amizade (Friendship Bridge)** into Paraguay. At the southern end of downtown, **Avenida das Cataratas** (BR-469) tracks southeast toward **Iguaçu National Park** and the falls. There are quite a few good hotels, some other attractions, and restaurants along this road. About 7km (4¼ miles) from downtown, there's a turnoff for the **Ponte Tancredo Neves,** which crosses into Argentina. Public buses take this route, and border formalities are minimal. The road to the falls, now called **Rodovia das Cataratas,** continues past the airport turnoff until, at 17km (11 miles) from the city, it reaches the gates of **Iguaçu National Park.**

GETTING AROUND

BY BUS City buses begin and end their routes at the **Terminal Urbana** on Avenida Juscelino Kubitschek (also called Av. JK—pronounced *Zho*-ta Ka) at the corner of Avenida República Argentina. Buses for the airport and the falls run along Avenida JK and Avenida Jorge Schimmelpfeng to the Avenida das Cataratas. Falls buses are marked CATARATAS (fare is R$2.20) or PARQUE NACIONAL (fare is R$2). They run every 20 minutes until 6:40pm. The trip to the park gate and visitor center takes 45 minutes. From the park gate, a free shuttle (departing every 20 min.) will take you the rest of the way to the falls. Getting to the Argentine Falls by bus is cheap but time-consuming. The one-way trip takes about 90 minutes. See review for Parque Nacional Iguazú (Argentine Falls), later in this chapter.

BY TAXI Taxi *pontos* (stands) are throughout the city, or you can flag a taxi on the street. A trip across town costs around R$20. A trip from the city center to a hotel on the Avenida

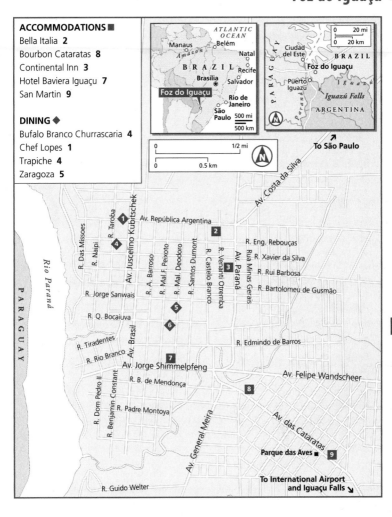

ACCOMMODATIONS ■
Bella Italia **2**
Bourbon Cataratas **8**
Continental Inn **3**
Hotel Baviera Iguaçu **7**
San Martin **9**

DINING ◆
Bufalo Branco Churrascaria **4**
Chef Lopes **1**
Trapiche **4**
Zaragoza **5**

IGUAÇU & THE FALLS

18

ESSENTIALS

das Cataratas costs between R$25 and R$35. A taxi from the center of town to the park gates costs R$45. Hiring a taxi to take you to the Argentine Falls and wait while you see them then bring you back costs about R$200, depending on your negotiation skills. **Coopertaxi** (✆ **0800/524-6464** or 045/3529-8821) has cabs available 24/7.

BY CAR   Renting a small car to travel to the Argentine Falls is a reasonable option. The cost is about the same as a tour, and rental and border hassles are minimal. You'll need a credit card, a valid state or provincial driver's license, and some other piece of ID (for example, a passport).

Iguaçu's tourist bureau employs excellent English-speaking attendants who have up-to-date and accurate information at their fingertips. They also give out free maps of the city. The main **tourist information center** is at Praça Getulio Vargas, Av. JK and Rua Rio Branco (© 045/3521-1455; www.fozdoiguacu.pr.gov.br; Mon–Fri 9am–5pm). Tourist information booths are at the airport and bus station, or you can call the Iguaçu tourist information service **Teletur** (© 0800/451-516 toll-free within Brazil). The service operates daily from 7am to 11pm.

(*Fast Facts*) Foz do Iguaçu

Banks & Currency Exchange **Banco do Brasil,** Av. Brasil 1377 (© **045/3521-2525**), has a 24-hour ATM. The HSBC branch is nearby at Av. Brasil 1151 (© **045/3523-1166**).

Car Rental Prices at **Localiza** (© **0800/979-2000**), **Avis** (© **0800/725-2847**), **Unidas** (© **0800/121-121**), **Hertz** (© **0800/701-7300**), and **Yes** (© **045/3522-2956**) are similar: about R$110 for a subcompact with air-conditioning for a 24-hour day with unlimited mileage, plus R$15 to R$30 for optional insurance. Gasoline is extra. Expect to spend about R$25 for a trip to the Argentine Falls. Both companies provide free hotel pickup and drop-off. With Avis, airport drop-off is free; Yes charges R$10.

Consulates **Paraguay,** Rua Bartolomeu de Gusmão 738 (© **045/3523-2898**); **Argentina,** Travessa Vice-consul E. R. Bianchi 26 (© **045/3574-2969**).

Dentist Try **Clinica Odontologica** (© **045/3523-5965**). On call 24 hours.

Hospital **Hospital Internacional** is at Av. Brasil 1637 (© **045/3523-1404**).

Pharmacy **Farmarede,** Av. Brasil 46, Centro (© **045/3572-1363**), is open 24 hours and will deliver to your hotel.

Weather In the summer Iguaçu is warm and muggy, but in the winter there's a very un-Brazilian chill. From April to September daytime temperatures drop to 10°C to 20°C (50°F–68°F). The falls are best seen in the summer from January to March when there is plenty of water.

---

2 WHERE TO STAY

Iguaçu has a wide variety of accommodations, with the more affordable options in town and the luxury accommodations found on the Avenida das Cataratas. High season is from December to February and in July; outside of these months you can usually negotiate a discount of 20% to 40%.

CENTRO
Expensive
Continental Inn ★★ (Finds)   Located in town, the Continental Inn is a real gem. The comfortable regular rooms feature firm twin or double beds, modern Art Deco–ish decor, good desk space, and showers with lots of high-pressure hot water. The suites are

outstanding; regular suites feature a separate sitting area, firm queen-size bed, and a large round bathtub. The top-quality master suites have hardwood floors, a king-size bed, fancy linens, a large desk, a separate sitting area, a walk-in closet, and a bathroom with Jacuzzi tub and a view over the city. Rooms for travelers with disabilities are available. *Note:* Make sure when reserving your room that you insist on staying at the Continental Inn. The hotel has another property, Recanto Park, which is not as nice and is often used in case the Continental is overbooked, even when the reservation was originally confirmed for the Continental Inn.

Av. Paranà 1089, Foz do Iguaçu, 85852-000 PR. © 0800/707-2400 or 045/2102-5000. www.continental inn.com.br. 124 units. R$280 double; R$350 suite; R$485 master suite. In low season 20% discount. Children 4 and under stay free in parent's room, 5 and over R$30 extra. AE, DC, MC, V. Free parking. **Amenities:** Restaurant; exercise room; outdoor pool; room service; sauna. *In room:* A/C, TV, fridge, hair dryer, Internet, minibar.

Moderate

Bella Italia (Value) Rooms at this midpriced hotel are pleasant enough—queen-size bed, writing desk, tub/shower combo in the bathroom, and a small balcony with a downtown view—but what makes the *Italia* so *bella* in terms of value is its packages. The Iguassu Passport package costs R$275 per person (based on double occupancy), and includes a night's accommodations with breakfast, plus the Macuco Safari boat ride, entrance to the Bird Park, lunch at Porto Canoas restaurant by the falls, and dinner at the hotel. Park entrance fees and transfers are not included. Still, given that the cost of just the Macuco Safari and Bird Park entrance is R$190 per person, that works out to R$85 per person for a good-quality room plus breakfast, lunch, and dinner. Check the website for other packages and rates. The only real drawback to the hotel is the traffic noise. The best rooms and suites face downtown, and though the glass provides good sound insulation, there is still some traffic murmur, especially during rush hour. However, if you're up early and out sightseeing all day, this shouldn't be an issue.

Av. República Argentina 1700 (corner of Rua Venanti Otremba), Foz do Iguaçu, 85852-090 PR. © 0800/45-4555 or 045/3521-5000. Fax 045/3521-5005. www.bellaitalia.tur.br. 135 units. R$155–R$250 suite. 20% discount for business travelers or in off season. Extra person add 30%. Children 7 and under stay free in parent's room, 8–12 R$30 extra. AE, DC, MC, V. Parking R$6 daily. **Amenities:** Restaurant; bar; small weight room; small outdoor pool and children's pool; room service; smoke-free floors; Wi-Fi. *In room:* A/C, TV, hair dryer, Internet, minibar.

Inexpensive

Hotel Baviera Iguaçu (Value) The Hotel Baviera provides a great low-budget option in town. Five of the rooms are suites with two bedrooms and a large closet area. These will easily accommodate four people and sometimes six. Other rooms are doubles, sometimes with a third twin bed. The German owners take pride in running a spotless establishment and serving up an excellent breakfast spread; the freshly baked goods, excellent breads, cheeses and cold cuts, and fresh fruit should keep you going well into lunchtime.

Av. Jorge Schimmelpfeng 697, Foz do Iguaçu, 85851-110 PR. © 045/3523-5995. www.hotelbaviera iguassu.com.br. 23 units, shower only. R$125 double. Children 6 and under stay free in parent's room, 7 and over R$40 extra. AE, DC, MC, V. Free parking. *In room:* A/C, TV, minibar, Wi-Fi.

ON THE PARK ROAD

Very Expensive

Hotel das Cataratas ★★★ Iguaçu's most famous hotel, and the only hotel located inside the national park, offers a variety of packages combining a 2-day stay with adventure sports or nature walks. Rooms have been recently renovated. Standard rooms are not overly large, but have nice hardwood floors and firm twin or double beds. (Some rooms have carpet instead of hardwood floors; state your preference when you reserve.) The superior rooms are slightly larger, but offer views of the forest or gardens. The deluxe rooms all have beautiful hardwood floors, dark-wood furniture, and bathrooms with large bathtubs; a few have balconies. Rooms are spread out over a number of wings, connected by spacious corridors. Guests also have use of a large pool complex and a forested area behind the hotel with nature walks and trails to explore. Perhaps the only drawback to staying here is that it's 25km (16 miles) from town. For many, this rather limited sacrifice is more than made up for by the magic of staying so close to the falls.

Parque Nacional do Iguaçu, Foz do Iguaçu, 85863-000 PR. (©) **0800/726-4545** or 045/2102-7000. www. hoteldascataratas.com. 200 units. R$500 standard; R$580 superior; R$660 deluxe. Check the website for Internet deals. Children 9 and under stay free in parent's room. AE, DC, MC, V. Free parking. Take the road to Iguaçu Falls, go straight toward the gate, do not turn left into the visitor's area. **Amenities:** 2 restaurants; bar; children's programs; large outdoor pool; room service; spa; tennis court. *In room:* A/C, TV, hair dryer, minibar, Wi-Fi.

Expensive

Bourbon Cataratas ★★★ (Kids)
The real draw of the Bourbon is its leisure space. True, all the rooms are beautifully appointed. In the original wing, the standard rooms look out over the front of the hotel, whereas the superior rooms have a veranda and look over the pool. The new wing houses the master suites—really just a room, but with newer furnishings and huge windows providing lovely views. Out back, there's a 2km (1¼-mile) trail through orchards and lovely gardens; keep an eye out for toucans, parakeets, and colorful butterflies in the aviary. The vast pool complex includes three large pools, one especially for children. In high season, activity leaders organize all-day children's activities. But wait, there's more: a top-notch gym and indoor pool, a climbing wall and tennis courts, a soccer field, and a beach volleyball court. Brazil Nuts often has specials at a low R$250 a night.

Rodovia das Cataratas, Km 2.5, Foz do Iguaçu, 85853-000 PR. (©) **0800/451-010** or 045/3521-3900. www. bourbon.com.br. 311 units. R$400–R$600 superior or master. Extra person R$140. AE, DC, MC, V. Free parking. Bus: Parque Nacional or Cataratas. **Amenities:** 3 restaurants; children's programs; huge pool complex (2 outdoor pools, 1 small indoor pool); room service; sauna (dry and steam); smoke-free rooms; outdoor lighted tennis courts. *In room:* A/C, TV, fridge, hair dryer, Internet, minibar.

Moderate

San Martin ★ (Kids)
Also located on the park road, the San Martin is near the park entrance, close to the bird park. Although the accommodations are slightly dated, the rooms are clean and pleasantly furnished and the rates are very affordable. Most of the superior rooms have been renovated and now feature hardwood floors and elegant, modern furnishings, quite an improvement from the '70s brown that still reigns in the standard rooms. The nicest rooms are the superior class rooms. These feature king-size beds and are much bigger than the standard rooms. Families will appreciate the two-bedroom suites that come with two double and two single beds. For kids, the hotel's vast grounds offer several play areas, a soccer field, a swimming pool, and gardens.

Rodovia das Cataratas, Km 17, Foz do Iguaçu, 85853-000 PR. (©) **0800/645-0045** or 045/3521-8088. www. hotelsanmartin.com.br. 135 units. R$180 standard; R$230 superior; R$320 family superior, sleeps 4–6 people. AE, DC, MC, V. Free parking. Bus: Parque Nacional or Cataratas. **Amenities:** Restaurant; outdoor pool; room service; sauna; smoke-free rooms; tennis court; Wi-Fi. *In room:* A/C, TV, minibar.

3 WHERE TO DINE

Don't come to Iguaçu for the culinary experience. Menus are rarely adventurous, but expect excellent Brazilian beef and fresh-caught fish from the Iguaçu or Paraná rivers. In addition to the restaurants below, most hotels outside of downtown also offer good dining options.

EXPENSIVE

Chef Lopes STEAK   Being just a hop and a skip from Argentina it is not surprising that you would find excellent Argentine steak dishes in town. Chef Lopes serves up a nice range of dishes, including salads, risotto, pasta, and fish, but most people come to feast on the fabulous juicy *bife de chorizo*. The well-chosen wine list includes some excellent Argentine and Chilean selections.

Av. República Argentina 632. ✆ **045/3028-3531.** www.cheflopes.com.br. Main courses R$42–R$60. AE, DC, MC, V. Mon–Sat 11:30am–11:30pm.

Zaragoza SPANISH   For those who are tired of eating steak, Zaragoza offers a wonderful alternative: international cuisine with a strong Spanish flavor. The menu is particularly strong on seafood such as prawns, lobster, and local fish served grilled or broiled. On Saturday, there's a traditional Brazilian *feijoada,* and on Sunday people come from far and wide to savor the paella for lunch. The wine list puts the emphasis on Spanish, Argentine, and Portuguese vintages.

Rua Quintino Bocaiúva 882. ✆ **045/3574-3084.** www.restaurantezaragoza.com.br. Main courses R$28–R$58. AE, DC, MC, V. Daily 11:30am–3pm and 7pm–midnight.

MODERATE

Bufalo Branco Churrascaria CHURRASCO   This is likely the best place in the city for *churrasco* (grilled meat). Appetizers from the grill include sausage, turkey breast with bacon, and chicken hearts. For the main course, waiters offer a range of popular cuts such as *picanha* (rump steak), *alcatra* (top sirloin), filet mignon, *maminha* (a fattier rump steak), and *contra filet* (entrecôte). *Surubim* (grilled fish) is also available, as are cold dishes, salads, and desserts.

Rua Engenheiro Rebouças 530. ✆ **045/3523-9744.** www.bufalobranco.com.br. R$42 per person, children 4 and under eat free. AE, DC, MC, V. Daily 11am–11pm.

Trapiche ★ SEAFOOD   For some excellent seafood try the Trapiche. The large menu includes everything from grilled fish such as tilapia, salmon, and trout to Bahian seafood stews such as *moqueca, bobó,* and *caldeirada* (with crab, shrimp, and octopus). The kitchen also takes pride in serving up high-end seafood such as lobster and oysters and local fish from the Paraná and Iguaçu rivers.

Rua Marechal Deodoro 1087, Centro. ✆ **045/3527-3951.** Main courses R$30–R$60. The more expensive dishes serve 2 people. AE, MC, V. Mon–Fri 5pm–midnight; Sat–Sun 11am–midnight.

4 EXPLORING IGUAÇU FALLS

Your first priority should be to visit the Brazilian Falls. The walk along the gorge starting from just below the soft-pink **Hotel das Cataratas ★★★** (see above) is spectacular.

Keep an eye out for the hundreds of colorful butterflies. Make the time to get up close and personal with the falls on a zodiac ride. (*Note:* In the zodiac, a motorized inflatable rubber boat, you *will* get drenched.) Time permitting, pay a visit to the Parque das Aves for a close-up of the many bird species that inhabit the park. Also worth a look is Itaipu Dam, the world's largest hydroelectric project.

THE FALLS

Parque Nacional do Iguaçu (Brazilian Falls) ★★★

The Brazilian Falls now have a newly renovated visitor center and a new restaurant—Canoas—above the falls. A new observation deck is also complete. The elevator is a work in progress. The **visitor center** is where you park your car or get off the bus and buy your entry tickets. The building has a gift shop and a small display area with some park history. From here, you board a shuttle bus and set off down the parkway for the falls. The bus will stop at the **Macuco Safari center** (from where rafting and zodiac trips depart, but do that after you've seen the falls), the pink **Hotel das Cataratas,** and then at **Canoas** restaurant before heading back to the visitor center. The hotel is the place to get off the bus. A small viewpoint at the foot of the hotel lawn is where you get your first magical view of the falls. From here, the pathway zigzags down the side of the gorge and trundles along the cliff face, providing views across the narrow gorge at water cascading down in a hundred different places. There are 275 separate waterfalls, with an average drop of 60m (197 ft.). While you walk, you'll see colorful butterflies fluttering about the trail and grumbling coati (a larger relative of the raccoon) begging for food. At the end of the trail an elevator will lift you up to the restaurant by the edge of the falls. Before going up, take the elevated walkway leading out *in front* of one of the falls. The wind and spray coming off the falls are exhilarating and guaranteed to have you soaked in seconds. (You can buy a plastic coat from the souvenir stand for R$5.) Allow at least a half-day.

Rodovia dos Cataratas, Km 18. ☎ **045/3572-2261.** www.cataratasdoiguacu.com.br. Admission R$22, R$7 children 2–6, includes transportation inside the park. Parking R$12. Daily 9am–5pm. Bus: Cataratas or Parque Nacional.

Macuco Boat Safari ★★★

Niagara Falls has the *Maid of the Mist.* Iguaçu has Macuco. I know which one I'd choose. Macuco participants pile aboard 8m (25-ft.) zodiacs, the guide fires up twin 225-horsepower outboards, and you're off up the river, bouncing over wave trains, breaking eddy lines, powering your way up the surging current until the boat's in the gorge, advancing slowly toward one of the (smaller) falls. As the boat nears, the mist gets thicker, the roar louder, the passengers wetter and more and more thrilled (or terrified), until the zodiac peels away, slides downstream, and hides in an eddy until everyone's caught his or her breath. Then you do it all again. Allow 1 hour for the entire trip.

Parque Nacional do Iguaçu. ☎ **045/3523-6475.** www.macucosafari.com.br. R$170 per person, children 7–12 half price. Mon 1–5:30pm; Tues–Sun and holidays 9am–5:30pm. Bus: Parque Nacional or Cataratas.

Parque Nacional Iguazú (Argentine Falls) ★★★

Visitors to the Argentine Falls arrive at a brand-new complex, which consists mostly of restaurants and gift shops. A small visitor center does have displays on the history and ecology of the falls, but text is exclusively in Spanish. (*No!* They do not, will not, cannot provide an English-language pamphlet.) Leave them then to their lonely pride, because the chief attraction of the new and improved Argentine park is the **Devil's Throat walkway ★★★**. To reach it, you take a free small-gauge railway, which departs every 30 minutes from 8am to 4pm, either from the visitor center station or from a second station located 600m (1,968 ft.) down a paved walking trail. The train takes about 20 minutes to trundle the 3km (2 miles) up to the Devil's Throat station, where waiting videographers will film your every move and later try to sell you a souvenir videotape. From here it's about a 1km (½-mile) walk along the steel catwalk to the falls, where you will once again find yourself accosted by photographers. Thankfully, all this crass commercialism fades in importance once you reach this viewpoint. There is something both magical and awesome in that much water falling in one place; nothing people do seems to mar it. The return train leaves on the half-hour, with the last departure at 5:30pm.

There are several other trails in the park. The **Circuito Superior (Upper Trail)** loops around the top of the falls. The steep **Circuito Inferior (Lower Trail)** ★★ has been much improved, to the point that much of it is wheelchair accessible. It leads down to the edge of the Iguazú River, offering some excellent views up toward the falls. It's the only way to reach **Isla San Martin** ★, an island that's surrounded on all sides by falling water—well worth the short boat ride (currently free of charge). The last boat back leaves at 5pm. Expect to spend at least 4 hours in the park, more if you take a boat excursion (see below).

Iguazu Jungle Explorer (✆ 03757/421696) operates a number of fast zodiac excursions. The **Adventura Nautica** (R$35) leaves from the bottom of the Circuito Inferior and blasts up as close as driver and passengers dare to one of the big falls on the Argentine side. The **Gran Aventura** (R$70) does much the same but starts 5km (3 miles) farther down the river, giving you a 4×4 drive through the forest and a bit more time on the river; the Aventura Nautica is better value. The **Ecological Tour** (R$20) begins at the Devil's Throat boardwalk above the falls. Passengers hop into rubber rafts and drift 2km (1¼ miles) downstream through the forest, then disembark and get trucked back to the visitor center. Please note that all rates are approximate as they are calculated from the Argentine peso.

Getting There: From Foz do Iguaçu take the PORTO IGUAZU bus from downtown. Customs formalities at the border are minimal. Stay on the bus, tell the Customs officer who boards that you're going to the Parque Nacional and—for citizens of the U.S., U.K., Canada, and Australia—you'll be waved through without even a stamp in your passport. The bus then goes to the main bus station in Puerto Iguazú. Go to stall no. 5, where a bus departs every hour between 7:40am and 7:40pm for the 20-minute trip to the park. Including connections, total trip time from Brazil will be at least an hour. The bus from Brazil to Argentina costs R$3, and the one from Puerto Iguazú to the falls costs R$5. A taxi to or from the Argentine side costs about R$80 each way.

Getting Back: The bus from Parque Nacional to the Puerto Iguazú bus station departs hourly from 8am to 8pm. Once back at the bus station, go to stall no. 1 and catch the bus marked FOZ DO IGUAÇU back to Brazil. Another option is to book a guided tour or transfer. See below.

Av. Victoria Aguirre 66, Puerto Iguazú, 3370 Misiones, Argentina. ✆ **03757/420-722.** www.iguazu argentina.com. Admission R$30 adults, R$15 children ages 6–11, free for 5 and under. Oct 1–Mar 31 daily 8am–7pm; Apr 1–Sept 30 daily 8am–6pm.

OTHER TOP ATTRACTIONS

Canion Iguaçu (Rappel and Climbing Park) ★★   This company has converted a part of the park into a delightful adult playground. Very popular is the *arvorismo* (tree-climbing) trail, an obstacle course made out of ropes, wires, and platforms attached to the trees. The lower portion of the course starts out at just 1m (3 ft.) above the forest floor; this lower section is appropriate for younger children 5 to 10 years of age. The more challenging higher obstacles will take you at least 7m (25 ft.) up into the trees. If that doesn't make your stomach flip there's the 37m (120 ft.) of rappel off a platform overlooking the falls. Maybe your thing is going up instead of down? The park offers a variety of climbing options. Beginners can try the artificial wall while more experienced climbers can explore over 33 different routes on the basalt rock face. And, last but not least, the company runs daily rafting trips over a 4km (2½-mile) stretch of the river. The run covers about 2km (1¼ miles) of rapids with a three-plus rating; the rest is calmer water that gives you a chance to observe the forest and the river. If you're traveling with children, be sure to check on minimum age and height requirements for certain activities.

Parque Nacional do Iguaçu. *© 045/3529-6040.* www.campodedesafios.com.br. Rappel R$70. Rafting R$90. Tree climbing R$80 for the higher part, R$60 for lower part only. Climbing R$50. Daily 9am–5:30pm. Bus: Parque Nacional or Cataratas.

Itaipu Dam ★★   The world's largest hydroelectric project stands 10km (6¼ miles) upriver from Foz do Iguaçu on the Rio Paraná. The project produces over 90 billion kilowatt hours per year, nearly 25% of Brazil's supply. Visitors are shown a 30-minute video on the dam's construction, featuring endless shots of frolicking children and nothing on the dam's environmental impact. Then you board a bus that crosses to an observation platform in the midpoint of the dam. For a much more in-depth look at the dam, which includes a visit to the Production Building and the Central Command Post, book the Special Tour. The Technical Tour (where you go inside the dam to see the turbines) is available only by prior arrangement. Contact the visitor center at least a week in advance. It is mostly of interest to engineers and people with a technical background who want to see the ins and outs of the dam. *Note:* No sandals, high heels, shorts, or miniskirts allowed.

Av. Tancredo Neves 6702. *© 0800/645-4645.* www.itaipu.gov.br. Regular guided tour R$19. Daily hourly 8:30am–4:30pm. Special in-depth 2-hr. tours R$36. Daily every half-hour 8:30–11am, and 2, 2:30, 4, and 4:30pm. Call ahead to check times with English-speaking guide. Bus: 110 or 120.

Parque das Aves ★★   Set in 4.8 hectares (12 acres) of lush subtropical rainforest, the Bird Park offers the best bird-watching in Iguaçu. A large number of birds are in huge walk-through aviaries, some 24m (80 ft.) tall and at least 60m (200 ft.) long, allowing visitors to watch the birds interact as they go about their daily routines. Highlights include the toucans and multicolored tanagers as well as a Pantanal aviary with roseate spoonbills, herons, and egrets. Signage is in English. The best time to visit is early in the day when the birds are most active. Allow 2 hours.

Rodovia das Cataratas, Km 17, 300m (984 ft.) before the national park entrance. *© 045/3529-8282.* www.parquedasaves.com.br. Admission R$18, free for children 8 and under. Daily 8:30am–5:30pm. Bus: Parque Nacional or Cataratas.

SPECTACULAR VIEWS

The confluence of the Rio Iguaçu and the Rio Paraná, about 7.5km (4½ miles) south of the town of Foz do Iguaçu on Avenida General Meira, is also the spot where Brazil, Paraguay, and Argentina all meet. Called the **Marco das Três Fronteiras,** it features a public viewing platform with good views up and down the Iguaçu and Paraná rivers.

ORGANIZED TOURS

BOAT TOURS   The **Iguaçu Explorer,** operated by Macuco Safari, offers a boat tour along the Iguaçu and Paraná rivers. Although there are no views of the falls, this leisurely tour is a great way to see the region from the water. Highlights include a view of the Tancredo Neves bridge that connects Brazil and Argentina, the tri-border marker, and a visit to a small regional museum on the Paraguay side. The vegetation along the way is quite nice but if you're going to the Pantanal or the Amazon I would skip this excursion. If not it's a good way to get a small taste of the country's natural wonders. Tours cost R$90, lunch included. Departure times vary. Details at ✆ **045/3523-6475** or www. macucosafari.com.br.

HELICOPTER TOUR   Taking the helicopter tour in the park involves a small moral dilemma. The noise from the helicopters does scare the wildlife. Park naturalists say that toucans appear only when it's rainy, windy, or fogged in—days that the copters are grounded. The helicopters are one of two issues over which UNESCO threatened to pull Iguaçu's World Heritage designation (the other was a plan to reopen highway BR-373, cutting the park in half). On the other hand the company has invested in the newest, quietest helicopters. And the view of the falls and canyon from the air truly is spectacular. Contact **Helisul–Helicopter Tours,** Avenida das Cataratas, Km 16.5, Foz do Iguaçu (✆ **045/3529-7474;** www.helisul.com; 10-min. flight over the falls and park R$180 per person, 3-person minimum; children are free if they don't occupy a seat; daily 9am–5pm; Parque Nacional or Cataratas).

GUIDED TOURS & TRANSFERS   A number of tour operators organize transportation and guides for visits to the falls. Trips can be customized to include visits to other attractions such as the bird park, Macuco Safari, or the Itaipu Dam. The most popular service is the 1-day visit to the Argentine Falls, which at most agencies costs around R$60 per person. Reputable companies include **Conveniotur,** Rua Rui Barbosa 820 (✆ **045/ 3523-3500;** www.conveniotur.com.br), **Central Tours** (✆ **045/3526-4434;** www. centraltours.com.br), and **Loumar Tourismo** (✆ **045/3572-5005;** www.loumarturismo. com.br). Loumar also offers a 1-day excursion to the shopper's paradise of Paraguay.

OUTDOOR ACTIVITIES

Just outside of Iguaçu Park is **Iguaçu Golf Club,** Av. das Cataratas 6845 (✆ **045/3521- 3400**), an 18-hole, par-72 golf course. In addition to the course, the club also has a 300-yard driving range and putting green, golf-club rental, a gift shop, and a large leisure area with a restaurant, lounge, sauna, and swimming pool. It's open daily year-round from 7am to sunset. Fees for visitors are R$70 for 18 holes, R$50 for 9 holes. Cart rental is R$70 for 18 holes and R$45 for 9 holes. To get there, take the PARQUE NACIONAL or CATARATAS bus.

---

5 SHOPPING

Foz do Iguaçu's *centro* is a popular shopping district. Most shops are concentrated around **Avenida Brasil, Rua Barbosa, Rua Almirante Barroso,** and **Quintino Bocaiuva.** You'll find many clothing and shoe stores, as well as excellent leather goods such as jackets and purses.

Tres Fronteiras ⓕ **Finds**   You can find anything here, from all regions of Brazil: T-shirts, carvings, carpets, hats, hides, semiprecious stones, precious stones, you name it; anything you ever considered picking up and didn't, it's here at reasonable prices. BR 469 Rodovia das Cataratas, Km 11 (just before the turnoff for Argentina). ✆ **045/3529-6565.** www.tresfronteiras. com.br.

6 IGUAÇU AFTER DARK

The corner of Avenida JK and Avenida Jorge Schimmelpfeng is Iguaçu's prime nightlife area, home to a number of restaurant/pubs, most with large patios. A favorite with locals and visitors is **Bar do Capitão,** Av. Jorge Schimmelpfeng 288 (© **045/3572-1512;** daily 6pm–1am, Fri–Sat until the last customer leaves). In addition to *cachaças* and great cocktails, the **Cachaçaria Agua Doce,** Rua Benjamin Constant 63 (© **045/3523-7715**), features live music on Friday and Saturday. Another popular downtown live music venue is the **Ono Teatro Bar,** Rua Rosa Cirilo de Castro 85 (Av. Paraná and Av. Venezuela; © **045/3027-5700;** www.onoteatrobar.com.br; Fri–Sat).

The Pantanal

It's a secret that, until recently, was known only to film crews: The best place in South America to see wildlife is not the Amazon but the Pantanal, a Florida-size wetland on the far western edge of Brazil that bursts with animals—capybaras, caimans, jaguars, anacondas, giant otters, colorful hyacinth macaws, kites, hawks, and flocks of storks and herons hundreds strong. In fact, many species that live in the Amazon and are next to impossible to see there can be viewed here in abundance. The Pantanal is home to over 700 species of birds, 100 mammal species, more than 250 fish species, and 80 reptile species.

The largest flood plain in the world, the Pantanal has a rhythm governed by its rivers. In the wet season (Nov–Apr), rivers swell and spill over to cover a vast alluvial plain for months. Millions of birds are attracted by this aquatic paradise, as mammals take refuge on the remaining few mounds of dry land. As the water drains (from May onward), the land dries up and the situation slowly reverses: Animals congregate around the few remaining water pools. Fish get trapped in these pools, and birds and mammals alike gather for water and food as they wait for the rains to start.

Most farmers use the land for cattle grazing in the dry season only, moving the cattle when the fields flood. Few roads of any kind exist in the Pantanal; the best way to explore the area is to make like the locals and head out on horseback. Many of the area's fazendas (cattle ranches) have slowly converted to tourism. Staying at one of these lodges is the best way to get a feel for the region.

A stay in a Pantanal lodge normally involves a number of activities—a boat trip to spot birds and caiman, a horseback trip through the fields, bird spotting by foot or in an open vehicle, and often a nighttime excursion to see nocturnal animals. Some lodges offer additional activities such as canoe trips, fishing expeditions, or specialized bird-watching outings. If you have a specific interest, it's a good idea to make contact ahead of time.

1 TOUR OPERATORS IN THE PANTANAL

Whether you decide to go to the North Pantanal or the South, whichever lodge you decide to visit, you may find it easier and often cheaper to arrange your visit through a tour operator, who can arrange not only your stay but your transfers to and from the lodge, and even help out with flights to the gateway cities. Sometimes there is a premium on top of the lodge costs for this service. Sometimes the operator can make up his costs through the discount he gets from the lodge, in effect passing this savings on to you. In any case, it's worth checking out what they have to offer. You can always book directly with a lodge afterward if you decide the service being offered isn't worth the money or effort.

Two particularly good operators offer expeditions to lodges in either the North or the South Pantanal. Located in the U.S., **Brazil Nuts** (© **800/553-9959;** www.brazilnuts. com) offers packages to a number of lodges, including the two pioneers of Pantanal

Gateways to the Pantanal

The best way to experience the Pantanal and observe its amazing birds and wild-life is by staying at a small lodge; depending on the time of year you'll either head out in a four-wheel-drive, canoe, boat, on foot, on horseback, or a combination of these. The Pantanal has three gateway cities: **Cuiabá,** which connects to the Transpantaneira Highway and gives access to the South Pantanal; **Campo Grande,** which leads in to the South Pantanal; and most isolated of all, **Corumbá,** which stands on a cliff top looking over the Pantanal itself, and provides access to lodges in the southwest of the ecosystem. None of these cities is really worth visiting in itself. Most lodges will pick you up at the airport and whisk you out into the swamp with nary a second glance at the city. The quickest access to the Pantanal is via the city of Cuiabá, just an hour and a half by car from the Transpantaneira Highway.

eco-tourism, **Araras Eco Lodge** ★★★ in the North, and **Caiman Ecological Reserve** ★★ in the South.

Located in Campo Grande, **Open Door** (© **067/3321-8303;** www.opendoortur. com.br) has some excellent packages for the Pantanal, Bonito, and combinations of the two. Open Door works with a wide variety of lodges in both the North and South Pantanal, including difficult-to-reach reserves such as **Fazenda Barranco Alto** ★★★.

In the individual sections on the North and South Pantanal below, we list a number of very good, but more regionally focused, tour agencies.

2 CUIABA & THE NORTH PANTANAL

1,576km (979 miles) NW of Rio de Janeiro, 1,321km (815 miles) NW of São Paulo

The capital of Mato Grosso state, Cuiabá is a modern, pleasant town of 430,000 that sits in the middle of Brazilian cattle country. The city serves as the main gateway to the northern part of the Pantanal—the Transpantaneira Highway starts just 98km (61 miles) away—and as the jumping-off point to the Chapada dos Guimarães.

ESSENTIALS

BY PLANE   Flights to Cuiabá are available on **TAM** (© **0800/570-5700** or 065/4002-5700; www.tam.com.br), **Gol** (© **0300/115-2121;** www.voegol.com.br), and **TRIP** (© **0300/789-8747;** www.voetrip.com.br). Most flights connect to Cuiabá's **Aeroporto Marechal Rondon** (© **065/3614-2510**) through Brasilia. Tours to a Pantanal lodge normally include pickup and drop-off at the airport, so there is no real reason to stay in Cuiabá.

BY BUS   Cuiabá's efficient bus terminal, **Engenheiro de Sá** (© **065/3621-1040**), is on Av. Marechal Deodoro s/n in Alvorada, just north of the city center. Buses to Campo Grande, gateway to the South Pantanal, depart daily at 7am, 8pm, and 9:30pm and take 10 hours. The overnight buses have comfortable reclining chairs. Contact **Motta** (© **065/ 3621-2514;** www.motta.com.br). The fare is R$85.

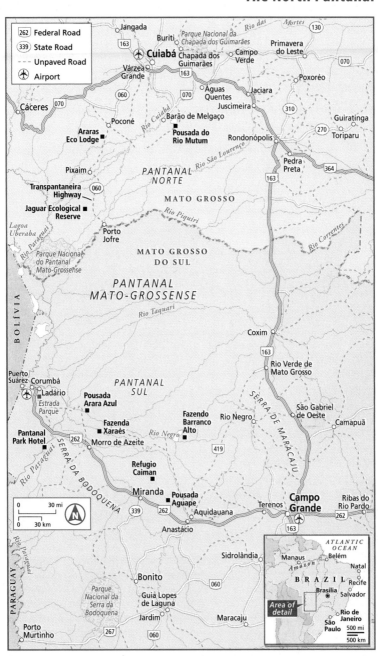

Jangada

262 Federal Road
339 State Road
--- Unpaved Road
✈ Airport

Buriti
Parque Nacional da
Chapada dos Guimarães

163

✈ **Cuiabá**
Chapada dos
Guimarães

Rio das Mortes
130
Primavera
do Leste
Campo
Verde

070

Várzea
Grande

163

060

070

Águas
Quentes
Jaciara
Poxoréo

Cáceres
070

Poconé

Rio Cuiabá
Barão de Melgaço

Juscimeira

310

Guiratinga

Araras
Eco Lodge ■

■ Pousada do
Rio Mutum

Rondonópolis

270
Toriparu

Pixaim

*PANTANAL
NORTE*

Rio São Lourenço

Pedra
Preta
364

**Transpantaneira
Highway** 060

MATO GROSSO

163

Jaguar Ecological ■
Reserve

Rio Piquiri

*Lagoa
Uberaba*

○ Porto
Jofre

*MATO GROSSO
DO SUL*

Rio Corrente

Parque Nacional
do Pantanal
Mato-Grossense

*PANTANAL
MATO-GROSSENSE*

Rio Taquari

B O L Í V I A

Coxim

163

Rio Verde de
Mato Grosso

Puerto
Suárez Corumbá
✈ ■Ladário
*Estrada
Parque*

**Pousada
Arara Azul**
■

*PANTANAL
SUL*

**Fazendo
Barranco
Alto**
■
Rio Negro

São Gabriel
de Oeste
Camapuã

**Pantanal
Park Hotel**
■

**Fazenda
■ Xaraés**
262
Morro de Azeite

Rio Negro

419

**Refugio
Caiman**

S E R R A   D E   M A R A C A J U

Rio Paraguai

SERRA DA BODOQUENA

Miranda
339

**Pousada
Aguape**
262
Aquidauana

Terenos

**Campo
Grande**
✈
262

Ribas do
Rio Pardo

0   30 mi
0   30 km

Anastácio

163

PARAGUAI

Sidrôlandia

Rio Paraguai

*Parque
Nacional da
Serra da
Bodoquena*

Bonito

060

Guia Lopes
de Laguna

Jardim

Maracaju

Porto
Murtinho
267
060

*ATLANTIC
OCEAN*
Manaus
Belém
Natal
Amazon
B R A Z I L Recife
Brasília ⊛ Salvador
**Area of
detail** Rio de
Janeiro
São
Paulo 500 mi
500 km

> (Tips) **A Health Warning: Yellow Fever**
>
> In this region of Brazil, yellow fever is endemic, and you should get a shot at least 10 days before you travel to the Pantanal. Health authorities may ask for proof of vaccination, so carry your vaccine certificate.

VISITOR INFORMATION The state tourist office, **Secretaria de Turismo** (© 065/3613-9300; www.sedtur.mt.gov.br), is located too far from downtown to be of any use.

(Fast Facts) Cuiabá

Car Rental **Unidas,** Av. Gov. João Ponce Arruda 920 (© **065/3682-4052**), and **Localiza,** Rua Mal Rondon s/n (airport; © **065/3682-7900**).

Currency Exchange & Banks **Banco do Brasil,** Av. Pres Getúlio Vargas 553 (© **065/3624-1944**), has a 24-hour ATM. *Tip:* Just outside the airport are 24-hour ATMs for all major banks that accept foreign cards. If you are going to a lodge there is no need to go into town. Although most lodges will let you run a tab for your personal expenses during your stay, make sure you have some cash for tips and souvenirs.

Hospital For medical needs, try **Hospital Santa Casa de Misericórdia,** Praça do Seminário 141 (© **065/3321-0166**).

Internet Access **Digitus Informática,** Av. Ten Cel Duarte 595 (© **065/3321-0166**), charges R$4 an hour.

Weather The state of Mato Grosso is hot and muggy in the summer; temperatures can rise to 35°C to 40°C (95°F–104°F). Most rain falls from December to March. In the winter (June–Sept) it can cool off significantly, with temperatures as low as 15°C (59°F).

THE PANTANAL

19

CUIABA & THE NORTH PANTANAL

WHERE TO STAY

All the Pantanal lodges will pick you up at the airport, sparing you the need to stay in Cuiabá. If you do find yourself stuck for a night (probably because your flight was delayed), you can grab a clean and decent room literally across the street from the airport at the **Hotel Diplomata,** Av. João Ponce de Arruda 678 or Avenida do Aeroporto (©/fax **065/3688-8500**; www.diplomatahotel.com.br). A double room costs around R$150. More pleasantly located, but a 20- to 30-minute cab ride into town, is the **Hotel Amazon,** Av. Presidente Getúlio Vargas 600 (© **065/2121-2000**; www.hotelamazon.com.br). The hotel is close to the city's shopping and restaurant area. Room rates range from R$140 to R$200.

WHERE TO DINE

Most of Cuiabá's better restaurants are located in the Goiabeiras neighborhood, conveniently located close to the city's hotels. **Peixaria Popular ★**, Av. S. Sebastião 2324 (© **065/3322-5471**), offers fish from the great inland fishery of the Pantanal. *Pintado,*

dourado, paçu, and *piraputanga* are served up grilled, fried, or in filets. **Getulio Grill ★**, <u>447</u>
Av. Getúlio Vargas 1147, across from Praça Santos Dumont (© **067/3624-9992**), offers
steak and excellent local fish dishes. At night, it's also a popular local tavern.

EXPLORING THE NORTH PANTANAL

Three days is the minimum reasonable itinerary for the Pantanal. With wildlife viewing,
the longer you spend in an area, the better your chances of seeing animals. Spend the
minimum possible time in Cuiabá, then take a slow wildlife-spotting drive out along the
Transpantaneira to a lodge. Take a guided hike, and after sunset, go for a spotlight drive
on the Transpantaneira to see the night creatures: capybaras, tarantulas, and (with the
most incredible of luck) jaguars. I also strongly recommend that you take the time to
explore the Pantanal as it was meant to be seen, on the back of a horse. Canoeing one of
the North Pantanal's small rivers is a great way to spot monkeys and giant river otters.

After exploring the Pantanal, consider a 1-day or overnight trip to the **Chapada dos
Guimarães** (p. 449), the highlands to the north of Cuiabá. The beautiful red-rock formations, plateaus, and canyons offer excellent hiking and fabulous views, great waterfalls
and swimming holes, and some excellent bird life, including red macaws.

Tour Operators in the North Pantanal

All tour operators work with one or more Pantanal lodges. These operators provide a
package itinerary—usually quite flexible—that includes transportation to a lodge plus
nature tours and guide services.

One of the best tour operators is **Pantanal Explorer,** Av. Governador Ponce de Arruda
670, Varzea Grande (© **065/3682-2800;** fax 065/3682-1260; www.pantanalexplorer.
com.br). Stays in the Pantanal are at the excellent Araras Eco Lodge. In addition, the
company offers trips to the Chapada dos Guimarães and boat trips in the Pantanal, as
well as eco-tours to the Mato Grosso part of the Amazon rainforest, excellent if you do
not have an opportunity to head up to the Amazon. All of these trips can be combined
with a Pantanal stay.

Another good tour operator is **Anaconda Turismo,** Av. Isaac Povoas 606, Centro,
Cuiabá (© **065/3028-5990;** www.anacondapantanal.com.br). This operator works
with a large number of fazendas and pousadas and can customize a package according
to your interests. It also operates in the Chapada dos Guimarães and can organize fishing expeditions.

Driving the Transpantaneira

There are a couple of ironies about the Transpantaneira. Though the name implies that
the road traverses the entire Pantanal, the highway stops in Porto Jofre, 144km (89 miles)

Three Ecosystems

The state of Mato Grosso features three different ecosystems within striking distance of Cuiabá. Visitors can explore the southern border of the Amazon rainforest, hike through the savanna landscape of the Chapada dos Guimarães with
lush waterfalls and beautiful rock formations, and observe the astonishing birds
and abundant wildlife of the flood plains of the Pantanal. Contact Pantanal
Explorer for more details on this 7-day program.

from where it began, and at least that far from the opposite edge of the Pantanal. The other irony is that the project, which if completed would likely have destroyed the Pantanal (by skewing the ecosystem's drainage pattern), has instead, in its unfinished state, become one of the great wildlife-viewing areas of the world. Ditches on either side of the roadbed have become favorite feeding grounds for kingfishers, capybara, egrets, jabiru storks, giant river otters, and caiman by the dozen. Spend but a day on the Transpantaneira, and you'll see more wildlife than you'd see in a week in the Amazon.

LODGES IN THE NORTH PANTANAL

Araras Eco Lodge ★★★   Araras Lodge is the best spot for exploring the North Pantanal. The location by the Transpantaneira is excellent, and lodge owner Andre Thuronyi has done extensive work to improve the local wildlife habitat. With only 19 rooms, the lodge is pleasantly small and rustic. No fancy rooms or amenities; each guest room comes with a private bathroom and a hammock on the veranda. The guides are usually knowledgeable. Activities include hikes along a rustic boardwalk through the flooded fields to the lodge's lookout tower. One afternoon as we watched the sun set over the Pantanal, a group of five hyacinth macaws flew right over us, attracted by our guide who sounded a credible macaw call. Other excursions include boat or canoe trips on a small local river known for large hawks and giant river otters (we saw both). On drives along the Transpantaneira, even in a 3-hour time span, you'll lose track of the number of birds you'll see. Fortunately the guide always seems to remember their names. Horse lovers will be in heaven riding through the flooded fields. If you know how to ride, the guides are happy to let you have some fun and gallop through the fields, startling caiman and snakes underfoot. The food is delicious and plentiful, often including excellent local fish. One of the most popular packages at Araras Eco Lodge offers a 3-night stay at the lodge and a 1-night stay in the Chapada dos Guimarães for some good hiking and swimming. However, packages and programs can be fully customized according to your preferences.

Transpantaneira Hwy. Reservation office: Av. Governador Ponce de Arruda 670, Varzea Grande, MT. 𝄃 **065/3682-2800.** Fax 065/3682-1260. www.araraslodge.com.br. 19 units, showers only. R$1,400–R$1,800 per person for a 3-day, 2-night package; R$3,000 6-day package (including the Chapada Guimarães), including airport pickup and drop-off plus all meals and guided activities. Extra person add about 25%. Children 10 and under stay free in parent's room. AE, DC, MC, V. Free parking. **Amenities:** Restaurant; bar; outdoor pool. In room: A/C, no phone.

Jaguar Ecological Reserve ★★   Wildlife viewing is always a matter of luck and patience, particularly when it comes to large predators like jaguars. But one of the best ways of improving your odds is to visit this lodge—the centerpiece of a private ecological reserve—where an astonishing one in four guests sees one of these huge South American cats. It's a long way (110km/68 miles) down the bumpy Transpantaneira, and the accommodations are expensive and only basic, but for a view of that big cat it may be worth it. For the 75% of guests who do not see jaguars, there is the usual vast array of caiman and colorful birds, so rare in the rest of the world, so common in the Pantanal. It's best to book your stay here through **Open Door Tours** (𝄃 **067/3321-8303;** www.opendoortur. com.br). The JER has been in operation for a number of years, and while operations in the field run smoothly, their booking operations have been a little on the amateur side. Better to deal with professionals.

Transpantaneira Km 110, Poconé, MT. 𝄃 **065/3646-8557** (office) or 067/9919-5518 (lodge). www.jaguar reserve.com. 9 units. US$750 per person 4-day, 3-night package, accommodations, transfers, meals, and excursions included. AE, MC, V. In room: No phone.

ⓜ Moments   A Birding Convert

I have to admit, I always thought birding was boring: Get up at dawn, sit in a blind, wear camouflage, and just be really quiet. But my first visit to the Pantanal opened my eyes. Just driving along the Transpantaneira for an hour I spotted parakeets, tanagers, hawks, egrets, and the amazing 1.5m-tall (5-ft.) jabiru stork. In less than 2 hours I counted at least 20 different species. That evening as I stood on a viewing platform to see the sun set over the flooded fields, I heard the unmistakable shrieks of a macaw. As my eyes adjusted to the low light I was able to spot three hyacinth macaws flying within a few feet of the platform. On a horseback ride the next day, splashing loudly through the wet fields, I still managed to log at least 15 species, including roseate spoonbills, toucans, egrets, herons, and cormorants. Not just one or two of each—great big flocks. Now there's a sport I can get in to!

Pousada do Rio Mutum   This pousada is highly recommended for those who enjoy fishing. The *pintado* catfish is a particularly prized catch, but anglers can also expect to hook *dourado, paçu,* or *piraputanga.* (The best months for fishing are Feb–Oct; there is no fishing Nov–Jan during spawning season.) For nonfishers there are tours of the Pantanal ecosystem by boat, foot, and canoe. The lodge also offers special bird-watcher packages, which do many of the same activities but are accompanied by a bird expert. Accommodations are in simply furnished rooms that come with private bathrooms and a veranda. All meals and activities are included. This region is a bit east of Poconé, and access is through the town of Barão de Melgaço.

Av. Isaac Póvoas 1177, Cuiabá, 78045-640 MT. ⓒ **065/3052-7022.** www.pousadamutum.com.br. 22 units, showers only. From US$720 per person 3-day, 2-night packages, including meals and pickup/drop-off at airport. MC, V. **Amenities:** Restaurant; bar; pool. *In room:* A/C, no phone.

3 A SIDE TRIP FROM CUIABA: CHAPADA DOS GUIMARÃES

74km (46 miles) E of Cuiabá

In appearance, the Chapada dos Guimarães has much in common with the desert buttes of Arizona or Utah in the States—weird, wonderful formations of bright red rock, and long beautiful canyons. Vegetation is dry and scrubby, except where the many river channels flow; then you get waterfalls streaming down into basins lush with tropical vegetation. Officially, more than 32,000 hectares (80,000 acres) of this vast highland were set aside in 1989 as a national park—the Parque Nacional da Chapada dos Guimarães. Only about half of the total area has been expropriated; much of the rest still lies in private hands, including the small town—also called Chapada dos Guimarães—within the park boundaries. It's a quiet, laid-back place with a slight counterculture feel, and the most convenient base from which to set off exploring. Hiking nearby is excellent; trails are clear even if—as ever in Brazil—they're completely without markers or signage. Most trails end at a viewpoint, a waterfall, or a natural pool (sometimes all three!). Wildlife is not up to the standard set by the Pantanal, but in the Chapada you do have the opportunity of seeing the gorgeous red macaw, often playing in the thermals by a cliff side.

GETTING THERE

BY CAR   The Chapada is 74km (46 miles) north of Cuiabá. The best way to get there is by rental car (see "Fast Facts: Cuiabá," earlier in the chapter). Roads are excellent. Follow the MT-251 to the park and the town of Chapada dos Guimarães.

BY BUS   Direct buses operated by **Viação Rubi** (✆ **065/3624-9044**) leave from Cuiabá's *rodoviaria* and take about 1 hour. Cost is R$8 and departures are daily at 9, 10:30am, 2, and 6:30pm.

VISITOR INFORMATION

The **tourist office** is at Rua Quinco Caldas s/n (✆ **065/3301-2045**). The park visitor center (✆ **065/3301-1133**) is located on highway MT-251 about 8km (5 miles) past the park entrance, and about 15km (9 miles) before the town of Chapada dos Guimarães. An excellent local tour operator, **Ecoturismo Cultural,** Praça Dom Wunibaldo 464 (✆ **065/3301-1693;** www.chapadadosguimaraes.com.br), arranges day trips with guides and transportation and can assist with accommodations.

All tour operators listed under "Tour Operators in the North Pantanal," above, can provide day trips or overnight packages to the Chapada, in combination with a visit to the Pantanal or as a separate trip.

EXPLORING THE PARK

Two days are plenty to explore the Chapada. Even if you only have a day, you can still see the "best of the Chapada"—take in the magnificent views, frolic in a few waterfalls, and get some hiking in, all before sunset.

Note: Due to park maintenance, some areas of the park are closed on Tuesdays and Wednesdays. Also, at the time this book went to press, trails to Cidade de Pedras and Morro São Jerônimo were closed, but were expected to reopen soon. Check with the park administration office (✆ **065/3301-1133**) or ask at your pousada.

Recommended Hikes

All times are one-way for the hikes listed below. Trail heads have sizable parking lots, but on weekends the sights closest to town can get crowded. There is no public transportation in the park or surrounding area.

CACHOEIRA VEU DE NOIVA   The tallest waterfall in the park is the gorgeous **Véu de Noiva.** The trail head is at the park visitor center, about 15km (9 miles) from the town of Chapada dos Guimarães. From the visitor center it is a short and obvious walk to the lookout (closed on Tues).

MIRANTE DA GEODESIA   This lookout marks the geodesic center of Brazil. The spot also happens to mark a fabulous lookout over the lowlands below the Chapada, with Cuiabá in the distance. Short trails below the lookout take you down some of the cliffs

> **Tips   Hiking Tips**
>
> Wear high-top shoes or boots—not sandals—as the rocks and sand are perfect spots for snakes (some may be poisonous). Be careful when sitting down and putting your hands on the rocks.

Tips **Where to Find Local Art**

For local art and crafts, visit **Artes da Chapada Artesanatos,** Rua Cipriano Curvo 464, Centro (✆ **065/3301-2739**). Open Monday through Saturday from 10am to 7pm. Around the Chapada's central square you will find a number of other arts and crafts stores.

with more views. The parking lot lies 8km (5 miles) east of the town of Chapada dos Guimarães.

CIDADE DE PEDRAS   The City of Stone is named after the beautiful eroded rock formations that look like the ruins of buildings. A short hike takes you through these rocks to the edge of a canyon, where the sheer cliffs drop 350m (1,148 ft.) straight down. To reach the trail head, go west from town on MT-251 for about 2km (1¼ miles), turn right (there's a small sign), and follow the smaller, rougher blacktop road straight on for 13km (8 miles). See note above.

PAREDÃO DO ECO   A 20-minute hike takes you to the edge of a mini Grand Canyon. Steep cliff walls and eroded rocks in various shapes form an amazing pattern, and on the far side where the walls are the steepest and sheerest you can often spot scarlet red *araras* (macaws). At sunrise and sunset the light bathes the rocks in a warm red glow. To reach the trail head, follow the same directions for Cidade de Pedra, above. About 12km (7½ miles) along the blacktop road, take the left turn on a dirt road and follow it for 3km (2 miles).

MORRO SÃO JERÔNIMO   The highest point in the Chapada, this tabletop mountain can be reached by a 4-hour hike. Bring water and sunscreen. The trail for the Morro begins at the visitor center parking lot. The peak is almost due south, but trails are poorly marked. Follow the signs to Cachoeira Véu de Noiva, then to Casa de Pedra, and then to Morro São Jerônimo. See note above.

WHERE TO STAY

Pousada do Parque ★★★ Kids   This pousada has a fabulous location, on the edge of a cliff looking out toward Morro São Jerônimo. The rooms are a bit small but very comfortable and several have heaters, great for the chilly fall and winter days. Guests can also warm up in the fireplace lounge or enjoy a glass of wine and an outstanding meal by the wood-burning stove. The owners are avid hikers and birders with lots of tips to offer. Ask the front desk for a copy of their detailed bird list. *Note:* Access is via a dirt road at Km 52 of the Cuiabá–Chapada dos Guimarães Highway. The gate is normally locked, so notify the staff of your expected time of arrival.

MT-251 Hwy., Km 52 (15km/8 miles from the center of town), Chapada dos Guimarães, 78065-010 MT. ✆ **065/3391-1346** or 3682-2800. www.pousadadoparque.com.br. 8 units. R$265 double. Seasonal discounts available. Children 5 and under stay free in parent's room. AE, DC, MC, V. Free parking. **Amenities:** Restaurant; bar; small outdoor pool; sauna. *In room:* A/C, no phone.

Solar do Inglês ★   This small but charming pousada with a lovely English garden (plus a very un-English pool) is the perfect couple's getaway. Rooms are lovingly decorated in antiques and bric-a-brac. In addition to a hearty breakfast, the pousada serves a proper afternoon tea, at 5pm on the dot.

Rua Cipriano Curvo 142, Centro, Chapada dos Guimarães, 78195-000 MT. ✆ **065/3301-1389.** www. solardoingles.com.br. 8 units. R$285 double. Extra person add 25%. AE, V. Free parking. Children 13 and under not accepted. **Amenities:** Bar; pool; sauna. *In room:* A/C (in 7 rooms), fan only (1 room), TV/DVD, hair dryer, minibar.

WHERE TO DINE

The town of the Chapada dos Guimarães doesn't really stand out as a culinary destination. Perhaps most visitors are so tired after a day of hiking that they can't be bothered to go out and prefer to eat at their pousada.

An excellent lunch spot is **Morro dos Ventos,** Chacara Morro dos Ventos, via Estrada do Mirante Km 1 (✆ **065/3301-1030**). Perched on the edge of a cliff, the restaurant offers fabulous views. With luck you'll spot red macaws flying along the rock faces. The menu offers regional home cooking. Try the chicken stew with okra, served in a heavy cast-iron pot with generous side dishes of beans, salad, *farofa,* and rice. Other options include the *pintado* or *paçu* fish. Open daily from 9am to 6pm.

4 CAMPO GRANDE & THE SOUTH PANTANAL

1,221km (758 miles) NW of Rio de Janeiro, 902km (560 miles) NW of São Paulo

Campo Grande is a fairly new town and an important transportation hub for the region. When Mato Grosso state was split in two in the '70s, Campo Grande became the capital of Mato Grosso do Sul. As with Cuiabá, there's nothing about Campo Grande that merits a visit, and most lodge packages will whisk you out of town right away. The Pantanal in Mato Grosso do Sul is less wild, more given over to cattle ranching, and significantly harder to access than in the north. That said, the avian life is still remarkable, and the lodges are larger, more established, and more luxurious by far.

As in the north, a stay in a Pantanal lodge normally involves a number of activities—a boat trip to spot birds and caiman, a horseback trip through the fields, bird spotting by foot or in an open vehicle, and often an evening excursion to see nocturnal animals. Some lodges also offer canoe trips, fishing expeditions, or specialized bird-watching outings. If you have a specialized interest, it's a good idea to make contact ahead of time.

The main road from Campo Grande to Corumbá, the BR-262, follows the southern border of the Pantanal, affording small inroads here and there, particularly around Miranda, Aquidauana, and toward Corumbá.

ESSENTIALS
Getting There
BY PLANE   TAM (✆ 0800/570-5700 or 067/4002-5700; www.tam.com.br), **Gol** (✆ **0300/115-2121;** www.voegol.com.br), **TRIP** (✆ **0300/789-8747;** www.voetrip.com. br), and **Azul** (✆ **067/3003-2985;** www.voeazul.com.br) all have flights to Campo Grande. The city's airport (✆ **067/3368-6093**) is 7km (4¼ miles) west of downtown. A taxi to downtown (the best option) costs about R$25.

BY BUS   The bus station in Campo Grande is at Rua Dom Aquino and Rua Joaquim Nabuco (✆ **067/3321-8797**). Buses connect Campo Grande to Cuiabá (approx. 10 hr.), Bonito (5 hr.), and Corumbá (7 hr.).

VISITOR INFORMATION   A **tourist information booth** is at the **airport** (✆ **0800/ 647-6050** or 067/3363-3116) and the **main bus terminal** (✆ **067/3382-2350**). Both staff. However, they can offer a few maps of the city, and some information on the Pantanal, Bonito, and other sights of interest.

(Fast Facts) Campo Grande

Car Rental Try either **Localiza** (© 067/3363-4598) or **Avis** (© 067/3325-0036), both at Campo Grande airport.

Consulates **Bolivian** consulate, Rua 13 Maio, 2500, Centro (© 067/3025-4453); **Paraguayan** consulate, Rua 26 de Agosto 384, Centro (© 067/3784-6610).

Currency Exchange & Banks **Banco do Brasil,** Av. Afonso Pena 2202 (© 067/3326-1064, is open 11am to 4pm Monday to Saturday; 24-hour ATM.

Hospital **Hospital Santa Casa** is at Rua Eduardo Santos Pereira 88 (© 067/3322-4000).

Internet Access Try **Virtual Cafe,** Rua 14 Julho 1647 (© 067/3384-0092). Daily 8am to 8pm; cost is R$6 per hour.

TOUR OPERATORS IN THE SOUTH PANTANAL (CAMPO GRANDE)

It's worth contacting both the lodge and a tour operator and comparing prices. Often (though not always) the tour operator can offer a lodge package with airport pickup and transfers for the same cost or less than you might get booking directly with the lodge.

Located in Campo Grande, **Brazil Nature Tours** (© 067/3042-4659 or 9258-6581; www.brazilnaturetours.com) has some excellent packages for the Pantanal, for Bonito, and for combinations of the two. The agency is quick in responding to e-mail.

If you're just interested in the Pantanal, a 4-day, 3-night package tour at a Pantanal lodge including all meals and activities, with transfer from and to Campo Grande airport, starts at US$800 per person. Trips to Bonito include admission to a few of the most popular activities, such as a visit to the blue lake cave and snorkeling on the Rio Sucuri. A 4-day, 3-night Bonito trip starts at US$650 per person, including accommodations and transfers from and to Campo Grande. A 6-day, 5-night combo tour, with a 3-night stay in the Pantanal and a 2-night stay in Bonito, including all transfers, starts at US$1,330 per person. Mostly geared toward backpackers, **Pantanal Trekking Tour,** Rua Jaoquim Nabuco 185, Campo Grande (© 067/3042-0508; www.pantanaltrekking. com), offers more rustic 3- to 5-day overland trips through the Pantanal—mostly along the Estrada Parque, a dirt road through the South Pantanal—between Campo Grande and Corumbá. Trips include guides and activities such as horseback riding. Price depends on itinerary and number in group, but starts at about R$250 per day per person.

EXPLORING CAMPO GRANDE & THE SOUTH PANTANAL

There's not much to keep you dawdling in Campo Grande. Those who are booked on package tours to Bonito or the Pantanal can time their arrivals to connect with their transfers onward, eliminating the need to stay in Campo Grande for a night.

THE PANTANAL

19

CAMPO GRANDE & THE SOUTH PANTANAL

Because of the distance and the difficulty of access, there is no 1-day option for the South Pantanal. Either commit to 3 days, or don't bother to come. The **Refugio Caiman** is one of the best ranches in the South Pantanal and a wonderful, cushy way to explore the ranch land and see some amazing wildlife. If you have a few extra days in this region, consider a 2-day side trip to Bonito to swim in the crystal-clear waters of the Rio Prata or Sucuri, and maybe try some rappelling or caving. If you need to spend the night in town, try to book a room at the **Bristol Exceler Plaza Hotel,** Av. Afonso Pena 444, Campo Grande (📞 **067/ 3312-2800;** www.bristolhoteis.com.br). This hotel offers top-notch amenities including tennis courts, a swimming pool, and a sauna. The rooms are spacious and comfortably furnished, with tile floors, firm queen-size beds, and a small desk area. A double room goes for R$170 to R$200 (children 7 and under stay free in parent's room).

WHERE TO DINE IN CAMPO GRANDE

Dining options include **Casa Colonial,** Av. Afonso Pena 3997 (📞 067/3383-3207). The house special is grilled chicken (delicious!), *picanha* beef, or roasted pork. At the popular Portuguese restaurant **Acepipe,** Rua Eduardo Santos Pereira 645 (📞 067/3383-4287), the house specialty is *bacalhau* (cod), served grilled or with egg and onion. Surprisingly enough, Campo Grande is also a good city for Japanese food, a legacy of the Japanese laborers who worked building the railroad through the state in the 19th century. For a full-menu Japanese restaurant, try **Kendô,** Av. Alfonso Pena 4150 (📞 067/3382-9000). Open Tuesday to Sunday 7pm to midnight.

LODGES IN THE SOUTH PANTANAL (CAMPO GRANDE)

Fazenda Barranco Alto ★★   This South Pantanal farm lies on the Rio Negro, in a region known for its landscape of small salt lakes (called *salinas*) and freshwater ponds, as well as its large populations of animals and birds. Hyacinth macaws are common, as are trogons, jacamars, toucans, raptors, and several hundred other bird species. There are also capybara and giant river otters. Jaguars are spotted now and then by the river (but no guarantees). The best time to visit is from March to October. For migrant birds the best months are July to October. Bird-watching is popular. Other tours include horseback riding to spot animals, or watching the daily work of cowboys on the farm, or trips by jeep in search of tapirs, anteaters, marsh deer, giant otters, and others. There is also swimming, fishing, and canoeing. Guesthouse rooms are simply but comfortably furnished with firm double or single beds. All rooms have a private veranda. The best way to reach the fazenda is by plane from Campo Grande. The pilot charges R$3,500, which covers the flight in *and* out, for up to three people. In the dry season (Mar–Oct) you can also come in by 4×4. The 6-hour drive costs R$1,500 (in and out) with room for four to five people. Brazil Nature Tours offers packages (4 days/3 nights), including the flight from Campo Grande airport for US$1,780 per person.

Caixa postal 109, Aquidauana, 79200-000 MS. 📞 **067/9986-0373.** www.fazendabarrancoalto.com.br. 4 units. R$440 per person per night, including meals, drinks (including beer), guides, and activities. Owner recommends staying 4 days, but there is no minimum. Children 5 and under stay free in parent's room, 6–13 50% adult rate. AE, MC, V. **Amenities:** Internet. *In room:* A/C, no phone.

Pousada Aguapé ★   Though still a working ranch, the Aguapé has largely transformed into a tourism and fishing lodge. It's located on 60km (37 miles) of dirt road from Aquidauana, itself 130km (81 miles) of paved highway from Campo Grande. Accommodations are in comfortable but simple rooms. Activities include horseback riding, trail walking, fishing for piranhas, a boat tour on the Aquidauana River, a nighttime search for caiman, and some time helping out with the cattle. The grounds are well equipped for downtime, with a pool, volleyball court, and soccer pitch. Avid fishermen can skip the eco-tourism activities and make use of the boats and drivers to fish the Aquidauana.

Rua Marechal Mallet 588, Aquidauana. ✆ **067/3258-1146** or 9986-0351 (cellphone). www.aguape.com. br. 15 units, showers only. Packages start at US$880 per person (double room), including excursions, meals, and transfers from Campo Grande. Children 3 and under stay free in parent's room. AE, DC, MC, V. Free parking. **Amenities:** Restaurant; bar; pool. *In room:* A/C, no phone.

Refugio Caiman ★★ (Kids) (Overrated)   The most luxurious lodge in the Pantanal, the Refugio Caiman is set on a huge cattle ranch outside the town of Miranda, about 250km (155 miles) from Campo Grande. We have given this place an overrated icon because it is by far the most expensive lodge in the Pantanal, and the staff really does its best to "hold your hand," making you feel, unfortunately, like just another tourist. However, the facilities are very comfortable and the wildlife population is still quite stunning. Huge jabiru storks, flocks of roseate spoonbills, egrets of all shapes and sizes, caiman, and capybaras can all be seen within steps of the lodge. Hyacinth macaws are frequently spotted. Soft-adventure activities here are very safe—perfect for families with young children. Excursions are geared to those who lack the fitness level for longer hikes or expeditions. Listed below are the rack rates; transportation from Cuiabá is not included. The lodge can arrange this for R$147 per person, one-way. Contact tour operators for less expensive packages that include transfers. *Note:* Children 7 and under are accepted only in December, January, and July.

Reservations: Av. Brigadeiro Faria Lima 3015, cj. 161, Itaim Bibi São Paulo. ✆ **011/3706-1800.** Lodge ✆ 067/3242-1450. www.caiman.com.br. 25 units. R$550–R$750 per person per night, including all meals, guides, activities, and insurance. Children 11 and under stay free in parent's room. AE, DC, MC, V. Free parking. **Amenities:** Restaurant; bar; outdoor pool. *In room:* A/C, no phone.

5 A SIDE TRIP TO BONITO

300km (186 miles) SW of Campo Grande

You have to admire Bonito. Though located in the middle of nowhere—it's 300km (186 miles) from Campo Grande, and Campo Grande is *already* the end of the earth for most Brazilians—this small town has turned itself into a prime eco-tourism destination for Brazilians and foreigners who come to snorkel, raft, and rappel. To accommodate these ecotourists, Bonito's tourism industry has created the kind of collusion that would make oil companies envious. All excursions cost the same, no matter where and how you book them. All trips are guided, numbers are capped each day, and transportation is not provided. Only taxis offer transportation and—you guessed it—they all charge the exact same fare. Brazilians first arrived after the town was featured in a nightly soap opera (if the moon had been featured in one of those *novelas,* the Brazilians would have been the first ones to land there), and more and more international travelers are drawn to Bonito as well.

The attraction is not the town. What people come for are the rivers; the numerous streams that bubble up from the substrate of limestone rock are so free of impurities that you get the kind of crystal-clear visibility normally found only in tropical oceans. You can see 21 to 30m (70–100 ft.) in these fast-flowing rivers, and they're full of freshwater *dourado* and *pintado,* not to mention the occasional anaconda. The area also has numerous caves and waterfalls. However, all of the prime terrain is on private land and you're only allowed on as part of an excursion.

Is the trip worth it? It's a long way to go, but the rivers are fun and fascinating. It's also instructive to see this little town in action, gouging tourists who fork over the bucks as a matter of course. A package tour with transportation and admission (such as the ones offered by Open Door in Campo Grande) is recommended; you will get no better prices once you get there, and at least it'll save the frustration of opening your wallet every time you want to do something.

ESSENTIALS

BY PLANE   The fastest way to get to Bonito is to fly. **TRIP** (© **3003-8747** or 0300/789-8747; www.voetrip.com.br) offers flights between Campo Grande and Bonito twice a week, on Sunday and Thursday, departing at 11:20am. Return flights from Bonito to Campo Grande depart on the same days, at 12:10pm. Flying time is 30 minutes and one-way airfare starts at R$159.

BY CAR   To reach Bonito take the BR-060 from Campo Grande to Guia Lopes da Laguna and then the MS-382 to Bonito. Count on a 4-hour drive.

BY BUS   From Campo Grande, take **Viação Cruzeiro do Sul** (© **067/3312-9710;** www.cruzeirodosulms.com.br/canais/passageiros/linhas). Tickets cost R$55, and the bus ride takes about 5 hours. Daily departures are at 7, 9, 11am, 4, 7, and 11pm (call to confirm).

VISITOR INFORMATION   The official **tourist office** is at Rua Cel. Pilad Rebuá 1780 (© **067/3255-1850**); open daily from 9am to 5pm. The Bonito tourist information site is www.portalbonito.com.br.

GETTING AROUND   Getting around Bonito without a car means getting gouged by taxis. Tour operators don't provide transportation; taxi companies all charge the same high rates. If you haven't come with a package tour, think seriously about renting a car. Contact **Agência Ar Bonito** to reserve a vehicle (© **067/3255-1008** or 3255-1897).

FAST FACTS   **Banco do Brasil** is at Rua Luiz Costa Leite 132 (© **067/3255-1121**). For Internet access, try **Rhema Cópias Lanhouse,** Rua Pilad Rebuá 1626 (© **067/3255-4271**). Open daily from 8:30am to 10pm; R$8 per hour.

EXPLORING THE AREA

All of the activities listed below (plus quite a few others) are sold through tour operators in Bonito. One operator with a good English website is **Ygarapé Tour,** Rua Pilad Rebuá 1823 (© **067/3255-1733;** www.ygarape.com.br). Every tour operator offers the same packages at the same price, so don't waste time shopping around. Numbers are limited, so it's key to book your excursions as early as possible. Avoid long weekends and high season in January, February, and July if you can; the popular trips fill up quickly.

All activities are guided. If you are a real outdoors do-it-yourselfer, Bonito will drive you insane. On the other hand, if you are a novice adventurer or are traveling with young children or older people, this is the perfect environment to try some rafting, snorkeling, or hiking. If you are driving, ask for detailed directions; some of these attractions can be tricky to find. The prices listed below are for the peak season. Some of the tours offer a small discount (up to 20%) in the low season.

Aquario Natural ★   The best known of the springs and rivers that people swim in is the Aquario Natural. Starting at the wellspring of the Rio Baia Bonita, you snorkel a

.5km (½-mile) stretch of crystal-clear river with amazing underwater views of fish. The downside is that this is also the busiest excursion, and your time on the river (an hour or so) is shorter than some of the others.

Road to Jardim, Km 7. R$99–R$125.

Cachoeira do Rio do Peixe   For a more mellow activity, take a visit to the waterfall of Rio do Peixe. Over 10m (30 ft.) tall with crystal-clear pools and caves to swim in, it's a great spot to spend a hot afternoon.

Road to Bodoquena, Km 35. R$75.

Floating the Sucuri ★★   First you walk through the forest to see where the Sucuri River gurgles up through limestone fissures. A bit farther down, once the river has gained some depth and momentum, you get in the water for your 2km (1¼-mile) snorkel trip. It's like floating in an aquarium with an amazing number of fish to look at. Drift and enjoy the view.

Road to São Geraldo, Km 20. R$100–R$125, includes lunch.

Gruta do Lago Azul   Tour operators promote this tour as a must-see, which is likely why it's always packed. Every 15 minutes a group sets off on the 351m (1,170-ft.) trail into the 69m-deep (230-ft.) cave. The calcium formations are certainly cool—amazing stalactites, stalagmites, stone flowers, and dish-shaped travertines. The lake at the bottom is an eerie clear blue; it's also fenced off to prevent people from sticking in their little fingers or toes. While you make your way back up, the next two groups will already be on their way down. From mid-December to mid-January, from 8:30 to 9:30am, the sun hits the lake directly—an impressive sight.

Road to Campo dos Indios (Fazenda Jaraguá). R$25.

Rafting on the Rio Formosa   The rapids are nothing to write home about, but it is a peaceful float. This 7km (4¼-mile) trip takes you over some small rapids, and you'll stop along the way for a swim in some of the waterfalls. Keep your eyes peeled for birds, monkeys, and butterflies.

Road to Ilha do Padre, Km 12. R$50.

Rappelling and Snorkeling in Anhumas Abyss ★★★   Book ahead for this most popular adventure, especially during weekends or holidays. If you have never rappelled before, you will learn how and be provided with all the gear for the grand descent of 72m (236 ft.) into an abyss packed with stalactites and stalagmites. At the bottom you can snorkel in the crystal-clear water.

Road to Campo dos Indios (Fazenda Jaraguá). R$360.

WHERE TO STAY

Aguas de Bonito ★   The Aguas is more like a small resort, with an outdoor pool and whirlpool, and lighted tennis courts. In addition to breakfast, an afternoon snack is included as well. The rooms are tile-floored and spotless, featuring a double or two single beds, plus a clean, functional bathroom. Each room comes with a small veranda and hammock. The best ones are on the second floor of the two-story chalets.

Rua 29 de Maio 1679, Bonito, 79290-000 MS. ℂ **067/3255-2330**. www.aguasdebonito.com.br. 30 units. High season (Dec–Feb and July) R$256–R$296 double; low season R$197–R$228 double. Extra person add 25%. Children 6 and under stay free in parent's room. MC, V. Free parking. **Amenities:** Restaurant; bar; Jacuzzi; outdoor pool; lighted tennis courts. *In room:* A/C, TV, fridge, minibar.

Santa Esmeralda ★★ Perhaps the nicest place in all Bonito, Santa Esperalda is located in a green piece of parkland on the banks of the Rio Formosa. Accommodations are in pretty, self-contained bungalows, each with a hammock and a broad front veranda. Guests can swim in the river, or lounge in the natural pools and small waterfalls, or go for a paddle in the complimentary kayaks. There's a pleasant outdoor restaurant, where both breakfast and dinner (included) are served. The only potential drawback is the location, a 17km (11-mile) drive out of town.

Rodovia Guia Lopes Km 17, Bonito, 79290-000 MS. ℭ **067/3255-2683** or 9986-4580. www.hotelsanta esmeralda.com.br. 16 units. R$280–R$335 double. Extra person add R$80. Children 5 and under stay free in parent's room. Rates include breakfast and dinner. AE, DC, MC, V. Free parking. **Amenities:** Outdoor pool; kayaks. *In room:* A/C, TV, fridge, no phone.

Wetiga ★★ This beautiful, modern hotel with an innovative design features extensive use of *aroeira* tree trunks in its structure. The hotel is built in a U around a central reflecting pool, so most units have pleasant balconies overlooking the pool. Rooms are new and modern, with tile floors and queen-size beds with nice linen. The restaurant (in the low season dinner is also included) serves innovative cuisine using local ingredients, with the option of outdoor dining by the pool.

Rua Coronel Pilad Rebuá 679, Bonito, 79290-000 MS. ℭ **067/3255-1699.** www.wetigahotel.com.br. 67 units, showers only. R$285–R$360 double. Extra person add 25%. Children 4 and under stay free in parent's room. MC, V. Free parking. **Amenities:** Restaurant (dinner included); bar; Jacuzzi; outdoor pool. *In room:* A/C, TV, fridge, minibar.

WHERE TO DINE

Aquária Restaurante SEAFOOD Dine on the main-street patio—you'll see all of Bonito file by. The food is simple home cooking, with lots of local fish such as grilled *pintado* or *dourado* served with a mushroom caper sauce. All dishes are served with rice, fries, and salads and are plenty for two. There are also individual *churrasco* plates such as the *picanha* with fries and salad for R$12.

Rua Pilad Rebuá 1883. ℭ **067/3255-1893.** Main courses R$22–R$35. No credit cards. Daily 10am–4pm and 6–11pm.

Cantinho do Peixe BRAZILIAN The best fish place in town serves up locally caught *pintado* and *dourado,* simply grilled and served with lots of *farofa* and fries on the side. The menu also includes chicken and various grilled beef dishes.

Rua 31 de Março 1918. ℭ **067/3255-3381.** Main courses R$18–R$28. No credit cards. Daily 11am–3:30pm and 6:30pm–midnight.

Taboa Bar BRAZILIAN Taboa is the nighttime gathering place. Sidewalk tables pack the street, and inside locals and visitors quickly fill up the tables. The drink of choice is *cachaça;* the house special is served with honey, cinnamon, and *guarana* powder. For food there are starters such as the *caldinho de feijão,* a tasty bean soup, as well as small plates with grilled fish, chicken, or beef.

Rua Pilaud 1837. ℭ **067/3255-1862.** www.taboa.com.br. Everything under R$25. No credit cards. Daily 5pm–2am.

6 CORUMBA & THE SOUTH PANTANAL

Corumbá looks like a city from a Jules Verne novel.
—Tristes Tropiques, Claude Levi-Strauss

351km (218 miles) NW of Campo Grande

I'm not entirely sure what the great French anthropologist had in mind when he set down that thought about Corumbá back in 1933. My guess is that it was a comment on the city's otherworldly setting. Corumbá clings to a low cliff top, at the bottom of which, beyond the docks and riverboats, there begins a vast brown and green prairie of water that swirls and broods its way over the horizon, constrained finally by a distant smudge of low gray hills. Looking up from the river, or out from the city, Corumbá appears as the sole outpost of civilization in an otherworldly landscape of water.

It's a difficult place to reach. For hundreds of years the only route to Corumbá was by water, either across the Pantanal by canoe or up the Paraguay River by boat through Argentina and Paraguay. A railway linking Corumbá to Campo Grande wasn't built until the early 20th century. A road wasn't built until the 1970s.

The isolation has left the Pantanal around Corumbá more pristine than in more settled places farther east. But the difficulty of access has been a challenge to the city's ecotourism operators. Though Corumbá is more truly a Pantanal city than either Cuiabá in the north or Campo Grande in the east, both of the latter get more Pantanal-bound visitors. Lodges located closer to Corumbá keep their offices in Campo Grande, where they also pick up and drop off most of their paying visitors.

Corumbá's one true forte is sport fishing. The Paraguay River offers larger, more varied sport fish than anywhere else in Brazil, as well as better fishing infrastructure. There are lodges, camps, and even floating lodges that cruise up the river, allowing guests to fish away the day and relax with a cold beer in the evening. Eco-tourism also exists. Many of the lodges have fishing and eco-tourism options, allowing visitors to combine the two.

Is it necessary to visit Corumbá? No. If you're visiting a local lodge, it's possible to land and leave the same morning. What is worth doing, if time allows, is a stroll along the cliff-top Avenida Rondon, where you can look out over the Pantanal and wonder if even Jules Verne would ever have thought of a city in a landscape so strange.

ESSENTIALS

Getting There

BY PLANE TAM (© 0800/570-5700 or 067/4002-5700; www.tam.com.br) and **TRIP** (© 3003-8747 or 0300/789-8747; ww.voetrip.com.br) offer daily flights to Corumbá via Campo Grande. Corumbá's airport is 5km (3 miles) north of downtown on Rua Santos Dumont (© 067/231-3322). A taxi to downtown (the best option) costs about R$25.

BY BUS The bus station is on Rua Porto Carrero (© 067/3231-2033) about 3km (2 miles) west of downtown. **Andorinha** (© 067/3231-2033 or 0300/210-3900; www.andorinha.com) has nine buses per day to Campo Grande (approx. 6 hr.). It costs R$82.

GETTING AROUND Corumbá is so compact you can walk pretty much everywhere in the center of town. There are taxi stands all over town. Taxis can also be hailed on the street, or by calling **Taxi Ponto One** (© 067/3231-4043). Taxis are more expensive than elsewhere in Brazil. A trip from the bus station to downtown costs about R$25.

VISITOR INFORMATION   The tourist information office, **Setur,** is on Rua Manuel Cavassa 275 on the waterfront (📞 **067/3232-5221;** www.corumba.com.br). Open Monday to Friday noon to 6pm.

⟮*Fast Facts*⟯ **Corumbá**

Car Rental **Localiza** is at Rua Cabral 22064, Centro (📞 **067/3231-6000**).

Consulates **Bolivian** consulate, Rua Cabral 1607 (📞 **067/3231-5605**).

Currency Exchange & Banks Try **Banco do Brasil,** Rua 13 de Junho 914 (📞 **067/ 3231-2686**). **HSBC,** Rua Delamare 1068, has an ATM (📞 **067/3231-5455**).

Hospital **Clinica Prontomed** is at Rua Major Gama 782 (📞 **067/3231-1301**).

Internet Access Try **Cyber Point,** Rua Major Gama 1387 (📞 **067/3232-4381**). Open Monday to Saturday 9am to 11pm; cost is R$8 per hour.

TOUR OPERATORS IN THE CORUMBA PANTANAL

Local tour operators can set up all the logistics of your journey, sometimes cheaper than you can do by contacting the lodge directly. It's worthwhile making contact, if only to compare prices. Operators in Corumbá have, in recent years, been eager enough for business to offer serous discounts (Pantur has been offering a two-for-one deal on airfare). **Pantur** (📞 067/3231-2000; www.pantur.com.br) offers day tours along the Estrada Parque into the Pantanal, and fishing expeditions along the Paraguay. **Perola do Pantanal** (📞 067/3231-1470; www.peroladopantanal.com.br) specializes in multiday fishing expeditions along the Paraguay, but also offers photo safaris along the Estrada Parque. **Canaá Viagens e Turismo** (📞 067/3231-3667; www.pantanalcanaa.com.br) also specializes in fishing expeditions, but offers a few eco-tourism options as well. Generally speaking, a 5-day, 4-night eco-tourism adventure includes accommodations at a Pantanal fazenda, horseback-riding trips, and wildlife-watching, and starts at about R$1,400 per person.

CITY LAYOUT

Corumbá is a small and pretty city, laid out in a perfect grid on a cliff top, overlooking the Pantanal toward the west. The center of the city is a green city square called **Praça da Independencia.** Bordering the square to the north and south are two of Corumbá's principal streets, the **Rua 15 de Novembro** and the **Rua Frei Mariano.** To the west of Praça Independencia, the 2 blocks of Rua Frei Mariano between **Rua 13 de Junho** and **Avenida Rondon** make up Corumbá's principal shopping district. North a block along Rua 13 de Junho is another, slightly seedy square called the **Praça da República.** On the east side of that square is the **Museu do Pantanal.** Avenida Rondon itself is a wide boulevard running along the edge of the cliff overlooking the Paraguay River and Pantanal. It's a pretty street lined with tall Imperial palms, where Corumbáianos like to stroll in the evening. At the intersection of Rua Frei Mariano and Avenida Rondon, a small street— **Ladeira Jose Bonifacio**—runs steeply downhill to the marina and port area, the **Porto Geral.** The port is currently about half-renovated; there are a number of outdoor cafes and a few restaurants on the waterfront. It's also the place to find the tourism office and fishing and tour operators.

EXPLORING CORUMBA & THE SOUTH PANTANAL

Though Corumbá is a charming enough city, the real attraction here is the Pantanal. The area around Corumbá offers wildlife viewing akin in quality to that found in the North Pantanal, and better than that found in areas closer to Campo Grande. Corumbá is also the best place in all of Brazil for sport fishing.

Though truly impressive, **Forte Coimbra** (no phone) is also 3 hours downriver from Corumbá. The fort was built in 1775 to protect Brazil's western frontier, and was occupied for several years during Brazil's 19th-century war with Paraguay. Access is by boat.

WHERE TO STAY

The nicest place to stay in Corumbá is the **Hotel Gold Fish,** Av. Rio Branco 2799 (on the road to Ladario; © **067/3231-5106;** double room R$120). The hotel is 8km (5 miles) outside of downtown, on the banks of the River Paraguay. Rooms are clean and simple, but the large outdoor pool and children's play area make this hotel worthwhile. The city's top hotel is the **Hotel Nacional Palace,** Rua America 936 (© **067/3234-6000;** www.hnacional.com.br; double room R$170). Rooms are clean and comfortable, with tile floors, firm single or double beds, and hot showers.

WHERE TO DINE

Fine dining is not the reason to come to Corumbá, but there are some good restaurants serving local Pantanal fish in traditional ways. The specialty at **Ceará,** Rua Albuquerque 516 (© **067/231-1930**), is *pintado à urucum* (baked with dendê oil and coconut milk and covered with mozzarella cheese) or *à pantaneira* (fried with banana and manioc). Open Tuesday through Sunday 11am to 2:30pm and 6pm to midnight. For steak and simple meat dishes, there's **Avalom,** Rua Frei Mariano 499 (© **067/3231-4430**), open Monday to Saturday 11am to 3pm and 5:30 to 11pm.

LODGES IN THE SOUTH PANTANAL (CORUMBA)

Note: The lodges listed below also regularly arrange transfers from Campo Grande. They also offer both eco-tourism trips and sport-fishing packages. Both lodges are located off the **Estrada Parque (Park Rd.)** a little-traveled dirt and gravel road crisscrossed by innumerable small watercourses that—much like the Transpantaneira in the North—offer tremendous wildlife-viewing opportunities.

Fazenda Xaraés ★ Located by the banks of the Rio Abobral, the Xaraés is very much a fazenda (ranch) experience, with visits to the corrals, rides in bullock carts, and outings to herd the cattle. In addition to horseback riding, guests can take advantage of the river to set out for self-guided paddles, as well as motorized bird-watching, night hunts for caiman, and 4×4 photo safari expeditions. Accommodations are in rustic but comfortable quarters by the riverbank. There's also a pleasant ranch-style main house, with bar and snooker table and small library. Access to the fazenda is over a rough 13km (8-mile) track, in a 4×4 provided by the hotel. Meals included.

Estrada Parque Km 17, Abobral, Corumbá. © **067/9906-9272.** Fax 018/9906-9282. www.xaraes.com.br. 17 units, showers only. R$300 per person, includes all meals and guided activities. Children 5 and under stay free in parent's room, children 6–12 50% of adult rate. V. Free parking. Access by 4×4 from Miranda. **Amenities:** Restaurant; bar; outdoor pool; canoes. *In room:* A/C, TV, fridge.

462 **Pantanal Park Hotel** ★   Set on the shores of the Paraguay River, this lodge specializes in fishing trips. For eco-tourists, there's horseback riding, bird spotting, piranha fishing, and nighttime caiman-spotting trips. Accommodations are in smaller chalet buildings, with four apartments per building. These vary in quality. The most basic ones—on the ground floor of the buildings—are clean and comfortable, with firm single beds and functional bathrooms. The more luxurious upstairs rooms have a screened-in sitting area with TV and couches and chairs. Common lodge areas include a large outdoor pool and restaurant/bar with nightly karaoke. All meals are included.

Reservations: ☎ **018/3908-5332.** Fax 018/3908-1333. Lodge 067/3275-1500 or 9987-3267. www.pantanal park.com.br. 41 units, showers only. R$640 per person 3-day package. Children 4 and under stay free in parent's room, children 5–10 years old R$480. AE, DC, MC, V. Free parking. Access by boat from the Paraguay River bridge in Porto Morrinho. **Amenities:** Restaurant; bar; large outdoor pool. *In room:* A/C, TV, fridge, no phone.

Fernando de Noronha

Fernando de Noronha may be the desert island upon which people dream of being marooned. On Noronha, verdant mountains descend to sheer cliffs, which in turn fall onto wide, sandy beaches that have known neither condo nor cabana. Beneath the waves live corals and colorful fish, manta rays, and lemon sharks. Sea turtles lay eggs by the thousands on the beaches facing the Atlantic. And then there are the spinner dolphins. Early in the morning, in a bay named, appropriately, Baía dos Golfinhos (Bay of Dolphins), spinner dolphins gather in pods of more than 1,000 to frolic and spin in the morning sunshine. Come afternoon, they set off on a daily circuit around the main island. It's an island ecosystem in all its tropical glory.

Noronha was Brazil's first national marine park. All of the water and 70% of the land on and around Ilha de Fernando de Noronha is national park, administered by the Brazilian environment agency IBAMA. Development is strictly controlled, and visitors must pay a daily tax that supports environmental preservation.

Even with the rules, there is plenty to do on Noronha. The archipelago is the best dive spot in Brazil, and one of the better ones in the world. It's also known as a surfing hot spot. Visitors can rent dune buggies and explore the island's pristine beaches.

For most of its history, of course, people have tried to escape from Noronha. From the 17th until the 20th century, Fernando de Noronha served as an inescapable political prison. This 21-island archipelago sits way out in the Atlantic, 360km (223 miles) from Natal, 545km (337 miles) from Recife, and 2,600km (1,612 miles) from the African coast. From the 1940s to the 1980s the island was under the direct rule of Brazil's armed forces, which used it as both a base and prison. (For a time in the 1960s the island also served as a satellite tracking station for the U.S. armed forces.) Not until 1988, when much of the island was incorporated in the new marine park, did Fernando de Noronha meet its destiny as a sought-after tropical paradise.

Unfortunately, now that everyone wants to get to Noronha—particularly after Brazil's movie-star glitterati discovered the island—prices for accommodations on the island have zoomed to ridiculous heights. Modest little pousadas offering little more than a room in the family home now charge upwards of R$250 a night—as much as some luxury hotels in other parts of Brazil. Prices for meals and tours haven't yet followed suit, though it may be just a matter of time. The islands do remain a special, even magical place. If you can accept being gouged with equanimity, by all means come and experience the magic. If coughing up such large amounts seems likely to stick in your craw, it may be best to plan your escape to somewhere else.

1 ESSENTIALS

360km (223 miles) NE of Natal, 545km (337 miles) NE of Recife

High season in Fernando de Noronha is in July, and December through March, especially the time between Reveillon (New Year's Eve) and Carnaval. Pousadas fill up, and prices for everything rise. In **low season** (all other times) prices are slightly more reasonable and bargaining is possible—though Fernando de Noronha is still pricier than the rest of Brazil.

GETTING THERE

Both **Gol** (✆ **0300/115-2121;** www.voegol.com.br) and **TRIP** (✆ **0300/789-8747;** www.voetrip.com.br) have flights to Noronha. The **Aeroporto Fernando de Noronha** (✆ **081/3619-1633**) is in the island's center, a R$25 taxi ride from anywhere.

ISLAND LAYOUT

The main island, Ilha de Fernando de Noronha, has two distinct sides, a gentle one facing the Brazilian coast and a rockier, rougher one facing the Atlantic. The inshore coast is the place for surfing and lazing on the beach. The offshore beach is for watching the waves crash in.

One paved road, **BR-363,** runs from Baía do Sueste at one end of the island to the port in Baía Santo Antonio at the other. The most settled area on Noronha is **Vila dos Remédios.** This is where you'll find the city hall, the church, the old fort, the only bar/disco, the post office, and the offices of **Atlantis Divers.** Up a small hill about 1km (½ mile) away is **Vila do Trinta.** This area has a couple of restaurants, the police, pharmacy, and main grocery store all together inside the walls of the old armory. **Porto Santo Antonio** has several watersports operators and a few restaurants and pubs. The hospital, school, and other services for locals are located on BR-363 in the middle of the island. The old American army base at **Alameda do Boldró** has boring necessary stuff like the power station and the water plant, but it also has the **Tamar Visitor Center,** which features a small museum where they hold nightly nature talks.

GETTING AROUND

BY BUS   Public minibuses depart at 30-minute intervals from opposite ends of the island, running along the main highway (BR-363) from Baía Sueste to Porto Santo Antonio with stops along the way. The bus runs from 5am to 10pm. Cost is R$3.25.

BY TAXI   Chances are, wherever you go on the island there'll be a taxi *ponto* with a buggy driver waiting for your business. Should you find yourself unaccountably taxiless, **NorTax** (✆ **081/3619-1314**) will dispatch a buggy from its fleet. Prices for all drivers are fixed according to a table, which the driver will be happy to flash in your face should

---

Renting a Dune Buggy ★★

Tooling around back roads to various beaches is one of the most fun things to do on the island. Buggies can be rented just about anywhere—ask at your pousada. **LocBuggy** (✆ **081/3619-1490;** www.locbuggy.com.br) provides 24-hour service, and also rents motorcycles, 4×4s, and powerboats. Other agencies include **Locadora Morro do Farol** (✆ **081/9967-8887;** www.locadoramorrodofarol.com.br) in Al. Boldro, and **Locadora Marlin** in Remédios (✆ **081/3619-1223**). A driver's license is not required. The price is currently R$125 per day, though if you rent for several days you can often get a 10% to 20% discount. The cost is the same with or without driver. Gas costs about R$5 per liter (about US$10 per gallon). A day of exploring around the island will eat up about half a tank, currently about R$75.

ACCOMMODATIONS ■
Eco Pousada Teju-Açcu **2**
Pousada do Vale **1**
Pousada Maravilha **5**
Solar dos Ventos **4**

DINING ◆
Ecologiku's **3**

Ilha do Lucena

Ilha da Rata

N O R O N H A

Ilha Sela Ginete

Ilha São José   Ilha Rasa

Ilha do Cuscuz

Porto Santo Antonio

Baía Santo Antonio

D E

F E R N A N D O

Praia do Cachorro
Vila dos Remédios
Morro do Francês
Vila do Trinta

Praia do Meio

A T L A N T I C

O C E A N

Praia do Boldró
Morro do Pico
Floresta Nova
Ponta da Pedra Alta

Praia do Bode
Tamar Visitor Center
363
Praia do Atalaia

Airport
Morro da Boa Vista
Ponta do Espinhaço

M A R I N H O

Baía do Sancho
Baía do Sueste
Ilha dos Ovos

Ilha Cabeluda

N A C I O N A L

Morro Branco

Ilha do Morro da Viuvinha
Ilha do Morro do Leão

Mar de Dentro

P A R Q U E

Mar de Fora

262 Federal Road
⊕ Airport
➤ Beach
- - - Trail

Ponta Cupim Açu
Ponta do Barro Vermelho
Ponta da Sapata

0   2 mi
0   2 km

ATLANTIC OCEAN
Fernando de Noronha
Manaus   Belém
Amazon
Natal
B R A Z I L   Recife
Brasília
Salvador
Rio de Janeiro
São Paulo
0   500 mi
0   500 km

you utter so much as a peep about the cost. The fare from Vila dos Remédios to Baía do Sueste on the far end of the island costs about R$35; from Vila Remédios to the Tamar Visitor Center is R$20; from Vila Remédios to the port, R$15.

VISITOR INFORMATION

The official government website, **www.noronha.pe.gov.br**, has an English-language version with much useful information. Free maps of the island (with English text) are available in pamphlet racks at the airport. An intermittently staffed and not very useful **tourist information office** is on the lower floor of the Palácio São Miguel (city hall) in the island's largest town, **Vila Remédios** (© 081/3619-1378). There's good information on the island's natural history at the **Projeto Tamar** office at Av. do Boldró s/n (© 081/3619-1171; www.tamar.org.br).

(*Fast Facts*) **Fernando de Noronha**

Note: For all its charm, Fernando de Noronha is essentially a small town, as lacking in services as the next village on a desert island in the middle of the ocean. If a service or resource isn't listed below, it means Fernando de Noronha doesn't have it.

Currency Exchange & Banks Bring *lots* of cash to the island. The only bank on the island provides absolutely no services to visitors. Dive operators and most pousadas take credit cards; so, increasingly, do many tour operators and restaurants. However, taxis and buggy rentals most often do not. In a pinch, you may be able to cash a traveler's check at Atlantis Divers (p. 470)—but don't count on it.

Hospital **Hospital São Lucas,** BR-363 s/n, in Vila da Floresta (© 081/3619-1377).

Internet Access **Companhia da Lua** (© 081/3619-1631) in Vila dos Remédios charges R$12 per hour.

Pharmacy **Lojinha de Mãezinha,** Vila Remédios (© 081/3619-1104), is open Monday through Saturday from 8am to 6pm. Selection is quite limited.

Police Contact Policia Civil (© 081/3619-1179).

Post Office The main post office in Vila Remédios (© 081/3619-1135), is open Monday to Friday from 8am to 12:30pm.

Taxes There is a special environmental tax—currently R$37, R$228 per week—payable (cash only) at the airport when you arrive, or in advance using the Internet. Go to www.noronha.pe.gov.br, look for the link reading "Preservation Fee," then fill in and print out the form. Pay the fee at any Banco do Brasil or Loterica (lottery selling booth). Make sure they stamp your form. If you decide to stay longer than anticipated, go to the airport and pay the extra days *before* your time expires. If you overstay and try to pay up at the airport upon leaving, you'll be charged twice the regular rate for your extension. Divers and boaters who enter the marine park are charged a day tax of R$18. As in the rest of Brazil, hotels normally add 10% to the bill.

Weather The weather is hot year-round, with an average daily temperature of 30°C (86°F). Ocean temperature is 28°C (82°F) year-round. The rainy season is February to July, the dry season from August to January. Surfing season is December to March.

2 WHERE TO STAY

Pousadas in Noronha used to be simple, even makeshift affairs, but at some point in the last few years Brazil's movie-star glitterati and their attendant national media discovered the island. Supply and demand have gone seriously out of whack, and prices everywhere have zoomed up into the red-line zone that economists label "just plain stupid." There is no longer anywhere inexpensive to stay on Noronha, but on a desert island in the middle of the Atlantic, there's not much you can do about it.

The pousadas listed below, while not inexpensive, at least offer something different or special. Given demand on the island they may well be booked. If so, try the **Dolphin Hotel** (© 085/3619-1100; www.dolphinhotel.tur.br), which offers small, clean rooms and a pool for R$625 a night, or **Pousada Sueste** (© 085/3619-1164; www.pousada sueste.com.br), which has a small pool and a view down to Sueste Bay, plus small, clean rooms with smaller bathrooms for R$350 a night.

The prices listed are for the high season—January through February and July through September, plus all holidays. In low season—March through June and October through December—most pousadas lower their prices by about 20% to 25%.

VERY EXPENSIVE

Pousada Maravilha ★★★   This brand-new hotel is built with exquisite taste in a Japanese-inspired style. Guests can stay either in self-contained bungalows (recommended) or in the main pousada building (not). The bungalows feature a spacious veranda with hammock and deck chairs, while inside are tile floors, a vaulted ceiling, and a king-size four-poster bed with firm mattress and crisp white linens. Bathrooms are large and lovely, with his-and-her sinks and mirrors, acres of counter space, and large hot showers. Rooms in the main building still feature tasteful decor, king-size futon-style beds, and lovely bathrooms, but are less spacious and luxurious, while almost just as expensive. The small "infinite-horizon" pool has a deck with gorgeous views down to Baía Sueste.

BR-363 s/n, Sueste, Fernando de Noronha, 53990-000 PE. ©/fax **081/3619-0028.** www.pousada maravilha.com.br. 8 units. R$1,910 bungalow; R$1,610 deluxe room. Children 6 and under stay free in parent's room. DC, MC, V. Free parking. **Amenities:** Restaurant; bar; pool; sauna. *In room:* A/C, flatscreen TV/DVD, minibar.

EXPENSIVE

Eco Pousada Teju-Açu ★★   Luxury is at least somewhat reconciled with environmental responsibility at these gorgeous self-contained bungalows in a forest setting. Showers in this "Ecopousada" are solar heated, while rain and sink runoff are recycled to water the gardens. Bungalows are light and airy, featuring king-size beds inside and a balcony with hammock outside. The bungalows are built around a small pool with wooden deck offering little shaded nooks for relaxing, and impressive views of Morro do Pico. The hotel restaurant is one of the better ones on the island.

Estrada da Alamoa s/n, Boldró, Fernando de Noronha, 53990-000 PE. © **081/3619-1277.** www.pousada teju.com.br. 12 bungalows. R$954–R$1,029 double. Children 6 and under pay 50% adult rate. AE, DC, MC, V. Free parking. **Amenities:** Restaurant; bar; outdoor pool; sauna. *In room:* A/C, TV/DVD, fridge, free Wi-Fi.

Pousada do Vale ★   Located in a lovely garden area just a short walk from Vila Remédios, the Pousada do Vale offers both quiet isolation and proximity to town. Rooms are bright and reasonably sized, featuring comfortable queen-size beds with good linens and clean and functional bathrooms. The best two rooms are the Marlim, which is somewhat larger and has a sizable balcony with a hammock, and the Golfinho room. The Golfinho is a tail fin smaller, but it also features a balcony and hammock. The two-story "bungalows" are tall and narrow, but bright and airy inside, with hammock-equipped verandas front and back, plus king-size beds and saunas. The beach is but a 250m (820-ft.) stroll away, and the pousada has beach chairs, umbrellas, and towels for its guests. Room rates include breakfast and a light afternoon tea.

Rua Pescador Sérgio Lino 18, Jardim Elizabeth (down the cobblestone street from Vila Remédios), Fernando de Noronha 53990-000 PE. ℂ/fax 081/3619-1293. www.pousadadovale.com. 5 rooms, 2 bungalows. R$630–R$720 double; R$882 bungalow. Children 3 and under stay free in parent's room. Transfer to and from airport included. AE, MC, V. **Amenities:** Restaurant. *In room:* A/C, TV, fridge, minibar, free Wi-Fi.

Solar dos Ventos ★★   These comfortable self-contained bungalows are on a green piece of land with a view down to Baía do Sueste. Each unit features a double and two single beds, a couch, a breakfast table, and a balcony with a hammock. The grounds are nicely landscaped, and each cottage is given a nice bit of space. The only drawback is the location at the far end of the island, a R$25 taxi ride from the restaurants and services in Vila Remédios and the port. But if you have a buggy, it doesn't matter.

Estrada do Sueste s/n, Fernando de Noronha, 53990-000 PE. ℂ 081/3619-1347. Fax 081/3619-1253. www.pousadasolardosventos.com.br. 8 bungalows. R$770 double. Children 11 and under pay 50% adult rate. DC, MC, V. Free parking. *In room:* A/C, TV, minibar.

3 WHERE TO DINE

There is one excellent and authentic restaurant in Noronha (Ecologiku's, below), and then there are the others. For prawns and other seafood, there's **Xica da Silva** in Floresta Nova (ℂ 081/3619-0437; Wed–Sun noon–4pm and 7:30–11:30pm). On the road to the beach at Praia do Boldró there's the new upscale pousada and restaurant **Teju-Açu** (ℂ 081/3619-1277; www.pousadateju.com.br; daily noon–11:30pm), which serves seafood plus the standard Brazilian steak and chicken dishes. **Trattoria di Morena,** Rua Nice Cordeiro 2600, above BR-363 near the school (ℂ 081/3619-1142; Mon–Sat 7–10:30pm), serves good seafood pastas in generous portions. For expensive fine dining, there's the restaurant at the **Pousada Maravilha** (ℂ 081/3619-1290; www.pousada maravilha.com.br; daily noon–3pm and 8–11pm). The menu leans toward Italian-inflected seafood dishes. For coffee and lighter fare, there's **Cacimba Bistrô,** on Praça Eurico Dutra in Vila Remédios (ℂ 081/3619-1200; daily noon–3pm and 6:30–10:30pm).

Ecologiku's ★★ SEAFOOD   The best restaurant on the island bar none, Ecologiku's features six plastic tables with checkered tablecloths on a patio in a garden in the house of the cook and owner. The kitchen specializes in seafood caught and cooked that day—simple but delicious. Lobsters are brought to your table, weighed, then taken back to be boiled, and served slathered in butter. The house special is the Sinfonia Ecologiku, a spiced and tasty hot pot of fish, octopus, shrimp, and sweet lobster, all in a rich seafood broth.

Estrada do Sueste, Sueste. ℂ 081/3619-0031. Main courses R$45–R$75. MC, V. Daily 7–10:30pm. Closed every other Sun.

4 EXPLORING FERNANDO DE NORONHA

Check with the **Projeto Tamar** office as soon as you arrive. If a turtle hatching is in the offing, rearrange your plans to see it—you won't be disappointed.

If your time is limited, find your pousada and then head out on a boat tour to see the island from the water. Go for an afternoon cruise to see the spinner dolphins or just to snorkel. If you have a bit more time, go diving or snorkeling around Baía do Sancho, saving time for a leisurely walk on the beach. Another great way to see the island is to rent a buggy and explore at will (see "Getting Around," above).

HITTING THE BEACHES

Baía do Sueste ★ is a pretty crescent beach with some good snorkeling. It's perfect for children, thanks to its large shallow areas and complete absence of waves. The beach has a snack stand and bathrooms.

Baía do Sancho ★★ is one of the prettiest beaches in all of Brazil. Access is via a series of precarious-looking iron ladders bolted into crevasses that somehow make it down through 30m (100 ft.) of sheer red cliffs. The beach features lovely red-tinged sand, cliffs with nesting seabirds, and crystal-clear blue water perfect for snorkeling.

Praia do Atalaia ★★ is a unique beach on the outer shore of Noronha. A thick shelf of volcanic rock extends halfway through the surf line, providing a bulwark for some quiet natural pools where tropical fish get trapped at low tide. Only 30 people are allowed in per day, and no suntan lotion can be worn when you swim in the pools. Access is through checkpoints monitored by IBAMA (Brazil's environmental agency), either on the trail from Vila do Trinta or the road from Baía do Sueste. If you don't know any better, you can also come in (as I did) on the uncontrolled trail from Enseada da Caieira. Arrive when the tide's coming in, and you can stand immersed to your waist by the outer edge of the rock shelf as huge waves come rolling in, only to smash themselves to harmlessness on the thick volcanic rock. It's reckless but a lot of fun.

The **surf beaches** are all on the inshore side of the island, facing back toward the Brazilian mainland. From west to east they are **Cacimba do Padre, Praia do Bode, Praia do Boldró, Praia da Conceição, Praia do Meio,** and **Praia do Cachorro.** Most have one or two small *barracas* (beach kiosks). They're good places to hang out for a morning or afternoon. Be careful swimming, and keep an eye on the shore. These beaches have currents that sweep parallel to the shoreline; it's easy to get carried along.

OUTDOOR ACTIVITIES & WATERSPORTS

DIVING ★★★ Walk into any dive shop throughout Brazil and they'll have a poster of Fernando de Noronha. It's the best place for diving in Brazil, and one of the better spots in the world. Water temperature is a constant 28°C (82°F), and especially in the dry season, underwater visibility approaches almost 30m (100 ft.). Underwater there's a wide variety of stunning sea life: rays of all types (mantas are not uncommon); sea turtles; lemon sharks and reef sharks; clownfish; and large schools of anthias, surgeonfish, parrotfish, and sweetlips. The coral formations are only average, but thanks to the island's volcanic heritage you'll come across numerous caves, including a number of terrific swim-throughs.

The only drawback to diving on Noronha is the tight control. You are not allowed to dive except with one of the island's three dive companies. All three companies have implemented a system in which four divers are shepherded underwater by a dive instructor. Exploring on your own is not possible.

Far and away the best diving outfit on the island is **Atlantis Divers,** Caixa Postal 20, in Vila Remédios (© **081/3619-1371,** or in Natal 084/3206-8840; www.atlantisnoronha. com.br); a distant second best is **Aguas Claras,** Alameda do Boldró s/n (© **081/3619-1225;** www.aguasclaras-fn.com.br).

For day use, **Atlantis** has a fleet of custom-built catamarans, all new and specially built for diving. Atlantis also recently inaugurated a live-aboard catamaran—the *Atlantis Voyager,* which cruises the best reefs, islands, and wrecks off the Brazilian coast. Aguas Claras uses 12-man open zodiacs or a converted fishing boat.

Atlantis charges R$220 for two dives, plus R$76 to rent a wet suit, BCD (buoyancy control device), and regulator. With the mandatory R$15 IBAMA tax, the total for two dives comes to R$311. Prices at Aguas Claras are comparable. Morning, afternoon, and night dives are offered. If you've never dived, both companies offer one-on-one escorted baptism dives for about R$270 plus IBAMA tax. You can also take a 5-day course to get your PADI diving certificate, for about R$1,000. Atlantis also offers nitrox courses and scooter courses, and for experienced divers, the Atlantis launch is available for custom excursions.

DOLPHIN-WATCHING ★★ Spinner dolphins congregate on Noronha in numbers virtually unmatched anywhere else. The best (and least obtrusive) way to see them is from the **cliff-top lookout** above Baía dos Golfinhos (Dolphin Bay). Monday to Saturday from 5:30am until sunset a researcher from the nonprofit **Projeto Golfinho Rotador** (© **081/3619-1846;** www.golfinhorotador.org.br) is on hand to answer questions and pass out binoculars between regular 15-minute counts of dolphin activity. Note that from 5:30 to 7am, the Projeto's binoculars are reserved for those who have come on the paid "Mirante de Golfinhos" tour offered by **Atalaia Noronha** (© **081/3619-1328;** www.atalaia-noronha.com.br). Cost is R$40. The dolphins usually arrive around 6am and depart between 3 and 5pm on their nightly feeding trip around the island. They're most active around sunrise, when they're just coming off an evening's feeding. In dry season the bay will have between 500 and 1,200 dolphins jumping and spinning about. In the wet season the bay will have between 5 and 300 dolphins. The bay itself is off-limits to all but accredited scientists.

Boat tours (see "Boat Tours & Operators," below) now cruise past the edge of Dolphin Bay, hoping to be surrounded by a spinner school coming out for the day. The afternoon tours offer the best odds of spotting dolphins.

HIKING Note that on trails within the national park you may be required to register with IBAMA and bring along a local guide. This has long been park policy; it's just never been enforced. Recently, however, the park has mooted plans to outsource the guiding and enforcing to tourism operators (mostly as a way of generating more revenue). A guide isn't really necessary, but if you want one contact **ACITUR,** the Ecotourism Guides Association of Fernando de Noronha, located at the TAMAR offices on Avenida Boldró (© **081/3619-1399**), or book one of the tours through **LocBuggy** (© **081/3619-1490;** www.locbuggy.com.br) or **Atalaia Noronha** (© **081/3366-6250;** www.atalaia-noronha. com.br). If you don't, your best bet is to simply show up at the trail head. Odds are no one will complain.

The **Trilha do Capim-açu,** which starts near the Dolphin Bay lookout and runs 7km (4¼ miles) as far as the lighthouse on Ponta da Sapata, is really not worth taking. The trail runs through dense forest from beginning to end, with only one small viewpoint on

the very first ridge. A much better plan is to hike along or above **Praia do Leáo.** The
territory is open so you can always see where you're going. More importantly, the beach
is wild and beautiful, and the views amazing. If you're happy jumping between rocks, you
can also reach the lighthouse on Ponta de Sapata on this route. One other good but tricky
trail runs from **Enseada da Caieira** near the port along the outer coast over a couple of
tall rocky headlands to **Praia de Atalaia.** For an easier hike with worthwhile views, try
the 2.5km (1½-mile) walk from the **Dolphin Bay Lookout** along the cliff top to **Baía
do Sancho.** Another nice walk—best done at low tide—goes from **Praia do Boldró**
along the beach east to **Praia do Cachorro** below Vila Remédios. This 2.5km (1½-mile)
walk features nature signs posted by IBAMA, but whatever was on them has long since
been erased by the sea.

HORSEBACK RIDING   There aren't any huge long beaches upon which to gallop on
Noronha, but there are some good trails, back roads, and shorter beaches to explore.
Three people offer horseback riding on the island: **Samuel** (✆ **081/3619-1141**), **Ron-
aldo** (✆ **081/3619-1250**), and **Valter** (✆ **081/3619-1764**). Going with them is a
matter of calling, saying what you're interested in, and seeing what's possible. Cost is
around R$35 per hour per person

KAYAKING ★   Tours depart Porto Santo Antonio at 9am and 3pm for a 3-hour paddle
along the island's sheltered coast, with a stop to snorkel at Praia de Conceição. A small
motorboat tags along with water and snacks. Cost is R$125. Call **Edlene** at **Remos da
Ilha** (✆ **081/3619-1914**).

MOUNTAIN BIKING   In Vila Remédios, **Pousada Solymar** (✆ **081/3619-1965;**
www.pousadasolymar.com.br) rents mountain bikes for R$30 per day.

PROJETO TAMAR ★★★   The Brazilian sea turtle conservation organization, Tamar
(Av. do Boldró s/n; ✆ **081/3619-1171**), has a site on Noronha with a shop, small lecture
theater, and cafe. It's worth checking in every day or so to see if any turtle nests are about
to hatch. Watching hundreds of newly hatched turtles scramble into the surf is an experience not to be missed. The shop is open Monday through Friday from 9am to 11pm,
Saturday and Sunday from 9am to 1pm and 3 to 11pm. Nightly nature talks in Portuguese start at 8:30pm.

SNORKELING ★   A number of operators offer organized snorkeling tours (see "Boat
Tours & Operators," below). For do-it-yourselfers, **Santuário** (✆ **081/3619-1247**), in
the port of Santo Antonio, rents masks and snorkels for R$18 per day for a mask, snor-
kel, and fins. Baía do Sancho and Baía do Sueste both offer good snorkeling. Tours are
also offered by **Alquimista Tour** (✆ **081/3619-1283;** www.alquimistanoronha.com.br).

SURFING ★   The surf season in Noronha runs from **December to March,** the opposite of that in the rest of Brazil. (Outside of this time there are *no surfable waves.*) Surfing
takes place not on the outer shore beaches, which are steep and rocky, but on the sandier
beaches facing Brazil's Atlantic coast. The best surf beaches are **Cachorro, Cacimba do
Padre, Bode, Boldró, Conceição,** and **Meio.** Waves average 2m (6½ ft.), but sometimes
reach as high as 5m (17 ft.). Bring your board and the gear you need. There are no surf
shops on the island, but **Pousada Solymar** (✆ **081/3619-1965;** www.pousadasolymar.
com.br) does rent boards.

ISLAND TOURS

TOUR OPERATORS   Formerly just a buggy rental company, **LocBuggy** (✆ **081/3619-
1490;** www.locbuggy.com.br) is evolving into a full-service tour agency, currently offering

a variety of tours including a dawn trip to see the spinner dolphins, a historic walk, an island tour, several hikes, trips to Atalaia beach, and planasubbing. Reservations can be made in advance via the company website. A similar range of tours is offered by **Alquimista Tour** (© **081/3619-1283;** www.alquimistanoronha.com.br).

BOAT TOURS & OPERATORS   You have several options for getting out on the water. You can go on a 3- to 4-hour **dolphin/snorkeling cruise.** Tours depart Porto Santo Antonio and run along the shore of Noronha, looking at the steep cliffs and seabird rookeries on Ilha do Meio and Ilha do Rata, before heading down to cruise the edge of Dolphin Bay, hoping to be surrounded by a spinner school coming out for the day. The 3-hour tours go as far as Ponta da Sapata and include a stop for snorkeling in Baía do Sancho. Afternoon tours have better luck with dolphins. Morning tours focus on snorkeling. The other alternative is a **planasub tour,** a strange but fun activity in which you get towed at a fast speed behind a boat holding on to a piece of shaped plastic. By tilting your board up or down you can dive way down and then shoot back up when your breath runs out. In the clear water it's a bit like gliding through a science fiction film (*Fantastic Voyage,* for example).

Abatur, in the building across the street from the port (© **081/3619-1360**), uses converted 7.5m (25-ft.) wooden fishing boats. They offer a dolphin-spotting and snorkeling cruise for R$70 per person, with departures daily at 8:30am and 1pm. Abatur's 2-hour planasub trips cost R$70 and depart daily at 9am and 1:30pm. They take six people, and each person is guaranteed 30 minutes of planasubbing. All prices include transfer to and from the port (cash only). Abatur also has moonlight cruises and tours to the offshore island, but these depend on weather and demand.

Santuário, on the dock at Porto de Santo Antonio (© **081/3619-1247**), offers planasubbing, snorkeling, and dolphin spotting on a modern speedboat. Planasub tours last 2 hours, depart at 9am and 2pm, and cost R$75 per person. Snorkeling tours leave in the morning and afternoon on demand. Cost is R$75 per person. Dolphin tours leave in the afternoon. Cost is R$70 per person. Cost includes transfer to and from the port.

Similar tours (often with a slightly different name) are offered by **LocBuggy** (© **081/** 3619-1490; www.locbuggy.com.br) and **Alquimista Tour** (© **081/3619-1283;** www.alquimistanoronha.com.br).

OTHER THINGS TO SEE & DO

In Vila Remédios, the most impressive structure is the **Forte dos Remédios,** built by the Portuguese in 1737. It's a wonderful crumbling ruin, with old cannons half-buried in the dirt and ramparts on the edge of collapse. Extending from the fort are a number of old stone roads, many built by convict labor. One leads back to the Vila Remédios plaza, a steep cobblestone square topped by the pretty yellow-and-white **Igreja Nossa Senhora dos Remédios,** built in 1772. Farther uphill is a bright red colonial building known as the **Palácio São Miguel.** It now serves as the island's administrative headquarters. At the bottom of the hill, a small history museum, the **Memorial Noronhense** (daily 8am– 4pm) shows the history of the island, from its discovery in 1503 by Amerigo Vespucci, through the years when the Dutch, Portuguese, and French all fought for possession, to its years as a political prison and then American army base from the '40s to the '60s.

Florianópolis

Florianópolis, aka the Island of Santa Catarina, is known throughout Brazil for its miles and miles of gorgeous beaches, excellent seafood (oysters especially), and traditional Azorean fishing villages. Figuring out the names may be the only tricky part of a visit to this most serene of Brazilian beach resorts. Florianópolis, the city, is the capital of the *state* of Santa Catarina. Florianópolis is also located on the *island* of Santa Catarina. Island and city together are usually just referred to as Florianópolis, which people often then shorten to Floripa. Confused? Don't worry, it's the beaches that matter.

The *city* of Florianópolis is small and pleasant but of no real interest except as a jumping-off point to the island's countless beaches.

Brazilians are infatuated with Floripa and flock here en masse in summer. Perhaps Brazilians see in Floripa a model of what their country could be—well-organized, well-run, calm, efficient, and law-abiding. Perhaps in a land with so much tropical exuberance, the opposite becomes exotic. In any case, when Brazilians rave about Florianópolis, they mention the fair-skinned, green-eyed residents, the affluent communities, the quaint Portuguese fishing villages, the pristine and unpolluted beaches.

There is more than enough variety on the island to customize a visit according to your interests. The northeastern part of the island is an urbanized, heavily visited beach scene, particularly in the high summer months of December, January, and February. Farther south in the center of the island there's the Lagoa da Conceição, a large partly salty lagoon partially surrounded by tall sand dunes. Nearby, the small quiet community of Lagoa da Conceição has some of the best restaurants in the region. Just to the east are the beaches of Galheta, Mole, and Joaquina—beautiful, wide, sandy beaches surrounded by lush green hills and blessed with large, surfable waves. Farther south toward Campeche, the beaches become more rugged and almost deserted. Even in the summer you won't find large crowds here. Finally, over to the west side of the island facing the mainland, you will find the quaint Azorean fishing village of Riberão da Ilha, accessible only via a gorgeous, narrow, winding, seaside road offering views of the Baia Sul and the lush hills of the mainland across the bay.

---

1 ESSENTIALS

742km (461 miles) SW of Rio de Janeiro, 488km (303 miles) SW of São Paulo

ARRIVING

BY PLANE   **TAM** (© 048/4002-5700; www.tam.com.br) and **Gol** (© 0300/115-2121; www.voegol.com.br) both have daily flights to Florianópolis from all major cities in Brazil. All flights arrive at **Aeroporto Hercílio Luz** (© 048/3331-4000). Taxis from the airport to the northern beaches (Praia dos Ingleses) cost R$60 to R$70; to the southern part of the island (Campeche) or Lagoa de Conceição, R$50; and to downtown, R$25.

BY BUS   Long-distance buses arrive at the **Rodoviaria Rita Maria,** Av. Paulo Fontes s/n (✆ **048/3212-3100).** **Auto Viação 1001** (✆ **021/4004-5001;** www.autoviacao 1001.com.br) offers daily departures to São Paulo for R$75 to R$115; the trip takes about 10 hours.

CITY/ISLAND LAYOUT

The city of Florianópolis straddles the narrow part of the straight about halfway down the island and is connected to the mainland by two bridges. The oft-photographed, scenic **Hercílio Luz suspension bridge** is currently closed for renovations. The historic downtown sits just a hop and a skip from the small but efficient Rita Maria bus station, the departure and arrival point for all long-distance buses. If you want to do a bit of shopping, just follow the elevated walkway across the main road for a short walk to the Praça XV, one of the city's main squares. The **Rua Felipe Schmit** and the **Rua Cons. Mafra** and its cross streets around the Praça XV are closed to traffic and packed with stores. A bustling indoor market is located at **Av. Paulo Fontees s/n,** almost on the corner of the **Praça Fernando Machado.**

The island itself is long and thin (approx. 70km/43 miles from north to south) and features a number of distinct regions. The most urbanized beaches are those near the northern tip of the island; **Praia dos Ingleses, Canasvieiras,** and **Jurerê** are popular and busy beach destinations in the summer. Farther south, facing the open Atlantic on the east side of the island, are the much less developed beaches of **Praia Mole** and **Joaquina,** and the clothing-optional **Galheta beach.** All are popular with locals on the weekends. The **Lagoa da Conceição** forms the center of the island. This large lagoon is the year-round nightlife and dining hub, attracting both locals and visitors. The southern part of the island is divided into two regions, the beaches (on the east side, facing the ocean) and **Riberão da Ilha** (on the west side, opposite the mainland). The ocean-facing beaches such as **Campeche** and **Armação** are mostly undeveloped, and even in the peak of the tourist season (Dec–Feb) it's easy to find a near-deserted stretch of sand. Farther south toward the tip of the island, the beaches of **Lagoinha do Leste** and **Naufragados** are only accessible by a short hike. Facing toward the mainland, **Riberão da Ilha** features Portuguese (actually Açorean [fishermen from the Azores]) settlements that have been beautifully preserved.

Access to the various parts is by well-paved state highways. From downtown Florianópolis there are three main roads: The **SC-401** goes north to the beaches of **Ingleses** and **Canasvieiras.** The **SC-404** cuts across the center of the island to the restaurant and nightlife area of Lagoa. The **SC-405** dips south toward **Ribeirão da Ilha.** A fourth highway, the **SC-406,** runs along the eastern side of the island, connecting to the SC-405 in the south and the SC-401 near the northern beaches.

ⓘ Tips Getting Around in Florianópolis: Rent a Car

To make the most of your visit you really need a car, allowing you to explore the more remote beaches and towns at your own pace. Floripa's roads are in great shape, speed limits and regulations are strictly obeyed, the island is easy to navigate, and you can safely park almost anywhere. Just remove all valuables from the vehicle when parking. See car-rental information in "Fast Facts: Florianópolis," below.

ACCOMMODATIONS ■
Ingleses Praia Hotel **2**
Pousada das Palmeiras **6**
Pousada da Vigia **1**
Pousada Penareia **15**
Pousada Vila Tamarindo
  Eco Lodge **13**
Praia Mole Eco Village **4**
Quinta das Videiras **10**

DINING ◆
Bar do Arante **16**
Bistrô D'Acampora **3**
Bistro Isadora Duncan **9**
Mar Massas **8**
Ostradamus **14**
Patagonia **11**
Pizzaria Basilico **5**
Thai Restaurante **12**
Villa Magionne **7**

Praia Lagoinha
Praia Ponta das Canas
Praia Cachoeira do Bom Jesus
Praia Brava
Praia Canasvieiras
Praia do Forte
Praia Jurerê
Praia Ingleses
Praia Daniela
Praia Sambaqui
Praia Sto. Antônio de Lisboa
Praia Moçambique
Praia Cacupé
Baía Norte
SANTA CATARINA
Praia Barra da Lagoa
BARRA DA LAGOA
FLORIANÓPOLIS
Lagoa da Conceição
Praia Mole
SÃO JOSÉ
CANTO DA LAGOA
Praia Joaquina
ATLANTIC OCEAN
Baía Sul
Aeroporto Hercílio Luz
Praia Campeche
Ilha do Campeche

Beach
262 Federal Road
339 State Road

0 — 3 mi
0 — 3 km
N

Praia Ribeirão da Ilha
ILHA DE SANTA CATARINA
Lagoa do Peri
Praia Morro das Pedras
Praia Armação
Praia Matadeiro
Praia Lagoinha do Leste
Praia Tapera
Praia Pântano do Sul
Praia Solidão
Praia Caieira da Barra do Sul
Praia Saquinho
Praia Naufragados

ATLANTIC OCEAN
Manaus   Belém
Amazon
Natal
BRAZIL
Recife
Brasília✴
Salvador
São Paulo   Rio de Janeiro
Florianópolis
500 mi
500 km

BY BUS   Local bus service on the island is slow and infrequent. In Florianópolis a vehicle is strongly recommended.

BY TAXI   Taxis are easily found in the city or at the airport, and hard to find elsewhere. To call a cab from anywhere on the island dial © **197** or call 048/3240-6009. Taxi fares add up; a one-way ride from Campeche to the bus station costs R$50. After two or three rides it's better to rent a car.

VISITOR INFORMATION

The state tourism board has an English-language website at www.santacatarinaturismo.com.br. The **main tourist information center** is in downtown Florianópolis, Praça XV de Novembro s/n, Centro (© **048/3244-5822**), open Monday to Friday, 8am to 6pm.

(Fast Facts   **Florianópolis**

Banks   **Banco do Brasil,** Praça XV de Novembro 321 (© **048/3216-6500**), is open Monday through Friday, 10am to 4pm, and has a 24-hour ATM. The **HSBC** is located on Rua Felipe Schmidt 376, Centro (© **048/3221-9000**).

Car Rental   Daily rental charges with unlimited mileage start at R$90 for a Fiat Palio (the smallest two-door Fiat) without air-conditioning. Insurance costs R$30 per day. Off-season discounts can cut the costs by 40% to 50%. Agencies at the airport include **Hertz** (© **048/3236-9955**), **Unidas** (© **0800/121-121**), and **Localiza** (© **0800/979-2000**); **Le Mans** (© **048/3222-9999**) will deliver and pick up from anywhere, including the airport and bus station.

Hospital   For medical needs, try **Hospital Governador Celso Ramos,** Rua Irmã Benvarda s/n, Centro (© **048/3251-7000**).

Weather   Florianópolis has a temperate climate; summers (Nov–Mar) are hot and sunny but fall and winter (May–Sept) can be downright chilly, with temperatures falling below 10°C (50°F).

---

2 WHERE TO STAY

The island offers great variety, everything from small pousadas to five-star resorts and high-rise hotels. The northern part of the island is very busy and urban in the high summer season. Out of season, restaurants and shops close and the area feels a touch dreary. Halfway down the east coast of the island, Praia Mole offers excellent accommodations in one of the nicest beach areas, only a short drive from Lagoa's restaurants and nightlife options. In the south, Campeche offers quiet accommodations on a beach that is often deserted and great for long walks. Note that the rates listed do not cover holidays such as New Year's, Carnaval, and Easter, when hotels and pousadas sell packages at a hefty markup, usually with a minimum stay of 3 nights.

NORTH ISLAND

Ingleses Praia Hotel ★ **(Kids**   Right on the beach, the Ingleses Praia Hotel offers a large outdoor pool and playground, making it perfect for kids. Deluxe rooms feature at least a partial ocean view, while the super-deluxe rooms and suites offer a full ocean view. The super-deluxe units are the best value: For a little extra (R$25 or so) you get a flat with full kitchen and small den that can accommodate four people comfortably. For luxury, book an oceanfront suite. These offer room for eight, with two bedrooms and two bathrooms as well as a sitting room and kitchen. The hotel is within walking distance of restaurants and shops in Praia dos Ingleses. Check the website for packages in the low season: a 3-night stay can cost R$95 per night.

Rua Dom João Becker 447, Praia dos Ingleses, Florianópolis, 88058-600 SC. ⊘/fax **048/3261-3300.** www. inglesespraia.com.br. 110 units. Apr–Nov R$195 double deluxe or super deluxe, R$500 suite; Dec–Mar R$385 deluxe or super deluxe, R$1,050 suite. Extra person R$75. Children 5 and under stay free in parent's room. AE, DC, MC, V. Free parking. **Amenities:** Restaurant; bar; exercise room; Jacuzzi; 2 pools (indoor and outdoor); limited room service. *In room:* A/C, TV, Internet, minibar.

Pousada da Vigia ★★ Literally on the northern tip of the island, this lovely pousada has one of the finest beach views around. All but one of the rooms feature an ocean view and all but one of the nine oceanview rooms come with a lovely private veranda. The rooms are beautifully appointed (though a tad on the small side) and the pousada offers top-notch amenities such as a heated indoor pool, beach service, sitting room with home theater, and spa treatments. The two best rooms are suite nos. 9 and 10. These feature a master bedroom with king-size bed, a deluxe bathroom with jetted tub for two, a living room with home theater and DVD, and a spacious deck with sauna, barbecue, and outdoor Jacuzzi. To reach the pousada from the airport, take the SC-401 to Canasvieiras, then follow the signs to Lagoinha. The pousada also offers a transfer service if contacted ahead of time.

Rua Con. Walmor Castro 291, Lagoinha, Florianópolis, 88056-770 SC. ⓒ **048/3284-1789.** Fax 048/3284-1108. www.pousadavigia.com.br. 10 units. Mar–Nov R$250–R$375 double, R$540 luxo suite; Nov–Feb R$300–R$560 double, R$830 luxo suite. Children 2 and under stay free in parent's room. AE, DC, MC, V. Free parking. **Amenities:** Restaurant; bar; exercise room; Jacuzzi; small indoor heated pool; limited room service. *In room:* A/C, TV, Internet, minibar.

MID-ISLAND

Pousada das Palmeiras ★ More Bali than Florianópolis, the Palmeiras offers high-end accommodations in a lush tropical setting. The six units are all beautiful split-level cabanas with verandas set in a lovely garden. All come with fully equipped kitchens, high ceilings, king-size beds, DVD and CD players, and views of the lagoon and gardens. All are charmingly furnished with lots of wood and bamboo, bright colors, and interesting artwork. The units *Ar, Bambu,* and *Lagoa* feature a Jacuzzi tub for two. The two-story *Bungalow Mar* is the largest unit and features a full kitchen, sitting room and Jacuzzi tub with fabulous views. Just a few minutes from the main village, the location is ideal for those who like to go out at night.

Rua Laurindo da Silveira 2720, Canto da Lagoa, Florianópolis, 88056-770 SC. ⓒ **048/3232-6267** or 9962-2900. www.pousadadaspalmeiras.com.br. 6 units. Mar–Nov R$380–R$420 double; Dec–Feb R$545–R$580 double. Extra person add R$75–R$125. Children 2 and under stay free in parent's room. AE, DC, MC, V. Free parking. *In room:* A/C, fan, TV/DVD, Internet, kitchen, no phone.

Praia Mole Eco Village ★★ **Kids** Set astride a piece of land between Praia Mole and the lagoon, this large hotel features beautiful large trees and lush gardens with tennis courts, a soccer field, and orchid park. Rooms are spread out over several buildings. The smallest building, overlooking the beach, has the feel of a small European seaside hotel. When reserving a room, make sure to request a *frente mar* and not a *vista mar;* the latter one has only a partial ocean view. The central building sits in the middle of the property, close to the swimming pool and leisure area. Request a *superior* apartment as it features a veranda overlooking the garden. The third large building, the Solar, sits closer toward the lagoon and rooms have either lagoon or garden views; in this building all rooms feature a veranda. Finally, for those who want a bit more privacy and space, there are 18 bungalows, with one or two bedrooms. These all have large balconies with views of the garden and lagoon.

Estrada Geral da Barra da Lagoa 2001, Florianópolis, 88062-970 SC. © **048/3239-7500.** Fax 048/3232-5482. www.praiamole.com.br. 98 units. May–Nov R$150–R$216 standard or lagoon-view double, R$250 oceanview or bungalow double; Dec–Apr R$290–R$400 standard or lagoon-view double, R$435 oceanview or bungalow double. Extra person add R$75. Children 5 and under stay free in parent's room. AE, DC, MC, V. Free parking. **Amenities:** Restaurant; bar; exercise room; Jacuzzi; large indoor heated pool; limited room service; tennis courts; watersports. *In room:* A/C, TV, hair dryer, Internet, minibar.

Quinta das Videiras ★★   The perfect spot for a romantic getaway, the newest boutique hotel in Florianópolis offers high-end comforts and colonial charm, in a quiet spot in the restaurant hub of Lagoa. Rooms come in luxo, plus, and premium. All offer high ceilings, parquet floors, top-quality bed linen, and a decor of colonial-era antiques, all carefully selected, cataloged, and arranged by the hotel owner. Luxo rooms have double beds, while plus and premium offer queen-size beds and a bit more space. The premium level San Giovese room has its own private *ofuro* (Japanese bath), on a small back patio. Though you wouldn't know it, the lovely "old" building is a new-built replica, giving it both charm and modern functionality, especially in the glittering new bathrooms. The master suite has a king-size four-poster bed plus an *ofuro* in the room. A full breakfast is served in the room, or in an outdoor solarium by the pool.

Rua Alfonso Luis Borba 113, Lagoa da Conceição, Florianópolis, 88062-040 SC. © **048/3232-3005.** www.quintadasvideiras.com.br. 10 units. Mar–Nov R$270–R$330 double, R$580 master suite; Dec–Feb R$310–R$440 double, R$610 master suite. AE, DC, MC, V. Free parking. **Amenities:** Small outdoor pool; small spa. *In room:* A/C, TV/DVD, free Wi-Fi.

SOUTH ISLAND

Pousada Penareia ★★   In a beautiful spot overlooking Armação Beach, this pousada is perfect for active, adult travelers. The owners are happy to lend you an inflatable kayak, soccer ball, or bike, or provide you with hiking tips. Inside, all rooms are bright and spacious; the beds are very comfortable, and even the standard rooms feature a private veranda with a hammock (but no air-conditioning). The special rooms are a bigger and come with air-conditioning. The top-level deluxe rooms come with a Jacuzzi, a DVD and CD player, and a large veranda with a barbecue. A few steps down from the pousada is a wonderful deck overlooking the beach, the perfect sunset spot!

Rua Hermes Guedes da Fonseca 207, Praia da Armação, Florianópolis, 88063-000 SC. © **048/3338-1616.** www.pousadapenareia.com.br. 12 units. Mar–Nov R$150–R$190 standard or special double, R$190 deluxe double; Nov–Feb R$200–R$240 standard or special double, R$270 deluxe double. Extra person add R$40. AE, DC, MC, V. Free parking. No children 11 and under. *In room:* A/C or fan, TV, fridge.

Pousada Vila Tamarindo Eco Lodge ★★   This lovely small pousada is just off Praia do Campeche, one of the nicest beaches of the southern part of the island. The beach itself is protected (no construction is allowed on its waterfront), so even in high season it's relatively empty. The 13 apartments are pleasantly furnished in bright colors and decorated with local artwork. All have ocean-facing verandas; if you leave your door open you can fall asleep to the sounds of the surf. The ground-floor "garden" suites have a fan but no air-conditioning. The first floor "ocean" rooms feature air-conditioning and better ocean views. For families or couples traveling together there are two two-bedroom apartments. The pousada also has two master suites offering a bit more luxury: Both feature a spacious sitting room and larger veranda. The "Eu & Voce" (you and I) suite comes with an *ofuro* for two facing out toward the ocean. ***Note:*** The region around Campeche is very quiet and a car is required to get around to restaurants and attractions.

Av. Campeche 1836, Praia do Campeche, Florianópolis, 88063-000 SC. ✆ **048/3237-3464.** Fax 048/3338-2185. www.tamarindo.com.br. 15 units. Mar–Nov R$150 garden double, R$190 ocean double, R$280–R$380 master suite double; Nov–Feb R$210 garden double, R$290 ocean double, R$380–R$480 master suite double. Extra person add R$70. Children 8 and under stay free in parent's room. AE, DC, MC, V. Free parking. **Amenities:** Outdoor pool. *In room:* A/C or fan, TV, minibar, no phone.

3 WHERE TO DINE

There are two seafood specialties for which Florianópolis is especially well known. The first is *sequencia de camarão* (shrimp in sequence), which consists of a number of shrimp dishes served one after another. Normally, there's *casquinha de siri* (baked crabmeat), followed by steamed shrimp, breaded shrimp, garlic shrimp, and then a fish filet with shrimp sauce. The other Floripa specialty is the oyster. Most oysters served in Brazil come from the area around Riberão da Ilha. Here at the source they're fresher and cheaper (R$12 a dozen). Always call ahead for opening hours during the low season, as many restaurants adjust their times during the quiet period.

NORTH ISLAND

Bistrô d'Acampora ★★★ FRENCH/ITALIAN   This cozy dining room–cum–art gallery makes for an intimate dining experience. The menu varies constantly, but normally includes three salads, five main courses, and three desserts, all made with fresh local ingredients and a mix of French and Italian preparation. Among salads, the mango stuffed with crabmeat on a bed of greens is a longtime favorite. Main courses can be *trés* French, such as the confit de canard or a sea creature of some sort (catch of the day, local oysters, prawns) in a bisque sauce served on Moroccan couscous. Desserts include the signature chocolate tort with pecans and crème anglaise. The restaurant also has a fantastic wine list with over 400 labels, including everything from outrageous R$1,000 bottles to many affordable options in the R$60-to-R$100 range.

SC 401 to Canasvieiras, Km 10 (Santo Antônio de Lisboa), on the northwest side of the island. ✆ **048/3235-1073.** www.dacampora.com.br. Reservations required. 3-course meal (without wine) approx. R$125. DC, MC, V. Tues–Sat 8pm–midnight.

LAGOA

Bistro Isadora Duncan ★★   BRAZILIAN/SEAFOOD   The perfect place for a romantic dinner, this lovely antiques-furnished house offers a tiny handful of tables in a dining room by a fireplace or on a veranda overlooking the lake. The menu is kept fairly small, offering a handful of seafood and meat dishes. In the land of the prawn you can't go wrong with the *camarões abençoados* (blessed prawns), served in a creamy Gorgonzola sauce with sautéed potatoes, or the *camarões encantados* (enchanted prawns), prawns flambéed in orange juice, served with wild rice. And if it is a romantic dinner, why not start off with a plate of local oysters au gratin? The wine list offers a few reasonably priced selections from Argentina and Chile.

Rod. Jornalista Manuel de Menezes 2658, Fortaleza da Barra. ✆ **048/3232-7210.** www.bistroisadora duncan.com.br. Reservations recommended on weekends and in high season. Main courses R$75–R$125. MC, V. Mon–Sat 7pm–midnight.

Mar Massas ★★ ITALIAN/SEAFOOD   This cozy Italian cantina sits perched on a hillside overlooking the southern end of the lagoon. The atmosphere is casual with paper place mats, checkered tablecloths, and chianti bottles for decorations. The menu offers a wonderful range of top-quality seafood pastas such as the *tagliatelle a Don Edson* with prawns, mushrooms, and a mustard-cream sauce, or the *tortelli Alleluia,* stuffed with sweet pumpkin and served with a generous helping of grilled prawns in pesto. Even the *piccolo*-size (small) plates are generous enough to serve two small appetites, especially if you are having an appetizer and dessert.

Rua Laurindo Januário da Silveira 3843, Morro do Badejo, Lagoa. (*©* **048/3232-6109.** Main courses R$75–R$100. DC, MC. Tues–Fri 6pm–midnight; Sat–Sun noon–11:30pm; Jan–Apr also Mon 6pm–midnight.

Patagonia ★★ STEAK   Large and succulent cuts of Argentine beef, lovingly prepared, are served in large sunny room with a peekaboo view of the lake. The highlight of the menu is the *bife de chorizo,* a thick contra-filet, served with red potatoes sliced and fried in extra-virgin olive oil. The wine list (surprise) hardly ventures forth from Argentina, leans heavily to reds, and offers both affordable and insanely expensive options. Don't come here if you're in a hurry. Patangonia's steaks take a minimum of 45 minutes to prepare.

Rua Laurindo Januário da Silveira 1233, Lagoa. (*©* **048/3232-5679.** Main courses R$50–R$75. AE, DC, MC, V. Mon–Sat 7pm–midnight; Sun 1–10:30pm.

Pizzaria Basilico ★★ PIZZA   The best place on the island for pizza, Basilico serves them in 30 different varieties, all thin-crusted and delicious. Order a large and you can choose three different flavors. The options include the Portuguesa, with ham, slices of boiled egg, and olives; the ricotta, with mozzarella, tomato sauce, fresh ricotta, and slices of tomato; or the spicy Maçárico, with tomato sauce, sausage, hot peppers, and onions. The patio sprawls out in several directions, and a roaring fireplace adds much-needed warmth on chilly evenings.

Rua Laurindo Januário da Silveira 647, Lagoa. (*©* **048/3232-1129.** Main courses R$30–R$60. MC. Daily 7pm–midnight.

Thai Restaurante ★★ THAI   A lovely wood room lit by candlelight, where traditional Thai favorites—accented with Floripa seafood—are served with style an panache. The menu runs from pad Thai, green curries of beef or chicken, red curries with locally caught fish and cashews, octopus in a Panang curry, or jumbo prawns grilled in an orange-and-ginger sauce. The wine list offers several good Argentine whites at a reasonable price. As the new "in" spot on the island, the bar is often graced by the local glitterati, sipping a drink, snacking, and being seen.

Estrada Geral de Joaquina 555, Lagoa da Conceção. (*©* **048/3232-4181.** www.bistroisadoraduncan.com. br. Reservations accepted. Main courses R$45–R$75. MC, V. Mon–Sat 7pm–midnight.

Villa Magionne ★★★ MEDITERRANEAN   Villa Mangionne is in a lovely small house overlooking a garden by the lagoon; you literally dine in the owner's living room. The menu includes salads, pastas, steak, and risottos. Make sure you start with one of the salads; the Moroccan salad is a delicious heap of crunchy lettuce hearts topped with toasted almonds, orange slices, and an orange vinaigrette. For a main course, stick with pasta. All are made from scratch with the freshest ingredients. Our favorite is the *ravioli de anatra,* a freshly made ravioli stuffed with tender duck served in a broth seasoned with mushrooms and cream. Also good is the *tonnarielli al filetto,* pasta served with a generous portion of filet

mignon strips flambéed in bourbon. The scrumptious desserts are made in-house. The *torta* **481**
romeo ande giuliett is a guava compote twist on the traditional cheesecake.

Rua Canto da Amizade 273, Canto da Lagoa. © **048/3232-6859.** www.restaurantevillamaggioni.com.br.
Reservations required. Main courses R$65–R$95. DC, MC. Mon–Fri 7pm–midnight; Sat noon–5pm and
7pm–midnight; Sun noon–5pm. In low season closed Mon–Tues.

SOUTH ISLAND

The southern part of the island, especially around Riberão da Ilha, is thick with oyster
farms. Looking out over the water you'll see the white floats that mark the locations of
the baskets that contain the various-size oysters. Numerous restaurants in this part of the
island serve up fresh oysters.

Bar do Arante ★ SEAFOOD   Located smack on the beach in Pantano do Sul, this
most authentic of local eateries is known for its seafood buffet, its delicious seafood
pastels (try the *pastel de berbigão*—steaming small mollusks wrapped in a pastry shell),
and the thousands of messages, notes, and poems festooning the walls and rafters. The
note-leaving tradition dates from the '70s, when visiting campers would leave messages
for friends on the walls. Inspired by shots of Arante's free homemade *cachaça* (another
tradition that continues), the utilitarian "behind dune number 3" note soon morphed
into art and poetry. Try a shot yourself, and release the poet inside.

Rua Abelardo Otacilio Gomes 254, Pantano do Sul. © **048/3237-7022.** Reservations not accepted. Main
courses R$25–R$65. MC, V. Daily 11:30am–midnight.

Ostradamus ★ SEAFOOD   This large waterfront restaurant serves up bivalves in a
variety of delicious ways: plain, steamed, grilled and topped with a béchamel sauce,
smoked, or served with garlic and olive oil. All are freshly harvested from the farms just
outside the restaurant's door. The menu also offers prawns, squid, clams, and grilled fish.
On Thursday night, the kitchen serves up oysters prepared in over 30 different ways—a
feast for oyster lovers.

Rodoviaria Baldicero Filomeno 7640, Riberão da Ilha. © **048/3337-5711.** www.ostradamus.com.br.
Reservations recommended. Main courses R$55–R$95. DC, MC, V. Tues–Sat noon–11pm; Sun noon–6pm.

4 EXPLORING FLORIANÓPOLIS

BEACHES

Florianópolis's main attraction is the more than 100 beaches scattered across the island.
Each has its own character. Starting clockwise from the northern part of the island, the
most visited beaches are **Daniela** ★, **Canasvieiras, Jurerê,** and **Praia dos Ingleses.**
Daniela, Canasvieiras, and Jurerê lie on the bay side of the island and have pleasant, calm
waters with almost no waves. Praia dos Ingleses faces the open ocean and often has
rougher surf. Daniela is the quietest of the four. The other three are very urbanized and
packed in the summer months when tourists flock here from all over Brazil. Jurerê is
popular with Brazilian celebrities, many of whom own houses or condos in the exclusive
subdivisions.

The northern part of the island has some places to escape the crowds (relatively speaking). At the very northern tip of the peninsula in between Praia dos Ingleses and Canasvieiras sits **Lagoinha** ★★, a lovely small beach backed by a small fishing village. This is

one of the best sunset spots on the island. A short drive south of Ingleses one finds **Praia do Santinho** ★, a small and pretty beach with a large beach resort at one end.

Moving clockwise along the eastern coast of the island you come to **Praia do Moçambique** ★, a vast 19km-long (12-mile) stretch of strand, protected along its entire length by an ecological reserve that forms a construction-free buffer zone of thick vegetation between beach and road. Moçambique is one of the best beaches for those seeking solitude. As it faces the open ocean, the waves are often substantial. It's not a beach for weak swimmers.

Heading south from Praia do Moçambique, you'll come to **Praia Mole** ★★★, the hotshot surf beach at the moment. Largely unspoiled, the beach is framed by green hills and rocky outcrops, and the sand is white and very soft. One of the island's prettiest beaches, **Praia da Galheta** ★★★ is only accessible on foot from Praia Mole. Look for the trails through the dunes at the north end of Praia Mole. Note that Praia da Galheta is also the island's clothing-optional beach and a popular gay cruising area. However, the beach is family-friendly and also popular with surfers.

Just south of Praia Mole is **Praia da Joaquina.** To reach this beach you drive past the shifting sand dunes east of the Lagoa. It was once the island's most popular surf beach, but these days Praia Mole seems to get most of the action.

Campeche ★★ is far enough south that even in high season it's not hard to find a quiet spot here. The beach is very wide, but large waves can make it dangerous for swimming. Another favorite surf destination (and a spot where one can often see dolphins) is **Praia da Armação** ★, just south of Campeche.

Following the SC-406 all the way to the end will lead you to **Pântano do Sul,** located on the eastern side of the skinny southern tip of the island. It's one of the main fishing communities on the island and has a busy, bustling atmosphere. However, the boat traffic (and dirty gray sand) make it less than ideal for swimming. It is the place to leave your car and set out on a hike.

One of the island's prettiest beaches, **Lagoinha de Leste** ★★★ sits on the outer shore of an environmentally protected headland, accessible only via a 4km (2½-mile) trail from Pântano do Sul. The trail takes about 90 minutes, one-way. The lovely wild beach sits nestled at the bottom of a large hill, with a small river at one that end that flows into the ocean.

The **Lagoa da Conceição** sits almost at the center of the island, to the east of the city of Florianópolis and west of Praia Mole. The lagoon is about 30% fresh water. The water temperature is balmy—in the summer it can reach 26°C (80°F). Watersports are allowed on the lagoon, but jet skis have been banned.

SIGHTSEEING

The main square in Florianópolis's city center, **Praça XV,** is a verdant, green space with intriguing mythological figures set into the cobblestones beneath the trees. Look especially for the Bernúncia, a unique bull-alligator hybrid endemic to Santa Catarina mythology. The centerpiece of Praça XV is an enormous fig tree, said to have magical powers. Circling it thrice clockwise is said to bring on matrimony, seven times counterclockwise divorce, while hanging upside down from its branches is said to be a shortcut to widowhood. Try it and see. Close by, the **Rua Felipe Schmit** and the **Rua Cons. Mafra** and its cross streets are closed to traffic and packed with stores; specialty items include shoes and leather goods such as belts and wallets. Thanks to the cooler climate,

the stores stock excellent boots and sweaters that will hold up to Northern Hemisphere
falls and winters. Also nearby, the **Public Market,** Av. Paulo Fontes s/n (Mon–Fri 7am–
7pm, Sat 7am–1pm), is packed with small stalls offering local arts and crafts and a vast
variety of fresh seafood. For a good quick snack, stop by **Box32** (✆ 048/3224-5588;
www.box32.com.br).

On the northwest coast of the island, the small settlement of **Santo Antônio de Lisboa** is a lovely collection of traditional Azores-style homes, plus some of the best and
cheapest oysters on the island. Stop by the **Cantinho das Ostras** (✆ 048/3235-2296;
Mon–Fri 8am–6pm) at the south end of the beach to watch as oysters are brought in,
cleaned, and shucked. Sample a few fresh and raw (R$5 per dozen) or for just a bit more
have them steamed and served with lemon (R$12 per dozen). Delicious.

In the southern part of the island, the western shore facing the mainland lacks beaches
entirely, but in compensation offers some fabulous driving and sightseeing. South of the
airport, heading down the SC-405 toward **Riberão da Ilha** leads to a small, winding
road that hugs the coastline virtually all the way to the southern tip of the island. Don't
miss a visit to this part of the island! It's a region of small villages with colorful Portuguese-style houses, settled by fishermen from the Azores. Their descendants still live in
this region and make a living fishing or raising oysters. Note that although Riberão da
Ilha looks like it's just a short drive away, the road is winding and there are viewpoints
and picturesque villages to distract you along the way. Plan to spend at least half a day,
with lunch or dinner at a seafood restaurant in Riberão da Ilha.

BOAT TOURS

The traditional schooner trips travel around the western side of the island. **Scunasul
Tours** (✆ 048/3225-1806; www.scunasul.com.br) leaves from downtown Florianópolis,
heading underneath the Hercílio Luz suspension bridge to the north bay. The tour visits
two beautifully preserved fortresses on small islands. A lunch stop and time for a swim
are included in this leisurely day on the water. Another great boat trip is a visit to the **Ilha
do Campeche,** located off Praia do Campeche, on the eastern side of the island. The boat
leaves from Barra da Lagoa on the east side of the island and cruises south. Once at the
island you will have time to hike, swim, or snorkel. Tours cost R$35 per person, free for
children 5 and under; 6- to 12-year-olds pay half price.

OUTDOOR ACTIVITIES

A vast range of outdoor activities available on the island are coordinated by the tour
agency **ViaFloripa** (✆ 048/3224-4668; www.viafloripa.com). They include horseback
rides on Moçambique beach (R$55 for 2 hr.); parapenting at Praia Mole (R$180, 20
min.); bird-watching tours (R$270, 5 hr.); canoe trips on the ocean or Lagoa de Peri
(R$140, 3 hr.); sandboarding (R$85, 2 hr.); snorkeling on Ingleses beach (R$60, 1 hr.);
surf lessons (R$75, 1½ hr.); rappelling (R$90, 3 hr.); mountain biking (R$85–R$225,
3–5 hr.); ATV touring (R$180, 1 hr.). All tours include a licensed guide or instructor.

Scuba Diving

Florianópolis is not a diver's paradise, but if you want to check out the waters, **Parcel**
(✆ 048/3284-5564; www.parcel.com.br) offers a number of dive tours depending on
the weather and group size. One regular trip heads out to the biological reserve of
Arvoredo. A 4-hour tour, including two dives and equipment, costs R$150.

Kite Surfing/Windsurfing

The prime kite-surf and windsurf spot in Florianópolis is the Lagoa da Conceição. Experienced surfers can rent gear from **Open Winds** (✆ **048/3232-5004;** www.openwinds. com.br) starting at R$45 per hour. For beginner kite surfers, a course of six 90-minute lessons costs R$1,200. The lessons can be spread over several days.

5 FLORIANÓPOLIS AFTER DARK

Every summer, bars and clubs come and go in the northern part of the island around **Praia dos Ingleses.** Most of the year-round nightlife options can be found around the **Lagoa da Conceição,** where locals and tourists mingle. To start the evening off with a fabulous view, head up to the Morro da Lagoa da Conceição, just west of the village. Follow the Rodovia Admar Gonzaga up the hill; the road will switch back until you get to the lookout. Just across from the lookout is where you find **Mandalla,** Rod. Admar Gonzaga 4720 (✆ **048/3234-8714**). This bar sits perched high above the road and offers spectacular views of the lagoon and the village below. On most nights, Mandalla has live bands starting at 10pm (closed Mon).

Back down in the village a couple of nightlife options are within an easy stroll of one another. **Drakkar,** Av. Afonso Delambert Neto 607, Lagoa (✆ **048/3232-9516;** www. bardrakkar.com.br), is a happening live-music venue with a varied program. Open as early as 6pm, it's perfect for an early-evening cocktail. The live music usually doesn't get started until 10pm. To dance the night away and listen to some great local bands, head out to Praia Mole's **Latitude 27,** Estrada Geral da Barra da Lagoa 565 (btw. Lagoa and Praia Mole; ✆ **048/3232-5841;** www.latitude27.com.br). Local bands appear on the stage, and a large dance floor provides plenty of space to dance Thursday through Saturday. Downtown is where you'll find popular **Bianco Lounge** (✆ **048/3209-3777;** www. biancolounge.com.br), a trendy restaurant and ultraminimalist lounge, with fancy cocktails and low-key DJ. Also downtown you'll find the **Scuna,** Avenida Beira Mar (underneath the bridge; ✆ **048/3225-3138;** www.scunabar.com.br), which features a menu of live music and snacks and booze 3 nights a week (Tues, Fri, Sat) starting at 10pm. The best features of the Scuna are the two large patios overlooking the city's waterfront.

Fast Facts

1 FAST FACTS: BRAZIL

ADDRESSES When writing addresses in Brazil, the street number follows the name of the street ("Av. Atlântica 2000" would roughly translate as "2000 Atlantic Ave."). Often in smaller towns a street name will be followed by the abbreviation "s/n." This stands for *sem numero* (without number), and is used when a building sits on a street but has no identifying number. Other words you might come across are *loja* (shop or unit), *bloco* (building or block), and *sala* (room or suite, often abbreviated "sl."). In mailing addresses, the postal code usually precedes the two-letter state abbreviation.

AREA CODES Brazil's country code is 55. For city codes, see "Fast Facts" in each chapter.

BUSINESS HOURS Stores are usually open from 9am to 7pm weekdays, 9am to 2pm on Saturdays. Most places close on Sundays. Small stores may close for lunch. Shopping centers are open Monday through Saturday from 10am to 8pm most places, though in Rio de Janeiro and São Paulo they often stay open until 10pm. On Sundays many malls open the food court and movie theaters all day, but mall shops will only open from 2 to 8pm. Banks are open Monday through Friday either from 10am to 4pm or from 9am to 3pm.

DRINKING LAWS Officially, the legal drinking age in Brazil is 18, but it's not often enforced. Beer, wine, and liquor can be bought on any day of the week from grocery stores and snack stands. Drinking is allowed in public places and in motor vehicles. Drinking is now prohibited in most soccer stadiums. For drivers, the legal alcohol limit is 0.00. This is now strictly enforced.

ELECTRICITY Brazil's electric current varies from 100 to 240 volts, and from 50 to 60Hz; even within one city there can be variations, and power surges are not uncommon. For laptops or battery chargers, bring an adaptor that can handle the full range of voltage. Most hotels do a good job of labeling their outlets, but when in doubt check before plugging in! Brazilian plugs usually have three prongs: two round and one flat. Adapters for converting North American plugs are cheap (R$3) and widely available.

EMBASSIES & CONSULATES All embassies are located in Brasilia, the capital. Australia, Canada, the United States, and Great Britain have consulates in both Rio and São Paulo. New Zealand has a consulate in São Paulo.

In Brasilia: Australia, SES, Quadra 801, Conjunto K, lote 7 (© 061/3226-3111; www.brazil.embassy.gov.au). **Canada,** SES Av. das Nações Quadra 803, lote 16 (© 061/3424-5400; www.canada.org.br). **Great Britain,** SES Av. das Nações Quadra 801, lote 8 (© 061/3329-2300; www.uk.org.br). **New Zealand,** SHIS QI 09, conj. 16, casa 01 (© 061/3248-9900; www.nzembassy.com/home.cfm?c=44). **United States,** SES Av. das Nações Quadra 801, lote 03 (© 061/3312-7000; www.embaixada-americana.org.br).

In Rio de Janeiro: Australia, Av. Presidente Wilson 231, Ste. 23, Centro (© 021/3824-4624). **Canada,** Av. Atlântica 1130, fifth floor, Copacabana (© 021/2543-3004). **Great Britain,** Praia do Flamengo 284, Flamengo (© 021/2555-9600). **United States,** Av. Presidente Wilson 147, Centro (© 021/3823-2000).

In São Paulo: Australia, CHEK Santos 700, ninth floor, Jardim Paulista (© 011/3171 2889). **Canada,** Av. das Nações Unidas 12901, 19th floor (© 011/5509-4321). **Great Britain,** Rua Ferreira de Araujo 741 (© 011/3094-2700). **New Zealand,** Av. Campinas 579, 15th floor, Cerqueira Cesar (© 011/3148-0616). **United States,** Rua Henri Dunant 500, Chácara Santo Antonio (© 011/5186-7000).

EMERGENCY NUMBERS For police dial © **190;** for ambulance or fire department dial © **193.**

GASOLINE (PETROL) Gasoline costs approximately R$2.80/liter. Most cars will also work on ethanol (alcohol) which costs only R$1.80 per liter. However, ethanol burns faster, so its effective cost works out to a bit more, close to R$2.20 per liter.

INSURANCE For information on traveler's insurance, trip-cancellation insurance, and medical insurance while traveling please visit www.frommers.com/planning.

LANGUAGE The language of Brazil is Portuguese. If you speak Spanish you will certainly have an easier time picking up words and phrases. In the large cities you will find people in the tourism industry who speak good English, but in smaller towns and resorts English is very limited. If you are picking up language books or tapes, make sure they are Brazilian Portuguese and not Portuguese from Portugal: big difference! A good pocket-size phrasebook is *Say It in Portuguese* (Brazilian usage) by Prista, Mickle, and Costa; or try *Conversational Brazilian Portuguese* by Cortina.

LEGAL AID In larger Brazilian cities there are special police detachments for dealing with tourists, called DEAT (Delegacia Especial Atendimento ao Turista). See the "Fast Facts" sections in each chapter for contact details. If you find yourself involved with the police, demand to be taken to the nearest DEAT station. DEAT officers speak English, and are normally better trained.

MAIL Mail from Brazil is quick and efficient. Post offices *(correios)* are found everywhere, readily identifiable by the blue-and-yellow sign. A postcard or letter to Europe or North America costs R$1.80. Parcels can be sent through FedEx or regular mail (express or common); a small parcel—up to 2.5 kilograms (5½ lb.)—costs about R$55 by common mail and takes about a week or two.

MAPS Good maps aren't Brazil's strong suit. Better to buy one before you come. In Brazil, your best bet for city maps is the *Guia Quatro Rodas—Mapas das Capitais;* this pocket book for sale at all newsstands (R$12) has indexed maps of all state capitals, including São Paulo, Rio, Salvador, Manaus, Brasilia, and Recife. Unfortunately it does not include any highways. The best highway map is sold with the *Guia Quatro Rodas Brasil* (for sale on newsstands for R$42), a Brazilian guidebook.

NEWSPAPERS & MAGAZINES There are no English-language newspapers or magazines in Brazil. Foreign papers and magazines are only easily found in Rio and São Paulo. The most popular Brazilian newspapers are *O Globo* and *Jornal do Brasil,* published out of Rio, and *Folha de São Paulo,* the leading business paper published in São Paulo. The most popular current affairs magazine (the equivalent of *Newsweek*) is *Veja,* published weekly. In Rio and São Paulo, *Veja* magazine always includes an entertainment insert that provides a detailed listing of nightlife, restaurants, and events.

PASSPORTS See www.frommers.com/ planning for information on how to obtain a passport.

POLICE For police dial ✆ **190.**

SHOPPING Clothing sizes follow the European numbering (36, 38, 40, and so on) or are marked P (*pequeno* = small), M (*medio* = medium), and G (*grande* = large); U stands for *tamanho único* (one size).

SMOKING Smoking is prohibited on planes and long-distance buses. It is also prohibited in restaurants in Rio and São Paulo. Other Brazilian cities are expected to implement restaurant smoking bans in the near future.

TAXES There are no taxes added to goods purchased in Brazil. Restaurants and hotels normally add a 10% service tax. In Rio, the city also levies a 5% tax on hotels. All airports in Brazil charge departure taxes; this is usually included in the ticket price but it's wise to check. Domestic departures cost around R$21 at most airports, and international departures are a hefty R$108. Payment can only be made in cash with U.S. dollars or Brazilian currency but not in a combination of both.

TIME ZONES Brazil has three time zones. The coast, including Rio de Janeiro, Salvador, and as far inland as São Paulo and Brasilia, is in one time zone. The ranching states of Mato Grosso and Mato Grosso do Sul, the Pantanal, and the Amazon around Manaus are in the second time zone, 1 hour behind Rio. The third time zone includes the state of Acre and the western part of the Amazon, 2 hours behind Rio. The time difference between cities in Brazil and North America varies by up to 2 hours over the course of the year as clocks spring forward and fall back for daylight saving time. From approximately March to September Rio de Janeiro is in the same time zone as New York City. From October to February, Rio is at least 1 and often 2 hours ahead of New York

(for example, noon in New York City is 2pm in Rio).

TIPPING A 10% service charge is automatically included on most restaurant and hotel bills and you are not expected to tip on top of this amount. If service has been particularly bad you can request to have the 10% removed from your bill. Taxi drivers do not get tipped; just round up the amount to facilitate change. Hairdressers and beauticians usually receive a 10% tip. Bellboys get tipped R$1 to R$2 per bag. Room service usually includes the 10% service charge on the bill.

TOILETS Public toilets are rare in Brazil, except in shopping malls. You'll do better seeking out hotels and restaurants. Toilets in Brazil can be marked in a few different ways. Usually you will see *mulher* or an M for women and *homem* or an H for men. Sometimes it will read *damas* or D for ladies and *cavalheiros* or C for gentlemen. It's not a bad idea to carry some toilet paper with you as in many public restrooms, the toilet attendant doles out sheets only grudgingly.

VISAS See "Visas," in chapter 3.

VISITOR INFORMATION The Brazilian national tourism agency, **Embratur,** has a good site at www.embratur.gov.br. The agency also has representatives overseas:

In the U.K.: London, 18 Greyhound Rd., London, W6.8NX (✆ **20/7396-5551;** fax 20/7396-5599; e-mail: ebt.uk@embratur. gov.br/assistant.ebt.uk@embratur.gov.br).

The **Brazilian Embassy** in the U.K. has an outstanding website including links to all the state and many city tourism websites: www.brazil.org.uk.

In the U.S.: New York (✆ **646/378-2126;** fax 646/378-2034; e-mail: ebt.us@ embratur.gov.br/assistant.ebt.us@embratur.gov.br). **Los Angeles** (✆ **310/341-8394;** e-mail: ebt.us2@embratur.gov.br/ assistant.ebt.us2@embratur.gov.br).

Other **Brazilian embassies** abroad also provide good tourist information:

In Australia: 19 Forster Crescent, Yarralumla, Canberra ACT 2600 (☎ **02/6273-2372;** fax 02/6273-2375; www.brazil.org.au).

In Canada: 450 Wilbrod St., Ottawa, ON K1N 6M8 (☎ **613/237-1090;** fax 613/237-6144; www.brasembottawa.org).

In New Zealand: 10 Brandon St., Level 9, Wellington 6001 (☎ **04/473-3516;** fax 04/473-3517; www.brazil.org.nz).

In the U.K.: 32 Green St., London W1K 7AT (☎ **020/7399-9000;** fax 020/7399-9100; www.brazil.org.uk).

In the U.S.: 3006 Massachusetts Ave. NW, Washington, DC 20008 (☎ **202/238-2700;** fax 202/238-2827; www.brasilemb.org).

WATER The tap water in Brazil is increasingly safe to drink. However, as a result of the treatment process it still doesn't taste great. To be on the safe side, drink bottled or filtered water (most Brazilians do). All brands are reliable; ask for *agua sem gas* for still water and *agua com gas* for carbonated water. However, you can certainly shower, brush your teeth, or rinse an apple with tap water.

---

2 AIRLINE, HOTEL & CAR RENTAL WEBSITES

MAJOR AIRLINES

Aerolineas
www.aerolineas.com.ar

Aeroméxico
www.aeromexico.com

Aerosur
www.aerosur.com

Air Canada
www.aircanada.com

Air France
www.airfrance.com

Alitalia
www.alitalia.com

American Airlines
www.aa.com

Avianca
www.avianca.com.co

British Airways
www.british-airways.com

Continental Airlines
www.continental.com

Cubana
www.cubana.cu

Delta Air Lines
www.delta.com

El Al Airlines
www.el.co.il

Emirates Airlines
www.emirates.com

Gol
www.voegol.com.br

Iberia Airlines
www.iberia.com

Japan Airlines
www.jal.co.jp

KLM
www.klm.com

Korean Air
www.koreanair.com

Lan Airlines
www.lan.com

Lufthansa
www.lufthansa.com

Méxicana
www.mexicana.com

Pluna
www.pluna.aero

South African Airways
www.flysaa.com

Swiss Air
www.swiss.com

TAAG
www.taag.com.br

TACA
www.taca.com

TAM
www.tam.com.br

TAP
www.tap.pt

Turkish Airlines
www.thy.com

United Airlines
www.united.com

BUDGET AIRLINES

Azul
http://viajemais.voeazul.com.br

Ocean Air
www.oceanair.com.br

TRIP
www.voetrip.com.br

Webjet
www.webjet.com.br

MAJOR HOTEL & MOTEL CHAINS

Accor hotels
www.accorhotels.com.br

Atlantica Hotels
www.atlanticahotels.com.br

Blue Tree Hotels
www.bluetree.com.br

Mercure Hotels
www.mercure.com

Othon Hotels
www.othon.com.br

Sol Meliá
www.solmelia.com

Windsor Hotels
www.windsorhoteis.com.br

CAR RENTAL AGENCIES

Avis
www.avis.com.br

Budget
www.budget.com.br

Enterprise
www.enterprise.com.br

Hertz
www.hertz.com.br

Localiza
www.localiza.com

LocarAlpha
www.locaralpha.com.br

Thrifty
www.thrifty.com.br

Unidas
www.unidas.com.br

Yes
www.yesrentacar.com.br

INDEX

See also Accommodations index, below.